VICTIMS AND SURVIVORS

VICTIMS AND SURVIVORS

Displaced Persons
and Other
War Victims in Viet-Nam,
1954–1975

LOUIS A. WIESNER

Foreword by Phan Quang Dan

CONTRIBUTIONS TO THE STUDY OF WORLD HISTORY,
NUMBER 14

GREENWOOD PRESS
New York • Westport, Connecticut • London

Library of Congress Cataloging-in-Publication Data

Wiesner, Louis A.
  Victims and survivors : displaced persons and other war victims in
Viet-Nam, 1954–1975 / Louis A. Wiesner.
    p. cm. – (Contributions to the study of world history, ISSN 0885–9159 ; no. 14)
    Bibliography: p.
    Includes index.
    ISBN 0–313–26306–X (lib. bdg. : alk. paper)
    1. Vietnamese Conflict, 1961–1975—Refugees. 2. Refugees,
Political—Vietnam. I. Title. II. Series.
  DS559.63.W54   1988
  959.704—dc19   88–15494

British Library Cataloguing in Publication Data is available.

Copyright © 1988 by Louis A. Wiesner

Library of Congress Catalog Card Number: 88–15494
ISBN: 0–313–26306–X
ISSN: 0885–9159

First published in 1988

Greenwood Press, Inc.
88 Post Road West, Westport, Connecticut 06881

Printed in the United States of America

The paper used in this book complies with the
Permanent Paper Standard issued by the National
Information Standards Organization (Z39.48–1984).

10 9 8 7 6 5 4 3 2 1

To the people of Viet-Nam—
those in their homeland and those scattered
to the ends of the earth.
May their long suffering not be in vain.

Contents

Maps and Illustrations

Tables

Foreword

There is no shortage of literature covering the military aspects of the 21-year period from the July 21, 1954, Geneva agreements, which practically divided Vietnam into Communist North and nationalist South, to the Communist takeover of Saigon on April 30, 1975. However, to my knowledge, Louis Wiesner's *Victims and Survivors* is the first scholarly study on the mostly forgotten yet more human subject of refugees made up of the little people uprooted by the war, who drifted from relief camp to relief camp and from resettlement site to resettlement site.

Louis Wiesner's career and, of greater importance, his dedication to the refugees, made him an international authority on refugees, especially in Vietnam. On behalf of the US Department of State and then the International Rescue Committee, he traveled the world over to assess refugee needs and demands. He had the rare opportunity of serving Vietnamese refugees, at the village, provincial, and regional levels, in close cooperation with Vietnamese authorities, as well as at the monitoring and funding level in Washington. This gave him well-rounded experience in refugee work.

His book, a project first conceived in 1970 and tirelessly pursued in the following 18 years, was based not only on his personal experience, but also on thorough research and analysis of available material from American, Vietnamese, and other international sources. With careful planning, Wiesner consulted a great many eyewitnesses and direct participants in the various refugee programs. *Victims and Survivors*, the fruit of these many years of sustained effort, is well-documented, objective, and accurate. At the same time, it is compassionate and moving in its discussion of refugees in South Vietnam. It contains an interesting chapter on North Vietnam, and presents occasionally striking views on the war itself, which served as the background to the refugee tragedy.

Facts were carefully checked. The 1972 destruction of the 1,000-bed Bach-Mai hospital was highly publicized by Hanoi as proof of indiscriminate bombing by the United States against civilian as well as military targets in North Vietnam. American visitors, taken to Bach-Mai by DRVN officials to see the ruins, took Hanoi's accusations for granted. However, Louis Wiesner points out that "the hospital was about a thousand yards from the Bach-Mai airstrip and military barracks." In fact, the airstrip was part of the hospital premises and was originally conceived of as a landing site for small aircraft transporting emergency patients from the provinces to Bach-Mai Hospital. From 1940 to 1944, as senior medical student in charge of leprosy and venereal disease services, I worked at Bach-Mai Hospital. In the early morning hours after long-duty nights, I used to stroll from the hospital to the airstrip, which was later expanded into a military base by Hanoi. Facts reported out of context, without sufficient investigation, lead to half-truths and misinformation. Louis Wiesner does not allow himself to commit such mistakes.

The 1956 Quynh-Luu peasant revolt in Nghe-An, Ho Chi Minh's native province, against Communist "land reform," which aimed at liquidating all peasants who owned land, be it just a few acres, and thus at stamping out any desire for private property, is forcefully depicted in a few paragraphs. Similarly depicted is the large March 1975 massacre in which NVA General Van Tien Dung's 320th Division showered Soviet bullets on the over 200,000 refugees, mostly civilians, fleeing the Highlands along Highway 7B towards Tuy-Hoa on the coastal plain, where hardly 45,000 arrived.

Victims and Survivors is much more than a piecing together of accurate facts. It has perspective and cohesion. The evolution and shape of events emerge powerfully, and their hows and whys become self-explaining. Louis Wiesner's book is a comprehensive study of refugee projects succeeding one another and spanning over two decades of Vietnamese political and social turmoil. Examining resettlement of refugees fleeing North Vietnam, Highlander resettlement, agro-villes, the Strategic Hamlet program, repatriation and resettlement of Vietnamese from Kampuchea, land development and hamlet building, it is a dramatic and sometimes dizzying but never confusing panorama of the entire history and spectrum of relief and resettlement projects in South Vietnam, remarkable in both width and depth. Furthermore, the reasons for the success or failure of each resettlement project are made crystal clear by Louis Wiesner's penetrating analysis.

I happened to be involved myself in refugee work. In 1954, I was asked by Prime Minister Ngo Dinh Diem to join his cabinet and be in charge of resettling refugees leaving North Vietnam. However, knowing Ngo Dinh Diem's mandarin background and penchant for nepotism, arbitrariness, and paternalism, I thought it more important to organize a loyal and constructive opposition, while standing ready to offer him advice on refugee work. Unfortunately, he tolerated no opposition and considered me an enemy for not cooperating with him. Then, from 1969 to 1975, after seven months of serving as Minister of State in charge of

External Affairs, I was put in charge of refugee relief and resettlement. My personal experience led me to conclusions very similar to those expressed by Louis Wiesner in his book.

Refugees should not be considered pawns to move around as part of military operations in the struggle against Communism. Forced relocations are bound to fail. Refugees who are badly treated may not become Communist, but they will likely turn against the non-Communist government insensitive to their needs and sufferings. At the very least, they will grow apathetic and will no longer care who wins.

Refugees should be treated with kindness and consideration, not with condescendence. There should be no discrimination against any religious community, especially in Vietnam, which is a multireligious society. There should be no discrimination against ethnic minority groups, especially highlanders who, far from being "primitive people to civilize," are sober, honest, hard-working, and proud people.

It is not enough that relief and resettlement be performed *for* the refugees. It should also be performed *with* the refugees who know their own problems best and could significantly contribute to finding and implementing the proper solutions.

In-camp idleness is the worst solution; it is no solution at all, no matter how comfortable refugee camps are. It is a waste of manpower, energy and talents. It leads to a rapid erosion of the sense of self-respect, enthusiasm, and determination to remake a new life. Refugees should be moved out of camps, the sooner the better, to new resettlement sites or back to their native villages wherever security and availability of land make it feasible.

Refugees should be fully reestablished economically, socially, and politically.

Close observers of Vietnam during the period 1954–75 will readily agree that the two most important developments to watch were how the war was fought and the way refugees were cared for. Though not dealing with the military events themselves, Louis Wiesner made an unusually perceptive remark for an American writer discussing Vietnam, saying in his preface:

The noncolonialist American providers of military and economic aid, advice, and combat troops . . . were largely ignorant of the languages, cultures, and societies within which they were required to operate . . . The insertion of the Americans, most of whom came with experience in military strategy and economic aid developed elsewhere under different circumstances . . . greatly complicated the counterinsurgency task.

This I fully endorse. It is fatal to the ultimate success of his venture, whether military or humanitarian, if a foreign expert assumes that his country's patterns of behavior, his country's particular standards, his country's values and priorities, and his country's ways of doing things can be transplanted full-blown into another nation's cultural soil. Such a plant may survive as long as the expert remains on the job to tend it, but it is bound to wither and die as soon as he departs.

The Americanization of the Vietnam War, based, maybe, on the generous assumption that American troops, powerfully equipped and well trained, could defeat Communist insurgency in a short time and then turn over a pacified Vietnam to the Vietnamese, was a wrong and fateful decision. It led to the longest, and most expensive and divisive war in American history. It confined the Vietnamese people to a secondary role, while they should have been led and inspired by true and independent-minded Vietnamese leaders to play the major role and fight wholeheartedly for their own freedom and survival. It propelled into artificial prominence unwarranted leaders who relied entirely on American protection, became defeatists after American withdrawal, and fled long before Communist invaders arrived, leaving behind disintegrated Vietnamese troops and defenseless Vietnamese people who are in the final analysis the main losers and victims of the war.

American direct and massive intervention was decided without the Vietnamese people being consulted. It was a paternalistic policy, the imposing of American will, no matter how well intentioned, on the Vietnamese people. This massive approach was followed by a precipitate withdrawal, dictated by American internal politics rather than by responsible consideration of the fate of the Vietnamese people.

However, in spite of sporadic unfortunate incidents, the overall good behavior of the American troops, while unable to mobilize the fighting spirit or the spirit of sacrifice of the Vietnamese people, did truly win their hearts and minds. This needs no other proof than the massive exodus of the boat people out of Communist Vietnam in the hope of reaching American shores.

The basic lesson of the Vietnam experience has also been learned. America is now refraining from direct intervention in regional conflicts, and is instead supporting authentic, freedom-loving patriots leading their peoples against Soviet colonialism which, in the post–World War II era, has replaced all previous colonial empires and generated, in the most ruthless way, miseries and refugees everywhere.

I personally found *Victims and Survivors* both fascinating and enlightening. I strongly recommend it to whoever wishes to acquire a better and more comprehensive understanding of the Vietnamese people, whose sufferings under Communist totalitarianism and Soviet colonialism are far from being ended, as the boat people continue on an international scale the saga of the internal refugees from 1954 to 1975.

                                                                        Phan Quang Dan

Preface

The insurgency and war in Viet-Nam, which ended in 1975 with the victory of the Communists, led to the displacement of millions of people in the two parts of the country and to a further toll in civilian war casualties. It is estimated that in South Viet-Nam close to 12,000,000 civilians, over half the population, fled from one side or the other or from armed conflict, or were evacuated or relocated, some of them more than once; about 250,000 were killed; and approximately 900,000 were wounded in the period from the Geneva accords of 1954 to the collapse of the non-Communist government in 1975. Except for the exile abroad of a few prominent political refugees, they did not leave their own nation but moved about within it. By way of comparison, it is as if over 120,000,000 Americans had been displaced within this country, 3,000,000 civilians had been killed, and more than three times that many wounded during a 21-year fight for our freedom. The social, psychological, and political consequences of such enormous trauma and its effects upon the course of the war were clearly profound, but were largely ignored during most of those years and are little understood to this day.

These displaced persons were generally referred to as refugees at the time, but they were not refugees in the sense of the international Convention of 1951 or the Protocol of 1967 on the Status of Refugees, in that they were not outside the country of their nationality or habitual residence. Hence, they did not fall under the mandate of the United States High Commissioner for Refugees and received no aid from his office.

In North Viet-Nam the dislocations were also enormous, though figures are hard to come by, and the totalitarian regime kept tight control over population movements.

People have been displaced by wars and persecution within their own countries, as well as across their frontiers, for thousands of years. What happened in Viet-Nam during the period covered by this book was unique in several ways, however. First, the sheer magnitude and duration of the displacements, which forced many away from their homes permanently, were unusual. This alone changed the social structure of South Viet-Nam and altered its history. Second, the United States was involved more closely and for a longer time in both the displacements and the relief of the dislocated people than it has been in any other part of the world. Third, several different systems of humanitarian assistance were developed within the country and were modified and adjusted over time.

This book examines how and why the various displacements and war casualties occurred, as well as the changes in official policies and military doctrines over time which affected the generation of refugees, evacuees, and civilian casualties; the evolution of policies and programs for the relief and reestablishment of the victims; the ways in which the dislocated and traumatized people adjusted or failed to adjust, and their economic and social behavior; and the effects of the dislocations upon their attitudes and actions toward the conflicting parties. It is hoped that this study will help to fill a gap in our understanding of ''people factors'' in what is now called low-intensity war, and that it may bring out some lessons that are transferable to such wars elsewhere. The effectiveness of the different systems and methods of providing humanitarian assistance, including the agencies and institutions that were involved, is analyzed.

A distinction is made between those who were dislocated by reason of flight from a conflicting party or relocation for purposes of social engineering or military security (the principal subjects of this book), and urban migrants for job-related or similar reasons. The borderline between these two populations was not always clear and statistical data were imprecise, but an attempt will be made to sort out the two categories.

The presentation is mainly historical. Statistical analyses of war victims are reported where they are available, but this method has limited applicability, since little scientific investigation was done at the time into some of the crucial factors with which this study is concerned, the human subjects who were affected are now largely inaccessible within their country, and those who have since become refugees abroad are scattered. Likewise, the records of the indigenous government and other local institutions that were involved up to 1975 are in large part not available for study. Fortunately, much policy and program documentation was acquired at the time by the US government and various libraries and archives. I have been fortunate in being able to correspond with, and in some cases to interview, many of the Vietnamese and Americans who were officially or as voluntary agency representatives involved in caring for war victims or who were themselves victims. Also, having myself been a member of the United States Refugee Division in Viet-Nam from January 1968 to July 1970, and a foreign assistance inspector visiting the refugee and public health programs in Viet-Nam twice in 1972, I acquired some personal knowledge of the problems and programs connected with both the generation and the relief of war victims. I was further involved from 1973 to August 1975 as director of the Office of Refugee and Migration Affairs of the Department of State; and from 1975 to the present as a member of the International Rescue Committee, a voluntary agency, I have been concerned with relief in countries of first asylum and resettlement abroad of Indochinese and other refugees.

The problems of war victims in both parts of Viet-Nam occurred in the context of Southeast Asian history and culture, and of the domestic insurgency and invasions from North Viet-Nam which were resisted by the indigenous government of the South. During the period covered by this study, the French colonial masters of Indochina were succeeded, except in North Viet-Nam, by the non-colonialist American providers of military and economic aid, advice, and combat troops, who, however, were largely ignorant of the languages, cultures, and societies within which they were required to operate. While the local government made its share of mistakes in dealing with its own people and the insurgents, the insertion of the Americans, most of whom came with experience in military strategy and economic aid developed elsewhere under different circumstances and thus were required to learn largely by on-the-job training, greatly complicated the counterinsurgency task.

It would make this book unmanageably large to set out the full context in which the problems of war victims were developed and coped with, though contextual factors of immediate relevance are discussed. Therefore, I commend to readers the study of a few works of general history of the area which are listed in the bibliography.

ACKNOWLEDGMENTS

I am indebted to many former associates and new friends who have spent many hours by correspondence or face-to-face interviews imparting information and interpretation and guiding my searches. It is not possible in this limited space to list them all, and I hope that those whose names are omitted here will not think that their contributions are not valuable and appreciated. The following are some of those whose recollections and thoughts have particularly helped in shaping this book:

Phan Quang Dan, M.D., who played a noteworthy part in the political and human development of Viet-Nam, both as an opposition leader and inmate of President Diem's jails and as Chairman of the Interministerial Committee for the Relief of Refugees from Cambodia in 1970, Secretary of State for Land Development and Hamlet Building (1972–75), and Minister of Social Welfare, concurrently Deputy Prime Minister (1974–75).

Tran Lu Y, M.D., Minister of Health, Social Welfare and Relief (1968–69).

Phieu N. Tran, M.D. (Tran Nguon Phieu), Deputy Minister of Health, Social Welfare and Relief (1968–69); Minister of Social Welfare (1969–74).

Ton That Niem, M.D., Assistant Minister of Health, Social Welfare and Relief

(1968–69), Senator in the Buddhist Faction (1971–75), and Minister of Health (1975).

Tran Quang Thuan, Minister of Social Welfare (1964 and again in 1965), Senator and leader of the Buddhist faction (1972–75).

Hung Thanh Huynh (Huynh Thanh Hu'ng), Assistant Minister of Social Welfare and of the succeeding Ministries (1964–75), who served under 10 Ministers as their valued expert and administrator.

Han Tho Touneh (Touneh Han Tho), a leader of the Montagnards; Secretary General of the Ministry for the Development of Ethnic Minorities (1971–73), and then of the Ethnic Minorities Council (1973–75).

Toplui Pierre K'briuh, R'Mah Dock, Y Yok Ayun, and Reverend Ha Cillpam, Montagnard leaders now in North Carolina.

Cuong Tu Nguyen (Nguyen Tu Cuong), whose assistance has been invaluable in arranging and interpreting for many of my interviews in the Washington area, and in researching source materials.

Lt. Gen. Nguyen Chanh Thi, Commandor of I Corps (1965–66).

Nguyen Thi Hue, employee in the office of Ngo Dinh Nhu (1956–63), and then in the Vietnamese intelligence service at Saigon City Hall; USAID (United States Mission of the Agency for International Development) Information Division (1966–67), CORDS (Civil Operations for Revolutionary [later Rural] Development Support) Refugee Division and Directorate and its successors in USAID (1967–75).

Kim Oanh Cook, employee of the CORDS Refugee office in Gia-Dinh province (1966–68).

Chau Thanh Pham, interpreter for the US Refugee Adviser in Military Region 4 (the Mekong Delta) (1970–75).

Hien Bich Vu (Vu Bich Hien), employee of CORDS Military Region 3 from 1970 to 1974.

Brig. Gen. (ret.) Edward G. Lansdale, Special Assistant at the American Embassy to Viet-Nam (1953, 1954–56, 1965–68).

Everett V. Bumgardner, US Information Agency (USIA) officer, Laos (1959–60), and Viet-Nam (1960–75), with details to the Viet-Nam Training Center in Washington.

William E. Colby, First Secretary of the American Embassy Saigon (1959–62); Chief of the Far East Division of CIA (Central Intelligence Agency) (1962–68); Assistant Chief of Staff, then Deputy to COMUSMACV (Commander, US Military Assistance Command; Vietnam) for CORDS (1968–71); Executive Director, then Deputy Director of CIA (1972–73); Director of Central Intelligence (1973–76).

John F. Thomas, Director, US Cuban Refugee Program (1963–68); Refugee Coordinator of US Operations Mission (USOM) Viet-Nam (1965); Chief, CORDS Refugee Division (1968–69); Director, Intergovernmental Committee for European Migration (ICEM) (1969–79). Mr. Thomas has set down on paper the account of his own distinguished service in Viet-Nam and, in numerous letters, has further answered my numerous questions.

Edward B. Marks, USOM Viet-Nam Refugee Coordinator (1965–66).

Clayton E. McManaway, Jr., USAID Program Officer (1965–67); Chief of CORDS Plans, Programs, and Policy Division and Directorate (1967–70); Deputy Director, Interagency Task Force on Indochina Refugees (1975).

Robert W. Komer, Deputy Special Assistant and Special Assistant to President Johnson for Viet-Nam Affairs (1965–67); Deputy to the Commander, US Military Assistance Command Vietnam, for Civil Operations for Rural Development Support, (1967–68); Under Secretary of Defense for Policy (1979–81).

L. Wade Lathram, Director, Office of Civil Operations (OCO) of the US Aid Mission Saigon (1966–67); Assistant Chief of Staff for CORDS (1967–68).

Graham A. Martin, Special Assistant to the Secretary of State for Refugee and Migration Affairs (1967–69); Ambassador to Viet-Nam (1973–75).

William K. Hitchcock, Director, CORDS Refugee Directorate (1969–70); Minister-Counselor for Political Affairs, US Embassy Saigon (1970–72).

Robert L. King, CORDS Refugee Division and Directorate (1969–71), USAID Chief of Social Welfare Division (1972–75).

Stephen F. Cummings, M.D., who was USAID Refugee Representative in Binh-Dinh Province, then in IV Corps Tactical Zone (CTZ) (1966–67); CORDS Refugee Division Liaison Officer with the Ministry of Social Welfare and Refugees (1967–69). Dr. Cummings, in a number of interviews, has provided valuable insights into how refugee assistance actually worked in the field, and has loaned many valuable papers.

Richard C. Holdren, USAID Refugee Chief in I CTZ (1965–67), then in IV CTZ (1968–75). Mr. Holdren has loaned or given me many of his own writings and, in numerous letters, has filled in many gaps in my knowledge and contributed valuable ideas and suggestions.

Raymond G. Fontaine, officer of the CORDS Refugee Directorate (1969–72); Chief of the USAID Refugee Division (1972–75).

Martha Barnhill, Administrative Assistant, CORDS Refugee Division I CTZ (1967–73).

Shepard C. Lowman, USAID and CORDS provincial and municipal representative (1965–70); Political Officer, American Embassy Saigon (1973–75).

Lionel A. Rosenblatt, CORDS (1967–69); Special Assistant to the Deputy Secretary of State (1974–75).

Moncrieff J. Spear, Consul General Nha-Trang (1973–75).

Paul M. Popple, Consul General Da-Nang (1973–74).

Wells Klein, Viet-Nam Representative of CARE (Cooperative for American Relief Everywhere) (1954); Viet-Nam Director, International Rescue Committee (IRC) (1965); Refugee Adviser AID/Washington (1965–66); Consultant to the Senate Subcommittee to Investigate Problems Connected with Refugees and Escapees (1967–75).

Gerald Cannon Hickey, member of the Michigan State University Advisory Group in the 1950s, and of the Rand Corporation Advisory Mission to CORDS and USAID until 1973; an internationally recognized authority on the highlanders.

Jerry Tinker, Researcher, Human Sciences Research, Inc. in Viet-Nam (1965–67); Consultant, then Counsel, Senate Subcommittee to Investigate Problems Connected with Refugees and Escapees (1970–81 and 1987–present); Minority Counsel (1981–87).

Leo Cherne, Chairman, International Rescue Committee (1951-present).

Msgr. Robert L. Charlebois, Director, Catholic Relief Services (CRS) in Viet-Nam, Laos, and Cambodia (1966–70).

Sir Robert G. K. Thompson, Head of the British Advisory Mission to President Diem (1961–63); occasional adviser to the Government of Viet-Nam and the United States Government (1964–73).

Carl Harris, Refugee Officer, Quang-Tin province (1967–69), then at Saigon (1969–71); Director, World Vision, Cambodia (1973–75).

The sharing of personal experiences by these and other participants in the events described in this book, and their helpfulness in examining and correcting my observations, have brought this account close to the reality of what happened, why it happened, and what it means.

Dr. Richard Hunt and Dr. Vincent Demma of the US Army Center of Military History were generous in making available to me a wealth of documents from MACV (Military Assistance Command, Vietnam), CORDS, and other sources.

Eugene Wu, Raymond Lum, and Phan Chan of the Harvard Yenching Library were most helpful in making available the unpublished papers of Joseph Buttinger. During my sorting and examination of these papers, I was in correspondence with Dr. Muriel Gardner (Mrs. Buttinger) until her death in 1985.

Wendy Thomas and David Paul of the Lamont Library at Harvard University greatly assisted me in finding source material from among the documents of the US and Vietnamese governments and foreign press translations, and they acquired additional material for this research.

Ronald E. Wealon and his colleagues at the John F. Kennedy Library were generous in guiding me through the numerous finding aids, making the relevant files available, and requesting mandatory review of some that are still classified.

Charles Sternberg and Robert DeVecchi extended the hospitality of the International Rescue Committee in giving me access to its Viet-Nam files. Mr. Sternberg, who was Executive Director during most of the period recounted by this study, and who had visited IRC's Viet-Nam projects on numerous occasions, shared his memory of the relevant events.

Claire McCurdy, the Archivist of Catholic Relief Services, assiduously searched out documents and the addresses of former relief workers.

Professor Hue Tam-Ho Tai of Harvard University has been most helpful in steering me to other knowledgeable people and in reviewing my manuscript.

I am grateful to the Ann and Erlo Van Waveren Foundation for its grant which enabled me to visit a number of the persons named above and in other ways to complete this study. The president of the Foundation, Olivier Bernier, an eminent historian and biographer, has been a source of moral as well as material support.

Executive Vice President Dr. James T. Sabin, production editor Todd Adkins, and copy editor Nicole Balant of Greenwood Press patiently encouraged and guided me through every intricate step of the publication process.

And finally my loving wife, The Reverend Elizabeth, steadfastly bolstered my sometimes flagging resolve and endured the long years of research and writing, while keeping our far-flung family together, pursuing her calling as an Episcopal priest, and writing her own book.

A NOTE ON PROPER NAMES

In Viet-Nam, the Vietnamese family name comes first, followed by the middle name and the given name. A person was customarily addressed by his or her title and the given name; thus, Dr. Phieu (Dr. Tran Nguon Phieu), or General Truong (Ngo Quang Truong). President Ngo Dinh Diem and President Nguyen Van Thieu were commonly referred to as Diem and Thieu, without the honorific title. Those usages are followed in the text of this book, including the index. However, many Vietnamese who have come to the United States have Anglicized their names, placing the given name first; thus Dr. Phieu N. Tran. When a person who has done this is cited as a source in my notes for information given after the name was changed, I have used the Anglicized name in the note. Because of the printing problem, Vietnamese diacritical marks on the names are not used in this book.

Some Montagnard tribes placed the given name first, while others placed it last. I have followed the usage of each person. Some highlanders also changed their names after arrival in the United States, and, when citing them in my notes, I have used the Anglicized name; thus, Han Tho Touneh (in Viet-Nam Touneh Han Tho).

NOTATION OF DATES

In my text I follow the normal American civilian practice of writing dates in order month-day-year. The US Department of State and American embassies abroad also use this style of notation. However, the US armed forces and their counterparts in some other countries, as well as civilians of British and many other nationalities, write the day first, followed by the month and year (for example, 3 May 1973). In Viet-Nam the American pacification agency CORDS, a part of the military command, used the military style.

In telegrams of the US military and some State Department messages, date-time group (DTG) notation is used to show when the message was transmitted. In this system, the first two digits indicate the day, the next four followed by the letter Z denote the Greenwich mean time using the 24-hour clock, and finally listed are abbreviations of the month and year. Thus April 4, 1974, at 11:04 P.M. Greenwich mean time appears as 042304Z Apr 74. Some messages are identified only by the DTG.

In the interests of accuracy and authenticity, when quoting or citing the writings of US or foreign authors and institutions, I note dates as they have done.

Abbreviations

AAR	After-action report (of a military unit)
ABC	Indicators of the Hamlet Evaluation System: A–fully pacified, B–largely pacified, C–fairly secure and with some development
AC of S	Assistant Chief of Staff
ACVA	American Council of Voluntary Agencies for Foreign Service
ADB	Agricultural Development Bank
ADP	automated data processing
ADWV	Associate Director of USAID for War Victims
AFB	(US) Air Force Base
AFVN	American Friends of Viet-Nam
AGILE	a research project code name
AID	Agency for International Development
AIDAC	AID action, a telegram indicator
APC	Accelerated Pacification Campaign
APC	armored personnel carrier
ARPA	Advanced Research Projects Agency, US Department of Defense
ARVN	Army of the Republic of Viet-Nam
ASEAN	Association of Southeast Asian Nations
CA	Civil Affairs
CAP	Combined Action Program (US Marines)
CAP	Country Assistance Program
CARE	Cooperative for American Relief Everywhere

CCSR	Central Committee for Supply and Relief of Evacuees and War Victims
CIA	Central Intelligence Agency (US)
CIDG	Civil Irregular Defense Group of the Montagnards
CINCPAC	Commander in Chief, Pacific (or his headquarters)
CIP	Counterinsurgency Plan for Viet-Nam
CJCS	Chairman, Joint Chiefs of Staff (US)
CMH	Center of Military History
COMIGAL	Vietnamese Refugee Commission, 1954–57
COMUSMACV	Commander, US Military Assistance Command, Vietnam
ConGen	Consulate General
CORDS	Civil Operations for Revolutionary (later Rural) Development Support, a part of MACV
CORDS/REF	CORDS Refugee Division (later Directorate)
COSVN	VC southern headquarters
CPDC	Central Pacification and Development Council
CRC	Central Recovery Committee
CRS	Catholic Relief Services
CSM	corn-soya-milk blend
CTZ	Corps Tactical Zone
CVT	Confederation of Trade Unions of Viet-Nam
CYSS	Christian Youth Social Service of Viet-Nam
DAMO	Department of the Army—Military Operations
DAO	Defense Attaché's Office
DepCORDS	Deputy for CORDS, in a military region or at MACV
DFC	Deputy for CORDS (I CTZ)
DGBFA	Directorate General of Budget and Foreign Aid
DIA	Defense Intelligence Agency (US)
DMZ	Demilitarized Zone
DOD	Department of Defense (US)
DRVN	Democratic Republic of Viet-Nam (North Viet-Nam)
DTG	date-time group, a telegram indicator
EA	Bureau of East Asia Affairs, US Department of State
E&E	Emergency and Evacuation
FAC	forward air control
FFV	Field Force Vietnam (US)
FMCPac	Fleet Marine Force, Pacific
FR	*Foreign Relations*

FULRO	Front Unifié de Lutte des Races Opprimées (United Struggle Front for the Oppressed Races)
FWMAF	free-world military assistance forces
GAO	General Accounting Office (US)
GRVN	Government of the Republic of Viet-Nam
G-3	Plans and Operations Staff (military); also, the chief of that staff
GVN	Government of Viet-Nam
HAC	Headquarters Area Command of the US Army
H&I	harassment and interdiction
HES	hamlet evaluation system
HEW	US Department of Health, Education, and Welfare
HOS	health opinion survey
HSR	Human Sciences Research, Inc.
HSWR	Health, Social Welfare and Relief
IATF	Interagency Task Force for Indochina Refugees, 1975–76
ICC	International Control Commission
ICEM	Intergovernmental Committee for European Migration
ICMC	International Catholic Migration Committee
ICRC	International Committee of the Red Cross
IGA	Inspector General of Foreign Assistance (US)
IIS	Institute for International Solidarity (of Germany)
INR	Bureau of Intelligence and Research
INS	Immigration and Naturalization Service (US)
IRC	International Rescue Committee
IRO	International Refugee Organization
IUE	US International Union of Electrical Workers
IVS	International Voluntary Services
JCS	Joint Chiefs of Staff
JGS	Vietnamese Joint General Staff
JPRS	Joint Publications Research Service
JUSPAO	Joint United States Public Affairs Office
LDC	land development center (under 1957–61 program)
LDHB	Land Development and Hamlet Building program
LICROSS	League of Red Cross Societies
LOC	line of communication
MAAG	Military Assistance Advisory Group
MACCORDS	Military Assistance Command CORDS
MACV	Military Assistance Command, Vietnam

MAF	Marine Amphibious Force
MDEM	Ministry for the Development of Ethnic Minorities
MEDCAP	visits by US military medical teams
medevac	medical evacuation
MHSWR	Ministry of Health, Social Welfare and Relief, 1968–69
MOBDES	mobilization designee
MOE	Ministry of Education
MOH	Ministry of Health
MR	Military Region
MSU	Michigan State University
MSUG	Advisory Group of Michigan State University
MSW	Ministry of Social Welfare, 1964–67, 1969–75
MSWR	Ministry of Social Welfare and Refugees, 1967–68
NCWC	US National Catholic Welfare Conference
NIE	National Intelligence Estimate
NLF	National Liberation Front
NODIS	No distribution beyond addressee
non-com	noncomissioned officer
NRM	the Can-Lao Party
NSC	National Security Council
NVA	North Vietnamese Army (term used by the United States)
OASD (SA)	Office of the Assistant Secretary of Defense (Special Action)
OCO	Office of Civil Operations
ORC	Office of Refugee Coordination
ORM	Office of Refugee and Migration Affairs, Department of State
OXFAM	Oxford Famine Relief, a voluntary agency
PAVN	People's Army of Viet-Nam (term used by North Viet-Nam)
PF	Popular Forces
P&D	pacification and development
PL 480	Public Law 480 of 1954 as amended, the basic United States statute authorizing food aid abroad
PMS	*Pays Montagnard du Sud*
POL	petroleum
Polwar	political warfare
PP&P	Plans, Programs, and Policy Division of CORDS
PRG	Provisional Revolutionary Government
PSA	province senior advisor
PSDF	People's Self-Defense Forces
psyop	psychological operation

PX	(US military) post exchange
RAD	Research and Analysis Division of CORDS
RD	Revolutionary Development
RDC	Revolutionary Development Cadres
RE	CORDS Research and Evaluation Division
REF	Refugee Division (later Directorate) of CORDS
RF	Regional Forces
ROK	Republic of Korea
RPDC	Regional Pacification and Development Council
RTV	return to village
RVN	Republic of Viet-Nam
RVNAF	RVN Armed Forces
SCA	Bureau of Security and Consular Affairs
SCR	Special Commissariat for Refugees
SDC	Self-Defense Cadres
SECDEF	Secretary of Defense
Sitrep	Situation Report
SOP	standard operating procedure
S/R	Special Assistant to the Secretary of State for Refugee and Migration Affairs
S/R:ORM	Special Assistant to the Secretary of State for Refugee and Migration Affairs: Office of Refugee and Migration Affairs
SSZ	specified strike zone
SW	social welfare
SWR	Social Welfare and Refugees
TAOR	tactical area of operations
TFO	Task Force Oregon
UNHCR	United Nations High Commissioner for Refugees
UNICEF	United Nations Children's Emergency Fund
USAID	United States AID Mission
USARV	US Army, Vietnam
USIA	US Information Agency
USIS	US Information Service
USOM	United States Operations Mission (predecessor of USAID)
USSAG	US Special Action Group
VC	Viet-Cong
VIS	Vietnamese Information Service
VNAF	Vietnamese Air Force
VNCS	Vietnam Christian Service

volag	voluntary agency
VPVN	Voluntary Physicians for Vietnam
VSD	village self-development
WIA	wounded in action
WRC	World Relief Commission
WSAG	Washington Special Action Group
WVD	War Victims Directorate of CORDS and then USAID
Z	Zulu, Greenwich mean time (indicator in date-time group)

North Viet-Nam

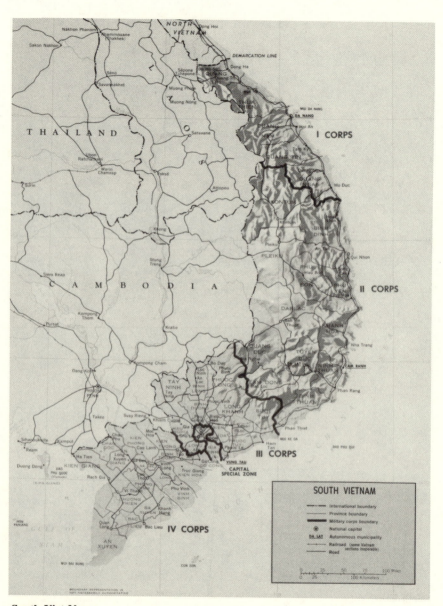

South Viet-Nam

VICTIMS
AND
SURVIVORS

1

Viet-Nam: Exodus from the North and Movement to the North, 1954–55

The flight of people from the Communist Viet-Minh or from French occupying forces and from the fighting began during the French-Vietnamese war, well before the Geneva accords of July 21, 1954, which ended that struggle and divided the country at the 17th parallel and the Ben-Hai River. Those who left Viet-Minh controlled areas for ideological reasons or because they could no longer stand the exactions in men and material support of the Communists generally settled in or near the cities. In the North, some strong Catholic parishes and dioceses, defended by the French Union forces and their own militia, kept the Viet-Minh out of certain areas, especially in the Red River Delta. A Catholic source estimated that in 1954 there were some 1,133,000 Catholics in 10 dioceses above the 17th parallel plus a section of Hue diocese, whereas there were only about 461,000 in six vicariates in the South.[1] Nam-Dinh, Bui-Chu, Phat-Diem, and Ninh-Binh provinces were areas of Catholic concentration in the North. There were also at least nine Catholic refugee villages outside these provinces which were being supported by the Bao Dai government and the United States Aid Mission, including Khoai-Lac, about 20 miles northeast of Haiphong port.[2]

In 1946, the revolutionary government of Ho Chi Minh forced many people to move to the countryside from Hanoi and other northern cities, and demolished their houses. However, as the fighting with the French swept over many rural areas, some of these evacuees moved back into the cities.[3]

About 55,000 Vietnamese from the North fled to Thailand during the period 1946–48; some were sympathetic to the Viet-Minh.[4] The Thai authorities, concerned for the security of their country, have been trying unsuccessfully to get them repatriated ever since. This was the only substantial group of refugees which left the Indochinese countries before 1975.[5]

After the defeat of the French force at Dien-Bien-Phu on May 7, 1954, the

Laniel government planned the withdrawal of troops from outlying areas of the Red River Delta, shortening their lines in order to protect Hanoi, Haiphong, and the connecting road. The withdrawal from Phat-Diem, Bui-Chu, Nam-Dinh, Phu-Ly, and Ninh-Binh occurred in late June and early July.[6] Laniel's successor, Premier Mendès-France, told Ambassador Douglas Dillon on July 2 that the French had offered to provide transportation for those of the local population who desired to move with them, but many had preferred to stay where they were. He added that since Dien-Bien-Phu, the Viet-Minh had behaved very well toward the local population, which might have been a temporary policy to facilitate the Geneva negotiations.[7]

Another group of people who fled from the Communists in North Viet-Nam before the end of the French regime was the Thai Dam ("Black Thai," so called because of their dress). Many of them had lived around Dien-Bien-Phu, near the border with Laos, and three or four major families had collaborated with the French. Some were then evacuated to Hanoi in 1952, and in 1954 about 5,000 were evacuated from Hanoi to Xieng Khouang, Laos. Later, another 5,000 fled into northern Laos.[8]

THE GENEVA ACCORDS AND THEIR IMPLEMENTATION

During the Geneva negotiations in June 1954, President Eisenhower, Secretary of State John Foster Dulles, and British Prime Minister Winston Churchill and Foreign Secretary Anthony Eden agreed on seven conditions under which their two governments would be willing to respect a settlement. The sixth of these was that the agreement: "Provides for the peaceful and humane transfer, under international supervision, of those people desiring to be moved from one zone to another of Vietnam."[9] During his conversation with Prime Minister Mendès-France on July 2, Ambassador Douglas Dillon took this up. His telegraphed report read:

Regarding the right of population transfer as contained in paragraph 6 of Deptel 4853, Mendes said that he was thoroughly in accord that this would be a good thing from the French point of view. He said that it had been mentioned to the Viet Minh in Geneva and that they had made no answer either favorable or unfavorable. When I reiterated the importance that we attach to this subject, Mendès made a note of it and said that he was writing Chauvel [the French delegate at the Geneva Conference] tonight and would include in his letter of instruction a reference to this subject. I think it would be useful if Johnson [U. Alexis Johnson, Deputy Undersecretary of State, the US delegate] would stress this subject in his next talk with Chauvel.[10]

Thus, it appears that the concept of allowing free movement of populations between the two zones originated in both the Anglo-American and the French governments more or less simultaneously. It was accepted by the Communist governments as well and appeared in the Geneva accords as article 14(*d*), as follows:

From the date of entry into force of the present agreement until the movement of troops is completed, any civilians residing in a district controlled by one party who wish to go and live in the zone assigned to the other party shall be permitted and helped to do so by the authorities in that district.

The Final Declaration of the Conference reinforced this provision in paragraph 8:

The provisions of the agreements on the cessation of hostilities intended to ensure the protection of individuals and of property must be most strictly applied and must, in particular, allow everyone in Vietnam to decide freely in which zone he wishes to live.

An International Control Commission (ICC) composed of representatives of India, Canada, and Poland, was provided to supervise implementation of the accords. Its Freedom Committee was made responsible for article 14(*c*), prohibiting reprisals against persons and organizations on account of their activities during the hostilities, and article 14(*d*).

The withdrawal of French Union troops from the Hanoi area was scheduled to end on October 11, 1954, from Haiduong on October 31, 1954, and from Haiphong on May 27, 1955. May 18 was the deadline for the movement of civilians. Similar schedules were agreed upon for the withdrawal of Viet-Minh forces from the South. This gave 300 days to transfer all civilians who wished to move from either zone.

The accords were subscribed to by France, England, the USSR, China, Cambodia, Laos, and the Democratic Republic of Viet-Nam (North Viet-Nam, henceforth referred to as the DRVN). The Bao-Dai government of South Viet-Nam, whose new Prime Minister, Ngo Dinh Diem, had just taken office in the middle of the Geneva Conference (July 7), had not been invited to participate, and protested the agreements, while accepting article 14(*d*). The United States also did not sign, but pledged to respect the accords.

The Government of Viet-Nam (GVN) actively discouraged migration from the South to the North, mainly by administrative obfuscation, and the United States targeted the Viet-Minh with a propaganda campaign against moving.[11] However, evidently under instructions relayed by Communist Party cadres in the South, somewhere between 130,000 and 140,000 armed soldiers, political cadres, and dependents moved to the North, and they were apparently not seriously impeded by the GVN authorities.[12]

About 90,000 armed Viet-Minh and 40,000 dependents were transported north by Polish and Soviet ships, while something over 4,000 went by other transport. 10,000 of the regroupees were highlanders and about 10,000 were children. Those who went were told that they would return to the South after the elections which, under the Geneva accords, were to be held in July 1956 (but which Diem, with US backing, refused to hold on the ground that democratic elections could not be held in the North).[13] According to one province-level Communist leader who later defected, Viet-Minh military forces, specialists, and those party members who had incurred the enmity of the people, were ordered by the party to go north, while political cadres and military personnel with political abilities were instructed to remain in the South.[14] This corresponds with other intelligence information. It was estimated that about 5,000 armed Viet-Minh, 3,000 political cadres, and an unknown number of dependents were left behind.[15] Many if not most of those regrouped to the North were reinfiltrated into the South after guerrilla warfare intensified in the 1960s.

In North Viet-Nam, after a few days of free movement to assembly points in Hanoi, Haiduong, and Haiphong demonstrated that many tens of thousands wanted to migrate to the South, the DRVN and the Viet-Minh applied increasingly brutal restrictions on movement, in violation of article 14(d). In some places, crowds of women and children were organized to stop trucks carrying refugees. Other obstructive actions included the distribution of tracts exhorting people not to evacuate, refusing to issue movement passes or requiring large payments for them, military blocking of roads, forcible separation of children from their parents, armed patrolling of coasts and firing in front of departing vessels, forbidding ferries, trucks, and buses from carrying refugees, blowing up bridges to prevent refugees from passing, forbidding the sale of property by persons wishing to depart, and torture and other forms of physical violence against those attempting to leave.[16]

In his book about the exodus, Thomas A. Dooley, who as a young US Navy lieutenant was put in charge of building and providing medical services to refugee assembly camps in Hanoi in 1954-55, recounted many instances of Communist torture and other atrocities committed on people trying to escape to freedom or simply practicing their religion.[17] For example, in November 1954, a boy came to the camp with a dangling ear which had been partly torn off with pincers for "listening to evil words." The evil words were the Lord's Prayer. The boy had come from the province of Bao-Lac, near the frontier with China. Dooley amputated the ear, one of several such cases. The next year, as he was disembarking at Hickam Field in Hawaii, Lt. Dooley was greeted by a group of Vietnamese Navy cadets, each without an ear, who were traveling to the United States for training as mechanics.[18] He had treated children who had had chopsticks driven into their middle ears and old women whose collar bones had been shattered by rifle butts, as well as a priest into whose head nails had been driven to make a crown of thorns. Dooley said that from December 1954 until the camps closed in May 1955, two or three atrocities a week came within his orbit. Priests, he wrote, were by far the most common objects of Communist terror.[19]

The ICC had inspection teams moving about both South and North Viet-Nam, but the Polish members systematically obstructed action to protect those attempting to flee. Dooley took horribly beaten refugees to the ICC team, where they told their stories but then were sent back to the camp, because the Polish team member wanted proof that was unobtainable.[20] Commander Menon, the Indian member and president of the ICC Fixed Team, told a US Embassy attaché in September 1954 that groups prevented from leaving on several occasions complained to the commission teams; the Polish members saw the complaints and then the group leaders would be murdered or disappear.[21] Nevertheless, the commission was able to publicize some instances of DRV efforts to prevent people from leaving, and sometimes these protests induced the DRV to allow people to depart.

Occasionally the Vietnamese National Army, the French forces, and the US Navy intervened to help the refugees escape. Major General Nguyen Duy Hinh told how, as a young commander of an armored unit stationed about 10 kilometers north of Hai-Duong, one week after the cease-fire he observed how a Viet-Minh cordon prevented the Catholic villagers of Kim-Bich from leaving; in order to deliver them, he maneuvered his unit through the cordon.[22] In cooperation with the Catholic underground organization of Bui-Chu, US and French Navy ships rescued about 18,000 from that province in an operation that lasted two nights and days, November 30–December 1, 1954, until Viet-Minh soldiers stopped the flow.[23]

It seems likely that many more people would have gone south had there been less harassment by the DRVN and the Viet-Minh.

Right after the conclusion of the Geneva Conference, the French declared that they would take complete responsibility for the transport of all Vietnamese who decided to rejoin territory controlled by the French Union.[24] However, both Diem and the local administration in Hanoi asked for American help, which the embassy endorsed. The embassy requested the urgent shipment of 2,000 20-man tents as a starter for emergency shelter.[25] Early in August, American Ambassador Donald Heath, after two days of visiting refugee camps and reception centers in Hanoi and Haiphong, reported his conclusion that the French had neither the transport nor the organization to live up to their promise to move all the Vietnamese who wished to take refuge in the South. They hoped to evacuate only 80,000 during August whereas, according to Vietnamese figures which he believed were probably roughly accurate, some 120,000 refugees were already in Hanoi, Haiduong, and Haiphong, with more coming in, not counting the residents of those cities who would want to leave. The Vietnamese refugee administration estimated that there would be at least 700,000 refugees. Prime Minister Diem orally on August 4 and the Foreign Ministry in a note handed to Health on August 5 asked that the US provide transport to bring the scheduled evacuation up to 160,000 by August 15. The next day, the French Deputy Commissioner General and the Chief of Staff to General Ely (the French Commander) formally requested US surface transport for up to 100,000 refugees a month above what the French could carry. Ambassador Heath recommended urgently that this request be met for two months, adding that more might be needed.[26] The Defense Department requested the Navy to direct CINCPAC (Commander in Chief, Pacific) to initiate evacuation action, and on August 12, CINCPAC reported that preparations were underway to lift 100,000 a month by sea.[27]

The US Navy thereupon formed Task Force 90 for the purpose of carrying out the evacuation. It was named Operation Passage to Freedom, and its deeds became legendary. Cargo vessels and tank carriers were quickly converted to accommodate the thousands of people who would be crowded onto them, and the task force proceeded on August 12 from Subic Bay, the Philippines, to Haiphong, finishing the ship conversions at sea. After serving on one of the first evacuation voyages, Tom Dooley and his corpsmen set up additional reception camps in Haiphong with the help of Mike Adler, head of the US economic aid organization (United States Operations Mission, or USOM) in the area. Rough American sailors tenderly carried the sick and injured on board the ships, calmed the fears of their simple peasant passengers, learned to prepare rice the Vietnamese way, played with the children, and endeared themselves to the people. There was close cooperation with the French Navy and Air Force, which, in addition to evacuating French troops and dependents, also carried most of the refugees. During the height of the movement, a French plane took off from Hanoi (later Haiphong) every 10 minutes, night and day, while American and French ships departed as fast as the refugees could be loaded aboard.

By the end of Operation Exodus (as the GVN named it), 768,672 refugees had been transported by allied carriers (213,635 by French planes, 235,000 by French ships, 310,848 by US ships, and 9,189 by British and other ships). About 109,000 escaped by their own means.[28]

RECEPTION AND RESETTLEMENT IN THE SOUTH

The Government of South Viet-Nam (GVN) had organized a Refugee Commission (COMIGAL) headed by Bui Van Luong, and the US Ambassador had appointed Military Assistance Advisory Group Chief Lieutenant General John W. O'Daniel to take charge of American support. He coordinated the US, French, and Vietnamese shore-based evacuation activities at Haiphong and the reception of the refugees at the port of Cap St. Jacques (later renamed Vung-Tau) and Saigon. The first arrivals in Saigon were housed in 100 tents at the Phu-Tho Hippodrome; then schools, warehouses, hospitals, churches, and other buildings were pressed into service, including the Municipal Theater in the center of the city (which later became the seat of the National Assembly). The USOM and the French provided tents and other supplies. The Vietnamese Army (Army of the Republic of Viet-Nam; or ARVN) was made responsible for operating the reception centers in Saigon; province chiefs were in charge of reception in their provinces.

There were daily meetings of the Joint Coordination Committee for Refugees chaired by Commissioner General Luong and including General O'Daniel; D. C. Lavergne, Deputy Director of the USOM Refugee Division; Most Rev. Pham

Ngoc Chi, former Bishop of Bui-Chu, appointed by the Vatican to be Bishop of the Refugees; General Gambiez of the French Army; and others.

Subsistence allowances of the refugees had been set at 12 piasters (p.) a day for adults and 5 p. for children in Haiphong (at 35.5 = $1 US). This was reduced to 10 and 5 p. in the South, where costs were less. On October 20, the system was revised to provide 100 p. on arrival and 700 p. when the refugees reached the resettlement area, and a final revision provided a lump sum of 800 p. upon arrival and an additional 200 p. for those settling in the Highlands. Rice was distributed for the first 7 to 10 days, and later during the resettlement process until the refugees became self-sufficient. The GVN's official report on Operation Exodus admitted that a few cases occurred of officials absconding with funds and that there was some fraud in the distribution of allowances, but said, "The important consideration, however, is that the refugees were fed and clothed and cared for throughout the emergency at a reasonable cost."[29] This seems to be an accurate appraisal of the operation.

Exact figures on the number of refugees are unavailable, because the head-quarters and files of COMIGAL were burned during the fighting between the GVN and the Binh-Xuyen in early May 1955. Commissioner General Luong provided a statistical summary in 1959, which, while open to some criticism, is probably "in the ball park" (table 1).

What were the motives of these refugees and migrants? Why would almost a tenth of the population of North Viet-Nam, attached to their land, homes, pos-sessions, jobs, and associations, leave all these behind after a victory which made the Viet-Minh so popular in the country that, in the opinion of at least one historian they would have won in any free elections?[30] First, the French Union forces, including the National Army of Viet-Nam, had to get out, under the provisions of the Geneva accords; and, unlike the Viet-Minh in the South, they did not leave stay-behind cadres, although some Vietnamese soldiers de-serted when their dependents could not or would not go with them.[31] Second, many Catholics were persecuted for practicing their religion, and others feared that they would be. Moreover, as the Pentagon Papers reported:

Almost as soon as the [1954] truce became effective, the Catholic bishops entered into a test of power with the Viet Minh, using their "self-defense" forces to balk DRV occupation. The response was predictably ruthless: Catholic villages were attacked by PAVN [People's Army of Viet-Nam] troops, and in two instances, inhabitants reportedly were massacred; churches were burned, Church property confiscated, priests tortured or jailed, and heavy taxes levied on Church lands and buildings. Among the consequences of that violence was a Catholic propaganda campaign against the Viet Minh—e.g., the-Virgin-had-gone-South theme—and mass migrations of whole parishes.[32]

As the statistics show, the overwhelming majority of those who left were Cath-olics. What about the others, those whom Luong labeled Buddhists and Prot-estants? (It is doubtful that all the refugees were adherents of organized religions.)

Table 1
Refugees from the North in South Viet-Nam

Total refugees in Free Viet-Nam	928,152
According to ethnic origin	
Vietnamese, living in the delta	913,358
Nung mountain people	13,306
Muong and Man mt. people	1,488
According to profession	
Farmers	706,026
Fishermen	88,850
Artisans, small businessmen, students, govt. employees, professionals	133,276
According to religion	
Catholics	794,876
Buddhists and Protestants	133,276
Total	928,152
These figures exclude military and quasi-military personnel, approximately	120,000

Source: Bui Van Luong, "The Role of Friendly Nations," in *Vietnam: The First Five Years, an International Symposium*, ed. Richard A. Lindholm (East Lansing: Michigan State University Press, 1959), 49.

Many of them also had reasons to hate and fear the Communists, especially if they had been wealthy or had collaborated with the French. A number of late-arriving refugees at the Haiphong reception centers told US Navy personnel that they wanted to leave less for religious reasons than because of the hard work which they were compelled to do without pay, high taxes, constant marauding and lawlessness, and intense Communist indoctrination.[33] Many of these pressures were experienced over and over again in subsequent years by refugees from Viet-Cong domination in South Viet-Nam. Wherever they ruled, the Vietnamese Communists were ruthless and demanding taskmasters. To these factors must be added one other: The overpopulation of the North, which for generations had pushed Vietnamese down to the underpopulated South, with its abundant land and shortage of manpower. Joseph Buttinger put it this way:

But they followed their desire because to move South has been for centuries the answer to the most terrifying social problem of Vietnam—the problem of local overpopulation. Vietnamese peasants have gone from the North to the South in search of land, and sometimes also in search of freedom, for at least one thousand years.[34]

Thus, although the 900,000 who moved south in 1954–55 were properly called refugees, in that they were fleeing Communist oppression and persecution, many were also economic migrants, in search of new opportunity and a new life.

They did not lose their identity in the South. They came in groups and were kept together as families and neighbors. Primarily responsible were the village priests, but the GVN also encouraged the preservation of their social structures. Even at the reception centers at Cap St. Jacques, signs were posted along the quay showing debarking refugees where people from their villages were congregating.[35] Generally they stayed together in the temporary camps and were later resettled together in the countryside or in cities.

In addition to intergovernmental assistance, principally from the United States, there was an outpouring of generosity from private voluntary agencies in aid of the refugees. The US National Catholic Welfare Conference (NCWC) was one of the first on the scene. Led by the dedicated and compassionate Monsignor Joseph J. Harnett, who was described by one of his colleagues as looking more like a decent dockworker than a priest—"something purely American and good"—the NCWC workers in the first ten months of their operation distributed to the refugees and other needy people food, clothing, medicines, and other supplies valued at $4,571,316 US. By the end of 1957, the value of the aid supplied by NCWC and its successor Catholic Relief Services (CRS) had increased to $35,000,000 US.

Supplementing the official resettlement program, which was slow in disbursing funds, CRS provided rice, trucks, tractors with farm implements, chain saws, water pumps, looms, and other necessities to the refugees clearing land. It organized a network of villages under the leadership of 30 specially trained priests and required them to submit detailed development plans, the format of which Msgr. Harnett said had been agreed upon with COMIGAL and the US Operations Mission (USOM). It helped villagers to acquire land titles from the government. By the end of 1956, CRS had assisted over 20 villages in resettlement projects, among them the villages of Hanoi and Phuoc Ly in Bien-Hoa province with over 50,000 refugees.[36] However, another participant/observer of the resettlement program reported that for many priests who had been leaders in settled communities in the North, the tasks of resettlement were too demanding; Msgr. Harnett had overestimated their capabilities, he said. USOM did not adopt all the plans prepared by the priests, some of which were too costly and not technically valid. The parishioners, however, quickly realized the doubtful performance of their priests as administrators, and the Church itself preferred that the priests limit themselves to spiritual work.[37] CRS also assisted in the establishment and maintenance of orphanages (some of which had moved as units from the North), hospitals, schools, and, of course, churches. It continued its humanitarian work throughout the ensuing years until 1975.

Scarcely had the Geneva accords been concluded than Leo Cherne arrived in Saigon to confer with Prime Minister Ngo Dinh Diem and to explore how the International Rescue Committee (IRC), of which he was chairman, could help. IRC, founded in 1933 to help victims of Nazi Germany, was much smaller than NCWC/CRS and was not equipped to handle large assistance programs involving procurement of food, tractors, and so forth. When Cherne reported to IRC's board, it decided to send the agency's vice chairman, Joseph Buttinger, to organize a relief program. The decision had consequences far beyond the modest assistance program that ensued. Buttinger, who had led the Austrian Socialist underground during the Dollfuss regime and fled to France and then the US during the Hitler years, had been IRC's first director in postwar Europe and later became increasingly active in many charitable and political causes in New York City. Upon his arrival in Saigon in late October 1954, he was immediately introduced to Diem, with whom he formed a close friendship which was terminated only in the early 1960s, when he broke with Diem's dictatorial repression of non-Communist oppositionalists. He also took an immediate liking to Msgr. Harnett.

On October 29, after visiting disembarking refugees, Buttinger wrote in his diary: "Remarkable faces, incredible misery, but no cold, and probably also no hunger—the two aspects of European postwar refugees I found worst in 45 and 46." After a subsequent conversation with Diem, Buttinger wrote:

He was very animated. Spoke much about his difficulties with the French, has a deep resentment which he has trouble to hide. The refugees are permanently on his mind. He said the French counted on 60,000 maximum. If there had been the kind of leadership that was provided in the catholic [sic] villages by the priests, he thinks there would have been 2 million, instead of 500,000 . . . . Only a direct appeal to Mr. Eisenhower by the president made the evacuation of hundreds of thousands of refugees from the North possible.

On November 7, Buttinger had dinner with Diem, his Secretary of State Dr. Tin, Msgr. Harnett, a bishop from the North, and another official; the conversation was mainly about the refugee problem and Communism. After the Vietnamese left, Diem kept Msgr. Harnett and Buttinger until 10:30, "talking all the time and smoking a whole pack of cigarettes."[38]

Buttinger found about 5,000 refugee secondary-school children in and around Saigon, and about 800 university students. He decided to concentrate IRC aid on these students and the Hanoi University professors who had escaped with them. Most were receiving small allowances from COMIGAL until their parents were resettled in other locations, at which time the allowances were cut off in Saigon. However, the students refused to go since they would be unable to continue their schooling in the country. Consequently, Buttinger found them working in the daytime and attending classes in the evenings, sometimes by candlelight in their crowded quarters in the Municipal Theater. He arranged to provide clothing, school supplies, and small allowances, and then IRC built a dormitory. In a speech to a gathering at his home on January 29, 1955, Buttinger said:

But when I met them I had this strange feeling of being confronted with a need which I've never noticed in any of the [other] countries where refugee work is done. With a spiritual and a moral need, primarily, and not of material, and once they felt that there was somebody whom they can see whenever they like—the theatre was fortunately just across the street from this place where our office was—they came every second day, a little delegation of three or four boys, excusing themselves very politely, pushing the one that speaks the best French forward . . . These people [were] desirous of study, and able to get the learning which they could absorb.[39]

In response to his appeal to the IRC Freedom Fund, shipments of food, clothing, medicines, and money began to arrive from the United States. Part of the appeal was for support to establish a Free University in Saigon, for at that time the only university in the country was in Hanoi but most of the students and professors had fled to the South. IRC did help to establish the University of Saigon. After a visit to the northern provinces, Buttinger also began assisting what became the University of Hue, and that support was continued for many years.[40]

After Buttinger's return to the United States in December 1954, he, Leo Cherne, and a number of others formed the American Friends of Vietnam (AFVN), with General O'Daniel as chairman and Buttinger as vice chairman.[41] At that time, the Diem government was besieged from all sides—by the army under a pro-French general, the religious sects, the Binh-Xuyen (a kind of Mafia which the French had put in charge of the police), and the Viet-Minh, which retained control of many areas where GVN presence had not yet been established. AFVN became in effect the Diem government's lobby in the United States. Its members were tireless in writing articles, making speeches, conferring with officials in Washington, countering negative newspaper reports (in many of which respected correspondents predicted the imminent fall of South Viet-Nam to the Communists or other enemies), and in other ways supporting Diem and his government. It was an influential group, which deserves much credit for overcoming hesitations at the highest levels of the US Government and winning its diplomatic, military, and economic support of the GVN. AFVN continued its work for many years, but Joseph Buttinger resigned from it in 1963 after several years of his growing disillusionment with Ngo Dinh Diem and his family entourage.

Operation Brotherhood, a program of the Philippine Junior Chamber of Commerce, was conceived when Oscar Arellano, Vice President for Asia of the International Jaycees, visited Saigon and had dinner with leaders of the Viet-Nam Jaycees, to which he also invited his old friend, Colonel Edward G. Lansdale, then an advisor on counterinsurgency at the American Embassy. The Vietnamese at the dinner included a doctor, a dentist, and a pharmacist. They described their concern at the health problems posed by the refugees coming from the North and the shortage of medical personnel in the South. Arellano offered to get Filipino medical volunteers to serve in Viet-Nam, an offer which was immediately taken up. Several weeks later, seven doctors and a nurse arrived and helped to set up a clinic in the main Saigon reception center. Jaycees in the United States also contributed funds, and soon there were 105 Filipino doctors and nurses. Then the International JCC (Junior Chambers of Commerce) adopted the project, and volunteers came from many other countries. They treated some 400,000 patients in the first year, and eventually established free clinics in many areas, serving not only refugees but others as well. They gave lectures in hygiene, nutrition, and home economics. The program was enlarged to include technical assistance in agriculture and fish culture. It was a tremendous success.[42]

Ninety-seven percent of the foreign-government monetary support of refugee relief and resettlement came from the United States, almost $56,000,000 in US Fiscal Year (FY) 1955 (ending June 30) and $37,000,000 in FY 1956. This was the largest component of US economic and technical assistance in FY 1955, and about 35% of such aid in FY 1956. In 1955, some $10,000,000 of the assistance went to reimburse the US Navy for its Operation Passage to Freedom, and additional amounts were used to finance temporary camps in both North and South Viet-Nam. Gradually, more and more of the aid went for permanent resettlement of the refugees, and this was granted through the International Cooperation Administration's usual project program system, which was slow, requiring as it did that projects be filtered first through the inexperienced bureaucracy of COMIGAL, then through the USOM.[43]

At the beginning, of course, resettlement sites had not even been selected; so the refugees were moved from the reception centers to quickly constructed villages, most of them in the greater Saigon area. There was land which would be suitable for settlement, but much of it was occupied or controlled by Viet-Minh forces and cadres who were to be moved north. When they had gone, the remaining population, who had been thoroughly indoctrinated, had to be brought under GVN control. Other areas, such as the Plain of Reeds (Plaine des Joncs) in the Mekong Delta, had been abandoned for years and the soil would have to be laboriously cleared and made suitable for cultivation. Also, it was impossible to know how many of the former owners and tenants would return to abandoned lands. Security would have to be provided, and that was not easy for a government whose position was tenuous at best. Thus, for example, one of the first permanent refugee villages, Phuoc-Ly, was completely burned out by the Binh-Xuyen on July 31, 1955—after their defeat in Saigon, destroying 190 houses and leaving 2,400 people homeless. The rebels took everything the refugees owned.[44] On account of such conditions, some refugee communities had to be moved to better sites where they could become self-supporting in relative security.

COMIGAL sent out prospecting commissions made up of experts and refugee representatives to the provinces in search of suitable resettlement sites. In co-operation with the province chiefs and local representatives, determinations were made. At first, project plans were drawn up by COMIGAL's Planning Office and, after approval by the Commissioner General, were sent to USOM. However, the Advisory Group of Michigan State University (MSUG), after making an extensive review in Saigon and the field in August and September 1955, rec-ommended a decentralization of the agency, creating provincial delegates in areas where there would be refugee concentrations to work with provincial committees for refugees and refugee village leaders in drawing up plans and supervising their implementation. This was done; provincial delegates were sent to Cho-Lon (then a municipality separate from Saigon), Gia-Dinh, Bien-Hoa, Dinh-Tuong, Tay-Ninh, and Binh-Thuan, where two thirds of the refugees set-tled, as well as to some other provinces. Generally, province chiefs allowed direct communication between the delegates and COMIGAL. Reviewing the program six months later, the MSU Group by random sampling found only a 7- to 12-day delay between the arrival of a project in Saigon and its submission to USOM. The Planning Division had used the interval to review and, if nec-essary, scale down projects. The MSUG also recommended that COMIGAL strengthen its own technical services, since the old-line Ministries and their field staffs only occasionally provided technical assistance, and that recommendation also was implemented. (This was the beginning of a trend that continued through-out the ensuing years, when successive Refugee Ministries—and also their Amer-ican advisory counterparts—hired their own experts and had their own budgets in food, building materials, sanitation, education and vocational training, small industry and handicrafts, agriculture, and other specialties, when the regular Ministries did not provide these forms of assistance, either because they were unable to or were simply not asked.) In June 1956, the Finance Minister finally decided to sweep away the antiquated and complicated payment procedures and to put responsibility largely in the hands of the refugees themselves; President Diem signed the necessary decree on June 12. The decree and details of projects and budgets were published in every refugee village.[45]

Jean Le Pichon, a French civil servant who served as a technical expert in COMIGAL from 1955 to 1957, wrote in retrospect that the Northern peasant was industrious and persevering but slow, stubborn, adjusted poorly to new methods, did not feel at home in the South, naively swallowed all propaganda lines. The farmers demanded that the government keep the promise made when they left home, granting, " 'a house, a hectare, a buffalo.' " He said, "A number of refugees developed a permanent 'social security' attitude. A few even became specialists in the art of 'freeloading' on official or private aid.'' However, the delays in disbursing American government assistance had a beneficial effect, according to Le Pichon: ''After the refugees saw that none of the administrative aid was materializing, they ceased to depend on it and had to make an effort themselves, which liberated many of them from the 'social security' complex, a serious obstacle to any resettling program.''[46]

Indeed, despite all obstacles, resettlement took place at an astonishingly rapid rate, and, unlike much of what was called refugee resettlement in later years, it was for the most part durable and viable. About 300,000 of the refugees, former government officials, and others either not entitled to official assistance or not willing to wait for it, resettled themselves, many of them in the greater Saigon area. By December 1954, some 271,208 others had been moved officially to relocation areas, a number that had been increased to 462,799 by April 1955. 150,000 of them were estimated to have adequate shelter, minimum essential public services, and employment. The population of Bien-Hoa province had doubled, to about 265,000, by August 1955, with 130,000 of them being refugees. The Province Chief had a committee made up of five priests paid by the province and five elected refugee representatives paid by COMIGAL. Each refugee village had a three-man committee elected by all residents over 18 years old. They in turn elected five sector committees. Honai, the most populous area, had 50,474 refugees in seven villages, named Hanoi, Haiphong, and so forth. Later, its population increased to 66,000, which was more than the area could support; so 16,000 were moved to other resettlement areas farther away from Saigon. Thai-Binh village with 11,500 was typical—overwhelmingly Catholic, with only 100 Buddhists. Father Pham Du Su was its recognized leader. The houses were mainly self-built, but government relief in money and kind had been received. The village had a 200-bed hospital, run by nine nurses and nine midwives, which was visited daily by doctors from Bien-Hoa town. Beri beri, a disease caused by a deficiency of vitamin B_1, was prevalent. There was occasional typhoid. Individual family latrines were the general rule. There was inadequate water during the dry season (October to May). The village had no land for farming, but there were extensive government-owned forests nearby. Six hundred men found work on a rubber plantation, others at an airbase 100 kilometers away, and still others in local small industry. At that time most of the 2,000 school-age children had no school, but 700 did. There were 132 blind and handicapped refugees. Thai-Binh means ''peace,'' and the village was peaceful.

There were many subprojects for clearing land by machine or by hand, building roads, digging wells, and so on. Hand tools, seed, and seedlings were provided. Fowl and piglets were given. There were long-term loans for water buffalo. (US AID spent $1 million for importing buffalo from Thailand; the animals quickly learned Vietnamese.) Sewing machines were given; loans provided sawmills, weaving looms, kilns, and so forth for small businesses. Loans were repaid to village funds controlled by province chiefs. Most subproject budgets included some maintenance assistance to the refugees until their first harvest or production of revenue. Fishermen presented the fewest rehabilitation problems. Grants and credits quickly turned them into productive citizens. Some had been initially settled away from the sea, but they were either relocated or moved themselves.

An example of a simple resettlement subproject was the movement of 1,036 refugees in 224 families from the south to Ba-Ngoi on Cam-Ranh Bay. The 150 fishermen were given the means to build boats. Seventy-four farm families were assisted with land clearance. The village quickly became self-sufficient and was integrated into Khanh-Hoa province. (When I visited it in 1969, Ba-Ngoi was prosperous. In the late 1960s, after the huge American air and naval base was built at Cam-Ranh, more refugees were moved there from overpopulated Binh-Dinh and provinces in I Corps Tactical Zone (CTZ) in order that they could work on the base.)

Go-Vap district, a partly urbanized area of Gia-Dinh province with over 30,600 refugees (of whom more than 20,000 were agricultural), was found to be overpopulated. Consequently, many were moved for resettlement elsewhere. Go-Vap was integrated into the province administrative and political system on June 30, 1957.

On December 21, 1955, President Diem announced the largest resettlement project in the entire program, the opening of a huge area of abandoned land named Cai-San for 100,000 people, mainly in Kien-Giang province from the Gulf of Siam extending back into An-Giang province. Each family was to be given 3 hectares (ha.) (7.5 acres) of land in tenancy, later to be bought by instalment payments, but the people would have to do most of the work to reclaim the smaller irrigation canals and clear the land. The offer was enthusiastically received. Within two years, beginning in January 1956, 100,000 did settle there, many of them from Honai, and they prepared 24,000 ha. (60,000 acres) for cultivation. After five years, the reclaimed land amounted to 77,000 ha. (192,500 acres). The project was the joint responsibility of five GVN Ministries under the supervision of the Director General of Plan. The Department of Land Reform took responsibility for land allocation and mechanical tilling. The Ministry of Public Works surveyed and dredged the major canals. ARVN provided security. President Diem visited the project often; he especially liked to hand out titles to land. In addition to rice, the secondary crops were bananas, sweet potatoes, and sugar cane.[47] Cai-San became a showpiece of the refugee resettlement program, and an anti-Communist stronghold. Bernard Fall wrote in 1959: "Every foreign dignitary, high or low, is given an opportunity to visit it. With its village-lined canals, its 90,000 inhabitants, its churches, hospital, tractor pool, motor launches, and airstrip, it is certainly one of the most ambitious undertakings of its kind anywhere."[48]

During 1957, emphasis shifted to the Highlands, and this turned out to be more controversial than resettlement in the lowlands. The approximately 15,000 northern highlander refugees, Nung, Muong, Yao, and Tai-speaking tribes, were resettled in the Central Highlands right away. However, Diem's objectives went well beyond that. He was concerned about integrating the Highlands into the new state, and one way to accomplish this was to settle Northern Catholic Vietnamese as well as people from the overcrowded Southern coastal plain in the mountains, to open them up and help "civilize" the tribespeople. About 17,000 lowland refugees in one Buddhist, one Protestant, and six Catholic villages were settled in the Blao area (which later became Lam-Dong province) 190 km. north of Saigon, where they raised tea, among other crops. Groups were planted in the Dalat and Ban Me Thuot areas, raising vegetables and coffee, and in other highland areas. They prospered with the help of Catholic Relief Services, but some were later attacked by the Viet-Cong and their inhabitants became refugees again.[49]

Bernard Fall reported that using refugees to "Vietnamize" the Highlands led to bitter complaints by the aboriginal population and, according to the MSU teams, there was evidence that it gave Communist propaganda a wider audience. However, Albert Cardinaux assessed the Central Highlands as "serving only as hideouts to hostile guerrillas," a view which Hickey, an eminent authority on that region, characterized as reflecting the prevalent lack of knowledge in Saigon.[50]

In all, 319 refugee villages with 605,000 inhabitants were formed under the aegis of the Refugee Commissariat. Two hundred eighty-eight of these were agricultural, 26 were fishing communities, and 5 were devoted mainly to artisanry. Two hundred seven of the villages were in the Mekong Delta, 50 in the central coastal lowlands, and 62 in the Highlands. The remaining 300,000 refugees had resettled themselves in the cities or the countryside. When the refugees in a village no longer needed government assistance, the Commissioner General handed the village over to the province chief who, taking into consideration its geographic position, population, and economic potential, let it stand as a village or incorporated it into an existing village. The administrative committee was thereupon dissolved, and the refugees elected a communal council or elected representatives to an existing village council. All expenditures for the refugees then devolved upon the province budget. Integration began in April 1956 and was completed in mid-1957. In the National Assembly elections of March 1956, there were already 12 refugee electoral areas.[51]

In sum, the movement of over 900,000 refugees from north to south and their resettlement in viable circumstances must be regarded as a tremendous success. It rescued a population that had been persecuted, and provided a valuable human resource to the underpopulated South. Much of the country's rapid economic rebirth in the late 1950s was due to the industry and hard work of the refugees. The emergency relief phase of the operation was carried on with commendable speed and efficiency by both the Vietnamese authorities and the international community, especially the United States. The resettlement phase was administered less efficiently, with delays in funding by both the US economic aid agency and the Vietnamese bureaucracy, but both finally became better organized. In

the meantime, the foreign and local voluntary agencies gave invaluable assistance, and their contribution to longer-term development of the refugees was
significant.

Many—some say too many—of South Viet-Nam's civilian and military leaders
in subsequent years sprang from the refugees, especially the Catholics. The
religious balance of Viet-Nam as a whole was drastically altered by the exodus.
In the North, the number of Catholics declined from 1,133,000 to 457,000,
while the number in the South jumped from 461,000 to 1,137,000, or one in
every 9.6 inhabitants. In 1956, the Diocese of Saigon had more practicing
Catholics than Paris or Rome, and about the same number as New York City.[52]
However, the transfer of so many strongly anti-Communist Catholics and others
who were embittered by their treatment at the hands of the Viet-Minh was a
significant factor in the political polarization of the two parts of Viet-Nam and
the unwillingness of the leaders on both sides to reach a compromise settlement
of their conflict. William K. Hitchcock, a senior Foreign Service Officer who
had been director of the US Refugee Directorate in Saigon in 1969–70, and then
Minister Counselor for Political Affairs in the American Embassy, put it this
way:

Hindsight suggests, however, that this concentration of Catholics in the South, educated
and intelligent as many of them were, provided a magnet which was a major factor in
the polarization of Northern and Southern views and fed the fire of the conflict for the
20 years after they arrived in SVN [South Viet-Nam]. This is admittedly a complicated
thought, and I don't want to be misunderstood. Certainly I am not suggesting that they
should have fallen down and let the Communists run over them. But I am convinced that
their presence in the South in such large numbers, associated with the success they had
in cornering so many of the levers of power, helped make VN a logical (and more
politically salable) place for an anti-Communist stand by the US. And at the same time
their strong role in the South strengthened SVN determination to resist while their departure from the North increased the resolve of the then purified Communist North.[53]

It is by no means certain that Ho Chi Minh and the other dogmatic Communist
leaders of the North would have been more flexible even if the refugees had
remained; the ruthlessness with which they killed peasants in the mid-1950s in
their drive to communize the countryside, their single-minded struggle for 20
years against what seemed like overwhelming odds to unite the country under
their rule, and their long-planned conquest of Laos and Cambodia after 1975
argue otherwise. However, we shall never know.

The presence of the refugees as an alien element throughout South Viet-Nam,
and their use by Diem and his successors as instruments to wipe out not only
Communists but also democratic oppositionists, also helped to polarize South
Vietnamese society, especially in the countryside. The authors of the Pentagon
Papers put it this way:

In the long run, however, Diem squandered the advantage the Geneva regroupment
brought him. His policies kept the refugees an unassimilated, special interest group,

which produced further distortions in an already stressed polity. They, in turn projected in rural areas an unfavorable image of the GVN, which probably figured in its eventual rejection by most Cochinchinese and non-Catholic Annamites: a government whose protection and largesse were extended preferentially to Catholics and northerners.[54]

I believe that the alienation of many peasants and city-dwellers alike from the GVN caused by the insensitive and fanatical methods of the government's officials and cadres, many of them northerners, weakened the cohesiveness of the country and furnished fertile ground for neutralism at best, and often for outright sympathy for the Viet-Cong.

2

Land Development, Highlander Resettlement, and Agrovilles, 1957–62

Even before the gigantic task of resettling the refugees from the North was completed, President Ngo Dinh Diem embarked on four experiments in social engineering, which had multiple aims. Diem's vision encompassed social, political-military, and economic restructuring of the country. He had long wished to integrate the Highlands into the state and to "civilize" the highlanders, or Montagnards, as both the French and the Americans called them. They comprised more than 600,000 people in over 20 ethnolinguistic groups living in the mountains from the 17th parallel (there were more north of that dividing line) for 750 kilometers to just north and west of Saigon. Some practiced swidden or slash-and-burn agriculture in the forests, rotating their fields every few years around their villages, but the largest tribes cultivated in a sedentary manner. For generations they had governed themselves, largely out of reach of central authority.[1]

Under the French, most of the Highlands had been Crown Domain, nominally property of the Vietnamese emperor but containing a number of French-owned plantations of rubber, coffee, tea, and other products, as well as the traditional lands of the highlander tribes. Diem envisaged economic development as a means of accomplishing integration, including bringing in Vietnamese from the over-populated coastal plain, where "there is too much sand and not enough soil." He got the Bao Dai to surrender his special powers in the Highlands, and on March 11, 1955, put the central Highlands (still called by their French name, *Pays Montagnard du Sud*, or PMS) under the administration of his government, appointing a delegate and replacing the French provincial officials with Vietnamese province chiefs. Diem drew heavily on a 1952 scheme of the Bao Dai, which among other features called for the settlement of highlanders in permanent villages, based on the erroneous notion that they were nomadic.[2] The Central Highlands officially became part of the Republic of Viet-Nam on October 23,

1955, the day of the election which abolished the monarchy and made Diem President of the Republic.[3]

Another important objective in Diem's mind was to create a "wall of [Vietnamese] humanity" along the borders with Laos and Cambodia and in the Communist-infiltrated areas both north and south of Saigon by settling loyal supporters, including refugees from the North, on lands that were thought to be little used. This would preempt the supply of Communist guerrillas from North Viet-Nam via Laos and Cambodia and inhibit raids against isolated farmers.[4]

Finally, Diem and his brother Ngo Dinh Nhu desired to consolidate the peasants of the Mekong Delta into large, defensible towns which would have schools, health facilities, other social amenities, and means of indoctrinating the people with the nationalist and "personalist" spirit.

THE LAND DEVELOPMENT PROGRAM

Late in 1956, a conference between Diem and Leland Barrows, the Director of the USOM (United States Operations Mission), developed the idea of the program. The American side saw it as an opportunity for the GVN, utilizing the skills acquired in the resettlement of the refugees, to open up the millions of hectares of supposedly idle land in the Highlands and other millions of hectares of abandoned land in the Mekong Delta. In April 1957, a project agreement was signed making $3,288,000 in dollar aid and 235,540,000 piasters (equivalent at the time to $6,729,742 US) of counterpart funds available, to which the GVN promised to add 44 million piasters (about $1,257,000 US equivalent). The purpose was stated as follows:

to assist the government of Viet-Nam in the permanent resettlement of 11,000 to 12,000 indigenous families (who are now in overpopulated areas of the country) on new lands or lands that were abandoned during the war. It will result, therefore, in putting into cultivation land that is presently non-productive. An additional, and important, factor is that the resettlement of loyal Vietnamese will greatly improve the security and stability of areas now, or recently subject to, anti-government influence.

Operations were started at high speed under military management, at Diem's order, without waiting for the conversion of the Commissariat for Refugees and Rehabilitation into the Commissariat for Land Development, which occurred in April 1957. (Bui Van Luong continued as the commissioner in the new agency.) Security demands outweighed considerations of economic and technical feasibility, and normal GVN administrative regulations were set aside in the haste to get moving. This resulted in a number of decisions that created hardship for the settlers and conflict with the USOM. Many villages were established during the rainy season, when houses could not be built or land properly worked. Some were established, usually for security reasons, on land that the American experts found unsuitable, and had to be subsidized when they could not be made self-supporting. Diem insisted on allocating only one hectare per family in the High-lands, as had been the practice in the Delta, though three to five were actually needed. Often hospitals, schools, and other facilities could not be used because equipment and supplies were not provided, maintenance was lacking, or permits were delayed. Centers in Pleiku, Ban Me Thuot, and elsewhere were used as detention centers for political prisoners, under army supervision. This broke into the open in June 1958, when the inhabitants of the village of Cu-Ty rose against its guards during a rainstorm, seizing weapons and vehicles and fleeing into Cambodia. After numerous attempts at resolving its differences with the GVN failed, and amidst recriminations on both sides, the USOM withdrew funds for the program in Fiscal Year 1958. However, the funds were reprogrammed for military assistance, and the Vietnamese government simply transferred its own military funds to land development. Curiously, once the US funding constraint had been removed, the Vietnamese paid greater attention to American technical advice and began to be more prudent in their own expenditures.[5]

By mid-1959, the program was considered fairly successful in economic terms. About 125,000 persons had been resettled on about 90 sites, including six centers for highlanders. About 50,000 hectares had been cleared, and over 20,000 houses had been built. Seventeen thousand of the settlers were refugees from the North, many of whom were relocated from overcrowded areas where they had originally settled. Some 6,000 were demobilized soldiers and their families. Where the land was not suitable for rice or the centers were too far from markets to make rice cultivation economical, industrial crops such as kenaf and ramie, which were not perishable, were grown. By 1960 there were 3,343 hectares planted to kenaf, 1,017 in ramie, 337 in cotton, 7,009 in rubber, 57 in lacquer trees, 379 in tea and coffee, and 134 in tobacco, almost all in the central Highlands. However, the most common crop in the resettlement centers was rice, with 45,323 hectares, mostly in the southern region; followed by vegetables, with 10,877, half of which were in the central Highlands. All told, 69,481 hectares were under cultivation. Most land was farmed communally, against the advice of the American experts, and this seemed to work. The villages were neat and orderly, with sanitary facilities much above the normal rural standard, health stations, and schools. Many had radios, information halls, and visiting theatrical troupes or movies. The centers were governed by appointed chiefs assisted by locally elected provisional administrative committees, pending integration into the regular village-hamlet system. Catholic Relief Services (CRS), CARE (Co-operative for American Relief Everywhere), and other voluntary agencies were assisting the settlers. As of October 1962, some 173 land development centers (LDCs) had been established with 210,460 people, 7,195 of whom were Mon-tagnards. Many of the LDCs were subsequently converted into strategic hamlets.[6]

The US consul in Hue reported early in 1959 and again in October of that year that three land development centers in Thua-Thien and Quang-Tri provinces had been singled out for special aid from the Can-Lao Party (NRM), which in Central Viet-Nam was under the tight control of Diem's younger brother, Ngo

Dinh Can. The NRM was directly in charge of the Nam-Dong center in Thua-Thien, and played an important role at Hoa-My in the same province, where Can himself maintained a house, and at Cua in Quang-Tri, which had the personal attention of the province chief. All three were partly funded from the province budgets, but were said to have received party funds also, as well as peasant labor for which the peasants "accepted" half-pay, rice rations, and other materials, whose source was unclear.[7]

However, the security goals were not always achieved. In some previously insecure areas in the Delta, the new settlers pushed Viet-Cong squatters off good rice land.[8] In other localities, goals had become confused when, in addition to moving loyal Christians to the Highlands, the government also moved from the coastal provinces which had previously been under Viet-Minh control families whom it considered unreliable. These settlements, though reinforced by some demobilized soldiers, were regarded as banishment camps, and many families slipped away.[9] Some of the best lands were not settled, awaiting action to secure them. By 1960, Communist assassinations were taking hundreds of lives each month, and people were fleeing the countryside.[10]

Did the settlers move to the land development centers voluntarily? Most evidently did, although those who had fled to the cities during the French war took some persuading. Henderson said, "It is to the credit of the Ngo regime that it chose on the whole to rely on persuasion rather than coercion." Some recruiting offices were besieged by applicants. Relatively few settlers abandoned their new homes, and there were long waiting lists of others to take their places. However, a few centers were detention camps for political opponents, who obviously did not volunteer to go.[11]

Moreover, the settlement of lowlanders in the Highlands caused concern to some members of the USOM. A report of January 22, 1957, prepared by a member of the Agriculture Division, recommended that "there should be a clear, just policy regarding Montagnard rights." It noted that there were traditional land rights, which had never been formally defined or recorded, and that failure to take the highlanders' claims into consideration could result in disaffection to the Communists. The report suggested that there should be payment for ownership rights, opening of new lands to the Montagnards as well as Vietnamese, and teaching of permanent cultivation methods through dialect-speaking agents.[12] These views were not widely shared in the USOM, however. Alfred Cardinaux's dissent has already been noted in chapter 1. Wolf Ladejinsky, President Diem's advisor on land reform, described the central Highlands as a wilderness, "little more than Bao Dai's hunting preserve," where "none but nomadic tribesmen lived."[13]

In May 1957, Dr. Gerald Hickey and Price Gittinger of the USOM Agriculture Division made a study of Rhadé tribal land tenure in the Ban Me Thuot area, where some of the first land development centers were to be established. In June they submitted two reports, both recommending that Rhadé land claims be honored and that compensation be paid to the guardians if Vietnamese were settled on their lands. Hickey also proposed that a joint Vietnamese-Rhadé commission be formed for the area, similar to one already set up by Colonel Le Van Kim, director of the land development program in the highlands. Diem was very upset by Hickey's report, which had included unfavorable quotations from representative Rhadé about the Vietnamese, and Ladejinsky was harshly critical of both reports. The American mission quietly agreed that land development would proceed without regard to highlander land claims. Diem also removed Colonel Kim, who had been paying compensation to the Montagnard land guardians.[14] Other Vietnamese moved into the region without settling in the centers. By 1963, some 40% of the population of Kontum, Pleiku, Phu-Bon, Tuyen-Duc, Lam-Dong, and Quang-Duc were Vietnamese.[15]

The incursions of the Vietnamese and their land grabbing were strongly resented by the Highland peoples, and this contributed to their disaffection from the government and made Communist propaganda more credible.[16] Some of the land which was taken in Tuyen-Duc, Lam-Dong, Darlac, Quang-Duc, and Lam-Dong provinces had been under sedentary agriculture for generations, as was the practice of the Jarai, Rhadé, Chru, Sre, Lat, and Bahnar tribes. They had been raising wet paddy rice, vegetables, coffee, fruit trees, and bamboo, and kept fish ponds.[17]

Some of the Vietnamese settlers were also unhappy, but for different reasons. The laterite soil required special care and was difficult to cultivate. Falciparum malaria, a particularly deadly variety against which lowlanders had built up no immunity, was endemic. Corruption deprived some of the settlers of the assistance that the government had promised them.[18] Last, the Highlands and some other land development areas were becoming increasingly insecure. After Diem's overthrow in November 1963, the land development program crumbled as many of the settlers fled. Dennis Duncanson, who had served in the British advisory mission to Diem, wrote that the only centers in the Highlands that remained were those whose inhabitants were ordered by the Communists to stay, continuing to draw subsidies and supplies from the government and passing on a share to the guerrillas. He added that the southern settlements were more durable, but were also complaisant to the Communists.[19]

THE HIGHLANDER RESETTLEMENT PROGRAM

The second of Diem's relocation efforts, the highlander resettlement program, regrouped the Montagnards into defensible communities, to decrease their vulnerability and ease the application of cultural uplift projects. Nominally part of the land development program, it was actually begun in 1955, when six settlements were founded. Highlander resettlement accelerated when land development was inaugurated. It made more Montagnard land available to the Vietnamese. Indeed, that seems to have been a principal reason for moving the highlanders. The Montagnards were regrouped along major roads, away from their traditional lands in the forest. The Jarai were put along Route 7B in Phu-Yen province, the Rhadé and some Roglai along Route 21 in Khanh-Hoa and Darlac; the Mnong, Maa, Cil, and Chru were moved to areas along Route 20 in Tuyen-Duc and Lam-Dong.[20] About 40,000 highlanders were regrouped in the fall of 1961 in Kontum province, equaling about half its tribal population. Some of the people refused to stay, but most remained in the new communities. At the end of 1963, there were 137 highlander centers with 90,000 inhabitants.[21] However, a number of the inhabitants in that year were refugees from the Viet-Cong and from the fighting which was intensifying in the mountainous areas. This program had effectively come to an end in 1962, however, when over 111,000 highlanders had become refugees by August.[22]

A particularly tragic relocation was that of some 6,000 Roglai from the mountains to the village of Tan-My between Phan-Rang and Phan-Thiet on Route 1. They were forced to live in houses built on the ground instead of their traditional houses on stilts, which had protected them against inundation during the rainy season. Over 600 died during the years 1957–59 from malaria, starvation, and the heat. Those who tried to leave were imprisoned. After propagandizing the people, the Viet-Cong attacked the village in 1961, rescuing its inhabitants, who went back into the Highlands. Many grouped together in Tuyen-Duc province, where the Chru helped them to resettle.[23]

A different approach was tried by Le Van Buong, chief of the newly created Binh-Tuy province in 1957. Finding that North Vietnamese cadres speaking the tribal language were living among the tribespeople in the mountains, he patiently visited the villages, learned their ways, and gradually got them to resettle, with the agreement of their priests, in four centers on 15,000 hectares of fertile land in the La-Nga River Valley. There he helped them to practice modern agriculture, improved sanitation, introduced education, and provided other assistance. The river was rich in fish. He was devoted to the people and genuinely desirous of bringing them into the modern world. An interviewer visited the Hieu-Tin center, where 1,139 persons were living. Some of the tribespeople went back into the mountains, but when they got hungry, they returned. The province chief was prepared for a long effort.[24]

Both the settlement of Vietnamese in the highlands and the efforts of the Diem regime to Vietnamize the highlanders alienated the Montagnards from the government. However, most were not driven into the arms of the Communists, although the Viet-Cong wooed them strongly. Instead, they formed their own nationalist movement, the Bajaraka, which demanded autonomy and equality with the Vietnamese.[25]

The Communists had their own program of relocating Montagnards as well as Vietnamese. After 1957, the Viet-Cong systematically relocated several thousand Katu in Quang-Nam into the jungles beyond the reach of the GVN. Embassy Saigon reported that the Consul at Hue, during a visit to Kontum in January 1960, was informed by the district chief of Dak Sut that during the three preceding weeks, the Communists had forced or persuaded three highlander villages to withdraw into the mountains out of GVN reach. They were used as labor on the

Ho Chi Minh Trail. In the fall of 1962, a contest developed between the government and the Viet-Cong in Quang-Tri for control of the Bru tribe; some came into government centers, while other Bru hamlets vanished into the VC-controlled jungle or into Laos. There were other such relocations by the Communists then and later.[26]

OTHER POPULATION RELOCATIONS

In February 1959, the GVN undertook a brief experiment, which had originated in the Interior Ministry, attempting to separate families with VC relatives or suspected of VC sympathies from loyal families while relocating villagers from indefensible areas. The former were placed in hamlets called *qui khu*, and the latter in *qui ap*. The criteria were vague, however, and were often only the opinions of local officials. Both those who were thus branded as disloyal (many of whom were highly placed) and the loyal families resented this clumsy forced movement. Diem appointed Major Pham Ngoc Thao, who himself had relatives in the North and was a deep-cover Communist agent, to study the problem. In his report, Thao said: "In the *qui khu* we grouped our enemies and gave them more reason to be against us. In the *qui ap* we grouped our friends without regard for economic and social considerations. We gave them reason to be unhappy with their lot and to turn against us." He suggested that, if there was to be consolidation, VC and nationalist families should not be labeled and segregated, and economic and social considerations should be seriously considered. Loans should be given to cover the hardships of moving. Hospitals, schools, and other amenities should be provided. However, by then the agroville concept (see below) had been adopted, and the *qui ap* and *qui khu* in Vy-Thuan were converted into the first agroville.[27] The program of segregated hamlets was abandoned.

AGROVILLES

By 1959, the insurgency against the GVN had reached a critical level, with 90 or more assassinations of officials and supporters of the government a month and spreading VC (Viet-Cong) control of the population. The programs of regrouping population were dominated by security considerations: to separate the guerrillas from the people and thus deprive them of labor, intelligence, and material support. The struggle against Communist terror had come to demand increasing resources and energies of the officials and was sapping effective government and economic activity. Many village and hamlet officials could no longer stay in their homes at night, and by day they went about with armed escort. It was in this atmosphere that a new regrouping program was conceived: to create large agglomerations of peasants beside major roads on which security forces could move, construct fences, establish guard posts, and control population movement; while providing schools, health facilities, and other services, including even electricity, and training the peasants in improved agricultural methods, to make the people's lives better.

On July 7, 1959, the fifth anniversary of Diem's assumption of office and an astrologically auspicious date (Double Seven Day), the President announced on the radio that:

This year I propose to create *densely populated settlement areas* (*khu thu mat*) in the countryside, where conditions are favorable to communication and sanitation and where minimum facilities for the grouping of farmers living in isolation and destitution in the back country exist. These settlement areas will not only improve the life of the rural population, but they will also constitute the economic units which will play an important role in the development of the country as a whole.

Not mentioned in the speech was the all-important security aim. This was spelled out in the instructions of the Minister of interior to province chiefs, the prefects of Saigon and Cholon, and the mayors of other large cities, as follows:

Following the President's Double Seven Day speech, one of the principal duties of 1959 will be the creation of agrovilles. The reason for this work is that the population, especially in the South, is living in such spread out manner that the government cannot protect them and they are obliged to furnish supplies to the Viet Cong. Therefore, it is necessary to concentrate this population, especially the families who have children still in the North or who are followers of the Viet Cong here. The echelons of government are requested to explain this policy to the people.

It was planned to group more than 500,000 people in the Mekong Delta between 1960 and 1963 into 80 *khu thu mat*, with whatever number of *ap tru mat* (hamlets) might be necessary, to develop competent cadres for village councils and administrative posts, replacing corrupt and inefficient officials who alienated the people, to improve village finance resources by developing public lands, increasing rice tax collections, encouraging taxable vehicles and so forth, and to form vigorous youth movements. Two years later, however, only 23 agrovilles had been built, with 40,000 people.[28]

The program was unpopular from the start. Peasants were required to move their houses, abandoning the tombs of their ancestors, and to live far away from their fields. In some cases they had to leave their farm animals behind. The work of digging canals and constructing fences and various facilities was unpaid and had to be done at high speed, sometimes during planting or harvest time, since higher headquarters imposed unrealistic timetables. Not even a food allowance was given. Some people were literally worked to death. Many villagers who were not to live in the new communities were drafted for forced labor. There was no US aid for the program, but the MSUG and other advisors pointed out that the government could use the counterpart of some of its large foreign exchange reserve to pay the workers. This was rejected by Nhu and Diem, who felt that the people should contribute their labor as a public duty. The Viet-Cong of course made the most of these negative factors and gained significantly from the popular disaffection. It burned and sacked some agrovilles, with little popular resistance, and assassinated unpopular officials and landowners.[29]

The American Embassy followed the agroville program closely and soon realized how its implementation was creating resentment among the peasants, which the Viet-Cong were exploiting. After a conversation with Diem on February 12, 1960, during which the President referred to the program and to what he called the success of the resettlement program in the high plateau and the Delta, Ambassador Elbridge Durbrow wrote:

Another factor which may explain in part the recent Viet Cong successes is the reported apathy of some of the rural population to the efforts being made by the Government to better their lot,—i.e., community development, resettlement and construction of "agrovilles." These reports indicate that bureaucrats have not properly explained the basic motivations and aims of the Government. Instead, they have concentrated on getting the job done by forcing the peasants to work excessively on community development projects or have in general been too autocratic in their dealings with the people. Thus, instead of winning over the rural population by these very worthwhile schemes, the bureaucrats have tended by their "get the job done" methods, to antagonize a considerable section of the rural population, who therefore are not cooperating with the Government in its anti-Communist campaign. It is possible, that the Communists are taking advantage of this growing attitude.[30]

In early March 1960, Ambassador Durbrow reported that signs of apathy and dissatisfaction among rural people had become more evident. Fear of the VC accounted for some of this, but so also did resentment of the GVN because of the coercive methods of officials. He continued:

There is a tendency to disregard the desires and feelings of the peasantry by, for instance, taking them away from their harvests to perform community work. The new agroville program requiring large numbers of "volunteer" laborers has accentuated this trend. Improper actions by local officials such as torture, extortion and corruption, many of which have been reported in the press, have also contributed to peasant dissatisfaction. Favoritism and fear of officials and members of the semi-covert Can Lao Party have likewise contributed to this situation.

Durbrow said that Diem was taking some actions to correct abuses, and that he evidently had ordered a slowdown in the construction of agrovilles. Diem told the Ambassador on February 22 that, while he must continue to create agrovilles, he was not planning to push too fast until one or two were in being, so that the peasants could learn of their advantages.[31]

On March 10, 1960, Ambassador Durbrow wrote that he had seen Diem the previous day and told him *inter alia* that the embassy was receiving an increasing number of reports of abuses by province chiefs and other officials, such as conscripting thousands of peasants to build agrovilles and other facilities, when only hundreds of workers were actually needed. Diem admitted that some excesses may have taken place and that he now found it necessary to slow down the construction of agrovilles.[32] On April 30, the Ambassador and several of his top aides, as well as officials of the GVN, visited the agroville at Vi-Thanh-Hoa-Luu, located about 60 kilometers southwest of Can-Tho in Phong-Dinh province. They found that this model community had required an enormous expenditure of labor and other resources for nonproductive purposes, much more than the already expensive land development centers. It was designed by an internationally recognized Vietnamese architect, and included a school, hospital, market, hotel, and elaborate artificial lakes, all visually attractive and substantial. This was probably due in part to the fact that Vi-Thanh was a demonstration project; some of the luxuries would not be duplicated elsewhere. The embassy despatch about the visit also contained the report that Diem had recently mentioned that the volunteers working on the agroville in Kien-Hoa province were receiving 10 piasters a day (equivalent to about 30¢ US in 1960) and that others working on future agrovilles would receive the same pay.[33] Evidently that was not done.

On October 14, Ambassador Durbrow saw Diem and read him a 14-page memorandum in French (a copy of which he gave the President) outlining a broad range of political problems which the US Government had found in the GVN's practices in meeting the increasingly serious Communist threat, and making suggestions for remedies. This démarche, originally proposed by Durbrow and slightly modified as a result of review by the relevant Washington agencies, represented the considered views of the United States Government. Diem received it as such. Most of the recommendations are beyond the scope of this book; the following ones, in section (9) of the memorandum, were intended to enhance support of the GVN in rural areas and are of particular relevance:

(d) Institute a system of modest Government payment for all community development labor whether on agrovilles or on other Government projects.

(e) Institute a system of limited subsidies to the inhabitants of agrovilles during the period of their readjustment. While the two situations are not completely comparable, the subsidies helped to bridge the period of adjustment for the settlers in the High Plateau. This should help to develop a favorable popular attitude toward the agrovilles by covering some of the expenses incurred in moving to and getting settled in the agrovilles.[34]

These suggestions were not adopted, and the agroville program was not resumed.

EVALUATION

All four of these programs failed or were abandoned. An important reason was the opposition of the Viet-Cong, which in a sense was a compliment since it meant that the VC considered them a threat. However, the principal causes of failure were otherwise. The programs were all conceptually flawed and badly managed, with little or no sensitivity to the customs, needs, and feelings of the people involved.

The land development program was basically sound in concept, to occupy abandoned and unoccupied lands, increase agricultural production, and spread security to the country's frontiers; but the policy was wrong in deliberately disregarding the land claims of the Highland tribes on whose territory a large proportion of the Vietnamese from the lowlands were settled. This error was concurred in by the USOM, and was not corrected when experience showed its damaging consequences. Instead, the GVN's director in the highlands, who had been paying compensation for land, was removed for his sin. The Montagnards, who were treated as ignorant savages, bitterly resented the intrusion on their lands and were alienated from the government as a result. They and the Vietnamese became lasting enemies, and they gave no help to the authorities or the settlers in resisting VC attacks on the land development centers. Moreover, against advice, Diem refused to allot more than one hectare of highland land to a family, a policy that ensured that the settlers in that region would have to remain on the dole, despite the new crops they were encouraged to cultivate. As Dennis Duncanson and Everett Bumgardner reported, at the end, only those settlements remained that suited the interests of the Communists. On the other hand, some of the settlements in the Delta seem to have become self-supporting; nonetheless, many succumbed to VC terror.

The highlander resettlement program, being based on the premise that the Montagnards needed civilizing, that is, Vietnamizing, as well as grouping for defense, flew in the face of the ancient customs of the tribes, and could not help producing further resentments. Moreover, to the extent that the regrouping required the highlanders to abandon their sturdy homes, treasured possessions, and land, it reduced their standard of living and quality of life. Administration, by insensitive lowlander officials, many of them northerners, was harsh. Some of the highlanders were induced or forced by the VC to move to Communist-controlled areas, and others simply returned to their former homes. Few Montagnards adopted Vietnamese ways, though some did take training in administration, agriculture, and other skills, which they then used to advance the welfare of their own people.

The segregated hamlets, *qui khu* and *qui ap*, were failures from the beginning, opposed by both the enemies and the partisans of the government, and that program was quickly abandoned.

Superficially attractive on economic, social, and security grounds, the agroville program could not work in the Delta. The flat, watery terrain and the pattern of land occupancy led to the spreading out of hamlets and villages along the rivers and canals, with the fields of each family stretching out in back of the houses. It was thus impossible to group more than a small number of families without forcing those at the edges to move far from their land. They then had the choice of abandoning their fields and cattle as well as their homes, or of walking or traveling by boat long distances to work their fields. The latter choice reduced the amount of time they could devote to cultivation, and also made them vulnerable to VC harassment while away from the defended community. It is true that at night they would theoretically be protected, assuming that the agroville was well guarded; however, since the VC political cadre and terrorists were not eliminated by the regrouping, even that was often not the case in practice. A number of agrovilles were destroyed by the VC, sometimes with little or no resistance. Moreover, the harsh requirements of unpaid forced labor, the corruption and inefficiency that deprived the settlers of the social and economic benefits that had been promised, and the general disruption of their lives attendant to moving, created lasting resentments on the part of the peasants which redounded to the benefit of the Communists.

Each of these programs was conceived in Saigon and centrally directed, usually by Diem himself and his brother Nhu. Their dogmatic misconceptions about the rural peoples, Vietnamese and Montagnards alike, with whose daily lives they had no contact and consequently no understanding, thus became the guidelines for the programs. Harsh, insensitive, corrupt, and inept administration in the provinces magnified the damage to the people whom the programs were supposed to help. Diem received considerable information and advice from some of his own officials, the American Ambassador, and others, who pointed out the unfortunate consequences of his policies; but this never shook his conviction that he understood his people better than his critics. So he deepened the crisis of confidence in the countryside and thus contributed to the growing power of the Communist-led insurgency.

3

The Strategic Hamlet Program, 1961–64

By the latter part of 1961, the Viet-Cong insurgency, now buttressed by rein-filtration from the North of cadres and troops who had been taken to North Viet-Nam after the 1954 Geneva accords, was reaching truly dangerous proportions. VC regular forces were estimated to have reached 25,000 and were being employed frequently in large units; the terrorist-guerrilla organization numbered about 17,000 by November; over 500 local GVN officials and civilians had been assassinated in the first half of the year, more than 1,000 had been kidnapped, and almost 1,500 personnel of the Republic of Viet-Nam Armed Forces (RVNAF) had been killed.[1] Arrayed against the insurgents were 150,000 troops of the Army of the Republic of Viet-Nam (ARVN) who had been organized and trained for conventional war, about 55,000 Civil Guards (later renamed Regional Forces), 40,000 members of the Self-Defense Corps (later Popular Forces) and 3,000 members of the National Police. Their superior numbers were no match for the fanatical and disciplined Viet-Cong, with their hit-and-run tactics and terror squads. Even earlier the VC already held the initiative in the countryside, controlled major portions of the population, and were drawing an increasingly tight noose around Saigon.[2] A series of high-level visits of American officials, beginning with Vice President Johnson in May 1961, and US-GVN conferences wrestled with the problem of how best to counter the threat. In September, the misfortunes of the Vietnamese people were further compounded by floods in the Mekong Delta, which created 320,000 refugees and destroyed 1,000 kilometers of roads and 4,000,000 hectares of rice and other crops. On October 19, President Diem declared a state of national emergency.[3]

The US Country Team in Saigon in late 1960 produced a Counterinsurgency Plan for Viet-Nam (CIP) setting out proposals for reorganizing both the civil and military sides of the GVN. It was augmented by the Geographically Phased

National Level Operation Plan for Counterinsurgency, which the Military Assistance Advisory Group (MAAG) issued on September 15, 1961, proposing a three-phase program for clearing and securing priority areas, reorienting the populace, and providing economic and social benefits to win its allegiance. First priority for 1962 operations was to go to six provinces around Saigon and to the Kontum area in the highlands. These plans did not arouse Diem's enthusiasm, despite intense selling efforts of Ambassador Durbrow and the MAAG Chief, General Lionel C. McGarr.[4]

SOURCES OF RURAL DISAFFECTION

One of the reasons for the increasing success of the insurgents was peasant resentment at the tactics of the RVNAF, partly taught by its American advisors, which involved using heavy firepower prior to ground assaults or as a sole means of attack, even in populated areas. Many observers pointed out that this was alienating the populations subjected to such damage and making new recruits or sympathizers for the enemy. One of the best informed wrote:

There is also considerable evidence to show that the South Vietnamese Army's response to the insurgency problems posed by Viet-Cong activities was frequently such as to alienate the traditionally suspicious rural people. Punitive artillery barrages on villages suspected of sheltering Communist agents, or the indiscriminate use of artillery and bombings have certainly played a part in Government operations. The Viet-Cong's execution of an official is an act of terrorism but it involves only one man and it can be cloaked in the guise of "people's justice." An artillery barrage is indiscriminate in its destruction of life and property. Furthermore, unlike the rebel's action it is damage inflicted by an outsider.[5]

Journalist Malcolm Browne accompanied an operation in Kien-Hoa province in December 1961 during which the troops of Province Chief Colonel Pham Ngoc Thao (the Communist agent) poured fire on two sets of hamlets until they realized that nobody was shooting back; then they moved forward. Encountering no VC, they pilfered ducks and chickens from the hamlets, prepared and ate lunch, and left on their landing craft.[6] During a visit to Viet-Nam, Roger Hilsman, then Director of the State Department's Bureau of Intelligence and Research, was invited by President Diem, along with Ambassador Frederick E. Nolting, to witness a large military operation, the attack against the VC at Binh-Hoa, near the Parrot's Beak of Cambodia, on January 21, 1962. Intelligence had reported that five days earlier some 300 VC had been spotted at a point about two miles from the border, and a full battalion was a few miles away. Air photos showed what looked like an installation for manufacturing VC munitions. The attack plan, which was prepared by the senior American advisor to the Vietnamese Third Corps, called for prepositioning troops on river boats the night before, and then at 0755 the next morning bombing and strafing a cluster of huts near the border, followed by air attacks on other targets, and paratrooper drops and troop landings. Through an error in map reading, a Cambodian village just over the border was bombed, killing and wounding a number of villagers. The other air attacks were on target. Hilsman said that, except for the error in map reading and the resultant bombing of the Cambodian village, the plan was efficiently executed, but was more appropriate to Europe during World War II than to guerrilla warfare (with which he had gained experience in Burma during the same war). Both the prepositioning of troops and the bombing had given the VC warning, and villagers reported that some 200 VC had moved out just before the air attack. He went on:

In any case, such elaborate traps will rarely work against guerrillas; the only way to "trap" them is to make contact by blanketing an area with a large number of guerrilla-size patrols, and then follow the contact by reinforcements and ambushes along the escape routes. The greatest problem is that bombing huts and villages will kill civilians and push the population still further toward active support for the Viet Cong . . . No one knows exactly how many Cambodians were killed because of the map-reading error, but in the bombing and strafing around the drop zone five civilians were killed and eleven wounded. A *Life Magazine* photographer, Howard Sochurek, who followed the parachutists in by helicopter reported that among the five civilians killed were a two-year-old boy, a five-year-old girl, and a seven-year-old boy . . . It seems obvious that an operation like that at Binh Hoa was not only fruitless but that it helped to recruit more Viet Cong than it could possibly have killed.

When Hilsman got back to Washington and reported on his visit, John F. Kennedy commented on the Binh-Hoa operation, "I've been President over a year, how can things like this go on happening?" He directed General Maxwell Taylor to find out without getting Hilsman in trouble with the Pentagon.[7] One could cite additional examples and expert comments like these, and indeed I shall do so in subsequent chapters, as such counterproductive tactics continued to be used by both the Vietnamese and American troops.

Many other practices of the GVN and its armed forces served to cause anger and alienation among the peasantry. Both the troop commanders and the civil officials appointed by Saigon, many of them Northerners, were city people totally unsympathetic to the uneducated peasants. Many were corrupt and extorted money and goods from those whom they were supposed to serve, as well as diverting to their personal use money and commodities appropriated for relief and public projects. Resentment caused by the forcible relocations, which were often carried out hastily and brutally, without permitting the people to take with them their most cherished possessions, has already been reported in chapter 2, and will be mentioned often again. Forced labor without pay on the agrovilles and other projects, frequently during the planting and harvest seasons, was another cause of disaffection.

There were also the grievances of the peasants about the lack of social and political reform. In the areas that the Viet-Minh had controlled during the French regime, landlords had been dispossessed and the land distributed to the peasants, without title to be sure, but for use without rent or payment, although new taxes were levied. The old system of village elections and autonomy (''The Emperor's writ stops at the village gates''), undisturbed by the French, had been altered by the Viet-Minh only to assure that ''exploiters of the people'' were not elected. The cadres and soldiers were of the people, living and working with them, and were under strict discipline. All this had been reversed wherever the authority of the GVN was established. The landlords came back, and were sometimes assisted in collecting back rents. Diem's land reform was shallow and did not benefit most of the tenants. His campaign of denunciation of Communists turned into a witch hunt and occasional personal vendettas in the villages, killing or driving into the jungle many of the peasants. In 1956, Diem abolished both village and municipal elections and sent strangers, many of them corrupt Northerners or his supporters from Central Viet-Nam, to take over local positions. The personalist philosophy that he and his brothers tried to instil through the Can-Lao Party and the Republican Youth had little appeal.[8]

For all these reasons, the Viet-Cong ''fish'' were able to swim in friendly waters, except in places inhabited by Catholic refugees from the North or by the Hoa-Hao and Cao-Dai. The counterinsurgency programs of the government and of the American military advisers did not address the grievances of the people, which were among the most important factors in the rebellion, but instead added new causes for resentment, even though Ambassador Durbrow, his successor Ambassador Nolting, Roger Hilsman, and others in the State Department and the White House, as well as friends of Diem like Joseph Buttinger, tried to get Diem and his brother Nhu to change course.[9] Indeed, Diem and Nhu became disgruntled with their American advisors and, to the limited extent that they felt the need for any advice at all, began to look elsewhere for their inspiration.

THE MALAYAN MODEL: SIR ROBERT THOMPSON AS ADVISOR

In 1960, Diem traveled to Malaya to study the successful program, New Villages, which had played a prominent role in overcoming the Communist insurgency there in the 1950s and 1960s. There were substantial differences between the two countries; not the least of which was that the insurrection in Malaya was largely carried on by Communist guerrillas among the Chinese in the countryside, who were a small minority and were disliked both as Chinese and as rebels by the Malay majority. In consequence, the New Villages regrouped many fewer people than would be affected by a similar program in Viet-Nam. Moreover, they had been carefully planned and were constructed so that life for the relocatees was truly better than in the squatter settlements where they had formerly lived. Diem thought that the Malayan example might have something of use for his country, and he invited Sir Robert Thompson, Permanent Secretary for Defense in Malaya, to establish a British Advisory Mission in Saigon. Much to the dismay of US MAAG Chief General McGarr, Thompson accepted and established his mission in September 1961. The next month he presented to the President an initial appreciation of the situation, which was well received. Diem asked him to follow it up with a specific plan, and he did so in November.

Sir Robert agreed with General Maxwell Taylor that the Communist objective was a political conquest as a result of combined political and military action, rather than a military takeover. He agreed with McGarr on the danger of VC attempts to control the unpopulated areas and to use them as bases, but he parted company with the US military advisors in viewing the VC threat to the populated rural areas as primary. The main government effort should not be the destruction of VC forces, he said, but rather the provision of an attractive alternative to Communist appeals by national reconstruction and development in the populated rural areas. Extensive security measures would be required, but these should be carried out mainly by the police, who could establish rapport with the people rather than the army, whose mission should be to keep the VC off balance and out of the initial pacification areas by mobile operations.[10]

The aim of Thompson's Delta Plan was to win loyalties rather than to kill rebels, so he emphasized clearing and holding areas rather than the American strategy of searching out and destroying the enemy; this was a fundamental distinction. The key to his security framework was the strategic hamlet (*ap chien luoc*), a settlement similar to those that already existed in many sections of the country, which was to be established first in relatively pacified areas, then extended outward progressively as security was spread. In less secure areas, the compact defended hamlet (*ap chien dau*), such as already existed in much of central Viet-Nam, would have to be established first. There were three objectives: The first, a prerequisite for the other two, was protection of the population. It required not only regrouping some outlying houses and surrounding the hamlet by a moat and barbed wire, but also a good radio network, the training and arming of a hamlet militia (meanwhile using territorial forces and the army to keep the VC out), and, what Thompson considered most important, the elimination of the insurgent covert organization (in later years called the VC infrastructure). The second objective was to unite the people and involve them in positive action on the side of the government. This meant instilling a sense of obligation and responsibility for the community and of national solidarity. The third objective, which would bring the peasants to see the advantages of the whole effort, was social, economic, and political development: the provision of water, schools, clinics, markets, improved agricultural methods, and improved communication with the wider world, followed by local and national elections. This was what Thompson called the "winning stage." The fundamental aim was to isolate the guerrillas physically and politically from the people. As Sir Robert put it to President Diem, "One must get all the 'little fishes out of the water' and keep them out; then they die."

It was estimated at the beginning of 1962 that about 11,000 strategic and defended hamlets would be necessary to blanket the country. Thompson thought that about half would require only minor regrouping of a few scattered houses;

about 30% would need major regrouping of half of the houses; about 15% would require moving considerably more than half of the houses; and 5%, in areas under VC control, would have to be moved to completely new sites. In all the first three cases, it was intended that no householder should be required to go more than three miles to work his land. Thompson advocated starting in a relatively pacified area in the Mekong Delta, proceeding under carefully developed plans, including allocating house sites in advance, providing free transportation, giving a subsidy, and feeding the people free until shops could be opened and normal supplies could be obtained, and, above all, explaining the plan to the people. He believed that each area should be fully pacified before spreading out to new zones.[11]

General McGarr was shocked at Sir Robert's proposal on a number of grounds, not the least of which was what he considered lack of prior coordination with the "physician" who was responsible for the "health" of the "patient." However, General Taylor, Roger Hilsman, and President Kennedy were favorably disposed to Thompson's plan. At the President's instruction, Hilsman produced a rewrite incorporating his own ideas called "A Strategic Concept for South Vietnam" and "sold" it to Robert Kennedy, the Attorney General; the heads of CIA and AID, and others. General Taylor pulled the Pentagon into line. Gradually consultations in Saigon brought about a measure of agreement between the British and American advisors, and, with the help of Secretary of Defense Robert McNamara, who offered to make resources available to start on one province, they presented their agreed-upon ideas to the GVN.[12]

Meanwhile, however, Diem and his brother Nhu had developed their own ideas, and these were not entirely consonant with what the foreign advisors were working up.

VIETNAMESE ORIGINS AND PRECEDENTS: THE NGO BROTHERS' PLANS

There was a long tradition of defended hamlets in Viet-Nam, going back to the period after the seizure of Annam from the Chams in the 15th century. During the war against the French, 1946–54, many of these hamlets, from Tourane (Da-Nang) down the coastal plain as far as Binh-Thuan, were controlled by the Viet-Minh, and remained in the hands of the Communists after 1954.

More recently in the far South, Father Nguyen Lac Hoa, a refugee from China (and a former colonel in the Chinese Nationalist Army) brought other refugees, the "Sea Swallows," to the Ca-Mau Peninsula in An-Xuyen province in 1959, armed them with US help, and created a group of defended hamlets which prospered right in the midst of a Communist stronghold area.[13]

Far to the north, another Father Hoa, a Vietnamese, formed similar defended hamlets in the Song-Cau district of Phu-Yen province to protect them against the Communists; there were others elsewhere. These projects received the approval and help of the Diem regime, as well as from elements of the US Mission.[14]

Ngo Dinh Nhu, whose task was establishing GVN control in the countryside, began the strategic hamlet program even before the United States and Great Britain had presented their plans, and he kept personal direction of it throughout. He and his brother Diem found their model in the compact hamlets of their native region, central Viet-Nam, which they believed produced a sense of community that was lacking in the sprawling hamlets and villages of the Mekong Delta. They were suspicious of the village as an obstacle to their ambition to exercise control over peasant life and to instil the personalist doctrine, which they felt was the best defense against the Communist insurrection. Each hamlet was to be surrounded by a ditch and fence along its administrative boundary, taking in rice fields as well as houses, in such a way as to cut it off psychologically and physically from other hamlets in the same village. Compulsory labor of both peasants and government employees was to build the fortifications. Nhu unabashedly borrowed from Communist practice in forming tight organizations of the youth, who would provide defense, capturing rifles from the enemy, the women, farmers, and so on. He was also determined that control should be exercised by the Palace through the Can-Lao apparatus, bypassing the regular Ministries, the Army, and the Americans, whom he disliked.[15]

The first project under Diem was by Colonel Khanh, the Province Chief of Ninh-Thuan, in 1960, when he organized several villages for self-defense, including armed voluntary militia and fences. In Darlac province, a Catholic priest had constructed defenses at the refugee village of Trung-Hoa and in May 1961 had asked for 30 shotguns. Nhu reportedly said later that Trung-Hoa was among the first strategic hamlets. In July 1961, three strategic hamlets were organized in Vinh-Long province. Then "hundreds" were reportedly formed in Quang-Ngai, and others elsewhere.[16]

BEGINNING OF THE OFFICIAL PROGRAM: OPERATION SUNRISE

Officially the program began on February 3, 1962, with the publication of Decree No. 11-TTP establishing the Interministerial Committee for Strategic Hamlets. The specific purposes were to: (1) provide security to the peasants, (2) enact political, economic, and social reforms that were meaningful to the peasants, (3) create a nationwide self-defense force at the hamlet level, (4) create the desire and will to resist Communist aggression, and (5) strengthen the peasants' image of their government.[17] Nhu used this committee to indoctrinate the bureaucracy, but he ran the program out of his own office, and he ordered that the hamlets throughout the whole country be completed in 14 months.

The government gladly accepted Secretary McNamara's offer to fund and supply a "pilot" project in one province, and, contrary to Sir Robert Thompson's advice, chose one of the least secure provinces, Binh-Duong, which included the VC base area, the Iron Triangle, and adjoined War Zone D in Phuoc-Thanh province. Even before receiving the offer of US aid, the GVN had begun planning and cadre training in August 1961, under Brigadier General Van Thanh Cao, for a rural reconstruction campaign to secure Tay-Ninh, Binh-Duong, and Phuoc-Tuy provinces. This was named Operation Sunrise. Most of the effort at first had been in the Cu-Chi district of Binh-Duong, where Xom-Hue hamlet of Tan-An-Hoi village was being converted into a strategic hamlet. Only 10 families were relocated out of a total population of 1,768 in the hamlet. The district chief asserted that he had paid 1,000 piasters per family. Farmers were compelled to work from 45 to 90 days from mid-December 1961 to mid-March 1962, with only a five-day break for Têt. In late March some were still doing communal labor. They said that their tobacco crops had suffered as a result. In addition, they had to contribute all their marketable bamboo, which takes three years to grow. Other strategic hamlets were built with the aid of other villages. The peasants who had to work outside their hamlets at first got no payment for their food.[18]

In their survey report on the civilian side of Operation Sunrise, John C. Donnell and Gerald Hickey of the Rand Corporation said that most families moved inside the security perimeters voluntarily, even while doubting that the sacrifices would yield satisfactory results. In Donnell and Hickey's opinion, farmers would participate willingly in security measures only if they saw evidence of improved economic, social, and political welfare. Diem and some of the American officials disagreed, holding that the rural population was basically hostile to the Communists. More information on attitudes was needed, said the two researchers. They had the following suggestions:

1. Expensive bamboo fences were of doubtful utility.
2. Promises of payment to villagers should be kept.
3. Paid public works would help farmers' incomes.
4. Agricultural credit and extension services were needed.
5. There should be special training for local government officials.
6. Central direction should be at the sub-Cabinet level, but there should be local autonomy.

They added that Self-Defense Cadres (SDC) should be given family allowances and, if possible, higher pay, closer to that of the Civil Guard and ARVN, especially because some SDC were used in offensive operations and many were stationed far from their home provinces. Finally, they recommended that the people be enabled to take a more meaningful part in political life and to participate in making the decisions affecting their welfare; also that GVN communications with the people be improved.[19]

General McGarr meanwhile was convinced that the GVN had decided that first priority for the program would be the area around Saigon, including War Zone D, as recommended by the MAAG. He reported on December 6, 1961, that some months previously his headquarters had "under the table" handed the

ARVN Field Command an outline plan for the area.[20] In mid-January 1962, however, Diem told General McGarr that he opposed his plan to conduct an operation in War Zone D, preferring to concentrate on pacifying Binh-Duong, where only 10 of 46 villages were under GVN control. Secretary McNamara ratified the GVN choice at the second Honolulu conference with McGarr on January 15, 1962.

The second, military, phase of Operation Sunrise began in March 1962, with substantial MAAG involvement. On March 16–17, an operation was conducted by an ARVN regiment minus one battalion in the southwest portion of Phuoc-Thanh sector in War Zone D to relocate civilians living in widely spread villages and hamlets into areas under GVN control. Approximately 600 persons in about 150 families were moved. A secondary objective was the destruction of VC forces and installations. There were two VC and no friendly casualties. The "Lessons Learned" report of the MAAG stressed the value of civic action teams, saying: "The importance of winning the people must be understood by all military commanders and the provincial authorities. Military civic action must be emphasized to insure an improved attitude toward the military by relocated civilians." The report also recommended that preliminary phases of similar operations include the initial layout and preparation of relocated villages, agricultural tracts, and even construction of family buildings. "Secrecy in this aspect is not important. The 'selling point' is that if civilians know that areas are already prepared, voluntary resettlement may result on the part of loyal citizenry, considerably easing the task during the military phase of the resettlement operation."[21]

The major military operation of Operation Sunrise began on March 22 in Ben-Cat district of Binh-Duong province, with a large force of ARVN and the Civil Guard, under the Commanding Officer of the Fifth Infantry Division (Brig. Gen. Van Thanh Cao). In addition, five civic action teams, some 80 civil servants from provincial agencies, various medical personnel, public works technicians, and laborers, (with vehicles and equipment for moving people and property, constructing temporary shelters, clearing land, and laying out roads and lots) were assigned. Three strategic hamlets were to be constructed. The mission was: "To eliminate VC control over the people; provide for a selective relocation and physical security of the population; enforce law and order; assist in rehabilitating village administration, economy and security; and assist in consolidating national control within the area of operations by enhancing popular support for the counterinsurgency effort."

The Viet-Cong did not stand and fight, but simply melted away into the jungle. However, few of the peasant families moved voluntarily; most were forced, and their homes were burned behind them. Some came with most of their belongings, others with little more than the clothes on their backs. There were few able-bodied men, which indicated that most had remained with the VC, willingly or unwillingly. By mid-May 1962, the three strategic hamlets had been constructed: Ben-Tuong, which was to be the showpiece, Ben-Dong-So, and Bau-Bang, with a total of 2,769 people in 546 families. One hundred seventy-four of the families had been there originally; the rest were moved. Only 43.5 hectares of land had been cleared, but 2,479 meters of moats had been dug, 6,036 meters of parapet had been built and enclosed by barbed wire, and 10,000 meters of new interior roads constructed. Three hundred thirty-five houses had been built by the residents and civic action teams. Two hundred ninety-seven thousand psywar leaflets had been distributed, mostly by air! At Ben Tuong, 80 Republican Youth members had been organized in two platoons, and 26 Republican Women in one platoon. Medical technicians and nurses were providing health care.

The VC did not take the relocations passively, however. Early in May there was a protest demonstration by women and children at Ben-Cat town. A psywar officer took the letters they had brought, talked to them, and sent them away. The VC sent them back again, whereupon General Cao ordered them sent to one of the hamlets to work on perimeter defenses for one month; the children were placed in the care of women cadres. Copies of VC directives on how to resist the strategic hamlets were captured. On May 8, an ambulance on the way from Bau-Bang, escorted by two infantry squads, was ambushed and five were killed. The nearby Self Defense Corps unit came to the rescue, killing a VC machine gunner and capturing his weapon. After that, the only VC activity in the first half of that month was the propagandizing of bus passengers stopped on the roads.[22] However, in mid-June a guerrilla force ambushed an ARVN convoy in full daylight near the Ben-Cat district town, killing 26 soldiers, several civilian public works technicians, and two American officers. The civilian population had not notified the ARVN posts of the impending attack. A year later the situation was uneven. Ben-Tuong was overrun and destroyed by the VC on August 20, 1963.[23]

There were further relocations during Operation Sunrise. One of these, from the 16th to the 22nd of July 1962, by elements of the Fifth Infantry Division, Fifth Airborne Battalion, and Binh-Duong sector (province), relocated 466 persons in 113 families in three "villages" (probably hamlets) from a portion of a VC stronghold in Long-Nguyen zone (the connecting link between Tay-Ninh and Zone D, Phuoc-Thanh) to Long-Cau strategic hamlet. The ambushes by the VC south of Ben-Cat on June 16 mentioned above and in Bau-Long on July 14 caused the deaths of three American advisors, among others. ARVN casualties were confined to five WIA (wounded in action), one of whom later died. There was adequate transport but, because of lack of civic action support, few of the people's belongings were moved before their houses were destroyed. The US after-action report noted, "In no case did the G5 [civil affairs] advisor witness ARVN soldiers assist the civilians in salvaging their belongings." Province and district authorities provided food, lodgings, and administrative control. There was a favorable reception at Long-Cau, and excellent shelter. The area had been secured by D + 1 (the day after its inception); when the people arrived on D + 2, several large structures had been erected, and water, food, and medical care were provided. There was an existing Catholic Church.[24]

In the 10 provinces encompassed by Operation Sunrise, 80 hamlets had been secured by the end of July 1962, of which 49 had received US defense materiel. Four hundred five others were under construction. The MAAG drew some significant lessons from the operation up to that point:

a) Logistical support requires close and continuing advisory effort. In spite of (GVN) presidential directives, required support from GVN agencies including the national Ministries was difficult to obtain, and in some cases was late and inadequate.

b) In an effort to maintain security of the [Ben-Cat district] plan, preparations to receive the people were not made at the new hamlet sites before relocation began. In spite of this precaution, the VC knew about the operation well in advance. Therefore, it appears practical in most cases to prepare the reception facilities and new living quarters early and secure them in advance. This avoids the requirement for temporary shelters for the people relocated and insures that troops are 'on site,' are familiar with the terrain and will be available for security duty once the relocation has been accomplished.

c) Properly executed psychological operations (psyops) are essential. Special efforts must be made to inform the people of what is taking place, why it is taking place and what progress is being made.

d) Medical care produces the greatest rewards. Many relocated people have never had access to medical care. Support from the Ministry of Health (MOH) was far less than planned and agreed. Province officials bore the burden.

e) Funding must provide for unanticipated expenditures. For example, since many able-bodied men initially avoided relocation, it was necessary to hire laborers to assist in building houses. Compensation for loss of personal property must be handled with dispatch and appropriate publicity.

f) Trained civic action cadres must be available.

g) Aerial photography is helpful in estimating the number of families in the target area.

h) Timing and speed are fundamental. It may be necessary to delay movement to permit harvesting, and then move people rapidly but not ruthlessly. Delay may permit families to escape or VC agents to infiltrate.

i) Relocation should be integrated with military operations. Prepare to have Civil Guard and Self-Defence Cadres participate.[25]

In his book *Defeating Communist Insurgency,* Sir Robert Thompson was harsher in his evaluation of the Ben-Cat part of Operation Sunrise. He wrote:

It involved the resettlement of all the inhabitants concerned away from their rice fields, which gave the unfortunate impression that all strategic hamlets were going to be of this type. This provided the Viet Cong with an excellent propaganda line. Considerable government forces were subsequently required to hold the hamlets, and the road to them from the provincial capital, running as it did through disputed territory, provided opportunities for frequent Viet Cong ambushes. These four hamlets [later five] remained hostages to fortune until they were lost to the Viet Cong in 1964.[26]

Douglas Blaufarb wrote: "It was highly inauspicious and not, in fact, typical of the program. But first impressions are lasting ones. The U.S. press found the spectacle repellant and said so; it questioned whether a movement to 'win the people' could succeed on such a foundation." However Blaufarb observed that operations like Sunrise were a minor feature of the program. "They represented the U.S. military's style and contribution. They did not, however, suit the style or goals of the GVN, which had little patience or capability for careful national planning."[27]

CAMPAIGNS IN OTHER PROVINCES

On May 6, 1962, Operation *Hai-Yen II* (Sea Swallow II) was launched in Phu-Yen province. It was similar in broad concept to Operation Sunrise, but with significant differences, some of them due to the fact that compact defended hamlets were native to the region. The US advisors and the GVN officials were united in their determination to give the people an interest and stake in their own well-being and the conduct of their affairs. The province chief, Major Duong Thai Dong, and his American advisor were anxious to avoid the mistakes of Sunrise, and to make the operation a genuine battle for the hearts and minds of the populace. Large sums of both economic and military aid were made available by the Americans. Those in charge insisted that people not be moved until houses were ready for them, and that they be compensated for their destroyed homes. The first-phase strategic hamlets were built in the relatively secure areas around Tuy-Hoa, the province capital; 90 days were allocated to that phase, and 157 hamlets were completed by August 8. After a short consolidation period, 60 days were allocated to the second phase, pushing out into less secure territory. It was delayed by floods in the coastal area. Indeed, both Phase 2 and Phase 3 goals were not met, because ARVN was unable to clear the Annamite mountain chain of VC insurgents.[28] Operation *Dang-Tien* (Let's Go) in Binh-Dinh had a goal of 328 strategic hamlets in one year, and Operation *Phuong-Hoang* (Royal Phoenix) in Quang-Ngai was to create 125 hamlets by the end of 1962.[29]

Kien-Hoa was one of the richest provinces in the Mekong Delta, and also home of one of the strongest guerrilla forces. By 1960, government presence had been virtually eliminated outside the provincial capital. President Diem sent Lt. Colonel Pham Ngoc Thao to be province chief. Thao had been a regimental commander and later chief of counterintelligence of the Viet-Minh in Cochinchina. He had not rallied to the French-sponsored Vietnamese government established in 1949, but had stayed with the Viet-Minh until the French defeat in 1954.[30] Upon his arrival in Kien-Hoa, he began to enlarge and improve the local military forces and to import a large number of Hoa-Hao troops, who by ruthless military operations and crude but effective psyops drove the Viet-Cong back from the edges of the principal towns and villages. However their tactics also alienated loyal citizens as well as VC sympathizers. In 1962, Diem sent Colonel Thao to the Command and General Staff College at Fort Leavenworth, Kansas.

The new province chief was a young major, Tran Ngoc Chau, who, as a member of the planning staff of the presidency had worked out details of the strategic hamlet program for Ngo Dinh Nhu. Beginning in May 1962, he visited every district and most of the accessible villages, and studied the history and the economic and social situation of Kien-Hoa. He also strengthened his intelligence system. In November he presented a strategic hamlet plan in Saigon for review by a committee representing Nhu's office, the USOM, and the Strategic Hamlet Division of the MAAG. John B. O'Donnell, one of the USOM members, was impressed by Chau's imagination and ability. The committee then visited the province, and authorized the major portion of the funds he had requested. USOM prepared a support budget and appointed O'Donnell as its representative to advise and assist the province chief in the implementation of the plan, along with the MAAG sector advisor. All expenditures of provincial rehabilitation funds had to be approved by the committee of these three men. Decentralization of authority was built into the strategic hamlet program, though the degree of independence varied with the province chief.

In Kien-Hoa, fiscal authority was further devolved to the district and hamlet level. Some cases of corruption were uncovered, and Major Chau took prompt action to correct them. The provincial administration was reorganized, and the eight districts (a ninth was created in 1963) were instructed to recruit candidates for cadres, all of whom were personally interviewed and selected by Chau. He then decided that 900 piasters ($12.37 US) a month was not sufficient salary for the work that these young men and women were to perform, and obtained the agreement of his tripartite committee to reduce the number of personnel and raise their pay. The cadres were trained under Major Chau's personal supervision, and then sent out in teams of 11. At the hamlets, they were broken down into three sections, to gather detailed information on all aspects of hamlet life; organize the inhabitants into work details and direct the construction of the moats and fences for defense; and explain the regime's philosophy and objectives, organize social and economic action groups, develop a hamlet charter, and arrange secret-ballot elections. The political-propaganda component of the team had the most important functions and, when its members had an understanding of the program and convincing personalities, the people responded. Where they did not, hamlet construction became an unpleasant, meaningless task, and the hamlet was vulnerable to VC subversion. A team would stay three to eight weeks in a hamlet, and when all basic steps had been accomplished to the satisfaction of the cadre, the village officials, and the district chief, a ceremony would be held, usually presided over by Chau (now a lieutenant colonel), to inaugurate the new strategic hamlet.

Lt. Colonel Chau had worked out a timetable for completion of the hamlets but, as his teams ran into difficulties in convincing people in areas long dominated by the Communists, he was flexible enough to give them more time. He resisted heavy pressure from Saigon to show rapid progress, and his courage paid off later, when the hamlets of Kien-Hoa resisted VC assaults while those in other provinces were crumbling. He instructed each hamlet's deputy chief for security to set up an interview schedule for all members of each family, so that they could air their complaints against the government confidentially and at the same time be asked about VC activities of which they might have knowledge. In some cases, he sent educated young people to help the hamlet officials with the task. Reports of these interviews were sent to the provincial complaints bureau, which gave condensed versions to Chau daily. He followed up the complaints and took appropriate action. A bimonthly newspaper was published, and a provincial theatrical team was formed. The US Information Service (USIS) helped. A radio transmitter was installed in July 1964. Self-help economic projects were supported with AID funds, Food for Peace commodities, excess property, and imported cement, roofing, and reinforcing rods. The provincial committee arranged to make up overdue back pay of health workers, and to upgrade their training. With funds from the Asia Foundation and AID commodities, a hamlet school construction program was carried out. International Voluntary Services (IVS) helped. Improved rice seed was distributed to about 15,000 peasants in 140 hamlets. Wells were dug. Roads were repaired, and new roads built. Most of these construction projects were accomplished by self-help of the people. The extended defense perimeters enclosing the spread-out hamlets were inappropriate for the Delta, however, as they were too long to be defended by the two squads of militia authorized for each hamlet.

In his province report for June-July 1963, O'Donnell recounted evidence of progress: In all districts, families were being moved in a planned manner as the strategic hamlets were created, and the relocated families were receiving food and money. Hamlet militia and the Self-Defence Cadres (SDC) were fighting off VC attacks; intelligence was coming in, permitting attacks on VC bases; and citizens were responding to increased security by building new homes and community facilities. Previously inaccessible areas were being traveled. Markets were busy. The VC still dominated large areas, but people had gained confidence in their ability to resist the Communists. Some hamlet militia were going out on night patrols and ambushes. Captured documents indicated that the program was hurting the VC: Young men were defecting, intelligence cadres were being arrested, VC tax collections were falling off, and travel was more dangerous for the VC. On the other hand, government tax collections and agricultural loan payments were increasing. Progress was uneven, as was to be expected, depending in large part on the quality of district and local officials.

In June 1963, Lt. Colonel Chau was reassigned by Diem as mayor of Da-Nang, and his military deputy, Major Le Huu Duc, was named to replace him. However, he was unhappy with the broadened assignment and, especially after the November 1 coup that overthrew Diem, things went downhill. At the end of January 1964, the same day as General Nguyen Khanh's seizure of power, the VC mortared Ben-Tre city. A week later a heavier barrage occurred. Morale sank. However, in February, Lt. Colonel Chau was reassigned as province chief. Shocked by the deterioration in the situation, he gradually turned things around but, with the confusion in Saigon and the casualties that had afflicted some of the best men in the province, it was a slow process.[31]

In Long-An province, where O'Donnell was also the USOM representative, it was quite a different story. There the province chief, Major Nguyen Viet Thanh, yielded to the pressure from Nhu's office to speed up the completion of strategic hamlets. He himself worked day and night and transmitted the pressure to his province and district staffs. The result was that standards were not observed. Eighty thousand people were relocated, many of them in April and May 1963, and their resentment was exploited by the Viet-Cong. By mid-1963, O'Donnell reported that the VC were attacking the hamlets, tearing down fences, kidnapping young men, assassinating hamlet officials, and generally destroying popular morale and the will to resist. In some hamlets, the people put up no resistance to VC incursions. The province capabilities were overextended. In July 1963, Major Thanh was assigned as the G-3 (chief of Plans and Operations) IV Corps, and Major Nguyen Ngoc Xinh took his place. O'Donnell made a number of recommendations for improving the program, but evidently it was too late.[32]

THE NATIONWIDE DRIVE

In August 1962, the GVN drew the various operations and province efforts together into a national plan. First priority went to the 11 provinces around Saigon, essentially the area of Sir Robert Thompson's Delta Plan plus Gia-Dinh and the original Operation Sunrise provinces. By the end of the summer, the government claimed that 3,225 of the planned 11,316 hamlets had been completed and that a third of the country's population was living in completed hamlets.[33] These statistics, like those that followed, turned out to be inflated.

The USOM reorganized itself to support the program, creating an Office of Rural Development under Rufus Phillips, who had served earlier in Viet-Nam and Laos; Bert Fraleigh, who had come with experience in mainland China, Taiwan, and Laos, was his deputy. In September, USOM gave the government $10 million worth of piasters purchased with dollars as a means of speeding the injection of funds without waiting for the usual time-consuming procedures of the Commodity Import Program. PL 480 surplus food and military excess property items were also furnished by USOM. The MAAG and the Defense Department in Washington likewise cut through red tape to get barbed wire, weapons, and other supplies delivered quickly.

The GVN's criteria for a completed strategic hamlet were: (1) a census and elimination of the VC infrastructure; (2) indoctrination and organization of civic groups and a work and disaster plan, assigning duties to all inhabitants; (3) organization of a civil defense system; (4) completion of physical defenses; (5) organization of secret guerrilla cells; and (6) election of a hamlet committee by secret ballot.[34]

Under forced draft, hamlets were stockaded all over the country. Ngo Dinh Nhu traveled extensively, publicizing and energizing the campaign and stressing "self-sufficiency," but at the same time, US-supplied resources were pouring in. By July 7, 1963, Diem reported 8,150,187 citizens in 5,917 completed hamlets; one week later, the official *Vietnam Press* put the figure at 8,737,613 in 7,205 completed hamlets. That would have been over half the people in the Republic. These figures included Saigon, where 661,086 of the 1,275,000 inhabitants were officially reported to be in 223 completed hamlets as of January 16, 1963. However, in relaying these figures, Milton Osborne cautioned that there were discrepancies and inaccuracies. He quoted approvingly a USOM report made after the program was reviewed in 1964, which said that the provincial officials, under intense pressure, were prepared to employ any measures, including false reporting, to achieve the quantitative targets that had been set. The USOM said that many good hamlets had been constructed, but that often the government's tactics were counterproductive. Colonel Thao admitted as much in an address at Cornell on May 20, 1964.[35]

A CIA memorandum for the Secretary of Defense, dated July 13, 1962, was cautiously optimistic about the prospects of the program, but said that a major weakness was hit-or-miss construction with insufficient integration into overall district and provincial security plans. The agency admitted that it was extremely difficult to come up with firm generalizations about popular attitudes, which varied from place to place depending on how the program was handled by the authorities.[36]

Sir Robert Thompson's memorandum addressed to Diem in September 1962 said that very great progress had been achieved over the last six months in the provinces he had visited. "There are, however, some gaps both inside the hamlets, in that all the ingredients for their success have not yet been completed, and outside, in that they have not yet been established in a sufficient block to achieve a solid security framework over a wide area." He recommended that the momentum be maintained, and offered a number of specific suggestions. He expressed worriment over the length of fences around some of the hamlets, where they could not be observed; four kilometers was the limit, he felt, even in government-controlled areas, and less in contested zones. This, he said, would require that more houses be regrouped, and he recommended that it be done firmly and promptly, and accompanied by measures to increase agricultural production and prosperity. He went on:

Generally there is less regrouping required in the rich and well developed rice-field areas of the Delta than in the villages of the coastal provinces in Central Vietnam and those to the east and north of Saigon along the jungle fringes in Phuoc Tuy, Bien Hoa, Binh Duong and Tay Ninh Provinces, where the soil is not as fertile as in the Delta.[37]

This statement revealed a curious misunderstanding by Sir Robert of the Mekong Delta, where the houses of a typical hamlet were strung out along the canals and rivers, with the rice fields behind them (see chapter 2) and the common mode of transportation was by boat. As the earlier efforts at regrouping showed,

these settlements were much more difficult to consolidate than the already compact hamlets of Central Viet-Nam. Maynard Dow reported that the Mekong Delta
was the only area where village and hamlet morphology was significantly altered
by the strategic hamlet program, with hundreds of thousands of peasants being
relocated. He cited among others the knowledgeable Colonel John E. Arthur,
the Viet-Nam action officer of the Joint Chiefs of Staff (JCS) in Washington,
who said in an interview in September 1963 that perhaps 20% of the strategic
hamlets resulted from relocation, mainly in the Delta.[38] Except in such places
as Kien-Hoa, where the purposes of the program were carefully explained to the
people and the relocations were handled sensitively, popular resentment of the
forced movements was the norm, and it redounded to the advantage of the enemy.
Dennis Duncanson, one of Thompson's lieutenants, was the only observer who
asserted that compulsory movement of houses was "a fatigue that the majority
seemed to undertake with gratifying cheerfulness."[39]

President Diem declared "open zones" in the highland areas near the frontiers
with Cambodia and Laos, where there was no immediate possibility of extending
GVN control, and took comfort in the unrestrained use of bombing and air strikes
to drive the people into the strategic hamlets closer to the coast. This policy was
a principal cause of the massive movement of highlander refugees in the summer
of 1962, which gave Diem the satisfaction of being voted for "with the feet."
However, it caused a refugee burden that nobody was prepared for and made
the government appear cruel to the victims of its policy.[40] Douglas Pike, however,
attributed this sudden migration, which he said may have encompassed 300,000
Montagnards, to the terror and exactions of the National Liberation Front (NLF,
the overt arm of the Viet-Cong).[41] Hickey reported Vietnamese Air Force
(VNAF) attacks on highlander villages, and attributed the exodus, which he said
involved more than 111,000 people, to those attacks as well as to VC terror. In
January 1963, Colonel Wilbur Wilson, the Senior Advisor to III Corps, transmitted comments by the ARVN 23rd Division, whose area of operations included
much of the Highlands, reporting that the exodus of Montagnards from VC-
controlled territory was due to increased VC demands for food and recruits,
increased government aid for the displaced tribes, and expanding self-protective
programs such as the strategic hamlets in Tuyen-Duc and Darlac provinces.[42]

The government claimed that 170,194 Montagnards were in strategic hamlets
in the Highlands as of April 1963, and 209,025 by July. These figures were
probably exaggerated. However, the concept of strategic hamlets was not alien
to the Montagnards, who had traditionally surrounded their villages with strong
fences, mainly to protect them against tigers and other wild animals. The CIA
and US Special Forces had helped many highlanders to relocate their villages
voluntarily near American military camps in the mountains and had armed and
organized them against the Communists.[43]

Roger Hilsman sent a comprehensive appraisal of the Viet-Nam situation and
short-term prospects to Secretary of State Dean Rusk on December 3, 1962,
with copies to the President and other members of the National Security Council.

He found that the GVN's strategic hamlet and pacification programs, with increased attention to political, economic, and social counterinsurgency measures and their coordination with more offensive-minded military campaigns, were paying off in slightly greater control of the countryside and improved peasant attitudes. However, the VC had also increased its strength, to about 23,000 elite fighting personnel plus 100,000 irregulars and sympathizers, controlling about 20% of the villages with 9% of the rural population and with varying degrees of influence over an additional 47% of the villages. He said the VC was prepared for a long struggle. Hilsman described the completed strategic hamlets as varying greatly in quality, praising those in the Binh-Duong Operation Sunrise area and in the Sea Swallow area of Phu-Yen. But, he said:

There are continuing reports that GVN officials have exacted too heavily from local resources and have not compensated the peasants for the material and labor required to build the hamlets, that the peasant's ability to earn a living has declined because of the time he is required to spend on construction, and that the government has been more concerned with controlling the hamlet population than with providing services and improving living conditions.

On balance, Hilsman said, the program appeared successful and had probably contributed to a reported slight increase in the number of persons and villages under effective GVN control. Nonetheless, the government must improve its counterguerrilla tactics and restrict the tactical use of artillery and airpower, which might otherwise contribute to the development of militant opposition among the peasants and positive identification with the Viet-Cong.[44]

The President then asked Hilsman and Michael Forrestal of the White House staff to go out to Viet-Nam. They arrived on December 31, 1962, just a few days before a strong ARVN force ignominiously and conspicuously failed to defeat about 200 guerrillas at Ap-Bac between the Plain of Reeds and the Mekong on January 3, Diem's 62nd birthday. The visitors found General Paul D. Harkins (who had replaced General McGarr) and Ambassador Nolting optimistic, in part because American military equipment and civilian supplies were beginning to arrive in quantity. They also were impressed with Nhu's drive in the strategic hamlet program. However, Hilsman saw that the progress was highly uneven and said that this was in considerable part due to lack of coordination among the American agencies. For example, some strategic hamlets enclosed Communists along with the other inhabitants, and there was no police program for rooting them out. The military was still oriented toward large sweeps that seldom made contact with the enemy and had little to do with the pacification campaign.

The two officials visited some coastal hamlets with Sir Robert and found some that were good, but saw others where the defenses were a sham, with long moats and walls around houses and fields guarded by a few old men with ancient weapons. Thompson, however, was optimistic, because his Delta Plan had evidently finally been adopted by Diem. From an aircraft over the Mekong Delta they could see traffic moving on the roads, bridges repaired, and new hamlets radiating out from a provincial capital. Some of the hamlets were isolated in hostile territory. Hilsman and Forrestal reported to President Kennedy that the war was clearly going better than a year ago, but that there were dangerous unevennesses. The attitudes of the peasants were largely unknown; some resisted the Communists bravely, others let them in or supplied what they asked for. VC strength had not diminished, and most of it came from local recruitment and captured weapons. The most serious lack they had found was the absence of an overall agreed-upon strategic plan. There were still too few clear-and-hold operations where troops remained to protect the population. It was going to be a long war, they concluded. In an "eyes only" annex, they were critical of the lack of coordinated strategic direction in Saigon. Still, in one of McNamara's Honolulu meetings in March 1963, General Harkins, after reeling off statistics, stated his thought that by Christmas it would be all over. The Secretary, wrote Hilsman, "was elated."[45]

Coincidentally, Thompson gave Diem another diplomatically worded report in March 1963. He said that the main emphasis in the first year of the strategic hamlet program had been on those areas that represented the basic infrastructure of the country, along the main roads and canals and around the district and province capitals. They were now linked and provided a firm base for expansion. In the Mekong Delta it was important in the next phase to clean out pockets still under VC control, which endangered the already secured hamlets. He warned against trying to extend outward too fast; action to improve the amenities was now called for. He made other recommendations, but was generally laudatory.[46] His recommendations were not followed.

Colonel F. P. Serong, chief of the Australian military advisory team, gave a more penetrating analysis in a report of March 14, 1963, to General Harkins: He believed that the allies were still winning the war. "However, there have now appeared clear signs that our main instrument, the Strategic Hamlet program, if continued on current lines (and there is no suggestion to the contrary), will unbalance our overall strategy, and create a situation favorable to the VC." The success of the program was largely statistical, he averred; points were awarded for numbers of hamlets and numbers of people in them. A steady advance had been made along main traffic arteries; now the laterals between them had to be filled in, and that was not being done. In the Delta, the intervening spaces between the axials were dominated by the VC, up to the suburbs of Saigon. Another malpractice was that of leaping over VC-infested areas, as in Operation Sunrise, which left a built-in ambush every time troops went on the Ben-Cat road. There were, he said, plans for more "Great Leaps Forward." On the high plateau, the plan for creating combat hamlets was not being followed. The reason was that the aim of Diem and Nhu was not "our aim," which was to create a strategic pattern leading to the destruction of the VC zone and control of the border. Serong found ample evidence that Diem and Nhu aimed at subjugation of the Montagnards, destruction of their ethnic community, and incorporation of the people and their land into the Vietnamese community. There was also an unwise program of food destruction in the high plateau. Both there and in the Delta, the program was bogging down, and was soaking up more and more of ARVN in static defense and garrison tasks. Most strategic hamlets, he asserted, did not meet 20% of the book requirements (the criteria). They were a leaky basket, from which the VC continued to draw adequate sustenance.

Colonel Serong set forth his ideas for remedying the situation, starting by working out of Saigon and cleaning up the VC pockets. He would give priority to Long-An, where less than 15% of the population was covered by the strategic hamlet program as of January 16, 1963, and move toward Binh-Duong and Tay-Ninh.[47]

Asked by Admiral H. D. Felt, Commander in Chief, Pacific, to comment on Serong's letter, General Harkins responded, "I agree with Serong that the situation here is growing progressively better[!]" He believed there should be continued emphasis on the strategic hamlet program, particularly in isolated areas between lines of communication. After a slow start, the GVN had recognized the primacy of the Montagnard in the plateau. Over 180,000 Montagnards had been relocated in strategic hamlets, "and have openly accepted government protection." Commenting on another passage, General Harkins said, "Here Serong is apparently speaking primarily of injury to innocent villagers through air strikes and gunfire . . . since it is President Diem's policy that all victims of GVN attack are, per se, VC. Nevertheless both the RVNAF and US forces take unprecedented measures to avoid this type incident." He concluded that he was delighted to have Colonel Serong's advice.[48] Clearly he and Colonel Serong were speaking different languages.

On May 15, Harkins addressed a letter to President Diem, reporting on the meeting he and Ambassador Nolting had had with Secretary McNamara the previous week, and summarizing the status of military programs. He continued:

As you are aware, there are over 6,000 strategic hamlets now completed in the country, with practically 8,000,000 people securely tucked away behind their fences. I believe this program, more than any other, has served to isolate the Viet Cong from the people. As it nears its completion in the coming months, it should prove one of the turning points in the war. Many of the combat units are involved in "clearing and holding" operations in support of the strategic hamlets. While I think this is vital, I believe that at the same time we must continue to have other operations which search and clear the Viet Cong bases that can be located.

Smaller operations are more effective; there had to be relentless pursuit of the enemy. "He is becoming a 'foreign legion' in a foreign country without support from the local population. . . . I am confident that 1963 shall be called the year of victory." The time for an all-out offensive was at hand.[49]

It is obvious that the MAAG had a different perspective on Viet-Nam than most other participants and observers.[50]

Beginning in July 1963, the Viet-Cong attacked the hamlets fiercely: tearing down fences, destroying construction work, assaulting militia posts, and forcing inhabitants to return to their previous locations. Roads were mined and communications with the more isolated hamlets disrupted.[51] In September, Sir Robert Thompson told Diem that the program had gone too fast and the provincial assets were overstrained. The VC had been presented with a number of soft targets, and the government had been unable to secure base areas. There had been a tendency for each province chief to fight a separate war. He thought the situation could still be retrieved, however.[52] By that time, Diem and Nhu were preoccupied with the struggle against the Buddhists, which had sharply divided opinion in the cities and was having some effect in the countryside.

From September 8 to 10, 1963, at President Kennedy's request, Marine General Victor H. Krulak and the State Department's Joseph Mendenhall traveled all over Viet-Nam to assess the situation. Krulak talked with 87 members of the military advisory team but not with any Vietnamese. He brought back an optimistic view of the shooting war. Mendenhall, who had talked mainly with Vietnamese whom he had known earlier, found fear and hate against the government in the cities and VC advances in the country. He concluded that the war could not be won unless Nhu was removed. After hearing the two officials, at a meeting of the National Security Council on September 10, President Kennedy remarked, "You two did visit the same country, didn't you?" At the meeting, Ambassador Nolting discounted Mendenhall's views, but two lower-ranking members of the mission staff sharply contradicted him. John Mecklin, head of the USIS in Saigon, said that in his opinion the regime's actions against the Buddhists had so alienated a large segment of the population that it could no longer hope to win a war in which public support was vital. He advocated applying direct pressure to change the government. Rufus Phillips, chief of the Rural Development Office of the USOM, started his report by saying he had known Diem, Nhu, and others high up in the government for 10 years and that he also knew the feelings of the rural areas. He said that there was a crisis of confidence between the people and both the government and the United States, which public opinion held responsible for keeping the regime in power. He agreed that the war was going well in the I, II, and III Corps areas, but asserted that it was going badly in the crucial Mekong Delta, which was as yet unaffected by the Buddhist crisis. The strategic hamlets there were being cut to pieces and were being overrun wholesale. He concluded by saying that this was not a military war but a political war, which was being lost. On that note the meeting ended.[53]

McNamara and General Taylor, who had become Chairman of the Joint Chiefs of Staff, General Harkins, and Henry Cabot Lodge, who had replaced Nolting as Ambassador, met with President Diem and his Secretary of State, Nguyen Dinh Thuan, on September 29, 1963, at the Gia-Long Palace. Diem spoke for two hours. He said the war was going well, thanks in large measure to the strategic hamlet program. The VC were having increasing difficulty finding food and recruits. US supplies were most helpful. The British, he said, had advised him to consolidate and hold firmly in one area before extending strategic hamlets to another; also to hold the coastal highway and consolidate the area to the seacoast before trying to secure areas farther inland. They advised that strategic hamlets should be limited at first to the most populous and productive areas.

Using maps, Diem explained that if he had disregarded the underpopulated Highlands, they would have become bases for VC attacks and a drive to the sea. He acknowledged that the program was overextended. The VC could overwhelm some hamlets, but others would grow stronger. He had taken calculated risks, such as opening highways before they were fully secure. The strategic hamlets affected all aspects of the war. Diem said that VC cadres returning from the North had been amazed. There was an increased propensity to defect. It now took larger VC units to get into the hamlets. Since the whole rural environment was more hostile, the VC had to group into larger units to survive. Moreover, land reform had won popular support for the government.

In their statements, McNamara and Taylor concentrated on political unrest in Saigon, caused by the repression. They said that there were serious political crises both in Viet-Nam and in America. McNamara called attention to the ill-advised statements of Madame Nhu. Diem rebutted these statements, and his manner was unshaken.

A White House press statement on October 2, 1963, said that Secretary McNamara and General Taylor "reported their judgement that the major part of the U.S. military task can be completed by the end of 1965, although there may be a continuing requirement for a limited number of U.S. training personnel." One thousand US military personnel could thus be withdrawn by the end of that year.[54]

A month later, Diem and Nhu were overthrown and killed, and the country sank into chaos. In 1965, President Lyndon Johnson found it necessary to send in US combat troops.

Years later, Stanley Karnow was told in Hanoi that the secret Communist agent, Colonel Pham Ngoc Thao, who (after his return from military training at Fort Leavenworth), had been named as Nhu's deputy for the strategic hamlet program, "had deliberately propelled the program ahead at breakneck speed in order to estrange South Vietnam's peasants and drive them into the arms of the Vietcong. Nhu had been duped."[55]

In fact, at least one political observer, Nguyen Ton Hoan, the leader of the Dai-Viet Party in exile, had anticipated Karnow's discovery. In a letter of April 29, 1963, to the historian Joseph Buttinger, Hoan, after sketching out the Communist strategy of sending some cadres to the North while keeping others in the South, named Colonel Thao as a concealed Communist, mentioning that his brother was a high official of the Hanoi Foreign Ministry, his father chaired Communist demonstrations in Paris, and his wife was the sister of an influential NLF member. This charge may have been dismissed at the time as guilt by association, to which Americans had become averse after the McCarthy years. Hoan also wrote that the most dangerous Communist infiltration was in the cadres of the strategic hamlets, except those inhabited by members of the religious sects. He turned out to be right on both counts.

In any event, the strategic hamlet program collapsed after the coup that unseated the Ngo family. Roger Hilsman wrote that the coup drew back the curtain that had been hiding the reality of how the war had been going. First, the VC had not been "compressed" into the Delta, but in the other regions had been lying low and infiltrating the strategic hamlets. Second, many of the attacks by government forces had been on targets where the VC were known to be absent.

Third, the statistics on the number of strategic hamlets and on the number of villages under effective government control were completely false. Vice-President Nguyen Ngoc Tho, for example, informed us that of the 8,600 strategic hamlets claimed under the Diem regime, only about 20 per cent actually met the standards . . . *Ah, les statistiques!"* one of the Vietnamese generals exclaimed to an American friend. "Your Secretary of Defense loves statistics. We Vietnamese can give him all he wants. If you want them to go up, they will go up. If you want them to go down, they will go down."[56]

Very soon after the coup, the VC destroyed most of the hamlets, and succeeding governments in Saigon abandoned the program. In 1964, the regime of General Khanh initiated a new program to build New Life Hamlets, which eschewed forcible relocation and placed the emphasis on creating a better life for the people while eliminating the VC infrastructure.

EVALUATION

Two highly qualified participant-observers, Dennis Duncanson and William E. Colby, maintained that the strategic hamlet program had been succeeding until the Diem regime was diverted by its struggle, first against the Buddhists in mid-1963, and then against the Americans, who finally acquiesced in the regime's overthrown. Duncanson put it this way:

Thus, by the spring of 1963, the situation was that the strategic hamlets had succeeded, in spite of maladroit propaganda but because of the prospect of personal safety for the average villager at last, in facing the Vietcong with an obstacle they urgently wanted out of the way, and at the same time bringing the authority of the regime into many villages for the first time. . . . . . . The only plot with guns to back it as well as American sympathy [in the fall of 1963] was that of the Generals; they took their time, for the prestige of Ngo Dinh Diem still stood high among their men and in the country, where hundreds of thousands of peasants, their hearts unwrung by denial of their human right to wave the flag of the World Fellowship of Buddhists on Wesak Days without the national flag, slept every night with new-found peace behind their hamlet fences and dutifully gave thanks to the patriarchy of Ngo Dinh Diem for it, as the Republican Youth told them to.[57]

William Colby felt that, though the Vietnamese government had proceeded too fast and had set up some hamlets in areas that could not be defended, it was mainly the Buddhist crisis and the overthrow of Diem that prevented the strategic hamlet program from overcoming its faults. As CIA Station Chief, he had been in agreement with Nhu's basic political approach and had been arming local communities for their defense. He was already aware in 1962 that a number of the hamlets were strategic only in a statistical sense, some enclosing a passive population that went on attending meetings that the Communists organized. The VC, however, saw the hamlets as a threat and began to attack them. But, he maintained, these were problems that could have been overcome with time. The Buddhist crisis, beginning in May 1963, caused time to run out.[58]

In my opinion, the weight of the evidence summarized in the preceding pages indicates that the strategic hamlet program was never successful, except in a few strongly Catholic localities, where the local priests and their parishioners created fortified hamlets and villages on their own; possibly for a time in such places as Kien-Hoa and the Operation Sea Swallow II area of Phu-Yen; and in some highlander villages. Even though massive VC attacks against the hamlets were delayed in Central Viet-Nam, it appears that the Communists had been enclosed along with everybody else in those areas which had for many years been under Viet-Minh and then Viet-Cong domination, so that they did not need to destroy hamlets which they in fact owned. In the crucial Mekong Delta, where hundreds of thousand peasants were forcibly regrouped and thousands of hamlets were enclosed by their unwilling inhabitants, the program was a tragic farce from the very beginning.

Why did the program fail? There were many reasons.

In the first place, the headlong haste that Nhu and his Communist deputy, Colonel Thao, forced made it impossible to fulfil all or even most of the criteria that the government itself had decreed, some of which were unrealistic for such areas as the Delta. Consequently, thousands of hamlets were declared complete when their defense perimeters were too long to be defended, when the defenders had no weapons and little training or motivation, when the people, resentful over being moved from their homes and rice fields and forced to labor long days without pay, did not understand the purpose of their sacrifices, when much of the resources allocated for social and economic benefits never arrived or were diverted for personal gain by the appointed officials, when the VC infrastructure was still in place behind the barbed wire, and when elections had not been held.

Of all the reasons why the program was doomed, the failure to eradicate the VC terrorist apparatus in the hamlets was surely one of the most important. When peasants and their own leaders were threatened with murder or kidnapping by Communist terrorists whom they knew (who, indeed, might be their relatives), and with no means of defending themselves, it is not surprising that they would be cautious about manifesting their loyalty to a regime that they in any case considered an alien exploiter. Sir Robert Thompson, Hilsman, and others repeatedly called for firm but sensitive police action to remove those terrorists from the hamlets and put them where they could no longer threaten the people. As these lines are written, many communities and business people in the United

States are faced with similar terror by racketeers and street gangs, whom they are not disposed to resist when they see that the criminal justice system does not keep them off the streets. In Colonel Chau's Kien-Hoa province, his hamlet interviewers gave the peasants opportunities to identify the VC death squad members, supposedly in secret; I have found no evidence as to how many took advantage of the opportunity or what happened if they did. In most localities, no credible opportunity existed, especially since the National Police were often corrupted themselves and distrusted by the populace. Under those circumstances, the VC needed only to ask and whatever they requested would be given.

Forced relocation throughout the Delta and other areas was, according to all the evidence, a universal cause of deep alienation. Some parts of Kien-Hoa, where well-trained and sensitive cadres were able to explain the necessity of moving, may have been an exception. I know of no other. The family graves and the land were the most precious things to the peasants. When farmers were forced to walk or otherwise travel such distances that cultivation of their fields was impaired, it is not surprising that they resented the agent of their economic loss. In too many areas the relocations were carried on brutally and hastily, not permitting the peasants to take their possessions and animals; and then their homes were burned. When the new locations were no more secure than those that they had left, their anger was intensified. Only the Viet-Cong could benefit from such foolishness.

Thus, many of the mistakes of previous unfortunate experiments in social engineering for security purposes were repeated in the strategic hamlet program, and, like its predecessors, it failed. This was the last nationwide governmental attempt to fit the South Vietnamese people into the Procrustean bed of rigid dogma until the Communists, after their victory of 1975, tried it their way.

4

The Beginnings of the Refugee Problem

For a year and a half after the overthrow of the Diem regime, that is, from November 1, 1963 until June 11, 1965, one government followed another with dizzying speed, each with less authority and presence in the countryside than its predecessor. This was a vacuum that the Viet-Cong were ready to fill. First they took over or destroyed the strategic hamlets, disbanding the elaborate controls imposed by Ngo Dinh Nhu and allowing or requiring their inhabitants to return to their homes. For most peasants, this was a welcome relief, and many were quite willing to cooperate with their new masters. In large parts of the country, GVN authority was soon restricted to the province capitals and district towns. Roads were interdicted or subject to VC tolls, and travel on them became unsafe for government officials, American advisors, and even the GVN military, except in heavily armed convoys which themselves were frequently ambushed. The guerrilla war was being converted into large-unit combat, as the Communists sensed victory at hand.

For a time it looked as if the VC, now reinforced by troops of the North Vietnamese Army, would be able to cut the country in two at its narrow waist, from the Highlands to the sea. President Johnson, however, was determined not to let South Viet-Nam fall into Communist hands. With the congressional authorization of the Tonkin Gulf Resolution, bombing of selected targets in North Viet-Nam began in 1964, and the first US combat troops, two Marine battalions, came ashore at Da-Nang on March 8, 1965. Those actions gave a much-needed lift to the morale of the Vietnamese. In June 1965, the game of GVN musical chairs ended when a military junta ousted the short-lived civilian government and named General Nguyen Van Thieu Chief of State and Air Vice Marshal Nguyen Cao Ky Prime Minister, thereby beginning a period of governmental stability during which Thieu gradually took possession of the instruments of power and remained in office until the final collapse in 1975.

FACTORS IN THE GENERATION OF REFUGEES AND CIVILIAN CASUALTIES

By no means did all the people in the countryside welcome or even tolerate the spread of Viet-Cong authority. Both during the Diem regime and after its overthrow, tens of thousands fled from the Communists. In the lowlands, the first to go were the landlords, Catholics, and devout members of other religions including Northern refugees who had been resettled in areas that could not be held, government officials, and village and hamlet chiefs who had been threatened with VC vengeance. They went to district towns, provincial capitals, sometimes to the strategic hamlets; some even moved as far as Saigon or other major cities, as will be seen below.

In the Central Highlands, some of the lowlanders who had been moved to the land development centers, including refugees from the North, were the first to go. The tribespeople, though they had many grievances against the GVN, were generally not eager to live under the harsh rule of the Vietnamese Communists, especially when doing so exposed them to bombing by GVN planes. As was reported in the previous chapter, the movement of up to 300,000 highlanders from the frontier areas in 1962–63 was a flight both from VC terror and exactions and from Diem's unrestrained air strikes.[1] As far north as Quang-Tri, some 3,000 "Mountaineers" who had escaped from VC exploitation were assisted by the provincial authorities and by Dan Whitfield of International Voluntary Services (IVS).[2]

In Tay-Ninh province, even though it was the center of the strongly anti-Communist Cao-Dai sect, the VC, whose southern headquarters, (called COSVN), were in the northern corner of the province, gradually came to control 90% of the land area; however, because of flight or relocation, 84% of the people lived in government-controlled "New Life Hamlets." The VC repeatedly attacked villages and hamlets, including strategic hamlets, and in the course of fighting, hundreds of houses were destroyed, creating new refugees and war casualties. The government could not provide security in that province, which was a terminus of the Ho Chi Minh supply trail from North Viet-Nam.[3]

In mid-June 1965, the VC attacked and overran the Vietnamese village of Dong-Xoai in Phuoc-Long province, creating more than 1,000 dead, wounded, orphaned, and homeless victims out of the total population of 3,000. They entered every home and cleaned out all the food and money of the inhabitants. The US Army civil affairs team immediately flew in rice which had been provided by USOM, and evacuated wounded children from there and from the provincial capital, Song-Be, to hospitals in Saigon. Leo Cherne, the chairman of the International Rescue Committee, who had just arrived in country, was asked by General William C. Westmoreland to visit the site. Cherne then bought dried fish in Saigon (with the help of the manager of his hotel), which the US Army flew up to the stricken village. An experienced leader of refugee aid, who had been visiting Viet-Nam since 1954, Cherne noted that there had been a profound change in VC tactics within the last year, resulting in total terror wherever the GVN had a presence. He recommended to the Senate Refugee Subcommittee, among other things, that US forces and the USOM be prepared to airlift thousands of victims of VC assault out of those areas that could not be held.[4]

The VC strategy in the 1964–65 period was to push anti-Communist refugees, especially Catholics, out of the land development centers and other villages into the towns and cities, in order to rid the Viet-Cong of a hostile element and overwhelm the capacity of the GVN to care for them. There was also evidence to indicate that the refugee flow enabled Communist forces to infiltrate government-controlled areas with Viet-Cong cadres.[5]

With the buildup of US combat forces, their military operations and those of the ARVN and the Koreans replaced flight from the Communists as the principal generator of refugees. However, there were various reasons for the refugee problem, as Deputy Assistant Secretary of State Leonard Unger explained to the Senate Refugee Subcommittee:

The motivation of the refugees is more complex. Most of them are fleeing from conditions of war which are becoming more intense as a result of generally increased military activity in the areas in which they lived. Many left their homes as a result of their unwillingness to accept further Vietcong terrorism and taxation. Many left at the urging of religious leaders, both Catholic and Buddhist, who know the fate of their religions in Communist areas. Some left as a result of last autumn's typhoons and floods.[6]

US military doctrine, shaped principally by World War II and the Korean War, both conflicts of massed uniformed troops with well-defined front lines, called for heavy use of artillery and air strikes to save the lives of soldiers, while decimating the enemy. US military advisors had been training the GVN forces in this doctrine for 10 years, and now American troops were practicing it themselves. When the enemy was an elusive part of the peasantry, however, such tactics were likely to inflict more damage and suffering on the people than on the guerrillas who, warned by the first shots if not before, could slip away to fight again. Indeed, the VC often deliberately drew fire upon inhabited places in order to kindle the people's anger against the forces responsible for it. However, angry or not, those who were wounded, bereaved, or made homeless by the bombardment, especially if it was repeated, usually had to move away from the conflicted area; and they almost always moved toward the GVN side. This did not represent "voting with the feet" for the GVN and its allies, as was sometimes claimed, so much as making a conscious decision that the side that had the heavy guns and planes was the safer place to be.

Anger and resentment were not simple phenomena. They depended on popular perceptions of who was to blame for the damage, and also on the treatment that the victims received afterwards. The peasants were well aware that in war people get killed and, when the VC hid among them and then drew fire from their enemies, it was the VC who were the cause of the injury. In those cases, the anger was often directed against the Communists, though it might have to be suppressed because VC retribution was always a threat. However, if the injury resulted from "friendly fire" when the VC was not present, sometimes because of map-reading errors, faulty intelligence, or because airmen traveling 500 miles an hour or even spotter-plane pilots could not distinguish ordinary farmers from guerrillas, then the resentment of the people would be directed against whoever fired on them. Also, when ground troops with their heavy tanks and armored personnel carriers tore up rice fields and then deliberately destroyed hamlets, killing or maiming old men, women, and children whom they suspected of concealing the VC, those troops and the country that sent them earned the hatred of the survivors. Unfortunately, these cases were the most typical of the war after the Americans and Koreans arrived. Their inability to understand or communicate with the people and their frustration at being killed by guerrillas who were indistinguishable from the peasants made the troops' sometimes savage conduct understandable, but it did not lessen the enmity of the victims, nor did it justify indiscriminate firing on civilians.

In 1971, General Westmoreland, then Chief of Staff of the Army, ordered a comprehensive study on the conduct of the war during the years 1964–68, when he was Commander of the Military Assistance Command in Viet-Nam (CO-MUSMACV). The study was intended to address the questions of whether US forces violated the laws of war or accepted norms of combat and whether high commanders were responsible for any such violations. The study listed some 40 directives issued by MACV and subordinate commands during those years setting out rules of engagement designed to protect the civilian population, and said that Westmoreland had taken a personal interest in seeing that they were observed. It acknowledged the international laws (the Geneva Convention of 1949 on Protection of Civilian Persons in Time of War) which, inter alia, prohibited deliberate attacks directed against civilians alone, but permitted attacks against defended places in which civilians are present so long as civilian casualties are not disproportionate to the military benefits obtained. It cited legal authorities to show that a town or village does not have to be fortified before it may be attacked if it is occupied by a combatant military force or if such a force is passing through. However, it did say: "On the other hand, no interpretation of the law would authorize deliberate attacks against unarmed farmers, women, or children engaged in normal civilian activities simply because they are found in a specified strike zone [commonly called free fire zone] or in other Viet Cong dominated or controlled areas." It pointed out that specified strike zones (SSZ) were cleared by the GVN authorities, and went on: "These SSZ, which are configured to avoid populated areas, include no known friendly forces or populace; they generally contain enemy base areas or infiltration routes. Unobserved fire may be directed against all targets and target areas located within an SSZ, after notifying the appropriate US/FWMAF [US/free-world military assistance forces] clearance authority.'' (It is not clear how unobserved fire could be directed so as to avoid hitting civilians who returned to SSZ's to cultivate or harvest their fields or to retrieve personal possessions, as they frequently did.) General West-moreland instituted compulsory classes for all ranks to instruct them in the laws of war in the light of the difficult and unusual circumstances of the Viet-Nam conflict. In September 1965, he convened a joint board to study the use of tactical air support.[7]

The evidence, however, is that all too often American soldiers and airmen failed to observe the rules of engagement that General Westmoreland laid down. ARVN and the Koreans were even less careful to protect civilian noncombatants. The American and Vietnamese press and other observers reported hundreds of cases in which inhabited places were destroyed from the air or by ground troops because of sniper fire coming from them or because they were suspected of harboring the enemy, and other instances in which people were shot simply because they ran or otherwise acted in a manner considered suspicious.[8] On the other hand, there were cases where American forces did act with restraint and sensitivity, even when destroying hamlets and forcing their inhabitants to move. These occasionally paid off in favorable attitudes and a boost to pacification. A few representative incidents of both kinds which took place during the years 1963–66 are summarized here.

The military operation in the Ba-Long Valley of Quang-Tri province during 1963 which brought in 2,500 refugees (mentioned above) was undertaken after the Vietnamese Air Force had unilaterally declared the beautiful, fertile valley a free fire area. It had been used by the VC as a medical and training center, and the only access to it by US and GVN personnel had been by air. This relocation operation appears to have been handled with sensitivity. By leaflets and aircraft loudspeakers, the people were offered resettlement. Those who came out were given a plot of land, food for six months, and money to help with house construction.[9]

On February 5, 1964, about 1,100 Viet-Cong overran Ven-Cau village in Tay-Ninh province, which had about 6,000 inhabitants. The Vietnamese military bombarded the village with artillery and air strikes, destroying 670 houses, damaging 200 others, killing 46 civilians, and wounding 60 others. Twenty-two ARVN soldiers were killed and 6 wounded. Eleven Viet-Cong bodies were counted. Two thousand refugees fled. They were fed and their wounds treated. Money was immediately authorized to pay compensation and rehabilitate the village, and compensation was paid. CARE, CRS, and AID relief supplies were provided, transported by US military and AID aircraft. In telling of this event to the Senate Refugee Subcommittee, USOM province representative Edmundo Navarro commented: ''Before this attack AID had assisted this village, it had given the people a better outlook on life. However, all our work was wasted by this one action by the military.''[10]

On June 2, 1964, US and Vietnamese Special Forces conducted an operation along the Cambodian border north of Tay-Ninh city and forcibly brought in 914 women and children—no men. By assuming personal responsibility, Mr. Navarro was able to get money immediately to provide housing, household items, food, and so on. He added that he and the province authorities had perfected the art of receiving refugees.[11]

In the last week of September 1964, a mistaken intelligence report was received in the Mekong Delta that 30 sampans on a canal were loaded with VC troops. An A1H air strike blew them apart. Then, several days later, it was learned that the sampans had contained only civilians, mainly women and children; 27 were killed and 30 seriously wounded. Malcolm W. Browne, in reporting this incident, commented:

The Air Force announced blandly that it would take steps to avoid a recurrence of such accidents. But similar announcements have been made after many of the hundreds or thousands of such incidents in the past, and basically nothing changes. The Air Force sometimes saturates areas with bombs weighing up to 500 pounds. Some of them go off immediately, but the others are timed to explode many hours later, presumably after the Viet Cong has come back. Or peasants who simply think it is safe to return to work. This kind of thing, regardless of whatever tactical advantage it may have, is to my mind little short of slaughter.[12]

A couple of months after the US Marines had established themselves at the Da-Nang air base in the spring of 1965, they occupied the nearby village of Le-My, drove out the VC in a firefight, and required the men to destroy punji traps (sharp stakes hidden in the ground) and bunkers, then turned the village over to Vietnamese territorial forces and moved farther out, saturating the area with patrols and ambushes. They trained the local forces, helped to prepare defenses, set up medical stations, and engaged in other civic action. This was a successful pacification operation, because the Marines stayed to provide security, but there were two hamlets northwest of the village that were in a VC area, whose inhabitants Lt. Colonel David A. Clement, the Marine battalion commander, wanted to bring into his security zone. They were reluctant to leave their homes and apprehensive about the coming rice harvest. As Clement recounted the events later:

I directed that H&I [harassing and interdiction] fire be brought close in to the hamlet, night after night. The attitude of the people about relocation improved in time and the relocation operation was scheduled . . . I had to convince the Vietnamese authorities of the necessity of this move since the official policy was to discourage refugees.

On June 18, the battalion and Vietnamese forces brought out 350 people, who moved into the Le-My complex.[13]

That August, the Marines attacked the VC village of Cam-Ne, destroying 51 huts, 38 trenches, and so forth. A CBS television crew with Morley Safer filmed the operation. Safer reported the burning of 120 to 150 houses and the leveling of the village. The impression left with the television audience was of senseless and wanton destruction and disregard for innocent civilian life.[14]

Operation Starlite, August 17–24, 1965, against fortified VC villages south of Chu-Lai (Quang-Tin province) was the first big battle of the Third Marine Amphibious Force, III MAF. It destroyed some of the villages, one of whose hamlets had been the command post of the First VC Regiment. Six hundred eighty-eight VC were reported killed, a number by air strikes or artillery, but only 109 weapons were captured. Forty-five Marines were killed and 204 wounded. The commander of the First Battalion, Seventh Marines, in his after-action report no. 1 of August 27, said: "More concern must be given to the safety of villages. Instances were noted where villages were severely damaged or destroyed by napalm or naval gunfire, wherein the military necessity of doing so was dubious."[15]

A civilian Front (VC) rallier, who had been deputy chief of a propaganda, culture, and indoctrination section in a district of Dinh-Tuong province in the Mekong Delta and was interrogated in July 1966, had a refreshingly different account of what happened in his area. In April 1965, the GVN dropped leaflets over Long-Dinh village urging the inhabitants to fill in their trenches with earth and to move out, because the village was going to be bombed. The people gathered up their belongings and went to live in huts along the highway. The Front guerrillas forced them back into the village, but they escaped again. Then the village was bombed and shelled for months, but there were no casualties. The VC reports concluded that, although the people were shaken, the shellings had deprived the Front of food, lodging, taxes, and manpower. International propaganda use of the incident was made, but otherwise the rallier saw no advantage to the Front. Asked if humanitarian considerations were put aside, whether he thought that the shellings were helpful to the GVN, he said they were indispensable. He said, "From experience, I realized that the Front is most strong in villages which haven't been shelled and that on the contrary it weakens there where shellings frequently happened." In his opinion, the peasants were losing faith in the Front and were eager to leave the insecure countryside for the towns. However, the GVN would have to help the people to settle and to make a living; then it could afford to shell their villages without having to fear resentment. It would have to keep its promises, however. In another case, this rallier succeeded in overcoming the fears of shelling on the part of the inhabitants of three deserted villages and inducing them to return and dig trenches.[16]

Operation Masher/White Wing of the US First Cavalry Division in northern Binh Dinh province from January 25 to March 6, 1966, evacuated 3,191 refugees from the An-Lao Valley by helicopter and brought out 10,000 more from Hoai-An district. It was followed by Operation Thayer I/Irving, in which Korean and ARVN units joined, and which ended October 24. Two villages were burned, and over 12,000 refugees generated. The town of Tam-Quan, which had been a VC headquarters, was captured, but few VC were killed or captured, and a tenuous security was established only in daylight hours.[17] Neil Sheehan of the

New York Times reported from the battlefield about "the appalling destruction wrought in Giahuu and about 15 other peasant hamlets on the central coast by artillery barrages and aerial bombardments." He said that "most of the destruction and the killing and wounding of civilians were, perhaps inevitable under the circumstances. The Vietcong and the North Vietnamese fought from an elaborate system of fortified bunkers and trenches built around and within the hamlets." Nevertheless, "some Americans here wondered whether the resentment and anger caused by the destruction might not thus create as many new Vietcong as the troops have managed to kill."[18]

Chemical defoliation, a purely American operation, was also a cause of refugee movement when it destroyed crops, which it frequently did, intentionally or because of drifting spray. A North Vietnamese company commander who rallied to the GVN on February 28, 1966, reported during his interrogation that he had seen crops destroyed by American defoliation spraying in two parts of Binh-Dinh during 1965 and had been told by cadres of other instances. The Front conducted active propaganda to get the people to hate the Americans because of the spraying, and it succeeded. The commander saw many empty houses in the defoliated areas and was told that the people had gone to the district town, though the Front had tried to keep them in place. Those who stayed said that they had not received any government compensation.[19]

During a second interrogation on August 24, 1966, this PAVN officer said that in long-liberated areas that had been subjected to repeated bombings and sprayings the people did not welcome the Front soldiers, and in more recently liberated areas they blamed the Front for the damage they had suffered. He reported: "The boys who herded the buffaloes said: 'You came and caused trouble to my family. My house has been burnt down, my parents are dead and that's because of you.' " He added that in the GVN-controlled areas, the people were faithful to the government, and the Front troops avoided the strategic hamlets and densely populated areas because they feared that the people would report their presence. However, those who had relatives in the Front complained about the GVN forces and said that the Koreans were inhumane. All, however, asked the Front troops not to fight or stay in their villages, so that they would not be attacked.[20]

Although there were undoubtedly other cases like the village of Long-Dinh where peasants were persuaded by the GVN to abandon their homes in advance of bombing and thus to escape injury, it was all too frequent that hamlets and villages were bombed while still inhabited, or that people were forcibly evacuated and then inadequately cared for. There were many voices at the time that pointed out how these practices caused unnecessary misery and worked against the war aims of the GVN and its allies. One who had the best credentials to warn his government was Father Nguyen Lac Hoa, who had founded and led a group of armed hamlets in the midst of VC territory in the Ca-Mau Peninsula (see chapter 3). When receiving the Ramon Magsaysay Award in Manila in 1964, the 75-year-old fighting priest said in his acceptance speech:

When fought as an international war, we have no chance to win. How can we explain to a mother when her child is burned by napalm? And how can we expect a young man to fight for us when his aged father was killed by artillery fire?

Indeed, how can we claim to be with the people when we burn their homes simply because those homes happen to be in the Viet Cong controlled territory?

Many have asked me why we are not wining in Viet Nam. My answer is simple. The misplacement of the order of importance. The Magsaysay way is: Winning the people first, winning the war second. I am afraid in Viet Nam today, the order is reversed.

I can talk plainly like this because I am a soldier as well as a priest. Fighting is necessary in order to protect the people from being physically harmed by the armed communists. But arms are useful only for defensive purpose.[21]

The joint communiqué of the Honolulu conference issued by President Johnson and Lt. General Nguyen Van Thieu on February 8, 1966, addressed this question in one paragraph, which said: "9. There was a full discussion of the military situation . . . They reaffirmed their determination to act with all possible regard for the rights of innocent civilians." The State Department's circular telegram 1520, February 16, 1966, to all diplomatic posts (worldwide) said: "9. FYI. If questions of prisoner treatment, bombing civilians, Cambodian involvement are issues in your country, your attention drawn to para. 9 of Communique."[22]

The Buddhist leader Thich Nhat Hanh, during a visit to the United States, issued a statement in Washington on June 1, 1966, the day the US Consulate in Hue was destroyed by Vietnamese youths. After assuring his audience that he was not anti-American and explaining the recent furor in his country, the Venerable Nhat Hanh wrote:

There are now more than 300,000 Americans in my country, most of them knowing and caring little about our customs and practices and many of them involved in destroying Vietnamese people and property. This creates friction which generously feeds the anti-American propaganda, and the fact that the war kills far more innocent peasants than it does Viet Cong is a tragic reality of life in the Vietnamese countryside. Those who escape death by bombings must often abandon their destroyed villages and seek shelter in refugee camps where life is even more miserable than it was in the villages. In general, these people do not blame the Viet Cong for their plight. It is the men in the planes, who drop death and destruction from the skies who appear to them to be their enemies. How can they see it otherwise?[23]

By the spring of 1966 some Army staff members in Washington were reevaluating the search-and-destroy strategy, and advocating greater emphasis on providing security to peasants in the countryside. This was resisted by MACV, but some experiments, which will be described below, were carried on in this direction.[24] It took another two years, however, before US and GVN strategy was significantly altered to reduce some of the damage and suffering inflicted upon the civilian population.

URBAN MIGRANTS OR REFUGEES?

Long before this period, indeed, going back to the French war, there had been movement of people from the countryside to the cities. Some observers attributed this to urban migration for economic or social reasons, as was taking place in most developing countries, but it appears that most of the migrants in Viet-Nam were internal refugees. That is, they were fleeing from military conflict or from the Communists. The eminent historian Bernard Fall wrote:

From the first day of the Indochina war, and particularly from December 19, 1946, until July 21, 1954, large numbers of hapless civilians left their houses and rice fields during actions of either the Communist or the French Union forces. The state of insecurity prevailing in the open country created a movement of large numbers of homeless refugees toward the urban areas. Even long before 1954, cities such as Saigon and Hanoi had seen their population increase five- to eight-fold in comparison to pre–World War II figures.[25]

Land Development Commissioner Bui Van Luong, replying to Fall, said:

In order to distinguish sharply between the diverse phases of the movement of Vietnamese during the period from December 19, 1946, to July 21, 1954, it should be said that two movements in opposite directions took place during the Indichinese war before the withdrawal of French troops from the southern provinces of the delta in north Viet-Nam. The first movement was that of city dwellers to the country, when the towns were to be destroyed in conformity with the Viet-Minh's policy of ''burnt land.'' The second movement was that to the cities of rural people who were aware that they had been deceived by the Communists, and left the villages to come and live in zones occupied by the French and nationalist troops, especially provincial capitals and large cities. It is this second movement that caused the enormous increase of the population of Hanoi and Saigon.[26]

About 175,000 refugees from the North who moved in 1954-55 did not settle in the countryside but remained in the Saigon–Gia-Dinh area. Many of these were government officials, military personnel, businessmen, skilled workers, academicians, students, and other urban dwellers.

After the Communist insurgency again turned to terrorism and armed conflict, especially after 1959–60, refugee flight from the countryside to the cities resumed. Individuals who had been living in insecure areas, including landowners, threatened local officials, and those ideologically opposed to the Viet-Cong, made up the vanguard of this exodus. Later, especially after the level of violence took a quantum jump following the arrival of American combat troops, whole hamlets and villages left their homes and became refugees.

A survey study of migration to Saigon–Gia-Dinh inquired into the reasons that motivated the migrants who arrived during the period 1964–72. It contains data from other sources on the increases in population of many cities, but not on the reasons for moving to cities other than metropolitan Saigon.[27] It found that the population of the smaller cities as a whole increased much more rapidly than that of Saigon from 1960 to 1970. Table 2 shows the figures for some of these cities.

Allan Goodman and his colleagues said that the rapid growth of Vietnamese cities could not be explained by the generation of refugees, because the migrants to Saigon did not have the characteristics found by some studies of Human Sciences Research to be typical of those they studied in provinces (for example, moving short distances, after having had direct experience with combat).[28] However, Goodman's sample survey of approximately 400 migrant respondents in various neighborhoods of Saigon and Gia-Dinh province showed that a clear majority came to the urban region for war-related reasons (table 3).

In reading this table, one should bear in mind that both 1964–66 and 1967–68 were periods of widespread insecurity and heavy combat in the countryside. In 1968, the Communist Têt offensive, beginning January 31, and the May offensive caused heavy fighting and a million war victims in Saigon and other cities as well. 1969–71 was the period during which territorial security was most widespread in the countryside, enabling about a million refugees to return home. 1972, which is not represented in table 3, was the year of the massive Easter offensive of the North Vietnamese Army, which generated over a million and a quarter new refugees. Goodman, analyzing responses from his sample for all of these periods, concluded that war-related factors accounted for 62.7% of the reasons given for migrating to the Saigon area, although other factors received secondary mention by some respondents. From the data reported in the study, one can infer that about 575,000 of the persons who migrated to the Saigon metropolitan area (excluding the refugees from the North but including all others who arrived before and after 1964 and were still living in 1972) had left their homes for war-related reasons.[29]

The war-related causes listed above would have qualified the migrants for GVN refugee assistance under the criteria laid down by the Ministry of Social Welfare and its successors. However, the official statistics never showed any refugees in Saigon and showed only a few in Gia-Dinh province (but did show many Têt offensive and May offensive war victims—a different category—in 1968). That this substantial number of migrants who were actual refugees was not counted or given government assistance appears to be due to a number of causes. The principal reason was probably that they either arrived before a formal GVN relief program for internal refugees began in 1965 or were not eligible because they were not in GVN camps but had settled among the general population. A former high official in the successive refugee agencies told me that they were excluded because (a) they had money and did not need assistance, an assumption that Goodman found to be contrary to fact in many cases, (b) they were not in camps, and (c) the government discouraged migration to the already overcrowded city.[30] The Senate Subcommittee on Refugees estimated in 1974 that there were about 2,000,000 unregistered refugees, including some 1,000,000 in Saigon who since 1964 were ineligible to register.[31]

Table 2
Population of Some Cities, 1960–70 (in thousands)

City	1960	1964	1966	1968	1970
Saigon, met. area	2,296	2,431	2,834	3,156	3,320
Saigon prefecture	1,400	1,600	1,518	1,682	1,761
Gia-Dinh city	69	80	110	151	156
Bien-Hoa	38	30	50	83	87
Da-Nang	104	149	228	334	385
Hue	103	110	114	160	184
Qui-Nhon	31	50	87	117	170
Nha-Trang	49	53	63	102	106
Cam-Ranh	NA	NA	31	66	76
Lac-Giao (Ban Me Thuot)	30	30	37	62	65
Dalat	49	55	73	85	79
My-Tho	40	63	73	80	110
Can-Tho	49	60	69	88	116
Rach-Gia	37	50	57	61	81
Vinh-Long	27	30	35	41	31
Long-Xuyen	23	25	30	47	73

Source: Allen E. Goodman, Lawrence M. Franks, and Nguyen Thi Huu, *The Causes and Consequences of Migration to Saigon, Vietnam* (New York: SEADAG, Asia Society, August 1973), 11–12.

Table 3
Causes of Migration to Saigon/Gia-Dinh, by Year Groups (percent)

Reason cited	1964-66	1967-68	1969-71
War related	55%	63%	36%
Military action in home area	14%	21%	15%
Damage/destruction of home/village	13	22	9
VC harassment	21	10	6
Village evacuated	3	4	2
Gen. lack of security	3	3	3
Defoliation	--	1	--
Combination of above	1	2	1
Job related	27%	24%	31%
Family related	13	11	12
Sugg. by religious leader	--	1	--
Misc. personal reasons	2	1	2
No answer	1	1	17

Source: Allan E. Goodman, Lawrence Franks, and Nguyen Thi Huu. *The Causes and Consequences of Migration to Saigon, Vietnam* (New York: SEADAG. Asia Society, August 1973), 137. Percentages may not add to 100 because of rounding. No reason was given for the high percentage of "No answer" in the 1969–71 column.

Many who came to other cities for war-related reasons were assisted by the GVN or US agencies, however, and some were counted as refugees, though before about 1967 refugee statistics were hardly more than informed guesses. Most of the population increase in Qui-Nhon up to the time of the US and Korean buildup in 1965–66 seems to have been accounted for by refugees, and a similar agglutination of refugees was occurring in and around Da-Nang, Gia-Dinh, and some other cities. Exact statistics are not available, however, because practices of recognizing and assisting refugees varied widely from province to province.

PACIFICATION AND REFUGEE POLICIES AND PRACTICES

Shortly after seizing power on January 30, 1964, General Nguyen Khanh issued the *Chien Thang* pacification plan (called *Hop Tac*, "cooperation," by the Americans). This plan consciously reversed many of the perceived evils of the strategic hamlet program and went back to Sir Robert Thompson and Roger Hilsman's concept of the "spreading oil stain." It proclaimed that "security must be completely restored in one area before proceeding to the next area." The plan laid out the precise duties of the regular forces, the territorial forces, and the self-defense corps in securing and protecting areas. It gave first priority to Gia-Dinh, Binh-Duong, Tay-Ninh, Hau-Nghia, Long-An, Dinh-Tuong, Go-Cong, and Bien-Hoa provinces. A Central Pacification Committee chaired by the Prime Minister and including all relevant ministries was established.

The plan was to create New Life Hamlets, not by regrouping people, except in carefully defined conditions, but by energizing and helping existing hamlets. Annex I of the plan, "New Life Hamlets," stated:

> 2. a. Relocation of people should be avoided, except in the cases of isolated houses which inflict obstacles on control and clearing, and the security defense missions. Psychologically, the people must be indoctrinated into such a group that they volunteer to join the movement. For this they must be compensated according to prescribed standards. However, in the case of distant moves, attention must be paid to care, help, land for cultivation, potable water, road and water lines, and other conditions in favor of the development of new life activities.

The plan specified that people must be kept free from collective development activities that bring them no direct advantage, such as the construction of highways, digging canals, and so on; these must be undertaken by the province. Nothing was said about assistance to refugees.[32]

MACV took a guarded view of the plan, regarding it as deficient in political measures such as land reform. However, the US Military Assistance Command and the US economic aid mission went even further than the government in eschewing forced relocation. A joint MACV-USOM directive said:

> When the population refuses to move in spite of our explanations, . . . we should not force them, but give them a free choice.
>
> a) Either they live in New Life Hamlets where they will have all the security guarantees and all the advantages of the New Life Construction Program.
>
> b) Or they live outside New Life Hamlets, and they will not profit from the advantages of the New Life Construction Program.

The principal deficiency of the new program was that it did not prevent the constant movement of army battalions from one locality to another, thus depriving the people of reliable security. The plan called for area saturation tactics and the need to clear *and hold* areas to be pacified, but with limited resources, military units were in fact moved for operational missions which were considered to have higher priority. Thus, people were reluctant to risk VC retaliation by visibly giving their allegiance to the government, and the VC took full advantage of this continuation of search-and-destroy tactics to reestablish control in undefended pacified areas. In fact, the "spreading oil spots" turned out to belong to the Communists rather than to the government, especially in the areas that had always had strong Viet-Minh or Viet-Cong controls such as the five provinces in coastal Central Viet-Nam: Quang-Nam, Quang-Tin, Quang-Ngai, Binh-Dinh, and Phu-Yen, where the proportion of the population in pacified areas sank from 22% in June 1964 to 12% in February 1965, while the proportion under VC control rose from 9% to 36%. In 20 provinces throughout the country that were analyzed from reports of US sector advisors, government control decreased from 41% to 36%, despite the fact that refugees increased the proportion in some provinces, while VC-controlled population rose from 29% to 35%, and population under strong VC influence remained almost constant, at 30% in June 1964 and 29% in February 1965.[33] The *Chien-Thang* plan was quietly abandoned in 1965.

However, the US Marines, although sometimes fully as destructive as the Army as we have seen, considered that the "spreading oil spot" strategy was preferable to search-and-destroy in densely populated I CTZ (the five northern provinces of South Viet-Nam). Lt. General Victor H. Krulak, Commander of Fleet Marine Force, Pacific (FMCPac), put it this way:

You can not shoot anything that moves in the rich area south of Da Nang, where the population runs as high as 1,000 per square mile . . . We have to root him [the enemy, who is mixed in with the civilian population] and separate him from the people; which is to say, fight a guerrilla counterinsurgency war, and clean up the area a bit at a time.[34]

Lt. General Lewis W. Walt, Commander of III MAF (Marine Amphibious Force), who had learned guerrilla warfare from men who had fought Sandino in Nicaragua and Charlemagne in Haiti, agreed. So it was that the Combined Action Program (CAP) was developed by the Third Battalion of the Fourth Marines at Phu-Bai in Thua-Thien province. A Vietnamese-speaking lieutenant hand-picked the volunteers. Each of four Marine squads was assigned to a PF (popular forces) platoon; the squad leader became the platoon commander, while the previous Vietnamese commander became his deputy. After joint training, the combined action platoons moved into hamlets and saturated the areas with patrols and night ambushes while protecting the rice harvest, for example, of the people who had moved into Le-My, and helping the peasants through civic action. Their presence, day and night, ended the accommodation that had char-

acterized many hamlets, and in time enabled the elimination of the VC infrastructure. For the villagers, the important thing was that the Marines made it
clear that their forces would stay and protect the people, so that they would not
have to become refugees. The program gradually expanded until by September
1967 some 75 hamlets were occupied by CAPs. They had helped to establish
intelligence nets, organize censuses and elections, denied resources to the enemy,
and continued to protect the people.[35] Unfortunately, the requirements of large-
unit warfare caused by the VC's 1968 Têt offensive, which struck Hue particularly hard, caused the withdrawal of the CAPs. However, at that time, a renewal
of pacification by combined action of US and RVNAF forces and the civilian
ministries took over.

A similar but shorter-lived program was implemented by the 25th US Infantry
Division under Major General Frederick C. Weyand in Long-An province, which
had largely reverted to VC control. Operation Lanikai was begun in September
1966 by the Fourth Battalion, Ninth Infantry Regiment jointly with ARVN, with
the mission being to secure a densely populated district. The movement of
refugees was discouraged and the Americans operated under very strict rules of
engagement, which limited the use of their great firepower. The battalion and
others assigned similar missions, lived among the people, developing local forces
and cooperation, so that the people could feel secure when American forces were
eventually withdrawn. However, the battalion was pulled out in November, well
before it could accomplish its mission, in order to join Operation Fairfax in Gia-
Dinh, and other units of the division were repeatedly withdrawn in 1967. ARVN
was not ready to assume the burden of area security, and so the VC were able
to return. During the last five months of 1966, MACV was investing 95% of
its combat battalions in search-and-destroy operations.[36]

If military and pacification policies and practices were often contradictory
during this period, so were policies and actions regarding refugees. Within the
GVN, the Ministry of Social Welfare (MSW) had responsibility for refugee
relief, while the Ministry of Rural Construction was responsible for resettlement.
However, neither ministry received any US money for this aspect of their work,
although USOM gave some supplies such as roofing, cement, and mosquito nets
to the Social Welfare Ministry in 1965. GVN budgetary support was pitifully
small. The result was that refugee assistance became largely a provincial matter,
dependent upon the attitudes of province chiefs, which ranged over the gamut
from benevolence and efficiency in Quang-Tri and Tay-Ninh, as has been recounted above, to indifference and hostility in Quang-Nam and many other
provinces. Moreover, arable land away from refugees' native villages was usually
already owned and cultivated by others; so opportunities for refugee peasants to
make a living at the only occupation they knew were almost nonexistent. Some
were able to take up jobs with the burgeoning American military installations
or near them. Around all these bases and in the neighboring towns sprang up
refugee shanty towns with laundries, car washes, tailors, shoemakers, taxis and
"cyclos," black market shops, bars, and prostitutes. Many a refugee daughter

earned far more at the world's oldest profession than her father had ever made growing rice. All this tore down the traditional family system and contributed to societal breakdown, but in the absence of adequate relief or the means of earning an honest livelihood, it was often the only way to survive. Until September 1965, there was nobody in the USOM assigned full-time to handle refugee matters, not to speak of social welfare in the cities.

Binh-Dinh, which had more refugees than any other province (as noted above) also had a remarkable Deputy Province Chief in 1965–66, Major Nguyen Bê, a former Viet-Minh leader who later became one of the fathers of the Revolutionary Development Cadres (RDC) and head of their training center, a program developed with CIA support through the Ministry of Revolutionary Development. On July 1, 1965, he sent a frank report to the International Rescue Committee and requested its assistance. At that time, he said, in addition to many victims of the typhoons of the previous November, there were 94,696 refugees from the Viet-Cong in this province of 804,000 people. He had established 26 sites in Qui-Nhon and the district towns for 4,845 families with 29,736 members, 7,238 of whom were children aged 17 and under. Only 799 were male youths 18 to 25, 12,252 were women 18 and over, and 9,447 were men over 25. This was a typical pattern, in which most of the young men and many of the older ones were in the forces of either the VC or the government (more likely the former). The remainder of the refugees in the province were living scattered in secure hamlets around the district towns (and hence probably not accurately counted). More camps were being built by the district authorities. Major Bê said that the refugees received 7 piasters a day (12¢ US at the official rate of 60 $VN per dollar in 1965), or 3 $VN plus 400 grams of rice; children under two also got five cans of condensed milk or 100 $VN per month. These were the official allowances established by the Ministry. He said, "The reason why to date we are continuing on the above rescue procedures is because we want to employ these refugees as a force for reconquering the countrysides." He asked IRC for 100 sewing machines to enable the women to make clothing for the Regional and Popular Forces.[37]

In December 1965, Binh-Dinh got the first USOM provincial advisor, Stephen F. Cummings, who came with experience with the American Friends Service Committee in Algeria and spoke fluent French (the second language of most Vietnamese officials). He found Qui-Nhon crowded with country folk who had come as refugees. It was also choked with American military and civilian goods which were warehoused in flimsy structures and freely stolen. During Operation Masher/Whitewing, when Tam-Quan was taken, Steve saw real malnutrition. The people were registered and fed to some degree; "there was such an arcane system that we never knew what got to whom." There was much corruption, he found. His counterpart, a young man from Hue who had graduated from the National Institute for Administration, refused to send relief money or commodities to some districts, because he feared that the district chiefs would syphon them off. At one point, the MACV team flew Major Bê out of the province because they considered that his life was in danger from the corrupt commanding general of the ARVN 22nd Division.[38]

The I Corps Commander, Lt. General Nguyen Chanh Thi, was reportedly antirefugee, and that naturally influenced the province chiefs, who were under his command—all except the chief of Quang-Tri, who was a member of the Dai-Viet Party and, at least under the Khanh government, had powerful friends in Saigon. The general feeling among GVN, US military, and AID officials in that region was that the refugees should not be pampered.[39]

The Province Chief of Quang-Nam was openly hostile to refugees. In a conversation in September 1965 with a USOM representative, he said there were perhaps 40,000 refugees who, for the most part, were "an uncontrollable mass. We don't want them." They were just a burden, he said; they just sat and received. The government could not control them, and the system was being abused by nonrefugees, cadres, and soldiers' families. And, "If we give them [refugees] something, they often give part of it to the VC." The Province Chief said that it was VC policy to drive the refugees into GVN areas to embarrass the government. The USOM man disagreed; he felt that 90% of the refugees were anti-Communist, and many had already joined the Popular Forces. He concluded his report: "But Colonel Tung is young and flexible. If he is given orders, a plan, guidance, funds without red tape, and in quantity, he is capable of directing a program.[40]

The journalist Philip Geyelin visited a number of provinces in the summer of 1965. At that time, it was estimated that 600,000 people had been displaced, of whom 200,000 were classified as resettled, which in many cases meant that they had moved in with relatives. Some, he reported, were relocated on new land. Near Nha-Trang, in Khanh-Hoa province, he found row housing for refugees that was superior to that of many local residents. On the other hand, in Quang-Ngai, where refugees were about half the population still under GVN control, conditions were "appalling," and the authorities were unwilling or unable to remedy them.[41]

These findings corresponded with the observations of two military civil affairs officers who were on temporary duty in Quang-Ngai for four months in the same year. They said that the majority of refugees had sought security from both friendly and enemy harrassment. An influx in June had increased their numbers from 20,000 to well over 90,000. During the VC offensive from May 29 to June 2, 1965, it was apparent that the Communists were trying to force large numbers of refugees into Quang-Ngai City. For the most part, the province prevented this. There had been a general lack of interest in the refugees until the province chief applied pressure. Payments were slow and incomplete, with much paperwork. Many refugees were demoralized by the inadequate and delayed supply of food. Some were without aid for four to six months. Montagnards were discriminated against, and some were malnourished. Meanwhile, large amounts of money and supplies were stockpiled in the province. The officers made a number of recommendations to improve the situation.[42]

The armed forces that generated refugees usually took no responsibility for them other than bringing them into district or provincial headquarters and dumping them onto local officials, usually without advance notice and never with advance planning or coordination with the civil authorities or their American advisors. Security was given as the reason for not sharing advance information on planned operations, although this frequently did not prevent the VC from knowing about them.

Winds of change were blowing, however, on both the military and the civilian sides. Although MACV was unwilling to change its refugee-generating search-and-destroy strategy and tactics, it did request 16 civil affairs teams in the summer of 1965 to assist in handling refugees. The first civil affairs company arrived in December.[43]

The Senate Refugee Subcommittee held three sets of hearings on Viet-Nam and Laos in July, August, and September 1965. Senator Edward Kennedy chaired them, and Senator Hiram Fong of Hawaii, the ranking minority member, was an active participant. They heard testimony from officials of the State Department, AID, the Department of Defense, Ambassador Henry Cabot Lodge, General Maxwell Taylor, voluntary agency representatives, Roger Hilsman (then a professor at Columbia University), Professor Wesley Fischel of Michigan State University, and others, and collected much additional material. It was a thorough review of the war victim situation. Some of the testimony has been summarized above. As of July 13, AID reported that there had been 530,000 new refugees in 1965. One hundred forty-five thousand of them had already been permanently resettled, and 13,105 were self-sufficient or cared for by their families; 371,895 were currently receiving aid.[44]

Ambassador Lodge ended his statement: "Let me say in conclusion that as Ambassador to Vietnam, this is the top of my list and I intend to do everything I can to be helpful with regard to the question of refugees and I pledge you my very best efforts."[45]

General Taylor was asked whether he saw the possibility that because of military necessity there would have to be the dislocation of large segments of the population. The testimony continued as follows:

General Taylor. Do I understand the question to be that we would have to evacuate population in order to conduct military operations?

Senator Kennedy. Do you see this as a possibility?

General Taylor. I don't think so as a deliberate decision. Obviously, when a war zone develops the population senses this in advance and that accounts to a large extent for the movement out of the area. They do not have to be told, they sense the danger. The Government thus far has not been obliged to deliberately evacuate people except in a few limited instances of border towns which are clearly vulnerable to Vietcong attack and which would be very difficult to defend or relieve. In a few cases, the Government has invited and assisted the population to move out, knowing, in the long run, they would be lost.

Senator Kennedy. Do you anticipate that other efforts would be made in order to secure various military objectives?

General Taylor. I think only in that very limited sense that in very carefully chosen places where the danger can be analyzed in advance and anticipated it may be necessary to move out population. But I would not anticipate it as a major problem.[46]

As it turned out, the Senator was more prescient than the General. Forced relocation of people did become a major problem in subsequent years.

Roger Hilsman, in his usual forthright fashion, had some pungent words to say about the way the US was conducting warfare in Viet-Nam. He warned that bombing a village, even though the enemy was using it as a shield for sniping, would recruit more VC than it killed. He asserted that refugees coming into the cities and towns were fleeing American and RVNAF bombs and shells, rather than voting with their feet for the government. Sometimes, he said, they blamed the Viet-Cong for causing the bombing, but at other times they blamed the GVN and the Americans. However, the refugees were people whose allegiance must be won—a symbol of whether the government cared. Hilsman advocated training the refugees, so that they could defend their villages when they were able to return.[47]

Wesley Fischel pointed out that thousands of peasants had to move because the Vietnamese sequestered their land for GVN and American bases. He advocated resettling refugees in a planned manner in South-Central Viet-Nam just inland, and in the Mekong Delta, where there were abandoned lands.[48] In later years this was in fact done, especially under Dr. Phan Duang Dan's land development and hamlet building program, which began in 1972.

The General Accounting Office (GAO), an agency of the US Congress, examined the refugee operations of AID and the GVN at the request of the subcommittee. It found, inter alia, that, of the 369,400,000 $VN allocated for refugees in 1965, only 24,400,000 $VN had been expended by July 28.[49]

These hearings had no efect upon American military strategy or tactics. However, they did lead to an administration determination that the war victims had to be helped. On August 30, President Johnson said that he was sending Dr. Howard A. Rusk, director of the Institute of Physical Medicine of the New York University Medical Center, to investigate the work of the voluntary agencies in Vietnam. AID announced that it was setting up a major program to assist the refugees. The New York Times, reporting these news items in an article that summarized some of the Senate Subcommittee testimony, said that according to US officials, the decision to make refugee aid a principal concern of the mission in Viet-Nam was in large part a result of the hearings conducted by Senator Kennedy.[50] AID Assistant Administrator for the Far East Rutherford B. Poats told a meeting of voluntary agencies that the refugee situation had become a "major crisis," referring to the Senate Subcommittee's attention, and admitted that there had been a "tendency" within the government to minimize the problem. He explained the new program, which would have a staff of 40 persons within the United States AID Mission (USAID).[51]

AID then temporarily borrowed the experienced refugee assistance administrator John F. Thomas, who was the director of the government's Cuban Refugee Program, and sent him to Viet-Nam to head the new refugee program with the authority and the assurance of resources to make it meaningful.

5

The Beginnings of a Refugee and War Victims Relief Program, 1964–67

Until 1964, social welfare, including refugee relief, was so low on the priority list of the Vietnamese government that it did not even rate a Ministry. The tradition in the predominantly rural society was that temporarily disadvantaged people were taken care of by their extended families. Thus, working-age adults looked after their aged parents, who in turn took care of the little children while their parents toiled in the rice fields. Minor children who lost their parents were brought up by grandparents or aunts and uncles. A family member who fell on hard times was helped by more fortunate family members. At most, the extended family looked beyond itself to burial societies. The government, even at the hamlet or village level, did not enter into the picture, but churches, the Red Cross, and foreign voluntary agencies provided supplementary assistance. The Catholic Church in particular instituted orphanages, which were often largely filled with poor urban children with one or both parents living.

After the transformation in 1957 of the Refugee Commissariat, which had resettled the refugees from the North (clearly a special case), into the Land Development Commissariat, a Directorate General for Social Welfare had responsibility to help victims of fire and flood and the few children who had lost all family. Its budget measured the perceived magnitude of the problem: 16,899,000 $VN ($478,000 US at the official rate of 35.35) in 1957, rising to 99,065,000 $VN ($2,802,000 US) the next year and gradually dropping back to 82,136,000 $VN ($2,324,000 US) in 1963. The Ministry of Health, which had responsibility for hospitals and clinics including the medical care of civilian war casualties, fared better; its budget in 1963 was 528,927,000 $VN ($14,963,000 US) in 1963. The total GVN budget during the latter year was 27,050,000,000 piasters ($765,205,000 US), the lion's share of which went to the Ministry of Defense.[1] In addition, the provinces and municipalities spent

276,277,000 $VN ($7,815,000 US) for social welfare and public health (together) in 1963.[2]

This combination of family support for ordinary hardships and GVN assistance
for natural disasters proved inadequate for the widespread displacement and
casualties resulting from the expanding insurgency and war. General Khanh,
shortly after taking power at the end of January 1964, appointed General Do
Mau (who had organized Khanh's coup) Vice Premier in charge of social welfare
and cultural affairs and named the Buddhist lawyer Tran Quang Thuan Minister
of Social Welfare, with the mandate to improve the care of both urban and rural
victims of societal disruptions.

THE MINISTRY OF SOCIAL WELFARE

Thuan organized his Ministry in three parts: Refugee Resettlement, Social
Institutions (orphanages, day care centers, old age homes, vocational training
schools, and so forth), and Social Activities (community development, social
services, and emergency relief). Most of his attention was devoted to the problems
of the festering urban slums. He tried to do something for newspaper vendors
and shoeshine boys. He got the Army and students involved in community
development in the poor districts of Saigon. He wanted to legalize prostitution,
but Catholic Church opposition prevented this. One day he went to the prostitutes'
prison in Cholon and released all over 16 years of age, sending the children to
a rehabilitation institute in Vinh-Long run by Irish Catholic sisters. This was
widely publicized. The Vinh-Long institute was a success. I visited it in 1968.
Thuan talked with his USOM advisor, Richard T. Evans, about building a
children's village like one he had seen in the Philippines to consolidate the
children who were in many orphanages, some of which were corrupt, claiming
more children than they had. This scheme could not be realized. However, he
cut off aid to orphanages that did not cooperate. He started a project that eventually became the National Institute for Social Service, which UNICEF (United
Nations Children's Emergency Fund) assisted.[3]

To assist refugees, Thuan set up provincial offices and sent some of his Saigon
staff out to train local recruits. Some of his officials complained about being
exiled this way. He also started training social welfare cadres, about 500 altogether. To head this program he appointed a remarkable young official, Huynh
Thanh Hu'ng, who had had no previous experience with social welfare but knew
administration and finance.[4] Hu'ng was to serve for 11 years, under 10 Ministers,
and he became the author of the growing body of regulations and procedures
that formed the framework of refugee relief and resettlement until 1975. He was
the consummate civil servant, but also a man of human compassion who did
not hesitate to go to some of the most dangerous areas in the field to see for
himself how the refugees were faring and to instruct officials in the regulations
he wrote. I worked closely with him in later years. Some of my colleagues

complained that he was unduly restrictive and obstructionist by his insistence on following the rules, but that was not my experience.

The budget of the Ministry more than doubled, to 188,472,000 $VN ($5,332,000 US) in 1964, which was still woefully inadequate to meet the needs of refugees and urban poor. Minister Thuan met with the foreign and domestic voluntary agencies twice a month. Since the Ministry's own funds were limited, he encouraged them to assist refugees directly.

In November 1964, Thuan resigned from the government in protest at what he considered General Khanh's dictatorial ways, but he came back when Dr. Phan Huy Quat was named Prime Minister on February 18, 1965. (Khanh was sent abroad a few days later as Ambassador-at-Large.) During his second term, he had to tackle the corruption of refugee relief in some provinces, including some of his own service chiefs. He found that some of the voluntary organizations, such as the Quang-Tri Buddhist chapter, were also corrupt, especially in the use of American Food for Peace commodities. This was a problem with which his successors and the USAID officials were to wrestle with over the years. Part of the difficulty was that, except for rice, the commodities that the US sent to Viet-Nam, such as CSM (a high-protein corn-soya-milk blend) and bulgur (cracked wheat enriched with soya) were strange foods which the refugees often sold or fed to their pigs.

During Thuan's second term, the number of refugees climbed rapidly and soon outstripped the capacity and resources of the Ministry, whose 1965 budget was a modest 210,784,000 $VN ($5,963,000 US). In later years he admitted that the program was not very successful. Thuan got some province chiefs to make land available for refugee resettlement, and his Ministry furnished farm tools and some money, but most of the refugees had to exist in miserable temporary camps with inadequate assistance. It was clear that a vast expansion of refugee relief and greater efforts to settle them in viable circumstances would be required. Minister Thuan resigned in June 1967 along with Dr. Quat, when the military took over the government with Air Vice Marshal Nguyen Cao Ky as Chairman of the Central Executive Council. Ky named lawyer Tran Ngoc Lieng Minister of Social Welfare.[5]

That was the situation into which John Thomas stepped in September 1965. Before he left Washington, he had worked out with AID a greatly expanded advisory and assistance program to mesh with what the GVN was prepared to do.

FORMATION OF THE US OFFICE OF THE REFUGEE COORDINATOR

John F. Thomas had spent most of his adult life helping international refugees. Beginning immediately after World War II, in the International Refugee Organization (IRO), which became the Intergovernmental Committee for European Migration (ICEM) in 1951, he worked mainly in Europe until being named in

1963 director of the US Cuban Refugee Program, which was an agency of the Department of Health, Education and Welfare (HEW). He was widely known to be a compassionate, nonbureaucratic, and versatile administrator of vast competence. So it was that, when AID was wrestling with the rapidly rising crisis of displaced persons in Viet-Nam, he was invited to sit in on its meetings as an informal advisor. The persons who were called refugees in Viet-Nam had not crossed international frontiers and were therefore not within the mandate of the United Nations High Commissioner for Refugees (UNHCR) or of ICEM, but their needs were the same and that was what mattered to Mr. Thomas. His policy was to assist those who had been forced to leave their homes, and to worry about definitions later. As he put it, "If a person fled from his home I never questioned his motives. I never got caught up in that 'fleeing from his home for economic reasons' bit of horseplay."[6] The worried AID officials accepted this view and gave Thomas the tools to make it work.

Shortly after meeting USAID Director Charles Mann and the few members of his own staff, Thomas went to Da-Nang and other places to see the refugee situation on the ground. He spent weeks visiting camps and speaking with Province Chiefs and AID Area Directors. He concluded that his previous thoughts about the problem had been correct:

1. It was not a traditional refugee problem in that the people had not crossed international borders;
2. The people were generally out of the same village and had preserved family ties;
3. The local people in whose midst the camp or camps had been located regarded the newcomers as "foreigners";
4. The displaced were homeless, destitute, and in need of immediate outside assistance.

Then Thomas reported to Charles Mann that there was little possibility of returning the refugees to their homes in the near future, and therefore new homes had to be built in secure areas. It appeared that in every camp at least 60% of the refugees were under age 14. That presented particular problems of schooling, medical care, clothing, and nutrition. Thomas found that:

Among GVN officials, US personnel and voluntary staff there was a great deal of semantics going on. Who was eligible for refugee services, who was responsible for providing them . . . All this led to a lack of positive action. Another strong principle in refugee work is to provide for the immediate needs of the refugee—questions of eligibility can be handled later."

In addition, there was a need for coordination between the USAID and GVN and for specialized US personnel in the provinces to advise and assist their Ministry counterparts. These observations were accepted.

Thomas built a strong staff to be on the ground by the time he had to return to Washington. Edward B. Marks, who had also served in IRO and ICEM and was pulled out of the AID Africa Bureau by Administrator William Gaud, was to be deputy, and then the successor as Refugee Coordinator. Eric Hughes, a Foreign Service Officer who had had refugee experience in Germany, came from his position as Consul General in Belfast to be Marks's deputy and eventual successor. Thomas persuaded HEW to release Jerry Ballanfonte from the Cuban Refugee Program. Wells Klein, who had been Director of the International Rescue Committee's Viet-Nam program, shifted to the USAID. Albert Cardinaux, on loan from the International Red Cross and with his background of having been head of the USOM refugee program in 1954–55, remained for a while. ICEM was persuaded to loan Porter Jarrell, who had been in Hong-Kong. Bert Fraleigh, Stephen Cummings and Richard Holdren have already been mentioned in chapters 3 and 4. George Beauchamp came over with John Thomas. Tom Hayashi was the logistics expert in the office. Others were added. Tina Kapsanis (who later served as Ambassador Komer's secretary) and two Vietnamese secretaries, Mrs. Thanh and Mrs. Sun, completed the staff. It was an extraordinarily experienced and competent group. At the same time AID/Washington named George Goss to be its Refugee Coordinator.[7]

For the first time since 1957, AID obtained a separate appropriation item for refugees in US Fiscal Year 1966 (July 1, 1965 to June 30, 1966), $10,400,000. Additionally, $7,900,000 in surplus foods and about $4,100,000 in medical and logistical support for refugees were included in other budget items.[8] Much of the dollar fund was used for the new staff; the rest went for commodities such as roofing sheets, cement, reinforcing bars, and so forth for the refugee camps. This did not help the pitifully small Ministry budget, however, which was only 280,000,000 $VN in 1966. John Thomas, with the help of a knowledgeable and sympathetic USAID program officer, Clayton McManaway, was able to tap the American Aid Chapter (AAC) of the GVN budget for this purpose. The AAC was that part of budget that was funded by the counterpart piasters paid to the Central Bank by importers of commercial commodities from the US financed by AID dollars—and that was a huge amount (over 15 billion piasters in US FY 1966, most of which went to the GVN military budget). Thomas got enough to raise the funds of the Ministry (and its successor) in calendar year 1966 to 1,016,600,000 $VN (equivalent to $12,582,000 at the new official rate of 80.80)[9] The supplementary amount was to fund the construction of 25 new temporary refugee camps and the improvement of old camps, the institution of training and work projects for the refugees, salaries and supporting costs for 100 new cadres to work in the camps of the most heavily burdened provinces, salaries and training of 600 camp health workers, salaries and training expenses of 2,000 school teachers, and for similar programs.[10]

These achievements set the GVN refugee program onto a more realistic level, assisted by a competent and effective US advisory staff. John Thomas went home in December 1965 and, after reporting to his old friend, Vice President Hubert Humphrey, Walter Stoneman and others in AID, and Senator Kennedy, he returned to the Cuban Refugee Program. Ed Marks took over in Saigon.

VIETNAMESE-AMERICAN HUMANITARIAN PARTNERSHIP

However, the Ministry of Social Welfare proved to be incapable of handling the greatly expanded resources and responsibilities that were now available—and that the rapidly increasing refugee population made necessary. By the end of 1965, Viet-Nam had over 735,000 registered refugees, of whom 282,000 were considered to have been resettled or returned to their homes.[11] Nguyen Cao Ky recognized that the refugee function would have to be strengthened. Late in January 1966, at breakfast with General Edward Landsdale, he said that he would be reorganizing the government during the next month and creating some new positions within his office; one of them would be put in charge of all refugee affairs.[12]

The Honolulu conference of February 8–9, 1966, between President Lyndon Johnson, Thieu, and Ky was largely devoted to the pacification program (now to be called rural construction or revolutionary development) as a means of winning the war, and for the first time the care of refugees was made an important element in that program. That gave refugee assistance a respectability within both the Vietnamese and the US governments that it had not previously enjoyed. It was clearly a subject in which President Johnson had an interest. Paragraph 8 of the Joint Communiqué issued at the end of the conference stated:

It was agreed that the refugees who have of their own free will come over from the enemy side must be adequately cared for and prepared to resume a useful role in society. The Government of Vietnam described its plans to meet this problem and the President assured them of full American support. It was agreed that a special effort would be made to provide good schools for refugee children.

The US record of Conclusions and Decisions for Further Action (classified Secret at the time) contained these items:

IV. B. Refugees

Consensus:

The care of refugees is highly important as a means of including in the social revolution now going on in South Viet-Nam the large numbers of people who have courageously, of their own free will, left the Viet Cong. The refugees must be prepared to resume a useful role in society. U.S. aid for refugees is an important demonstration of the humanitarian aspects of U.S. aid to Viet-Nam, and the U.S. will provide full support for GVN plans in this area.

Further Action:

1. Special effort will be made to provide schools for refugee children. (Resp.: GVN, AID with HEW).

2. In addition to the school effort, the President urged special attention to other

refugee projects such as vocational training, small loan programs and the like. (Resp.: GVN, AID with HEW).

3. Refugees should be given employment in light industry and given training in handicrafts. (Resp.: GVN, US Mission).

IV. F. Economic and Social Programs

1. *Health*

Further Action

g. Increase assistance to refugees, including surveillance, immunization, etc. (Resp.: GVN, US Mission).

It was clear from the above passages that President Johnson was concerned not only with helping refugees as part of the counterinsurgency strategy, but also with getting them back into productive life so as to avoid having them as a festering sore within the society. After the conference, he wrote several letters expressing his wishes. The letter to General Westmoreland said:

I know that you share my own views on the equal importance of the war on social misery, and hope that what we did at Honolulu will help assure that we and the Vietnamese move forward with equal vigor and determination on that front. As I have told Ambassador Lodge and am telling Thieu and Ky, I hope that in June I can have a report of real progress in that field. With continued progress in the military field, we should by that time be able to see ahead more clearly the road to victory over both aggression and misery.[13]

The State Department did make periodic reports on follow-up to the conference decisions, and both AID and HEW Secretary Gardiner monitored progress which, however, was not as rapid as President Johnson had wanted.

On February 22, 1966, Ky created the Special Commissariat for Refugees (SCR) in his office and appointed his friend and supporter, Major Nguyen Phuc Que, a medical doctor in the Marines, as Commissioner.[14] Dr. Que, a soft-spoken and modest person, brought with him some very capable military and civilian aides, such as Major Le Van Ba, and quickly extended the SCR into all the provinces. He himself traveled a lot, finding out the needs and aspirations of the refugees and persuading reluctant province chiefs that refugees should be considered a national asset rather than simply a burden. It is fair to say that a new era in refugee assistance began with Dr. Que. However, at first Ky placed responsibility for both refugee resettlement and return to home villages in the Ministry of Rural Construction (Revolutionary Development), which caused considerable confusion, and it was not until the beginning of 1967 that Dr. Que got the refugee program all together under his office.

The SCR also had to build its own field staff, although Que had some social welfare personnel transferred. This, plus the continued reluctance of some province chiefs to help refugees, largely accounted for the fact that only 56% of the

1966 funds were expended; even that was a better record than in 1965.[15] The SCR was subject to the financial and logistical procedures and controls of the Revolutionary Development (RD) program, which meant that funds and commodities were released to the province chiefs, who in turn disbursed them in concert with the service chiefs, while not relinquishing control. This meant that representatives of the provinces (usually district chiefs) as well as the SCR service chiefs personally had to be present when refugees were paid, and to sign the payment or distribution accounts. These requirements, which in part were intended to satisfy the AID auditors, greatly slowed down the disbursement of relief. It was only some years later that the procedures were simplified and control decentralized.

Dr. Que issued a series of guidelines and regulations covering all aspects of the refugee program, from the construction of temporary shelters (with blueprints—long houses with 10 family units, each three by seven meters), latrines, wells, classrooms, and so forth, to the payment and accounting rules, and other factors such as reporting, and hiring of personnel. These were translated by the Office of Refugee Coordination (ORC) and issued to its field personnel. When Stephen Cummings became the USAID liaison officer to Dr. Que, he systematized and extended this parallel communications system so that mutual exchange of information and ideas occurred at all levels. The regulations were compiled in a loose-leaf procedural manual; amendments and new issues were substituted for superseded ones or added as required.[16]

Refugees were being generated at the rate of about 20,000 a month during the six-month period from October 1965 through March 1966, while about 18,000 were counted as resettled or returned to their home villages each month. In April, as the level of military activity increased, the refugee flow doubled to about 40,000 a month, while some 31,000 a month were resettled or returned home. Of the approximately 450,000 refugees registered in temporary status at the beginning of 1966, most were in four provinces Binh-Dinh, Quang-Ngai, Quang-Tin, and Quang-Nam; this continued to be the case throughout the year. Because of the widespread insecurity in those provinces and the lack of arable land in the GVN-controlled areas, "resettlement" became a largely cosmetic term. The SCR regulations allowed the conversion of temporary camps into resettlement camps upon the payment of six months' rice allowance at the rate of 500 grams per adult person per day, 300 grams for children under two plus a house construction allowance of 5,000 $VN, about $62 US, for those not living in SCR-built quarters. Dr. Que placed much emphasis on health facilities, schools, vocational training, cottage industries, and other development projects, but it was not possible to make the refugees self-sufficient by these actions alone.[17] As was mentioned in the previous chapter, many of the refugees, both male and female, took jobs with the US and Korean forces or established trades and shops near the bases. Others lived somehow by hook or by crook—frequently the latter—and some of the remainder continued to receive temporary relief or help from the voluntary agencies. Neither I nor my colleagues saw evidence of malnutrition, except in rare instances.

Dr. Que knew that many refugees were VC dependents or sympathizers. However, he obtained the approval of President Thieu and Vice Marshall Ky for a policy that refugees were to be helped regardless of their origins or political opinions. He traveled widely, explaining the policy to military commanders and province chiefs, some of whom had black lists of those whose male relatives were on the other side. He pointed out that even many refugees who did have relatives in the VC were not Communists. In any case, he said, the GVN had to help those who lived in its territory without discrimination. It had to show them that it had a good policy and gain their confidence. If it didn't help the refugees, they would hate the government and help the other side with information and in other ways.[18] In October 1966, Que issued policy guidelines for assistance to refugees. After recounting the history of refugee movements beginning in 1954, and the reasons for movement, the paper set out in quite objective terms who the refugees were and how they were to be aided. The following is a summary:

The people who migrate to secure areas can be divided into two main classifications:

Those fleeing from circumstances of the war:

1. Persons migrating for a few days waiting for military operations to end, so that they can return home.

2. Those living in insecure areas who fear bombing or fighting. Their period of migration may be two or three months.

3. Persons living in VC base areas who flee with their entire families because of continual air or ground attacks against the bases.

4. Those who have moved to towns or other areas where allied armies are in order to find employment.

5. Persons who may be in one of the above groups but also have relatives among the VC or have pro-Communist inclinations.

Apart from entire family groups in category 3 above, most people have no intention of permanent resettlement. Some leave someone behind to look after their house and fields; some have relatives in the VC. For this reason, emergency relief assistance should be extended "along with all the measures which tend to attract people back to the just national cause."

Those fleeing from Communist oppression:

1. Civilians without political inclinations who are not able to endure any more the harsh VC regime.

2. Persons who previously supported the VC but have become disillusioned by the harsh and dictatorial VC measures.

3. Dependents of VC cadres or soldiers who have come out under the *Chieu Hoi* (open arms) program.

4. Persons who believe in the national cause but leave their homes in insecure areas.

These people wish to settle in GVN-controlled territory in order to be protected. Relief "should be accompanied by all other measures which encourage people to contribute to the pacification plan for their country." Relief is not only intended to satisfy needs.

It is also intended to win the population away from the VC and to transform the refugees into a positive element, a political force which will support the government at local levels and participate actively in the entire pacification program. This is an essential goal of the refugee relief policy . . .

However, social assistance is of a temporary character designed to assist people at the initial stage, when they still feel lost and far away from their homes. In order to avoid that people become demoralized or dependent, the authorities concerned should create favorable conditions so that refugees will have employment and be transformed into a productive element.

The rest of the directive set out the practical measures to achieve these goals. It pointed out that the programs previously divided between two Ministries were now brought together under the SCR. Priority was to be placed on return to home villages when security was restored or permanent resettlement. Coordination with the other services at the province level and with voluntary agencies and youth and students groups was enjoined.[19]

This instruction defined refugees so broadly that the limited resources of the SCR could not possibly reach all who were theoretically entitled to assistance. In practice, only those who went to SCR camps were registered. Many displaced people and migrants were unaware of the conditions for eligiblity and, as reported in chapter 4, those who fled to Saigon were excluded. Moreover, within both the GVN and the USAID there were still officials who regarded the refugee program as a boondoggle that existed only because of political interest. Some considered that the refugees were all VC dependents and took the attitude "To hell with them." It was also noted that the refugees themselves were not vociferous as a group in organizing and demanding their rights, as had been the case with postwar refugees in Europe.[20] Nevertheless, the Special Commissariat did its best to provide registered refugees with at least temporary relief, although implementation was always dependent on the province chiefs.

At the end of 1966, according to official GVN statistics, there were 560,937 registered refugees in temporary status, that is, they had not received all their resettlement assistance. A year later, 867,963 were counted in that status, after 390,918 had been resettled or returned to their homes; 195,998 of the temporary refugees at the end of 1967 were in Binh-Dinh, 169,695 were in Quang-Ngai just to the north, and 169,057 were in Quang-Nam, while 55,577 were in Quang-Tin, and 42,127 in Phu-Yen.[21] These figures reflected the rising intensity of the war and the shortage of resettlement opportunities with widespread insecurity, especially in the three southern provinces of the I Corps Tactical Zone (I CTZ) and Binh-Dinh.

In November 1967, President Thieu merged the SCR with the Ministry of Social Welfare to create the Ministry of Social Welfare and Refugees (MSWR), with Dr. Que as the Minister.[22] This eliminated the confusion of roles between the two agencies, and increased the influence of the combined Ministry. Trinh Viet Tam, who had been with Dr. Que in the SCR, was named Assistant Minister for Refugees, and Mr. Hu'ng became Assistant Minister for Social Welfare. At the beginning of 1968, Dr. Tran Nguon Phieu was appointed Deputy Minister. Shortly thereafter, Mr. Hu'ng became Assistant Minister for Refugees, and Dr. Ton That Niem, a Buddhist leader, was made Assistant Minister for Social Welfare.

US-supplied resources for the refugee program expanded to help meet the greatly increased burden. AID had dollar appropriations totaling $29.8 million for refugee relief in US Fiscal Year 1967 and $35.6 million for FY 1968. These included portions of other programs that were to be applied to refugee assistance. In addition, the equivalents of $6.8 million and $12 million in counterpart funds were allocated to the GVN's refugee budget, which then became 1,452.9 million piasters in Vietnamese fiscal year 1967 (the calendar year), of which 1,253.6 million piasters were counterpart funds, including 450 million in unexpended 1966 funds carried forward. The US Refugee Division was authorized 96 American personnel, of whom 27 were to be in Saigon and 69 in the field. Seventy-two were on board as of November 1967.[23]

In May 1967, following President Johnson's authorization, Ambassador Ellsworth Bunker announced a reorganization of the US pacification staffs in Viet-Nam, placing the civilian as well as military personnel and programs under General Westmoreland. He was given a second Deputy Commander, Robert W. Komer, who had been Special Assistant to President Johnson for Vietnamese Affairs, to be head of Civil Operations for Revolutionary Development Support (CORDS) with the personal rank of Ambassador. This was truly an unprecedented change. Ambassador Komer, a civilian, became the chief of over 6,000 military personnel and about 650 civilians in the new staff, in Saigon and the field, and had charge of military assistance to the Vietnamese territorial (Regional and Popular) forces as well as other paramilitary operations and all the field staffs of the USAID. The Refugee Division, then headed by George Goss, was transferred from USAID to CORDS. There was a good deal of uneasiness among some civilian staff members and others at this militarization of a humanitarian program, but it placed at their disposition very substantial material and personnel resources from the military side that were additional to the budget figures cited above. Komer was a dynamic and demanding chief—just as demanding of his commander and military colleagues as he was of his subordinates. Not for nothing had he earned the sobriquet, "the blow torch." Although evidently he was not at first able to change the search-and-destroy strategy, he obtained General

Westmoreland's support to effect a quantum leap in the priority of pacification as part of the war. He also raised the consciousness of US military commanders to the importance of providing prompt assistance to refugees as a means of winning their support for the GVN, and he gradually impressed upon them the necessity of reducing the generation of refugees. Goss was one of his senior staff members, and his program became an integral part of pacification, entitled to help from the other staff divisions, and in turn expected to help them. Komer was equally vigorous, though in a more diplomatic manner, in his advice to President Thieu, successive Prime Ministers, and the other Ministers of the GVN.

As the assistant chief of staff (AC of S) for CORDS, Westmoreland and Komer chose L. Wade Lathram, a Foreign Service Officer who had been director of the USAID Office of Civil Operations. Calm, unflappable, and knowledgeable, Lathram was an ideal support to his chief and at the same time the confidant of often-bruised division chiefs. When he was transferred to Korea in the spring of 1968 as Deputy Chief of Mission, William E. Colby came out from Washington to succeed him—and six months later took Komer's place as Deputy to COMUSMACV for CORDS.

Among the new assets that the CORDS Refugee Division acquired were three US Army civil affairs companies and one detachment, with a combined strength of 439 men. These well-trained young men had the mission of assisting military units during and after combat in their relations with the indigenous civilians, providing short-term relief and other aid, and reporting on matters that could affect military operations. Most of their complement were generalists, but it also included specialists in agriculture, public health, small industry, and so forth. The 29th Civil Affairs Company in I CTZ was assigned exclusively to refugee assistance; the other two companies worked mainly on refugees. Their help was invaluable.

Temporary Camps and Resettlement Sites

By 1966–67, the coastal areas of Central Viet-Nam and some parts of the Highlands, especially Darlac, Pleiku, and Kontum provinces, were dotted with temporary and resettlement camps for refugees. Most of these were pretty squalid places, but there were exceptions; some looked no different from the neighboring hamlets. These camps were not generally enclosed with barbed wire, even for defense, and their inhabitants were free to come and go. This marked a significant difference from the former strategic hamlets, and also from many camps in other countries for refugees who had crossed international frontiers. These refugees were Vietnamese nationals and, even when looked upon as intruders in some already crowded areas, they were among their own people. Improvements were being made in many camps, in accordance with SCR plans. Thus, for example, of 269 temporary classrooms authorized for 1966, some 104 had been completed by June 30, and 60 more were under construction. Short-term vocational training for refugees was underway at five polytechnical schools of the Ministry of

Education.[24] Some of these camps and shanty settlements were to become famous—or infamous—because they were often visited by news reporters and investigators for the Senate Refugee Subcommittee.

The Hoa-Vang district of Quang-Nam, especially Hoa-Khanh village on the outskirts of Da-Nang, had over 30,000 refugees in a string of shanty towns on the sandy beach, some next to the sprawling garbage dumps of the US air base. Their wretched houses had few latrines, little potable water, few schools or dispensaries, and no shade from the merciless sun or protection from the blowing sand; yet the people found employment on or in connection with the huge base and the headquarters of the US Marines. There were also a few camps, some equally unattractive, within the city of Da-Nang.

Tam-Ky, the capital of Quang-Tin province, became notorious as the site of a crowded, unsanitary reception center whose population was constantly replenished by new refugees dumped there by US, Korean, and ARVN troops.

The beautiful sandy beaches of Quang-Ngai were lined with one refugee camp after another, and there were others inland, 32 in all at mid-1966. However, there were dispensaries or aid stations at 18 of them, and another three received regular visits from district health workers. Fourteen additional dispensaries were scheduled.[25]

Right against the wall of the Qui-Nhon Catholic Cathedral was a horrible refugee slum, with open sewers, an inadequate water supply, swarms of flies, rats, and hordes of unschooled children; this was the Cathedral camp, which became a tourist attraction for visitors looking into the refugee situation. USAID Director Mann had recommended to both Lieng and Que that this camp be closed, and this was decided. Yet, the inhabitants, many of whom worked for the American military logistical headquarters or stole from its warehouses, resisted all efforts to move them to more salubrious camps elsewhere. When I visited in 1969, the camp was still as crowded as ever.

On the outskirts of Qui-Nhon was the Ghenh-Rang resettlement camp, which could hardly be a greater contrast. Looking like a middle-class American suburb of the 1920s, its rows of red stucco houses on neat streets were supplied with ample well water, a school, and other amenities. This camp, largely inhabited by Catholics, had invited the people of the Cathedral camp to come there but got few takers.

In An-Khe district of Binh-Dinh there were several quite good resettlement camps for Montagnards and Vietnamese, each built in the style of its inhabitants—that is, with Montagnard houses on stills and Vietnamese houses on the ground. The two Dong-Che camps and the Hoai-Cu camp had some abandoned agricultural land around them, which the refugees were clearing and cultivating when I visited on January 25, 1968.

Inland, the Ca-Lui Montagnard resettlement camp in Phu-Bon province, which I visited first on January 26, 1968, was really a return-to-village site. The VC had destroyed the village in 1965 and taken the inhabitants away to be production workers. In 1966 they were able to come back, and others had joined them, to make a total population of about 6,000. They were being assisted by a Revolutionary Development Cadre 59-man team and a Truong-Son Cadre team, and protected by a company of the tough Montagnard Civil Irregular Defense Group (CIDG). This illustrated the integration of pacification forces and cadres to help refugees which Komer and the GVN had brought about.

Down the coast, alongside an abandoned railroad track in Tuy-Hoa, the capital of Phu-Yen province, was Chop-Chai, one of the worst camps I ever saw in Viet-Nam. Its few long-houses were falling in ruins. There were no latrines and only one well for water. It had no community facilities or school. However, it was used to house temporary refugees year after year.

However, in mid-May 1966 the first interprovincial resettlement occurred, when 852 refugees from Phu-Yen were moved to the outskirts of Cam-Ranh. Both the GVN and the US forces wanted workers for the huge air and naval base being constructed at Cam-Ranh. Three hundred more families from the same province were moved shortly thereafter to the Dong-Lac settlement in Cam-Ranh, in a project sponsored by the GVN, AID, the Vietnamese Confederation of Trade Unions (CVT), and the US International Union of Electrical Workers (IUE).[26] The trade union project was not successful and was later abandoned by many of its refugees, but the first project, in which Catholics had moved under the leadership of their priest, did succeed, and the community was prosperous when I visited it in 1969. It had cultivated land, in addition to the employment opportunities on the base.

In 1966, another interprovincial resettlement project moved refugees from Binh-Dinh to two hamlets, Binh-Son and Son-Hai, on sandy soil near the coast of Ninh-Thuan province. Agricultural experts from the USAID and the Vietnamese Ministry of Agriculture had found the land and said that, with water and fertilizer, sugar baby melons, onions, garlic, and other crops could be grown. When Edward Marks took Dr. Que to see it, the Commissioner was skeptical, but a delegation of refugees was prepared to recommend it to their people. At first only about 50 families moved. Within a few months, the settlement was a success.[27] With the help of the SCR and AID, deep wells with pumps were drilled, and both chemical fertilizers and manure bought from the Chams in the area were used. (The Chams, unlike their Vietnamese neighbors, kept their cattle in pens.) When I visited in 1969, these two settlements were prosperous, even though each refugee family had only half a hectare of land. They were supplying onions and garlic to the Saigon market and furnished water to President Thieu's native village. Casserina pines and eucalyptus trees were growing around the houses as windbreaks and sources of shade. A Filipino community development worker employed by CORDS was helping the people with their agriculture and the beautification of the hamlets.

In the Mekong Delta there were few refugee camps; most refugees lived with their relatives or in scattered houses in the ordinary hamlets and villages. There were some temporary camps, but generally the people moved out of them quickly. Even the places that were formally designated as resettlement camps were usually hamlets or subhamlets, where the refugees were allocated sufficient land to make a living. Thus, for example, in one resettlement camp in Go-Cong province which had the elegant name, *Ba-Le* (Paris), and which I visited in 1968, each family had three hectares of land, and there were many fish ponds; the settlement had its own local social welfare cadres.

THE HOLDREN REPORT, JULY 1967

Although much progress was made by the SCR in 1966 and early 1967, aided by the Americans in the USAID, there remained substantial deficiencies. Many refugees were not registered or counted, especially those who were not in recognized camps. Payments were often delayed or not made at all, sometimes because funds were slow in getting from the SCR through the bureaucracy, but more frequently because province chiefs and their service chiefs hoarded or misused the money. The same was true of rice and other commodities allocated for refugee relief. A CORDS evaluation report of May 1967 showed that of 573,546 refugees eligible for daily allowances, 244,498 had not received them. The proportion of nonreceivers was highest in IV CTZ (probably reflecting the scattered location of most refugees there) but second highest (63.5 percent) in I CTZ. A number of CORDS Refugee field personnel had been assigned to other duties. Camp facilities were frequently not provided.[28] In a frank conversation with a CORDS representative in July 1967, Dr. Que expressed the view that on the American side the priority for refugee assistance had been lost in the succession of reorganizations since January. His own problems within the GVN remained: Refugees were still given low priority and were often distrusted as VC elements. Assistance to them was minimal, despite the prodding and instructions of the SCR. Though the III Corps commander had a positive attitude, those in I and II Corps were particularly negative. Que had asked for a meeting with General Hoang Xuan Lam, the I CTZ commander, after the elections early in September, hoping to show him some captured documents from Phu-Yen which showed VC concern at the loss of population.[29]

These faults were particularly hard on the refugees in the five provinces of I CTZ, which were more frequently hit by VC attacks and allied military operations than most other areas and had less secure land on which to put their displaced people. Richard C. Holdren, the Regional Refugee Advisor of CORDS, had been reporting regularly on the situation, but evidently without effect. He decided to call attention to the problems in his scheduled briefing of the Commander of the Third Marine Amphibious Force, Lt. General Robert E. Cushman, Jr., who was also the MACV Senior Advisor to the Vietnamese Corps Commander, on July 26, 1967. He submitted a short paper and then briefed the general and his staff orally. His main points were: There were an estimated 234,500 refugees in 204 camps and 236,750 scattered refugees, a total of 451,250. (These were the first statistics, to my knowledge, which included the large out-of-camp population, who in that region were just as much in need of aid as those in camps.)

The SCR had a commendable program (he listed the benefits that refugees were to receive) and a fine leader in the person of Dr. Que, but implementation was hampered by shortages of experienced personnel and vehicles, overcentralized control from Saigon, and lack of interest by many provincial officials. CORDS/REF, the Third Marine Division, and the voluntary agencies were rendering valuable assistance. However:

Overall, there is a highly visible failure of the announced GVN refugee assistance program. Less than 50 percent of the refugees have received temporary relief payments; less than 25 percent the resettlement assistance. Some have received one payment or the other. Many have received no assistance at all. The program is too little to be really meaningful, and sorely delayed. Thus, among this group of possibly 20 percent of the people under GVN influence there is widespread disillusionment. The psywar loss to the Allied cause is incalculable, not only among refugees, but on the other side credence is given to the VC claim that the GVN is not interested in the rural people.

Holdren made a number of recommendations, principally that the US military impress upon ARVN and the GVN the critical refugee problem and the need for a greatly increased effort to meet it. He suggested that the 29th Civil Affairs Company might be asked to set up a coordinating center, with qualified ARVN personnel assigned, to help the SCR catch up the arrears with a crash effort. General Cushman received the briefing favorably and talked with Holdren for 20 minutes afterwards.[30]

Two days later, while the Refugee Advisor was out of his office, his Vietnamese interpreter, who had typed the paper, gave a copy to Richard Critchfield, a reporter for the *Washington Star*. Since it was not classified—most papers prepared by CORDS advisors had to be typed by their Vietnamese assistants in the absence of American secretaries—this was not a breach of security.[31] On August 6, liberal quotes from the report appeared in American newspapers and on television from coast to coast. The *Washington Post* headlined it, "Refugee Project Called a Failure in U.S. Report." The *Chicago Tribune* said, "Viet Refugee Aid Program Called a Flop, Red Tape, Disinterest are Blamed."

The effect upon official Washington was what so often happens when news of failures of programs for which US Government agencies are responsible surfaces. The squeaky wheel gets the grease, as my father used to say. After transmitting the text of the *Washington Post* report on August 8 and reports of other media shortly thereafter, James Grant, the AID Assistant Administrator for Viet-Nam sent an Eyes Only telegram to Komer saying that he would be seeing Senator Kennedy and was sending Wells Klein for a short trip to Saigon, and asked that a plan be prepared to strengthen the refugee program. The same day, Komer alerted the Deputy for CORDS of I CTZ. Then he sent a telegram to Washington expressing agreement that action must be undertaken and saying that he had laid on a trip to I CTZ with Goss and possibly Dr. Que.[32]

On August 15, the day after he had made a quick survey on the ground,

Komer sent a letter to Dr. Que saying he was afraid the refugee problem in I Corps was outrunning GVN capabilities. The US was strengthening its staff and giving high priority to the airlift of supplies. Ambassador Komer recommended the prompt release of SCR funds allocated but not disbursed, emergency release of US-supplied rice, and the appointment of a senior ARVN officer as the SCR Inspector in the region. He said he would gladly provide a plane to get Dr. Que up there. Two copies of the letter were sent to General Cushman, one of them marked for General Lam. Komer mentioned the matter also to Prime Minister Ky.[33] The next day, a telegram from Grant reported that he had met with Senator Kennedy, who had reacted favorably to Komer's initiatives and to his own. The Senator had asked the GAO for a report and was sending the subcommittee's counsel, Dale De Haan, to Viet-Nam. Grant was sending Wells Klein in advance.[34]

The first weekly situation report from I CTZ, dated August 17, reported that approximately 150,000 refugees had been generated since April 1, of whom 20,000 had been uprooted by military operations within the last two weeks. The pace was expected to continue. Roofing and canvas were exhausted. Five thousand sheets of aluminum roofing were to be flown from Saigon to Quang-Ngai for the expected relocation of civilians by Task Force Oregon. The 29th Civil Affairs Company had been augmented. An SCR mobile team had arrived in Thua-Thien August 15. A CORDS/REF officer was on temporary duty.

On August 22, Dr. Que replied to Ambassador Komer. He said that the provinces had been urged to pay allowances promptly and I Corps had been requested to release funds to Quang-Nam. Fifteen new vehicles had been allocated to the region. He had requested the Minister of Commerce to allow the SCR to buy 2,400 tons of rice from the Da-Nang warehouse, and he had asked for a meeting with General Lam. In turn, Dr. Que requested that his office be informed in advance of the estimated number of refugees to be generated by military operations. He said:

I think military officials should take into consideration the factor of time set for migration. A hurriedly-performed migration will possibly reach the military target but not surely the pacification objective. Refugees ought to be given enough time to bring over with them some of their belongings. There are, in most cases, only usual things but bear a great spiritual value for some.

He requested that two C-123 or C-130 aircraft be put at the SCR's disposal and that cadres in the provinces be provided helicopter transport to bring payments and commodities to mountainous areas.[35] The request for assigned aircraft was not granted, but helicopters were often used to transport GVN refugee personnel and commodities when the US advisors went along.

The second weekly situation report from the region reported that 6,347 refugees had come in within the last week; they had received only minimal support, due to shortages in the CORDS warehouses. However, 1,744 of them had been carefully relocated by Task Force Oregon, bringing their house frames and all their possessions.

On September 9, Dr. Que and General Lam got together, and the general announced that he regarded the refugee situation as the number one priority to which he expected the province chiefs to give attention. The commissioner for his part announced that all displaced persons were to be regarded as refugees, no matter what their origin, in other words, whether VC or not. He was simplifying payment procedures and would attempt interzonal resettlement of some refugees. Dr. Que then visited Thua, Thien, Quang-Nam, and Quang-Tin with George Goss and some of their respective staff members; he announced increased allowances.[36]

Thus, for a while there was a flurry of activity and the care of refugees improved in I CTZ. Holdren was not pilloried for the leak of his report; instead, Ambassador Henry L. T. Koren, the I CTZ DepCORDS, and the Refugee Division in Saigon were grateful that he had stimulated some belated action. He wrote: ''The fall of 1967 was truly productive for the I Corps program. Achievements in cash payments, food distribution, housing construction, plus all other programs ranged from double to triple the previous rates. Another benefit was the new attention given to refugees by the [US] military.[37]

In October 1967, Luther McLendon took over as I CTZ Refugee Advisor, and Holdren became the action officer for the region in the CORDS Refugee Division. There he experienced the frustrations of dealing with the dual bureaucracies of CORDS and USAID to get funds and commodities allocated, as well as the equally complex bureaucracy that SCR had become—frustrations that I myself was to experience some months later.

NEW KENNEDY HEARINGS

In May, August, September, and October 1967 the Senate Subcommittee to Investigate Problems Connected with Refugees and Escapees held nine days of hearings, following up those it had held in 1965. Most of the new sessions were devoted to civilian war casualties and will be discussed in chapter 6. However, William S. Gaud, Administrator of AID, Assistant Administrator James P. Grant, Assistant Secretary of State William P. Bundy, Dean James R. Dumpson of the Fordham University School of Social Work, Professor Roger Hilsman, and representatives of voluntary agencies testified on refugees and social welfare problems. The record of proceedings included also the GAO reports on refugees and war casualties, and the Senator questioned Mr. Gaud about the Holdren report. Much of the information brought out has been summarized above.

A new element was the testimony of Dean Dumpson who, together with Dean Kindelsperger of the University of Louisville School of Social Work, Mrs. Susan Pettiss of HEW, and Dr. Martha Branscomb of AID, had visited Viet-Nam in July and August at the request of AID and with the approval of the President. He pointed out the miserable condition of refugees who had exhausted their SCR benefits, as well as of the many displaced people who did not go to refugee camps and were not registered. These victims of the war were technically the responsibility of the Ministry of Social Welfare, which, however, did not have the resources or the staff to care for them. He said that the GVN and the US in its supporting role

must accept and act on the fact that failure to deal promptly, efficiently, and humanely with displaced persons in Vietnam is destroying the effort of nation building, is supporting the efforts of the Vietcong to weaken the will of the Vietnamese and their faith and confidence in the GVN, in their own Government, and is contributing to defeat the goals sought by all our military activity.

He called attention to the disruption of families caused by dislocation and the absence of resources to help them, which, he said, was "threatening the very fabric of Vietnamese life." Special attention should be devoted to the youth, he believed.

Family dislocations have driven them to the urban centers. Already there are wandering gangs of youth in the areas of Saigon. The presence of large numbers of foreign troops has resulted in the mushrooming of bars and bar girls and prostitution... Now, this may be a natural and unavoidable consequence of war but, nevertheless, it is one more factor ripping apart the fabric of the Vietnamese social structure.

Dean Dumpson found a lack of understanding of social welfare as a factor in nation building or of the need to integrate social welfare with economic development. He urged that USAID and CORDS acquire the resources and staff to deal with the problems with some adequacy.[38]

These hearings, like the earlier ones, had the effect of further stimulating US Government action in the refugee and public health fields. In January 1968, Senator Edward Kennedy made a personal trip to Viet-Nam, his first since 1965. He visited more than 25 refugee camps and talked with hundreds of people. When he returned, he summarized his findings in an important speech before the World Affairs Council of Boston on January 25. It marked the Senator's growing conviction that not only were US and GVN actions toward refugees misguided, but that the war itself was wrong. He had found much of the countryside ravaged and 25% of its population refugees with a great deal of resentment toward the United States. He said:

It is apparent to me that it is the refugees in Vietnam, and their brothers in the hamlets, whom we must win over... But all too often this task may be almost impossible, because of that one forgotten and seemingly insignificant act in a fast-moving war, the destruction of a home or a hamlet—and that most significant fact, that we displayed no compassion thereafter. One further impression—and perhaps the strongest and most depressing—is the impression of the Vietcong themselves... The determination of the Vietcong is awful to behold. They are capable of great cruelty. They often attack positions using the peasant and his home as a shield...

While I was in their country I tried to assess the spirit with which the Vietnamese on our side conduct their part of the war. For we are in Vietnam because they are in peril; it is their country, their war, their future. Every other time in our history when we have gone into battle to help others to stay free the other nations have been dedicated to the cause. When they were threatened, as Britain and Russia and South Korea were, they fought valiantly . . . But at this stage of the war in Vietnam, I believe the people we are fighting for do not fully have their hearts in the struggle. And I believe as well that the government that rules them does not have its heart in the cause of the people. So we are being forced to make the effort for them and take the risks they should be taking themselves . . .

I say that the explanation for this terrible situation is not cultural but political. I say that most of the officials in Saigon do not care about these stricken people; that they are more interested in maintaining their own positions of power than in helping the victims of the war; and that the way they look upon the people outside Saigon and the way they treat the peasants elsewhere, they have become much like the colonialists who trained them. They are truly colonialists in their own nation . . .

In the field of refugee care and in many other fields the Government of South Vietnam has been engaged in the systematic looting of its own people . . .

So it should be made clear to the elected Government of South Vietnam that we cannot continue, year after year, picking up the pieces of their failures. We should as a nation do all that is necessary to prepare that government to take over their true responsibilities. But if they are unwilling to accept them, they should be aware that the American people, with great justification, may well consider their responsibilities fulfilled.[39]

Senator Kennedy tended to see things in black and white. He was wrong in not distinguishing Dr. Que, most of his top lieutenants, and other honest and compassionate GVN officials in Saigon and the provinces from the corrupt and indifferent ones he was condemning. He should have pointed out that millions of ordinary Vietnamese did have their hearts in the struggle to remain free, that their underpaid soldiers fought bravely, especially those in the underequipped territorial forces, and that hundreds of thousands of youth and other plain people were helping their fellow citizens, often at great personal sacrifice. Nevertheless, this powerful speech contained much painful truth. It undoubtedly made an impact upon its influential audience. Ironically, the Communist Têt offensive that began five days later, while intensifying the antiwar feelings of the American people and their Congress, turned much of the Vietnamese government and people around, and with the help of Ambassador Komer and his staff, caused the correction of many of the negative features that the Senator had so penetratingly observed. However, by then the United States was irrevocably committed to withdrawal.

VOLUNTARY AGENCIES AND RELIGIOUS ORGANIZATIONS

Vietnamese and foreign voluntary agencies, religious organizations, and youth groups played a major role in supplying the aid to refugees and other war victims—and, more importantly, in providing that humanitarian, people-to-people contact that official agencies often neglected. Thus, for example, Vietnamese Catholics, Buddhists, women's clubs, and private citizens, aided by such voluntary agencies as Catholic Relief Services (CRS) and the International Rescue Committee (IRC), set up and ran orphanages and day care centers for thousands of children, some of them with parents too poor or tired to care for them, and their personnel held and loved the babies and children who had nobody else to show them tenderness and love. Those agencies and several others, including the Philippine Civil Affairs Group, also sent medical teams into various provinces, with some of the teams staffed by doctors and nurses who themselves had been refugees from persecution in other countries. International Voluntary Services (IVS) sent agricultural experts who spoke Vietnamese or one of the Montagnard languages into the most exposed country villages to work with the peasants, including refugees, to improve their farms and introduce new seeds and simple tools. Project Concern set up and operated a hospital for Montagnards at D'ampao in remote Tuyen-Duc province, where American medical personnel trained tribespeople to be nurses and barefoot doctors. Outside Kontum city, Dr. Pat Smith on her own, gathered support where she could and founded a hospital that attracted far more Montagnards than the nearby Province Hospital, which discriminated against them.

Vietnam Christian Service, a coalition of the Mennonites and other Protestant denominations, helped the slum dwellers of Saigon and refugees in three I CTZ provinces to improve their miserable sanitary facilities and to provide supplementary feeding to malnourished children. The American Quakers built and operated a rehabilitation and prosthesis center in Quang-Ngai, a dangerous province not reached by the GVN rehabilitation center in Da-Nang. In the same province, the American Red Cross entirely took over refugee feeding and care in two districts, later extending its activity into Quang-Tin province. The New Zealand Red Cross operated a wonderful pediatric clinic in Qui-Nhon. The German Red Cross stationed the hospital ship *Helgoland* in the Da-Nang River for years, providing the most modern surgical and medical care to all who needed it; then, when operating the ship became too costly, they built and staffed a splendid hospital in the city to replace it. The Vietnamese Christian Youth Social Service (CYSS), aided by the World Relief Commission, established a fine vocational school and agricultural experiment station mainly for Montagnards just outside Hue, and another school and bakery in Da-Nang. CYSS was also ready at a moment's notice to accompany CORDS Refugee personnel, including me, to remote areas where new refugees were brought in, and to supply food and medicines as needed. Students from the Universities of Saigon and Hue, including medical students, spent their vacations aiding refugees. In 1968, one student group was given governmental responsibility in a district of Saigon, where they organized the slum-dwellers, mostly victims of the Tết offensive, to rebuild or improve their houses, sanitation, and water supply, and to engage in other forms of self-help. These examples represent only a handful of many.

By the late 1960s, over 30 foreign voluntary agencies were operating, providing several million dollars worth of goods and services annually, as well as distributing tens of million dollars worth of food furnished by the US government under PL 480 to refugees, school children, and others. Some of the agencies were under contract to CORDS or USAID to furnish specified services, but most operated on their own. A voluntary agency council was established, but it was not very successful in coordinating the activities of the agencies, which jealously guarded their independence.

Some of the voluntary agencies, such as CRS and IRC, supported the GVN/US war effort. Most others kept their opinions to themselves and, since they were dependent on CORDS and USAID for air transport, movement of their commodities, and sometimes housing and military post exchange (PX) privileges, dissent was not encouraged. A few, however, such as IVS and the Quakers, openly expressed their opposition to the war and gave their help equally to needy VC and those under GVN control. In 1967, Don Luce, the Viet-Nam director of IVS, and several of his colleagues resigned in protest; and IVS gave up its AID contract and decreased its staff in the country. Don Luce and representatives of the American Friends Service Committee were frequent witnesses before the Senate Refugee Subcommittee.

The humanitarian role of the Vietnamese and foreign private voluntary organizations was a splendid part of the assistance effort for the war victims and the poor of Viet-Nam.

6

Mounting Combat as a Generator of War Victims

In the period up to late 1966, most of the Vietnamese who had an ideological enmity to the Viet-Cong or who by virtue of their economic and social position (for example, landlords, government officials and their dependents, Catholics, Cao-Dai, and others) felt threatened by Communism left VC-controlled and contested areas as refugees. To their numbers were added many thousands who had been generated by Vietnamese and Allied military operations, as described in chapter 4. In the contested areas, thousands of local officials and leaders owing allegiance to the GVN had been assassinated or had fled.[1] Thus, the measures of pacification, such as the hamlet evaluation system (HES), could show an ever-increasing percentage of the population under GVN control, but much of the increase represented refugees who had come in voluntarily or involuntarily. Large areas of the countryside were abandoned to VC control and were declared free fire zones, even though many villages and hamlets were still inhabited by peasants who for one reason or another could not bring themselves to leave the land and the family graves.

By the end of 1964 to mid-1965, the VC had ceased driving people into GVN areas as refugees. Instead, anxious to preserve their manpower base of military recruiting and labor as well as the source of their food supply and taxes, they prohibited movement into GVN territory. Some peasants, especially those who had benefited from the Communist redistribution of land or who had family members among the cadres or fighting forces, stayed voluntarily. Others remained because they could see no other form of existence than the one that their families had followed for generations. Still others may have wanted to leave but were held by the threat of retribution. For these, Allied military operations often furnished the opportunity to escape. In most of the VC or contested areas it therefore gradually became inevitable that by 1967 the generators of refugees and civilian war casualties were almost exclusively the military forces of the GVN and its Allies, especially the Americans and Koreans. They were increasingly inclined to use military operations, including artillery and air strikes, as a means of driving the people out of their homes and into GVN territory in order to deprive the enemy of their manpower and food. These forces tended to regard all who remained in such areas as VC partisans and, as such, fair game. In a number of operations, they forcibly relocated whole villages and made free fire zones of their former homelands.

On the other hand, in GVN-controlled areas, VC and NVA attacks and harassment generated both war casualties and what came to be called "in-place war victims." Many of these attacks consisted of random mortaring, rocketing, or grenading of populated places, intended to terrorize the people and convince them that the government could not protect them anywhere. Refugee camps were often subject to propaganda, ground attack, and destruction, to induce the refugees to return home. Both pressure-detonated and command-detonated mines were placed in roads to interdict travel into or out of GVN market areas. No form of attack or harassment was too grisly to be employed to teach the government servants and troops and the people that the VC would punish those who defied its commands and that there was no escape. Several in-depth investigations by both private and official analysts and reporters revealed how people became refugees and war victims, and how this affected them and the contending parties.

In 1966–68, under contract with the US Defense Advanced Research Projects Agency, a think tank called Human Sciences Research, Inc., made a series of carefully researched and objective studies of refugee and evacuee populations in various provinces, which for the first time revealed who these people were, why they had left their homes, how well they were assisted, and what impact they made upon the communities within which they settled. The studies were made at the request of the US military, which was concerned at the counterinsurgency aspects of the problem, but were assisted by the Refugee Coordinator of the USAID and his field staffs. The first to be published were conducted in three widely separated provinces: Phu-Yen in Region II, Dinh-Tuong in Region IV, and one district of Quang-Nam in Region I, where almost all the surveyed refugees had come out on their own, although many were prompted by military operations or bombardment in their home areas.

THE REFUGEE SITUATION IN PHU-YEN PROVINCE

In the summer of 1966, 1,193 heads of families in 25 resettlement areas and temporary camps, representing 9,845 refugee families with about 51,000 members that were accessible (out of a population of 327,500) were surveyed by trained Vietnamese interviewers using a prepared questionnaire.[2] Ninety-six percent of the refugees studied were ethnic Vietnamese, the remainder being Rhadé and Hroi tribesmen. Forty-five percent were Buddhist, 39% ancestor worshipers, 8% Catholics, 5% Cao-Dai, and 3% animists. There were more children and old people than in the general population and both males and females in the 15-to-35 age group were greatly underrepresented (a finding that was typical of refugees throughout the country). In the 15-to-29 age group there were only 69 males per 100 females. The analysts attributed this to non-conflict-related migration of rural young people to cities, military recruitment and conscription by both the GVN and the VC, war losses, and evasion of conscription. The detailed data brought out the fact that the dominant factor in the Phu Yen situation appeared to be military recruitment and conscription. Each refugee of productive age (15–49) had to support 2.7 others, compared with 1.3 among nonrefugees. This was also due to the smaller numbers of persons in the able-bodied age group who came out as refugees. The mean household size was 5.2, which was smaller than among nonrefugees. One fourth of the respondents reported separation from one or more family members at the time of moving. Nearly 40% of the refugees considered themselves to be literate. Sixty-five percent of the families had owned agricultural land, and 75% had access to land. Distribution of land was relatively egalitarian, with a mean holding of 2.4 hectares and a mode of 1.5.[3]

Each respondent was asked at length what factors influenced his decision to move. Respondents could cite more than one factor, and so 2,185 citations were recorded by the 1,193 respondents. Ninety-three and eight-tenths percent said that they had not been physically forced to move, and some of those who said they were added that they had wanted to move before but could not, because of the VC controls. The causal agents and reasons for movement are shown in table 4.

Of the 18.7% who gave artillery and bombardment as a reason for moving, most said that their houses or possessions had been destroyed, and some specified that family members or neighbors had been killed or wounded. The Allies were the principal causal agents associated with this reason, but 3.5% said that the VC had caused the bombardment. Seventeen percent of the refugees said that ground military operations had served as the opportunity or catalyst for movement, some adding that they had wanted to move and had done so in response to warning from Allied forces that their area would be attacked and that aid would be furnished in GVN territory.

Almost all who cited terrorism or coerced activities as their reason identified them with the Viet-Cong. Many found the forced labor making punji stakes, digging tunnels or ditches, and serving as porters to be particularly irksome, often preventing the peasants from working their own land. (These complaints are reminiscent of those levied against the GVN during the agroville and strategic hamlet campaigns.) The compulsory political education sessions were also resented. Fear of being conscripted by the VC was another reason for moving. However, 20% of the Korean citations and 7% of the GVN citations were in the category of coercive acts. Among the economic and social reasons was general dissatisfaction with living under the Viet-Cong. Some left when Allied troops and GVN troops abandoned their villages.

Some nonrefugee heads of families in Phu-An and Dong-My hamlets, from

Table 4
Causal Agents and Reasons for Refugee Movement, Phu-Yen Province (1,193 respondents, 2,185 citations)

Causal Agent	Frequency of citation (%)
Viet-Cong	84.9
GVN	24.4
Allies (unspecified)	26.5
Korean troops	10.9
US troops	6.1
Viet-Cong vs. GVN	16.4
Viet-Cong vs. Allies	5.4
Other (relatives, friends, religious leaders)	8.0

Summary

Viet-Cong	84.9
Allies	67.9
Interface	21.8
Other	8.0

The cited reasons for movement were as follows:

Reasons	Percentage of citations
Forced to move	3.4
Artillery and bombardment	18.7
Ground military operations	24.1
Terror and reprisals	16.4
Coerced activities and levies	21.0
Fears/hardship from VC activity	8.2
Economic and social factors	7.2

Source: A. Terry Rambo, Jerry M. Tinker, and John D. LeNoir, *The Refugee Situation in Phu-Yen Province, Viet-Nam* (McLean, Va.: Human Sciences Research, Inc., 1967), 31, 33.

which refugees had moved, were surveyed. They expressed roughly the same reasons for refugee departure as the refugees. They themselves generally said they had not wanted to abandon their land, homes, ancestors, and livestock, and feared that life would be harder in exile. About half of those respondents in Dong-My hamlet had been refugees and had returned. They thought that security had become adequate, and they said that farmland had not been available when they were refugees and living conditions had been hard. Their hamlet was in fact near the edge of the zone where Korean troops were expanding their secure

area. Only 15% of the refugees interviewed reported that they had been discouraged from leaving their homes; this was by the VC in all cases.[4]

Relatively small refugee movement had occurred in Phu-Yen as early as 1961,
but it was not until 1965 that a significant flow occurred. The earliest to move
as VC terrorism began were wealthy persons and higher officials fleeing to district
towns and the provincial capital. After the destruction of the strategic hamlets
began, hamlet-level GVN civil and military cadres and their relatives fled. Then
the VC consolidated their control and restricted out-migration, allowing only the
old and weak to leave; some GVN adherents managed to escape also. Only 9.6%
had left before 1965. (The report noted that the pre-1965 movers may have been
underrepresented in the sample by reason of assimilation into the general population or return to their home villages.) As American and Korean troops were
introduced in 1965 and began a series of spoiling operations into NLF "liberated
areas," people could escape at will, and mass refugee movement occurred. There
were two peaks, in October-November 1965 and January-February 1966, when
41.9% of the refugees moved. The second peak in the migrations coincided with
the "rice harvest protection campaign" in Hieu-Xuong and Tuy-Hoa districts.
The campaign was successful in safeguarding the rice and reducing VC control
in the Tuy-Hoa valley, but it caused extensive property damage and generated
a considerable number of refugees. Fifty-one and six-tenths percent of the total
refugees migrated during the first six months of 1966.

Refugee movement throughout the province was almost all for short distances,
usually within the same district. It had the effect, however, of greatly increasing
the population in Tuy-Hoa and other urban areas and of decreasing (but by no
means emptying out) the people in VC areas. The reporters wrote:

All but a few villages retain large civilian populations which can be exploited by the
guerrillas. Refugee migration in Phu-Yen has not yet reached proportions sufficient to
eliminate all effective VC population resources, as some Vietnamese and American
officers had hoped it had, nor in planning Allied firepower can those who do remain be
considered Viet-Cong.[5]

On the basis of its interviews with hamlet and district officials, Human Sciences
Research (HSR) estimated that there were 54,455 refugees in the province at
the end of July 1966. The official GVN figure was 44,689, while the USAID
refugee representative estimated 73,788. Only 61.2% of the HSR sample reported
receiving any government aid, while 38.8% said they had received nothing at
all. Living conditions in the refugee camps were squalid: they were refugee
slums. Only 14% of the children between 5 and 19 were attending school. Thirty-
three and four-tenths percent of the people were unemployed, and very few of
the remainder were employed in the same occupations (mainly farming) as before.
Most reported receiving lower income than before moving, but some previously
low-income persons had improved their lot. The refugees had an adverse effect
upon the communities where they were settled; hamlet chiefs blamed them for

increasing inflation and unemployment, as well as overstraining local facilities, and posing a security problem.[6]

On the other hand, the refugee migration represented a major loss to the Viet-Cong and a potential gain to the GVN. The HSR study estimated that it drained an estimated 5,000 men of military age and a total of about 21,000 from the labor force accessible to the VC, as well as reducing the tax base. It made it more difficult—but by no means impossible—for the VC to propagandize the refugees. The movement of people into GVN areas offered a corresponding potential political-psychological gain to the government which, however, the researchers found was not exploited, except by recruiters of ARVN and the territorial forces. Although the Saigon government pointed out that refugees were a potential asset to the national cause, that lesson had evidently not penetrated among the officialdom of Phu-Yen.[7]

THE REFUGEE SITUATION IN DINH-TUONG PROVINCE

Two hundred seventy-two heads of refugee families were interviewed in eight locations by trained Vietnamese university students in the summer of 1966, a few weeks after the interviews in Phu-Yen. Two of the seven districts in the province, one in the extreme west and one in the South, could not be reached because of insecurity. According to USAID estimates, there were 5,177 refugee families (with an average of 5.9 members each, HSR found; thus 30,544 refugees) in this rich agricultural province of some 530,000 inhabitants. The 272 inter-viewed families contained 1,617 people, 736 males and 881 females. This works out to about 84 males per 100 females, a lower ratio than the 90:100 in Phu-Yen. Each refugee of productive age, male and female, had to support two others. Of the 736 males, only 126 were in the 15-to-34 age group. An additional 46 were reported as separated from their families, and 17 were reported killed, but even when these are added, the male population in that age group would still be less than the normal pattern. Jerry Tinker, the author of the study, thought that the difference was accounted for by failure to report family members in the VC. Fifty-four and four-tenths percent of the refugees were Buddhists, 14.1% ancestor worshipers, (Confucianists), 15.4% Catholics, 15.4% Cao-Dai, and 0.7% Protestants. Fifty-four percent considered themselves literate. Sixty-five percent had been engaged in agriculture before moving, but only 38% owned land (contrasted with 65% in Phu-Yen).[8]

In contrast to Phu-Yen, where 99% of the refugees came from within the province, only 73.3% of those in Dinh-Tuong were natives of the province; 19.1% came from Kien-Hoa, which was the neighbor on the southeast, 4.4% from Kien-Tuong on the northwest, and the remainder from three other provinces. Officials stated that Giao-Duc district, which could not be surveyed, contained many refugees from Kien-Phong. That district contained part of the Plain of Reeds, a VC stronghold. It was thought that some Dinh-Tuong refugees had gone into neighboring provinces, but probably fewer than the number that had come in. All the refugee movements were over relatively short distances.[9]

The causal agents and reasons for movement cited by the refugee sample are shown in table 5. Eighty-eight and nine-tenths percent of the refugees cited the GVN and the Allies as the causal agent, and only 38.6% cited the VC, a distinct reversal of the citations in Phu-Yen. On the other hand, the citations of VC vis-à-vis the GVN were higher in Dinh-Tuong.

In the Mekong Delta during the summer of 1966, the war was more static than in Phu-Yen, and the Allies relied heavily on artillery to spoil VC activity. Twenty-nine and four-tenths percent of the refugees said that their houses or possessions had been destroyed by artillery, 19.8% said that family members or neighbors had been killed or wounded, and 12.1% said that bombardment had disrupted their source of livelihood. Eleven and four-tenths percent of the refugees (3.5% in Phu-Yen) said that VC presence was the cause of GVN bombardment, 19.8% expressed a general fear of future harm from artillery, 7.6% said that family members or neighbors had been killed by ground operations, and 4.7% reported loss of their houses or possessions. VC coercion and terror were minor factors in movement, by contrast with Phu-Yen.

A quarter of the refugees reported that their movement had been encouraged; 76.5% of their citations said that GVN forces had encouraged it. However, 8.8% said that the VC had encouraged the migration; in Phu-Yen there was no VC encouragement. Twelve percent said that their movement had been discouraged, in all but one case by the VC.[10]

Minor refugee movement in Dinh-Tuong began in 1961–62, and movement before 1965 may have been underrepresented in the sample because of assimilation or return to home villages. Sixty-two and six-tenths percent of the refugees moved in 1965, the first peak occurring in February-April and the highest peak in June-July. That was earlier than the peaks in Phu-Yen. Substantial movement occurred from October 1965 through February 1966; there was little thereafter through the first half of 1967. The high points coincided with intensifications of military operations by both the VC and the GVN, although at a much lower level than in Phu-Yen. The GVN abandoned several outposts in the northern part of the province in July 1965, warning the people beforehand.[11]

Refugees were not a great problem in this economically prosperous province. Whole hamlets and even villages sometimes moved together. Most of the refugees settled with or near relatives and friends. However, 26.4% reported losing all their possessions when they moved (36% in Phu-Yen). Formal camps were few. Only 43% of the sample reported receiving government aid, and most of those received it only after four months or longer. Forty-seven and four-tenths percent of the children were in school. Most of the adults became general laborers, small merchants, or craftsmen. Ten percent were recruited by the GVN military (8% in Phu-Yen). Only 8.6% were unemployed.

The GVN officials displayed a positive attitude toward the refugees, and also used them as assets in the pacification effort. For example, they settled many

Table 5
Causal Agents and Reasons for Refugee Movement by Causal Agent, Dinh-Tuong Province (272 respondents)

Causal Agent	Frequency of citation (%) n=272
Viet-Cong	38.6
GVN	33.8
Allies (GVN & US)	53.3
US Troops	1.8
VC vs. GVN	28.3
VC vs. Allies	9.1
Other	7.3

Reasons by causal agent	Percentages (470 responses)[*]
Forced movement	
GVN	1.8
VC	1.8
Artillery and bombardment	
GVN	16.0
VC	6.5
GVN vs. VC	0.2
Allies	31.0
Ground military operations	
GVN	1.7
VC	3.1
GVN vs. VC	10.0
Allies vs. VC	1.4
Coerced activities and levies	
VC	9.6
Terror and reprisals	
VC	7.0

Note by Mr. Tinker: Only 418 of the 470 citations are shown in this table; the remaining 52 are spread among other categories of causal agents.

Source: Jerry Tinker, *The Refugee Situation in Dinh-Tuong Province*, Field Research Memorandum no. 6 (McLean, Va.: Human Sciences Research, Inc., August 1967), 15, 16.

along the principal roads, and attached them to existing "new life" hamlets to strengthen their self-defense capabilities. However, no special propaganda efforts were directed toward them, it being taken for granted that they were already pro-GVN.[12]

REFUGEE MOVEMENT IN THUONG-DUC DISTRICT, QUANG-NAM PROVINCE

This survey was conducted a year later than the preceding two, in mid-1967, when 1,633 refugee heads of family were interviewed in the three hamlets around the district capital where approximately 10,000 had settled.[13] Eight high school students recruited in Hoi-An, the province capital, and three senior interviewers who had worked with Jerry Tinker in Dinh-Tuong in 1966 did the survey. It encompassed 97% of the identifiable households. The refugees had come from 23 hamlets. Only about 350 were from out of the district. Most had moved voluntarily.

The principal thesis was that refugee movement was an adaptive response to the stresses of revolutionary warfare. The villagers were caught between two equally implacable forces, each of which demanded total commitment, and threatened the people in one or more ways. Revolutionary warfare had wholly abolished the dividing line between combatants and civilians. A guerrilla pressure mine made no distinctions. Air strikes were occasionally equally indiscriminate. Economic dislocations affected everybody. The data indicated that the refugees moved primarily out of fear or dislike of the VC, including the economic and social hardships they inflicted, or fear of GVN military activity. There was a buildup to a peak by 1966, with the inception of large-unit warfare. Fear of the VC lessened in the latter phases, as most of its targets had left.[14]

The data supported seven hypotheses:

1. Literate persons tended to move earlier than illiterates.
2. Owners of large plots of land tended to move earlier than owners of smaller plots.
3. The landless tended to move earlier than landowners.
4. Refugees with family members with the government tended to move earlier than nonassociated refugees.
5. Persons with skills tended to move earlier than farmers.
6. Catholics, Protestants, and Cao-Dai tended to move earlier than Buddhists and ancestor worshipers.
7. Younger persons tended to move earlier than the elderly.

The categories of war-induced stresses which were the reasons for movement, and their agents are shown in table 6.

Thuong-Duc district was the largest, least populated, and most isolated in the province. The capital, Ha-Tan is at the end of the Vu-Gia River Valley, which

Table 6
Reasons for Refugee Movement and Causal Agents, Thuong-Duc District, Quang-Nam Province (1,633 family heads, 2,862 citations)

Reasons and agents	Percentages of responses
Fear of reprisals or ideological dislike of	
GVN	0.0
VC	23.6
Economic or social hardship from activities of	
GVN	10.3
VC	19.6
General economic or social disruption from war	16.2
Fear of military activity of	
GVN	20.7
VC	3.8
General fear of war	5.9

Source: A. T. Rambo, Gary D. Murfin, and David DePuy, *Refugee Movement in Revolutionary Warfare: A Study of the Causes and Characteristics of Civilian Population Displacement in Viet-Nam* (McLean, Va.: Human Sciences Research, Inc., 1968), 10–13.

opens eastward. West of the town are forested mountains extending into Laos. The insurgency went back to the war against the French, but there was a period of peace from 1954 to late 1958. Then guerrilla warfare resumed. The strategic hamlets in the district, from 1961 to the end of 1963, were characterized by the authors of this study as poorly conceived and hastily implemented, but many appeared to have increased security by the end of the period. Phase II, the expansion of VC control, lasted from 1964 to early 1966. Then came phase III, Allied countermeasures and large-unit warefare, beginning with Operation Orange of the US Marines in April 1966 to disrupt the VC and enable US Army Special Forces to establish a camp at Ha-Tan and recruit and train a native strike force. Guerrilla defections climbed. By mid-1967, the VC were reduced to an understrength company. There were frequent Allied air strikes and bombardment.

Then large NVA units were introduced, and the situation stalemated, halting pacification.

In mid-1964, the population of the district under GVN control had been 18,579, made up of Vietnamese and Katu Montagnards. That year, refugee movement was mainly to Hoi-An and Da-Nang. The movement of the 10,000 refugees encompassed by this study began at the same time.[15]

Thus, although there were wide variations among these three locations in the perceptions of the refugees as to the principal reasons and causal agents of their movements, there also appear to have been some uniformities. The listing of time differences between the movements of different social and religious classes of the refugees seems to be valid for all three areas. Of those who moved because of terror or coercion, almost all identified these phenomena with the VC. Those who cited bombardment or ground military operations tended to associate these mainly with the GVN and its Allies; bombardment was largely the product of the superior firepower of the GVN, Americans, and Koreans. The studies did not attempt to ascertain the emotional reactions of the refugees to their experiences or the degrees of resentment against the causal agents. Evidently these factors were ruled out of bounds by the sponsors of the research.

Late 1966 and all of 1967 saw an intensification of US and Korean military operations, and ARVN participated in many of them. The heavy use of firepower in populated areas to prepare for troop landings, to suppress enemy fire, to eliminate suspected VC hiding places, and to induce the people to move into GVN areas, caused much destruction of civilian dwellings, the killing and wounding of noncombatants, and population movement. The I Corps area suffered most, but no part of Viet-Nam escaped completely. As of November 1, 1967, there were 790,000 refugees registered in camps and temporary shelter, of whom 402,000 in I CTZ, 191,000 in II CTZ, 91,000 in III CTZ, and 106,000 in IV CTZ. By the end of the year, the total had risen to 867,963.[16] More than 2,000,000 had been displaced in the previous three years; most were considered resettled or returned to their home villages but, as reported in the previous chapter, resettlement was often no more than a statistical manipulation.

TASK FORCE OREGON IN QUANG-NGAI AND QUANG-TIN

The campaigns of Task Force Oregon (TFO) in Quang-Ngai and Quang-Tin provinces were fairly representative of the way American troops fought in Viet-Nam at that time. Because TFO received considerable attention from evaluators and journalists, its operations can be summarized with some precision, although the various observers had significant differences in their views.

Before 1967, the only parts of Quang-Ngai that were under some semblance of GVN control were eastern Tu-Nghia and Nghia-Hanh districts along the central coast, small enclaves around the Mo-Duc and Duc-Pho district towns, and the port of Sa-Huyen in the South. The rest of the large province belonged to the VC, as it had belonged to the Viet-Minh during the French war. Then a portion of the Seventh US Marine Regiment began operations in northern Binh-Son district, mainly to protect the large airbase at Chu-Lai in neighboring Quang-Tin province. There were also eight combined-action platoons of the Marines and the Popular Forces, which had secured their hamlets in an otherwise insecure district. In southern Binh-Son and Son-Tinh districts, three infantry battalions of the Republic of Korea (ROK) Marine Brigade won some major victories over VC main force units in February, but then settled down to static defense of their bases, allowing the VC free run of the area including the Batangan Peninsula, which was a VC access route to the sea. In the next two districts, the only pacification (revolutionary development) activity in the province was making slow progress under the unreliable protection of the Second ARVN Division. In late January 1967, the Third Battalion of the Seventh Marines established a tactical area of operations (TAOR) around the Duc-Pho district town. Then in March, the First Cavalry Division began operations in the district along the border between the I and II Corps Zones.

On April 6, 1967, COMUSMACV ordered the execution of Operations Plan Oregon, and TFO headquarters arrived at Chu-Lai on April 20. The 196th Light Infantry Brigade also arrived and relieved the Seventh Marines. Two days later, the Third Brigade of the 25th US Division relieved the First Cavalry Division. In May, additional units augmented the task force, including the First Brigade, 101st Airborne Division, in the Duc-Pho area. It was later sent to western Quang-Tin and was relieved by the Third Brigade of the Fourth Division, which also covered southern Mo-Duc district. The missions of the TFO were to protect the Chu-Lai complex, seek out and destroy VC and NVA main force units, and support revolutionary development. Generally, ARVN and RF/PF (Regional/Popular Forces) units were used as blocking forces during operations, sometimes furnishing interpreters also.

Task Force Oregon had been established without any coordination with the pacification planners for the two provinces, with the result that its search-and-destroy operations could not be followed up by other units to stay and secure the areas through which it swept. So, although the VC/NVA lost over 1,700 KIA (killed in action) in Duc-Pho district alone and its main force units were decimated everywhere, small VC units and cadres quickly reinfiltrated, even into hamlets that had been evacuated and destroyed. Often the enemy simply evaded the sweeps. Friendly troops were frequently subjected to fire and minings from hamlets recently "cleared" or "cordoned and searched." The hamlets were then destroyed, after the remaining inhabitants were removed. The 12 RD teams in the TFO areas of Binh-Son and Duc-Pho at opposite ends of the province were subjected to 14 VC attacks, or 1.2 per team, between the beginning of June and August 24, while the remaining 31 teams in the province sustained only 17 attacks, or 0.55 per team. In Binh-Son district, on the night of August 8, the VC overran and burned New Life Hamlet My-Yen which was only 300 meters from the district town, suffering no losses. Moreover, the VC infrastructure evidently sustained no significant damage.[17]

The operations of TFO and its immediate predecessors caused widespread destruction of villages, particularly in Duc-Pho district, reflecting the near-conventional warfare that was conducted there. The area had been laced with VC fortifications, and a series of major battles had been fought in April and May; it became virtually depopulated. About 160,000 of the province's 712,000 people had become refugees, overwhelming the capability of the provincial services to care for them. CORDS evaluators wrote:

It is doubtful whether an effective RD program can be instituted in Quang Ngai Province as long as a fifth of the population exists as uprooted refugees constituting an economic burden, a potential source of political disaffection, and as VC support rather than a productive asset. . . . Besides the political, social and economic disadvantages of refugees indicated above, there are also security drawbacks. As hamlets are evacuated, the informant net is disrupted. Often the refugees are not fully screened and all or part of the VC infrastructure goes with the people to the refugee center. Thus, support is given to VC local forces by caring for them and/or their dependents in refugee camps. . . . However necessary it may be for tactical reasons to destroy hamlets and relocate the inhabitants, the creation of refugees can conflict with the techniques and aims of pacification. Refugees in camps or "squatting" precariously are not suitable candidates for pacification. At the same time, areas cannot be pacified if there are no people living in them.[18]

Another CORDS evaluator, Jerry L. Dodson, focusing on the refugee problem and measures to cope with it, reported that 250,000 people in the province had been displaced during the past year, of whom 160,000 were still in refugee status, but less than half in camps. He said that the refugees had developed a dependent mentality. The camps were dirty, crowded, and unpleasant. No evidence had yet been found that the discontent was political, but elements of the VC had moved into the camps. The province SCR Service Chief, an able man with a staff of 20 assisted by a dedicated CORDS Refugee Advisor, was not able to cope with such a huge population. The American Red Cross had a team of five, working with a five-man medical group; and Vietnam Christian Service (a coalition of American Protestant denominations) and the Quakers were also assisting. There was a refugee vocational training school in Quang-Ngai city, but very few jobs. Medical care was adequate. A 22-man CORDS Public Health staff was serving at the province hospital. Mr. Dodson recommended that liaison officers from TFO and the Koreans be detailed to the province, that the SCR and American staffs be augmented, that graft and corruption be investigated, and that alternate military tactics which would generate fewer refugees be explored. He appended a memorandum from the Sub-Sector MACV Advisor of Binh-Son district recommending that screened, trained, and armed refugees, initially secured by the RF/PF, be put back on the land as a pilot project.[19]

One relocation, conducted by the Fourth Battalion, 31st Infantry, on the Batangan Peninsula in Binh-Son district on August 21–23, was considered by the CORDS evaluators to have been a constructive alternative to simply dumping refugees into miserable camps. It moved 2,300 people from the fishing-farming hamlet of Tuyet-Diem to the former site of Son-Tra II hamlet, six kilometers away, together with their livestock, most of their possessions, and many house doors and thatched roofs. They were no farther from their fields than before. Mr. Tri, the Vietnamese evaluator, reported that most of the people had long wanted to escape the VC but had been unable to do so until this operation. A 12-man team from the province SCR, a Red Cross representative, a culture-drama team, and several national police assisted. The screening, however, did not appear to be thorough. The evaluators said that advance planning and co-ordination with district and province officials and advisors were the keys to success but "the Tuyet Diem operation is the exception rather than the rule."[20]

Jonathan Schell, a reporter for *The New Yorker* who accompanied the American troops on the Tuyet-Diem/Son-Tra operation, was not as complimentary as the CORDS evaluators, but he said that Ernest Hobson, the CORDS Refugee Advisor, acknowledged that it was the most carefully planned move thus far. Schell observed that the people had not been given sufficient time to dismantle their houses, some of which were of stone in any case, and so had to live for several weeks in makeshift shelters at the new location.[21]

The Japanese daily *Asahi Shimbun* published a series of reports in the fall of 1967 by its reporter, Honda Katsuichi, who had accompanied elements of Task Force Oregon on some of their operations.[22] One of these was Operation Baker in Duc-Pho district, by the Third Brigade of the 25th Infantry Division, whose objective, he wrote, was to start at the district town, "and, working northwards up the coast, wipe out the farming villages on the way, leaving them in ruins." Another objective was to prevent the VC from carrying away the maturing rice crop. He observed a company of the Brigade pound the village of Van-Ha into dust with bombs and shells before entering it; then the soldiers threw grenades or smoke shells into all the bomb shelters, but did not burn the remaining houses. He speculated that the presence of his photographer deterred the troops, since an NBC television crew had filmed soldiers burning houses the previous week and the film had been aired. He wrote: "Wherever the American soldiers go, villages become infernos: furnace after furnace: hell upon hell." Coming from a small country where every square meter of cultivated soil is sacred, he was especially dismayed at the way the American armored personnel carriers (APCs) in which he was riding chewed up the fields of rice and other crops, as well as destroying fruit trees, family altars, and so forth. He described house-to-house searches, during which the troops turned food containers upside down and trampled the contents, and then, finding nothing suspicious, shoved a group of women into their helicopters and took them away for questioning.[23]

Jonathan Schell spent weeks with Task Force Oregon, interviewing its personnel and observing operations, mainly from forward air control (FAC) planes, and described in detail what he saw in a series of *New Yorker* articles, which were later republished as a book.[24] It was his conclusion that the US Marines, the Army, the Korean Marines, and ARVN together had destroyed approximately 70% of all the houses in Quang-Ngai province. In some instances, the people had been forcibly removed; thus, some 5,000 inhabitants of the Song-Ve Valley in Duc-Pho district had been removed by the beginning of September, as well as another 5,000 in Binh-Son district along 10 kilometers of the coast south of the former village of Tuyet-Diem. He described many air strikes, both preplanned and "immediate," in which populated areas were ruthlessly attacked and whole hamlets destroyed because enemy fire had been sighted from them, or simply because they were considered VC territory, on the justification that the people had been warned by leaflets or loudspeaker to get out. The FAC pilots had various empirical ways of deciding when people on the ground were VC and could therefore be killed, for example, hiding, "pretending to be working" in the fields; "There's a V.C. havin' his supper. There shouldn't be anyone down there. He shouldn't be there." "In the mountains, just about anything that moves is considered to be V.C. No one has got any reason to be there."[25] The ground troops were equally indiscriminate in deciding who was a VC and in calling for air strikes against areas from which they observed or suspected enemy fire, including in one instance two churches that were in the middle of a preplanned strike area but from which no fire had been observed. The FAC pilot double-checked with the ground commander before calling in the strike against them, and later Schell observed the airmen to be visibly embarrassed about the strike. The churches were listed as two permanent military structures in the FAC pilot's bomb damage report to the Chu-Lai headquarters.[26]

Schell found that the TAOR of the ARVN Second Division was almost un-damaged, by contrast with the areas in which the American units fought. (This may have been because of the passivity of the division, which was noted by the CORDS evaluators.) An ARVN captain complained bitterly to the reporter about the destruction wrought by the American units. He said:

The Americans are destroying everything. If they get just one shot from a village, they destroy it . . . They bomb villages with the families of our troops living in them. A soldier comes back from Saigon and finds that his family has been killed. They bomb the rich and the poor. The rich man is the V.C.'s enemy. We should protect him. But now he has two enemies: the V.C., and the Americans who bomb all the houses. They even bomb the houses of the local militia. Who has made this policy? The Americans never try to protect a village. Just one V.C.—*just one*—can enter any village with a machine gun and the people are helpless against him. What can they do? Nothing. He shoots, and then their village is bombed.[27]

Schell's account, like that of Katsuichi, was powerful because it simply set down what he had seen and what he had heard directly from the participants in Task Force Oregon's war (plus the province chief of Quang-Tin, the CORDS province senior advisor of Quang-Ngai, and a few others). There is no indication that he talked with policy-makers or with generals. There was little analysis until the end, and that was not profound. The reader was left with the inescapable impression that the gigantic American war machine on the ground and in the air was in the hands of men with no understanding of or interest in the longer-range consequences of their enormously destructive actions, with no interest in—but rather, contempt for—the people whom they were there to help defend, to say nothing of concern for the relationship between the feelings and reactions of the people and the ultimate outcome of the war. The soldiers, airmen, and their officers with whom Schell was in contact were engaged in a bloody but mechanical series of repetitive operations that left the countryside barren and the people forlorn and helpless, and by his account they were insulated from any perception of what that meant.

When Schell got back to the United States, he briefed Secretary McNamara among others. According to Paul Nitze, who was Deputy Secretary of Defense at the time, McNamara put Schell in an office and told him to write the article.

He read the draft before it was even submitted to *The New Yorker*. He was horrified by its stories of meaningless and random bombings by our airforce, by the cynical attitude toward human life which, it purported, permeated our forces. He circulated the draft in the Pentagon and to the commanders in Vietnam and asked for comments on what was wrong with it. Obviously, there were things wrong with it; it wasn't wholly accurate. But still the essence of it appeared to be valid. I think this brought him to the realization that we had not been fighting the war correctly; we were using firepower too indiscriminately, with insufficient discipline and in a manner which was often counterproductive.[28]

The text of the articles was sent to Ambassador Ellsworth Bunker, who distributed a copy to General Westmoreland in December 1967 and, upon the general's request, had some of his staff check out the facts. James D. Hataway, Jr., a senior officer of the embassy, spent six hours overflying Quang-Tin and Quang-Ngai on December 9 and, though critical of Schell for giving the impression that vast areas were destroyed "when in fact the area described is only a few square kilometers," he agreed that there was a very large number of destroyed houses in both provinces. He found that many hamlets were completely destroyed, and the process was continuing. A detailed study, perhaps using a combination of aerial photography and population surveys, would be necessary to determine the exact percentage of destruction. He went on, "That percentage, however, would in my opinion be large enough to be useless or actually damaging on a public relations basis."

Hataway then examined 10 areas in comparison with Schell's assertions; in seven of them he did not dispute what the reporter had said. In one other, Son-Tinh district east of Route 1, he was at a loss to explain Schell's statement that all but two hamlets had been demolished; he found dozens of hamlets that appeared virtually untouched. In Mo-Duc and Duc-Pho districts, where Schell said between 90% and 100% of the houses had been destroyed except for three small areas, Hataway noted that the bulk of the population resided in a fairly narrow band of the coastal plain and that the three "small exceptions" included some 24 of the 57 kilometers of Route 1. Even excluding those exceptions, he estimated that only 30% to 40% of the houses had been destroyed. In Quang-Tin, where Schell estimated 70% destruction, Hataway found a great deal of destruction but guessed it was less than 50%. He was unable to check the two churches near Chap-Vum. He had observed VC trenches, fighting positions, and bunkers, often in hamlets.[29] An unsigned draft embassy memorandum of December 16, 1967, titled "Comments on the Schell Manuscript," said that, because of time limitation, the inquiry was confined to the TAOR of the Americal Division and the two provinces, and to US troops now serving. The author of the memorandum found that the descriptions of destruction by Schell were "overdrawn but not to such degree as to discredit his statements. Two civilian officers have recently overflown the areas in question and have reached essentially the same conclusion as Mr. Hataway; Mr. Schell's estimates are substantially correct." However, what Schell failed to explain,

probably because he did not understand, was that there are some very important political and military reasons for the scope of the destruction in this area. Quang-Ngai, particularly the districts of Duc Pho and Mo Duc, have been redoubts of Viet-Minh-Viet-Cong strength for more than a generation. The population is totally hostile towards the GVN and is probably nearly in complete sympathy with the NLF movement.

There was savage fighting in both districts. Every house was part of the VC defensive system. The VC were therefore partly responsible for the damage; they had chosen to fight from "combat hamlets." The memorandum then examined the rules of engagement, finding that they differed widely from unit to unit. Some commanders had a good understanding of them; others evidently did not. With regard to refugees, the writer found that since the arrival of the Americal Division, forced relocation was now eschewed wherever possible. He cited the Son-Tra relocation as good, saying that even the houses were dismantled in order to set them up again in the new village.

Every stick of furniture, every possession was moved to the new site in order to minimize the trauma of relocation as much as possible. Today the new village is a healthy, functioning community, free of the apathy and spirit of discontent which often pervades less fortunate but "voluntary" refugee settlements elsewhere.

However, the writer found an astounding and callous lack of interest in the refugee problem that seemed to be endemic among GVN officials at the district level, where paper plans must be translated into reality. The problem was not just at that level; in Quang-Ngai province, only 5,726,965 $VN out of the budgeted 23,614,000 $VN for the year had been expended as of November 30. American officials had explained all these problems to Schell. The writer admitted that his impression of FAC pilots was similar to Schell's. He wrote: "While not actually violating the current rules, they tend to take maximum license within those rules. If there aren't supposed to be friendlies in an area, then all people—regardless of what they are doing—are enemy." In conclusion, the memorandum said that Schell's "incredible bias and his unwillingness to accompany troops in the field make refutation of the manuscript exceedingly difficult."[30]

On January 26, 1968, Mr. Hataway addressed another memorandum to the Ambassador summarizing a research project conducted by the Americal Division. He expressed the view that in general MACV policy on civilian casualties and destruction of property was enlightened and sensitive—certainly a far cry from the 1,000-plane raids on cities during World War II. However, the study revealed the wide variations in the rules of engagement at different command levels and in different units. On November 24, the Americal Division had issued new rules limiting deliberate destruction of buildings and reserving to itself the decision on destruction of entire hamlets or large groups of buildings.[31]

There was a defensive tone in all these memoranda. They tended to take at face value the assertion that the total population of the damaged areas was hostile to the GVN and was VC-oriented, ignoring the finding of the CORDS evaluation (cited above) that the inhabitants of Tuyet-Diem, for instance, welcomed the chance to escape the VC, and the statement of the ARVN captain to Schell that ARVN dependents and local forces were among the victims of American bombing. There was no mention in the three memoranda of the political and psychological effects upon the people who were subjected to such treatment. There seemed to be a wide gap between the reasoning of the embassy analysts and the politically sensitive views and policies of Dr. Que and his superiors as well as those of Ambassador Komer and his pacification experts. One wonders how Ambassador Bunker, a wise and culturally insightful person, reacted to these papers.

General Westmoreland, after reading Hataway's reports, felt that the *New Yorker* reporter had exaggerated the destruction. "Because the countryside between Route 1 and the sea was uninhabitable salt flats, there had never been any houses between the highway and the sea," he claimed. However, he considered that "there was nevertheless truth enough in Schell's article to prompt me to go to Quang Ngai and talk with the commander of the Americal Division." He spoke about precautions aimed at careless and indiscriminate use of firepower.[32]

EFFORTS AT CHANGE—AND THEIR LIMITS

Ambassador Komer took a pragmatic position on refugee generation, but he was insistent that refugees be given prompt and adequate care. On August 7, 1967, he sent a brief memorandum to George Goss transmitting a copy of the Human Sciences Research study on Phu-Yen summarized above, and asked: "What do you think of the attached study? It shows that we can make money inducing refugees—at least in selected areas. You should consider this aspect in your action plan." The memo also referred to another study on what was done to attack the VC infrastructure during the evacuation of the Demilitarized Zone (discussed in the next chapter).[33]

Komer's actions to get more adequate relief to refugees, in response to the Holdren report, have been summarized in chapter 5. Jerry Dodson's report on refugee handling in Quang-Ngai aroused his ire. He wrote to the MACV Chief of Staff:

1. It's ridiculous to expect a 20 person SCR refugee staff to handle 160,000 refugees in Quang Ngai. Yet a lid is on SCR strength. Even if SCR could get more staff, the organization isn't large or strong enough to handle this number of refugees.

2. I agree with the recommendations in the evaluation. However, one possible solution is overlooked, namely, making the military forces involved in an operation that generates substantial numbers of refugees responsible for temporary handling up to the time the refugees are returned to their homes or settled in a permanent camp. The military forces (RVNAF, US, and FWMAF [free-world military assistance forces]) already do much of the work. Please have the staff analyze this alternative also.[34]

The Chief of Staff referred the memorandum and the Dodson report to the US Senior Advisors in the four regions (who were also commanders of US forces) and got negative responses from all of them on making the military responsible for initial refugee handling. However, with the exception of Lt. General Cushman (Senior Advisor, I CTZ, and Commander, III MAF), the Senior Advisors believed it was practical to reduce the generation of refugees and said that they were doing so.[35]

In fact, some of what Dodson and Komer were advocating was translated into policy mandates. The Combined Campaign Plan for 1968, which was drawn up by MACV and the Vietnamese Joint General Staff (JGS), had a refugee support annex that set out the overall responsibilities of the SCR and the province chiefs, pointed out that, when cared for properly, refugees could become an asset to the national cause, and said:

Some refugees leave VC dominated areas voluntarily; others are generated by military operations. Persons in VC dominated areas should not be encouraged to come to GVN controlled areas as refugees except in conjunction with ongoing military or pacification operations *and when the GVN is capable of caring for such refugees when they arrive in the GVN controlled area.* (Author's emphasis)

The annex then stated the tasks of the Vietnamese Corps commanders and US field force commanders in identical terms: (1) Emphasize to all subordinate commands the value of the refugee to the GVN pacification program and the necessity for fair, timely handling and support of refugees regardless of their political or religious affiliations or ethnic background. (2) Make provision for handling refugees so that they are cared for properly and do not interfere with military operations, and for early turnover to GVN refugee officials.[36]

In a telegram to Washington on October 14, Komer reported: (1) It is correct to say that it is MACV policy that US forces will provide temporary care of refugees on an emergency basis and then assist GVN agencies. (2) "It is not repeat not MACV policy deliberately to generate refugees, except in those few cases where to leave civil population in areas of planned intensive operations would create great hazard to them. When such cases occur, . . . US military forces and CORDS make special arrangements with the GVN for refugee resettlement." . . . In many other cases, refugees simply take advantage of US or ARVN operations to flee to more secure areas away from VC control.[37]

Late in November, in a memorandum to General Westmoreland entitled "Refugees," Ambassador Komer, referring to a quick visit for consultation in Washington, said that he had been "hit very hard, both on Capitol Hill and in State/ AID." He sought to assuage Senator Kennedy, but sensed that Kennedy was determined to make an issue of refugees and civilian casualties when he came to visit January 1968. Komer then listed the actions he had taken, including a request to the J-3 of MACV (General Chaisson) to do a quick analysis of why there were so many refugees in I CTZ, and an instruction to Goss to redouble efforts to get relief disbursed speedily by the SCR. He said that the problem was concentrated in I CTZ, where 500,000 of the 800,000 registered refugees were located. In IV CTZ, resettlement and return to home villages were exceeding refugee generation. Consequently, Komer said, they must concentrate on alleviating the situation in I Corps.

I do not yet feel qualified to say, but perhaps some alteration in our tactics might serve to reduce unplanned refugee flow. When we generate 20,000 refugees in a three week period and 10,000 in one week in Quang Nam alone, it may create more problems in this political war than direct military results would justify.

He enclosed a message of the same date to Lt. General Cushman, saying (in summary):

Greatly concerned about heavy influx refugees in I Corps. Koren's (the DepCORDS in region I) latest figures show 20,016 coming in 1–23 November and 12,300 generated by military operations in 17–23 November alone, of which 10,348 in Quang Nam. Refugee problem most painful of those raised with me in Washington last week. Senator Kennedy is hot on trail and asking whether US operations not creating much popular antipathy for this reason in countryside. Coming out in January. Other Congressmen and press building up head of steam. Since great bulk of problem is in I Corps, focus will be there. Recognize that CORDS, volags (voluntary agencies), and Marines all doing their best, bottleneck is GVN, "but I also consider it important that we carefully analyze causes of refugee generation which may suggest means of reducing inflow." Would appreciate your views and look forward to coming up and discussing this and other matters with you. Hope you will keep urgency of problem before General Lam.[38]

General Cushman replied on December 1, saying that in his opinion, the current influx of refugees was due to two basic causes: (1) terrorism and taxation by the enemy, increased due to continuing military pressure, and (2) an unknown percentage leaving home to avoid battlefield hazards. He thought that a majority were moving voluntarily, but he had requested General Lam to conduct sampling interviews with the refugees. He added, "To take any action to reduce flow of refugees voluntarily leaving VC areas of influence would be inconsistent with our often stated goal of winning the people as opposed to winning terrain."[39]

Charles T. Cross, a retired Marine colonel who was a senior Foreign Service Officer and Acting DepCORDS in I CTZ, then sent a personal memorandum to Komer on December 7, expanding on their telephone conference of the preceding day and giving some arguments that Komer might find useful to have tucked in the back of his mind. He agreed on the seriousness of the problem, but thought that all elements including the GVN were improving. The approximately 15,900 refugees who came in during Operation Foster 13–30 November were not expected. There had been 10 major and seven minor operations in the previous year, generating far fewer refugees altogether. "This time unit commanders report that the overwhelming majority of refugees were ready and even eager to move. These facts would seem to indicate that operations per se are not the main reason for refugees." They were conducting surveys to determine motivating factors. (He may have been referring to the Human Sciences Research studies.) The initial assessment was that people simply took the opportunity to escape from VC control. The rice-denial operations throughout I CTZ had been very effective, as shown in numerous intelligence reports reflecting VC/NVA food shortages; the VC had "put the screws" on the people. Recent terrorist acts against refugee camps had been one reason for Operation Foster, to relieve pressure on the Quang Nam camps. Cross believed it would be difficult to devise operations that would not generate refugees, but said that the handling of refugees should be improved and means would have to be found to enable them to return home in security. However:

Since this is a war for population those people who come over to the GVN side whether willingly or not theoretically are a net gain. It is how they are taken care of that will make the difference as to whether they turn out to be so in fact as well.[40]

Ambassador Koren followed this up with a memo saying that III MAF was reviewing its rules of engagement and population control procedures in major operations, and was pressing General Lam to name a representative to a joint task force.[41]

It appears that there was little change in US military strategy and tactics or in attitudes toward the generation of refugees at that time. A member of the Joint Staff in Washington, returning from a field trip during which he had spoken with Komer's Assistant DepCORDS Major General G. I. Forsythe and a number of officials in the four regions, reported that the GVN attitude toward caring for refugees had undergone a constructive change under Dr. Que, and that the number of refugees deliberately generated by military operations was less than one percent of the total. However, he continued:

Although the policy to create refugees for military purposes does not, in so many words, appear in any MACV document, the necessity is openly recognized as a realistic requirement which will be acted upon on a case-by-case basis. This is also true on the GVN side. . . . The forced generation of refugees not only is a realistic fact of life in attacking the VC on all fronts but, conceivably, could become a more productive strategy as the position of the GVN strengthens in the country-side. In any event, the proposition offers considerable potential as a means of negating sizeable pockets of hard core resistance.[42]

ABORTED SOCIAL SCIENCE STUDIES

The Human Sciences Research studies discussed above had reportedly been useful to the US military in Saigon. For a time from late 1966 to mid-1967, social science studies reached a peak of popularity, and the military requested more research investigations of special interest. The research community also felt emboldened to propose additional studies. General Westmoreland asked the Advanced Research Projects Agency (ARPA) to undertake a study of psychological warfare, with some specific questions. Seymour Deitchman, who was director of ARPA's Project AGILE (so-called because it could respond rapidly to urgent requests), assembled a team of the best known experts, including military psywar specialists. The group thought that Westmoreland's questions were too narrow, that they must explore the entire impact of military operations by both sides. Deitchman's account of the sequel is illuminating:

The group pointed out, for example, that it did little good to paint a stark picture, on leaflets, of the Viet Cong as vicious monsters (a common practice), when the recipients of the leaflets knew many of the Viet Cong as their relatives and friends. . . . And they indicated that any attempts of the Saigon government to say that it acted in the best interests of the population would be negated if the conduct of the war, with such activities as bombing of villages, in response to Viet Cong groundfire (even though there might be a deliberate effort to draw fire) were destructive of the population and its possessions.

They made a number of suggestions for improving psyops and also for affecting popular attitudes by changing the conduct of the war. The report ran into a "buzz saw." The officials at MACV felt that the findings and recommendations were gratuitous and inappropriate. General Westmoreland signed a letter saying that the report was not responsive, was overtaken by events, and that "we're already doing what it recommends."[43]

The subject, however, did not go away. Almost all the social scientists who were in contact with the Vietnamese people, on the basis of scattered conversations with villagers and with some American advisors, had come to the conclusion that more was being lost in terms of loyalty and respect for the GVN and the Americans than was gained in hurting the VC by bombing and shelling of villages, even where they were VC strongholds and fighting bases. Ithiel de Sola Pool, who had excellent relations with the military, proposed a field study of the rules of engagement, to be based on extensive interviews. It would attempt to determine the impact of operations upon the people and the enemy and the gains and losses, and would make recommendations to reduce the negative effects and increase the positive factors. General Westmoreland made it clear that the subject was not for study, and the matter was dropped. Thereafter, the popularity of social science research declined among the military.[44]

COMMUNIST TERROR AND ATTACKS ON CIVILIANS

Both because most of its assassinations and attacks were small and swift and because the world press was not invited to witness, the Communist assault on human life and property received only a fraction of the attention that the larger operations of the GVN and its Allies did. A few atrocities, such as the VC attack on Dong-Xoai in 1965 were publicized. Another of these was the VC/NVA attack on the Montagnard refugee village of Dak-Son in Phuoc-Long province in December 1967, when the Communists went from house to house, systematically killing the people in their shallow bunkers with flame throwers. Two hundred fifty-two died and nearly 50 were wounded, 33 of them with severe burns.[45] I visited that village shortly afterwards; the people were busy rebuilding, and this time they also organized a defense force, which the American advisors helped to arm. It fought off subsequent attacks. There were other such VC attacks on a smaller scale, but generally the VC only fired a few rockets or mortars into villages, marketplaces, churches, schools, and other populated places; mined roads; placed bombs; and assassinated individuals loyal to the GVN. The bombing of the floating restaurant My-Can in Saigon occurred in 1967, when it was crowded with Vietnamese and foreign patrons. It was one of my favorite eating places. All told, 15,502 incidents of harassment by indirect fire, mainly against civilian targets, were recorded in 1967. That was a high point: the numbers declined through 1972. However, 7,566 other incidents of VC harassment and terror were recorded in 1967; the numbers went up subsequently until they reached a peak of 12,056 in 1970, and then declined.[46]

CIVILIAN WAR CASUALTIES

There has been considerable disagreement about how many civilians were killed or wounded during the war and about the division of responsibility between the two sides. All the estimates start from the figures of the Ministry of Health on admissions to GVN hospitals, including those run by the 44 provinces, but even here there were differences. The *Vietnam Statistical Yearbook* showed 39,678 war injury admissions of inpatients and 42,389 war injury outpatients in 1967. These figures compare with 23,663 and 47,970 the preceding year.[47]

However, US officials considered that the GVN reports of civilian war casualty admissions (by which they meant patients who stayed 24 hours or longer) were inaccurate. They believed that about 3,800 civilians a month were admitted during the first 10 months of 1967.[48] In a later statement before the Senate Subcommittee on Refugees, Robert Nooter of AID gave figures of 46,783 civilian war casualty admissions to GVN hospitals in 1967, and 1,951 additional civilians admitted to US military hospitals, for a total of 48,734 that year, out of 473,140 admissions from all causes.[49] In May 1967, Brigadier General James W. Humphreys, Assistant Director of the USAID for Public Health, said that in the last six months, admissions had gone up from about 2,000 to 4,000 a month; he expected the total for the year to stabilize at about 50,000, although the various facilities could take care of up to 75,000. He thought that no more than 1 injured person was not treated for every 10 who were, although he had seen estimates of up to 5 to 1.[50] A distinguished team of physicians commissioned by the Department of State to look into the US-supported health programs in Viet-Nam estimated that there were about 75,000 civilian war casualties a year, of whom two thirds were admitted as inpatients for 24 hours or longer.[51] However, two private physicians who had visited Viet-Nam for three weeks on behalf of the Committee of Responsibility and the Shriners, looking for severely injured children patients who might need treatment in the US, estimated that at least double the number admitted to hospitals never made it. Some of those were killed. The physicians admitted that their estimate was little better than a guess.[52] These discrepancies indicate a good deal of uncertainty as to the absolute numbers, especially in the earlier years of American combat participation, but all agreed that they were substantial.

As to causes, General Humphreys had figures to indicate that about 20% to 25% of the casualties were caused by mines and booby traps, which were mainly VC; 15% to 20% by artillery and air strikes, almost entirely Allied, and up to 60% by ground gunfire, which could come from either side.[53] Other statistics for the full year 1967 showed that 15,253 of the casualties admitted to hospitals were suffering from mine or mortar wounds, 9,785 from gun or grenade wounds, and 18,811 from injuries caused by shelling and bombing; the total was 43,849.[54] These breakdowns are striking in view of the enormous use of firepower by the Allies and the necessarily parsimonious expenditure of munitions by their enemy. The Allies destroyed many more houses and other structures than the Communists, and in the process killed or wounded many civilians, but much of their ordnance was expended in or over jungles and mountains, which were sparsely populated. Much of it was wasted; the amounts that were expended for each VC/NVA soldier killed were staggering. By using mines and booby traps that had to be triggered by road vehicles or humans, and grenades and rockets that were deliberately fired into populated places, the VC achieved a grisly economy of ammunition.

Both AID and the US military as well as voluntary agencies and other nations provided substantial assistance to the GVN's health programs, not restricted to the care of civilian war casualties. The need was enormous. Disease, much of it exacerbated by malnutrition, crowding, and unsanitary conditions, was a far more widespread problem than war wounds. Viet-Nam had endemic tuberculosis, cholera, plague (it was the only country in Southeast Asia where plague was dangerously prevalent), small pox, measles, malaria (including falciparum malaria in the mountains), tetanus, and typhoid, not to speak of parasites, scabies, and other diseases that were not necessarily lethal but were debilitating all the same. AID was supporting about 1,200 foreign medical personnel in 1967, a sixfold increase in three years. There were 43 US and other foreign medical teams working in province hospitals. Equipment and supplies were provided to upgrade hospitals. A modern plastic and reconstructive surgery suite was being built in Saigon; it was known as the Barsky Unit, after its founder. Assistance to medical, dental, and nursing schools included the provision of visiting professors under contracts with the American Medical and Dental Associations. The AID and US Department of Defense budgets for public health totaled about $47 million in FY 1968.[55] A system of rural dispensaries, clinics, and maternities was spread throughout the country. The hospitals and clinics treated all who came, including VC partisans, with the result that the VC sent their more difficult cases to GVN facilities, especially the hospitals.[56]

Although the Communists and the Allies generated about the same number of civilian war casualties in the years up through 1967, their behaviour toward the survivors was diametrically opposite. The VC/NVA made no distinction between soldiers and civilians; people were either on their side or they were the enemy. Those who refused allegiance to the Front must be killed or made to suffer until they learned. Hence, wounded victims of Communist terror were not aided or treated by the terrorists; instead they were left to die or to the care of their own society. The Allies, at least in their official doctrine, did make a distinction between enemy soldiers and noncombatants, even though recognizing that many civilians in VC areas were, willingly or unwillingly, assistants to the guerrillas. That distinction, derived from the 1949 Geneva Conventions, of which both the GVN and its Allies were adherents, was embodied in the military rules of engagement, and it was GVN doctrine with regard to the care of refugees. As recounted above, crass and cruel violations occurred, but sincere efforts were made to enforce these rules, and performance did improve over time. Quite apart from this, the humanitarianism that animated most people on the Allied side, including the soldiers, motivated them to care for the sick and wounded, regardless of their origin or beliefs. Thus, for example, US military medical evacuation (medevac) choppers carried wounded soldiers, American and Vietnamese alike, as well as wounded or seriously ill Vietnamese civilians, to hospitals—frequently to US military hospitals. As mentioned above, GVN and US hospitals were willing to accept and treat referrals even of VC guerrillas. Out of humanitarian concern—and perhaps a certain amount of guilt feeling—thousands of Americans volunteered for medical and other noncombatant service in Viet-Nam. Among them were hundreds of doctors who spent two months each without salary under the Voluntary Physicians for Vietnam (VPVN) program of the American Medical Association, serving in remote and poorly equipped hospitals. Many from the United States and other countries who were opposed in principle to the Allied war effort were eager to help alleviate its catastrophic effects. The Canadian government, for instance, built, equipped, and helped to staff a splendid rehabilitation and prosthesis center in Qui-Nhon. The medical and rehabilitation work of the American Friends Service Committee in Quang-Ngai has already been mentioned in chapter 5. One could cite many other examples.

7

Once Again, Planned Forcible Relocation of People

The history of the war records many instances of forced relocation of civilians and their unfortunate results for the anti-Communist cause. Those of the highlander resettlements, agrovilles, and strategic hamlets that were involuntary (chapters 2 and 3) are examples. Then, beginning in 1964, this method of attempting to extend security fell out of favor, though the 1965–67 campaigns in Binh-Dinh, Quang-Ngai, and elsewhere employed it on a largely unplanned basis. In 1967, however, US forces revived the practice of planned population relocations as a means of denying people to the enemy, bringing them to GVN territory, and making free fire zones of their previous homelands. Some of the most significant of these forced movements produced settlements whose subsequent history was followed in detail, so that the consequences of this aspect of war making were documented. The beginning stages of several forced movements will be recounted here, and the sequels will be told in later chapters.

OPERATION CEDAR FALLS—THE VILLAGE OF BEN-SUC

Northwest of Saigon in Binh-Duong province, extending from just outside the province capital of Phu-Cuong in an area bounded by Route 13 on the east, the Saigon River on the west, and the line from the village of Ben-Suc to the district town of Ben-Cat, was the Iron Triangle, an important VC base area that contained the headquarters of its military region IV. That was the VC region that encompassed the Saigon–Gia-Dinh area. Extending to the north and west of the Iron Triangle was War Zone C, and to the northeast was War Zone D. Part of the Iron Triangle and the territory just to the west and south of it had been the locus of Diem's Operation Sunrise, planting strategic hamlets that were resisted from the beginning and that succumbed in 1963–64 to the resurgent Viet-Cong. ARVN had been driven out of its outpost in Ben-Suc in 1964 and, except for short operations, had never returned. That village and the others in the Iron Triangle, although bombed from time to time, were prosperous under Viet-Cong control and supplied a surplus of rice for the guerrillas. Most of the Triangle was thick jungle, sheltering deep tunnels and underground installations. This, then, was the target of Operation Cedar Falls, the first multidivision US/ARVN operation of the war. It was planned late in 1966 and began in early morning January 8, 1967. The mission was to attack the Iron Triangle and the Thanh-Dien Forestry Reserve to destroy enemy forces and the MR IV headquarters, evacuate the civilian population, and establish the area as a specified strike (free fire) zone to preclude its further use as a VC support base.

Because so many operations jointly planned with ARVN had been leaked to the enemy in advance, this one was planned entirely by the US forces and not revealed to the Vietnamese until D-day minus 2 (January 6). ARVN units were to be used primarily as police, for screening of villagers, and for assistance in evacuating refugees and receiving them at the reception camp. John Paul Vann, the Director of the USAID Office of Civil Operations (OCO) for III CTZ, was the only US civilian official who was privy to the plan; he in turn mobilized his staff to prepare for the reception of refugees, but they were not permitted to preposition supplies or coordinate with the SCR.

The operation did in fact achieve surprise. There had been no preparatory fire on Ben-Suc, though the adjacent jungle was bombed—a not unusual occurrence. The troops that occupied Ben-Suc and three other villages were lifted in by helicopters. Seven hundred fifty of the enemy were killed but, as Jonathan Schell reported, some of these were unarmed civilians. Two hundred eighty prisoners were taken; there were 540 VC "Chieu-Hoi" ralliers to the GVN side; and 512 VC suspects were detained. Thirty-seven hundred tons of rice, and 23 crew-served and 550 individual weapons were captured. Five hundred nine buildings, 424 underground shelters and tunnels, and 334 boats were destroyed. US forces lost 72 killed and 337 wounded. ARVN lost 11 killed and 8 wounded. Eleven square miles of jungle were cleared, and a network of tunnels and installations was destroyed with heavy equipment and bombing. Over 500,000 pages of documents were captured, as well as many supplies. The operation concluded on January 26. However, this was a search-and-destroy mission; the Allied troops did not remain, and within two days the base area seemed to be alive with renewed enemy activity.[1]

Some 5,987 refugees were evacuated by helicopter, truck, and river boats; five hundred eighty-two of them were men (a number well below the usual proportion, even among refugees), 1,651 women, and 3,754 children. Two hundred forty-seven water buffalo, 225 cattle, 158 oxcarts, 60 tons of rice, and countless pigs and chickens were taken out with them. The US and ARVN troops helped the villagers to take their possessions, a process that took some days, and the villages were not destroyed until the methodical evacuation was complete.

At first, the villagers thought that their relocation was temporary; when they realized that it was not, many women asked to return to dig up their buried gold and money, and this was allowed. One has to say that the evacuation was handled in a humane manner.[2]

On January 13, 1967, while the operation was still going on, General Westmoreland met with General Nguyen Van Thieu to discuss a variety of subjects. In his memorandum on the conversation, Westmoreland wrote:

Thieu is pleased with the operation in the Iron Triangle but regrets that it was necessary to evacuate Ben Suc Hamlet. Rather than moving people to the vicinity of populated areas, he feels that security forces should move out to the people in the outlying areas to provide them security. He feels that a large military post should be established at Ben Suc to provide security for the people. I replied that this might be possible at a later date but that the VC controlled this area and were using the hamlet as a major operations base.[3]

Here General Thieu, who was Viet-Nam's Chief of State, was saying, ''Bring security to the people, not people to security,'' and the top American commander was saying, ''It can't be done.'' This memorandum is the only record we have of this conversation, and I have found no evidence of further discussions of the subject, so we do not know whether the GVN ever suggested that its forces might protect the people of the village and keep the VC out if they were returned to their homes, which in any event would have had to be rebuilt. At any rate, this was not tried.

The evacuees were brought to a large lot in Phu-Loi, near Phu-Cuong, and the Fifth ARVN Engineer Battalion and elements of the US First Infantry Division erected shelters over the following days, with the materials furnished by OCO and the First Infantry Division. Two RD Cadre teams arrived. Rice was distributed; many of the evacuees already had rice of their own. The US forces provided purified water for drinking and cooking in a 5,000-gallon tanker, with water distributed to twelve 400-gallon trailers. Two existing wells were augmented by a US drilling rig, but there was insufficient water for washing and bathing. Likewise, latrines were inadequate and often not used. This is always a problem when people are snatched from their villages, where all such necessities have been built and furnished by the families themselves, and put into crowded quarters in small areas. ARVN medical teams, assisted by the Philippine Civil Affairs Group and Korean medical teams, provided health care, including immunizing against cholera, typhus, and plague. Psyops broadcasts over a public address system were continuous and noisy, and television, movies, and culture-drama teams played, but how effective they were is not known. Local Buddhist, Catholic, Boy Scout, and other groups pitched in to help. The reception and initial care were necessarily ragged, because the site could not be prepared in advance, so there was a good deal of grumbling by the evacuees. Their main complaint was that they were away from their land and had no occupation. The US Embassy and MACV congratulated themselves on a successful evacuation, evidently not realizing what trauma the dislocation had inflicted on an already hostile population.[4]

Gradually, with much effort by OCO, SCR, and other agencies, both Vietnamese and American, conditions improved. An attitude survey taken after the first week had shown that the principal aspiration of the people was education for their children. A school structure was erected. The ARVN Engineers and the MACV advisory team made desks for the pupils out of ammunition crates and blackboards from 4' by 8' plywood. Teachers were found among draftees of the ARVN 5th Infantry Division and women social workers of the ARVN Political Warfare (Polwar) Directorate. The province Education Chief provided textbooks, and CARE furnished school kits. The whole effort was arranged by the OCO Psyops Representative. By such improvisations, some semblance of normalcy was achieved, but the place was still an unsatisfactory temporary camp.[5]

Most of the evacuee families decided, with GVN approval, to join relatives or to establish themselves in Ben-Cat town, Tu-Duc in Gia-Dinh province, or Binh-Long province. For the remaining 2,600 people in 480 families a permanent site was located in Lai-Thieu district of Binh-Duong province, and both the GVN and the Americans determined to make it a model resettlement area. While the evacuees were still in the temporary camp, virtually all able-bodied men and women were employed making "cinvaram" bricks (mud-cement blocks compressed in a simple machine and dried in the sun) and wooden frames, which were transported to the new site by trucks of the ARVN Fifth Division. The division's engineers supervised house construction; each house had two cinvaram brick walls and an aluminum roof, leaving the other two sides to be filled in with woven bamboo or other material by the evacuees themselves. The workers commuted between the camp and Lai-Thieu. By April 10, people started moving into Ap Doi Moi (New Life Hamlet) Binh-Hoa. Later, a second hamlet, Binh-Phuoc, was occupied. An overcomplicated water system was installed by the International Drilling Company, with pipes threading through the hamlets, ending in one spigot for every two houses; these were quickly disabled or twisted off by the people. Objectively speaking, the housing and facilities at the new hamlets were probably better than in Ben-Suc.

SCR mobile cadres, ultimately 34 in number, were stationed in the settlement, as were an OCO advisor and a team from the International Rescue Committee. IRC adopted the two hamlets as a major project, and kept personnel there for the next two years, often under conditions of extreme danger. The YMCA and other voluntary agencies also had projects there. A dispensary was set up, with an IRC medic and a Danish nurse. Medical personnel from the US 1st Infantry Division frequently assisted at sick call, and GVN public health officials visited. There was also a school.

On May 13, Prime Minister Ky promised six months of rice at 700 grams per day. As of late September, most families had received one month's ration, 60 families had received two months', and none had received the six months' ration. The refugee cadres had reported this to the SCR Service Chief, but without result. Nobody was overly enthusiastic about the quality of the refugee cadres, however. CORDS had distributed bulgur.

The prospects for self-sufficiency seemed good. The settlement was near large cities. Some evacuees were hired to work on new houses, others at a small power plant or in Phu-Cuong or Saigon. Little shops were set up in homes. Each family that asked was assigned 1,600 square meters of land. Some rented rice fields. However, while 92.5% of the households had cultivated land in their home villages, according to a Human Sciences Research (HSR) survey taken in 1967, only 4.2% did so at Lai-Thieu. A higher proportion of the evacuees was employed at skilled labor than previously, but 35.5% were unemployed, compared with 12.8% (a rather high percentage) in their previous villages.

Security was provided by one PF company and by roving patrols of the US 1st Infantry Division. Nevertheless, small bands of VC guerrillas occasionally detained refugee wood cutters.

If many things, including security (there were no more bombings and no ground attacks) were objectively better at Ap Binh-Hoa and Ap Binh-Phuoc (indeed, those hamlets were rated by the surveyors as the best of the nine evacuee and refugee sites tested), the people didn't think so. The HSR interviewers asked whether the present was better, the same, or worse than the past. Only 2.5% of the sample of 120 family heads thought that the present was better, 3.3% said there was no change, 83.3% thought that the past was better, and 10.8% did not answer. The survey then used the Cantril Self-Anchoring Striving Scale, which meant that the respondents themselves defined conditions on a ladder for the best (10) and worst (0) possible lives and then rated their past, present, and future lives on this scale. Although Vietnamese were accustomed to assign the number 1 to the best of anything and 10 to the worst, the survey designers were satisfied that the Cantril scale, which they had used in many countries, produced a reliable result. The Cedar Falls evacuees rated their past lives at 5.95, the highest of the nine evacuee and voluntary refugee sites studied. However, they rated their present lives at only 1.65, the next lowest among the sites; and they rated the future at 2.48, again the next to lowest (surpassed only by the Lam-Son 87 evacuees in Thua-Thien province).[6]

The American authorities and voluntary agencies did not give up. however, and sometimes the GVN agencies helped. IRC was able to obtain scrap lumber and nails and to borrow trucks from ARVN (in return for part of the lumber), and the evacuees were overjoyed to be able to finish their houses. IRC also distributed over 400 banana trees, which the refugees eagerly planted. With help from the SCR and labor volunteered by the villagers, IRC built a temporary dispensary in July. Charlie Cowden, a retired Army medic, staffed it, scrounging medical supplies from US units and the province health agency. A garden project and chicken raising were started, but both had difficulties until IRC experts arrived in 1968. However, evidently because of the shortage of able-bodied men and the inability of the women with small children to leave their homes, little of the arable land was cultivated. Two-hundred thirty families had requested and received titles to farmland but, as of mid-November, only 20 had started to clear it. The land became overgrown, offering cover to the VC, and only strenuous resistance from OCO prevented the military from defoliating it, which would have killed the vegetables and banana trees being grown in small gardens. The IRC team asked its New York headquarters for money to build a day care center like many which that agency was supporting elsewhere. At the end of November, 78 new families, genuine refugees, moved in, having fled their homes voluntarily.

For all these efforts, the two hamlets remained a settlement of VC dependents, and the attitudes of the inhabitants remained hostile. An important reason was that, for all the attention paid by the US agencies to the material welfare of the refugees, the GVN was visibly less concerned, and there was a lack of political work in the two hamlets. In their former location the VC had organized the people into tightly controlled associations of farmers, youth, women, self-defense forces, and so forth; and trained cadres among the people had engaged in continuous political education with a combination of anti-GVN, anti-American, and socialist appeals. No doubt some of this was carried on in the new location. On the other hand, once the RD teams had completed their short-term tasks and departed, there was no GVN or nationalist political party counterpart to the long-term Communist indoctrination, organization, and control of the people at Ap Binh-Hoa and Ap Binh-Phuoc. Hamlet elections gave the refugees a semblance of democracy, but did not change their attitudes or allegiance. Lack of GVN political work was a common failing in the refugee program throughout the country.[7]

The Communists had reinfiltrated the surrounding countryside as well. By early December it was estimated that three Communist battalions (two of them North Vietnamese) and a number of smaller units were in the area between Lai-Thieu and the province capital of Phu-Cuong. They threatened to assassinate any refugees working for the Americans. The evacuees commonly made invidious comparisons between the SCR cadres, who were certainly not the best, and the VC cadres.[8]

EVACUATION FROM THE DMZ—RESETTLEMENT AT CAM-LO

As the war intensified, the Demilitarized Zone (DMZ), a 10-kilometer band along both sides of the 17th parallel and the Ben-Hai River, became less and less demilitarized. There was constant infiltration of men and supplies from North Viet-Nam, and increased fighting. In March 1967, the GVN and MACV decided to evacuate all civilians living in and just below the southern side of the DMZ, in Quang-Tri province, in order to turn it into a free fire zone and to build a barrier with electronic surveillance and obstacles to movement. No attempt was made to keep the evacuation secret. Advance planning was done jointly by GVN and US military and civilian authorities. On the US side, the Mission Council, chaired by Ambassador Ellsworth Bunker and including General Westmoreland and the heads of the civilian agencies, had discussed the project. A relocation site was selected at the junction of National Highways 9 and 558, a short distance from the village of Cam-Lo, which was the headquarters of the district of the same name. Unused agricultural land was nearby, and the area could be made secure. The people were to be informed in advance by their district, village, and hamlet officials where possible, and by airplane loudspeaker and leaflets in contested areas; a 45-man ARVN psywar platoon, divided into 15 teams, was to explain the reasons for the movement. A temporary school was to be built; culture-drama teams, movies, loudspeakers, and a weekly newspaper were planned.

Supplies were stockpiled in a school near the Cam-Lo district headquarters. ARVN sent an engineer company to begin construction of the camp and a medical team. The US Marines and Army supplied trucks for the move and tents, and OCO provided aluminum roofing, cement, and food. The evacuation was planned to begin on May 16, moving 120 families a day for at least a month before the Marines and ARVN would clear the area in a military operation. It was estimated that as many as 23,000 people would have to be evacuated. The people were to be allowed to take all their possessions, including livestock, house frames, and furniture. They were to be screened at the camp by security forces. The SCR was to register the refugees and provide temporary relief.[9]

The notification process began at least a week before May 16. One Catholic hamlet had learned of the move even earlier and, led by their priest, took all its possessions and had already built 86 houses at the new site by mid-May. Other residents, stimulated by intense VC propaganda, were reluctant to move, especially before the rice harvest. On May 16, the province chief had to intervene personally to restore order in some hamlets of Gio-Linh district, where some 200 people demonstrated against the move. At the suggestion of OCO, the hamlet chiefs were taken to Cam-Lo to see the preparations, and upon return they conveyed their favorable impressions, with the result that two thirds of the demonstrators were said to be ready to relocate. Then, without warning, on May 18 the US Marines and ARVN launched Operations Hickory, Lam-Son 54, and Beau Charger to clear the DMZ; this was a month earlier than planned. This required the evacuation of all the people in 10 days instead of over a month; almost half had not been notified and could not bring their possessions, and great confusion resulted. However, only 48% of the 120 respondents in the HSR survey felt that their own movement had been forced. Not more than 12,000 people were moved to Cam-Lo, and evidently not all stayed. When the HSR study team did a complete census of the camp population, its final count as of August 7 showed 2,252 families with 10,644 people, 4,704 of whom were males and 5,940 females. There were only 852 males, compared with 1,975 females in the 20-to-49-year age group.[10] Another 500 families were moved to the Gio-Linh district headquarters in the extreme east of the province, and 200 Buddhist families were moved to Quang-Tri city.[11]

One wonders how the foul-up occurred, especially as General Westmoreland was a member of the Mission Council, which had approved the original plan. If circumstances had developed that required a speedup of Operation Hickory and its companion operations, why wasn't the relocation started earlier? Furthermore, why weren't those responsible for the relocation notified? The available evidence does not answer these questions. The CORDS evaluators had this to say under the heading ''Conclusions'':

a. *Planning*: The premature activation of Operation Hickory resulted in several unfortunate consequences.

(1) The refugees being moved before the people had harvested their rice.

(2) Contrary to the original plan, most of the refugees did not have an opportunity to bring all of their belongings with them.

(3) The refugees were moved before adequate arrangements for water had been made.

(4) In the confusion, the best land at Cam Lo was used for home sites rather than farming.

(5) In general, carrying out the plan was more difficult because of the premature activation and hence many important sections of the plan were not carried out.

The evaluators recommended that in the future, planning should include not only military considerations but also factors such as harvest time, planting season, land, availability of water, and economic potential.[12]

The bringing together in May 1967 of civil and military pacification staffs into CORDS under the military command was supposed to end this kind of uncoordinated action. To some extent it did, but many instances of uncoordinated US military relocation of people occurred thereafter.

To help care for the unexpectedly rapid influx of evacuees, the 29th Civil Affairs Company was mobilized, the Third Marines sent a medical team, the Da-Nang Naval Support Activity sent six immunization teams, and the SCR sent a mobile team to augment the two RD Cadre teams. However, only about half the refugees had been immunized by June 5, the temporary school and entertainment activities never materialized, and only one issue of the newspaper appeared. The Third Marines helped with the acute water problem. Eventually the evacuees were all registered, and 80.2% of the respondents in the HSR survey reported that they had received money and food from the GVN.

That the VC considered this relocation damaging to its cause was shown by the intense propaganda they directed to the people before the move and by their numerous attacks on the site afterwards. About 60 VC had attacked and driven out the ARVN Engineers during the initial construction.[13]

The province SCR chief spent little time at Cam-Lo and was considered ineffective, as were the two RD Cadre teams, and the ARVN psyops platoon was generally inactive. Here again, no real effort was made to organize or motivate the refugees politically or to replace the Communist political apparatus that had previously controlled them. On the other hand, the SCR mobile team and the Vietnamese Information Service (VIS) personnel were active and helpful.

A student work camp was established under the auspices of the Ministry of Youth; the students came from Saigon, Da-Nang, Hue, Dalat, and Quang-Tri, and worked in two-week shifts. They helped the refugees build their homes, worked at the dispensary, planned construction of a school, and comforted and talked with the evacuees, establishing a genuinely good relationship with them. This project was valuable to the middle-class students as well as the refugees. However, on July 20 a message came from Saigon ordering them to leave the resettlement area immediately; the Political Bureau of the Youth Ministry had decided that their presence was not in the best interests of the GVN, since they might engage in political activity and the security situation was not good. The CORDS evaluators wrote:

By pulling the students out in the middle of the project, the GVN succeeded in alienating the most dedicated portion of the Vietnamese student population, stopped construction on a school for the refugees, halted the student medical program, removed an effective counterweight to the Viet Cong, and antagonized the refugees who already were skeptical of the GVN.[14]

Aside from the lack of political work among the people, the most serious deficiency of Cam-Lo was that it had little potential to make the refugees self-sufficient. Almost all of them had been farmers. Because of the hasty move, the small amount of good land on the site was used for housing, instead of putting the houses on the surrounding hills, as had been planned. The planners of the relocation had said that there was sufficient untilled land around the camp, but it turned out that some of the land was cultivated by local peasants, and the rest was abandoned because of insecurity and lack of water and hence could not be used by the refugees. The site was not near any city, so employment opportunities were few, despite the efforts of the Americans to develop income-generating projects. Forty-seven-and-a-half percent of the family heads were unemployed. Only the Catholic hamlet of Gio-Mon managed to eke out a living. By late summer, 150 families had already left Quang-Tri city and other areas in search of employment.[15]

The sympathies of the evacuees remained overwhelmingly pro-VC, because most had come from VC-controlled areas and had been required to leave their land and family graves, although most understood why; they felt that the GVN had done little to help them, and they faced an uncertain but not promising future. However, the evacuees felt that the Americans had done much to help them. On the Cantril Self-Anchoring Striving Scale (10 - best and 0 - worst) they rated their past lives as 5.55, their present existence as 2.42, and their future prospects as 4.96. Though their rating of the past was below what the Ap Binh-Hoa evacuees had scored, their evaluation of the present was somewhat better, and their expectation for the future was much higher. Ten and eight-tenths percent thought that their present life situation was a little better than the past, 2.5% said there was no change, 23.3% found the present a little worse, and 63.3% found it much worse. Almost all expected future government assistance of various kinds, and felt dependent on it.[16]

Don Luce, who had resigned as Viet-Nam Director of International Voluntary Service in protest against US war policy, felt that the evacuation from the DMZ was necessary because of the bitter fighting which was going on there.[17] The American military and pacification personnel worked manfully for over four years to improve the miserable Cam-Lo resettlement center—and lost not a few lives to VC attacks in doing so. They achieved some notable improvements, such as a superb water system, schools, health facilities, community centers, and small income-producing projects. However, as subsequent chapters will show, the people never became self-sufficient, and their pro-VC sympathies were not changed. The relocation did not halt infiltration from the North across the DMZ, despite the freedom of allied forces to fire on it, and pacification was not advanced.

THE HUMAN SCIENCES RESEARCH STUDY OF EVACUEES AND REFUGEES

For 15 months during 1967–68, Human Sciences Research interviewed 498 heads of families who had been forcibly relocated to four sites and 593 heads of voluntary refugee families in five centers to develop a comparison between forced evacuees and voluntary refugees. HSR published the results in mid-1968.[18] The surveyed sites of the two categories were:

Forced Movement

DMZ Resettlement (Cam-Lo) *and Cedar Falls Resettlement* (Binh-Duong province)

These sites were described above.

Lam-Son 87 Resettlement (Thua-Thien province)

In June 1967, in a four-day operation, the ARVN 1st Division and the ARVN Airborne Brigade evacuated 13,000 people from a strip of land on the southern side of the Phu-Tan Lagoon, across from the "Street Without Joy," and took them to the Phong-Dien and Quang-Dien district headquarters, where no preparations to receive them had been made because the GVN officials had not been notified until two days before the operation began. The HSR survey was made in four areas of the Quang-Dien district town, where the evacuees were living in a high school, a pagoda, a primary school, a semipublic school, some deserted houses that had been bombed by the Americans during a VC attack, and some additional houses. One hundred twenty-eight families were surveyed in September 1967; 63.3% of them felt they were forced to move; the other 36.7% said they were encouraged to relocate. No family was able to bring all its possessions, and most had to leave large valuable items such as livestock and furniture behind. The SCR paid temporary relief to 1,956 families. No other GVN assistance had been provided, but roofing sheets had just arrived from Hue. Fifty-three percent of evacuees were unemployed, and none had access to agricultural land; they did have access to community facilities. As was typical of evacuees, the ratio of males to females in the 15-to-49 age group was 37 to 100; for the entire evacuee population it was 85-to-100. Only 18.2% of the men and 16.4% of the women were functionally literate. This was the worst of all the nine sites surveyed for this study.[19]

Hung-Quang Regroupment (Quang-Nam province)

In February 1967, the 51st ARVN Regiment regrouped people from a number of scattered hamlets in the eastern and western parts of Hoa-Vang district into three "peace hamlets" close enough to their former dwellings that the farmers could continue to work their fields. However, they were required to be within the fences of the new hamlets at night. The SCR was not involved in the operation or resettlement of the evacuees, but ARVN had coordinated with the district chief. CORDS supplied cement and roofing. The HSR surveyed 130 of the 209 families in Yen-Ne and Le-Son peace hamlets on the west side of the district in September 1967. They had had ample opportunity to move all their possessions, but some had moved from other locations earlier, had few or no possessions, and had lost their land in the earlier moves. Thirteen and four-tenths percent of the evacuees were unemployed in the new location. Many houses in Yen-Ne peace hamlet were under construction before the move, and ARVN soldiers helped the evacuees to build their houses. They were also building a new school to replace one that had been bombed by the VC. A GVN dispensary was available and used. Other GVN services and a market were also available. The two hamlets had elected chiefs. Thirty-one-and-a-half-percent of the respondents felt that they had been forced to move, 28.5 percent said they were encouraged, and 40 percent felt that their move was voluntary. A few genuinely voluntary refugees had moved in with the evacuees. Of the 59 who said they had moved voluntarily, 52.5 percent cited insecurity (VC activity) as their reason; 6.8% cited VC taxes, conscription, or imprisonment; 44.1% cited bombing or artillery; 47.5% cited GVN-US war operations; 23.7% cited house destroyed; 28.8% cited fear of stray bullets or general fear of death; and 3.4% no jobs, couldn't farm. (People could cite more than one reason.) The Second Battalion of the ARVN 51st and US Marine CAPs (Combined Action Platoons) provided security, and 93.3% of the evacuees reported that the area of their new homes was always secure. The male-female ratio in the 15-to-49 age group was 30 to 100; in the entire population,

84 to 100. There were no males in the 20-to-24 or 25-to-29 age brackets. Thirty-four and six-tenths percent of the men and 16.9% of the women were literate.[20] These two peace hamlets were the best of the forced relocation sites (in my opinion) because they were close to the farms of most of the inhabitants.

Voluntary Refugee Movement

Ngoc-Thanh Camp

This camp held 482 families, of whom 118 were surveyed. The Ngoc-Thanh camp, in Quang-Nam province on the outskirts of the provincial capital, Hoi-An, was in Cam-Kim village, most of which had been on the south side of the Hoi-An River, a contested area. Refugees had been coming to the camp for more than five years, but it was officially declared a refugee camp only in October 1965. The Cam-Kim village chief served as chief of the camp; he registered the refugees with the SCR. However, 36.4% of the refugees reported that they had received no GVN assistance. Refugees who had lived there more than six months had the vote. Camp facilities included a market place, consumer cooperative, a five-room school, dispensary, VIS, and four potable water wells. The German Knights of Malta (Maltheser Hilfsdienst) assisted the refugees. The sandy soil on which the camp was built was unfit for farming, but only 3.4% of the refugees were unemployed.[21]

Quang-Nam Settlement (Vinh-Dien hamlet, Vinh-Xuong village, Dien-Ban district)

This hamlet, on Highway No. 1 and the Vien-Dien River, had experienced a heavy refugee influx from outlying districts over the previous five years, and had 281 families at the time of the survey. All the usable land was claimed by native residents; some of the refugees were employed as agricultural laborers, others in local industries. Wages had gone down because of surplus labor, and prices had increased. However, the residents had evidently accepted the refugees as people in need. Only 8.8% of the refugees were unemployed. Despite the presence of security forces, the VC reportedly were able to infiltrate and kidnap a few refugees. However, because anti-Communist refugee men were recruited into local forces and ARVN (10.5%, compared with 5.5% before their move), the officials believed that security had improved. The procedure for getting SCR aid was long and complicated since Vien-Dien was not considered a camp, with the result that little or no assistance was provided. However, the hamlet was a village and district center, so many facilities, including three schools, a dispensary, VIS, and so forth, were available to the refugees.[22]

Most of the refugee respondents in both the Ngoc-Thanh camp (74.1% of 108) and Vinh-Dien hamlet (63.8% of 116) cited insecurity arising from VC activity as their reason for moving. Also cited were bombing/artillery, GVN/US war operations, VC taxes, conscription, imprisonment, fear of stray bullets or general fear of death, and so on. Some 40.3% of both groups reported that the VC had attempted to prohibit their movement. The male-to-female ratios in the 15-to-49-year age group, 58 to 100 in the camp, and 59 to 100 in the settlement, while low, were above those in the forced movement sites.[23]

Da-Nang An-Cu Camp

Nine hundred seventy families lived in the three sections of this camp, which had been built by the refugees with the assistance of the mayor and USAID in 1966. The dwellings were concrete, and in the opinion of the HSR surveyors they represented the finest refugee housing in I CTZ. Cement and roofing were furnished by the GVN, and loans up to 14,000 $VN (at 80.80 = $1 US in 1966) were available for construction and for starting a garden or small business. Each section of the camp had a dispensary and a school, but the schools were not open at the time of the survey. HSR commented:

An Cu is a model of how refugees could and should be resettled. The housing is more than adequate and school and medical facilities have been provided. But what is more important, an attempt has been made to enroll refugees in vocational training and to employ refugees with American agencies. Furthermore, loans were made available to the refugees so they could start a small business or a small agricultural enterprise.

However, 16.8% of the people were unemployed, and only 2.3% were in the police or military, compared with 4.2% before they moved.[24]

Da-Nang Settlement, Ap Mot (Hamlet 1)

Near the camp, along Cach-Mang Street and the road to the bridge to West Da-Nang, was a narrow strip of land that was a native hamlet of 70 resident families, into which 124 refugee families had settled themselves. The refugees were unregistered, because the city government was trying to discourage further influx, even going so far as to disband the local SCR from January 1967 to late in the year. Ap-Mot was only one of the refugee squatter areas within the city. Employment with the Americans and ARVN was available, and the HSR researcher observed several brothels in Hamlet 1. He found that most of the refugees were doing reasonably well. They had access to electricity, schools, and health care, and were in a secure area. Eight percent were unemployed.[25]

A somewhat higher proportion of refugee citations of factors that caused their movement in both the camp and the settlement mentioned the VC as causal agent (48.3% and 41.0% respectively) than mentioned the GVN/US (23.4% and 37.3%), while 21.7% and 28.4% mentioned other causal agents. However, the overwhelming majority of those living in the camp (82.2%) relocated there because the site was arranged by the government. In the age group 15-to-34, the male-female ratios were 49 to 100 in the camp and 56 to 100 in the hamlet. However, a surprising 65.0% of the males and 41.2% of the females in the two sites combined were tested as literate.[26]

Quang-Tri Settlement, Khu N

This was a subdivision of Thach-Han hamlet, Hai-Tri village, Mai-Linh district, on the outskirts of Quang-Tri city. It had 278 refugee families at the time of the survey, 45.4% of whom had come between October 1966 and September 1967. They had access to the superior schools and other facilities of the city, but poverty kept many of their children out of school. Only 6.5% of the respondents reported that they had been forced or encouraged to move; 62.5% of their citations of causal agents for their move cited the VC, 21.0% the GVN/US, and 16.5% other agents. "No security" (VC activity) got 62.3% of the citations of specific reasons, with VC taxes, conscription, or imprisonment at 46.5%, bombing/artillery at 26.7%, GVN/US war operations at 9.9%, fear of stray bullets/general fear of death at 15.8%, "house destroyed" at 3.0%, and "no jobs, couldn't farm" at 3.0%. Some 38.9% of the respondents reported that the VC had tried to prohibit their movement. Most of the refugees had received no GVN assistance. They built their own houses, which were crowded together on land which they rented. About half had been farmers before moving, but they had no access to agricultural land in their new site. A surprising 19.5% were in the police or military, compared with 14.2% before movement. Thirteen and seven-tenths percent were unemployed (1.8% before movement). The ratio of males to females in the 15-to-34 age group was 42 to 100, but when the 29 men reported to have been away in the GVN armed forces were added, the ratio became 96 to 100, which was higher than that for the entire refugee population. From this the surveyors concluded that few were in the VC forces. However, their population table showed an abnormally low number of both males and females in the 15-to-19 and 20-to-24 age groups.[27] Similar but less extreme shortages of females in these age groups were evident at some of the other sites also.

Comparisons Between Evacuees and Refugees

On the basis of the survey data, HSR made a number of comparisons between forced evacuees and voluntary refugees in the nine sites.

1. Objectively, 57.1% of the evacuees lived in better houses than before their movement, 41.1% experienced no change, while 1.6% lived in worse houses. The refugees were not so fortunate: only 35.5% lived in better houses, 54.8% in houses that were about the same, and 9.7% in houses that were not so well constructed. This reflects the special effort that was made, except in the Lam-Son 87 operation (after which no qualitative evaluation of housing was attempted), to make conditions as good as possible for the evacuees.

2. Except for the Hung-Quang evacuees, 60.0% of whom continued to cultivate land (compared with 93.8% before their movement), almost none of the evacuees and refugees had land to cultivate after their movement.

3. Among the evacuees, 38.2% were working at unskilled trades after move-

ment, 12.9% were working at skilled trades, and 48.8% were unemployed (compared with 6.9% unemployed before evacuation); while 23.4% of the refugees were employed at unskilled work, 37.6% were employed at skilled work, and 39.0% were unemployed (compared with 11.4% before movement). Both groups had suffered a diminution of their employment status.

4. The evacuees owned only 39% of their previous capital stock, that is, livestock, fishponds, tools, vending stock, and vehicles; while the refugees owned 57%. Only in the Hung-Quang peace villages did the evacuees own more than 50% as much as they had previously, because they were close to their former homes.

5. All had improved access to health facilities.

6. Refugee households had a higher percentage of children in school, but in two relocation sites the new schools were not yet open.

7. Because they were near existing communities, the refugees were considerably better off than most of the evacuees in markets, water supply, electricity, cooperatives, transportation, and entertainment. However, the Cedar Falls evacuees had an excellent, if oversophisticated, water system.

8. Both evacuees and refugees in great majority turned to their local chiefs for advice and aid.

9. A surprising 98.4% of the evacuees reported receiving some GVN assistance, while less than 60% of the refugees were helped by their government.

10. Ninety-four percent of the evacuees said that their sites were fully secure; 99.2% of the refugees felt secure. In the case of the evacuees, HSR questioned whether this enhancement was more than illusory, given the inadequate defenses observed at the sites. It was doubtful that VC cadres had been denied free access to the evacuees.

11. There was little change in exposure of either group to GVN propaganda.

12. The data were insufficient to measure the sociopolitical integration of either group. The refugees showed a somewhat higher degree, measured by attendance at religious and other ceremonies and travel, probably because they generally lived near existing communities.

The aggregate score for these 12 factors, or objectives as HSR called them, on a scale of 0 (very bad) to 9 (perfect), was 4.77 for the evacuee sites and 5.18 for the refugee centers. However, Hung-Quang was 6.33 and Cedar Falls was 6.42, the highest score of all.

The evacuees were a somewhat older population, with a mean age of 23.8 years, compared to 20.6 years for the refugees.

All respondents were asked to name their hopes and fears for the future, as the anchoring points on the Cantril scale. The refugees placed more weight on peace, happiness, and an easy life (62.5% of their responses) than the evacuees (53.6%), while the evacuees placed more emphasis on food, clothing, and housing (49.8%) than the refugees (31.4%); but otherwise their hopes were similar. The Lam-Son 87 evacuees, who had been left on their own, and the Cedar Falls evacuees, who had received inadequate food and poor shelter during the first few days, were especially concerned with food, clothing, and housing. Money and education for the children were the other major hopes. Only 5.2% of the evacuee hopes and 3.4% of hopes of the refugees were for land.

The evacuees' most pressing fear for the future was of having no food or clothing (66.2%); the refugees also had this fear (52.9%). Eighty-five and eight-tenths percent of the responses from the Cedar Falls evacuees cited this fear, but it was cited in only 41.7% of the DMZ evacuee responses, while 37.6% of the evacuee responses and 42.9% of those from refugees expressed fear of misery and no education; 35.0% of the evacuee responses and 40.0% of those from refugees expressed fear of sickness; and 28.4% of evacuee expressions and 21.5% of those from refugees were fear of war. Other fears were minor.

Asked to rate the past, present, and future in terms of these hopes and fears, on a scale of 0 (worst) to 10 (best; the respondents were actually shown a ladder and asked to indicate the places on it), the family heads came up with the mean scores shown in table 7.

In the 14 other countries where Cantril administered this test, no national group rated its present lower than its past. Among Vietnamese peasants associated with the RF/PF, only the women felt that the present was worse than conditions five years earlier, but not by the order of magnitude shown by the evacuees and refugees. The HSR authors commented:

Vietnamese refugees (volitional) in the present study rate themselves significantly lower at present than five years earlier (a discrepancy of 1.90 scale points, significant at well beyond the 99 percent level of confidence in statistical terms). And forced evacuees in the Viet-Nam sample show a discrepancy between past and present mean ratings nearly *double* that of volitional refugees. There can hardly be any more dramatic proof that, first, all Vietnamese displaced persons are far from satisfied with their present conditions, and that, of the two types of displaced persons, forced evacuees are significantly less satisfied than are volitional refugees. In fact, the lowest mean rating for a voluntary movement is higher than the highest mean rating for any single forced movement site.[28]

When the respondents were asked directly whether the present or the past was better, 11.3% of the refugees but only 1.4% of the evacuees considered the present better, 11.4% of the refugees and 4.0% of the evacuees felt that there had been no change, 74.6% of the refugees and 85.8% of the evacuees said the past was better, and 2.7% of the refugees and 8.8% of the evacuees gave no answer. When asked to rate the future by comparison with the present, over half of each group gave no answer, but 27.6% of the refugees and 17.6% of the evacuees thought that the future would be better. Thus, both groups were pessimistic, the evacuees more so than the refugees.[29]

HSR explored the extent to which displacement separated the insurgents from the civilian population and mobilized new population resources for the counter-insurgents. It found that in Phu-Yen province (see chapter 6) the relocation of farmers from the edges of the hills to more secure valleys had markedly reduced the flow of rice to the VC. This could happen only when alternative sources

Table 7
Evacuee and Refugee Evaluations of Their Past, Present, and Future on the Cantril Self-Anchoring Scale, 1967–68 (0 = worst to 10 = best), in Four Evacuation Sites (n = 498) and Five Voluntary Refugee Sites (n = 593)

		Mean Scale Ratings	
Sites	Past	Present	Future
DMZ Evacuees	5.55	2.42	4.96
Hung-Quang Regroupment	4.57	1.90	3.00
Lam-Son 87 Evacuees	4.79	1.33	2.24
Cedar Falls Evacuees	5.95	1.65	2.48
Quang-Nam Refugee Camp	4.72	3.08	5.05
Quang-Nam Refugee Settlement	4.55	2.51	5.00
Da-Nang Refugee Camp	4.81	3.11	4.13
Da-Nang Refugee Settlement	4.64	2.87	3.17
Quang-Tri Refugee Settlement	4.96	2.53	3.58
All Refugees	4.78	2.86	4.39
All Evacuees	5.19	1.81	3.20

Source: A. T. Rambo, D. Brown, and P. Estermann, *A Study of Mass Population Displacement in the Republic of Vietnam* (McLean, Va.: Human Sciences Research, Inc., 1968), Part I, 48.

could not be found, which was not the case at Ben-Suc, where the VC brought in other people to cultivate the fields. Also, the VC had access to the Cedar Falls evacuees, and the VC infrastructure was not eliminated from their midst. There was no appreciable increase in the GVN manpower pool from the evacuees, but some increase from the refugees. However, the only resettlement sites of either group that had the potential for self-support were the Hung-Quang peace hamlets. No direct measurement of political attitudes was attempted, but it was believed that there were few GVN adherents and many enemies among the evacuee population, and the experience of forced relocation was not likely to produce pro-GVN attitudes. Economic and social betterment actions appear to have been totally ineffective in changing the attitudes of the evacuees. The Cedar Falls site, where the most had been done to improve the living conditions, showed the second lowest on the Cantril scale, while Cam-Lo, where objective factors were the second lowest, had the highest Cantril rating among evacuee sites.[30]

HSR drew the following conclusions:

Despite its evident efficacy in other counterinsurgency campaigns [in other countries] forced relocation has not in the balance been an effective and efficient pacification tactic as it has been employed in Viet-Nam. The material costs to the GVN and the U.S. have been vast, the material and psychic costs to the evacuees beyond measure, and the evident damage inflicted on the Viet-Cong relatively slight. This is not to say that population regroupment is never justified; there are specific tactical situations where carefully planned and implemented relocations can be of real value to the pacification effort. But, on the basis of the evidence presented in the preceding chapters, forced relocation of civilians on a massive basis does not appear to offer a viable solution to the problems of rural pacification in Viet-Nam.[31]

My experience indicates that the HSR conclusions were conservative. The forced relocations that I have studied and whose victims I was engaged in helping were, almost without exception, counterproductive to pacification objectives.

This thorough and well-reasoned study, which had been commissioned by the Defense Department (ARPA), seems to have had little immediate effect on the strategy and tactics of the US forces and even less on ARVN. It was reviewed in draft by the Refugee Coordinator of AID/Washington, but not by the CORDS/ Refugee Division in Saigon, which did not even receive the finished product. There is no mention of it in the Komer or Colby papers, and it is not known whether MACV received it at the time (mid-1968). In any case, many of those who would have been most concerned were occupied with repairing the damage wrought by the VC's Tết and May Offensives.

RELOCATION OF PEOPLE IN THE HIGHLANDS—EDAP ENANG

In the fall of 1966, the US Fourth Division, commanded by Major General William Peers in concert with General Vinh Loc, Commander of II Corps, began planning the first organized, large-scale relocation of highlanders since 1961. The idea was to move about 10,000 Jarai in Pleiku province from the area along Route 19 near the Cambodian border and from the Ia-Drang Valley, both in Le-Thanh district, in order to deny manpower and foodstuffs to the enemy, bring more people under GVN control, and create a free fire zone at a terminus of the Ho-Chi-Minh trail. The plan called for three stages: cordoning of some 48 Jarai villages and removal of the people by helicopter, boarding the evacuees in temporary housing, and finally, movement to permanent housing and development of the resettlement site near the district town of Thanh-An (formerly Le-

Thanh). The planners chose the name Edap Enang for the relocation site, which in Rhadé (not Jarai) means "peace and security".

The operation got under way on April 1, 1967. Units of the Fourth Division cordoned off each village; then a Vietnamese platoon accompanied by GVN officials and usually an American advisor entered to inform the people that they had to leave. Chinook helicopters carried the people and what few possessions they could gather up. They had to leave their sturdy houses, precious jars and gongs, cattle, and newly planted rice fields. The villages were burned even before the people had left. At the new site, GVN officials registered the refugees and assigned them to tents or tin and bamboo temporary houses. By mid-July, 8,100 had been moved.

General Vinh Loc had engaged a corrupt contractor to build the permanent houses; the contractor had received 24 sheets of roofing for each house but used only 20 and collected poor wood from the neighboring forest. Nevertheless, he demanded from each family most of the 5,000 piasters (at 118 = $1 US), and the 60 shoddy houses he constructed in the Vietnamese style, on the ground instead of on piles, were soon falling down. The CORDS province officials appealed to Lt. Col. Nay Lo, the province chief, who canceled the contract and allowed the evacuees to build their own houses, giving them the 5,000 $VN and 24 sheets of roofing. Truong-Son cadres cut and hauled wood for the people. Rice, bulgur, salt, powdered milk, cooking oil, and blankets were distributed. Major Kiem, a capable officer, was made camp commander with a staff of 20 plus 70 Truong-Son cadres. The chiefs of the 46 villages met regularly with GVN officials. Security was provided by the 11th ARVN Ranger battalion, which abused the people, the 143rd RF company, and two PF platoons. However, 40 to 50 VC propaganda and intimidation agents operated in the settlement at will.

General Peers insisted, even a year later, that the people had left their old homes voluntarily. That does not appear to have been the case. Jerry Dodson, the CORDS evaluator who visited the camp in July and talked with the tribesmen, reported that none of the people liked leaving their own homes; they resented being crowded in with 8,000 others, and complained that the land was not fertile and that the bulldozers were scraping off the topsoil. They were forced to move during the planting season, couldn't bring their livestock and poultry, and had to leave some family members behind. Those who were moved were almost exclusively old people and children. Some of the younger members had been forced to work for the VC, whom the people disliked as much as they did the Vietnamese. One elder said that many had died during the last few months because of disease, weakened condition from food shortages, harassment by the VC, and the forced migration. He wrote:

Despite their complaints, the tribesmen expressed neither anger nor bitterness at the Americans or the GVN. They understood the situation well, and realized that the Americans and the GVN had moved to create a free-fire zone and to remove them from VC control. A fatalistic "what will be, will be" attitude was pervasive.

However, at the time of Dodson's visit, 116 families had left.[32]

A lot of effort by the GVN, the Americans, and the evacuees was going into improving the camp. There was an excellent medical program, with four GVN personnel including one Jarai and two medics from the 41st Civil Affairs Company. All the evacuees had been innoculated against cholera and plague. Two schools, the dispensary, a playground, and a market were under construction. Lieutenant Khoa of ARVN psyops was very active in distributing commodities, caring for lepers, and talking continuously with the people. The Jarai themselves built a spillway on the stream flowing through the site with USAID cement. They were using four old spillways, and were digging wells. However, Dodson found that a mendicant mentality was developing among this traditionally proud and independent people. He questioned whether military necessity justified the relocation, which had not denied manpower to the VC since most young people were still in the old area. He recommended that a permanent government should be established in the community, American civil and military advisors be kept there, an economic base be created, informational activities be increased, defense be improved, and the performance of the 11th Rangers be reevaluated. He also proposed that in the future, US officials be given sufficient time to prepare if such operations again took place.[33]

Wade Lathram transmitted this excellent evaluation to Ambassador Komer on July 27, and the next day Major General George I. Forsythe, Komer's second in command, sent back a memorandum suggesting that it be sent to Washington with an action program and given to the GVN. He also said that several policies should be staffed and adopted, to wit:

a. Massive resettlement without adequate preparations should, except when militarily necessary, be avoided.

b. US units should not be involved in resettlement operations unless Vietnamese forces are unavailable. US forces could take over other security missions to make Vietnamese forces available.

c. Vietnamese Rangers should not, under any circumstances, be used for operations in which close, sympathetic dealings with the people are involved.

d. After initial movement of people into resettlement areas, CORDS should assume the total advisory function.[34]

Except for the recommendation concerning the Rangers, General Forsythe's memo really gave no guidance at all, probably because he did not want to antagonize his tough, unbending colleague, General Peers.

In August, the GVN's Thanh-An district took over responsibility for the refugees, superseding Major Kiem, and conditions rapidly deteriorated. The 41st Civil Affairs company bulletin characterized the district chief as demonstrating a lack of administrative knowledge and leadership, and greedy. At one point the evacuees went without food rations for two weeks, subsisting on bamboo shoots and leaves. Security was poor. The dispensary was inadequately supplied. Some pigs for raising which had been shipped from Saigon were eaten. Wells dried up. Banana trees for planting during the dry season died for lack of water. Teachers were frequently absent from the new school. In November, bulldozers cleared about 1,000 hectares for the next planting season, but took off the trees, brush, and topsoil, leaving the laterite subsoil to harden in the sun. When the Jarai were allowed to visit their old villages to harvest what little rice they could find, most did not return. By January 1968, Edap Enang had only 2,700 inhabitants. ARVN was ordered to bring them back, and rounded up about a thousand, most of whom left again. VC propaganda teams were active, and found the people receptive.[35]

The American military in II CTZ remained convinced that they had done the right thing. In a message of January 11, 1968, to Komer, Lt. General William B. Rosson, Commander of I Field Force, said of the Edap Enang operation. "This movement was made at the request of the local tribesmen because of attacks on their hamlets by enemy forces." He estimated that US casualties had decreased by at least half in the areas from which refugees were removed (including the An-Lao valley of Binh-Dinh, from which 5,000–6,000 Vietnamese inhabitants were evacuated).[36] That, at least, was some justification for the suffering inflicted upon the Jarai, although whether it was sufficient remained an open question.

On January 12, 1968, Peter Rosenblatt, a brilliant young man who had been Komer's assistant at the White House, visited Edap Enang, and later talked with numerous people in the province. He reported that the Jarai were not nomadic, as was commonly assumed, but were very much attached to the land (a finding that Hickey confirmed). Therefore, the prospect of becoming refugees distressed them at least as much as it did Vietnamese in similar circumstances. They traditionally lived in small villages. The military had informed CORDS only a week before the operation, which took place in the middle of the planting season. When some of the villagers were later permitted to go back and recover their rice, only 150 tons ever got back to the camp. There had been a food crisis in December 1967, he said, because of a dispute between Dr. Que and General Vinh Loc, and between then and mid-January almost two thirds of the residents decamped. There were conflicting estimates of the population remaining: A team from Saigon found that it had declined from 5,400 on January 1 to 2,682 January 18. On the other hand, the deputy PSA (province senior advisor), Robert Burke, told Rosenblatt that 7,000-8,000 were still there and that everything was under control; his refugee advisor said sotto voce that this was not so. Rosenblatt summed up the situation in the conclusion of his report:

Edap Enang can safely be described as a classical resettlement blunder. This resulted from lack of information about the people involved, compounded by hasty and ill-conceived execution, sagging follow-through and poor administration. I can only suggest that if such massive forced population movements are found necessary—and I personally doubt their utility—the CORDS and GVN authorities who must bear the brunt of making them a success should be consulted long enough beforehand to permit them to make adequate advance arrangements. GVN follow-through remains a problem. This simply points up the value of selecting a site and moving the people at a time which will enable them to be independent of outside assistance at as early a date as possible.[37]

In view of the fact that Generals Westmoreland and Creighton Abrams and Ambassador Komer were deeply disturbed by the apparent mass exodus from Edap Enang, Wade Lathram after talking with the Chief of Staff of I FFV (First Field Force Vietnam), sent Colonel A. H. Ringler, the Chief of the Evaluation Division, George Goss and Stephen Cummings of the Refugee Division, and Jay McNaughton of the Ethnic Minorities staff to look into the situation and confer with General Peers, who had in the meantime become deputy to General Rosson, Commander of I FFV and Deputy Senior Advisor to the Corps Commander. (I had just been appointed to succeed Goss as chief of the CORDS Refugee Division, but Lathram told me that he did not want me to start my tenure by getting into a dispute with General Peers. He was wise. I did see the general later.)

The team reported on January 21: The OCO senior advisors in Pleiku and the SCR had expressed strong reservations about the move when they were first notified, pointing out that there was insufficient time to prepare, the Jarai had just planted a crop, the people would not consent to remaining tightly clustered together, and there were insufficient water and farmland. "Contrary to popular misconception, the Jarai are not nomadic but very deeply and religiously rooted to the land on which they live. There are Jarai villages over 100 years old in Western Pleiku Province." Swidden agriculture takes the Jarai far afield, but they remain anchored to their villages. The operation did seem to get off to a good start, however, with an effective II Corps administrator and much help from the SCR and American units. However, after a new administrator without full authority was named in August, the situation deteriorated. Whole villages left. In October-November many were permitted to leave to harvest rice, with security provided by the Fourth Division, and many did not return. The camp population, which had been 8,639 on April 1 and 7,987 on October 1, declined to 7,520 by December 1, to 5,401 by January 1, and to 2,682 by January 18. However, the people who left had moved, not to their destroyed villages along the Cambodian border, but to new lands about 18 kilometers south and west of Edap Enang. Colonel Nay Lo, at the direction of General Vinh Loc, was rounding them up and returning them forcibly to the camp. The report concluded that the project had not enhanced the position of the GVN or the US with the Montagnards, and was ill-advised. It recommended that the US authorities seek to stop further forcible return of those who had left and allow the people to resettle in the new location, and that the GVN be asked to relieve the province chief if he could not be moved to take action. At the same time, Robert E. Matteson, the DepCORDS of II CTZ, in a memorandum to General Rosson, reported that only one-third of the villages remained, that three elders were being held hostage by

Colonel Nay Lo, and that a conversation with one of the three revealed that the VC were not responsible for the departures; living conditions were.[38]

The investigating team met on January 22 with General Peers, Matteson, and Lt. Col. G. G. Gibbs, PSA of Pleiku, and handed them copies of the report. Peers said that he was not in agreement with it. Specifically, he indicated that 75% of the Montagnards initially resettled at Edap Enang had done so at their own volition. The project was successful, he maintained, until mid-December, but declined when Major Kiem left and the administration was turned over to the province. If conditions had continued as originally promised by the GVN, the people would not have left. Peers was not opposed, however, to letting the people resettle in areas north, east, or south of the camp, where they would be less susceptible to VC control. That afternoon, General Peers and Matteson met with General Vinh Loc who, according to Matteson, agreed to the appointment of a new manager and to letting the refugees resettle in alternate locations if the district chief concurred. He also said that if Paul Nur, Minister of Ethnic Minorities Affairs would release Mr. Ya Ba, one of his assistants, the Corps Commander would appoint him province chief, replacing Colonel Nay Lo.[39] On January 23 Komer sent a message to all US Force commanders, saying he desired a report as soon as possible whenever any group of 500 or more people was relocated. The report was to show need for the move, initial care, ongoing plans, and problems.

As part of my orientation tour, I visited the Pleiku CORDS team and then Edap Enang on January 26. Mr. Burke told me that he had just been at the camp and that people were definitely being held there against their will. He and Colonel Gibbs added that General Vinh Loc had not agreed to the plan to allow the refugees to resettle 15 kilometers away. Colonel Nay Lo, they said, was forcing people to stay. The Corps Commander had said that he would not force people to return but would make the camp a success by magnetic attraction. When we were at the camp, Lt. Schaffener of the 41st Civil Affairs Company told me that ARVN had brought back 500–700 people on trucks within the past week. A Chinook helicopter had returned some more the preceding day. After Têt (which was to begin on January 30) there would be additional operations to bring people back forcibly. Lt. Low added that people in outlying villages in the free fire zone were ready to come back and had all their belongings ready to move. Instead, however, the people of Plei Ya Ho village, who had never been in Edap Enang, were brought in by force on January 19 and 20. Major William Schuler, the district senior advisor, estimated that there were about 3,000 in the camp; he said most would stay if they were given security and basic necessities. As it was, the VC were coming in at night and kidnapping hamlet chiefs; two "patrons" (elders) were at that moment being held as hostages by the VC. All the wells were dry and had been for at least one and a half months. Colonel Nay Lo wrote a note for me saying that 4,595 people were presently in the camp, and that he planned to bring in an additional 2,822 from the vicinity of the Plei Me Special Forces camp. Later, Colonel Gibbs, Robert Burke, Major Schuler, and refugee advisor George Shepard all gave me their recommendations that General Vinh Loc should be told that the US would not support any forcible movement to Edap Enang, including Nay Lo's planned movement from Plei Me, and that people must be allowed to settle freely along the Edap Enang–Plei Ya Ho axis. They thought that we should go all the way to back up our stand, that is, actually cut off support if necessary. They were going to work toward getting an effective camp manager appointed and solving the practical problems of the camp, and wanted to have an SCR (actually MSWR [Ministry of Social Welfare and Refugees] by that time) mobile team to help.[40]

Colonel Gibbs sent a message on January 29 to Matteson, info copy to Saigon, saying that people were still being returned against their will and that there was no indication that General Vinh Loc had issued orders to the contrary. On January 26, Colonel Nay Lo had told a group of the returnees that they had "sinned" but that he would forgive them. However, he said, if they left again, he would put them in jail. He had become agitated when the Deputy PSA (Burke) had tried to discuss the matter. The message concluded, "From all of the above it is abundantly clear that a policy of forced retention of the population in E.E. continues to be followed." Komer sent this message with a handwritten note: "GIF[Forsythe] Check out with AC/S Cords and Matteson. I'm not sure we ought to be this high handed." K.[41]

Komer followed this up with a telegram to General Rosson for Matteson saying, "When time is right you should inform General Vinh Loc that MACV strongly opposes forcible retention of Montagnards in Edap Enang." He asked what Matteson thought of a recommendation to the Minister of Social Welfare and Refugees that he be prepared to cut off funds to Edap Enang unless the policy of forcible return was dropped. He further recommended that camp improvements be undertaken, but that people be allowed to resettle in nearby, relatively secure areas.[42]

By March 1968, the United States had spent $900,000 on the resettlement site and improvements had been made, but the camp was still not self-sustaining. The CORDS province senior advisor commented in his monthly report for May: "This project has cost more than all other provincial refugee projects and has had less success than any. This should be a lesson that forced resettlement does not work." In April, two operations were conducted to "police up" over 2,000 refugees who had left the camp; the province CORDS team at first thought that they came willingly, since they lacked food. We in the Refugee Division of CORDS also thought so, but evidently we were mistaken. By the next month, over 1,000 people had left. Most of them were the April returnees, but 285 were from a hamlet that had been in the camp since the summer of 1967. In May 1968, an operation to clear an area south of Route 19 brought in 1,200 more Jarai, mostly old men, women, and children. Seven hundred eighty-five of them left and returned to their homes. However, according to a report of the 41st Civil Affairs Company's Team 9 in July, there were no more departures after May 9, and 400 new settlers came in voluntarily, bringing the population to

3,780 (of whom less than 420 were males). This seemed to indicate that those who remained had become resigned to their fate. Major William Reiff of CORDS/ REF Saigon reported in late June that further voluntary arrivals had raised the population to 5,122 by June 20, including young males. The reasons were that the area was relatively secure (although still under VC threat), medical aid was available, and commodities were being distributed regularly, while the areas from which the newcomers migrated had been the scenes of military activity. All refugee families had their house lots plus one hectare of land, 90% of which was planted at the time of Reiff's visit. So it seemed that what could not be accomplished by forced relocation was gradually being accomplished by voluntary refugee movement.[43]

On May 11, General Peers, then Commanding General of I FFV and Senior Advisor of II Corps, called a meeting of his staff and Region II CORDS to consider Edap Enang. The meeting concluded that an area south of Thanh-An district headquarters would be cleared of its population. New centers would be created for the evacuees. The PSA commented: "I for one can see no sense to this continued movement of the Montagnard people."[44] Thus, the sad story of military insensitivity to "people-factors" and forced relocation of highlanders would be continued.

8

The Communist Têt and May Offensives of 1968

At the end of 1967, although intelligence was already available that the enemy was planning a general offensive, an air of optimism pervaded the US military and CORDS headquarters.[1] The CORDS Refugee Division, in collaboration with the Ministry of Social Welfare and Refugees (MSWR), had estimated for planning and budgeting purposes that about 800,000 new refugees would be generated in 1968. Ambassador Komer, aware that the estimate had been motivated primarily to ensure adequate funding, rejected it. He pointed out that a rising proportion of the population was living in relatively secure areas; only 2.7 million were estimated to be still under VC control. General Westmoreland and Komer believed that military operations in the coming year would shift increasingly to sparsely populated or essentially uninhabited areas, thus reducing refugee flow. Komer's tentative view was that new refugees in calendar year 1968 were not likely to exceed 250,000–350,000.[2]

In his year-end summary of the refugee situation, issued on December 28, 1967, he said that refugee generation had peaked in 1966 and that the trend was downward since then, while resettlement and return of refugees to their home villages was running much higher than the flow of new refugees. After he and the GVN had checked with their field staffs, the GVN estimated about 300,000 new refugees in the coming year, while his estimate was about 340,000.[3] The CORDS Refugee Division adopted these estimates and, starting from a figure of 794,000 refugees in temporary status as of December 31 (a figure which itself was underestimated by about 74,000) calculated that the total number of refugees to be dealt with in 1968 would be about 1,100,000. The division presented a plan and budget for temporary relief, resettlement, and return to village based upon those figures; it had been developed jointly with the MSWR.[4]

Both the GVN and CORDS, as it turned out, were wide of the mark, because

of the massive Tết offensive of the VC and NVA which began late in January
and large-scale fighting during much of the rest of the year. About 1,000,000
urban war victims and almost 800,000 new rural refugees were generated in
1968, an overwhelming burden on the GVN and US staffs, which had prepared
for a much smaller number.

Until the Tết offensive, the large cities and many of the smaller towns had
been safe havens from the war which had ravaged the countryside for many
years. As reported in earlier chapters, many, indeed, probably most of the new
inhabitants of the cities had been refugees from the insecure rural areas. They
were strongly anti-Communist, and their very presence had helped to make the
cities nominally secure. However, in those cities a well-developed VC infrastructure had never been recognized or seriously attacked. Consequently to the
city dwellers war meant an artifically induced prosperity, based on providing
goods and services to the armed forces of both the GVN and the allies.

Even when the US Mission on January 5, 1968 published the full text of a
captured order to the People's Army of Viet-Nam (PAVN, which Americans
called the NVA) and party cadres, saying that strong military attacks and a
popular uprising were to take over towns and cities (and there was confirming
evidence) not many South Vietnamese or Americans paid attention.[5] The optimistic view of the future prevailed. Until the last few days, almost nobody
expected the enemy to violate the Tết truce, which had been declared by both
sides. Tết, the oriental New Year, is like the American Christmas, New Year,
and Fourth of July all rolled into one. Officially it lasts three days; in 1968 it
began on January 29, but in fact celebrations begin several days ahead of time,
and normal work doesn't resume until a day or so after the official end. Both
soldiers and civilian employees are granted generous leave. President Thieu was
in My-Tho with his wife's family. Homes, villages, and towns are cleaned and
decorated. People go to visit their relatives and to venerate their ancestors, living
and dead; gifts are exchanged, debts are paid, and a new beginning is made. To
celebrate the Year of the Monkey, for the first time in many years the government
allowed firecrackers to be set off, and the people took full advantage of the
opportunity. On their part, the American authorities allowed holiday visits to
Viet-Nam of wives and children, who were settled in safe havens in Manila,
Taipei, and Bangkok.

I myself received an indication that something was amiss during my orientation
tour in II CTZ. On January 25, I flew into Kontum City, where the CORDS
team refused to let me go out into the countryside because it was not safe to
travel anywhere without a military escort, which was not available. We had to
be content with conferring with US and GVN officials in the isolated city. When
I arrived in Pleiku late in the day, the people in the CORDS staff told me that
the city and the adjacent Camp Holloway (the headquarters of the US Fourth
Division) had come under heavy attack the previous night by the NVA and VC
troops. After dinner, we settled down to a relaxed evening in the CORDS
compound, only to experience another such attack across the neighboring fields.

It lasted most of the night and pinned us down in the steel, sand-bagged bunker under the house, with weapons at the ready. Fortunately, the CORDS house itself was not attacked, and we were able to visit Edap Enang the next day. Similar attacks had occurred in other cities of II CTZ.[6] These experiences cast some doubt on the forecasts of a widening area of GVN control which was going to reduce refugee flow in the new year.

As the Têt holiday grew closer, the indications multiplied that the Communists might be planning to violate the truce. The 1st ARVN Division in I CTZ and the 23rd Division based at Ban Me Thuot canceled all leaves. Some other units did likewise. Some US forces were drawn into the Saigon area. On January 29, General Cao Van Vien, the chief of the Joint General Staff instructed his J-3 to warn all corps commanders of an imminent enemy attack and to order defensive measures.[7] However, most military units and the civilian ministries did not cancel leaves; it would have been difficult to recall the many thousands who had already scattered to their homes across the country; and President Thieu remained in My-Tho.

THE GENERAL OFFENSIVE

Early in the morning of January 30, Da-Nang, Hoi-An, Ban Me Thuot, Kon-tum, Pleiku, and Qui-Nhon were attacked. Most assaults were quickly repulsed, including the attack on Qui-Nhon, which had been considered a Communist hotbed, but the fighting in Ban Me Thuot lasted nine days and caused heavy damage.[8] It is not clear why these attacks occurred 24 hours before the general offensive was to begin, since they should have warned the GVN and US military leaders; but in fact, the element of surprise was scarcely diminished.

At about 3 A.M. on January 31, the VC and NVA attacked over 100 cities and towns, including Saigon, Dalat, and Hue, 34 of the 44 provincial capitals (five others had been attacked the previous day), and 71 district towns, in a superbly coordinated general offensive.[9] Again, almost all the assaults were quickly repulsed, and in no place did a popular uprising occur. Only in Saigon and Hue did the fighting continue for more than a few days. However, the general offensive inflicted terrible damage to the civilian population and property every-where, much of it quite deliberate on the part of the VC. It ended with the decimation of the Viet-Cong, whose best cadres and forces were slaughtered or captured. More than that, it brought home to most Vietnamese some elemental facts about the Communists and caused widespread revulsion against them. In places where the GVN forces and civil officials performed well, the offensive enhanced their standing among the populace; where they performed badly, the GVN's reputation suffered, but throughout the country there was a realization that strong measures and greater sacrifice would be necessary to defeat the forces that were now recognized as the enemy.

In the United States the effect was the opposite. The credibility gap between what US leaders had been telling the people about the progress of the war and what was perceived to be occurring widened greatly, and the process undermined confidence in the government and its war policy. This monumental event, which was brought into the living rooms of all Americans by television, caused both opinion makers and a majority of the public to decide irrevocably that the cause was not worth the sacrifice, that the United States had to get out. It drove Lyndon Johnson from the presidency. Ironically, this happened just as the South Vietnamese were galvanized into undertaking the constructive measures that set them onto the road of winning instead of losing.

On February 1, Ambassador Komer appointed me the Disaster Relief Coordinator of the US Mission, with responsibility to work with all its elements and the GVN in providing emergency relief to the rapidly increasing number of Vietnamese war victims. I set up a small operations center in the crowded offices of the Refugee Division and borrowed people from other parts of CORDS and USAID. Edward Lawrence, the experienced deputy chief of the Refugee Division, became deputy coordinator. Randy Bomar was chief of operations, in contact by the sporadically functioning military telephone network with CORDS and other units in the field—and the recipient of their urgent requests for tents, tarps, blankets, food, cooking utensils, and so on, to supplement the rapidly exhausted stockpiles of these commodities already in the regions and provinces. Peter Boyle came over from USAID Logistics to replace Preston Hogue of our office in taking charge of getting these supplies to the field and to the MSWR, using mainly US military assets and the contract airline, Air America.

William Luken, the division's reports officer, now became responsible for satisfying the insatiable demands of MACV and other parts of the mission for information on what was happening. Norman Firnstahl, unflappable veteran of both military and civilian bureaucracies, was put in charge of administration, which included obtaining money rapidly from the regulation-bound USAID Program Office. Steve Cummings remained at the Ministry for the same long hours as the Minister and the few key personnel who were able to get there with passes issued by the military. At first, our own loyal Vietnamese staff could not get to work because of the security situations where they lived and the rigid curfew imposed by the GVN. The voluntary agencies (volags) stationed representatives in the operations center, headed by Abner Bataldan of Vietnam Christian Service, the chairman of the Voluntary Agency Council. Virginia Callahan of UNICEF took charge of fanning out volag personnel to survey refugee locations and facilities and preparing reports for the Ministry and the mission. The Disaster Center put out a situation report, at first twice daily, and then daily.

In the first days, we in CORDS and MACV had virtually the only functioning communications and transportation systems in the country; the Vietnamese civilian systems were shut down by both the fighting and the absence of personnel, who were unable to get back to their jobs. Once the American dependents had been evacuated to their safe havens, the US facilities were used freely (subject to overriding military priorities) to support both our needs and those of the GVN, as well as those Vietnamese who had urgent need to travel. Air America and

US military aircraft never flew with empty seats or cargo space. In addition to carrying our passengers and cargo, they were filled at each stop with those Vietnamese, including ordinary peasants and their families, who had valid travel orders from their authorities. We never knew who our companions in the hard bucket seats would be, or what goods and chattels would be loaded on with them. We ourselves shipped the cargo that the MSWR considered urgent, including *nuoc-mam*, the fermented and very pungent fish sauce that was a staple of the diet. This was put up in theoretically unbreakable plastic containers, but sometimes they did break; a plane on which that happened carried the olfactory evidence for weeks.

Information on the magnitude of the crisis was slow coming in, even from the outlying districts of Saigon, where fighting was going on. Our Situation Report (Sitrep) of February 3 carried these items:

Numbers of Refugees: 20,000 registered in Saigon, receiving commodity assistance and medical services. No information available from MSWR field staff. On 2 Feb. IV CTZ reported Chau-Doc with 25,000 refugees and 5,000 houses burned. III CTZ reported 1,500 refugees. *Voluntary Agencies*: (gave the three locations and activities known). *Logistics*: 10 trucks with drivers and armed guards available from military. MSWR and CORDS personnel directing use to distribute commodities in Saigon and to Tan-Son-Nhut airport (TSN) for shipment to provinces. Will be available also on 4 Feb. *Funds*: [MSWR authorized each provincial service chief to spend up to one million piasters (about $8,500 equivalent in 1968); if those funds were insufficient, each province in I and II Corps was authorized to utilize three million piasters, and each province in III and IV Corps four million, from a special fund. Regional CORDS refugee officers were to monitor expenditures from the latter fund].

Flash Reports: Bien-Hoa reports 11,800 persons departed their homes in city and neighboring villages. 1,000 houses destroyed. Being sheltered in schools, etc. 10,000 pounds of rice distributed, 9,000 gallons of potable water provided. Mellon, PSA, coordinating. Local GVN officials not yet effective. Military situation quiet. II FF Hq. has been hit. USARV [US Army, Vietnam] never touched.

Pleiku city, approximately 2,300 refugees, mainly from areas VC occupied. Extensive civilian damage and casualties. 31 Jan. 42 civil casualties with large number not yet recovered.

III CTZ reports 18,000 refugees in Gia-Dinh, 650 Phuoc-Tuy province, 780 in Vung-Tau from Phuoc-Tuy. CRS [Catholic Relief Services] and 101st Airborne troops supplied commodities. Sufficient food for 2–3 days.

IV CTZ reports estimated 125,000 require temporary care and 50,000 need aid in resettlement. Soc-Trang (Ba-Xuyen) 3,000 homes destroyed, 15,000 require assistance. Chau-Doc 4,000 houses damaged or destroyed, 25,000 people require care. My-Tho 700 houses destroyed. Can-Tho 300 homes destroyed, 5,000 require care.[10]

There were many examples of heroism and selflessness on the part of both GVN and US troops and civilians. In Saigon, the MSWR headquarters office personnel, assisted by the mobile cadres, Boy Scouts, and other Vietnamese and foreign volunteers, loaded trucks with supplies and distributed them at the refugee centers, which were in schools, temples and churches, and open fields under hastily erected canvas or plastic shelters. The mobile teams of the Ministry, led by retired US Army sergeant William (Bill) Thompson, extracted frightened people from areas under attack by the VC or about to be bombed by allied forces. These teams and Bill Thompson were among the authentic humanitarian heroes of the Têt offensive. Similar deeds of bravery and compassion were performed all over the country. Dr. Herbert Froewys, an Austrian physician under contract to IRC and assigned to CORDS Public Health in I CTZ, flew into besieged Hue, where bitter fighting went on for 25 days and nights, to treat the wounded and look after elementary sanitation and other health needs throughout the battle. Other voluntary agency medical personnel treated the wounded and sick in hospitals and clinics across the country, often in the midst of battle. Some missionaries were kidnapped or killed by the VC. In Saigon, on February 6, Dr. Que warned the voluntary agencies through our office to keep their American employees out of the refugee centers because of the danger of VC assassination. In the meantime, Vietnamese officials, military personnel, and volunteers ran the risks to which Dr. Que did not want to expose the Americans. Only on February 15 did he inform the voluntary agencies that it seemed safe to send their representatives into the camps, provided they kept on the lookout for VC terrorists.

Nearly 3,000 Têt victims sought refuge in a Hoa-Hao village of about 9,000 people, probably in Vinh-Long province. The religious leaders and village council members organized a "Charity Committee" to take responsibility for the welfare of their new guests. Within weeks, the men of the village were building houses for the refugees, providing food and clothing, and finding places for the children in the schools, overcrowded as they were. Each refugee breadwinner was provided with a job, and every native farmer gave up some of his land for the refugees to cultivate. Almost all the residents donated one day's wage to build up a welfare fund. Professor Samuel Popkin, who discovered this example of generosity during his research stay in Delta villages, commented: "Protected from dishonest GVN officials by a church hierarchy with enough power to enforce civil law, TQ village has been able to hold together as a community and even transform the fanaticism of Têt into constructive work in institutional development."[11]

The obverse situation was that there were also examples of shameful cowardice, callousness, and brutal acts against the people and their property.

The province chief of Vinh-Long had been paralyzed by fear during the attack and could not even respond to a CORDS officer in the tactical operations center who had asked him whether he had called on the Rangers to defend the city, as the commander of the ARVN Ninth Division had ordered. The Rangers finally did appear, but only to engage in wild looting for a day and a half after most of the population had fled. Then the Viet-Cong resumed their attack, and were met by fire from US gunships and river boats, which devastated much of the city. The battle raged for two more days and nights. On February 5, about a

Illustration 1

Hue during the Têt offensive of 1968. Refugees fleeing across a broken bridge over the Perfume River (Joint United States Public Affairs Office [JUSPAO] photo).

Illustration 2

Saigon residents picking through the ruins of their former homes (JUSPAO).

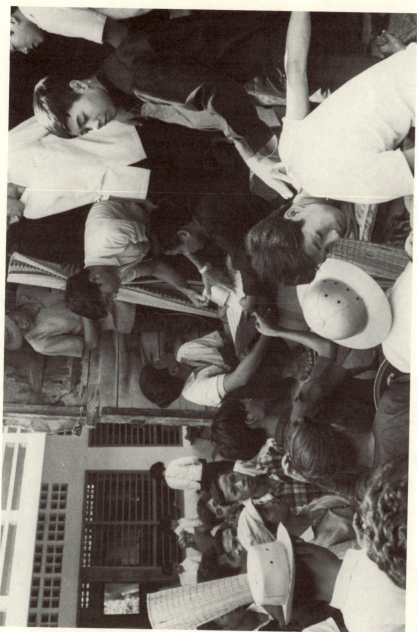

Illustration 3

Youth groups distributed food even while fighting in Saigon continued (JUSPAO).

Illustration 4

John F. Thomas, US Refugee Coordinator in Viet-Nam (1965); Chief, Refugee Division, Civil Operations for Revolutionary Development Support (CORDS) 1968–69); Director, Intergovernmental Committee for European Migration (ICEM) (1969–79) (ICEM photo taken at an Indochinese refugee camp in Thailand, after 1975).

Illustration 5

House construction at the Ca-Lui highlander refugee village, Phu-Bon province, April 13, 1969. Minister Tran Lu Y is in the floppy hat (Louis A. Wiesner [LAW] photo).

Illustration 6

Buon Ale A highlander refugee village, Darlac province, May 1969. This was a village of the Front Unifié de Lutte des Races opprimées (FULRO) (LAW photo).

Illustration 7

Refugees who had just returned to Dinh-Tri, their home hamlet, Hoai-Nhon district, Binh-Dinh province, September 1969. The hamlet chief is in the peaked cap at center. To the chief's right in the white shirt is Bui Liem, social welfare assistant at CORDS II CTZ, with Tom O'Keefe, district senior advisor, on his right (LAW photo).

Illustration 8

Binh-Son refugee hamlet, Ninh-Thuan province, September 1969. This and a companion hamlet were built on sandy land considered worthless. Casserina pines and eucalyptus trees were planted as wind breaks (LAW photo).

Illustration 9

With deep wells, compost, and fertilizer, the refugees prospered, growing onions, garlic, melons, and other crops on sand. The Filipino community development expert shown here helped them (LAW photo).

Illustration 10

Chau-Son I, Quang-Nam province April 1970. This forced-relocation camp, whose 740 people were crowded into seven tents, had much sickness (LAW photo).

Illustration 11

The marketplace of Loc-Vinh village, Thuong-Duc district, Quang-Nam province, June 16, 1970. It had been destroyed by the Viet-Cong (LAW photo).

Illustration 13

Dr. Phan Quang Dan, Deputy Prime Minister in charge of land development, hamlet building, and social welfare (photo made in Saigon 1974, furnished by Dr. Dan).

Illustration 12

Mushrooms being grown on rice straw in a peasant house in Quang-Nam province, June 1970, with the advice of "Chuck" Fields, shown here with his assistant and a child. This was a good cash crop for refugees without land (LAW photo).

thousand US troops were committed and finally, the next day, the VC were driven out. The American troops then withdrew and ARVN established a defense perimeter. Refugees filtered back into the smoldering city and pulled 100 dead civilians out of the rubble. Fourteen hundred more had been wounded, and 15,000 of the original 40,000 inhabitants were homeless.[12]

In Kien-Hoa there also was looting by ARVN troops, and the province chief had lost all control. CORDS evaluators reported: "Actual social degeneration was visible in Kien Hoa where the plundering of ARVN soldiers and the almost complete abdication of responsibility by GVN officials was being well exploited by the aggressive VC." There was looting by troops also in Sadec, but the province chief and his officials performed well. In Chuong-Thien province an ARVN division (probably the Ninth) imposed restrictions on the use of artillery. Security in the countryside, however, was so tenuous in late February that travel outside the province and district towns was impossible. In Kien-Giang province, roughly half the previously secure rural areas had reverted to VC control; most GVN forces had been pulled in to defend Rach-Gia and the district towns. The province chief had sandbagged himself in and appeared to have little concern except for his own protection. A similar situation was found in Ba-Xuyen, where the VC took advantage of it to recruit youths. On the other hand, the province chief of An-Xuyen (at the bottom of Viet-Nam) and his troops performed admirably. The people in that Communist stronghold saw the VC run, but feared that they would return. They did. They had warned the people that if they returned to their homes, they would burn the town. On March 5 it was discovered that the town of Ca-Mau was again under siege by the VC. The regional CORDS refugee advisor, Gene Chiavarolli, asked that emergency commodities be shipped to Can-Tho for him to forward as soon as possible.[13]

Although in few other places was there the same paralysis combined with wanton abuse as in Vinh-Long and Kien-Hoa, the indiscriminate employment of American and Vietnamese firepower was the preferred method of rooting out the Communist attackers everywhere. The statement made by an American officer during a press visit to Ben-Tre on February 7, "It became necessary to destroy the town to save it," could be applied to many locations throughout the country.[14] However, to defeat the fanatical determination of the elite Communist troops, ground assaults were also necessary, especially in Saigon and Hue. All this caused heavy military and civilian casualties as well as property destruction.

A significant sidelight was that the Lai-Thieu refugee settlement for the villagers of Ben-Suc had become one of the staging points of the VC on their way to and from Saigon. This had been observed by the IRC team, which had been pinned down in the village. Two of them, Charles Cowden, a retired Army noncom (noncommissioned officer) and Richard Thrams, made their way to the Saigon office of their voluntary agency on February 24. William Vale, the IRC director, described their conversation in a letter to his New York headquarters:

All around Lai Thieu there is considerable military activity, yet the hamlet itself is relatively free of menace. In fact it has not been attacked at all. Now we are not professionals and someone says, "Oh for Pete's sake, anyone can see that it's a staging area for personnel traffic to and from Saigon. There were hundreds of such points in the Alps and Pyrenees in the last war." So the boys say that no one knows who is in the village at night and no one is about to investigate, but it's a fact that 35 males have left (abducted or seduced) during the Tet offensive. An early riser may see new young faces leaving the village. I put the question directly to Cowden and Thrams, "Are you in fear of your life?" And with equal candor they reply, "Sometimes, but is it any better here?" They returned to Lai-Thieu the next day.[15]

Gradually we in the Disaster Office were able to take the measure of the largest man-made disaster in the history of the Vietnamese Republic up to that time. As of February 7, the coordinating center had reports of 280,000 Tết refugees, 10,603 houses destroyed, 769 civilians killed, and 8,234 civilians wounded; but data from many provinces and cities, including Thua-Thien and Hue, Quang-Ngai, Tuyen-Duc and Dalat, Tay-Ninh, and 8 of the 16 provinces of IV CTZ, were missing. On February 8, the voluntary agencies presented to Dr. Que the first results of their survey of 51 temporary shelters in Saigon-Gia-Dinh, only to be told that it was incomplete. The next day, he said the number of refugees in the metropolitan area was still increasing, both because of continued VC harassment of the population, particularly in Cholon, and on account of rising food prices, which were inducing people to come to the shelters for assistance. Nonetheless, almost all the genuine refugees in the area (120,000) had been registered.

The first report from Hue, received on February 10, estimated 30,000 refugees within the city and another 9,000 who had fled from the city and Phong-Dien district to Phu-Bai, where there was a large US base. (Months later, final figures showed that almost 136,000 people had fled their homes in Hue–Thua-Thien.) Five MSWR mobile teams were sent to the beleaguered city, along with a platoon of the 29th Civil Affairs Company and two CORDS public health teams to innoculate against cholera and typhoid. Blaine Revis from the Saigon staff was detailed to supervise refugee operations, assisted by Thomas Killeen from Quang-Nam. Twenty-nine youths from Saigon, mostly pharmacy and medical students from the university, went to Hue early in March to help the victims, treating over 2,000, distributing medicaments, innoculating, and spraying insecticide. They returned to Saigon on March 12 and were replaced by a second group.

By February 11, the Tết refugee total was 527,339 and still rising. However, some of the war victims had already begun returning to their homes, and a week later only 411,324 were still recorded as being in camps. Then the number began rising again, it was 599,858 at the end of the month. As of February 29, there were 121 temporary centers in the Saigon–Gia-Dinh area, with 240,000 refugees.

The Sitrep of February 14 recorded that refugee camps in Quang-Ngai province were being burned and the inhabitants captured by the VC. Five hundred ninety-nine refugees were taken from one destroyed camp, and 248 families (probably over 1,250 people) from seven other camps were believed to be under VC control.

Whether these were Têt victims or old refugees was not reported. The same sitrep said that several thousand houses in Darlac, Kontum, and Quang-Ngai were destroyed in post-Têt attacks.

By the end of February, commerce had resumed in most of the country, and thousands of refugees had gone home. Others were still waiting for their resettlement payments or for security to improve. The National Police Directorate General urged the war victims to return to their homes as soon as possible, except for those whose homes had been destroyed. The next day, the VC attacked refugee camps in Phu-Yen province and hamlets in Quang-Duc, and mortared two camps in Quang-Nam.

It was only toward the end of April 1968 that we were able to get a reasonably accurate picture of the total number of evacuees generated by the Têt offensive: 863,158 had been registered, of whom 538,359 had not been resettled or enabled to return home by April 26; 108,115 houses had been destroyed by over 50% and 102,308 damaged less than 50%. At the same time, it was possible to get a count of regular refugees: 1,043,133, of whom 678,099 were in camps and 265,034 out of camp.[16] During the Têt attacks and the resultant fighting, 12,607 people were killed and 21,253 were wounded. Total property damage was estimated at about $173.5 million US, of which approximately 46% was to housing, 34% to private industry, 10% to agriculture and fisheries, and 10% to public facilities.[17]

As the GVN authorities and CORDS personnel were able to get out into the country, they discovered that the Communist offensive had not been limited to the cities and towns. In Binh-Dinh, for instance, the VC and NVA complemented their attack on Qui-Nhon by intensifying their activity in the surrounding Tuy-Phuoc district during the first half of February. The CORDS evaluator commented:

Reaction by friendly forces was a tragic duplicate of the national pattern: pursuit to the edge of an enemy occupied hamlet, destruction of enemy and homes with air strikes and artillery, then further pursuit to another hamlet and renewal of the same cycle. Almost 400 houses in eight formerly pacified hamlets were destroyed and nearly 12,000 persons were temporarily displaced.

However, some were able to return to their homes by March 1.[18]

In Phong-Dinh province almost every rural hamlet, as well as the capital, Can-Tho, suffered some damage during the Têt offensive. The banks of over 60 kilometers of canals were devastated. It was estimated that over 10,000 peasants were made refugees.[19]

COMMUNIST MASSACRES

The Communists killed a number of Vietnamese and foreign civilians in cold blood at various centers throughout the country. For example, a maid at the IRC house in Quang-Ngai told of the VC killing a child, cutting off the head, arms, and legs, and tossing the torso back to the mother.[20] In a Rhadé village near Ban Me Thuot, North Vietnamese troops killed five missionaries of the Christian and Missionary Alliance, a sixth died of wounds, and two more were led away and never returned.[21] Other foreign medical and missionary people were killed or abducted and never heard from again.

The worst massacre occurred in Hue, where at least 2,800 persons whose names were on carefully prepared lists of enemies were executed in accordance with a party plan that had been drawn up in advance, with the objective of not only punishing "spies, reactionaries . . . scoundrels, hoodlums, robbers, and . . . cruel tyrants," but also to "destroy and disorganize the enemy's restrictive administrative machinery from the province and district levels to city wards, streets and wharves." Those murdered included police and other officials; Catholics, including several foreign priests; three German physicians; and members of the CORDS staff. Some were buried by their families, but most were put into mass graves outside the city and found only months later.[22] My friend Philip Manhard, the PSA, was taken captive, and was released only in 1973 along with the military POWs.

Truong Nhu Tang, a wealthy Saigonese who had been a GVN administrator while concealing his Communist activities, was told by Huynh Tan Phat, the President of the Provisional Revolutionary Government (PRG) after Têt that discipline in Hue had been seriously inadequate.

Fanatic young soldiers had indiscriminately shot people, and angry local citizens who supported the revolution had on various occasions taken justice into their own hands. According to Phat there was absolutely no policy or directive from the Front to carry out any massacre. It had simply been one of those terrible spontaneous tragedies that inevitably accompany war.

Tang continued, "I did not find this explanation particularly satisfying. But I must admit that neither did I pursue the issue." However, Tang's reflection upon the Hue massacres was a factor in causing him to accept the position of Justice Minister in the PRG, in order to make a strong statement against "revolutionary justice."[23] Phat's explanation is not plausible. The accounts by Don Oberdorfer (*Tet!*, 232) and others (for example, Karnow, *Vietnam*, 530–31) make it abundantly clear that the killings had been part of a carefully developed plan of the party leaders, at least on a provincial level. Given the tight discipline of the Lao-Dong Party, it is highly unlikely that such a plan would have been produced and carried out without approval at a higher level. It fit perfectly with the systematic assassinations of popular as well as unpopular leaders that the insurgents had been carrying on throughout the country since at least 1959. Similar plans may have been developed in other areas as well, but Hue was the only city where the VC were in control long enough to carry out a program of liquidating their enemies.

As more and more mass graves were uncovered in subsequent months and other evidence of these horrors came to light and was publicized, the Hue massacres changed public attitudes toward the Communists fundamentally. In the city itself, which had long been a hotbed of Buddhist-led opposition to successive Saigon regimes, by 1969 all the members of the 1966 Struggle Coordinating Committee were social welfare officials eager to cooperate with the government. Unfortunately, the GVN only rarely reciprocated their offers.[24]

Even before the revelations concerning the massacres, many people became convinced that the VC were not only cruel but also weak. In the Mekong Delta, where most villages had televisions, people witnessed the fighting in Saigon and elsewhere. In the villages where Professor Samuel Popkin lived, people thought this was a total collapse of the Communists. Before Tết, 18-year-olds had lied about their age to avoid the draft. Afterwards, 13- and 14-year-olds magnified their age in order to be drafted before the Communists got to them. Also, however, the events of Hue instilled a fear and horror of the Communists which caused mass flight before them in subsequent offensives, including the final offensive of 1975.[25]

RELIEF AND RECOVERY

The Tết victims differed from ordinary refugees in that almost all were urban residents. They had to flee a few hundred meters from their homes because of the fighting, but almost all remained within their own cities or towns and intended to return to their home locations as soon as possible. It was expected that these areas would soon be secured, and they were. Those whose homes were destroyed needed temporary shelter for some time, until they could rebuild their houses or, in some areas of Saigon and Hue, until permanent apartment blocks could be built for them. Except in the case where some factories (for example, Vintexco on the outskirts of Saigon) were destroyed, they did not lose their means of livelihood, even though most lost property and possessions. They were not dislocated from farms or fisheries, and could rapidly become self-supporting citizens again when the economy was able to function. Thus, while suffering grievous losses, they were in a much better position than most rural refugees and evacuees.

As described above, the MSWR and the municipalities, with help from many volunteers and from CORDS, began providing improvised shelter and commodity relief from the first day of the disaster. On February 3, the Ministry issued a circular authorizing temporary relief in accordance with existing allowances for refugees. Resettlement allowances would also be the same, except where the local governments decided to reconstruct destroyed areas themselves. However, pending their full reestablishment, all victims would get the normal six-month rice allowance at the rate of 500 grams per person per day.[26] This message was supplemented on February 14 with another circular specifying the resettlement allowances, to be financed from the resettlement budgets allocated to the provinces and cities, authorizing the construction of temporary camps in order to free up schools and other public buildings, and asking the provinces to loan money to the SWR services if their imprest funds were inadequate; loans were to be repaid by the Ministry.[27]

However, just taking care of the war victims was not enough. The intricate economy and commerce of the whole nation had been disrupted, and unless they were quickly restored, people would run out of food and other necessities. Because of the general lack of refrigeration and their custom of going every day to market, ordinary city dwellers did not keep large stocks of rice or other foods, as peasants did. That meant that hunger threatened as long as the markets could not open. CORDS and GVN officials felt that there was a real possibility of food riots which, with VC encouragement, could be made to look like the general uprising the Communists had been proclaiming. In the Saigon area it happened that most of the private rice warehouses were in Cholon and the principal government warehouses were at Thu-Duc. Strong VC forces were entrenched in both areas. Consequently, a close coordination of rapid GVN and US military and civilian actions was called for to avert an even greater disaster and to get the country back on its feet. Thus was born Operation Recovery.[28]

On February 2, President Thieu announced the formation of the Central People's Relief Committee (later renamed Central Recovery Committee), to be chaired by Vice President Nguyen Cao Ky, with General Nguyen Duc Thang, Minister of Revolutionary Development (RD), as Secretary General. The members were the Ministers of Interior, Social Welfare and Refugees, Defense, Revolutionary Development, Health, Economy, Public Works, and Information, the Chief of the Joint General Staff, and the Director General of the National Police. Similar committees were to be organized at corps, province, district, village, and hamlet level.[29] After a time, Ky and General Thang resigned, perhaps because Ky was being extolled in a CIA report and the American press as "the man of the hour," to Thieu's discomfiture.[30] Prime Minister Nguyen Van Loc and Doan Ba Cang, First Minister to the Prime Minister, succeeded them. Colonel Do Kien Nhieu was chief of the CRC (Central Recovery Committee) staff from February 4 until June 9, when he was appointed mayor of Saigon. The object of the committee was to get all relevant authorities working together—something they didn't ordinarily do—and to mobilize all necessary resources in a national effort.

The US counterpart to this committee was headed by Robert Komer, at first with General Forsythe as his operating deputy, but after Forsythe was called away for other duties, with Clayton McManaway, Chief of the CORDS Plans, Programs, and Policy Division (PP&P) succeeded him. Major Harry T. Johnson of that division was stationed full-time at the Prime Minister's palace; he and his chief attended the meetings of the committee. The logistics chiefs of USAID and MACV were active members. Sometimes we in CORDS/REF were invited to participate.

According to Johnson, the coordination within the GVN and between it and the Americans was achieved mainly at the subcabinet level. Instead of using up-down channels within each Ministry and formal communication between them, the Secretaries General talked with each other and with the JGS staff heads, and got things done face-to-face. It worked. One of the first actions was to send US troops in to reinforce ARVN in Cholon and Thu-Duc, liberating the warehouses and providing armed escort when needed to convoys of commodities. Food got to the market places, as well as to the supply lines of CORDS/REF and the MSWR; there were no food riots, and no general uprising. The vital Route 4 from the Delta was opened early in February and kept open. The hours of curfew were shortened as soon as possible; in the meantime, dock workers and other essential personnel were given curfew passes.

The urgent tasks of Operation Recovery were stated as follows:

1. Return Saigon, the province capitals, and district towns to normal.

2. Open, secure, and repair lines of communication (LOCs).

3. Develop a national spirit of unity.

4. Put radio stations back in operation.

5. Prevent looting.

6. Provide food, clothing, and shelter to the victims.[31]

These tasks were accomplished. President Thieu declared a national mobilization ending most fraudulent draft evasion, and the people accepted this in good spirit. Donations for Tết relief poured in from the public, as well as from foreign governments and organizations. The draft, however, took many of the best officials of the MSWR and other Ministries; we had some of them reassigned to their old offices, and we persuaded the Ministry to hire more women.

There was some overlap between Operation Recovery and the Disaster Relief operation, consisting mainly of exhortations by Cang and his deputies to the Ministry and the provinces, and parallel exhortations by McManaway to me, and later to John Thomas. Both sides sent inspectors, sometimes the Secretaries General, and evaluators into the field; they uncovered bottlenecks and were able to open them, and they discovered incompetent officials but were rarely able to do much about them. The Ministry and its SWR service chiefs were responsible for both temporary relief and issuing 10 bags of cement and 10 sheets of aluminum roofing per family, as well as cash payments (10,000 $VN per family in Saigon and Hue, and 5,000 $VN elsewhere).

The Central Recovery Committee (CRC) had decided that these standard allowances would be paid generally, so that the refugees could rebuild on their own as they were accustomed to do; but that in certain districts of Saigon some 6,000 apartment units and in Hue 4,000 units would be constructed to replace totally destroyed slum areas. In the meantime, the people waiting for the new apartments or houses would be lodged in temporary camps to be built by the government, and they would not receive the building materials and cash payments. The CRC was responsible for getting the cement and roofing out to the provinces, and it augmented the MSWR funds by one billion piasters, taken from the American Aid Chapter. On March 4, in a ceremony attended by several Ministers and other members of the CRC, Prime Minister Loc presented the "10–10–10" disbursements to 10 families of Saigon District 8, thus inaugurating the resettlement program in the city. In Hue, many evacuees were returning to their own homes from Phu-Bai and the south side of the Perfume River.[32]

A 15-hectare wooded lot had been acquired in the Petrus-Ky area of Saigon, next to the compound of the International Control Commission (a body set up by the 1954 Geneva accords) in District 5, and the MSWR decided to make it a model temporary camp. Petrus-Ky proved to be a highly visible magnet for volunteer assistance from many quarters. Colonel James E. Bodine, head of the US Army Headquarters Area Command (HAC) Civic Action Force, became Dr. Que's advisor. US and Korean military civic action groups graded the site. At first, tents were put up by ARVN and US troops. Nguyen Tam Nam, a sugar mill operator, volunteered to supervise the carpenters and helpers building roofing trusses and frames for the 1,315 housing units, which were to be built of good hardwood lumber on concrete pilings, with fibrocement roofs (which are much cooler than aluminum sheets).

The CORDS disaster office borrowed Walter E. Pierce from the USAID Forestry Branch as construction advisor and William Coster as project coordinator. Pierce fought manfully, and largely successfully, to save the trees from the bulldozers. A Vietnamese student work group of 100 set up camp on the premises; the students, helped by International Voluntary Service, made concrete foundation forms and did other work. The Têt victims themselves did much of the work. The 33rd Vietnamese Air Wing donated 10,000 board feet of lumber and erected 60 of the 200 20-person tents. CORDS delivered more lumber, and USAID supplied the cement.[33] Completion of the sewage, drainage, latrines, and electricity systems was delayed, but by June 27 some 8,500 people in 1,289 families (an average of 6.6 people per family) had moved into the completed units.[34] In short order they had set up many shops, small restaurants, and other enterprises. Dispensaries, meeting rooms, and other amenities were created. Petrus-Ky was not only a commodious and sturdy camp; it was fun to build for everybody involved and became a genuine community center. Three smaller camps of the same type were built elsewhere in the city.

We and the Ministry had shipped and issued some thousands of tons of food, blankets, tents, sleeping mats, cooking utensils, mosquito nets, cotton cloth, used clothing, and other supplies. However, the aim of getting all victims under permanent roofs before the rainy season began in mid-May was not achieved. As of April 25, only 32,237 families had received their home damage indemnities, 29,943 families had received the 10 bags of cement and 10 sheets of roofing, and 25,020 had received the cash resettlement allowances.[35] The CORDS evaluations and other reports told a mixed story of what was happening in the provinces.

Of the 31 provinces (out of 44) and 2 autonomous cities (out of 4) from which information collected from February to June has been examined, 14 provinces and the 2 cities (Saigon and Hue) were rated as good in the performance of their authorities in providing relief and resettlement assistance to the Têt victims; 6 were poor; 7 had mixed records, usually improving with time; and in 4 provinces no victims or very few were generated. One of the 4 latter provinces was An-Giang, a completely secure Hoa-Hao province, which received thousands of refugees from its neighbors. A number of province chiefs, including those in Thua-Thien and Vinh-Long, as well as several SWR service chiefs, were replaced after the offensive. Also replaced were three of the four corps commanders.

There was constant pressure from both the Americans and the Vietnamese in the Central Recovery Committee to do better, in particular to get as many people as possible into permanent homes before the rainy season began in the south in mid-May. On April 29, Clayton McManaway recommended a number of measures to Minister Doan Ba Cang, including wide publicity about the program and its procedures and allowances, paying all allowances at once in accordance with President Thieu's decision, simplifying payment procedures, closer inspection and monitoring of performance at each camp and resettlement area, and use of RVNAF and RD Ministry transport to get commodities to outlying areas.[36] Many of these recommendations were implemented, but bureaucratic habits died hard.

THE MAY OFFENSIVE

On May 5, the VC/NVA again assaulted Saigon in force. They attacked other places as well, but not nearly as many as during Têt. This time there had been intelligence about the Communist Phase II, and preemptive operations had been mounted in advance. However, the devastation in crowded areas of Saigon, including some pagodas, was worse than during the earlier fighting. The enemy deliberately chose these places to dig in. In the Phu-Lam neighborhood of Saigon, for instance, the VC occupied houses, and it took two days and the support of armor, artillery, and tactical air to root them out. A battle raged from May 9 to 12 around the Y-bridge in a heavily populated part of the city. Many people had to cross the bridge to escape the fighting and were trampled or caught in cross fire. About 100 refugees were killed there. Bill Thompson and the mobile teams extracted many others under fire. The US Army newspaper *Stars and Stripes* published a front-page picture of Thompson, whom it erroneously called a soldier, carrying two youngsters across the bridge. Others were caught in the streets by strafing gunships or VC fire. ARVN troops laid planks across their barbed wire in some places so that the people could cross. The offensive was defeated by May 12, but a smaller attack occurred on May 25.[37]

On May 5, the first day of their offensive, the VC killed my friend Baron Hasso Ruedt von Collenberg, First Secretary of the German Embassy, in Cholon. He had planned to accompany the German IRC team to select a site in Binh-Duong province.[38] Nobody knew why he was murdered; he was widely mourned.

The office of the Saigon Mayor reported as of May 14 that 103,354 persons had been displaced, an estimated 9,000 houses had been destroyed (including some that had been rebuilt after Têt), 127 civilians had been killed, and 2,950 were treated in the city's hospitals. Gia-Dinh reported 38,796 displaced, an estimated 8,000 houses destroyed or damaged, 53 civilians killed, and 100 injured. The refugees were sheltered in some of the same centers as had been used for the earlier evacuees.[39]

One village in Binh-Duong province, which had lost 212 houses during Têt, suffered the loss of another 420, due to US artillery and air strikes, during the period May 5–15.[40]

This time, the excessive use of US and ARVN firepower caused such adverse public reaction that remedial action had to be taken. During a luncheon meeting with CORDS and USAID officials on May 16, Dr. Ho Van Minh, Vice Speaker of the Lower House of the National Assembly, told them of the immense psychological damage that had been done to the people of Saigon's District 8 by American artillery and bombing the previous week. "He stated that many of the people are very bitter and particularly over the fact that a number of people were killed and wounded at the Chanh Hung area market. He stated that the people are now afraid of US soldiers who are still in the area."[41] Colonel Hoang Ngac Lung wrote:

By this time, however, the use of tactical air and artillery to support [military] relief operations in Saigon had begun to incur some adverse opinion among the urban population about their destructive effect. To soothe popular sentiment, the newly designated prime minister, Mr. Tran Van Huong, issued instructions to the effect that our forces had to curtail the use of firepower in the densely populated suburbs.

However, on June 2 misfired rockets from an American gunship killed the Saigon police chief, Col. Nguyen Van Luan, Col. Dao Ba Phuoc, commander of the Fifth Ranger Group, and the Fifth Precinct police chief, and wounded Saigon Mayor Col. Van Van Cua and the military governor of Saigon, Col. Nguyen Van Giam.[42]

Shortly thereafter, Dr. Tran Lu Y, who had been named Minister of Health, Social Welfare, and Relief in the Huong cabinet, approached Ambassador Komer and asked that the US forces take steps to limit the use of firepower in populated areas in order to minimize the creation of refugees. He said his Ministry was overwhelmed by the huge numbers of persons who had been displaced by the recent fighting. Komer forwarded his memorandum of this conversation to General Abrams, who had just succeeded Westmoreland as commander of all US forces (COMUSMACV), together with a draft message to the field commanders. After the objections of some staff elements had brought about a compromise, the message was sent on July 29. Its subject was limiting new refugees, and it began by saying that there were currently 700,000 refugees in temporary camps; the new Minister intended to alleviate problems but was close to the saturation point. "Therefore, I wish to reiterate MACV policy concerning limiting new refugees:

a. Commanders will make every effort to avoid creating new refugees by proper development of plans, judicious use of combat power in inhabited areas, and appropriate psyops beamed at the local people. Annex C of AB 143 [the Combined Campaign Plan for 1968] applies . . .

b. Some operations cause civilians to be displaced from their homes either through fear or because of military necessity to move people from combat areas. In such cases, providing temporary assistance in the form of shelter, food and medical care is the responsibility of the US tactical commander controlling the operation. AB 143 applies . . .

3(C) During this period when refugee population is already very large, MHSWR capabilities are declining, and the world spotlight is on US activities, I require US commanders to take all appropriate and prudent measures to limit creating new refugees and to care for and return all temporarily displaced persons so that they will not become refugees or be less friendly to the GVN and US . . .

4(U) Commanders down to Battalion level will be instructed in these policies and will incorporate them in unit SOP's.[43]

This was only the latest in a long series of MACV directives regarding the use of firepower in populated places, but it was the first (to my knowledge) specifically relating friendly fire to the generation of refugees and requiring its control for that reason. It seems to have had somewhat more effect on US forces than previous instructions. On the other hand, Prime Minister Huong's instruction appears to have had little effect on the Vietnamese forces.

THE CONCLUSION OF OPERATION RECOVERY

The Central Recovery Committee on May 17 approved a plan, called Operation Dong-Tam, to use American and ARVN troops to construct 1,500 units of prefabricated housing, primarily for victims of the May offensive, in Districts 6 and 8 of Saigon and in metropolitan Gia-Dinh. The two forces worked together on land clearance and on much of the construction. The US Engineers also repaired war damage to the District 8 dispensary and a school. Early in June the ARVN engineers were temporarily withdrawn from District 6 and 3,500 post-Tết evacuees were transferred to District 5 because of poor security. However, they later came back, and by mid-September the GVN and US forces had completed the 1,500 units and all auxiliary works. On September 19, the joint task force was deactivated. The 46th US Engineers then restored the Phu-Tho race track, whose stands had been used for temporary shelter during the emergency.[44]

Many Vietnamese youth groups were involved in self-help projects, especially in Districts 6, 7, and 8, where 1,500 housing units were reconstructed under the auspices of the New Life Construction Project. The Saigon Student Union had assumed responsibility for running five temporary centers with 12,000 residents. Eleven other youth groups took responsibility for centers with another 30,000 inhabitants, transporting rice, giving medical care, clearing debris, and assisting in rebuilding houses. Many continued their work at Petrus-Ky. Similar projects were carried on in other cities.[45]

In April construction had begun on several of the modern apartment projects. Nine hundred units were built near the An-Quang pagoda. The Ban-Co project was to have 1,307 units. These attractive apartment blocks were built by the GVN and were scheduled for completion in November; they were actually completed and occupied by Têt 1969. The Canadian government built a 74-unit block. USAID contracted to build 2,000 units at Nguyen-Kim; largely because of the elaborate AID procedures, they were completed a year later than the Vietnamese and Canadian apartments.[46]

By early October, Project Recovery was officially completed. It had accomplished much, but not as much as its authors had planned. About 1.6 billion piasters had been allocated for payments to the victims, mostly from the American Aid Chapter (counterpart funds); some of that had not been disbursed, but the people went ahead and rebuilt anyhow. In some outlying areas, money had to be paid in lieu of cement and roofing. (That caused prices to rise and created some hardship.) Over six million (US) dollars' equivalent (in 1968) had been donated by 24 foreign countries and organizations.[47]

The final count showed the peak number of registered Têt offensive victims as 892,454, and of May offensive victims as 179,164. The total was 1,071,618, which included an unknown number of people who had been displaced or injured in both assaults. All but about 30,000, who were destined to move into as-yet unfinished Saigon apartments, were resettled by the end of 1968.[48]

It needs to be said, however, that the successful resettlement of the Têt and May offensive victims was achieved in some provinces at the expense of the regular refugees, whose numbers had increased from about 868,000 at the end of 1967 to 1,176,000 by September 30, 1968.[49]

In my opinion, the principal value of the Central Recovery Committee was that it brought the various GVN and US agencies, civil and military, together to cut through normal channels in order to accomplish a job that was too big for any of them working by the traditional methods. The infusion of military assets on both sides was a significant factor in getting relief to the victims and in helping with reconstruction. It was much more than a refugee assistance program, which the Refugee Ministry under its two incarnations and successive Ministers developed and implemented admirably. Recovery involved getting the entire governmental machinery and the economy of the country back into operation. That was done, and the Vietnamese people participated wherever they were made to feel welcome. A new sense of national unity and pride was created. It set the stage for the military and civilian successes which followed.

9

The Coming of Age of the Refugee–War Victims Program

The Tết offensive of 1968 stopped the regular refugee relief and resettlement programs for a couple of months in those provinces that were most affected by the Communist attacks, and slowed them down everywhere, as GVN efforts and resources were concentrated on assisting the Tết victims. It was not even possible to gather statistics on the refugee population until the third week of March, at which time the 1967 year-end figures (which themselves turned out to have been understated) were more or less repeated. The total as of March 21 was given as 794,912. However, those figures showed no regular refugees at all in six provinces where refugees were known to be present, and fewer than were believed to exist in several others.[1] A week later, the total had jumped to 914,543 (in addition to 568,611 Tết evacuees), including 42,880 in Phu-Yen, which had reported only 10,564 a week earlier, and 30,789 in Bien-Hoa, where there had reportedly been none on March 21. By May 2, the number of regular refugees had grown to 1,095,654, of whom 581,956 were in camps and 513,698 out of camp.[2] Even then there were substantial differences between figures from some provinces reported by the CORDS refugee advisors and those obtained from other sources.

The various discrepancies were noticed in Washington, and a Saigon telegram of May 8 from Ambassador Komer for Grant attempted to explain them. It pointed out that the December 31, 1967, figures showing 793,944 refugees, which had been obtained from the Ministry, had included 402,942 in I CTZ, whereas the data that had been jointly reported by the CORDS advisors and the province SWR chiefs from the region totaled 533,619 at the end of the same month. As of May 2, 1968, I CTZ reported 623,272 regular refugees. We considered that the increase was real, due to continuous and extensive military action, especially in Quang-Tri and Thua-Thien for the previous four months, (quite apart from the Têt fighting), and to an increase of 47,612 in Quang-Nam during the same period. Likewise, from December to early May the in-camp refugee populations of II and III Corps were reported to have grown by 144,329 refugees, which we thought was largely a genuine increase. We admitted that the reality was not as precise as these statistics implied, but said that we would use the May 2 data as a base and would continue refining and reconciling statistics with the MSWR.[3]

During the remainder of 1968, what with new refugee generations, resettlement, return to home villages of some, and refinements in data collection and analysis, the monthly figures never again dipped below 1,100,000, and ended the year with 1,328,517 refugees on the rolls. It was not a good year judged by statistics alone. However, those figures represented a more accurate count of those who were displaced and in need of assistance than had been the case previously, and by the latter part of the year the refugees were receiving better care than the somewhat hit-or-miss relief and resettlement system had earlier provided.

JOHN THOMAS AS LEADER AND GUIDE

President Lyndon Johnson was mindful of the acute suffering being inflicted upon the Vietnamese people by the Communist offensives and the war in general, which he called "social misery," and so in the second week of March he designated John F. Thomas to return as chief of the CORDS Refugee Division. Mr. Thomas resisted the move at first, saying that he had plenty to do taking care of Cuban refugees, but when Walt Rostow, the President's Assistant for National Security Affairs, told him that the next step would be a telephone call from the President, who was noted for his persuasive powers, he gave in. It was an earnest show of the US government's determination to see that the wretched victims of the war were properly assisted, and John Thomas regarded that as his mandate. He was also convinced of the need to impress upon the GVN, the US military, and USAID, "the important role the treatment of refugees could play in winning over the hearts and minds of the Vietnamese people."[4]

When Ambassador Komer told me of this decision and asked me to stay on for at least six months as John's deputy, I readily agreed. What with the concentration of both the GVN and my office on Têt relief and Operation Recovery, neither the MSWR nor CORDS/REF was doing justice to the regular refugees, whose needs in many cases were greater than those of the Têt victims. I didn't have the budgetary skills or the influence to obtain the additional human and material resources required to care for all the war victims at the same time, and I was not an expert in refugee assistance. Although I had not yet met John Thomas, it seemed evident from what Komer told me that he was a successful refugee administrator and would come with support from the highest level. Ted Lawrence, the division's deputy chief, did know Thomas, and agreed.

Prior to coming to Viet-Nam, John Thomas was assured by AID officials of their full support. He met in New York with the American Council of Voluntary Agencies for Foreign Service (ACVA), and on Capitol Hill in Washington with Senator Kennedy, Representative Peter Rodino of the House Judiciary Committee, and others. On his way to Viet-Nam he stopped in Hong Kong to be updated on the remarkable systems of refugee care and social welfare in that tiny but prosperous Crown Colony.

Upon his arrival in Saigon in mid-April, John made an excellent impression on everybody, including the Refugee Division staff. We were delighted to have as our chief a man who not only had a worldwide reputation but also knew Viet-Nam and was a warm and concerned human being. In the staff meetings of Ambassadors Bunker and Komer, while defining the differences between international refugees and the people in Viet-Nam who were displaced within their own country, he stressed that all US entities, military and civilian, should understand how important it was for the Vietnamese war victims to receive the same attention they would have received as international refugees.[5] He took special care to cultivate good relations with the military, who had enormous resources and was often helpful in applying them to refugee assistance.

John was quite prepared to see the GVN-US Recovery staff handle the reestablishment of Têt victims, with help from me and others in our staff, while he himself set about improving both the American and the Vietnamese capability to help all refugees and other war victims.

EXPANSION AND ANCHORING OF STAFF AND BUDGET

The CORDS refugee field advisory staff had key roles in the GVN program. They and their superiors controlled US-supplied commodities and often also controlled the transport to get them out to the refugees. The CORDS communication network was the fastest and sometimes the only means of two-way information exchange between the Ministry and the SWR personnel. The reports of our advisors were the basis for planning and budgeting in the American Aid Chapter. They could mobilize US military assets. They frequently motivated their counterparts.

For US fiscal year 1968, the Refugee Division had an authorized strength of 96 American civilian personnel plus 15 military personnel, but in May 1968 many civilians were not on board. Some of the vacancies were caused by the assignment by regional DepCORDS and province senior advisors (PSAs) of refugee officers to other duties. This was a perennial problem, which I had tackled with little success, and which John Thomas was determined to resolve. In some cases the refugee officers in provinces were uninterested in the job and were attracted to more prestigious positions such as district senior advisors. In other instances the DepCORDS and PSAs asserted their right under the CORDS command structure to assign officers to what they regarded as the highest priority jobs. They were in command of all personnel in their areas, and they wrote or approved their efficiency reports. That was vital, especially to the young career State Department or AID foreign service officers. In contrast, REF and the other CORDS staff divisions had only a technical channel to their field personnel. Some regional DepCORDS, especially John Paul Vann in III CTZ in 1968 (later in IV CTZ and finally, in 1971–72 as senior advisor in Military Region II) were sensitive to the political and humanitarian considerations in refugee aid, but even they felt that their judgment of the needs and appropriate responses was more realistic than that of the "bureaucrats in Saigon." John Thomas was sometimes compelled to use his White House sponsorship and the command position of Robert Komer and his successor, William E. Colby, to bring about reforms in the field.

The four regional refugee advisory chiefs held key positions. They were the division's point men in convincing their DepCORDS, military region senior advisors, and through them the corps commanders, of the importance of providing prompt and effective care to the refugees. In this and other tasks they were the allies of the Ministry's regional inspectors, who were dedicated and able officials. The strong advisors in I CTZ (first Dick Holdren, then Luther "Mac" McLendon) and IV CTZ (Gene Chiavarolli, followed by Dick Holdren) had considerable success. They were also the models for the province refugee advisors and exerted influence in keeping them active in their work.

The regional advisor in III CTZ, a cowboy-like character with little interest in refugees, was a friend of John Vann, who was not at all convinced that he needed a refugee expert to advise him. However, in the spring of 1968 I saw that the refugee work in the region was being neglected, even though in most of its provinces Têt victims were not numerous and the SWR service could do more for the regular refugees. George Klein in our office, who had worked for Catholic Relief Services, was eager for a field assignment, so I proposed him to Vann. He wouldn't hear of it. After John Thomas arrived, I reported the situation to him. It happened that he had known George Klein from his service in Austria during the Hungarian crisis of 1956–57, and had a high opinion of his work. He told Vann that Klein was the man for the job. As Thomas put it,

I stood by my guns, saying that President Johnson had sent me to Vietnam to put some teeth in the refugee program and I wanted to have on my staff the kind of people who could follow my ideas. John finally bought the deal and became an admirer of Klein's work. Once I had John Vann on my side the other Area Directors caused less difficulties.[6]

At that time most of the refugee advisors in the provinces were young State Department or AID officers who were in no sense refugee experts when they were assigned. Some had been tagged for the jobs while they were still training in Washington, in response to criticisms of the program by the Senate Subcommittee. Upon arrival in Viet-Nam, they had to become familiar with the complicated regulations and procedures of the Ministry and with the real conditions, needs, and aspirations of the refugees themselves. Furthermore, they had to gain the confidence and respect of their counterparts, the SWR service chiefs and their deputies, some of whom were competent and dedicated and others who did little without tactful but persistent prodding. To acquire that knowledge, confidence, and respect took time and leadership. When a good officer had become proficient it was certainly not the time to move him into another job, either leaving the SWR service chief without a counterpart or bringing in a new refugee advisor who had to build a position de novo. Nonetheless, the very qualities that made a good refugee officer also fitted him for increased responsibilities, and some of our people were resentful when they were denied those promotions. The fact that civilian tours of duty were only one and a half years added to the pressure on the career-minded individuals. It required difficult management decisions to do the right thing both for the job and for the man.

We leaned over backwards to be fair to the young officers. If they wanted to move on, generally we let them do so, although we asked that they stay until replacements were on board. However, John Thomas was very tough when regional DepCORDS or PSAs reassigned refugee officers against their will and over the objections of our regional advisors. Ambassador Komer gave strong support.

We had some excellent refugee officers, both young and older ones, in the provinces. Carl Harris in Quang-Tin was one of the best. He was an ordained Episcopal priest. Feeling called to serve in the wider field of humanitarian relief, he had resigned from his suburban Virginia parish in order to volunteer for work in Viet-Nam as a refugee officer. He and I trained together in "CORDS V" (the fifth course at the Foreign Service Institute preparing officers for service in Viet-Nam) in the autumn of 1967, along with Norman Firnstahl and others who became our colleagues. He elected refugee work in a province, and was assigned to one of the most hazardous provinces in the entire country. Not infrequently, its capital, Tam-Ky, took as many as 200 VC mortar and rocket rounds a night. As part of my orientation tour, Carl took me to the Pineapple Forest a few kilometers from Tam-Ky, which was projected as a refugee resettlement area. During the Tết offensive it fell back under Communist control and was not retaken until late 1969. He was tireless in supporting the SWR service chief in bringing relief to refugees—resettlement was out of the question after Tết—and in improving their miserable temporary camps. We had to bring Carl and others serving in especially dangerous areas to Saigon from time to time for rest and recuperation, usually over their protests. When Carl came in, he often celebrated mass at St. Christopher's Church across the street from the US Embassy, with Ambassador Bunker, John Thomas, and me in the congregation. Carl has made his career in humanitarian assistance ever since.

In Kontum, Bill Egan, an agricultural expert from Tennessee, worked mainly with the Montagnard tribesmen who were the majority of the refugees. Since they no longer had sufficient secure land to engage in their traditional swidden agriculture, Bill set up some experimental farm plots to test high-value crops, using refugees as helpers, and invited village leaders to observe them. He then provided seed, fertilizer, and hand tools to the refugee communities that were interested. This assistance did not make them self-supporting, but it supplemented the Ministry's rice allowance and added variety to their diet. Joe Veasman, who followed Bill, was cast in the same mold and continued this valuable assistance and cordial relations with the refugees.

There were many other fine refugee advisors, some of whom came back for several tours of duty. One of them, Edmund Sprague in Phu-Bon, learned the languages of his hill-tribe clients, and stayed with them until the collapse of the GVN in 1975.

Even if all the positions authorized the Refugee Division had been filled, the numbers were not sufficient, especially in I CTZ and those provinces elsewhere such as Binh-Dinh that were heavily impacted by both regular refugees and Têt victims. The personnel shortages became more evident as pressures increased for more rapid responses to refugee emergencies and at the same time for greater accountability for US-supplied commodities and funds. American refugee officers had to sign for withdrawals of food, tents, cement, roofing, farm tool kits, and so forth from both GVN and US warehouses, and they frequently had to obtain trucks and accompany the goods to their destinations, with or without SWR officials. Moreover, when Dr. Tran Lu Y (who became Minister in May 1968) required that CORDS refugee officers witness payments of refugee allowances and sign along with the SWR officials as an anticorruption measure, this became a welcome but burdensome additional duty.

John Thomas obtained an increase of slots to 116 for FY 1969, including social welfare personnel taken over from USAID, by his appearance before the AID Washington budget committee for the Country Assistance Program (CAP) review in October 1968, as well as more piaster funds for the Ministry to acquire land for resettlement and to meet other requirements. Table 8 shows the evolution of CORDS/REF and Ministry budgets from US fiscal year (FY) 1968 through FY 1971 and (for the Ministry) calendar years 1968 through 1971.

Of the Ministry's 1968 budget, 2.36 billion piasters, the equivalent of $20,000,000 US, came from the American Aid Chapter; almost double the 1967 AAC contribution, due to the extraordinary demands of Têt and May offensive relief and reconstruction. Thereafter, the AAC portion continued to increase until calendar year 1971, when it went down slightly.

TRAINING OF MOBILE CADRES

Impressed by the utility of the 10-person mobile teams, which were under the direct control of the Ministry and could be quickly deployed where needed (as they had been during the Têt and May 1968 emergencies), John Thomas and Dr. Lu Y signed a contract with the Community Development Foundation to conduct formal training courses. They included a one-month field training practicum, and were quite successful in turning the young recruits, including a number

Table 8
International Support and MSWR/MHSWR Budgets, 1968–71

A. Millions of US Dollars, Actual (US Fiscal Years)

	1968	1969	1970	1971
AID Budget	17.9	9.5	5.9	3.8
PL 480 Title II (programmed)	32.2	33.9	24.2	10.0
US Vol. Agencies	22.4	25.9	22.4	19.4
Other Donors	3.1	3.1	3.1	3.1
Totals	75.7	72.4	55.6	36.3

B. In Millions of VN Piasters, Actual (calendar years)

	1968	1969	1970	1971
GVN Budget	507.4	424.8	896.8	1,026.6
Counterpart funds	2,360.0	3,351.2	3,787.8	3,717.0
Totals	2,867.4	3,776.0	4,684.6	4,743.6

Source: Statement of Robert H. Nooter. Deputy Coordinator, Bureau for Supporting Assistance, AID, submitted to the Judiciary Subcommittee on Refugees, US Senate, May 8, 1972, 39.

of hill tribesmen, into versatile and effective cadres. Both John and I took pleasure in helping to hand certificates to the graduates. The goal of 500 members was achieved in 1969. The teams were helpful in registering newly discovered refugees and screening out ineligibles as they were insulated from the corruption that sometimes afflicted provincial services. They were also invaluable in the many refugee emergencies all over the country, when they brought prompt relief to the victims.

DEFINITION OF A REFUGEE

From the beginning of refugee assistance in 1964–65, there had been some confusion as to who was eligible for GVN aid. At first this had been left up to the individual province and district chiefs or the SWR services to decide, and when they were uncertain, it was referred to Saigon. Dr. Que's splendid policy guidelines of October 1966 (chapter 5) had outlined the categories of people migrating to secure areas, including those seeking employment, and stated that all of them who entered GVN territory to ask for help, regardless of their political allegiance, should have their immediate needs satisfied. However, that part of the instruction could not be carried out, and it was not included in the MSWR Basic Procedural Documents in 1967–68. Moreover, it contained no guide as to when people ceased to be refugees.

The situation was further complicated with the 1968 Communist offensives, which created over a million urban war victims. These people did not come into GVN areas from insecure territory; they had already been in GVN areas and in most cases remained there, but some, especially in Hue, fled from what had been GVN territory to the surrounding countryside and the American base at Phu-Bai. A special regime was devised for their care, and a procedure for emergency relief was put in place for similar occurrences in the future.

John Thomas considered these ambiguities sufficient cause to develop and present to the Ministry a unified definition of a refugee, which would be the basis for assessing the magnitude of the problem, deciding who was eligible for GVN assistance, and determining when the aid should be terminated. He directed his staff to work on the matter. On May 22, he sent a letter to Dr. Que saying that he had found considerable confusion in the provinces, that he understood that the Ministry had formerly included a definition in its handbook but had subsequently dropped it, and that he believed it would be helpful if a definition could once again be part of the procedures. He enclosed a draft for the Minister's review.[7]

Shortly after the letter was delivered, the Vietnamese Government changed, and Dr. Tran Lu Y became Minister of Health, Social Welfare and Relief. It was a couple of months before he gave attention to the question; on August 13 he issued a communiqué addressed to the mayor of Saigon, all chiefs of province and autonomous cities, and all SWR service chiefs. It referred to the former SCR definition, cited the new problem of urban refugees and the special measures for their relief, and concluded that both types could be considered '' 'anti-communist refugees' because the present war is initiated by the Communists, and these people are moving out to escape from either VC influence or bombardment for the same reasons, that is, to keep away from VC control or VC terrorism actions.'' For this reason, the MHSWR defined the word ''refugee'' as follows:

Refugees are persons who leave their places of abode for one of the following reasons:

a. Escape from Communist terrorists;

b. Fleeing from artillery or bombardment; or

c. Evading or being evacuated from military action areas.

Persons who fall into the category of "refugees" may enjoy relief procedures *within the framework of the Refugee Program* until:

a. They have been returned to their original place of abode after benefiting from prescribed relief payments;

b. They have been resettled at a new location after receiving prescribed relief payments due to them; or

c. They have become self-supporting before being formally resettled by the GVN.[8]

Quite apart from dealing with internal rather than international refugees, this definition is very different from that which is embodied in the Convention of 1951 and the Protocol of 1967 on the Status of Refugees. The key concept in the latter definition is "well founded fear of persecution" on account of race, region, nationality, political opinion, or membership in a particular social group. Persecution or the fear of persecution might or might not play a role in a decision to escape from "Communist terrorists" in Viet-Nam, but it had nothing to do with flight or evacuation from artillery, bombardment, or other military activity. In other words, the MHSWR definition was broader. The question of whether a claimant for refugee status in Viet-Nam was in fact an economic migrant (which has plagued applicants to the US Immigration and Naturalization Service) would arise only if the *sole* motive for moving was to seek employment. It is not surprising then, given the pervasive nature of this war without front lines, that the number of people counted as refugees was enormous. The definition was an appropriate description of an all-too-real situation.

However, the provisions for terminating relief had the potential to cause trouble. The proposed definition that John Thomas had submitted on May 22 had said that persons cease to be refugees when *all* of the following conditions had been met: when they have returned to original places of abode or provided alternate but suitable permanent housing, received all allowances due them, *and* have become self-supporting. The Ministry's provision, "Or they have become self-supporting before being formally resettled by the GVN," required a judgment by officials as to whether and when a person had become economically viable—a sort of means test, as a condition for receiving the prescribed allowances. It was a license to provincial officials to strike refugees from the rolls.

I took this matter up with Mr. Hu'ng and Major Le Van Ba at the Ministry on September 10, 1968. Mr. Hu'ng said that this provision was intended to apply only to war victims or refugees who resettled outside of MHSWR-designated settlement sites. Steve Cummings's memorandum of the conversation reported: "In no way does Category (3) apply to regular refugees in MHSWR approved sites, nor may it be construed to deny full resettlement benefits to the latter. This interpretation has not yet been communicated to the SWR Service Chiefs, pending a revision of communique N.528." I mentioned that I would be visiting some provinces in the delta later that week to look at problems of refugees who had received only partial payments but had achieved self-sufficiency. The situation was most conspicuous in Kien-Giang and Phong-Dinh provinces. I asked about the tools by which the Ministry determined whether a service was living up to its responsibilities. Mr. Hu'ng replied that inspector reports, monthly province reports, and field visits by Ministry officials brought deficiencies to light, and appropriate instructions were then issued.[9]

In actuality, these provisions did cause some confusion in the provinces about categories, and the refugee population figures varied somewhat. The official definition did not seem to have resulted in disqualifying significant numbers of refugees. However, it did cause many refugees to be dropped from the rolls after receiving their payments but before they had become self-supporting or their sites had been brought up to standard.

MEASURING THE REFUGEE POPULATION AND LIVING CONDITIONS

Mr. Thomas, together with the two successive Ministers, set in motion three new measures to develop an estimate of the refugee caseload and conditions in the camps: a refugee site census, a monthly automated data processing (ADP) reporting system, and registration of out-of-camp refugees.

A site census card in English and Vietnamese, approved by Minister Que, was distributed late in May 1968, to be filled out jointly by the CORDS advisors and SWR personnel, with one card for each site. In addition to information on name and location, it recorded the type (temporary center, resettlement hamlet, or combination; existing hamlet or new site), population, predominant religion, number of primary-school-age children, classrooms available and number built on site, health clinics, wells built, latrines built, number of able-bodied workers: men and women; number of men and women employed, and number in vocational training. ADP printouts were prepared from the returns and sent back to the provinces by the end of June with instructions to correct and return them by July 15. A month later, new corrected printouts were to be sent to Saigon, indicating the planned future status of each site: to be converted from a temporary camp to a resettlement site; to be abandoned if it could not be made viable; or, if the site was complete with all prescribed facilities, all refugee benefits paid, and the inhabitants required no further assistance, to be declared finished. A check list by which to judge each site was enclosed; it asked for data on security, the principal planned occupation of the residents (agriculture, fishing, employment at a nearby facility, or other); amount of farm land available and requirements to cultivate it; for a fishing village, boats, motors, and nets required; and so forth. The memorandum transmitting these instructions said their purpose was to pinpoint action areas needed ''to resettle the refugee in a situation where he becomes self-supporting and is thereby removed from the category of refugee.''[10]

Drawing from his experience with electronic processing of data on Cuban refugees, John Thomas used his contacts with the ADP experts of MACV/ CORDS to obtain their help in developing a comprehensive system for refugee reports. No attempt was made to do this on an individual case basis, which would have exceeded the capabilities of the MACV computers and their staffs. Instead, the camp census and the checklist were to be the starting point, and they would be updated every month; only the changes would have to be noted by the province advisors. Through the summer and early fall of 1968, CORDS/ REF, especially Bill Luken and John Hayes, worked with MACCORDS/RAD and the Ministry to refine the system. It was interfaced with the hamlet evaluation system (HES) and other periodic reports.

The first ADP forms were sent out to the field in September, and experts from CORDS/REF and the Research and Analysis Division (RAD) fanned out to explain them to our refugee officers. I went with one of the teams to IV CTZ and thereafter maintained close contact with our advisors in all regions to encourage and assist in making the reports meaningful, particularly in collecting realistic data about the economic activities and prospects of refugees in camps and hamlets.[11] The advisors were by no means unanimously in favor of the new system, even after the experimental period ended in November and the old manual tabulation was discontinued. Especially in thinly staffed provinces, where they were confronted with frequent emergencies caused by VC attacks or allied military operations as well as fires, floods, and other disasters that required prompt relief, and with the need to press their counterparts to make payments to refugees who had been on the rolls for many months, they sometimes didn't see the urgency of careful examination and reporting on wells, latrines, and so forth which in their view were unlikely to receive attention in the near future. Most camps everywhere were deficient in many respects, and many refugees were no more helpful than the service chiefs in fixing them up. John Thomas created a camp clearance task force late in the year, whose members traveled with their MHSWR counterparts developing and expediting plans to upgrade camps and resettle refugees; this achieved limited results.

However, the lack of secure, arable land and other employment opportunities in rural areas that were not near cities or US bases was a continuing barrier to successful reestablishment of many thousands of refugees. Even when camps got all the dispensaries, wells, latrines, classrooms, and proper housing units, and temporary and resettlement payments were completed, hundreds of camps were not economically viable.[12] In those cases, resettlement became a statistical exercise, and assistance in one or another form, often provided by voluntary agencies, had to be continued. John Thomas got the Ministry's agreement to introduce the category, "in resettlement process," for reporting on refugees who had not received all payments and whose camps were not complete; the concept was sometimes stretched to encompass refugees in unviable sites, so that they were not simply dropped. He also badgered MACV, USAID, and the GVN to secure and to make available additional land for resettlement.

It had long been known that thousands of refugees never entered formal camps or even registered with the local authorities for assistance. This was particularly the case in the Mekong Delta, with its plentiful land and rich crops. Most refugees had settled in with relatives or on their own. In the Saigon metropolitan area and the central provinces, squatter towns grew up in or on the edges of cities and around military bases, and the refugees somehow managed to survive. They were included in the statistics, largely as "guesstimates," if at all, and most GVN and US officials were content to ignore them. Mr. Thomas, however, saw that some of these people might need and be eligible for assistance and that most would require help at such time as security was extended outward, enabling them to go home to destroyed hamlets and villages. Early in August, Dr. Lu Y accepted Thomas's proposal to use the Ministry's mobile teams to conduct surveys.[13] At Ministry request, it was planned to start in Binh-Dinh and Kien-Phong, two provinces with large numbers of displaced persons. After radio broadcasts had alerted the people, the surveys began on October 9 in Binh-Dinh and October 15 in Kien-Phong.[14] Other provinces were rapidly added to the list; in those with few refugees, the regular SWR staffs did the surveying.

On November 4, Dr. Lu Y incorporated the out-of-camp survey into a Ministry program of national registration of in-camp, out-of-camp, and resettled refugees and their sites.[15] A special form was used to count the out-of-camp refugees, including a notation by the census-takers saying whether in their opinion a family should be recognized as refugees.

Going out into the countryside and the cities to look for and register refugees was a new departure in Viet-Nam—and, indeed is rarely done in any country. Many of those who were surveyed were already settled one way or another and did not need help, but the fact that the government was interested enough to seek them out evidently was a source of gratification. As will be seen below, it turned out to be a useful device for identifying those who would return to their native villages when security permitted and who would need help in reestablishing themselves. However the survey was not conducted in metropolitan Saigon.

Robert Allen, the chief CORDS refugee advisor of Binh-Dinh, obtained the cooperation of the US Army's Qui-Nhon Support Command to put the survey results onto data processing tape. About 150,000 names and other identifying data were key-punched and recorded on one reel in the early months of 1969. Processing then revealed over 30,000 duplicate registrations, leaving 118,000 genuine refugees. This saved the Ministry considerable money in allowances and assisted in later tracking of the refugees. It was, however, the only instance when individual displaced persons were the subjects of machine data processing. Had it been possible to generalize the Binh-Dinh system, many more duplicate registrations and "ghost refugees" would have been eliminated, removing one source of corruption.

How Many Refugees?

The definition and the surveys were tools to ascertain the magnitude of the regular refugee problem and to guide the relief and resettlement programs. Table

Table 9
Refugee Movements and Population, 1968

Summary of Refugee Movements

Refugees at beginning of year	867,963
Returned to home villages	90,729
Resettled	235,043
New refugees	786,326
Refugees at year-end 1968	1,328,517

Refugee Population at December 31, 1968, by Corps Tactical Zones

CTZ	Temporary refugees	In resettlement process	Outside centers	Totals
I	271,547	126,340	283,869	681,756
II	88,906	48,308	236,078	373,292
III	14,310	56,851	9,574	80,735
IV	89,929	38,823	63,982	192,734
Totals	464,692	270,322	593,503	1,328,517

Source: Refugees at beginning of year, from National Institute of Statistics, *Vietnam Statistical Yearbook 1969*, 379. All other figures from CORDS Refugee Division. *Assessment of Refugee Program 1968*, 1, 11. "New refugees" is a residual figure. These statistics are in accord with the reports of provincial SWR chiefs and CORDS refugee advisors, but are probably not precise. Different, less credible data on returned to home villages and resettled had been presented by the Ministry of Social Welfare in the *Vietnam Statistical Yearbook 1969*, 379.

9 shows what reportedly happened in 1968. Even with reservations about some of the data, the table makes it clear that the GVN was confronted with an unprecedented dislocation of people in 1968, almost the same as in the three preceding years together. Some of the growth in the regular refugee numbers was due to more accurate counting and the new category, "in resettlement process," but the displaced population was nonetheless real. Some of the out-of-camp refugees were already resettled, though it is significant that none of those shown in the above table had been disqualified under the definition as

being self-supporting. Indeed, as the surveys progressed, the number went on increasing. At the end of February 1969, the total had reached 1,449,036, of whom 730,189 were not in camps.

At that point, the Ministry moved to limit the number of out-of-camp refugees by narrowing the criteria; in order to be counted, they must: (1) have moved after January 1, 1964, (2) have left insecure hamlets within the same province, and (3) be living in controllable groups of 20 or more families. The SWR service chiefs were instructed to review the survey cards and to decide who met all three criteria and who met only the first two. Those who met all three criteria were entitled to a one-month temporary relief payment at 15 $VN per day for each member of the family. They, and those who met only the first two criteria, were issued the "white card" and were eligible for assistance at such time as they could return to their original villages. In the meantime, the three-criteria refugees after payment and the two-criteria refugees immediately were considered as resettled and were no longer counted. Those who were classified as "emigrants in search of a living" were to be eliminated from the lists.[16] By April 30, the refugee total had declined to 1,325,312, of whom 630,440 were out-of-camp. Thereafter, resettlement and return to village accelerated in keeping with the expansion of territorial security, as will be recounted in the next chapter.

DR. TRAN LU Y, A CHARISMATIC LEADER

Dr. Lu Y, who had been Minister of Health in the previous Cabinet before that Ministry was combined with the MSWR by Prime Minister Tran Van Huong on May 25, 1968, outdid even Dr. Que in his energy, rapport with the refugees, and willingness to go anywhere at the drop of a hat to inspect a new situation and institute prompt assistance. He often said, "We will go there and settle the matter on the spot." Then we would obtain an Air America plane or helicopter, and he would go, usually with John Thomas, sometimes with me, and always with Steve Cummings.

In his manuscript, John wrote:

One problem was that Dr. Lu Y who always wore a field jacket, kept a revolver under his chair cushion. He would stick the gun in his pocket, reach under the chair to pick up a short Swedish Sten gun which was an automatic rifle and take off out the door. I always either tried to get well ahead of him or stay well behind, thus keeping out of the line of fire should shooting begin. On one occasion he found that people were not getting their rations because all the goods were still in the warehouse. (This was a constant problem. Rations were piled up in the warehouse. Subsidy funds remained in the safe of the province clerk. There was such a lack of belief in the Central Government that province staff acted like hamsters hoarding away what they had received in the fear that no more would be coming.) Anyway, when Dr. Lu Y reached the warehouse, he saw the bags of rice stacked up. To his utter chagrin, he noted that some of the bags had not been placed on platforms and brown rings showed that water had seeped into the bags. In answer to his demand as to why this had happened, the warehouseman meekly explained that there was a small hole in the ceiling where some water had trickled through. But it was a very small hole according to the man. My attention had been directed to another part of the warehouse but I hit the floor at the first burst of fire. When things quieted down I was told that Dr. Lu Y pulled out his revolver, fired a series of shots into the ceiling, and shouted to the frightened warehouseman: "Now the hole is big enough to be fixed!" He was a man of action to say the least.

But people listened to Dr. Lu Y. At one camp where some unrest had been reported Dr. Lu Y called the whole camp to meet with him. He had found that the people had not been given the monthly payment offered by the GVN; so he brought the Province Chief and some of his staff with him. He told the people why the Viet Cong should be overcome and outlined the merits of the Central Government in Saigon. When he had finished speaking, the people lined up to receive the monthly allowance due to them. After that Dr. Lu Y met with the elders of the camp. There is a great respect for age in Vietnamese society. . . .

In May 1975 I was in Camp Pendleton, California, to check on the work ICEM [of which Thomas was then the Director] was doing in bringing Vietnamese from Guam to the United States. I was walking down a corridor . . . glanced through a door where some Vietnamese were sitting at school desks filling out forms. Their backs were towards me but it did not take more than a second glance for me to recognize the army field jacket that Dr. Lu Y always wore. I went into the room and greeted him. He looked up with a wry smile and said: "Ah, Mr. Thomas, I am just one of your refugees now." He finally went to France where he is practicing medicine today. A great human being![17]

Dr. Lu Y instituted the practice of taking along news reporters and members of the National Assembly from the area concerned. This was done both as a politically astute event and in order to curb corruption. In July 1968, he sent a message to all provincial SWR chiefs instructing them to publicize the distribution of assistance for at least one week in advance, using local radio and news bulletins prominently posted, specifying the kind and quantity of commodities and money each refugee was to receive and the date, time, and place of the distribution. (One of the Ministry's top officials said later that such notices were visible when the Minister came to visit but were frequently taken down by province chiefs after he left.) Following each distribution, a comprehensive report was to be sent, including the namelist of the recipients with signatures or thumb prints, and names of deputies, local notables, and other witnesses.[18]

Dr. Lu Y maintained two separate branches in the combined Ministry, heading the health branch himself. He appointed Dr. Tran Nguon Phieu as his assistant in charge of the social welfare and relief branch. Under him there were three blocks: emergency relief under Mr. Hu'ng; refugees, administered directly by Dr. Phieu; and social welfare, under Dr. Ton That Niem, previously the delegate of the Ministry of Health in II Corps.[19]

VOCATIONAL TRAINING AND HANDICRAFT DEVELOPMENT

Both Dr. Lu Y and we in CORDS/REF looked upon vocational training as a means of fitting some rural refugees, now without land, for the many skilled and semiskilled jobs that were going begging in cities and on military bases. The Ministry began by transferring 22 million piasters ($186,441 US equivalent in 1968) to the Ministry of Education (MOE), which instructed the directors of all technical schools to open classrooms by August 15, 1968; SWR chiefs submitted lists of eligible refugees. Sixteen schools declared themselves ready to accept refugee trainees in the first cycle, which was to close in mid-October to allow teachers to receive nine weeks of military training. In provinces without technical schools, eligible students could receive 1,000 $VN per month as a living allowance for three months if admitted to the nearest school.[20]

Thirteen of the MOE schools did teach 1,285 refugee students in Da-Nang, Quang-Ngai, Qui-Nhon, Tay-Ninh, Phuoc-Tuy, An-Giang, Cao-Lanh (Kien-Phong province), Go-Cong, Can-Tho, Ben-Tre (Kien Hoa province), My-Tho, Rach-Gia (Kien-Giang province), and Vinh-Long. In addition, 120 students received training at the old French hospital in Tam-Ky, which was renovated for use as a vocational school, funded directly by the MHSWR with help by the American Red Cross. Another vocational school was built near Da-Nang with funds and equipment donated by CARE, OXFAM, and US military units. In October, two more schools were opened in Hue and Phu-Tho (Saigon). The most popular courses in all the schools were mechanics, sewing, carpentry, and electrical systems.[21] Other courses were in metal working, welding, masonry, typing, and heavy equipment operation and maintenance. Refugees graduated from the GVN schools numbered 1,370 in 1968 and 1,898 others took courses organized by voluntary agencies and provincial SWR services.[22]

The World Relief Commission (WRC), an Evangelical voluntary agency, in cooperation with Christian Youth Social Service (CYSS), a Vietnamese organization, established a vocational school and agricultural experiment station near Hue for both Vietnamese and Montagnard refugees. They established a second school in Hoa-Khanh village, a refugee squatter settlement near Da-Nang, with help from US Navy SeaBees.[23] The US Seventh Air Force at Tuy-Hoa, Phu-Yen province, helped set up an advanced auto mechanics course at the Dong-Tac refugee resettlement site, donating condemned vehicle engines and sending motor pool personnel to advise.[24] In subsequent years, both the GVN and unofficial vocational and technical training programs for refugees were expanded until they encompassed most of those who desired to advance their economic prospects by that route.

A number of refugees, including Montagnards, were encouraged and assisted in their traditional handicrafts by voluntary agencies and the US military PX system, which marketed their products. Montagnard cross bows, which were quite powerful weapons, were popular with American soldiers and others (I have one), while the intricate hand-woven cloth, with both traditional and new patterns, was eagerly bought by both men and women. Vietnam Christian Service imported some color-fast dyes and taught Montagnard women to use them in place of the natural dyes, which were not color-fast when washed in hot water.

The International Recreation Association, an American voluntary agency under contract to our division, had classes in many locations teaching handicapped persons including refugees to make little toys and decorative articles out of coconut shells, bamboo, aluminum beer cans, cloth, and paper.

All these efforts were helpful in providing employment and business opportunities to the refugees and others in need. Their vulnerability was that they, like the jobs on and near the military bases, were dependent upon the huge and affluent American military and civilian presence. After the Nixon administration began to phase down the American presence in 1969, the parlous economic situation of many refugees in and around the cities and bases was increasingly revealed. However, this effect was mitigated by the extension of territorial security and the consequent return of many refugees to their homes, as will be described in the next chapter.

Within the refugee sites there were many projects, organized by voluntary agencies, CORDS advisors, and SWR service chiefs, growing vegetables, pigs, poultry, rabbits, mushrooms, and other food items. These had both immediate and more lasting results, improving the refugees' diet as well as earning supplemental income. International Voluntary Services (IVS) and the International Rescue Committee (IRC) were outstanding in promoting these endeavors.

SOME RESETTLEMENT PROJECTS

The Social Welfare Service staffs and the CORDS refugee advisors in the provinces devoted ever-increasing efforts to upgrading those of the more than 500 refugee camps in the country that had the prospect of becoming viable and to resettling elsewhere some or all of the inhabitants of those camps that could not be made self-supporting. Extraordinary attention was devoted to some projects, with mixed results, and both the Vietnamese and we on the American side learned some painful lessons. The case histories of a few of these projects recounted below extend into the period of pacification and other programs that are the subjects of later chapters, but rather than fragmenting the narratives, I have kept each of them together for the sake of continuity.

The Cua Valley of Quang-Tri

In April and May 1968, GVN authority was reestablished in the fertile Cua Valley in that part of Cam-Lo district that contained Huong-Hoa district-in-exile, to the south of Khe-Sanh, from which most of the Bru Montagnards had fled to Cam-Lo the previous year when the Communists took over all of their original district except a few US fire bases. About 5,000 Bru and 1,000 Vietnamese were resettled in the valley at adjacent sites, which we in the CORDS Refugee Division were told had been carefully planned, called Cua-Thuong and Cua-Kinh.[25] The latter village, settled by the Vietnamese, had no difficulty integrating with the Vietnamese neighbors. However, the provincial authorities had not provided sufficient secure agricultural land for the Bru, whose numbers kept increasing, and the Vietnamese objected to expanding the Bru territory. The SWR service, the ARVN Tenth Polwar Battalion, CORDS, and the 29th Civil Affairs Company devoted much attention to making both of the new settlements a success. In the course of his inspection tour of the DMZ area on August 16, 1968, President Thieu stopped by the Bru settlement, assured the people of support to improve their farming and animal breeding, and granted them some seed and wheat flour.[26] The I CTZ CORDS refugee agricultural advisor, Charles Fields, Jr., spent much time there teaching the tribespeople new methods of cultivation and introducing new crops on the 142 hectares allocated to the inhabitants. There was more land around the camp, but it was insecure. A large dispensary had been built, and many of the Bru had latrines.[27]

After becoming the chief of the I CTZ Refugee Division, I visited the settlements in late December 1969 with Major Powell, the district senior advisor; John B. Swanson, the agricultural expert of the CORDS province team; and Lt. Steve Visher of the 29th Civil Affairs Company, who was living there. According to the November ADP report, Cua-Kinh had 972 resettled Vietnamese refugees, 75% of whom were Buddhist. Its medical facilities were still not adequate, but there was sufficient good water. It had no latrines. Physical security was adequate. One hundred fifty of the 300 school-age children were attending school in neighboring communities. Only 15 of the 336 families were without an employed adult. Many of those from Khe-Sanh were soldiers, while those from Ca-Lu lived on their refugee payments. They had gardening tools but did not garden.

The nine villages of Cua-Thuong had 6,966 resettled refugees in 1,872 families, adequate medical facilities and water, 998 latrines, adequate physical security, 200 of the 1,000 school-age children in school, 1,000 able-bodied men, and 1,500 able-bodied women. The number who were employed was shown on the printout as unknown. Lieutenant Visher said that vocational training in agriculture, veterinary subjects, and small motor maintenance would be advisable. There had been some women weavers, but they had gone to Laos. The people had pigs and poultry, and were interested in upgrading their swine. They were busy with their gardens and small rice fields. Many had banana trees. The tribespeople welcomed the help the Americans were providing. There were 227 hectares of additional land on the edge of the settlement, and the province team was trying to get help from the US XXIV Corps to plow it, but it was learned later that the district and provincial officials were unable to make a firm commitment to allocate the land.[28] The Bru villages had been "localized," that is, integrated into the local government structure of the province, which made their inhabitants voters and entitled the settlement to receive village self-development (VSD) funds. However, although 36 projects and 3,600,000 $VN had been authorized in 1969, the Bru villages got nothing that year because they did not have a literate finance commissioner. For 1970, the province chief authorized the district chief to act as finance commissioner for the tribespeople.[29] He also named Cua-Thuong as one of only two refugee sites for development programs in 1970.[30]

However, conditions then deteriorated and, beginning in April 1970, a number of families left the settlement, some to return to Cam-Lo, others going to Thua-Thien province. There were several reasons: Recent enemy action in the area, including an attack on the Bru villages on May 31 that killed 10 people, wounded 29, and destroyed 12 houses, had made the Bru anxious about their security. Ever since they had first arrived, tribespeople who had gone out looking for food and firewood were frequently met by VC, who told them that unless they left Huong-Hoa, they would be destroyed; evidently the threats were now being taken more seriously. Some connected the threats with the obvious resentment of their presence on the part of local Vietnamese. Also, a number of the people had no continuing source of income once the resettlement allowances were paid, and even those with members in the military or civilian GVN service were having increasing difficulty obtaining food on account of rising prices.[31] Those who had given money in advance to An Ya, the deputy district chief, to pay for food deliveries complained that the deliveries were late and short, in one instance causing a six-week period of hunger. That delay was evidently caused by lack of transport, but there was no reasonable excuse for the repeated tardiness of rice deliveries that had been paid for in advance. Another cause of the exodus, which had risen to 274 families by June 19, was the indiscriminate firing into the Bru villages by the CIDG and Delta forces in the area, which went on for weeks. Meanwhile, the 14th US Army Engineers were plowing part of the 227 hectares, but the Vietnamese told the Bru that if they occupied it, they would be subject to reprisals when the Americans left. The province chief had promised to send a team to distribute land titles on June 15, but the team never showed up. There was general disillusionment with the treatment the Bru were receiving at the hands of the Vietnamese.[32]

On June 22, the acting regional inspector of social welfare, Vo Trong Khoa, and I visited the area with the SWR chief, Hoang Duc Thac, and the Ethnic Minorities chief, Le Van Nghiem, to seek a solution. The Vietnamese officials said that the Bru were leaving because of insecurity, the short rounds of "friendly fire," threats from the Vietnamese, inability to go into the forest to cut wood, and lack of land, seed, and tools. The other CORDS officers in our party added that PL 480 food intended for the Bru was being distributed to purported widows and orphans or simply sold by the deputy district chief An Ya. We agreed that a special development plan was necessary, and CORDS refugee advisor Ellsworth M. Amundson said that he had presented a plan; the province chief had approved but had done nothing to follow up. We then met with the Bru village chiefs, who told us particularly about the danger from the VC. The Vietnamese officials told them that they would ask the province chief to allocate land to them. The previous night, about 200 Bru had been delivered back to the valley from Cam-Lo, having been persuaded by the district chief and CORDS; however, more than 560 Bru who went to the Nam-Ho district of Thua-Thien province were still there, and the chief of that district was planning to allocate land to them. Some of the people had gone into VC areas. Father Neyroud, a Belgian who had ministered to the Bru for many years, said that the first problem was the transport of rice, which the province chief had promised to assure. The second problem was security; he said 14 people had been killed in one night. The third problem was the Vietnamese-Bru land problem. Upon my return to Da-Nang, I urged Deputy for CORDS Alex Firfer to press for implementation of the reforms and the development plan that the province service chiefs, CORDS team, and the 29th Civil Affair Company had proposed.[33] He did so.

After I left Viet-Nam in July 1970, my successors continued their efforts on behalf of the Cua Valley Bru. For a while the situation worsened, especially after the VC abducted 55 villagers including their chief. Bru political leaders who were long-time residents of the Cam-Lo area exacerbated the problem.[34] However, a month later 220 hectares of land were allocated to the Bru, and cultivation was begun. Although this was welcome news, it brought the amount of land available to the refugees to only a small fraction of the several thousand hectares that were needed to make them self-supporting. Fifty thousand manioc cuttings, 240,000 sweet potato cuttings, and some other vegetables were planted on the new land. There were some problems, but the agricultural advisors were helping with them. VSD funds were used to purchase 71 water buffalo and 33 cattle. Security improved when Vietnamese Marines were deployed. In February 1971, the ARVN operation into Laos brought out 24 families of Bru, who were sent to the valley.[35]

By the 1972 new year, the Quang-Tri Ethnic Minority service was distributing PL 480 commodities to 3,999 Bru in Huong-Hoa and Cam-Lo. However, the CORDS War Victims and Community Development directors in Saigon, having learned of a proposal from 9,000 Montagnards in Quang-Tri and Thua-Thien who wished to move to Region 2 as soon as possible, called on Nay Luett, Minister of Ethnic Minorities. He told them that he had visited the areas the preceding week and found the refugees very poor, with no means of making a living except producing charcoal; security conditions, he added, made even that endeavor almost impossible. He said that his Ministry had few resources, but he offered to make 800 cadres available.[36] American civil and military planes did move 3,000 Bru from the Cua Valley to III CTZ under Dr. Phan Quang Dan's Land Development and Hamlet Building program just before the North Vietnamese Easter Offensive of 1972.[37]

The history of this resettlement project revealed some painful truths. The Bru were induced to leave Cam-Lo for what was held out as a better future in a fertile valley, but the province officials failed to secure the necessary land to enable the refugees to become self-sufficient, even with sedentary agriculture. Moreover, they did not take the trouble to gain the acceptance of their project by the Vietnamese peasants into whose midst they were planting the Montagnards, who were looked upon by most Vietnamese as savages. This was, ironically, the reverse of the usual pattern in Viet-Nam, whereby Vietnamese had been transplanted into tribal lands without the agreement of the tribespeople.

Security in the valley was never adequate, and it was made worse by the barbarous behavior of some of the Vietnamese troops. Negligent and in some cases corrupt officials delayed and sabotaged the provision of both food (for which they had been paid) and such land as was available. By the time these grievances were remedied, the Communists were again in the ascendancy, and the belated good works were lost. We have no scientific attitude data from the Bru, but it is difficult to imagine that their hearts and minds were won to the national cause by their treatment.

Interzonal Resettlement—Quang-Ngai to Cam-Ranh

As early as 1967, during Dr. Que's tenure, consideration had been given to moving some of the refugees from the over-crowded camps of I CTZ to more abundant land in Region II, but these thoughts were abandoned because of fear that such a move would be interpreted as preparation for giving up territory to the Communists. With the enormous increase of war victims in 1968, and strong indications that the new American air and naval base at Cam-Ranh would welcome refugees as workers, Dr. Lu Y decided to take the risk. In July, he wrote to Lt. Gen. Hoang Xuan Lam, Commander of I Corps and I CTZ, asking his opinion of a plan to move about 2,000 families with over 8,000 refugee members, mostly poor farmers, from Quang-Ngai province, with others possibly to follow later. General Lam concurred but asked for details. Dr. Lu Y replied that there was plenty of agricultural land available in Lam-Dong and that in Cam-Ranh the refugees could make a living in other ways. He said that 3,356 families with 15,946 members from the three southern provinces of I CTZ and 80 families with 400 members from Binh-Dinh were ready to move.[38]

Since any such move would require extensive US military and civilian support, CORDS/REF made contact with MACV, which put us in touch with the Seventh Air Force. The USAID Mission objected that there was a water problem in the Cam-Ranh area, which would make it inadvisable to bring in additional people. John Thomas assigned Major William Reiff of our staff, who was a water expert, to the problem, and he was able to show that there was the potential of sufficient water at the site, which was some kilometers from both the city and the base.[39] Thereupon, planning went forward on the Cam-Ranh project, in consultation with all the GVN agencies concerned including the mayor of Cam-Ranh, and with the US base officers. In mid-October, 15 representatives of refugee camps in Quang-Nam, Quang-Tin, and Quang-Ngai spent three days in the area and approved the move. Long houses for temporary stay, wells, and other facilities were constructed. The Ministry decided to give the usual cement, roofing, and money to the refugees, who would build their permanent houses, plus an extra 1,000 $VN per person and six-months' rice ration.[40]

On December 19, 1968, Mr. Hu'ng and Bui The Canh of the Ministry and I accompanied the first 100 families from Quang-Ngai to the US Chu-Lai base and from there to Cam-Ranh. A festive departure ceremony with many speeches was held by the province chief and other officials at the gaily decorated Quang-Ngai airport; the refugees were dressed in their best clothes, and their baggage was already palletized. Then we climbed into US military planes (De Haviland Caribous and C-123s) for the short trip to Chu-Lai, where we and the baggage were transferred, with the help of the 29th Civil Affairs Company, to giant (and incredibly noisy) C-130s. At the Cam-Ranh airport, the refugees and the accompanying officials and newsmen were met by the mayor, the base commander, and many others. The speeches there were shorter, and soon military buses conveyed us to My-Ca, the resettlement site, which was set in a broad, wooded area. Reception tents had been set up, and sisters of Catholic Relief Services and the local churches served punch to the tired but excited refugees. They were then shown their temporary quarters. The next day, another 94 families arrived. The whole move went like clockwork, thanks to the cooperative efforts of the many Vietnamese and Americans involved.

However, this move of 1,000 refugees had taken many people months of preparation to organize, straining the resources of both the Ministry and our office as well as the cooperating US military units. During a meeting on another subject which Major Reiff and I had with Dr. Lu Y on the last day of 1968, I suggested that, with the newly opened opportunities for return of refugees to their home villages (which will be discussed in the next chapter) and the camp clearance effort on which he and Mr. Thomas had agreed, we should not initiate any more projects like Cam-Ranh, since they took a disproportionate amount of time and work. (I had in mind Lam-Dong, about which we in CORDS/REF had misgivings, since it would have transplanted Vietnamese refugees to a Montagnard area.) Dr. Lu Y agreed.[41] It was only several years later, with a special administration that Dr. Phan Quang Dan set up as the Secretary of State for Land Development and Hamlet Building (which will be described in chapter 13) that it became practical to move large numbers of refugees interzonally and resettle them on new land.

My-Ca was only marginally successful. When I visited it three months later, some 191 families with 1,035 members were living on 100 hectares of land. They had received the 10 bags of cement, 10 roofing sheets, 5,000 $VN for each family, and four-months' rice rations, plus 20 truckloads of lumber from the US base, and had constructed quite pleasant and well-spaced houses. The base had also donated two tons of canned food. One hundred sixty-five of the 235 school-age children were in four classes held in the temporary buildings, while US and Korean military civic action teams were building permanent classrooms. There were 40 latrines, and I was asked to (and did) send a booklet describing the construction of single-family latrines, the only kind that the refugees were willing to use and keep clean. There were five wells, one of which needed cleaning out; hand pumps were supplied shortly. One hundred seventy-five men were being trained at the air base in various occupations, but only 50 of them were hired. The rest of the people were raising vegetables and cutting firewood. CRS had a team stationed at the site, and there was a MHSWR mobile team.

Near My-Ca were the Dong-Lac refugee settlement founded in 1966, sponsored by the Vietnamese Confederation of Trade Unions (CVT) and a relatively new one, Vinh-Cam, intended for refugees from Quang-Duc province and led by their Catholic priest.[42]

It had originally been planned to send up to 1,000 families from I CTZ to Cam-Ranh. In October 1969, as the DEPCORDS for II CTZ, James Megellas, was visiting My-Ca, the mayor of Cam-Ranh had been informed that 111 additional families were to be moved from Quang-Tin. Megellas sent a message to the CORDS Refugee Division reporting this and saying that only about 50% of the refugees had found employment on the base, which was even then phasing down its jobs. Consequently, there was no prospect of employment of newcomers, except a few with special skills. The settlement looked good, but had no irrigation for its gardens and little other means of support. The inhabitants planned to make the site their permanent home, but realized the difficulties. Megellas recommended that the additional refugees be cared for in their own region. William Hitchcock, who had meanwhile replaced John Thomas, replied that Dr. Tran Nguon Phieu, the new Minister, had decided to stop any further movement to Cam-Ranh. He had also stopped the Lam-Dong project, to which Hitchcock added: "This news will elicit warm support from many longstanding opponents of this proposal in both I and II CTZ."[43] These decisions of the Minister ended interzonal transfers of refugees until Dr. Dan's program began in 1971.

Cam-Lo and Ha-Thanh, Quang-Tri Province

Cam-Lo

The evacuation from the Demilitarized Zone (DMZ) and the establishment of the Cam-Lo refugee camp have been described in chapter 7. After about 7,000 Bru refugees had come from the Khe-Sanh area, of whom over 5,000 were transferred to the Cua Valley in the spring of 1968, the population of Cam-Lo stabilized at approximately 12,000, living on 200 hectares of land. It was not a viable site.

A major effort by both the GVN and US forces went into providing an elaborate system providing water for drinking, washing, and irrigation. This project was constantly harassed and sabotaged by the VC. By the time the concrete-lined reservoir, dam, and canals had been completed in July 1968 by the refugees, the US Army and Marines, and the US Navy Seabees, 12 refugees and 1 US Army advisor had been killed, and 44 refugees and at least 9 US Marines had been wounded.[44] Thereafter, the pump periodically broke down and the system was sabotaged repeatedly as late as May 1971.[45] Wells were dug to supplement the system.

Quang-Tri finished all refugee payments by the end of November 1969 and thereafter reported no refugees in its caseload. The statistics were deceiving. Cam-Lo and a number of other camps, including Ha-Thanh (as will be shown below) were by no means self-supporting. Moreover, neither the SWR service nor the American advisors knew how bad the situation was. I was not satisfied with this state of affairs and insisted on keeping these sites on the active list. In December I visited Cam-Lo. The November 1969 ADP printout for the Trung-Gio resettlement camp (its proper name) of Cam-Lo district showed 12,210 resettled refugees in 2,750 families living in that number of houses. Sixty percent were Buddhists. There were inadequate medical facilities but, what with periodic "MEDCAPS" (visits by US and ARVN military and public health service medical teams), health care was adequate. In addition to the main system, water was supplied by seven wells. Seven hundred of the 1,500 school-age children were in school—19 classrooms. The printout showed an unknown labor force and unknown employment: That was inexcusable. Personnel resources to conduct a scientific labor survey were not available but, as I had shown in many camps, one could get a pretty good idea by sitting down with the camp and elected village officials (the camp had been localized, that is, integrated into the village-hamlet system). I urged the provincial and district advisors to do this. Thirty-three refugees were in vocational training. Many others were engaged in various shops and small enterprises, such as carpentry and basket weaving, and there was constant traffic to and from the district and province capitals.

The US advisors told me that there were about 1,000 hectares of fallow land around the camp, some of it public. Moreover, Cam-Huong village volunteered to give some land to the refugees. The problem was to get it plowed and, according to Major Nguyen Van Rao, the district chief, to protect the farms against jungle pigs. He had requested barbed wire for this purpose. He had also requested authority from Major General Ngo Quang Truong, commander of the 1st ARVN Division, for the people to venture farther from the camp to cut wood. There were 800 Regional and Popular Forces (RF/PF) and 1,500 Peoples Self Defense Forces (PSDF), of whom 800 were armed.[46]

As a result of pressure from the CORDS advisors at province and regional levels, including me, a program of "Plowing for Peace" was set in motion by US forces in Quang-Tri. It was slow, because first priority went to land clearing for military purposes. However, by April 1971, some 700 additional hectares had been made available to the refugees, and 200 of them had been plowed. The Ministry budget had included money to purchase 2 tractors, rice seed and fertilizer, and 10 cattle-raising projects.[47]

All this was of course insufficient to support over 12,000 refugees on such a small area. How did they live? Not very well, although this was considered one of the better camps in the region. The small enterprises mentioned above furnished income to some residents. The province continued to send rice and PL 480 foods to the settlement, although there were some complaints of unfair distribution.[48] Voluntary agencies supplemented the official aid. Nonetheless, there continued to be an air of hopelessness among many of the people, as well as receptivity to VC propaganda.

In April 1970, the Rural Survey Program of CORDS I CTZ did a study of 12 refugee camps including Cam-Lo, at my request, using carefully trained Vietnamese interviewers under the supervision of Vietnamese-speaking Americans.[49] (A full report on the survey and its follow-up will be given in chapter 11.) The survey found the following in Cam-Lo: It was considered a relatively good camp. The population was 14,185, of whom 5,934 were male and 8,251 female; 1,908 of them had come in 1964 and 1966 from as far away as Quang-Tin, but the rest had been moved to the site in 1967. Fifty-seven and eight-tenths percent were ancestor worshipers, 35% were Buddhist, 7% were Catholic, and 0.2% were Protestant; 77.8% were laborers, and 85% were considered poor by the surveyors, but only 9% were found to be totally unemployed. There were 1,850 pupils in 28 classrooms (a much higher number than reported in November 1969). The interviewing team found that there was a lack of economic life and a lack of public facilities. The external security situation was good, because ARVN and US forces were located around the camp and it had PF and PSDF of its own. However, there was a hidden VC structure, and the people were characterized as "showing enmity, would conduct struggle" against GVN. A quarter of the refugees were "Pro-Red, like VC," 40% were neutral, and 35% were "Energetic Nationalist." The team concluded that, "Due to economic situation and VC's incitement, refugees would cause trouble to GVN."

These observations were based on interviews with camp officials and 103 respondents in a sample of the refugees, including 21 Montagnards. Eighteen came from Gio-Linh district (on the eastern side of the province), 31 from Cam-Lo, and 54 from Truong-Luong (in the DMZ). If the sample was representative, only a little more than half of the refugees were the original evacuees from the DMZ. Fifteen of them said they came to the camp fleeing VC oppression, 46 fled fighting and bombing, 5 said they were evacuated by US troops, and 37 were evacuated by ARVN. Eighty said they could not or did not want to return to their homes because they were insecure; 22 said the GVN would not let them return, and 1 said it was too far, no transportation. Only 8 said they had not received the assistance to which they were entitled. Ninety-seven said their present life was much worse than when they had lived in their home hamlets; 6 said it was a little better. Thirty-three said they would like the war to end in a clear GVN victory, 20 in a peace that brought both sides together, and 55 did not care so long as it ended soon.

Early in January 1972, some 851 families from Cam-Lo who had volunteered were transported, with their household and personal effects, to Phuoc-Tuy province in III CTZ by Air America and settled at Soui-Nghe under Dr. Dan's program (1,150 people from Ha-Thanh were also in the party). Temporary shelters, water supply, electricity, latrines, a dispensary, a reception center, and marked home sites were already in place. Two thousand hectares of land had been set aside by the provincial officials, and the Catholic church had agreed to sell another

665 hectares.[50] Other transports followed, and by June there were 3,200 Quang-Tri refugees and 800 from other provinces at Soui-Nghe. That settlement was attacked by the VC on June 17, causing the inhabitants to flee, but they soon returned. When I visited it on October 11, 1972, as head of a State Department inspection team, every house in the settlement was surrounded by a lush garden including banana trees, all the refugees had received their payments, land was being cleared (but had not yet been distributed), there was a deep tube well, and other community facilities were being used. The refugees were the only ones I had ever talked with in Viet-Nam who did not want to go back to their original homes.

The North Vietnamese Easter Offensive of 1972 overran Cam-Lo and other localities before many of the inhabitants could escape. Those who could went first to Quang-Tri city, where I visited them in April, and then to Hue and Da-Nang. Twenty-three hundred were moved to MR 3 in April, 75% of them to Soui-Nghe.[51] Others followed. Most, however, remained for some months in Da-Nang, where during late September I visited them in camps that had formerly been occupied by US military units. They were crowded together and miserable. However, within a year almost all had been relocated to Soui-Nghe and many other settlements in the south under Dr. Dan's program.

Ha-Thanh

This camp in Gio-Linh district, to which over 18,000 refugees had come from five villages in the same district in 1967 and 1968 (mostly staying within the same villages but not being able to till their land), was spread out on barren sand dunes bordering the South China Sea. This was an area nobody else wanted. The people had fled from military action and the VC, but even in mid-1969 there was not sufficient allied military priority to advance the few kilometers to secure their home hamlets. When the 29th Civil Affairs Company surveyed the site in August-September 1969, it estimated that 80% of the able-bodied people in Gio-Ha village were employed, and 30% in Gio-Son were working, as were an unknown number in the other three villages. The November ADP printout showed 18,213 resettled refugees in 2,996 families, 65% of whom were Buddhist. There were inadequate medical facilities and services, 20 wells (which were inadequate), substandard physical conditions, and adequate security; only 250 of the 4,210 school-age children were in school, employment was unknown, and 75 were in vocational training.

When I visited on December 28 and 29, 1969, I found the camp not unattractive. The houses were shabby but well spread out, most with kitchen gardens, including sweet potatoes, taro, squash, garlic, mustard, and banana trees. Eucalyptus trees provided by Chuck Fields seemed to be doing well. There was a large Catholic church, a Protestant church, and a Buddhist temple, all with schools. A cinvaram brick factory across the street from the bus station was unused since its roof had been blown off by a typhoon in October. Six hundred hectares of land north and west of the settlement were to be plowed as soon as equipment became available. The village chief of Gio-Ha (7,200 inhabitants) said most people wove baskets and sleeping mats of rice straw, which they sold in Dong-Ha town and neighboring villages. There were many tailors, carpenters, and mechanics with no place to work; some did not have tools. Protestant Pastor Phien, whose congregation comprised 300 souls, said people collected reeds to make baskets. There were many widows. Vietnam Christian Service (VNCS) had given sewing machines, which I saw; classes had been going for two years. There were 40 people in the class at that time. The pastor had a breakfast program for 300 to 400 children—corn meal gruel. Money for that came from the SWR service and VNCS. Father Giao, the Catholic priest, and his assistant, Father Nam, said there were about 2,000 Catholics. Six hundred fifty children were in their school, including one secondary class. Although the people had received their six months' rice allowance, they still needed rice and also clothes. The priests were planning to move some of their people back home as soon as land was reclaimed. There were 800 armed PSDF and four PF platoons in the immediate area.

Just how precarious the living conditions at this huge but isolated camp were was revealed by a visit on February 2, 1970, by Dr. Herbert Froewys, our refugee public health advisor, and Henry Webb, our Food for Peace officer. They went into 25 houses selected by the village chiefs as belonging to particularly poor people, and in almost all they found cases of severe malnutrition and possibly starvation. One child was so sick and probably malnourished that Dr. Froewys brought him to the Quang-Tri hospital in the party's helicopter. The child died half an hour later. In another house they found five malnourished children whose mother was in the hospital and whose father was out attempting to find food. There was no food in the house and no adult. Another house where four people had lived was vacant, the family having gone elsewhere looking for food. Based on those observations and comments of the village chiefs, it appeared that 12% to 15% of the residents of the camp were seriously underfed. There was no plan to help them. The GVN had no feeding program at all, and Catholic Relief Service, the other agency with responsibility for PL 480 feeding, had a plan on paper only, according to Mr. Webb. Dr. Froewys and Mr. Webb called on the Catholic, Protestant, and Buddhist clerics with Captain Cramer, the district senior advisor, and got their agreement to form a group to visit all houses to evaluate needs.[52]

The Quang-Tri refugee advisor, "Butch" Amundson, followed up on this disturbing report. In January, the province had sent 36 tons of rice and a quantity of PL 480 food to Ha-Thanh, and additional quantities to Cam-Lo; on January 26–27, acting SWR regional inspector Khoa, Webb, and Frank Bruno of CRS had visited in General Lam's chopper. However, when two men from the province SWR service arrived at the Ha-Thanh camp on February 4 to supervise distribution of the food, they found that the district chief was in Quang-Tri and that a different plan had been decided; so they went back without fulfilling their mission. At a meeting of the Joint GVN-US Coordinating Committee of the province on February 12, Amundson reported that 350 bags of corn meal sent 10 days earlier were still sitting in the warehouse. The district chief was reluctant to use a religious committee and had asked the SWR service chief to send a representative to distribute the food. The military medical team opined that dysentery and parasites, compounded by lack of sanitation, were the main causes of debilitation and death. After Têt, some rolled oats were distributed on February 12–13.[53]

During a visit to the camp in mid-April, Mr. Webb found that the situation had improved somewhat. Both the Christian ministers were feeding children, and the SWR service was feeding the poor on a regular basis. Its cadres were at that time making a census of the whole province to determine who were poor, widows, orphans, and disabled veterans, and consequently should be fed. Rice was also more abundant on the market. However, Webb recommended that another rather thorough survey at Ha-Thanh be conducted to ascertain whether the really needy had been selected.[54]

The attitude survey conducted in April 1970 found that Ha-Thanh had 18,266 refugees, of whom 6,738 were male and 11,528 female. All were from five villages in the district, 12,366 having arrived in 1967 and 5,900 in 1968. Forty-four and five-tenths percent were ancestor worshippers, 40% were Buddhist, 14% were Catholic, 0.5% were Protestant, and 1% had no religion. Five percent were unemployed, the others being laborers, farmers, merchants, and so on. Seventy-six percent were poor. Only 120 children were reported in school (this was probably understated). Security was only 60% at night because "VC infra structures lead their exterior units to operate at night (Gio-My and Gio-Ha)." The people's politics was reported as "Pro-Red, still like VC." The refugees' attitudes toward the GVN were: "Show enmity, lack of confidence"; toward the Allies: "expecting U.S. help (economic)"; toward the VC: "Majority hate, some like." Thirty percent were rated as energetic nationalists, 45% as neutral, and 25% as pro-Red. The team considered that the camp had "prosperous land, good climate," but a bad economic condition, and predicted that if the situation was not improved, the populace would bear more enmity and even less confidence toward the GVN.

There were 102 respondents with various occupations, half men and half women. Seventy-nine said they had fled fighting and bombing, 21 had fled VC oppression, and 2 had moved because their home hamlet was cleared for the electric fence (the McNamara barrier). Ninety-three believed that their home hamlets were still insecure; 9 said the GVN would not permit them to return. Ninety said their present life was much worse than previously, 10 said it was a little worse, and 2 said it was the same. Thirty-three wanted the war to end in a clear GVN victory, 24 wanted a peace that brought both sides together, and 45 didn't care so long as it ended soon.

The Ha-Thanh story had a temporarily happy ending. By mid-May 1970, almost 7,000 of the refugees had been able to return to their home villages in Gio-Hai and Gio-Ha. Others followed; by early March 1971, some 10,681 had

"RTV'd (returned to village) and received all their return-to-village payments. A month later, the population of the camp was down to 6,000, with another 2,000 slated to return home. The rest had elected to stay at the settlement.[55] As mentioned above, 1,150 were moved to Soui-Nghe in January 1972. All who had remained in Quang-Tri province became war victims again during the Easter Offensive of 1972, and many ended up in Dr. Dan's III CTZ hamlets.

Although one could have wished that more land had been made available earlier at both Cam-Lo and Ha-Thanh, the nature of the war and the large population of the small province made that impossible; this was a condition that afflicted most of I CTZ. What caused unnecessary suffering and intensified adverse reactions at both sites—and at many other sites throughout the country— were the rules of the Ministry, stemming from that part of the definition of a refugee pertaining to termination of refugee status, which it had adopted. The definition provided that people ceased to be refugees, and hence the responsibility of the Ministry, when they had been resettled after receiving all prescribed benefits. John Thomas's proposal, which was not adopted, added to this, "and have become self-supporting." Had his draft been accepted, most of the refugees at the two camps would have been kept on the rolls; as it was, they became nonrefugees, integrated into the regular population but not budgeted for by any of the regular Ministries. The government attempted to correct this situation with a communiqué in August 1969 directing that plans be made for refugees who were returning to their home villages and those who were to be permanently resettled. All relevant Ministries were tasked to participate in the process of reestablishment but they were not given extra funds to do so. The Ministry of Social Welfare followed up with a communiqué of its own directing that resettled refugees were to benefit from site development programs.[56] For many months neither instruction had appreciable effect.

In our monthly reports from I CTZ, we had warned about the consequences of this lacuna. For example, this from our report of November 21–December 20 1969: "We have mentioned previously that the payment of resettlement allowances by no means represents the full reestablishment of most refugees in this region, since many are still living in crowded, unsanitary camps, with little land and few employment opportunities." Using the ADP data, we concluded that 214,339 refugees who were counted as resettled and therefore off the rolls were living in sites that were substandard because of inadequate employment, schooling, or deficiencies in physical conditions. In all, some 166 sites with 355,713 refugees fell into the deficient category. Every month we updated these figures, and little improvement could be claimed, especially in the employment situation.

As part of the 1970 pacification and development program, the Central Government once again instructed the provinces to make development plans for all villages; this included localized former refugee sites. The CORDS Refugee Division and its regional advisors pressed strongly for the preparation of such plans, but with limited success. Quang-Tri was particularly disappointing. My final monthly report as chief of the I CTZ division had this to say:

Although the overall record of Quang-Tri with respect to relief and payment of refugees is good, things like the neglect of the Bru mentioned above and the failure to make development plans for the huge (and restless) refugee concentrations at places like Cam-Lo and Ha-Thanh mar the record. The Province authorities have ignored instructions of their Government to make such plans and have done very little to raise the economic levels of these sites. The renovation of the Cam-Lo irrigation system has been largely an American operation, as has been the plowing of land in the Cua Valley.[57]

A staff report of the Senate Subcommittee to Investigate Problems Connected with Refugees and Escapees quoted from this passage in asserting, somewhat unfairly, that, "Indeed, it would appear that the greatest success achieved in the Vietnam refugee program this past year was the reclassification campaign, which, in effect, 'solved' the refugee problem by reclassifying refugees out of existence."[58]

Return to home villages and movement to more open spaces in Region 3 partly remedied the defects of refugee resettlement in I CTZ, but the progress came only after years of privation suffered by the helpless victims of war, VC attacks, and allied policy.

Lai-Thieu—Binh-Hoa Village

American official and voluntary agencies continued the efforts begun in 1967 to make a viable settlement for the pro-VC evacuees from the village of Ben-Suc (See chapters 7 and 8). In the spring of 1968, the International Rescue Committee (IRC) brought in a poultry expert, Jackie Heggeman, who developed a program whereby families could borrow from the Agricultural Development Bank (ADB) to buy 200 one-day-old chicks, which she imported, plus the feed, vaccines, and other items. She taught them how to build pens and raise the birds for 8 to 12 weeks, after which they were marketed at about 1.5 kilograms each, realizing an average profit of 20,000 $VN (about $169 US equivalent). This was the first time, to my knowledge, that anybody had been able to get the ADB to help refugees. The program was extraodinarily successful; by September, 117 families were participating, at least 25 of which were headed by widows. Miss Heggeman and her colleague Charlie Cowden, as well as Dr. Froewys, were decorated with the Ministry's Social Welfare Medal in November. A Lai-Thieu District Broiler Raising Association was formed in order to assure continued growth of the program, and Miss Heggeman was invited to advise on a similar project in Sadec province.[59] Brother Peter Leonard, a Catholic monk and agricultural teacher from the Soloman Islands, joined the IRC team in September to initiate a pig raising project. The next year another member founded a carpentry training shop, all of whose graduates were able to find jobs upon graduation from their six-month course. IRC also operated a dispensary.[60]

However, the settlement continued to be a dangerous place. In May 1968, about 100 VC held a daylong meeting in Ap Binh-Hoa. Charlie Cowden's trailer was full of bullet holes, and the VC prowled around at night. Jackie Heggeman slept at the house where US military officers lived. The US Seabees took a mortar or rocket round in June, and a refugee was killed in the village.[61] On the other hand, among the worst harassments was the damage wrought by US and ARVN military vehicles. The IRC director wrote:

Although tanks and the like are not supposed to travel through the hamlet, they continue to do so and frequently smash culverts, damage plants, hurt livestock, etc., sometimes accidentally but as often as not deliberately. They think it is a great joke. On one occasion, the US military provided new culverts for the ones smashed. The ARVN just laugh. You can imagine how the villagers react to this attitude. I raised the problem with Mr. Thomas and he will take it up through channels.[62]

Since the community was approaching self-sufficiency, in October the IRC director recommended that the team phase out by June 1969 and be redeployed.[63] That was done, leaving only the head of the carpentry school. For the next two years or so, the community's economic status improved. However, with the phase-down of the US military presence, jobs diminished and despondency again crept in.

A massive study of defoliation in Viet-Nam in 1972 included an investigation of attitudes in Ap Binh-Hoa. One hundred two of the 120 family heads who had been interviewed using the Cantril Self-Anchoring Scale in 1967 (see chapter 7) were again given this test. Their average rating of their present situation was 2.4, while their situation five years earlier was given a rating of 4.9 (compared with 1.65 and 5.95 in the 1967 test). Thus, the refugees felt that their life was somewhat better in 1972 than they had felt in 1967; it is not clear whether their evaluation of the past was made with the preevacuation status in mind or not. However, even the 2.4 rating contrasted with identical 4.6 scores indicated in 1969 by two groups of villagers in An-Xuyen province, one in an NLF area and the other in a GVN area, and with the average ladder rung of 6.4 in 1972 selected by 1,800 respondents in the United States. In 1972, the rating of present life given by the Binh-Hoa respondents was lower than those in 14 other countries, including India and Nigeria. Only the Dominican Republic was lower (1.6). In another test, the health opinion survey (HOS), the Binh-Hoa sample scored 32.7, compared with 22.8 in Nigeria, 24.9 in the United States, and 27.4 in Senegal; the higher scores indicated greater stress. The researchers commented:

Thus, our interpretation of the HOS results is that the people of Binh Hoa *are* suffering and that the degree to which they are laden with symptoms marks them off as different from most people living in normal communities and as similar to groups whose need is sufficiently great that they seek out sources of relief.

The surveyors added:

We know that the war experiences of the Binh Hoa people were homogenous to a remarkable extent. All had lived through Operation Cedar Falls; all had had their homes destroyed; all had been evacuated; all had shared five years of marginal existence as refugees; most had been landed farming families and now were either unemployed or working as farm laborers. This similarity of stressful experiences has been offered as an explanation.

Twenty-four members of the sample mentioned herbicides during the Cantril Scale test, and 34 said that they had suffered health symptoms in connection with defoliation spraying, but this was only one of the stresses they had endured.[64] The investigators concluded that the Binh-Hoa evacuees continued to suffer from the psychological aftermath of the traumatic upheaval of Cedar Falls, and that these feelings might continue into the future.[65]

The survey showed that all that had been done by others *and by the refugees themselves* to make their life better had not been sufficient to overcome the injury of their forcible relocation and economic-social degradation. Now, in 1972, the people of Binh-Hoa were again in difficult economic straits, but they were perhaps no worse off than many of their neighbors who were not evacuees. The researchers did not test an adjacent control group, but I have no doubt that such a group would have shown a much more positive evaluation of its situation than the Binh-Hoa evacuees. The fact that the evacuees had been, and probably still were, VC partisans, who had been exposed to little contrary political influence by the GVN, was undoubtedly a factor.

The foregoing case histories deal with only a few of the many refugee groupings that had received special attention from the GVN and (especially) the Americans to bring them to viability and integration into the Vietnamese society and body politic. Others could be named, including the notorious Ly-Tra camp in Quang-Tin, whose refugees were finally moved to a better location; Edap Enang in Pleiku, which finally became a success; Bon Kri Montagnard settlement in Phu-Bon, which had plenty of farm land and where Tracy Atwood of International Voluntary Services had stimulated a successful project of raising chickens on wire mesh; Paradis Montagnard camp in Kontum, another success, stimulated by CORDS refugee advisor Joe Veasman; and Soc-Son in Kien-Giang province, astride a terminus of the Ho Chi Minh trail, which American advisors tried for years to make into another Cai-San. However, they were frustrated by the Communists, who eventually forced its abandonment.

All of the more than 500 temporary and resettlement refugee sites in the country received some attention by the SWR service, if only to make payments, and often got continued help from the American advisors, military units, and voluntary agencies. The ADP reporting system, by confronting the CORDS advisors and the SWR services in the provinces each month with a large printout, which contained conspicuous blank spaces for each site, tended to compel some attention to the missing elements, which usually related to the facilities and viability of each place. The voluntary agencies frequently made the difference between life and death for many refugees who were in difficult sites or who had been declared resettled before becoming self-supporting. All in all, the Vietnamese refugee assistance system, with much help and encouragement from the American advisors, Civil Affairs companies, and private voluntary agencies, did a remarkable job of caring for the largest body of displaced persons in the nation's history. However, given adverse security and economic conditions as the American forces were withdrawing, the wrong-headed actions of many insensitive US and Vietnamese military commanders and troops, and Vietnamese prejudices against minorities, the Ministry and its foreign helpers could restore only a fraction of the refugees to self-sufficiency and the dignity of being respected members of society and the body politic.

SOCIAL WELFARE

Although social welfare problems were scarcely less pressing than those affecting refugees, neither the GVN nor the US Mission made much progress in addressing them in the period 1966 to the middle of 1968. At that time there were 341 institutions: orphanages, day care centers, boarding houses for students, rehabilitation and vocational guidance centers, old peoples' homes, low-cost restaurants, and community centers. The orphanages and day care centers were almost all privately run. The other institutions were mainly state-run. The Ministry of Social Welfare had 200 employees, not one of whom had advanced training, plus 100 female social welfare workers trained by the Catholic charitable organization Caritas and 500 female graduates of ARVN training who had served in the army.[66] In addition, USAID had a small branch of the Local Development Directorate, to which it paid little attention.

John Thomas had envisaged the refugee problem as just one facet of the total social welfare picture. Distressed by what he found, he gladly accepted the offer of the USAID to transfer the social welfare staff and function to his division, and that was accomplished on June 1, 1968.[67] Then he tackled the budget problem, seeking increased funds from the American Aid Chapter. When the GVN budgeteers cut one item after another at a meeting, he gathered up his papers, said that President Johnson had sent him out to help the GVN do something for the common man but that he would have to tell the President that he had failed, and started to walk out. Clay McManaway whispered something to the chairman, who asked John to come back; money was then found for three of the projects. William Colby also persuaded President Thieu to approve a national school for social work. With that, a new approach could be set in motion.[68]

Thomas selected social welfare advisors for each of the four CORDS regional staffs. Hugh O'Neill in II CTZ was particularly outstanding. He made a complete inventory of social welfare institutions, public and private, with details about each. This was much appreciated by the Ministry, as well as by the voluntary agencies which could plan their programs in the light of what was already available and where there were gaps. He developed a close and effective collaboration with the volags and helped them to coordinate with each other and the SWR service. Furthermore, he had a brisk sense of humor and rapport with Vietnamese, Montagnards, and Americans alike. In III CTZ, George Klein, himself a social worker, took over the additional function with aplomb.

Bill Bacon, the experienced chief of the Social Welfare Branch of our division; Dave Beecher, the urban social planning advisor, and Mrs. Pham Thi Nguyen Ninh of the Branch, one of the few trained social workers in the country, along with their assistants, set about developing a new program to move from custodial care, which the country could not afford and which was wasteful of human beings in any case, to preventive and rehabilitative social welfare. Dr. Lu Y, Dr. Ton That Niem, John Thomas, and Ambassador Komer fully backed this approach. Contracts were negotiated with Catholic Relief Services for a comprehensive child welfare program, with IRC for increased day care centers, and with Goodwill Industries for vocational rehabilitation, tying in with the prosthetics and physiotherapy work of the National Institute of Rehabilitation. The Salvation Army was helped to start a program for rehabilitating prostitutes in Saigon, supplementing the work of the Irish Sisters in Vinh-Long. The Canadian voluntary agency, Foster Parents Plan, was encouraged to expand its program whereby contributions from abroad helped keep poor children from being separated from their families. Other voluntary agencies willingly participated in the new approach.

Dr. Lu Y got an American Aid Chapter social welfare budget of 133,000,000 $VN (about $1,127,000 US equivalent) for Vietnamese Fiscal Year 1969, far more than the Ministry had ever had for this function. It was programmed mainly for the school of social work (which had other funds from UNICEF and the Dutch government, and a prefabricated building from the Australians), day care centers, and other projects to put orphans and old people back into their family homes.[69]

A more informal activity was visits to orphanages by CORDS members of various nationalities. We had noticed that many of the children in those understaffed institutions had become withdrawn for lack of personal caring and love, and some had died from that cause. In September 1968, our division laid on transportation, acquired some balloons and candy as ice-breakers, and invited all the personnel in our building to go out to hold and play with the children. The response was overwhelming. Within a month, over 90 people were devoting their lunch periods to such visits, and they kept on with them.[70] It is hard to estimate how many children's lives were made a little better by this example of human kindness and love.

The German voluntary agency Institute for International Solidarity (IIS) built a children's village at the Juvenile Delinquent Reeducation Center in Thu-Duc, near Saigon, which was dedicated on October 25, 1968 in a ceremony attended by Dr. Lu Y, the German Ambassador, and other notables, together with the proud and happy children. The village consisted of a number of houses for 10 children and a house father or mother, surrounding a community building with classrooms and recreational facilities. Vocational training facilities were also augmented. It moved the center toward a more human approach to rehabilitating these young men and women.

CORDS/REF inherited a certain number of AID participant grants for training in the United States. David Beecher and Mrs. Ninh arranged for Thich Nhat Thien, Director of the Buddhist Social Welfare Center, to go on a training visit using one of these grants. After a brief period of orientation at AID and the Department of Health, Education and Welfare (HEW), he went for a month to Our Lady of the Lake College in San Antonio, Texas, visiting a number of local institutions as part of the training.[71] Upon his return, he became our fast friend and collaborator. His organization had branches in the regions and many of the provinces.

Ambassador Colby was much taken by the Singapore system of community centers, which not only brought people together for recreation, education, and health care (including family planning), but were also a means of cementing allegiance to the government. He and a number of other CORDS officials, including me, made pilgrimages to Singapore in 1969 and 1970. We were briefed by, among others, Arieh Levy, an Israeli who was the youth advisor to the government. (It happened that Charles Cross, who had been the I CTZ Dep-CORDS when I had first arrived in Viet-Nam, was the US Ambassador when I visited in 1970. He was eager for news of our programs and the region, which he missed.) After much effort, complicated by interagency jurisdictional disputes within the GVN and political party rivalries, some community centers were established in Viet-Nam. They were not a great success.

The social welfare program never achieved the effectiveness of the refugee program, but it did help many disadvantaged and handicapped people and gave many children a better start in life.

CHANGING OF THE GUARD AT CORDS AND THE GVN

In November 1968, William E. Colby, who had been the Assistant Chief of Staff for CORDS, succeeded Robert W. Komer as Deputy to COMUSMACV for CORDS. Colby, who had been in Viet-Nam on and off since 1959 and knew all the leading figures intimately, was a quiet and modest but very strong man who gave the same effective support to the refugee program as his fiery predecessor and tied it even closer into pacification. George D. Jacobson, the former Mission Coordinator (who had shot one of the Viet-Cong guerrillas at the bottom of the stairs in his house during the attack on the US Embassy at Têt 1968) took Colby's position as AC of S, CORDS.

In January 1969, John Thomas was elected by the 33 member nations of ICEM, his former agency, to be its director. He left early in February. He felt, rightly, that he had strengthened both refugee care and social welfare, in collaboration with Dr. Lu Y. William K. Hitchcock, formerly Consul General in Calcutta, where then-Ambassador-at-Large Ellsworth Bunker had often been his house guest, was chosen by Bunker to succeed John. He stayed until March 1970, when he became Minister–Counselor Political in the embassy. Wells Klein, who visited Viet-Nam often for the Senate Subcommittee, considered that John Thomas and Bill Hitchcock had been extraordinary leaders who had made exceptional contributions to the refugee program.[72] He was right.

It was considered inappropriate for two State Department Foreign Service Officers to occupy the top jobs in CORDS/REF, so Colby suggested that I become chief of the II CTZ Refugee Division, which needed strengthening. He told me frankly also that I was too much the Saigon administrator and needed some field experience. I was not at all happy with the idea, which in my view was a demotion, but I accepted it, and worked well with Jim Megellas, my chief, and with the province teams, as well as with the regional inspector of the Ministry. Six months later, Alex Firfer asked me to join his staff in I CTZ, which had by far the largest and most intractable refugee problem in the country. Consequently, I exchanged places with Luther McLendon. The field experience was indeed a blessing in disguise; it deepened my perspective as well as giving me experience in the practical problems of helping refugees within two large bureaucracies. When Bill Hitchcock was about to transfer to the embassy, he offered me his job, with Colby's concurrence, provided I would agree to stay at least a year. Though I was flattered, I felt that I had been away from my family too long and regretfully declined. However, the Viet-Nam experience changed my life fundamentally. Except for a brief period as a Foreign Assistance Inspector (which brought me back to Viet-Nam twice in 1972), I have been involved with refugees ever since.

In January 1969, fearing that Dr. Lu Y would be replaced in a cabinet reshuffle, John Thomas recommended that Ambassador Bunker approach President Thieu and Prime Minister Huong asking that this effective and compassionate man be retained in his important post.[73] I do not know whether the Ambassador made the approach, but in any case Dr. Lu Y remained in the cabinet until September 1969, when the new Prime Minister, General Khiem, separated the two parts of the Ministry and appointed Dr. Tran Nguon Phieu Minister of Social Welfare. Dr. Phieu continued in that position until March 1974, the longest tenure of any person who had headed the Ministry.

10

The Flowering of Pacification, 1969–72: Military Doctrine and Civil Administration Support People's War

The Tết and May offensives of 1968 drew both Viet-Cong and allied forces from the countryside into the cities. In some provinces, such as Thua-Thien, Kien-Hoa, and Vinh-Long, the VC were strong enough to extend their control in the rural areas while attacking the cities; but in most a political and military vacuum was created in the countryside. After the emergency was dealt with, Ambassador Komer was determined that the GVN and its allies should fill that vacuum; President Thieu and General Abrams agreed with him. That was the origin of the Accelerated Pacification Campaign (APC), which began officially on November 1, 1968, and lasted through January 31, 1969.[1] It was the first of a series of pacification programs that extended territorial security to the farthest parts of the country, weakened Communist influence, addressed some of the people's grievances, and enabled a million and a half refugees to go home. The progress was by no means uninterrupted or complete; there were many weaknesses, as will be shown in this chapter and the next. Furthermore, too much of its success was dependent on the US military presence. Nonetheless, the few years until the North Vietnamese Easter Offensive of 1972 were happy ones for most of the people.

Even before the official start of the APC, the province chief of Thua-Thien, Colonel Le Van Than and his American advisor, Colonel Thomas Bowen, aided by General Melvin Zais, Commander of the 101st Airborne Division, and ARVN, planned to retake Vinh-Loc district, a long island that had been inhabited by about 50,000 progovernment peasants and fishermen, mostly Catholics. Most of them had remained in or fled to a narrow strip still under GVN control. The plan was executed in mid-September with speed and minimum use of air strikes or artillery. The operation was successful in wiping out or capturing the VC forces and infrastructure. The concept of minimum destruction resulted in the burning of only three houses and little other civilian damage. The provincial and local forces had been integrated into US and ARVN units, which facilitated contact with the populace. Sufficient US and Vietnamese troops were kept in the area to secure it. By the end of the month, almost 10,000 refugees had returned to their homes.[2]

The Accelerated Pacification Program had interrelated numerical targets, which it more than achieved. Thirteen hundred sixty-seven hamlets were pacified, increasing the population under GVN control by 1,317,288 at the end of January 1969. Over 10,000 members of the VC "infrastructure" (political and security cadres) were exterminated by capture or killing, and 8,400 VC rallied under the Open Arms program. Over 1,100,000 persons were enrolled in the People's Self Defense Forces (PSDF) and 170,000 of them were armed. Three hundred forty village administrative committees were elected and another 232 were appointed. It was the same with hamlet boards.[3] In order to ensure participation of all agencies, civilian and military, the Central Recovery Committee, which had successfully coordinated Têt relief and resettlement, was converted into the Central Pacification and Development Council (CPDC).

ASSISTANCE TO REFUGEES RETURNING HOME

There were no targets specifically related to refugees in the Accelerated Pacification Program, although the Prime Minister's communiqué said that they should be encouraged to return to their home villages and hamlets after the Communist infrastructures had been exterminated, and directed that each province prepare a resettlement plan. It also ordered that qualified officials among the refugees be given priority for employment. Dr. Lu Y followed this up with his own communiqué setting out the return-to-village (RTV) benefits and other assistance to be provided.[4] It provided that each returned refugee family should receive for housing construction 5,000 $VN, 10 bags of cement or 2,500 $VN, 10 large roofing sheets supplied by CORDS, and six months' rice ration at 15 kilograms or 225 $VN per person per month. These allowances were to be provided in two installments. Additionally, Montagnards were to be provided a six-months' salt ration at the rate of 200 grams a day. RD cadres were asked to help in civic action, and other teams were to be organized to help in the return process. The provinces were to draw up lists of pacified villages, namelists of refugees who desired to return, and plans for the movements.

The refugees were eager to return home when they were satisfied—and they had very sensitive antennae—that their home villages were in fact secure. Thua-Thien continued in the forefront, but other provinces were not far behind. Sadec in the Mekong Delta was an example. That small province had three areas under VC control, one of them going back 20 years to the time of the Viet-Minh. They were free fire zones and had lost their populations. The land had been laid waste; all buildings, bridges, and roads had been destroyed. The trees had been defoliated or shot up. Two of the VC areas were selected for pacification, and were invaded by GVN troops, with their former inhabitants close behind. Fourteen hundred seventy families returned home in December 1968. The SWR service chief sent the Ministry a list of 570 returned families who had never been registered as refugees, but when Mr. Hu'ng took the matter up at the CPDC on December 26, urging that the people receive help, Minister Huynh Van Dao cautioned about the possibility of people moving from place to place, collecting money fraudulently. On the last day of 1968, together with Major Reiff, I met with Minister Lu Y and argued that the GVN should by all means take advantage of the Accelerated Pacification Program to give prompt and generous assistance to returning refugees. Sadec was only one of a number of provinces, I said, where previously unregistered refugees had returned home and been denied aid. Dr. Lu Y said he came from Sadec himself and, in his characteristic manner added, ''We will go there and settle the matter on the spot.'' The date January 4 was agreed on for the visit; Dr. Lu Y asked that we not notify the province chief, because he did not want elaborate ceremonies but wished to get right down to business. Before concluding the meeting and wishing the Minister a happy New Year, I handed him a memorandum proposing changes in communiqué 919 to make previously unregistered refugees eligible after verification that they had in fact left their hamlets to escape VC terrorism or military action.[5]

On Saturday, January 4, 1969 Dr. Lu Y with his personal assistant and Mr. Hu'ng, three of us from CORDS/REF, and a free-lance reporter flew to Sadec, where we were greeted by a small Vietnamese/American party, and were immediately taken by bus to the Duc-Thanh district headquarters. From there we traveled by sampan long-boats (narrow wooden craft powered by small motors) down the Hau-Giang River to the village of Phong-Hoa. In the village square, the Minister talked to the people and their village chief. The villagers, including inhabitants of two neighboring hamlets, had left in 1965, some of them settling in Vinh-Long province, a short distance away. In the second half of November 1968, a two-week operation had cleared out the VC and their booby traps, whereupon the people returned, cut down the brush, and began rebuilding their homes. After verifying the facts, the Minister decided that the refugees would be registered by an SWR mobile team already in the province and another team would be sent down from Saigon. They would then receive the 919 allowances in two installments. On the return trip we traveled by long-boat on the Muong-Khai Canal past the two outlying hamlets, where the refugees, each family flying the yellow and red RVN flag, were rebuilding, while RF and PF soldiers patrolled. We went ashore at one point so that Dr. Lu Y could speak with the refugees. At the province capital, the Minister and Mr. Hu'ng briefed the province chief, promising to send a telegram confirming the arrangements and to have everything in order to assist the returnees within two weeks.[6] It was a productive and satisfying way of doing business, which I have no doubt won many friends for the GVN.

A smaller number of refugees returned to their APC hamlets in Chuong-Thien province at the same time, while over 1,000 left a VC stronghold in the U Minh

Forest during an APC military operation. Most of the latter group apparently came out voluntarily.[7]

AREA SECURITY CONCEPT REPLACES SEARCH AND DESTROY

Without explicitly saying so, the Accelerated Pacification Campaign represented a turning away from the search-and-destroy strategy to a doctrine of clear and hold. This was made explicit in the Combined Campaign Plan (AB 144) for 1969 and the Pacification and Rural Development Program which began on February 1, 1969. The important word was "hold." Security for the people was to be extended outward from already secure areas, with ARVN and allied forces pushing and holding the enemy's main forces away from the populated areas, which were to be secured by the Regional and Popular Forces (RF/PF) and PSDF. The objective was to bring 90% of the population under GVN control by the end of 1969 without evacuating people from VC-controlled territory. The refugee annex (Annex IX) to the 1969 Pacification and RD Plan criticized past practice in these words:

Due to military requirement and territorial security, instead of launching military operations for pacification, a number of Provinces forcefully regrouped people from insecure areas to "establish refugee hamlets." This action both loses the people's heart and creates a heavy load for the Government in relief assistance because of the ever-growing number of refugees.

Refugees might in the future be created by military operations themselves, but then the generating military force was responsible for their reception, care, and control until they could be turned over to the civilian authorities. Military operation plans must include provision for such care, including advance notification of US and GVN officials, within security limitations. The military was also made responsible for providing security to refugee concentrations. Conditions were to be created for the people to return to their home villages. The watchword became: Bring security to the people, not people to security.[8]

In contested areas, ARVN and US forces were broken down into small units co-located with the RF/PF. Thus, for example, in the fall of 1968, Major General Ellis Williamson, Commander of the 25th Infantry Division, assigned a battalion to each district of Hau-Nghia province, working with Vietnamese units. However, some brigade and battalion commanders regarded pacification as a charade, and there was friction with ARVN, the provincial government, and the province senior advisor (PSA). Security improved in 1969, but the VC still remained strong.[9]

A better result was achieved in Binh-Dinh and neighboring provinces in 1969. In mid-April, the US 173rd Airborne Brigade stationed one battalion in each of the four northern districts of Binh-Dinh, under the operational control of the district chief. They were broken down into platoons, each working and fighting with an RF or PF unit. Within a month, the combined units had entered 48 target hamlets under the pacification program. They had organized day and night hunter-killer teams that patrolled and set up ambushes, thus "taking the night away" from the VC. Two ARVN regiments were also located in the area; the headquarters of one was at Landing Zone English, co-located with the 173rd. The effect upon area security was dramatic. Even in Tam-Quan district, which had been so insecure in March when the regional deputy for CORDS, James Megellas, and I had visited it (9% ABC hamlets) that we could not go beyond the district town, refugees were returning, and the brigade was helping to rebuild a church in one hamlet. More had returned in the other northern districts. Of the 345,000 people in the four districts in mid-May, 150,000 were in hamlets rated D, E, or V; most were expected to be pacified before the end of the year. In the southern districts, similar dispositions were made by part of the 173rd, ARVN, and the Korean Tiger Division. Another battalion of the 173rd was assigned to Task Force South in Lam-Dong province. The key to territorial security and the return of refugees, and what distinguished these combined operations from earlier ones, was the assurance that the 173rd Airborne would remain indefinitely.[10] This was also the case with the Marine CAPs in I CTZ. Thus, the people gradually gained confidence that they would be protected. When the Koreans had pulled a regiment out of Phu-Yen province in April, General Corcoran, Commander of I Field Force and Senior Advisor to the GVN Corps Commander, had the regiment returned. About 9,500 refugees had returned home in that province by early May.[11]

In October 1969, shortly after I had taken over as Refugee Division Chief in I CTZ, I sent a memorandum to Alex Firfer, the Deputy for CORDS, telling about the Binh-Dinh military dispositions, which had by then resulted in the return of over 75,000 refugees to their homes, and said:

I realize that the conditions of warfare in this region are quite different than those in II CTZ; however, I wonder whether it may not be possible to utilize some of the lessons of the Binh Dinh experience to push out further with territorial security in support of pacification in some parts of the three southern provinces of this region.

A week later Firfer's deputy reported that the Commanding General of III MAF (Lt. General Nickerson) had been pressing the US divisions to do something like the CAPs. The American Division had broken two of its companies down in Quang-Ngai, and they were working in hamlets with the RF/PF.[12]

One could multiply these examples around the nation. The 1970 and 1971 pacification plans continued the emphasis on durable and expanding area security and other conditions that enabled refugees to go back to their homes. This persisted for some months even as US troops were phased down under President Nixon's Vietnamization plan.

The Minister made clear his determination that return to home villages must

be voluntary. When Colonel Hoang Dinh Tho, the province chief of Quang-
Tin, told Dr. Lu Y during a visit that he was determined to move refugees back
to their homes areas as soon as he felt that security permitted, the Minister
interjected firmly that under no circumstances were refugees to be forced to
return home. Return to village was not mandatory, he added. The Ministry itself
had originally set a limit of three months after a village was pacified during
which refugees must return in order to be eligible for the 919 allowances, but
then had second thoughts and did not insist on a rigid time limit.[13] It seems
probable that some refugees were pressed to return home before they were
convinced that security had in fact been restored. The Senate Refugee Subcommittee staff report that I have cited claimed that many refugees receiving RTV
payments never made the final move but were nonetheless reported as having
returned to village.[14] Their numbers do not seem to have been large, however.

THE OBJECTIVE: FULL REESTABLISHMENT
OF REFUGEES, ECONOMICALLY, SOCIALLY,
AND POLITICALLY

The program measures developed by John Thomas and Dr. Lu Y enabled the
Ministry and CORDS/REF to take advantage of the opportunities opened up by
the new pacification programs to help refugees to become self-supporting, either
by returning to their homes or by resettlement in more viable circumstances. We
knew that we had an enormous caseload, but now there would be more room
for refugees to live in. I was particularly concerned to help bring about that
economic viability that was a prerequisite to full reestablishment of the refugees
socially and as citizens. The efforts in that direction (described in the preceding
chapter) were not enough. Now the doors could open wider.

William Hitchcock, Ambassadors Bunker and Colby, and Dr. Lu Y broadened
our horizons to include the political dimension. They were conscious that the
huge numbers of refugees could be a critical factor, not only in supporting or
opposing the GVN, but in winning or losing the people's war. Hitchcock often
said that our objective must be to make the refugees viable and willing members
of an essentially participant society. This should be accomplished by melding
them into the general population. In his view, if this job were not done well,
resettling refugees in a way that satisfied them, the GVN might not be able to
contain such a large group of dissident people.[15] Dr. Lu Y never lost sight of
the fact that the refugees were voters, and this was recognized also by President
Thieu. The Minister urged his service chiefs to realize the strategic value of
active assistance to the refugees because they had abandoned Communism to
return to the national cause. (Dr. Lu Y was not naive about the fact that many
of them had been coerced into moving to GVN territory, a practice that the new
pacification programs discouraged.) His watchword was, "Spirit of community
collaboration."[16] Both the American and the Vietnamese leaders were also conscious that, largely through the Senate Subcommittee and the voluntary agencies,

the refugees had a constituency in the United States that could influence the amount of support provided to the total war effort.

The first objective of the refugee relief program stated in Annex IX of the 1969 Pacification and RD Program was "Fostering the refugees' anti-communist spirit." The second objective was assisting them in attaining self-sustenance. The program document listed several defects in refugee relief as it had been implemented up to then, including neglect by local administrations. Annex IX required that 300,000 refugees be returned. Plans for resettlement and return to village should be made in each province, assigning duties to all related government agencies.[17] This was a reiteration and strengthening of the policy that sites containing resettled or returned refugees were to be "localized," that is, incorporated into the regular village-hamlet structure, which made them the responsibility of the line Ministries and their provincial services, gave the vote to the refugees, and entitled their settlements to share in village self-development funds.

Although there was no opposition to accepting returned refugees into the system, many villages resisted incorporation of resettled refugees from other localities because they diluted the funds and other resources available to the natives. Also, as mentioned in the previous chapter, the regular Ministries had not budgeted for the assumption of these increased responsibilities in 1969, and were accordingly unwilling to stretch their funds and personnel to care for the refugees. Dr. Phieu told a meeting of the CORDS regional refugee officers in July that for the first time the whole government was giving attention to the refugee program, and Dick Holdren reported that in IV CTZ a page on refugees and return to village had been added to the handbook of the RD cadres, thus giving them responsibilities in this field. In Darlac province various other services were helping with the return to village. However, Bob Allen reported that in Binh-Dinh the service chiefs of most Ministries had not received instructions to cooperate in the effort and were not doing so. The II CTZ Deputy for CORDS said that although the Refugee Ministry needed assistance from other Ministries, resources of those other Ministries were not greater and bureaucracy was hampering progress.[18] Consequently, the MHSWR had to continue carrying responsibility for many thousands of refugees who were no longer on its rolls, with the result that a number of them received little assistance from any source. The problem was made worse by the pacification plans' increasingly stiff requirements to reduce the numbers of refugees. The plan for the second phase of 1969, for example, required the resettlement or return to village of 1,030,000 refugees, and this had been initiated by Minister Lu Y. He admitted that it was unrealistic, but did hope to achieve 600,000 by the end of the year.[19]

In an effort to cope with these problems, Mr. Hitchcock had his staff develop a draft CPDC directive on the reestablishment of the rural community, which would state in clear terms the responsibilities of the various GVN Ministries. This was discussed with MHSWR personnel while in preparation, and late in June Hitchcock took it up with Dr. Lu Y, who asked to present a document based on it to the CPDC, of which he was a member.[20] The directive was issued in August. After noting that the goals for phase one of the 1969 P and D plan had yet to be accomplished, the CPDC stated that the provincial P&D (pacification and development) councils had the mission of planning for both the permanent resettlement and the return home of all temporarily resettled refugees. The plans should include local government organization, security, construction of public facilities, and economic development. For the economic development task, specialists in such areas as agricultural business and animal husbandry were to help families to obtain credit, seed, fertilizer, and farm machinery, and to form cooperatives. The plans were to include funding from village and provincial budgets and which agencies were to support the effort. CPDC specifically tasked the MHSWR and Ministries of Interior, Land Reform and Agriculture; Public Works, Communication and Transport; Education and Youth; Revolutionary Development; National Defense; Information; and Ethnic Minorities Development with various aspects of the reestablishment process.[21]

The Ministry of Social Welfare followed this up with a communiqué outlining the various categories of refugees who were eligible for temporary, resettlement, or RTV assistance; it included people who, after January 1, 1969, left insecure hamlets that were not included in the 1969 pacification program. The directive specified when refugee sites were to be localized and the inhabitants normalized, that is, made full citizens again.[22] As stated in the previous chapter, it was some time before these instructions resulted in appreciable cooperation of other Ministries in the resettlement of refugees. However, their performance in helping refugees who had returned home was better. In both cases a strong and concerned province chief could enforce participation, as was the case in Thua-Thien.

The pacification programs did make provision for voluntary relocations of people from insecure areas, provided that they had advance approval in Saigon, and some of these occurred. One of the most successful, in Quang-Tri under the Accelerated Pacification Program, was the consolidation of about 12,000 fishermen who had lived under VC control for about 12 years in 14 hamlets from the border of Thua-Thien north to the Cua-Viet River. They were moved to a central location, screened for VC members, and then reestablished in Gia-Dang village with fishing privileges restored, boats licensed, and a new road to Quang-Tri city, so that they could market their catch. President Thieu presided over the dedication ceremony on December 19, 1968. On February 17, 1970, I accompanied Dr. Phieu to a ceremony in which he presented new boat motors to the refugees. Military civic action built two schools, three dispensaries, two marketplaces, and latrines and wells. Two RF companies remained to protect the village; contact with the enemy was rare.[23]

Refugees returned in record numbers (officially 488,220 of them) to their home villages in 1969, as territorial security returned. They were not transported by the GVN or US forces, but went on their own, carrying their meager possessions. Once at their home villages, they received the allowances and varying amounts of development assistance. They had no difficulty in reclaiming their land.[24] Thua-Thien led both in numbers of returnees (over 128,000) and in the imaginative ways by which they established themselves. The refugees, at the suggestion of Province Chief Colonel Than, decided to use half of their monetary allowances to buy 232 Kubota garden tillers, two each for their 116 hamlets. Each of the machines had the power of eight water buffalo (which had all been lost when the people had fled from their homes), and they were equipped to cultivate flooded rice paddies. The US Navy had carried them without charge from Japan to Da-Nang; they reached a demonstration farm near Hue late in November, where operators from the villages were trained by provincial experts. At a ceremony early on December 7, 1969 they were turned over to representatives of the hamlets. Ambassador Colby took off his shoes, rolled up his pants, and steered one of the tillers around a rice paddy.[25] The farm vehicle maintenance center, located in the Hue citadel, stocked spare parts for the Kubotas and trained farmers in their repair.

More refugees went back home in 1970 to areas that had been in VC hands for many years, including the infamous Street Without Joy, so named by the French who had been defeated there by the Viet-Minh. These returnees bought not only the Kubota tillers but also four large Minneapolis-Moline tractors with disc plows. In company with Colonel Than, Mr. Firfer, and others, including AID/Washington refugee advisor Johannes Hoeber, I saw these at work in May 1970. As we visited hamlet after hamlet, we met many busy and happy people who were rebuilding their lives from scratch. We traveled without military escort, as the province chief, dressed in peasant black pajamas, was wont to do; he was recognized and warmly greeted by his people. On other occasions I flew over this and other RTV areas, which one could distinguish by the sparkling aluminum roofs on the widely spaced houses and the newly plowed fields and rice paddies.[26]

Farther south in I CTZ, especially in Quang-Tin province, there was a tendency by province officials and the US military to require returning refugees, as well as those declared resettled, to live in tight little hamlets surrounded by barbed wire, much like the strategic hamlets of the early 1960s. While those configurations may have been militarily necessary, they probably dampened the allegiance of the inhabitants to the GVN.

Alex Firfer was the author of a plan, conceived in the fall of 1969, to retake from the Communists Go-Noi Island in the Vu-Gia River near Hoi-An, Quang-Nam province, and return up to 27,000 refugees to their home villages there. The refugees were then living in various temporary camps in Dien-Ban district. The island was totally deserted and was a wasteland. Just north of a VC stronghold in the Que-Son mountains, it was a very dangerous place. Colonel Tin, the province chief, requested from Corps Commander General Lam permission to recruit four new RF companies, and he wanted a company of US Marines to break down into small units working with the RF/PF to secure the area, beginning late in December. The province senior advisor agreed. The province submitted the "Dong-Tien" plan on October 30, and it was approved by General Lam. However, it took many months to bring it to realization. The MSW initially approved allowances for 11,928 returnees, but refused to allow direct extraction of funds for agricultural machines from the allowances. Both ARVN and US military units, as well as the ROK Marines, provided security and substantial civic action support. In May 1970, the first refugees moved into what was to become Phu-Ky village at the eastern end of the island, and by June 3, some 1,115 people were settled there. By October, 2,500 refugees were building their homes and public facilities in two villages. Then Typhoon Kate inundated the island, forcing the evacuation of its inhabitants with only such possessions as they could carry. It meant that they had to start over again.[27] The project was a success, but it had involved an inordinate amount of effort by both GVN and US civilian and military officials.

With much less hoopla, about 10,000 other refugees returned home elsewhere in the province during 1969, and many more in the other two provinces in southern I CTZ; 47,206 of them returned in Quang-Ngai, 23,280 in Quang-Tin, and 18,759 went back home in Quang-Tri.[28] That progress continued in 1970.

Next to Thua-Thien, Binh-Dinh province had the largest number of returnees in 1969, over 90,000. However, they had a much more difficult time getting reestablished, because of inadequate resources to cope with the immense destruction and delays in receiving their RTV allowances. The same was true of Phu-Yen province. In many areas the brush was so thick that it could not be cleared by hand or plow. Roads were in poor shape, and most bridges were destroyed and wells choked up. As stated above, the regular Ministries and their services had made no provision for assisting the newly pacified hamlets. The 173rd Airborne and the Koreans had helped greatly in their areas of operation. My II CTZ refugee report for June-July 1969 added this comment: "One fact which the reoccupation of these hamlets has highlighted is that the VC did nothing for the people when they were in control."[29] There was almost no return to home villages in the mountain provinces.

IV Corps was scarcely behind I CTZ in the number of refugees who returned home in 1969—184,080.[30] In that lush region, much had to be done in clearing abandoned canals, rebuilding houses, and clearing rice fields, but it was easier and more quickly accomplished than in the harsher provinces to the north. In Region 3, few people went home because security remained tenuous in the western provinces and many refugees were satisfactorily resettled elsewhere.

In 1969, aside from the return of 488,220 refugees (by the official statistics, actually about 581,000) to their home villages, the GVN paid resettlement allowances to 586,388 refugees and dropped them from the rolls, ending the year with 268,252 refugees in the active caseload.[31] Since the official count was 1,328,517 refugees at the beginning of the year, that would indicate that only 14,511 new refugees were generated during the whole of 1969. That is not credible. Even using the unofficial but probably more accurate figure of 581,264 refugees returned home yields a figure of 107,553 new refugees during the year. As we shall show in chapter 11, that also was an understatement because many people who were brought out forcibly from insecure areas were not recognized by province chiefs as refugees. Moreover, some of those who had returned to their home villages had already been resettled; so an unknown number were double counted. Another 476,000 were registered during the year for out-of-camp benefits, but had not been shown in the statistics at the time. Getting an accurate count of refugees was truly a tricky business.

The 1970 Pacification and Development Program aimed at bringing 100% of the population into A, B, C hamlets. Once again, this was to be done by bringing security to people, not people to security. It was not realistic and caused many abuses. The emphasis of the program was on the village, both rural and urban, stressing meaningful community participation in decision making through elections, control of village self-development funds, self-defense, and self-help.

The refugee portion of the plan was called "A Brighter Life for War Victims." This assimilated refugees formally into the broader category of war victims, reversing the terminology of the August 1968 communiqué, "Definition of a Refugee." The MSW was more cautious than in the preceding year in setting numerical targets for return to village, recognizing that return had to be voluntary, but aimed at 500,000 returnees, resettling 200,000 pre-1969 refugees and all who had been generated in 1969. The Minister released 220,000,000 $VN of 1970 resettlement funds to the provinces early in December 1969, so as to avoid some of the delays that had plagued the 1969 effort. In addition, the MSW planned to take care of 15,000 war victims turned over by the Ministry of Defense.[32]

This time, the province refugee plans were supposed to be built up from plans for all sites, aimed at completing their facilities and making them viable. After the astonishing successes of the previous year in returning about 581,000 refugees to their homes, and with the continuing extension of territorial security, this became a realistic objective in all except the three southern provinces of I CTZ and such places as Cam-Lo and Ha-Thanh; even there, progress was possible. Some provincial social welfare (SW) service chiefs did prepare good plans. For example, Le Dam in Quang-Ngai was already preparing his 1970 plan in October 1969. He listed all families that did not have fully employed adults, that is, those who were indigent for some reason, and presented the welfare cases to the Red Cross. He agreed that refugees who were still in unsatisfactory sites should continue to receive development assistance from his service and be kept on the rolls, even if they had received all their allowances.[33] Other service chiefs were not as conscientious, and traveling delegations from the MSW and CPDC in the winter and spring of 1970 made them revise their plans.[34]

However, as late as the end of April, when President Thieu said in a meeting that temporary refugee centers must be turned over to regular administration or the individuals must be resettled elsewhere as soon as possible, Dr. Phieu asked that the other Ministries include in their budgets provisions to help such communities. The President replied that the province chiefs could twist certain of his other programs to give such assistance; and to the Minister's complaint that the province chiefs were frequently reluctant to accept hamlets as resettled, he directed that the MSW develop special programs for those hamlets, involving the province chiefs and other Ministry assistance.[35] This was not a very helpful instruction.

As refugees continued to return to their homes and others were technically resettled, there was a growing contradiction between rapidly decreasing refugee numbers and the continuing need for money and other support for refugees who officially did not exist. There had long been a reporting category, ''In resettlement process,'' for refugees who had not received all their allowances, but it did not cover those who had been paid but were still in unsatisfactory sites. In Region I we instructed our refugee advisors to keep the sites in the ADP reports, even though their inhabitants were no longer counted as refugees. As of April 1970, still another category was added, ''In return-to-village process,'' which meant those who had not received all their RTV allowances. That added 239,570 refugees to the April figure, bringing the total on the rolls to 584,794. By June, the total was 602,024, after which it declined slowly.[36] The 1970 year-end figures showed 129,000 new refugees plus 281,000 generated in previous years but newly registered for out-of-camp or RTV benefits, 388,000 returned home, and 228,000 paid resettlement benefits, leaving 137,000 in the active caseload.[37]

VIETNAMESE REFUGEES FROM CAMBODIA

The refugee figures above do not include 200,000 ethnic Vietnamese refugees who came from Cambodia in the spring and summer of 1970. Until the Vietnamese conquered a portion in the middle of the eighteenth century, all of the Mekong Delta had been part of Cambodia.[38] For generations thereafter, Vietnamese and Cambodians had lived on both sides of the border, with about a million ethnic Cambodians in Viet-Nam, comprising the majority in some provinces, and about 400,000 ethnic Vietnamese in Cambodia, principally in the cities. After about 1960, the North Vietnamese used a strip of eastern Cambodia as part of the Ho Chi Minh trail and also used the road from Cambodia's only port, Sihanoukville (later Kompong Som) as a supply route for their forces and the VC in South Viet-Nam. After the overthrow of Cambodia's Prince Sihanouk in March 1970, the new Lon Nol government had systematically stirred up resentment against the ethnic Vietnamese, believing that they were infiltrated by the Communists. Soon bodies began floating down the Mekong, and those who could moved to Viet-Nam via commercial airliner to Saigon and across the border. After the beginning on April 30 of the combined US-Vietnamese operation against the VC/NVA sanctuaries on the Cambodian side of the border, during which both armies were responsible for much destruction of villages and some soldiers committed atrocities against the civilian population, hatred of the Vietnamese increased and massacres occurred. By late May, almost 75,000 Vietnamese from Cambodia had entered the III and IV Corps areas. Another 125,000 were evacuated after negotiations that Dr. Phieu conducted with the

Lon Nol government of Cambodia. Having been Surgeon General of the RVN Navy, he was able to get Navy vessels to move the refugees.[39]

The GVN put Dr. Phan Quang Dan at the head of an interministerial committee in charge of the relief and resettlement of these people. They were not classified by the GVN as refugees, but rather as Vietnamese repatriates. This caused considerable confusion at first, since they did not fit the MSW categories of refugees or war victims; and the new arrangements delayed relief payments and other GVN assistance for a while. However, temporary camps were set up in Tay-Ninh (which I visited in July), Chau-Doc, and other provinces, including the Dong-Tam army base in Dinh-Tuong, which the US Ninth Division had just left. On July 9, Dr. Dan issued Decree 311 which eased the procedures for registering and paying the refugees. The local people of the Delta area were hospitable, helping to build houses, donating food, offering jobs, and so forth. Many of the refugees were skilled workers, who had no difficulty finding employment. There was an upsurge of national pride, especially in IV CTZ, on account of ARVN's successful foray into the Communist sanctuaries and the success of ARVN and the GVN in handling the reception and resettlement of their compatriots. Interestingly, after the ARVN troops returned in July, the pace of pacification picked up, and normal refugee return to village increased in Kien-Hoa, Vinh-Binh (a province with a majority of ethnic Cambodians), Dinh-Tuong, An-Xuyen (much of which had been VC-controlled), Bac-Lieu, and Kien-Phong.[40]

Since these were in fact international refugees in the sense of the Convention and Protocol (although most had Vietnamese nationality), in April the GVN requested the assistance of the United Nations High Commissioner for Refugees, who allocated $50,000 and sent a chargé de mission to Saigon.[41] This assistance was largely of symbolic importance.

Dr. Dan took considerable pride in this resettlement effort, and it set the stage for his later assumption of responsibility for interzonal resettlement, which will be the subject of chapter 13.

LAND TO THE TILLER, A MOST IMPORTANT REFORM

Law 003/70 passed by the National Assembly and signed by President Thieu in March 1970 was perhaps the most important reform in the pacification process. Unlike the weak and aborted land reform instituted by Diem, this measure distributed titles to 1,136,705 hectares (over 2.8 million acres), 45.8% of the total rice-land in the country over the next several years, and virtually wiped out tenant farming, especially in the Mekong Delta, where it had been most prevalent. During the law's development, some influential people had urged that priority be given to supporters of the government, but the drafters, supported by President Thieu, decided that the land should go to the persons who were then tilling it, even though some of them had previously been installed by the VC. Fortunately, most of the refugees who wanted to return to their land had done so (except for thousands of Montagnards who had been forcibly relocated) by the time titles were actually issued, and there were evidently few cases where squatters or VC partisans received land that had previously belonged to Vietnamese refugees. Moreover, unlike the Communists, who had given only provisional ownership contingent upon continued loyalty, the GVN gave permanent titles—free. The measure was a clear political, economic, and social success.[42] The refugees for once also participated in something that was a benefit to them.

CONTINUATION OF THE REFUGEE–SOCIAL WELFARE PROGRAM

The 1971 pacification program pretty well exhausted the possibilities for returning refugees to their home villages, mainly because it extended territorial security as far as the GVN could now that US combat troops were for the most part gone. That still left large areas, especially in the mountains, in the hands of the enemy or insecure, but one could drive in safety through almost all of the coastal plain and the Mekong Delta, at least in the daytime. In 1971, some 566,000 refugees were reported as returning home, but this included 300,000 in the process of receiving RTV allowances, who may actually have returned in previous years. Another 127,000 were paid resettlement allowances, leaving an active caseload of 94,000 on the rolls.[43] All told, about a million and a half refugees had returned to their home villages since the Accelerated Pacification program began in 1968, a remarkable achievement. It was by far the best way of reestablishing displaced persons economically, socially, and politically, akin to the voluntary repatriation of international refugees. Development work continued on both resettlement and RTV sites, and now this represented more than merely completing latrines and wells. For example, some Quang-Tri refugees decided to purchase livestock with development funds. In Thua-Thien the P&D Council made 18,640,000 $VN available to purchase 13 large tractors for refugee sites.[44]

On the other hand, in order to meet their pacification targets, many province chiefs and military commanders, especially in Military Regions 1 and 2, forcibly moved large numbers of people into supposedly secure areas in 1969, 1970, and 1971, usually without getting the required advance approval of the CPDC. This was the dark side of pacification "progress," which will be discussed in the next chapter.

AID budgetary support of refugees and social welfare peaked in 1969, but remained substantial in 1970, declining in 1971. One would like to believe that support of other aspects of pacification picked up the slack, but that could not be demonstrated. Total AID support was higher in all years than had previously been planned because, although direct dollar amounts were lower, PL 480 commodities were increased over previously budgeted amounts until FY 1971, and the piasters available to the Ministry were considerably greater. This had the effect of shifting more responsibility for day-to-day management from CORDS to the Ministry. In addition to these amounts, voluntary agencies put in substantial assistance, and foreign donors contributed lesser sums. All in all, the refugee and social welfare program received adequate resources through the Ministry, but other parts of the GVN did not give sufficient support when the refugees became ordinary citizens again.

11

The Dark Side

While the pacification successes described in the previous chapter were being achieved, the dreadful business of killing went on. Indeed, a necessary condition of extending territorial security was more efficient identification of Communist forces and cadres and their elimination by killing, capture, and induced surrender. For the most part, the GVN and its allies improved their observance of the laws of war, but there were some grievous lapses. The Communists on the other hand intensified their targeting of civilians, including refugees, for both selective and indiscriminate murder. Both sides violated the human rights of the people; the Communists by terror, the US and GVN by forced mass relocations and re-grouping of populations. This, then, was the dark side of the seemingly endless war.

MY-LAI AND OTHER AMERICAN ATROCITIES

On March 16–17, 1968, the worst atrocity committed by US forces occurred in Son-My village, Son-Tinh district of Quang-Ngai province. In My-Lai 4 and some adjacent subhamlets, units of the 11th Brigade of the Americal Division gunned down in cold blood between 175 and 347 noncombattant women, children, and old men after raping some of the women. They also killed their livestock and burned their dwellings. The US units had been briefed that they would encounter a VC battalion, but in fact they received no enemy fire and suffered no casualties except one self-inflicted wound.

The incident was covered up at all levels including division headquarters until it was revealed a year later by a Viet-Nam veteran. Only one officer, Lt. William L. Calley, a platoon commander, was convicted in a court martial; others, including Major General Samuel H. Koster, commander of the Americal Division, received letters of censure or no punishment at all, a fact which General William R. Peers, who headed an official inquiry for the US Army, deplored.[1]

A factor that contributed to this atrocity, General Peers found, was lack of proper training of soldiers and officers alike in the law of war, the safeguarding of noncombatants, and the rules of engagement. The Americal Division had not adequately communicated or enforced its own policies regarding the protection of civilians. Peers found evidence that well before the My-Lai operation there had been instances of mistreatment, rape, and unnecessary killings in the task force concerned and perhaps in other units as well. Even more important was the attitude of some soldiers and officers toward the Vietnamese people. General Peers wrote:

The most disturbing factor we encountered was the low regard in which some of the men held the Vietnamese, especially rural or farming people. This attitude appeared to have been particularly strong in Charlie Company [the unit that was responsible for the worst atrocities], some of whose men viewed the Vietnamese with contempt, considering them subhuman, on the level of dogs. . . . Some of the men never referred to Vietnamese as anything but "gooks," "dinks," or "slopes." During my time in Vietnam I had never heard these terms used so universally, and I think I lived fairly close to the troops. . . . Undoubtedly, this attitude was partly the result of the mines and booby traps that had killed or maimed so many men in their units. Many of the men thought that these devices had been laid by the women, children, and old men or that if Vietnamese civilians had not actually planted them they at least knew where the devices were, but never warned the American troops.[2]

Charlie Company in particular was in a state of fear and tension before the operation, having suffered 20 casualties from mines and booby traps in the area, without ever being able to establish contact with the enemy. The general added that it was difficult to distinguish combatants from noncombatants, an observation that was shared by all American fighting men in the country. Moreover, in this particular case, the GVN officials considered that all the inhabitants of the area were VC or sympathizers and didn't care what was done to them.[3]

My own view, based on two and a half years of experience on the ground, is that the inability of the American troops and most of their officers to communicate with the Vietnamese people in the countryside contributed greatly to a sense of alienation and fear. The village scene in the movie "Platoon," whose producer had been a combat soldier, admirably illustrated this isolation and frustration and its tragic consequences.

That My-Lai was by no means the only wanton killing of civilians by American troops was frankly admitted by other soldiers who talked with newsmen, and by one who later wrote a book about his experiences. They asserted that murder, rape, and robbery were commonplace, and the reasons they cited were similar to those General Peers had found in the Americal Division.[4] Some soldiers and officers have said the same thing to me. However, I have no specific information about other such incidents.

My-Lai and the trial of Lieutenant Calley were widely publicized in the United States and undoubtedly contributed to the growing antiwar sentiment among our people. Some reforms were instituted in the practices of the US Army with regard to indoctrination of troops and officers, according to General Peers, but how effective they have been is a matter of conjecture.

In Viet-Nam there was no large public outcry about the incident. General Tran Van Don, who, as Chairman of the Defense Committee of the Vietnamese Senate, had conducted an on-site investigation, explained it this way: "Our people had been quite accustomed to such wanton destruction of life. This was only one of many similar cases where innocent people were killed during a long war going back to 1940. Both sides were guilty of this kind of conduct."[5]

COMMUNIST ATROCITIES

Even though it was not unique among violations of the law of war by US forces, the My-Lai massacre was something that official policy condemned and top commanders tried to prevent. This cannot be said of the Viet-Cong or the North Vietnamese Army (NVA). Their attacks on civilians were deliberate and frequently indiscriminate, intended to terrorize the survivors and bend them to the Communist will.

In the period 1968 through 1971, many of the VC/NVA attacks were on refugee sites, with the objective of forcing the inhabitants to return to Communist-controlled territory. Thus, for example, in the four months from May through August 1968, there were 45 such attacks in I and II CTZ alone. In the last two of those months over 1,725 houses were destroyed, over 53 refugees were killed, more than 112 were wounded, and over 36 were abducted.[6] The attacks continued through the rest of 1968 and into 1969, despite the fact that the VC had been considerably weakened by the Têt and May offensives of 1968.[7]

VC booby traps killed and wounded many innocent people. For example, on December 30, 1968, in Thua-Thien province, one booby trap tripped by a water buffalo killed a 12-year-old boy walking beside the animal; another killed one civilian and wounded another who were clearing around a grave site.[8]

In late February and early March 1969, the VC staged a post-Têt countrywide offensive, concentrating in I CTZ. Refugee sites bore the brunt of the offensive. As of February 28, the attacks had killed 228 civilians, wounded 596, destroyed 2,334 houses, and made 18,457 war victims. By March 10, the number of victims of the attacks had climbed to 23,877, with 4,104 houses destroyed. At least 81 separate attacks by fire and on the ground were listed in the admittedly incomplete CORDS reports.[9] A few of the most serious incidents were:

- A VC mortar attack on the Voung-Lai refugee camp in Tam-Ky, Quang-Tin province, on February 23, killed 18, wounded 59, destroyed 25 houses, and damaged 11 more.

- That same day, in an attack on Phuoc-My hamlet, Tien-Phuoc district, Quang-Tin, the VC murdered 20 children.

- A VC attack on the Kon Horing highlander refugee camp in Kontum province on February 24 killed 68, wounded 67, burned 177 long-houses (multifamily dwellings typical of Montagnard areas) and made 2,698 people homeless. Most of those killed and injured had been in their bunkers and could not escape.

- On February 22, VC attacks in the Song-Be area of Phuoc-Long province destroyed 644 houses and made war victims of 877 families with 5,686 people. The number of casualties was unknown at the time of the report.

- Two rocket attacks on Saigon on March 3 and 6 killed 55 people, wounded 117, and destroyed 91 houses.

- A VC attack on My-Tho town on February 25 killed 10, wounded 84, and made 200 people homeless.

- VC attacks in three districts of Chau-Doc province during February 22–28 wounded 83 people and made 6,575 homeless.

The response of both the SWR services and CORDS to Communist assaults was rapid and effective. As early as June 1966, the GVN had placed refugee relief imprest funds which could be used without prior Saigon approval in the hands of province chiefs.[10] The system of emergency response was improved in subsequent years, especially after the Têt offensive of 1968. The imprest funds as well as commodities stockpiled by CORDS and the Ministry in province warehouses were used after VC attacks. Generally, GVN and US personnel, including some from military units, were on the afflicted sites within hours. This was important to the survivors, who were usually in a state of shock and exposed to the elements. Tents, tarpaulins, and other shelter materials, along with blankets, food, and household utensils were the standard relief items. Voluntary agencies in the areas were equally prompt in responding; coordination among the various elements was good.

After the February–March 1969 attacks described above, Dr. Lu Y visited Kontum, Da-Nang, and Quang-Nam on March 2 and 3, dispensing checks to the province chiefs and promising further relief assistance if needed. Mr. Hu'ng, together with the National Assemblyman from the province, visited Chau-Doc on March 5, releasing funds for assistance.[11]

As a result of the tragic happenings at Kon Horing and some other places (where people were trapped and suffocated in their bunkers), the Refugee Division and the Community Development Foundation, which was training the Ministry's mobile teams, disseminated information on the proper construction of bunkers under houses, primarily to provide air supply and outside exits. The help of CORDS community development personnel was enlisted to get these guidelines out to the general population.[12] Since both US forces and ARVN were prone to assume that houses with sturdy bunkers must belong to VC families, CORDS/REF through MACV told those forces what it was doing.

There was another spike in the number of VC attacks on refugee sites in May 1969, which was concentrated in Quang-Ngai and Quang-Nam. Two Ministry mobile team members were abducted on May 13 near Quang-Ngai city; one of them was later found dead, while the other was missing and presumed killed. In Binh-Dinh, Darlac, and Long-An there were attacks against the general population.[13]

Communist Party Decision No. 9 of 1969 directed that refugee camps were to be main targets for attack in the new year.[14] A rash of attacks on refugee sites and others on the general population in I CTZ did occur during late December 1969 and January 1970, killing 101 people, wounding 254, abducting 14, and making 282 homeless.[15] Similar assaults continued in subsequent months. One of these, on April 10, destroyed twin refugee camps in Quang-Nam province, Ngan-Cau and Tu-Cau, which had been created by the forcible relocation of their inhabitants. GVN officials and the province senior advisor reacted with speed, visiting the sites and sending food and roofing, as well as a culture-drama team (a troupe of Vietnamese entertainers presenting government themes in a light manner), and information service (VIS) personnel.[16] Less than a month later, there were 15 attacks on civilian targets in the same province, including Hoi-An City, two refugee camps, and a civilian bus (destroyed by a mine which killed 25 and wounded 5) in a four-day period.[17]

I visited a number of places after these attacks, especially in I CTZ. One such visit was to Ba-Ren hamlet in Que-Son district, Quang-Nam, with acting SWR regional inspector Pham Huu Nhan and the CORDS province refugee and development chief Jim Ready, a day after a VC mortar attack at about 2 A.M. June 11, 1970 had killed 70 civilians, wounded 83, and destroyed 345 houses. This was one of the worst man-made disasters I had ever seen. The survivors were silent in their grief and shock. They had already buried their dead and were picking up bits and pieces of their possessions. The SWR service had sent cloth and soap. Christian Youth Social Service had brought a truckload of PL 480 bulgur and rolled oats, and a US military civic action team had arrived with lumber and more bulgur. The province was preparing to pay the surviving victims. It was hard to gauge the attitudes of the people, but my belief was that they were full of resentment and fear of the VC and silently appreciative of the help that their government, CYSS, and the Americans had brought, while perhaps wondering why the powerful US and GVN military forces could not protect them.[18]

A few days later (on June 16) I accompanied the assistant SWR inspector to the capital of Thuong-Duc district, the most remote in Quang-Nam province, where, at the order of the Prime Minister, he was to inspect three refugee camps that had been burned by the VC within the past month. Virtually the whole town seemed to be in ruins, including what had been an attractive market. Some rice and bulgur had been delivered, but the people needed more food urgently. The local price of rice had gone up to 2,500 $VN (over $21 US in 1970) for a bag of 100 pounds of American rice, or 5,000 $VN for a 100-kilo bag of Vietnamese rice; for most people that was unaffordable. The district chief had also requested roofing sheets. Bulgur and roofing were to be sent the following day.[19]

A year later, CORDS/REF I CTZ reported that in the first six months of

Table 10
Hospital Admissions Summary

CY	All causes Totals	Civilian war casualties		
		Totals	GVN hosp.	US mil. hosp.
1967	473,140	48,734	46,783	1,951
1968	456,972	84,492	76,702	7,790
1969	525,772	67,767	59,223	8,544
1970	574,814	50,882	46,247	4,635
1971	597,423	39,395	38,318	1,077

Source: Statement of Robert H. Nooter, Deputy Coordinator, Bureau of Supporting Assistance, AID, presented to the Senate Refugee Subcommittee, May 8, 1972, 40.

1971, enemy attacks and terrorism had again increased, generating 54,329 war victims, 1,049 of whom had been killed and 1,367 wounded; 8,404 homes had been damaged, most of them by over 50%. The demands for emergency relief were such that the normal resettlement and return-to-village program was temporarily suspended. This occurred after 889,520 refugees and war victims had returned home, most of them in the previous two and a half years.[20] Clearly, despite all the progress of pacification, the Communists were still inflicting grievous harm to the population, especially in the three southern provinces of Military Region 1.

CIVILIAN WAR CASUALTIES

Table 10 summarizes civilian war casualties as measured by admissions to GVN and US military hospitals. These statistics show that, while total hospital admissions went up during the period under review, civilian war casualty admissions peaked in 1968, the year of the Têt and May offensives, and declined thereafter. They were still high in 1971, despite the progress of pacification and the fact that most of the large-unit fighting had been pushed away from populated areas. However, as the above section on Communist atrocities makes clear, VC terrorism in the populated centers had not by any means stopped. These statistics of course do not include the war victims who were killed outright, nor do they take account of those who were only slightly injured or who, for other reasons, could not get to hospitals.

The Ministry of Health collected data from its hospitals on principal causes of war-related injuries; these could be attributed to the opposing sides as follows: mine and mortar, generally the enemy; gun or grenade, either side; shelling or bombing, usually the allies. Table 11 shows the trend. The figures indicate that in every year the Communists accounted for more war-wounded civilians than

Table 11
Civilian War-Related Casualties, by Cause of Injury

Cause of Injury	1968	1969	1970	1971	1972
Mine or mortar	34,500	27,464	35,989	24,891	33,044
Gun or grenade	16,292	13,298	9,876	7,528	10,676
Shelling or bombing	28,454	16,696	9,163	7,241	10,061
Totals	79,246	57,458	55,028	39,660	53,781

Source: "Followup Review of Refugee, War Casualty, Civilian Health and Social Welfare Problems in South Vietnam," by the Comptroller General of the United States, printed in the hearing record of the Senate Refugee Subcommittee, *Humanitarian Problems in Indochina*, July 18, 1974, 154. The data were obtained from the revised annual statistics of the Ministry of Health relating to GVN hospitals; those are considered more precise than the figures in Nooter's statement of two years earlier.

the allies, and that their margin increased as the United States phased down its combat troops and limited air strikes. It will be recalled (chapter 6) that in 1967 the allies accounted for somewhat more civilian casualties than the Communists. As reported above, 1970 was a year of particularly intense VC terrorist attacks on the civilian population. In all years the VC and NVA expended much less ammunition than the allies, but deliberately targeted the civilian population as well as the opposing troops. All the figures increased from 1971 to 1972 because of the NVA Easter offensive in the latter year, which will be recounted in the next chapter.

RELOCATION OF PEOPLE

Despite the often restated principle of the 1969 and following pacification plans—bring security to the people, not people to security—many mass population relocations, most of them involuntary, were conducted in those years. However, the CORDS refugee officers and Ministry officials, who previously had passively accepted and tried to care for whatever refugees the military forces brought in, were becoming increasingly insistent on having a voice in relocation decision making. Gradually, with strong support from Ambassador Colby, we were able to bring about some modulation of the most objectionable practices.

The problem was not simple. In some cases the people themselves were anxious to escape from Communist terror and exploitation but could not. They managed to get word to GVN or US forces, and operations were mounted to extract them. Some of these, for instance in Phu-Bon province, were well planned; sufficient new land was made available for cultivation, and they were successful. However, too often the SWR service and CORDS had not been notified or consulted in advance, for security reasons, so the many preparations necessary for a successful relocation, such as providing food, shelter, land, or employment opportunities for a viable settlement could not be carried out. Those relocations might be intrinsically desirable, but the result was often that the refugees were miserable and resentful of the authorities, which vitiated a principal potential benefit of the operations. In other cases the military commanders conceived relocations as means of denying the people and their resources to the enemy, bringing them under GVN control, and making free fire zones of their former dwelling places. However, what they usually did not take into account was that they were disrupting the lives of people, breaking up intelligence nets, and bringing a disgruntled mass, often including VC cadres and sympathizers, into GVN territory, without preparation for their care, and where means of enabling them to make a living were absent. Again, the result was most often increased resentment and disaffection. The more hastily they were executed, the worse the effect. Sometimes the very areas from which the people were relocated were scheduled for pacification in later months. In the cases of both voluntary and involuntary movement, lack of careful thought and planning in advance all too frequently botched what might have been successful resettlements, or caused relocations which did not need to take place at all.

The Ministry and some of the higher levels of the GVN, as well as CORDS, had learned some lessons from many previous unhappy relocations such as those described in chapter 7. In February 1969, the Prime Minister's office issued instructions on the implementation of the 1969 Pacification and Development Plan listing as the first of eight objectives that 90% of the population was to be under GVN control by the end of the year, but also under that heading addressing the relocation problem:

1. a. (3) Evacuation of people should not be advised because of following disadvantages:

   (a) Political disadvantage because evacuation of people entails desertion of land.

   (b) Evacuation of people entails a relief problem for the province.

   (c) Evacuation of people entails trouble in daily activities of those subject to evacuation. In case an evacuation is needed, concerned provinces must report to the Central Pacification and Development Council and will not carry out the evacuation until approval by this Council.[21]

Vice Premier Tran Khiem followed this up with a stronger message in April, and General Cao Van Vien, Chief of the Joint General Staff, sent instructions to all RVNAF commands specifying the procedures which were to be followed in all population movements.[22]

The key points of these instructions and the increasingly stringent ones that followed were that relocation of people should generally be avoided, but when it was considered necessary, plans for resettlement had to be made *and submitted to the CPDC for approval in advance*. Unfortunately, for most of the next two years these directives were honored more in the breach than in the observance. I took the lead in calling attention to many poorly conceived and unauthorized forced relocations, especially in I CTZ, and a number of my colleagues in the provinces all over the country did likewise.

Relocations in the I Corps Tactical Zone

Operation Russell Beach

One of the first operations undertaken under the Accelerated Pacification Program, code-named "Russell Beach," was conducted in January 1969 on the Batangan Peninsula of Quang-Ngai and part of Son-My village just to the south. It had been carefully planned by the US forces, with some help from the SWR service and the American Red Cross. Billed as a large "county fair," it swept the Communist-controlled area, killing some hundreds of VC and destroying their fortifications and tunnels as well as all the houses, gathering over 12,000 inhabitants into a tent encampment called "Resurrection City," where they were screened for VC cadres, after which they were to be returned home. The promise of returning the refugees to their home villages after about a month was what got the approval of the GVN and CORDS/REF. John Thomas took his successor, William Hitchcock, Johannes Hoeber of AID/Washington, and Alexander Firfer, ICTZ Deputy for CORDS (DFC)–designate, to visit the site late in January. The SWR service dug wells and latrines, and provided food, cooking utensils, and paper blankets. The children, equipped with CARE kits, went to school in tents, taught by teachers supplied by the Ministry of Education and the RD cadres.[23] However, since the operation was conducted in the middle of the rainy season in that region, when it was quite cold, both shelter and blankets were insufficient, and five infants died of exposure. Additional blankets had to be rushed to the tent city. The Refugee Division report commented: "Urgent requests for unprogrammed support underscore the need for more exhaustive coordination regarding the refugee aspect of military operations, particularly large-scale cordon-and-search efforts."[24]

By the latter part of February, the Quang-Ngai province plan for returning the refugees was complete, and 42 million piasters had been approved in principle to provide rice, milk, and reconstruction allowances. RD cadres and US Marine CAP teams had been introduced to the refugees and were stationed in the areas to which they were to be returned. The operation was to be terminated by April 20.[25]

The initial RTV allowances were paid. However, it turned out that the people were not allowed to rebuild on their old homesites but were clustered tightly together in poor houses in new hamlets, guarded by three CAP teams, two RF companies, 400 men of the Americal Division, and 400 ARVN soldiers. Some 2,000 refugees who came from Son-My village were put behind a fence of sharpened bamboo stakes on the edge of a barren hill. Only My-Lai 4 was safe enough to permit cultivation of the land.[26]

From October 23 through December 10, 1969, Le Dam, the able SWR service chief of Quang-Ngai, distributed PL 480 corn meal and rolled oats, a small quantity of rice, and the remainder of the returnees' RTV payments. He reported that the people were not starving but were very poor, earning their living day by day, and had to have the district headquarters buy and transport rice to them. When the weather was bad, they ate manioc, sweet potatoes, and corn.[27]

In January 1970, Tong Quyen, the able and aggressive I CTZ Social Welfare Inspector sent a comprehensive report on the status of the returnees, who numbered 12,196. The 6,411 inhabitants of three former villages in the Tam-Son area were now concentrated in two of the villages, so there was a shortage of farmland. Those from Son-Quang village who were at Son-Hai village could not earn a living and were starving, he said. The fishermen in Son-Hai were in their original location and had over 200 boats with motors, so they were all right. The inhabitants of the third village, Son-My, had recently been permitted to return home, and their lives had improved somewhat. In the Tam-Binh area, the 5,785 inhabitants of three villages were concentrated in one of them, Binh-Duc; those from the two other villages were starving, he said. In the Phu-Chi hamlet of Binh-Duc village, 275 families with 1,026 people were confined within a barbed wire fence and were starving; they had to eat manioc in place of rice. A few of them collected seaweed for sale to the Americans. Many of them did not have the customary straw sleeping mats and used sandbags. There was a lack of blankets. Transport of foreign-supplied food by air and sea was erratic because of the weather. The inspector recommended that the province return the people to their original hamlets after they were pacified, or at least to locations where they could work their land, and that the security perimeters be opened to permit access to the land. He further recommended that an additional month's food allowance be given, and that breeder pigs, chickens, and other animal husbandry and agricultural supplies be furnished, along with technical help, sleeping mats, and blankets.[28]

Four days after this report was sent, Tong Quyen and I went to Quang-Ngai, where Le Dam and Roger Kelling, the CORDS refugee officer, joined us, and we discussed the situation with Lt. Colonel Nguyen Van Binh, the province chief. The basic problem was that the refugees were not able to get back to their own land because of insecurity and mine fields. Colonel Binh said that he would try to station additional RF companies in the area and that, if the people would point out to the soldiers where the mines were located, the soldiers would remove them. Then we went in a US military helicopter, with door gunners, to the peninsula, which we flew over at a low altitude; I could see and photograph much abandoned land and some cultivated plots pockmarked by small bomb craters. The pilot gave me a smoke bomb, dropped us and immediately ascended several thousand feet and hovered until I signaled him to come and fetch us. This was the only time in my stay in the country that a pilot had been unwilling to stay on the ground. This area was very close to My-Lai and was considered VC territory. We visited three hamlets.

Chau-Thuan was a fishing hamlet with a large number of boats and nets. The people also raised vegetables and gathered firewood. They were not badly off, although subject to frequent VC attacks and mortaring. They had received one 100-lb. bag of rice for each three families at a subsidized price (to last one month), and had to buy other rice on the free market at 45 piasters (38¢ US equivalent in 1970) a kilo.

Phu-Chi (see above) was an inland settlement surrounded by three ridges topped with barbed wire, with some vegetable-growing land around it. People did not seem to be undernourished, but a number of the children had skin blotches that Tong Quyen said indicated malnutrition. They had nothing to sell to buy food or other commodities. They had received the same amount of rice as those at Chau-Thuan.

Ky-Xuyen camp, also called An-Ky, was on the beach and composed of long-houses constructed entirely of CORDS aluminum roofing and very close together. One hundred eleven families of refugees from Russell Beach had been living there, but 303 new families had been brought in during the five days prior to our visit. Thus, probably over 2,000 refugees were living in a camp that had already been inadequate for 550. (The number more than doubled in the next months.) It had some fishing boats, but obviously not enough to support all those people. The American Red Cross had supplied some blankets, tinned sardines and similar provisions, which were being distributed while we were there, but the new people had almost no rice. We saw children eating uncooked white rice and paddy (unhulled rice). There was inadequate water. The children were very dirty. A CAP team was living at the camp. One soldier said that the people were hard workers; give them materials and they would build new houses.

Nobody whom we saw in the three sites appeared to be starving, and it amazed me that the people were so friendly, not only to Tong Quyen and Le Dam, but also to Roger Kelling and me. Of course, they realized that we were genuinely concerned with their condition and were there to help them.

Henry Cushing, the PSA, said to us later that priority was being given to opening up the road to the peninsula (Highway 521) and providing additional territorial security. He knew of a source of captured rice, and said he and the province chief would visit the next day, along with Le Dam and Kelling, and bring relief commodities. Mr. Quyen directed Le Dam to give seven days' commodity ration and to pay one month's temporary allowance to the Batangas refugees. Upon learning of the plight of the people, General Lam ordered the 2nd ARVN Division to furnish 36 tons of rice that had been confiscated from the VC in the province.[29]

In the next two months, a large GVN military campaign relocated some 5,400 people in Binh-Son district. For the people of Chau-Thuan, this represented a return to their original village; the others were moved away from their homes, some allegedly voluntarily.[30]

Son-Hai village appealed for a food-for-work project in the summer of 1970 to construct a dike 1,600 meters long behind the village intended to prevent salt water intrusion and open up about 100 hectares to rice farming, salt beds, and

fish spawning grounds. After irrigation and engineering experts determined that
the project was feasible, Le Dam supplied 390 bags of cement and the villagers,
750 families of them, paid themselves with PL 480 food and did the work.
Floods in August and September washed out part of the dike, but it was rebuilt.
The project was completed in April 1971. The main dike was branched into
secondary levees with cement flood gates. The mud banks were planted with
grass and small trees to prevent erosion. The people were leveling the new land,
and some salt beds were in operation.[31]

Russell Beach was an operation that betrayed its promise to the people and
to the MHSWR and CORDS/REF, with grievous consequences. Had the Refugee
Division known in advance that the people were not to be returned to their home
villages but instead were to be confined to crowded new sites, where many of
them would not be able to resume cultivation of their land, we would surely
have asked Ambassador Colby to have the operation changed or abandoned. As
it was, it did not pacify the Batangan Peninsula, it caused unnecessary suffering
to the people, and therefore could not have made friends for the GVN. A year
later, as summarized above, CORDS, the provincial and regional authorities,
and the people were still trying to repair the damage. They were achieving some
success, because the area was finally being pacified.

Other Involuntary Relocations

There were numerous operations by both US and ARVN units, especially in
the three lower provinces of I CTZ, from late 1968 right through 1969 and into
1970. These had the express purpose of bringing people from insecure areas to
GVN territory. Only one of these had advance CPDC approval, the relocation
of 1,200 Vietnamese and Montagnards from Ca-Lu near the Vandergrift fire
base in Quang-Tri to the Cua Valley in September 1969. When I took over the
I CTZ Refugee Division in late September 1969, I began reporting these unauthorized relocations and asked Saigon to take action to stop them. My year-
end report of 1969 said that until that year, military generation of refugees had
been largely "accidental," that is, a by-product of the fighting and resultant
destruction. The COMUSMACV instructions of mid-1968 had been effective in
reducing this, but deliberate bringing in of refugees had increased greatly, beginning with the Russell Beach operation of January. The orders of the CPDC,
General Vien, and the Combined Campaign Plans, I said, had been honored
more in the breach than in the observance, especially in the three southern
provinces. The report then listed 10 such unauthorized relocations by American,
ARVN, and Korean units, which together had generated about 22,500 refugees,
not one of whom had been registered, mainly because the provinces and the
military units did not want it known that they had violated the orders. Among
the instances cited were the operation by the Quang-Nam province chief in
August–September which had brought 3,500 refugees to Ngan-Cau and Tu-Cau
(which the VC destroyed on April 10, 1970, as recounted on above), and consolidations of over 5,000 people from scattered hamlets of the Thang-Binh district

of Quang-Tin into new settlements with houses crowded together behind barbed wire on open sand close to military posts; these were reminiscent of the strategic hamlets of Diem's time. Another 7 smaller relocations brought in about 2,300 additional refugees, and we said that there were undoubtedly many other incidents that had gone unreported. (All told, there were almost 78,000 unrecognized refugees in I CTZ, most of them generated by US military operations.) We said:

The GVN authorities in this Region have gotten themselves into a box on this matter. On the one hand, their forces and Province authorities evacuate people and approve FWMAF [free-world military assistance forces] evacuations in violation of their Government's instructions. On the other hand, they cite these same instructions as authority for denying the evacuees refugee status and benefits.

We asked that the GVN and US enforce the orders or repeal them, and concluded: "We are presenting to top command of CORDS and III MAF certain proposals for improving US compliance with GVN policies within the Region. Clarification and indoctrination from GVN Saigon to its officials here is, however, a prerequisite for compliance on that side of the house."[32] Shortly thereafter, CORDS I CTZ asked the commanding general of III MAF to permit me to brief General Lam on the refugee problems in his presence.[33] It was decided that Alex Firfer would do the briefing.

In my travels around the region I constantly reminded the PSAs, province chiefs, and unit commanders of the joint policies governing this matter. However, the relocations continued in 1970, and General Lam refused to permit the evacuees to be recognized as refugees.

NEW POLICY DIRECTIVES—LIMITED EFFECT

Bill Hitchcock used the Hoffman newspaper article "Statistics Are Hiding Refugees" (see footnote 26), which had been picked up by Kennedy, along with the visit of two staff members of the Senate Foreign Relations Committee as the occasion to remind Ambassador Colby of the problem. He said that the previous orders of the GVN and MACV were not being adequately implemented, and recommended (a) that Colby urge General Abrams to send a message to all field commanders, and (b) that he seek a parallel reiteration of policy by the Prime Minister.[34] Both recommendations were adopted.

On February 8, 1970, General Abrams sent a comprehensive guidance memo to all subordinate commands on the subject of generation of refugees. It started with references to CPDC Circular 142 and other instructions, including General Abrams's own message of July 29, 1968 (chapter 8). Then it said:

1. (U) The policy of the GVN and this command requires that the relocation of people to regroup them for greater security or to remove them from enemy control be kept to an absolute minimum. Such relocations generally work against US and GVN policy

objectives. Not only do the people become a burden on the Government, which must house, feed, and resettle them, but their allegiance or potential allegiance to the GVN is undermined by the hardships which they undergo. At the same time the hamlet structure is destroyed and usable land is taken out of cultivation. It is therefore GVN policy that civilians are not to be relocated, except when special circumstances exist, and then only after approval by the Central Pacification and Development Council.

After briefly summarizing what each of the references said and explaining the distinction between relocations for extended periods, which required CPDC approval, and temporary displacements for screening or to remove civilians from battle areas, the message gave detailed guidance, which may be summarized as follows:

a) The appropriate province senior advisor and Corps headquarters are to be notified, so that a request for approval can be sent to the CPDC, and the operation is not to be carried out until approved.

b) If the CPDC approves, the US unit conducting the operation notifies the province chief and PSA prior to the operation so that plans and preparations can be completed.

c) In operations only temporarily displacing civilians the unit conducting has primary responsibility for logistic support and care, including returning the people to their original homesites.[35]

The message had been drafted by R. L. King of the Refugee Directorate, a fact which was not shown on the electronically transmitted copies. Even so, it evidently aroused considerable consternation among its recipients. Five months later, at Alex Firfer's Fourth of July party, Firfer introduced me to Major General White, Commander of the Americal Division, saying that I was to explain the MACV message on generation of refugees, and then gleefully went away. The general thundered, "We can't fight a war with these restrictions!" After some minutes of discussion, during which I explained why forced population movements were counterproductive to the aims of the war and reminding him that General Abrams, who was not inexperienced in fighting wars, had issued the message, he grudgingly admitted that his division might be able to abide by his superior's instruction.

The Prime Minister issued his own circular on March 2, 1970.[36]

Ambassador Colby took advantage of a III MAF change of command ceremony on March 9 to speak with General Lam about relocations of people. The general said that the Corps was carrying on several new programs of moving people a short way to security, which they frequently welcomed, allowing them to cultivate their fields during the day, and also developing other areas for people like those at Ha-Thanh. He stressed that the word not to generate more refugees clearly came from the Central Government, and he looked to Colby as being partly responsible. The Ambassador said that he and the GVN had urged a reduction in the number of refugees by finally paying their allowances, and that they preferred not to move people but that he realized that this might be almost essential to establish security. In that case, he said, the people should be recognized as refugees and given their benefits. General Lam said that he had no great problem with these thoughts, but that he was under instruction not to generate refugees. Colby agreed to speak with the Prime Minister.[37]

In our I CTZ monthly report for February–March 1970, we said:

CPDC Circular 657 of 2 March 70 has not in any way curbed the propensity of GVN authorities in the three southern provinces to move people around like pieces on a chess board [listing four such operations displacing 1,600 civilians], but it has created further confusion about the status and entitlements of the evacuees. A correction of this part of the circular is badly needed.[38]

The Prime Minister issued another circular on April 18 dealing with three types of cases in which evacuations might be proposed. The latter circular, which had all the earmarks of having been drafted by Mr. Hu'ng, probably arose out of Colby's representations as well as some movements in II CTZ. It reiterated that evacuations of people were to be restricted, and that they must have prior CPDC approval. In the case of people voluntarily leaving or being evacuated from insecure areas that were not in the 1970 pacification plan, they were to be considered anti-Communist refugees and entitled to temporary, resettlement, and development assistance, upon approval by the MSW. However, under the Ministry's Circular 8924 of September 23, 1969, province chiefs could themselves decide to grant temporary allowances. In the case of temporary evacuations, the people were entitled to immediate commodity rations for seven days, one month's temporary allowances, and RTV assistance. In the case of moving people permanently from hamlets included in the 1970 pacification plan, that is, the "gathering of people for hamlet building," this must be avoided in principle. However, one such request (from Darlac province) was submitted to the President, who decided that if the corps commander agreed with it, the relocation would have to be funded solely by P&D money, without any support from the MSW. Even a request for relief under the war victims regulations would have to be submitted to the CPDC.[39]

This instruction was somewhat helpful in clarifying who was entitled to what allowances, but it scarcely deterred General Lam and his subordinates from relocating numerous unfortunate people in the region. Alex Firfer sent a long memorandum to Hitchcock on May 14 detailing some of the involuntary movements, including one then being conducted in Quang-Ngai by the Second ARVN Division with help from Americal Division choppers to relocate 2,000 Montagnards in the Song-Ve Valley. On June 13, Colby wrote to Prime Minister Khiem calling attention to the I CTZ problem. He said that General Lam was apparently still under the impression that GVN policy did not permit the generation of refugees; hence CPDC approval was not requested for movements, and evacuees were not registered as refugees. Within the last six months, 22,500 people had been moved in Quang-Ngai along. The social welfare chief had added 12,000 of them to his rolls, but was then directed by the province chief to remove them and cease giving assistance. The Ambassador recommended that General Khiem and possibly President Thieu talk directly with the I Corps commander.[40]

In the absence of a coherent GVN policy permitting assistance to relocated people, CORDS, US military units, and voluntary agencies had to redouble their efforts to aid the unfortunate evacuees. Phu-Lac (6) in Duy-Xuyen district, to which 1,500 people were moved in January-February 1970, and Chau-Son (2) in Que-Son district, to which almost 1,200 people were moved in March (both in Quang-Nam province) were cases in point. When GVN and US units relocated the people, they provided some tents, a bit of food, and nothing more. The social welfare chief was forbidden by the province chief to report to the Ministry and request authorization for relief. Jim Ready, the province refugee and development chief, moved rapidly to assist, and voluntary agencies, including IRC and Christian Youth Social Service, were literally lifesavers. On March 5, the VC fired mortar rounds into Phu-Lac (6), killing one inhabitant and wounding 47. More than half the people went back to their homes in VC territory. An operation late in March brought some of them back. Jim Ready and I visited that camp a number of times. On April 25, I took Carl Fritz, the acting DFC, Paul Brown of my office, Dr. Fred Zerzavy, the Public Health chief, and Reverend Nguyen Van Do of CYSS in a chopper to visit Chau-Son (2) via Hoi-An, where we picked up Jim Ready and the deputy SW chief, Nguyen Quang Tan. There were no latrines or wells; the people had only a few blankets or sleeping mats. There were many sick people in the tents, and Dr. Zerzavy sent a badly dehydrated child to a hospital in our chopper. Reverend Do had already delivered canned food and clothing in CORDS choppers, and continued to send supplies in the next days. A few days later, the province delivered five truckloads of commodities.

Over the next months, combined US and province aid effected gradual improvements in these and other wretched camps. At the end of May, 883 refugees at Phu-Lac (6) were finally issued their green registration cards and paid temporary allowances. Those refugees were completely paid off in December, and some 2,000 optimistic people were living in a pleasant hamlet, with land for cultivation. Several VC attacks had failed to daunt the people. The inhabitants of Chu-Son (2) were to be recognized and paid early in 1971.

However, at Phu-Lac (6), VC harrassment increased after the people had received their final payments. A serious mortar attack at the end of February 1971 destroyed 50 houses, and the people left the settlement. By April it was a deserted ruin.[41] It seems likely that some and possibly most of the inhabitants went back to VC-controlled territory. If so, the Communists had achieved their aim, and all the effort to bring the people to "security" was in vain.

In May 1970, after we had learned about the Song-Ve Valley relocation being conducted by the Second ARVN Division with American Division help and a contemplated relocation of 4,000 people in Mo-Duc scheduled to begin on May

15, my deputy, Tom Estrada, flew to Quang-Ngai with Major Chinh of the Regional Pacification and Development Council (RPDC) and two other CORDS officers. Nobody at the GVN province headquarters, in the absence of the province chief, professed to be aware of this operation. The party then flew to Mo-Duc district, where they learned that the district chief had developed the plan to move the people to Nui-Ong-Do, already the locus of over 3,100 refugees who had been forcibly relocated in 1969. Major Chinh pointed out to the district chief that the plan could not be carried out without approval of the RPDC and the CPDC.[42]

Tom's report of the actual and proposed relocations was forwarded to Lt. General Melvin Zais, whose Army XXIV Corps had taken over military responsibility in the region from the Marines. He was angry and intended to speak severely to the Americal Division commander at the forthcoming commanders' conference. Alex Firfer directed me to attend the conference, and I did. I do not recall what words were said there. In any event, CORDS sent a memorandum (drafted by our division) to the RPDC giving reasons why the proposed Mo-Duc relocation would be counterproductive, and the RPDC ordered it canceled.[43]

On June 24, President Thieu made a statement that the provinces were not to receive any more refugees and that military forces were not to relocate more people. That statement produced further confusion as to the recognition of refugees, but did not stop military movements of population. On the very day that the Quang-Tin province chief reported the President's remarks to his own P&D council meeting, US choppers deposited 100 new refugees at the Tam-Ky reception center.[44]

REFUGEE ATTITUDE SURVEY

The refugee attitude survey that was made at 12 sites in April 1970 at my request by the Rural Survey Program office of CORDS I CTZ (chapter 9) was intended to explore how the attitudes of the refugees were affected by (1) the conditions in the camps and the adequacy of assistance to their inhabitants, and (2) the manner in which the refugees were generated. I chose sites in two groups, those which were relatively good (recognizing that almost no camps in I CTZ were viable) and those in which conditions were clearly unsatisfactory. In the relatively good group, only one camp of the seven, Ky-Tan in Dai-Loc district of Quang-Nam, was composed largely of people who had been forcibly evacuated. The second group had also been planned to include seven sites, but two of them could not be reached for security reasons. Four of the five sites were inhabited largely by forcibly relocated people. The sites were:

A. *Control Group—Relatively Good Sites*

1. Cam-Lo, Quang-Tri, population 14,185.

2. Chon-Tam, Hoa-Khanh village, Quang-Nam, pop. 6,554.

   3. Ky-Tan, Dai-Loc district, Quang-Nam, pop. 2,761.

   4. Loc-Chanh, Dai-Loc district, Quang-Nam, pop. 2,374.

   5. Hiep-Duc, Hiep-Duc district, Quang-Tin, pop. 3,583.

   6. Thanh-Tam, Ly-Tin district, Quang-Tin, pop. 2,574.

   7. Cao-Dai B, Quang-Ngai, pop. 3,183.

B. *Relatively Poor Sites*

   1. Ha-Thanh, Gio-Linh district, Quang-Tri, pop. 18,266.

   2. Phu-Lac (6), Duy-Xuyen district, Quang-Nam, pop. 599.

   3. Ngan-Cau, Dien-Ban district, Quang-Nam, pop. 1,758.

   4. Ky-Xuyen, Son-Tinh district, Quang-Ngai, pop. 4,838.

   5. Nui-Ong-Do, Mo-Duc district, Quang-Ngai, pop. 3,179.

A great deal of detailed information was collected in each of the camps, by direct observation and talks with camp and hamlet leaders and others, and by interviews with random samples of the refugees. The carefully selected and trained Vietnamese interviewers did not identify themselves as CORDS employees, although this may have been suspected. We felt that some of the most sensitive questions could not be asked directly, but instructed the interviewers to judge the attitudes of the respondents toward the GVN, the allies, and the VC. Thus, this part of the findings lacked scientific rigor, but after talking with the teams at the end of the survey, the Rural Survey Program head and I were confident in the validity of their appraisals. Table 12 summarizes significant parts of the findings.

The survey found that in only two of the seven camps in the control group (Loc-Chanh and Hiep-Duc) did 90% or more of the refugees have a poor standard of living. That situation prevailed in four of the five camps in group B. However, at least 50% of the refugees in all the sites were poor. Unemployment was high in all camps except Cam-Lo, Cao-Dai B, and Ha-Thanh. Housing, education, and health facilities were inadequate in all the camps. However, some sites in the control group (Cam-Lo, Chon-Tam, Thanh-Tam, and Hiep-Duc) were relatively privileged. All sites in group B were relatively underprivileged. In general, more GVN assistance had been given to the group A camps than those in group B, but it was not sufficient for their basic needs, and large numbers of families in all sites said they had received no assistance at all. All camps had good security by day, but in Ky-Tan and all group B sites night security was less than 70% effective.

As to political attitudes, "energetic nationalist" meant to the surveyors that the people supported the GVN to the extent that they would fight for it if able and if they thought it had a chance to win. Many of them had relatives in ARVN or the territorial forces. Neutralists were those who did not particularly care for either side, but were not antagonistic to the VC and would perhaps cooperate with them if that seemed the most advantageous course. "Pro-Red" meant those

Table 12
Survey of 12 Refugee Sites in I CTZ, April 1970

A. Relatively good sites

Why at this location	Cam-Lo n=103	Chon-Tam n=50	Ky-Tan n=50	Loc-Chanh n=50	Hiep-Duc n=50	Thanh-Tam n=50	Cao-Dai B n=50
Fled VC	15	27	--	10	4	11	30
Fled fighting and bombing	46	23	--	18	14	9	19
Evacuated by US troops	5	--	50	22	13	11	--
Evac. by ARVN	37	--	--	--	--	--	--
Other reason	--	--	--	19 (returned)	19(seeking job)	--	1(afraid of being VC laborer)

Political Standpoint	%	%	%	%	%	%	%
Energetic nationalist	35	45	30	45	70	60	80
Neutral	40	47	40	50	20	38	18
Pro-Red	25	8	30	5	10	2	2

B. Refugee Sites classified as Poor

Why at this location	Ha-Thanh n=102	Phu-Lac(6) n=50	Ngan-Cau n=50	Ky-Xuyen n=50	Nui-Ong-Do n=50
Fled VC	21	--	--	--	--
Fled fighting and bombing	79	--	--	--	9
Evac. by US troops	--	50	9 ARVN and US (probably should be 47)	50 (hamlet occ. by VC 1964-69. ARVN and US troops evac. people)	10
Evac by ARVN	--	--			31 (Some said they followed ARVN and US forces)
Other reasons	2 (Hamlet cleared for electric fence)	--	--	--	--
Political standpoint	%	%	%	%	%
Energetic nationalist	30	10	20	20	10
Neutral	45	60	50	50	50
Pro-Red	25	30	30	30	40

Source: Rural Survey Program, special Assistant to the Office of the Deputy for CORDS, I CTZ, *Survey of the Attitudes of Refugees in Twelve Selected Camps in I Corps (April 11–27, 1970).*

who had Communist ideas and would fight the government openly if a good opportunity presented itself. Many in this group had relatives in the VC, and most attempted to maintain contact with the VC and worked actively as cadres for them.

Geography and the standard of living did not seem to be the primary factors accounting for the political attitudes of the refugees, nor did the degree of insecurity of the environment. The manner in which the refugees were generated was more important. The report concluded:

With the exception of Cam-Lo (Quang-Tri province), in all cases in which half the respondents or more in the Control Group said they left home to escape VC domination or avoid the bombing generally, VC influence was only slight. Conversely, in all cases in Group B in which most respondents said they were evacuated by US or ARVN troops, sometimes seeing their homes burned and not being allowed to take along their possessions, VC strength is considerable. [This was also true of Ky-Tan in Group A.] With the exception of Cam-Lo and Ha-Thanh camps, both of which are located in Quang-Tri province, the correlation between the reason the refugees left their home hamlet and their present loyalties is a constant in this survey.[45]

The principal limitation of the survey was that it "froze" the attitudes of the refugees within a thin slice of time, without comparison with earlier times or an indication of what if anything had modified them. The study made it clear that forced evacuations had produced masses of dangerously pro-VC refugees within GVN territory. Since the sites where this occurred were representative, it meant that such islands of pro-Communist strength probably existed in all the numerous places where forcibly relocated refugees were settled—a rather frightening prospect. However, the survey could not tell us whether those attitudes had been softened or hardened by what had happened to the people after they had been moved. We should have been conducting such attitude studies periodically, all over the country. In only one of the surveyed sites, Cam-Lo, did we have the advantage of earlier studies, the CORDS evaluation and the Human Sciences Research study of 1967 (chapter 7). The CORDS evaluators had found that the sympathies of the evacuees at that time were overwhelmingly pro-VC. The later improvements in the camp and the influx of people who were not forcibly evacuated (chapter 9) had evidently diluted pro-VC attitudes somewhat, but had still left a hard core of sympathizers and cadres.

As to the other sites, we and the surveyors knew their histories, and that gave us some sense of their evolution. Phu-Lac (6), for example, was at a low point in its population at the time of the study, most of the pro-VC inhabitants presumably having gone back to their homes. The fact that 30% of those who remained were "pro-Red" indicates that the site was a hotbed of potential insurgency. The later improvements and increase of population recounted above perhaps made the people more amenable to living under GVN "protection," but that they all departed after the VC attack of February 1971 indicates that they had little confidence in the government. The inhabitants of many other refugee camps and hamlets had been subjected to equally frequent and damaging VC assaults and had not left. The net of this was that forcible evacuations brought VC partisans into GVN territory and made other evacuees disgruntled with those who had moved them, that poor treatment exacerbated the ill will, and that among many of the evacuees the hostile attitudes were lasting. Flight from bombing, as in the case of Ha-Thanh, and poor conditions in the resettlement site, evidently produced similar though less pronounced hostility. In none of these settlements did the GVN conduct the kind of constant political organization and indoctrination that the inhabitants had experienced under the VC. The fact was that, even with the RD teams, the GVN did not have the numbers of trained and dedicated leaders and cadres living and working among the people who could match the Communists. Quite the contrary, many if not most Vietnamese in the countryside distrusted the Saigon government and had little regard for its civil and military officials. Forcible relocation intensified that alienation, as well as bringing more VC partisans into GVN territory.

The survey report's conclusions bore out what we had been saying, giving our views concerning the counterproductive nature of forced relocations a new basis in fact. We distributed the survey widely, including the other corps areas, but kept it within channels, since it was classified *For Official Use Only*.

On June 13, Ambassador Colby sent the report to Prime Minister Khiem along with a long letter analyzing its findings. He said that

In view of the clear indications that refugees represent an element in the population whose faith in their government has been severely shaken, it is obviously of primary importance, from a pacification as well as a humanitarian standpoint, to keep the generation of new refugees to an absolute minimum.

He praised CPDC Circular 1166, but said that violations continued, particularly in I CTZ, about which he had written separately. The reported lack of confidence in Social Welfare and other GVN personnel led to the suggestion that the decentralization of authority to the people in nonrefugee villages might be extended also to refugee camps. He called for an increase in psychological operations and information dissemination. Finally, he reiterated that all Ministries should participate in the reestablishment of the refugees.[46]

The Senate Foreign Relations Committee asked for and was given a copy of the report, after it was upgraded to *Confidential*.[47]

The *New York Times*, in an article by Tad Szulz on March 13, 1971, reported the survey results, highlighting the correlation between forced relocation and pro-Communist sympathies. Citing that article and some figures on new refugees generated in Viet-Nam, a Pentagon memorandum said that the Pacification Attitudes Analysis Staff report, "does in fact substantiate the allegation that Vietnamese *forcibly* relocated do feel bitterness toward their government, while those voluntarily dislocated and assisted by their government were sympathetic to the GVN."[48]

I CTZ AFTERWORD

In the spring of 1971, at the order of Major General Nguyen Van Toan, commander of the Second ARVN Division and deputy commanding general of I Corps for territorial security, military operations were conducted in Nghia-Hanh and Son-Tinh districts of Quang-Ngai (including the Song-Ve Valley, where some Montagnards had been relocated in 1970) to move up to 12,000 people to secure areas. Henry B. (Hank) Cushing, the PSA, had defended many of the forcible relocations in that province in 1969–70, but by 1971 he was convinced that they should be limited and conducted in accordance with the GVN instructions. He voiced strong objection to this operation, since there had been no prior submission of a resettlement plan to the CPDC, and he allowed his objection to be recorded in the refugee report from the province. Lt. General Cao Hao Hon, Secretary General of the CPDC, visited the province on April 9 and gave retrocative approval for temporary refugee status of the evacuees.[49]

Cushing wrote up the operation for the CORDS War Victims Division and Ambassador Colby, saying that it was inconsistent with both the national and provincial pacification plans. Henry Kamm published the story in the *New York Times* in a long article about refugees in Viet-Nam, Cambodia, and Laos (''Hopes Dim for the Millions Adrift across Indochina''). According to Cushing, the Prime Minister reversed both General Toan and the corps commander, General Lam, who complained to the American Senior Advisor, General Dolvin. The result was that Cushing and the district senior advisor in Nghia-Hanh were relieved. Cushing was transferred to IV CTZ, where he was promoted several times, ending up as the Deputy Consul General.[50]

POPULATION RELOCATIONS IN II CTZ

Plei Ring De and Plei Ia Lou

Even before the situation at Edap Enang had been stabilized, General Peers had agreed in May 1968 to move Jarai villagers in southwest Pleiku province to a more secure area. The CORDS Refugee Division was informed that the Jarai were willing to be relocated. On June 18, Major Reiff and Steve Cummings accompanied Dr. Phieu and a representative of the Ministry for the Development of Ethnic Minorities (MDEM) to Pleiku, where they toured a proposed site, to be called Plei Ring De, near the Catecka tea plantation. There was some land for cultivation, but the thought was that many of the evacuees would be able to work on the plantation. Dr. Phieu and the MDEM representative returned to Saigon to study the plan.[51]

The project was to relocate 23 hamlets with approximately 1,200 people from the Ia-Drang and Ia-Muir River valleys. However, when the movement took place in December 1968–January 1969, only 832 people, mostly old men, women, and children were found. Eight of the 23 hamlets had disappeared, evidently forced by the VC. At the resettlement site, a corrupt building contractor defrauded the evacuees of much of their allowances, but the provincial officials did their best to reestablish the people. However, by mid-March only 279 people remained. The refugees expressed dissatisfaction at the forced movement, some of them having been thus relocated twice before with their old hamlets burned behind them. The province officials were discouraged, and the deputy PSA, John Rogers, agreed with them that the project should be abandoned.[52]

I visited Plei Ring De on April 25, 1969, together with Bob Pooley, the province refugee advisor. Only 105 people were left. Lieutenant Wiechman, chief of the Civil Affairs team, said that 80 to 90 refugees had worked on the Catecka plantation but that all had left within the previous few days. He doubted that any refugees would stay in the settlement, and requested reassignment of the team. Lieutenant Dois, commander of the 446th RF company, agreed, and thought that his company also should be reassigned. There were several reasons for the failure: First, the people who had been brought there had previously been taken involuntarily to Edap Enang and had escaped at least once. Second, after being told that bombing and other operations would be conducted at their former home sites, the refugees learned that no bombing had taken place and that the military operations did not harm those who had remained. Third, Plei Ring De was close to another Montagnard village whose inhabitants were pro-VC, and was vulnerable to VC penetration and attack; several houses, the school, and the administration building had been heavily damaged in a recent assault. More-over, the settlement was quite distant from the main road, making it difficult for the refugees to go to work and to market. When we talked later with Colonel Ya Ba, the province chief, he also agreed that the project should be abandoned.

My report on the visit said: "I have rarely seen a more forlorn site than Plei Ring De with its many skeletons of houses, a monument to the futility of poorly conceived involuntary movement of Montagnards."[53]

The next day John Rogers took me to Plei Ya (or Ia) Lou, a site on Highway 14 to which 2,300 Montagnards had asked to be moved in September–October 1968 from an insecure area north of Pleiku City. The area ARVN commander had originally rounded up the men, mostly VC, kept them a while with good treatment, and then released them. They persuaded their families that they would be treated well, and they were. Fifty tents had been set up by the SWR service, with help from Pooley, and commodities were ready for the reception. When I visited, the community consisted of very neat, quite commodious single-family houses with CORDS aluminum roofs. There was a stream below the hamlet, and a well had been dug. Land was being cleared beyond an RF outpost. Weaving of cloth seemed to be a prevalent occupation of the women. During our visit a number of parties seemed to be going on all that afternoon—it was Hung Vuong Day, a national holiday.[54]

Other Relocations

Consolidation of hamlets and Montagnard villages was a favorite practice of some province chiefs and military units in the mountain provinces of II CTZ.

The principal motivation was to facilitate the maintenance of security; a secondary reason was to enable the provision of better community services, such as schools, dispensaries, and markets. By mid-1969, some lessons had been learned from Edap Enang and Plei Ring De, and most people were not moved far from their homes and lands. However, the hill tribes were accustomed to living in small, scattered villages, surrounded by their swidden farm plots, so grouping them together disrupted the familiar patterns of life.

In Pleiku, the US Fourth Division was responsible for most of the consolidations. I visited two of the consolidated villages in April 1969. Plei Gao Thong, in Le-Trung district, with about 420 people in 90 families, had brought three Jarai villages together involuntarily in February 1968, shortly after Têt. A civil affairs team was at the site, commanded by Lt. Lyons. The people were farming their original fields, but one of their farming areas was almost four miles away from the consolidated village. The CA (Civil Affairs) team was assisting the people to grow more and better paddy rice and was helping to install an irrigation system. There was a school, built by self-help, with 58 pupils. The team was also helping with sanitation. There seemed to be minimal contact between the team and the people, except for the lieutenant, who was learning Jarai and met regularly with the hamlet chiefs. Some 9 to 12 RF and CA team were the only security forces for the settlement. The VC had occasionally mortared and stolen rice. Lieutenant Lyons thought the village was too small for security. My judgment was that it was not a success; it had been undertaken without consulting the province or district, and was still not coordinated with the GVN.

Mr. Pooley and I visited another consolidation village, Plei Bong Huot. This was the product of voluntary movement, with 1,900 inhabitants in four hamlets. Each hamlet was dominated by a traditional ''happy house,'' a tall building used for ceremonies and parties. New people had come in early January to escape VC taxation and obtain more security. The SWR service had paid temporary allowances and given roofing and resettlement allowances. A CA team of the Fourth Division from the nearby Black Hawk fire base had helped to move the people's houses and assisted in other ways. The people, who were farming their own lands, seemed prosperous and happy. There was a cordial atmosphere as we walked around, in contrast to that in Plei Gao Thong.

Before visiting Plei Ring De and the two consolidation villages, I had briefed the regimental and battalion officers of the Fourth Division on the refugee program. I explained the GVN policy to bring security to the people, not people to security, and went over the disadvantages of relocation. I said that when relocation was necessary, CPDC approval should be obtained in advance. The officers listened politely and asked some questions, but it was obvious that they were not impressed by my remarks concerning the movement of people. The contrast between them and the officers of the 173rd Airborne Brigade in Binh-Dinh was marked. These men were sincere and undoubtedly competent but, as I said in my report, the refugee program in the province, which was good, ''would go even better if the 4th Division would be induced to work somewhat more closely with the Province Team and the GVN.''

Colonel Ya Ba approved of the program of consolidating villages, but said that it was finished, except for the possible bringing together of seven more hamlets into Plei De Groi, southeast of Pleiku city.[55] As we shall see, this movement took place a year and a half later, with unfortunate consequences.

Relocation and consolidation on a systematic basis in Kontum was begun by the province chief as early as 1965, and continued over the next five years, regrouping about 94% of the people in relatively secure areas. However, this narrowed the economic opportunities of the hill tribesmen who were moved, and by the end of 1970, the approximately 10,000 who had been resettled around the Dak To district headquarters were in deteriorating straits. An effort was made to clear additional land, in part by using village self-development funds to purchase tractors, and the use of fertilizer and improved seeds was expanded. In December, allegedly at the request of the people concerned, plans were made to move the remaining hamlets.[56] It might be added that in the consolidation process, much of the territory of the province had been abandoned to the VC and the North Vietnamese Army, which used it as a base to attack the remaining areas, including refugee settlements.

In Tuyen-Duc province it was the CORDS refugee advisor, Bernard Salvo, who as early as 1966 originated the idea of consolidating hamlets, including refugee settlements, in order to improve security, provide adequate schools and other government services, and save money from the province budget that had been used to pay many chiefs of small hamlets. Salvo admitted to me during my visit on June 28, 1969, that the consolidations were not entirely voluntary and sometimes brought different tribes together, but that applications for approval and funds were always made to the Ministry. President Thieu then directed that the abandoned hamlets be abolished.

Together with Salvo, I visited four of the consolidated settlements. Dagun, made up of five former Chru hamlets, had 1,209 resettled and 93 temporary refugees. Hamlet elections had been held the previous week. A new program was getting under way to upgrade its HES rating from a low C to B. A Son-Thong cadre team (the Montagnard equivalent of RD cadres) of 70 men was to begin work among the people. Village self-development funds were being made available. There was plenty of agricultural land. The crops were in the ground. (Summer was the rainy season.) Two hundred twenty bags of fertilizer were being distributed while we visited.

Soui-Thong A, made up of three tribes, was strongly Protestant in faith and anti-Communist. It had suffered a VC attack the previous week, which killed several people, destroyed 11 houses, and damaged the school. The people's self-defense forces (PSDF) stood off the attackers, as they had in several previous attacks. Plans were being made to increase their number, and Truong-Son cadres were to be deployed. Roofing had already been distributed for rebuilding. The people were friendly.

M'lon had 1,098 refugees in the resettlement process. They had received the housing allowances and were to get three months' rice payments within the next week or so. The houses were quite close together, but well-constructed, clean, and neat. We were invited into the village chief's house. The deputy province chief for ethnic minorities had tried, without success, to interest the people in vocational training. They were working their old lands and had some 60 hectares of new land also. They had held hamlet elections. Children were in school, and two new classrooms were being built alongside the existing five-room village school.

Kado was the newest consolidation, made up of nine small hamlets brought together next to a large old hamlet. It had 103 families with 472 people. There were 1,330 people in the two hamlets. The new hamlet had received roofing and seven days' rice allowance. The houses were good. The people were working their old lands. Truong-Son cadres showed us charts of the entire village. In the old hamlet there were Catholic and Protestant churches. The people in the two hamlets got along well together, said Salvo. Applications had gone to the MHSWR for approval of three more consolidations of refugee hamlets.[57]

"GATHERING PEOPLE FOR HAMLET ESTABLISHMENT"

The 1970 pacification plan set a target to eliminate all D, E, and V (insecure and VC-controlled) hamlets by October 31, that is, to bring all the people in Viet-Nam under GVN control. This was an utterly unrealistic goal. We have seen what extremes of forced relocation of people resulted from this target in I CTZ. The same thing happened in II CTZ, affecting especially the hill tribes-people. General Ngo Dzu, the II Corps Commander, launched a massive reset-tlement of the Montagnards and Vietnamese throughout the vast region. This was a purely Vietnamese campaign; American combat troops and their helicopters were gone. Except for the province senior advisors of Darlac and Binh-Thuan, the CORDS advisors were unanimously opposed to this sweeping dislocation of people, which was set in motion without any application to the CPDC. Some of the people were relocated before they could harvest their rice, and many of the moves were conducted so hastily that the people had to leave behind some of their most cherished possessions. The Montagnards in most cases could not take their hardwood furniture, ceremonial gongs, heavy house frames which they had spent years building, or cattle. Many of their villages were burned, sometimes including rice stocks. The Vietnamese troops hauling their possessions occa-sionally stole them.

The largest relocations were in Pleiku (14,766) and Darlac (23,532), but significant groups were moved in Kontum, Phu-Bon, Tuyen-Duc, and Binh-Thuan. The grand total was 54,782 as of March 1971. By the latter part of August, the number had climbed to about 62,500.[58]

In some cases, Vietnamese were allowed to cultivate lands from which Mon-tagnards were forcibly evacuated on grounds that the lands were insecure. This was especially the case in Darlac province. Examples were the lands from which tribespeople were moved to Buon Gram, Drai Si, and Buon Ea Sah in Darlac province. Vietnamese from Ha-Lan village with large tractors also took over the lands assigned to Montagnards who had requested to be relocated from 16 villages in Buon Ho district. The district chief ordered the Vietnamese off the land, but they refused to leave. Ha-Lan, some 15 kilometers northwest of Ban Me Thuot on Highway 14, was a village of some 800 North Vietnamese Catholics who had been moved there in 1956. With the help of International Voluntary Services (IVS) under an AID contract, it became probably the richest village in the province, boasting 60 tractors. When the Montagnards were relocated, the villagers quickly took over all the available land, including that surrounding the relocated centers. Other Vietnamese also began cultivating land allocated to the relocated Montagnards: altogether, this occurred in about 15% of the relocated hamlets in Darlac, Pleiku, and Tuyen-Duc. This was most serious in Darlac, where most of the hill tribespeople were moved from fertile lands to crowded areas on much poorer land. A survey commissioned by the USAID showed that 77% of the relocated people in that province overwhelmingly wanted to return to their previous homes. In the other two provinces, the relocated people had better land, and in Pleiku they could also get urban jobs. Sixty percent and 40% respectively of the evacuees in the latter two provinces wanted to go home.

Vietnamese lumbermen were logging the former lands of people moved to Buon M'Bre, Buon Kli B, and several other locations, also in Darlac, and to Bon Blech in Phu Bon province.[59] Some observers believed that a prime motive for the forced moves was to get the Montagnards off the land so that the Vietnamese could claim it.[60]

The relocations were extremely traumatic for the Montagnards, particularly those made during the cold winter months. About 208 of the 2,050 people moved to Plei De Groi and 56 of the 760 relocated to Plei Bang Ba (also called Plei Ia Maih) died between mid-December 1970 and April 1971. The high death rate became a cause célèbre, and many medical teams and high-ranking officials, including Colby and General Hon, visited the camps during those months and afterwards. There were congressional inquiries. Extra food, medicines, and other supplies were rushed in. The deaths were attributed to exhaustion, exposure, physical and psychological trauma during the moves, pneumonia and other respiratory diseases during the early period, and enteric infections and malaria during the later months. Malnutrition, both primary at first, and secondary (to diarrheas), was a factor. The sick were treated at the camps; few consented to medical evacuation.[61] What happened at these two camps was probably duplicated, although perhaps in a less severe fashion and with less public notice, at many other relocation sites.

In February 1971, the Assistant Commander of II Corps sent letters asking that CORDS and the voluntary agencies support the program, and giving specifics of some relocations. The Council of Voluntary Agencies sent a strong letter to Dr. Phieu expressing its dismay over the manner in which the forced movements had taken place, giving many concrete facts and asking a number of questions.

The council's letter pointed out that 872 of the 1,407 Montagnard hamlets in the whole country (62%) had been relocated, 150 of them since July 31, 1970.[62] Gerald Hickey had estimated that close to 65% had been relocated since 1965. He said:

In the past programs plagued by these problems [of forcible resettlement] the result has been a bitter and discontented population that physically may be under GVN control but whose loyalties are dubious. . . . If these poorly implemented resettlements continue there is a strong possibility that the Montagnards will be left a poverty-stricken population living on the fringes of Vietnamese society.[63]

The relocations received wide publicity in the United States, and were a principal subject of the Senate Refugee Subcommittee hearings on April 22, 1971.

Both Dr. Phieu, Minister of Social Welfare, and Nay Luett, Minister for Ethnic Minority Development, protested to General Dzu and also spoke up in the cabinet, but to no avail.[64] The actions of the CPDC were weak and vacillating in the face of General Dzu's determination, as they had been in I CTZ also. Although frequently reiterating the policy of bringing security to people, not people to security, in visits to the Second Region in March and April 1971, General Hon retroactively approved the relocations by ordering that assistance be given to the evacuees.[65] At President Thieu's request, General Dzu discussed the relocations on February 19, 1971, with Dr. Hickey, who advised him that, if such movements were still considered necessary, both national and local Montagnard leaders should be consulted in advance, in order to plan the displacements to accord with the aspirations and customs of the people. The II Corps Commander expressed his determination to protect the land claims of the Montagnards and to push for land titling.[66]

At the urging of Ambassador Colby, the Prime Minister issued a new communiqué on May 12, 1971, requesting all provinces to halt any relocations that did not have CPDC approval. It also contained new guidelines for planning, including the provision of adequate farmland to ensure self-sufficiency within one year.[67] Colby distributed this message to all regional DepCORDS and PSAs, saying that the CPDC intended to enforce the new rules. Whether as a result of the communiqué or more direct intervention by the President, General Dzu did not carry out his plans to move an additional 38,000 people in 1971–72.

In Pleiku, ARVN extracted 82 people in August 1971, but after receiving their emergency rice allowance, all but six returned to their old hamlets. Binh-Thuan went merrily ahead with its relocations through September, but then evidently stopped.[68]

Thus ended one of the most disgraceful and tragic chapters in Vietnamese history. The II Corps Commander and his underlings had virtually completed disrupting the main Montagnard society, causing untold suffering and irrevocably alienating its members, as well as dislocating many Vietnamese in the lowlands. These actions did not advance the cause of pacification; rather, they retarded it.

Some of the afflicted people took their revenge during the final offensive of the North Vietnamese in 1975. One wonders how the covetous people of Ha-Lan, who did not love their neighbors, fared in that debacle.

THE U-MINH FOREST OPERATION

A greater contrast to the movements of refugees in the I and II Corps areas could scarcely be found than the operation into the U-Minh Forest at the southern tip of Viet-Nam beginning in December 1970. That large area, taking in parts of An-Xuyen, Chuong-Thien, and Kien-Giang provinces, had been a Communist stronghold since the French war period. Efforts had been made sporadically to penetrate it, but had always failed because insufficient force was applied and the GVN troops did not remain. Agricultural production had remained relatively high and provided a reasonable standard of living for the people, although the exactions of the VC were burdensome. Frequent air strikes forced many to spend much time in their bunkers. However, beginning in 1969, pacification was gradually extended into the area, and some 20,000 people came out as refugees.

It had been estimated that the 1970–71 campaign would generate about 12,000 refugees, and that the job would be completed in 90 days. Both forecasts proved to be conservative. The massive insertion of the 21st ARVN Division and other units induced 63,800 people to come out. Their principal means of transport were their boats, which were frequently loaded with food, house frames, and other personal belongings. The SWR services were slow to render assistance, but in that lush region the people managed. Probably the most important help the GVN gave was allowing some of them to return home to harvest their crops. One district chief even organized RF operations escorting the returnees and providing security while they harvested. Some were injured by VC booby traps, but they got their rice before Têt. About 15,000 were enabled to return home to live. The operation continued into May 1971. RD teams were sent into the newly occupied areas, and village governments were constituted. Elections were scheduled for later in the year.

In mid-May, the CORDS Pacification Studies Group conducted an attitude survey among the refugees, interviewing 181 respondents in five widely separated locations. The respondents were much older than the norm, 60% being over age 40, and the number of females was higher, 42% compared with 33% in the general population. (This presumably refers to female heads of household.) Many young men had been with the VC, and a large number had been killed during the Têt offensive. Only 3% had any formal education, compared with 40% to 50% in the normal samples. Almost all were farmers or farm laborers. Forty-seven percent were Buddhist, 41% ancestor worshippers, 8% Cao-Dai, 2% Catholics, and 1% Hoa-Hao.

Slightly over half the respondents had neutral feelings about the VC; only a few had anything good to say about them. One third had left their homes before the December operation. GVN bombings and artillery were the major cause of movement, with troop entry being an important secondary cause. Twenty-eight percent of the respondents said that government troops or officials forced them to move. The VC had tried to prevent exodus.

The refugees reported that GVN assistance was usually late and inadequate. Almost half had returned to their former homes and fields, normally once a month. One third had been forbidden by the authorities to go back.

A crucial question was whether their attitudes and understanding of the GVN and life in government areas had changed since leaving their homes; 54% chose the answer, "Yes, the life in government controlled areas is *much better* than I thought before," 33% said life was a little better, 6% said their attitude had not changed, 3% found life much worse, and 4% had other answers or did not want to respond.

Only 1% of those questioned thought that the VC were winning the war; 2% said the war would continue for many years, since both sides were strong and had popular support; 2% expected it to end soon with a coalition government. However, 25% said the government forces were winning because of strong American support, and 48% thought the government was winning because of strong support of the people and the Americans. Twenty-two percent didn't know or didn't want to respond, and 1% gave other (unspecified) answers. Most of the nonresettled refugees wanted to return home as soon as they thought it would be safe and the authorities gave permission.[69]

Thus, the U-Minh operation had produced a large number of refugees who in an overwhelming majority felt that their lives had improved and that the GVN was winning the war. That is an astonishing result for a population that had lived under Communist domination for decades.

12

The North Vietnamese Easter Offensive of 1972

The massive conventional military offensive of the North Vietnamese Army (NVA), which began on March 30, 1972, cast aside the fiction that the conflict against the Republic of Viet-Nam was still a civil war. Ten NVA divisions, with accompanying artillery and other support units, together with almost the entire military force of the Democratic Republic of Viet-Nam (DRVN), were thrown against the GVN forces in assaults on Quang-Tri and Hue in Military Region 1 (MR-1), Kontum and Binh-Dinh in MR-2, and Binh-Long province in MR-3, with secondary attacks in many other localities. Viet-Cong military units and cadres were largely absent from the fighting and from the administration of conquered territory, except in MR-4. On the GVN side, ARVN and the territorial forces were the only elements involved in ground combat. The United States provided effective air and logistical support, but its combat infantry troops were already gone. Heavy fighting went on for more than eight months, although the weight of the offensive was largely defeated by mid-year.

The Communist offensive had as its objectives both the weakening of the already waning US resolve to defend South Viet-Nam militarily and the strengthening of the Communist presence in the South in preparation for the expected agreement that was being negotiated between the United States and the DRVN in Paris. Despite President Nixon's determination that the North Vietnamese should not win, evidenced by renewed US bombing of the North, mining of Haiphong harbor, massive air support of the GVN's forces, and generous logistical support, the offensive achieved both its objectives. Popular revulsion in the United States against the war increased, as did the feeling that the only thing that was important was to get the American prisoners back, and that Viet-Nam's future could be sacrificed if necessary. However, it is the question of Communist versus GVN strength within South Viet-Nam and how it was affected by population displacement that particularly concerns us here. In previous chapters I have shown how the voluntary movement of refugees from insecure to GVN territory tended to increase the government's population base, while involuntary relocation more often than not weakened it. In both cases, however, such refugee flows abandoned territory to the enemy. The large-scale return of refugees to their home villages as territorial security was extended in the period from late 1968 to March 1972 reinforced that security at the time in much of the country, while continued forced relocations in Military Regions 1 and 2 defined and contracted the boundaries of GVN control and influence.

The Easter offensive diminished GVN territorial security markedly, driving over a million and a quarter refugees into shrunken areas, and keeping perhaps half of them there indefinitely. At the end of the offensive, a significant additional portion of South Viet-Nam remained in Communist hands, especially northern Quang-Tri, most of Kontum, and much of Binh-Long. Northwest Tay-Ninh, from which the Communist headquarters for the South and its front organizations had fled to Cambodia in the spring of 1972, became so safe for the Communists that those headquarters returned in October.[1]

The offensive caused enormous destruction and refugee generation, in addition to the tens of thousands of civilians who were killed by the NVA. Refugee care was assumed totally by the GVN, and was generally adequate, although some egregious instances of corruption and mismanagement were uncovered.

THE OFFENSIVE IN MR-1

Three NVA divisions, coming straight across the Demilitarized Zone (DMZ), swept through the northern part of Quang-Tri down to the Dong-Ha bridge over the Mieu-Giang River by April 2, while others advanced on a broad front from Laos on the west. So rapid was the advance that thousands of people, including many of those at Cam-Lo and Ha-Thanh, were overrun. A few went north voluntarily, while others were marched to labor camps on the outskirts of North Vietnamese towns, where they were still held more than a year later.

There had been no ARVN plan to evacuate civilians from the battle area, even dependents of the troops. Some Third Infantry Division troops followed their families to the South as refugees. That division had been organized only six months earlier and was still being trained when the offensive began. Thus, when a stream of refugees came down Highway 1 (QL-1) across the Dong-Ha bridge on April 2, this deeply affected the morale of the 57th Regiment soldiers, whose families were among the refugees, and they broke ranks in panic. The commander of the Third Division flew to the position and restored confidence, inducing the soldiers to return to their units. The Marines, who were more experienced and without families, rolled back before the assault in good order.[2]

The "family syndrome" was to affect South Vietnamese troop morale and cohesion on many occasions, including the 1972 battles and during the final NVA offensive of 1975. It was a serious weakness of the GVN military forces.

The families of the North Vietnamese troops, on the other hand, remained in the North and frequently were not reunited with their sons and husbands for years. Although this was a hardship, it meant that the soldiers were free of concern for the safety of their loved ones during battle.

By April 7 approximately 100,000 inhabitants of Quang-Tri, almost one-third of the province's population, had become refugees. An interministerial committee in charge of relief, headed by Dr. Phan Quang Dan, had been formed. Eight reception centers had been set up in schools, pagodas, churches, and other public buildings in Quang-Tri City, and three in Phu-Van district on the border with Thua-Thien. About 60,000 refugees had been counted at checkpoints going into Hue, where 28 reception centers had been established. Large stocks of rice, flour, bulgur, cooking oil, canned fish, and other foods were sent from Da-Nang to Hue and Quang-Tri. Blankets, tarpaulins, and other supplies were flown up to Phu-Bai base near Hue.

About 10,000 refugees continued going south at that time (since NVA units were threatening Hue from the west) but were held back by the crack First ARVN Division. Two reception centers had already been set up in Da-Nang by April 7. Several base camps that had formerly been occupied by US troop headquarters in the Da-Nang area were being prepared to receive refugees. Much of their equipment had been removed, but their barracks and kitchens were largely intact.[3] By April 21, an estimated 150,000 people of Quang-Tri had become refugees. Thirty thousand of them were being cared for at the eight centers in Quang-Tri city, about 82,000 were in 66 sites in Hue and the surrounding area, another 8,000 were staying with relatives and friends, and about 12,000 were in the Da-Nang area. Approximately 2,000 Bru tribespeople were brought from a temporary site near Hue to Ban Me Thuot in Air America planes on April 19-21 and settled at Buon Jat, a site selected by the MSW and the Ministry for the Development of Ethnic Minorities (MDEM).

I visited Quang-Tri city on April 25, along with members of the province CORDS team who spent each night in Da-Nang. We traveled in the military helicopter assigned to John Gunther Dean, the regional DepCORDS, on that dreary, rainy day; fixed-wing aircraft could not be used, since the city's airport across the Thach-Han River was already in enemy hands. We went to several crowded refugee centers in schools. The people seemed calm and even cheerful and had been provided with the bare necessities. The city itself seemed almost normal. Within a week it had been captured by the NVA. On the way back to Da-Nang we stopped in Hue and saw more refugee centers, also crowded but filled by people who were coping competently, as many had done previously. The GVN relief program in both cities was as good as could be expected in the enormous emergency.

The heaviest fighting took place north of Quang-Tri city from April 8 to May 1, when the city fell. As the ARVN troops fell back, the flow of refugees on and alongside QL-1 south to Hue increased, with civilians and soldiers all mixed up together. Military equipment was abandoned, but the NVA took the whole column under fire on May 1 and 2, slaughtering thousands of civilians as well as soldiers. It has been estimated that as many as 20,000 perished in those two days. The full horror of it was not revealed until September, when the southern part of the province and the city itself were recaptured. At that time, that stretch of QL-1 was named "Terror Boulevard." The shock of the tragedy, like the VC's massacres at Hue in 1968, was long remembered, and it influenced the panicked flight when the same kind of invasion recurred in 1975.[4]

By May 5 it was estimated that the offensive had generated almost 700,000 refugees nationwide, of whom over 500,000 were in MR-1. Some 250,000 to 290,000 were said to have left Quang-Tri, out of its 320,000 population; approximately 200,000 escaped from Hue and Thua-Thien. North Vietnamese broadcasts and leaflets warned people to leave Thua-Thien. The Vietnamese Navy was ferrying people from a port near Hue to Da-Nang, but most were arriving by bus, truck, and on foot. Seven former US camps were being filled, and Philco-Ford, under a US contract, was operating the water systems as it had when US forces had occupied the camps. Schools, pagodas, the National Police training center, and other buildings were also used. The regional pacification and development council was coordinating the reception and relief effort. Food, medical care, and other services were adequate. It was an astonishing achievement to receive and care for the hordes of panic-stricken refugees who had poured into the city within a short time.

Eighteen hundred sixty former inhabitants of Cam-Lo and Ha-Thanh who had already planned to join friends and relatives at Soui-Nghe in Phuoc-Tuy province were flown south from reception centers in Hue and taken to the resettlement site. Another group was carried to Vung-Tau from Quang-Tin province on a Vietnamese Navy ship.[5]

By the end of May, the NVA offensive in the northern provinces had been checked, and some refugees were cautiously filtering back into Hue and Thua-Thien. The officially registered refugee population in Da-Nang was then about 280,000 in 137 centers. Several thousand people from Quang-Tri and Thua-Thien had taken refuge in Quang-Nam and Quang-Tin.[6]

A counteroffensive to retake Quang-Tri province was launched by General Truong on June 28, and by July 7 it had reached the outskirts of the capital. However, it took more than two more months of bitter fighting to recapture the city on September 16, and by then it was nothing but rubble.[7] That was as far as the GVN forces could go; more than half the province remained in North Vietnamese hands. Almost 22,000 refugees returned to their home hamlets in the first half of 1973.

However, at that same time Henry Kamm, the perceptive East Asia reporter of the *New York Times*, wrote that the actual number of refugees who had come from Quang-Tri was somewhere between 75,000 and 160,000 less than the number for whom relief had been provided, since at least a quarter and perhaps half of the province's population had remained behind or been killed. Especially in Cam-Lo and Gio-Linh districts, the NVA advance had been so rapid that many were overrun, while others were pro-Communist and stayed voluntarily. He asserted that refugees were still compelled to make kickbacks to the camp officials for the excess family members whom they claimed.[8] In response to a similar article that appeared in the *Washington Star*, the Saigon Mission reported that as of March 22, 1973, the official count of Quang-Tri refugees in camps totaled 319,200 (which was virtually the whole population of the province), made up of 252,000 in Da-Nang, 57,400 in Hue, and 9,900 in Chu-Lai (Quang-Tin). It was estimated that about 65,000 had remained behind during the offensive. Thus, the current number of "ghosts" and ineligible recipients was approximately 64,000. There had been surveys in the past, and a new survey was going on at that time.[9]

Thua-Thien like Quang-Tri had been a thoroughly pacified province. It was less affected by the 1972 Communist offensive. I attribute that to a number of factors: the presence of the ARVN First Division, the best in the country; the fierce anti-Communism of its population, engendered in large part by what the VC did during the Têt offensive of 1968; and the superb reestablishment of refugees in their home villages beginning in 1968, for which Colonel Than and his province administration deserved much of the credit. All this created a loyal and defensible people. According to GVN statistics, the Easter offensive generated 110,000 refugees in the province.[10] Virtually all had returned home by the end of 1972.

Quang-Nam accounted for 59,000 war victims from March 30 to the end of 1972, and 29,500 were still in camps at the end of the year. Fifty-nine thousand Easter offensive victims were generated in Quang-Tin, of whom about 20,000 still remained in identified centers at year-end (after deducting the 9,900 Quang-Tri refugees at Chu-Lai). Two hundred four thousand Easter offensive victims were registered in Quang-Ngai during 1972, a number exceeded only by Quang-Tri; 70,100 were still in camps at year-end. Those three provinces remained dangerous places throughout the war, as the history of refugee generation recounted in this book has already demonstrated.

MR-2

The NVA attacks in Military Region 2 came somewhat later than the assaults in MR-1. GVN positions in northwest Kontum province came under attack in mid-April, but the attempt to take Kontum city did not begin until mid-May. It was defeated in two weeks.[11]

The delayed attack on Kontum provided the opportunity to remove refugees in an orderly manner, beginning early in the month. As of May 5, there were about 7,000 refugees in Kontum city, but thousands of others had fled to Pleiku, Nha-Trang, and even Saigon. Other thousands were trying unsuccessfully to move down QL-14 to Pleiku; the enemy had interdicted the road. Twenty-two hundred thirty Montagnard refugees from Kontum were moved on US Air Force planes from refugees sites in Pleiku to temporary sites in Ban Me Thuot on May

24.[12] Altogether, 45,300 Easter offensive victims were generated in the thinly populated province. Thirteen thousand nine hundred were still in Kontum camps at year-end; others were in Pleiku. Some refugees returned from Pleiku to Kontum's Mary Lou camp near the capital in the first part of 1973, but few were able to get back to their home villages. Most of Kontum remained in enemy hands.

Fifty thousand five hundred war victims were generated in Pleiku from March 30 to the end of December, of whom perhaps 10,000 remained in camps. (The Pleiku camp figures included many from Kontum.) Only 6,200 refugees were generated in Phu Bon, of whom 3,750 were still in camp in December.

When the NVA's 711th Division took the Hoai-An and Tam-Quan districts of Binh-Dinh without resistance early in May, some of the people, whose pro-VC sentiments had been hardened by the brutal Korean occupation that had just ended, welcomed the North Vietnamese. They were to be bitterly disillusioned. GVN officials were hunted down and tried in kangaroo courts. A hundred GVN-village and -hamlet cadres in Hoai-An were summarily executed. In Tam-Quan, 48 people were buried alive. Able-bodied inhabitants were taken for forced labor into the jungle, where an estimated 80% died. Younger women were permitted to volunteer ''for promotion of soldiers' morale.'' By the time the ARVN 22nd Division liberated the area three months later, all the goodwill with which the Communists had been received was gone; the lesson of northern Binh-Dinh was not lost in Saigon and elsewhere.[13]

At least 80,000 inhabitants of Binh-Dinh had been registered as refugees by early June, but the total may have been twice that number. They did not all stay within the province; some went to Nha-Trang and Cam-Ranh. When the northern districts were liberated, another 25,000 came out.[14] One hundred seventeen thousand five hundred refugees were counted as still in camps on December 29, 1972.

Phu-Yen counted only 9,500 new war victims, 3,750 of whom were still on the rolls in December.

MR-3

The NVA offensive in Region 3 began on April 3 by overrunning a fire base in Tay-Ninh province near the Cambodian border. Thereupon, III Corps ordered the evacuation of all such bases along the border. This turned out to be significant, because the territory thus surrendered included areas from which COSVN and the headquarters of the NLF and the Provisional Revolutionary Government (PRG) had fled earlier, after repeated B-52 attacks, resettling in Cambodia. Those headquarters returned in October.

The NVA attack in Tay-Ninh province was a feint to conceal the real objective, An-Loc, the capital of Binh-Long province, which was intended as the capital of the PRG. First, Loc-Ninh district in the north of the province was taken on April 6, sending thousands of refugees down QL-13 to An-Loc and on south.

By April 7, the city was encircled, and a three-month siege began. However, unlike the defenders of Quang-Tri, the GVN troops defending An-Loc, including many territorial force units, were well-led and determined, even though they took incredible punishment from the artillery and ground assaults of the attacking forces and were supplied only by air drops during most of the siege. The NVA occupied about half the city but never managed to take it all. The people, including many trapped refugees, and the defending soldiers established a close rapport, sharing food and other necessities; the civilians did soldiers' laundry, administered first aid, and helped in many other ways. The 81st Airborne Rangers and the First Airborne Brigade particularly earned the admiration and affection of the population, and refugees interviewed in a camp praised the Fifth Infantry Division as well. The 21st Division, however, which was the relieving force, got bad marks from the refugees for looting, robbery, indiscriminate firing, and other reprehensible actions. The siege of the city was ended on June 18 after three excruciating months.

Most of the city's residents were prevented by the enemy from leaving, and some said the province chief had also barred their exit; however, two groups, one led by a Catholic priest and the other by a Buddhist monk, managed to escape and headed down QL-13. After about 10 kilometers they were stopped by the invading troops, who impressed the able-bodied people into moving supplies, and took away the GVN officials, who were identified by an ARVN captain who was a Communist agent. They abandoned the women, children, and aged. These victims suffered from hunger and crossfire, and were rescued only later by an ARVN relief column.[15]

A month after the attack on Binh-Long had begun, that province accounted for 30,000 refugees, more than half those in MR-3. The number later increased to 45,000, three-quarters of the province's population. About 15,000 were in camps in and around Phu-Cuong, the capital of Binh-Duong province. Some 4,200 residents of Binh-Duong had fled to Tay-Ninh province, joining 6,000 refugees generated there.[16]

Seven thousand six hundred refugees fled from Phuoc-Long province.

In Hau-Nghia province, long a VC stronghold, the 101st NVA regiment occupied Trung-Lap, a refugee resettlement village with a large number of pro-Communist inhabitants, in late April. The North Vietnamese urged the people to leave to avoid heavy fighting that would occur, and then lured the ARVN 25th Division into flattening the village with air strikes. Three hundred houses were destroyed. Captain Stuart A. Herrington, a Vietnamese-speaking officer in the district CORDS team, visited afterwards with his GVN counterpart. A woman searching in the ruins shook her finger at a Vietnamese captain and launched into a bitter denunciation of the Americans for destroying her home. Herrington replied angrily that the Americans had nothing to do with it, but realized that "To that woman, all airplanes came from America, and she didn't care who the pilots were." He felt that the disciplined militia of the area probably could have cleared out the NVA without air strikes. In another village, the militia, police, and PSDF decimated a whole NVA company on May 11. That victory changed the outlook of the province and the local troops. By the end of the month, the North Vietnamese had been pushed out of the district.[17] Twenty thousand two hundred inhabitants of Hau-Nghia became refugees, but all had left the camps by year-end.

Binh-Duong, a province literally on the outskirts of greater Saigon, was host to many of the refugees from Binh-Long, which undoubtedly raised the percentage of population under GVN control but did not benefit outlying hamlets. Twenty-two thousand of its inhabitants became war victims. At the end of the year, its camps held 28,900 refugees, most of whom evidently came from Binh-Long.

In Long-Khanh, which had become sufficiently safe to be chosen as one of Dr. Dan's land development areas, 10,300 inhabitants became refugees, with 4,300 still in that status at year-end.

MR-4

The fighting in the Mekong Delta began on March 22 on the Cambodian side of the border, and throughout the offensive was concentrated on both sides, with NVA units in Cambodia, Dinh-Tuong province and other nearby areas, and mainly VC local-force units in Chuong-Thien. Since the ARVN 21st Division and a regiment of the Ninth Division were redeployed to Binh-Long province to relieve the pressure against An-Loc, GVN forces in Cambodia and Military Region 4 were stretched thin and frequently relied on B-52 and other air strikes. Heavy action continued through the summer and, after a lull in September, Communist attacks resumed in October-November 1972 and again after New Year's Day, 1973. They were all defeated; no district town fell into enemy hands, even temporarily, and vital communication lines remained open. General Truong wrote: "Despite some ups and downs in the pacification effort, the enemy was unable to achieve any additional gains in population control."[18] He was over-optimistic.

Whatever the military necessity, use of such a blunt instrument as the B-52 bomber in the densely populated Delta caused grievous damage to the civilian population. *Time* magazine's investigation in Dinh-Tuong province during September 1972 revealed that farmers, including children, working in their fields, as well as some inhabitants of places where Communist troops had been, were struck down. In the month of July alone, more than 125 B-52 missions were flown over that small province.[19]

Chuong-Thien had long been an insecure province. The heaviest fighting in MR-4 during the Easter offensive occurred there. Nonetheless, relatively few of its hamlets were abandoned. Twenty-nine thousand one hundred of its people became refugees, the largest provincial total in the region, but none were in camp in late December. Few refugees in the Delta needed to live in camps. When our IGA (Inspector General of Foreign Assistance) team visited the province in October 1972, we found a number of refugees living on their boats and in the hamlets where they were moored.

Vinh-Binh, with an ethnic Cambodian majority, had been another risky province. Only 2,000 refugees were generated by the 1972 offensive, none of whom were in camp.

There had been heavy fighting in Kien-Giang, which generated 17,000 refugees; in Dinh-Tuong, with 7,000; and in Kien-Phong, with 22,000 war victims. Only 5,600 new refugees came from An-Xuyen, far fewer than during the U-Minh Forest campaign of 1970-71 (chapter 11).

All told, the NVA offensive and the ensuing fighting had generated 1,288,800 refugees by the end of December 1972; 732,000 of them were in MR-1, another 291,500 in MR-2, some 158,100 in MR-3, and 107,200 in MR-4. Six hundred seventy-four thousand seven hundred refugees were still in identified locations, about 400,000 had returned home, and the remainder were living with friends or relatives, or caring for themselves.[20] The offensive had caused great suffering to a population that had grown to expect a better future after all its previous dislocations, and imposed an enormous new burden on the country's economy and its refugee and social welfare capabilities.

RELIEF AND REESTABLISHMENT

By 1972, the GVN had developed a smoothly functioning refugee–social welfare structure in Saigon and across the country, which had handled many emergencies that occurred even in the best of times, as well as restoring millions of refugees to productive lives in their former homes and new resettlement sites. In the Central Pacification and Development Council (CPDC) it had a coordinating mechanism which, while sometimes performing weakly in enforcing its own policies on recalcitrant corps commanders, was competent in mobilizing both civil and military resources for both emergency assistance and rural pacification and development. The Easter Offensive disrupted pacification and ongoing refugee programs in many parts of the country, but it did not overstrain the existing capabilities to care for large numbers of newly displaced people. Commodities were stockpiled in regional and province warehouses, and both GVN and US transport was available to replenish them.

However, on April 5, at the begining of the offensive, the government established the Central Committee for the Relief of War Victims, with Dr. Dan as chairman. A month later, a delegation headed by the Prime Minister and including Dr. Dan and Major General Cao Hao Hon, Secretary of the CPDC, visited Da-Nang. The DepCORDS of MR-1, John Gunther Dean, recommended strongly that a military man be put in charge of war-victim relief in the region, and the Prime Minister asked the Minister of Chieu Hoi to take on that assignment. However, he begged to be excused, and ultimately the Prime Minister decided that he and his Cabinet would take charge of relief throughout the country. At

Dr. Dan's suggestion, General Hon was named as the executive agent. This was ratified by the Prime Minister's Decree of May 15, establishing the Central Committee for Supply and Relief of Evacuees and War Victims (CCSR). It is unclear why Dr. Dan was replaced after only five weeks. In an interview with an American journalist, he hinted that there was too much interference by others in the government in his management of the program. While he was in charge, he had planned to move about 150,000 of the refugees from Da-Nang to Regions 2 and 3, but General Hon canceled that plan as soon as he had taken over. The general then explored the possibility of moving the refugees temporarily to some islands off the coast of MR-1, but that was found to be infeasible, so the refugees remained in the Da-Nang camps.[21]

Within the US Mission, an ad hoc committee was formed, chaired by Norman Firnstahl, Associate Director of CORDS for War Victims (ADWV), and including representatives of other CORDS units and USAID Public Health and Engineering officials.[22]

In Washington, a similar interagency committee was formed, chaired by John Arthur, Director of Vietnam Affairs, AID Bureau of Supporting Assistance; and including representatives from other AID bureaus; the National Security Council; Office of Management and Budget; and the Departments of State, Defense, and Agriculture. The two US committees in Washington and Saigon were able to arrange funding of the emergency relief, the provision of PL 480 commodities, and the use of military assets. AID personnel ceilings were relaxed to permit CORDS and USAID to keep refugee and public health advisors slated for rotation or termination.[23]

As was the case in the Têt emergency of 1968, the initial GVN-US emergency relief effort was effective. Temporary shelters, including the former US base camps, were quickly put in order by the authorities, voluntary agencies, and the refugees themselves. Food and other supplies were provided promptly and in most cases distributed fairly. The USAID released one billion piasters (at 420 = $1) on May 23, 1972, for a special fund. At first, the former separate benefits for refugees and war victims were applied, but a new system, unifying the two programs under the heading "war victims," was introduced early in August.[24]

However, coordination in Saigon turned out to be something less than perfect. On June 20, John R. Mossler, the USAID Director, rejected a CORDS request for additional piaster funds, saying that this should be budgeted by the GVN, and then, without informing Firnstahl, told the GVN that after September 1 there might not be any more American Aid Chapter funds for war victims assistance. As a result, General Hon placed tight restrictions on expenditures from the one-billion-piaster fund, and reduced the rice ration. ADWV objected, and urged the MSW and General Hon to continue adequate support of the displaced people. In mid-August, President Nixon announced that the United States would make available an additional $15 million (equivalent to 6.45 billion $VN) for refugee relief, and the crisis was over.[25]

In September, Dr. Dan was brought back into the refugee picture by being named chairman of a small interministerial committee responsible for finding resettlement sites. He was authorized to go to Da-Nang to persuade the war victims in the camps to resettle to the south.[26] One reason for this was that President Thieu was exerting increased pressure to get the refugees out of camps, and General Truong had written to the Prime Minister asking that as many as possible be taken out of MR-1. Dr. Dan had found some new land, and Nay Luett, Minister for Ethnic Minority Development, was urging that up to 90,000 highlanders then in camps, most of them from Kontum north of Dak To, be resettled in Darlac. The Ministry of Land Reform had found two sites with over 19,000 hectares in the latter province. The Bru settlement there was already successful. One of Nay Luett's motives was reportedly to reestablish a Montagnard majority in Darlac.[27]

Communist attacks against refugee sites continued during much of 1972. One of the most serious occurred during the early morning hours of September 9, when sappers killed 27 refugees and wounded at least 120 at two sites near Da-Nang. Twenty of the dead were at Camp Books, the largest center, where four buildings housing some 200 families were destroyed. At the Khai-Quang site, a section of Camp Haskins, seven refugees were killed and about 50 injured.[28]

Communist activity in and around the land development settlement of Dong-Tam II in Xuan-Loc district of Long-Khanh province from October 28 to November 2 killed two people and destroyed 80 houses. The people fled to Dong-Tam I but returned after a few days, when the settlement was secured. In December, a VC unit attempted to destroy two bulldozers clearing land at the first of Dr. Dan's land development centers, Soui-Nghe, and held an operator for a short time.[29] That site had sustained a more serious attack in June 1972.

A serious case of corruption relating to the purchase and distribution of rice in Da-Nang surfaced in September. At the CCSR meeting of September 25, the representative of the Ministry of Economy reported that some bad rice bought from local merchants by the Da-Nang city administration was being refused by the refugees. Jim Ready, Acting Chief of the regional CORDS War Victims Division, had already reported this to the regional P&D Council and to Saigon. At the CCSR meeting, General Hon authorized the Quang-Tri province administration-in-exile to purchase rice in the future from GVN warehouses. Mr. Hu'ng of the MSW urged an investigation.[30]

This was the second time in recent months that substandard rice had been distributed to the refugees. The first time had been in August, when 700 tons had been bought; the refugees threatened to riot then, and the matter had been aired by Vietnamese newspapers and CBS television in the United States. The chief of the regional P&D Council and Refugee Program Coordinator, Colonel Pham Cao Dong, had demanded and received authority to buy rice from government warehouses. Later, however, the Prime Minister's office had ordered a return to the practice of buying from local merchants.[31]

An investigating team was appointed in September, chaired by a representative of the Justice Ministry and including representatives of the Interior Ministry,

Directorate General of National Police, and MSW (Huynh Thanh Hu'ng). In Da-Nang the team inspected sample bags of rice, finding some mixed with plastic pellets. On the voyage up from Saigon, some bags of rice and other bags of the plastic had burst; the loose cargo was swept up and rebagged. There was not much of this, and the plastic was not poisonous. Much more serious was that a lot of red, broken, and insect-infested rice that was ordinarily fed to animals had been bought from local merchants at prices very close to that charged for no. 1 rice. The delegation recommended sanctions against the mayor and deputy mayor of Da-Nang, as well as the chief of the city's economy service and the deputy chief of the SW service, all of whom had been involved in the corruption.[32]

At just that time (early October) a foreign assistance inspection by the IGA team headed by me was in Da-Nang. We visited a number of the camps, where angry refugees showed us some of the bad rice, and I discovered that the plastic pellets had been destined for a small factory near one of the camps. We found, as had the GVN team, that the poor rice had been bought at a high price by city officials for the ration period September 1–10; there were 1,300 tons of pink rice and 530 tons of broken white rice, all of it dirty. The refugees had been afraid to complain, but five camp leaders had refused to accept it, even though no rice at all had been provided for the succeeding ration periods and the refugees had received no milk, salt, or fish sauce for many weeks.

Three rice merchants were jailed, and the accused officials, except for the mayor Colonel Nguyen Ngoc Khoi, were suspended in mid-October and dismissed the next month. The mayor, who had high political connections in Saigon, was eventually removed as well but was transferred to another position.[33] It had been estimated that in the first two months of the crisis alone as much as the equivalent of $10,000 a day had been siphoned off from rice purchases for the refugees.[34]

THE US FOREIGN ASSISTANCE INSPECTION

The Inspector General of Foreign Assistance (IGA), who reported directly to the Secretary of State, was mandated by federal law to conduct periodic examinations of all programs, civil and military, funded under the Foreign Assistance Act. Our IGA inspection team which was in Viet-Nam from September 24 to October 14, consisted of Robert J. Carroll, a young Foreign Service Officer who spoke fluent Vietnamese, Donald B. Kraft, an experienced auditor, and me. We visited refugee sites in all four regions. Bob Carroll and I were familiar with the programs and problems that we were to inspect, and Don Kraft had no difficulty looking into the intricate financial records of USAID, CORDS, and the relevant GVN agencies.

We found that, although both Vietnamese and American agencies had done a splendid job of coping with the emergency after the initial NVA attacks, there had been a deterioration of attention and refugee care as the months wore on. The statistics of refugee numbers, based as they were on incomplete but sometimes padded registrations, were unreliable and an invitation to corruption by both GVN officials and the refugees themselves. In the more than a score of camps that we visited, in only one, in Pleiku, did we see the official green cards that were supposed to be issued to all recognized camp refugees, now called war victims. The refugees themselves did not know why they had not received the proper documents. Food distributions were recorded in various ways of differing credibility, the lists sometimes showing utterly implausible family data. Thus, for example, Camp Books, outside Da-Nang, claimed 68,000 war victims receiving rations, but when the MSW's Inspector General arranged a one-day police survey without notice, after sealing the camp early one morning, only 50,000 were counted. Nonetheless, the camp officials continued claiming many more refugees than that. The CORDS War Victims advisors in MR-2 told us that the name lists in Binh-Dinh, which totaled 115,200 in-camp and 41,600 out-of-camp war victims as of October 4, were inflated so that some of the SW cadres could steal commodities. Repeat surveys were conducted from time to time to eliminate "ghost refugees," but seldom succeeded.

The condition of the refugees in camps in the Da-Nang area and the three camps we visited in Binh-Dinh were worse than those that had been experienced by the Têt victims of 1968. Their circumstances were more difficult to start with, in that, unlike the Têt victims, most of whom had remained in their home cities and villages near their jobs, the 1972 victims were generally at some distance from their home villages and away from their rice fields or other sources of livelihood. Their camps, some of which were huge, were terribly overcrowded, with poor sanitation, often insufficient potable water, inadequate schools for the children, and poor security. Clothing and blankets were often inadequate, although we found blankets in MSW warehouses. Worst of all, the camps offered little opportunity for employment or other activity, although the refugees themselves often set up little shops. As a result, most refugees simply vegetated, and thereby lost their self-respect. We found that there was poor camp leadership and sloppy administration in the Da-Nang camps under the control of Quang-Tri officials, and that, even apart from the rice scandal, commodity distributions were usually late and incomplete. The regional CORDS agricultural advisor, Charles Fields, had started some excellent chicken and vegetable garden projects in the limited space available, but they were only a drop in the bucket of need. In the three Phu-Tai camps of Binh-Dinh province, which together claimed to house almost 82,000 refugees, we encountered evidence of widespread diversion of rations and other supplies by the camp officials. The ARVN major who had been in charge of Phu-Tai I was removed as a result of our findings. Others should have been removed as well.

On the other hand, we were greatly encouraged by a visit to a village in the northern part of Thua-Thien province, where returned refugees were cheerfully rebuilding their houses with lumber from ammunition boxes, bought at 20 $VN each, assisted by local officials and with security provided by both ARVN and territorial forces.

We found a mixed situation in Darlac, where we saw an excellent Bru settlement but also visited a temporary camp for 6,000 war victims which was overcrowded; and the SW service chief was no better than the one in Binh-Dinh. Hugh O'Neill, the CORDS refugee advisor, was one of the finest officers I had ever encountered; he had been my social welfare advisor when I was the II CTZ refugee chief in 1969. O'Neill was a real bundle of energy, with excellent rapport with the Vietnamese and Montagnard leaders.

Pleiku was in a rather chaotic state when we visited, with a new service chief expected momentarily. Records were not in order, and the people were not getting their rice rations. In the eight camps in Kontum city, some of which were located in schools, the situation was confused. The province chief wanted to move the people out of the city, and they were anxious to go; however, Saigon was opposed.

When I reported these findings at Mr. Firnstahl's meeting on October 10, the CORDS and USAID officials were already at work on the Da-Nang rice scandal, but said that the other information we brought back had not reached them from the field.[35]

The officials in MR-4, including Lt. General Nghi, the Corps Commander, had much difficulty with General Hon over the eligibility of the out-of-camp war victims, who were the majority in that lush region. Our inspection team made a suggestion to solve that problem, and in some provinces a satisfactory solution was found.[36]

We found that after AID/Washington had sent a telegram on May 9 authorizing the retention of both public health and refugee advisors whose positions were stated for abolition, the USAID had requested the extension of six public health officers but had made no move to delay the planned reduction of CORDS/WVD (War Victims Directorate) personnel to 25 by the end of FY 1973, and indeed had decided to immediately abolish the positions of refugee personnel whose tours of duty were ending. We recommended that at least 30 to 32 refugee advisors be retained.[37]

We also recommended improvements in the financial and logistical management of the program, especially on the GVN side, and that attention be given to longer-range planning under various assumptions as to the course of the war. In view of the fact that US military involvement in refugee care was continuing to decline, while resettlement and development could be expected to be of increasing importance, we proposed that the War Victims Directorate be transferred from CORDS to USAID.[38]

Many of our recommendations were adopted even before we left Viet-Nam, and others were implemented shortly after our return, when we briefed AID and State officials.[39] One reason for this was undoubtedly an extraordinarily blunt report submitted on November 8, 1972, by two AID officials, William Mulcahy and Donald Goodwin, who were much less polite than we were in describing the serious flaws in both GVN and US management of the relief and resettlement effort. They found that the essential requirements of the refugees were not being met; specifically, water, sanitation, and housing were below minimum standards in most camps. While they said that food tended to be sufficient in the larger camps (this did not accord with our findings), they found that the quantity and variety in the smaller camps was much less. The Mission (by which they meant CORDS and USAID) was not taking effective action to correct these deficiencies. Though funding had been increased, the two officials considered that it was still insufficient, particularly in those line items necessary to upgrade camps. They wrote:

Despite repeated demonstrations of poor management, poor communications, poor programming, and poor execution, together with a complete lack of visible evidence of the high priority and degree of management attention claimed by the Mission for refugee relief, the Mission still attempts to maintain the fiction that CORDS and USAID have a closely coordinated, effective, top-priority program to meet essential refugee needs. . . . With rare exception, the U.S. personnel reacted immediately to the discovery of each new deficiency by demonstrating a concern for posterior protection so overwhelming in its importance as to completely eclipse the first priority need to take immediate remedial action.

The Mission ad hoc refugee committee, they found, did not exercise executive authority. They recommended the establishment of a single directive authority over all USAID and CORDS elements involved in refugee assistance, the setting of minimum standards and resource requirements, and the formation of joint US-GVN mobile inspection and direction teams with authority to remove administrative obstacles and take action as necessary. AID Assistant Administrator Robert Nooter transmitted this report in an *Eyes Only Confidential* letter to DepCORDS George Jacobson and USAID Director John Mossler, saying, ''I believe we have a serious problem on our hands which deserves your most urgent attention.'' He said that the report differed from the official reporting, which indicated that the two directors were not receiving the full story from their staffs. He himself would be in Saigon shortly to discuss the matter further.[40]

The effect of our briefing, which was followed by a formal IGA report on December 8, combined with that of the Mulcahy-Goodwin report, was to bring about some long-delayed action. One of the most important steps was the creation of two GVN-US ''impact teams,'' each containing 10 members with responsibility for war victims, Food for Peace (PL 480 food), public works, public health, and regional affairs, and with authority and funds to hire labor, purchase supplies, and do whatever else was needed to correct problems in MR-1 and -2 refugee sites. The MR-2 team suffered an air crash in December, which killed a Vietnamese brigadier general and ''Mac'' McLendon and injured several others, including Lt. Colonel Le Van Ba of the MSW. However, another team was quickly put together, and it continued the work. The Ngok Long site in Kontum province, formerly the US Mary Lou base, was found to be a model camp, with plenty of room, adequate water, and so on for its 13,000 refugees who had recently moved from other camps.[41]

AID/Washington requested that the War Victims and Community Development Directorates, including Ethnic Minorities Affairs, be transferred from CORDS to USAID effective February 1, 1973, and that was done.[42]

At the same time, the US Mission sent comments on the IGA inspection, agreeing with its recommendations and reporting on their implementation by both the GVN and CORDS/USAID. Among the most important measures were the allocation of substantial funds for employment-generating projects (principally camp upgrading), the provision of additional classrooms and Ministry of Education teachers, an order by the Prime Minister that all refugee camps were to be adequately protected, the replacement of SW service chiefs in Quang-Tri and some other provinces, additional emphasis on distribution and clearance of land, accelerated auditing of piaster accounts, and the establishment of a mission refugee committee cochaired by the DepCORDS and the USAID Director.[43] The formal AID reply to our report, setting out in detail what was being done, was transmitted early in March, and we were able to close the investigation.[44]

THE AFTERMATH

Recognizing the intractable size and conditions of the residual refugee population in Region 1, the Prime Minister once again turned to Dr. Phan Quang Dan. On March 14, 1973, he issued a decree establishing an Interministerial Committee in Charge of Return-to-Village and Resettlement of War Victims, with Dr. Dan as chairman and Minister of Social Welfare Dr. Phieu as vice chairman. The committee was given responsibility to provide relief assistance to war victims in temporary camps, clear those camps as soon as possible by return to village or resettlement, carry out necessary reconstruction, and coordinate aid for recovery of war victims.[45]

The first officially sponsored return of Quang-Tri refugees to their home villages began on March 16, and about 6,000 went back to Hai-Lang district in four days. There lay before them the huge job of rebuilding their lives in the shattered province. Rice and other food, tents, lumber, and roofing had been brought to the area in advance. GVN soldiers checked the land for booby traps and unexploded ordnance. Twelve tractors were provided.[46] That was almost two months after the cease-fire agreement of January 27. By the end of May, 21,800 refugees from the camps in Da-Nang and Thua-Thien–Hue had been able to return home to Quang-Tri.[47] Additional numbers came later, but the northern half of the province remained in NVA hands and the capital city was in ruins and off-limits to civilians. As of mid-June 1973, the official population of the Da-Nang camps was 239,200 and of those in and around Hue 47,400, consisting almost entirely of refugees from Quang-Tri.[48] Even after Dr. Dan eliminated the ghost refugees, many real refugees remained who would have to be resettled elsewhere if they were not to remain in the miserable camps indefinitely.

Several hundred thousand more refugees, many of them generated in the post–"cease-fire" fighting, were in other recognized centers. The official total was

521,000 in all regions (including the Quang-Tri war victims) as of mid-June 1973.[49] There were thousands of others not in camps. They all needed to be reestablished. The labors of Sisyphus were to begin again.

The Easter offensive had inflicted a blow to the non-Communist forces and people of South Viet-Nam from which they never recovered. An innovative study by Professor Richard Shultz of the Fletcher School of Law and Diplomacy analyzing provincial HES (hamlet evaluation system) aggregates by hamlets instead of by population, revealed that even before the Easter offensive (and despite the pacification successes recounted in chapter 10), large numbers of hamlets in many important provinces were under dangerous degrees of Communist influence or control, or were abandoned outright, during the period from January 1970 through 1971 and into 1972. In much of the country GVN control and territorial security regressed further during the Easter offensive and remained low at the end of 1972.[50] This revelation would have come as no surprise to the hundreds of thousand refugees who had fled from those areas and felt unable to return home, but it contradicted the conventional wisdom that pacification had succeeded throughout the nation. Unlike the situation after Têt 1968, when VC cadres and troops had been decimated and there was a vacuum in the countryside that aggressive American and GVN forces could and did fill, this time the territory abandoned by ARVN was occupied by badly mauled but still operational NVA and VC units, and on the margins the struggle for control went on. Moreover, Soviet and Chinese support of the North Vietnamese continued at a high level, while US support of the South was being steadily eroded. The cease-fire agreement of January 1973 ratified the changed balance of power and entrenched the NVA and its puppets legally on what had been GVN territory.

13

Resettlement and Return of Refugees to Home Villages, 1972–74

As the hopeless condition of most refugees in I CTZ despite all efforts at camp upgrading became apparent in 1971, the Vietnamese government reverted to an experiment it had rejected in 1967 for political reasons and then had tried, with limited success two years later—interzonal resettlement. This time the GVN realized that the complex and arduous work of preparing and carrying through such long-distance movements and reestablishment was beyond the capacity of any single Ministry and would require a full-time authority that could mobilize the resources of several agencies, both civil and military, Vietnamese and American. However, the CPDC, already occupied with the pacification task and, none too successfully, with trying to discipline recalcitrant corps commanders who were relocating people in violation of its directives, could not take on this new job. Consequently, in late 1971, the Prime Minister turned to one of the country's most remarkable politician-administrators, Dr. Phan Quang Dan, appointing him Secretary of State (a rank higher than Minister) for Land Development and Hamlet Building (LDHB) and creating an interministerial committee to assist him.

Thus began a program which in the next few years transformed the process of refugee resettlement, giving new prospects for a productive life to many thousands of uprooted people who had been condemned to hopeless idleness in wretched camps. Toward the end of 1972 Dr. Dan and Dr. Tran Nguon Phieu, the Minister of Social Welfare, were given responsibility to find new homes for the new refugees generated by the NVA Easter offensive of 1972. Then came a second wave of new refugees, generated by the protracted warfare arising from the ill-fated "cease-fire" agreement of January 1973. In some cases, the generals and province chiefs used those unfortunate people as pawns in their misguided struggle for territorial control. However, the great majority of the war victims too came under the ministering wing of the refugee resettlement programs.

Although availability of secure agricultural land remained the major problem, the humanitarian resettlement efforts had achieved some successes just as the North Vietnamese were beginning their final offensive in 1975.

WHO WAS THIS DR. DAN?

We have met this man earlier in this book, when he was made responsible for resettlement of the Vietnamese refugees from Cambodia in 1970 (chapter 9) and of the 1972 Easter offensive victims (chapter 12). He was a Northerner, born in 1918 in Nghe-An province, which was the birthplace of Ho Chi Minh, and was a classmate of Vo Nguyen Giap at Hanoi University. In 1939, while a medical student, he joined clandestine nationalist organizations to fight colonialism. Just as he was finishing medical school, famine struck the Red River Delta in 1945, and Dr. Dan organized an association for collecting leftover food for the hungry people who flooded into the city. It was successful and spread to other towns, altogether feeding 300,000 people. When the Communists took over Hanoi in 1946, Ho Chi Minh offered Dr. Dan the Labor Ministry in a coalition government, but he refused and left the country for China, where he worked as a physician in Shanghai. For over two years he was political advisor to Bao Dai and for a brief period Minister of Information, but he resigned when the emperor agreed with the French on terms that left Viet-Nam still their vassal. He later repeatedly refused the position of Minister of National Defense which was offered by Bao Dai and the French. He cooperated actively with Tunisian, Moroccan, and Algerian nationalists in the struggle against French colonialism. Dan took a second medical doctorate at the Sorbonne and then a doctorate in public health at Harvard. In 1955, he returned to Viet-Nam, practicing medicine among the poor, first near the Saigon docks, then in Gia-Dinh. In addition, he started to create a loyal opposition to Diem. Dr. Dan was overwhelmingly elected over the Diem candidate in the 1958 elections for the National Assembly, but the government prevented him from taking his seat.

In 1960, after supporting an abortive coup, Dr. Dan was arrested, and spent the next three years in jail, being released only after Diem's fall. He was elected in May 1965 to the Gia-Dinh provincial council, and became its chairman. In 1966 he was elected to the Constituent Assembly, where he strongly advocated land reform and turning provincial administration over to civilians, which would have allowed ARVN officers to devote the best of their time to fighting the Communist insurgency. From September 1969 to March 1970, as Minister of State in charge of External Affairs, he brought Viet-Nam into the Association of Southeast Asian Nations (ASEAN) as an observer member. He also restored relations with Indonesia, which had been broken under Diem. In April 1970, the government put him in charge of flood relief in central Viet-Nam and then in charge of the settlement of repatriates from Cambodia. It was during these assignments that he conceived the idea of putting refugees and others on the vast tracts of abandoned or unoccupied land that he found, much of which was owned by the government. He started by settling the Vietnamese from Cambodia on some of this land.[1]

Dr. Dan has been a democratic nationalist and a humanitarian all his life. He applied his principles forcefully to every job he undertook, which did not always make him popular with his superiors or colleagues, but nonetheless he rose to the highest ranks of his government. There was one position he was denied in the GVN: Minister of National Defense. He was incorruptible and, almost uniquely among most high officials, he did not send his son abroad to escape military service. Air-captain pilot Phan Quang Tuan was shot down by Soviet missiles over Cam-Lo on April 6, 1972, after having destroyed seven Soviet-built tanks. Dr. Dan received condolences from every embassy in Saigon, but not from his own government which, as he put it, "considered me stupid for not having sent my son to France or the USA as all of them had done."[2] In 1975 Dr. Dan escaped, first to mainland US, then to St. Thomas, the Virgin Islands, where he practiced medicine and, through his writings and in other ways, actively supported freedom for Viet-Nam, Laos, and Cambodia. At present, living in the mainland United States, he is even more active in this cause.

THE BEGINNINGS OF LAND DEVELOPMENT AND HAMLET BUILDING

Soui-Nghe, in Phuoc-Tuy province, was the first LDHB settlement. Several thousand inhabitants of the Cam-Lo and Ha-Thanh refugee camps were moved there in January 1972. By October of that year, when I visited it, the people were the only refugees with whom I had ever spoken who did not want to return home (chapter 9). In planning that move, Dr. Dan firmly established and enforced the principle that such relocations must be entirely voluntary; he never thereafter deviated from that rule. Dr. Dan would move no refugee unless he had a request for the relocation signed by the family head. His program had nothing in common with General Ngo Dzu's "Gathering People for Hamlet Establishment" (chapter 11). A delegation of the refugees had come down from Quang-Tri on November 27, 1971, and was met by Dr. Dan, officials of CORDS, the province chief, a representative of the Land Reform Ministry, and Lt. Colonel Ba of the MSW. They visited two possible sites in the province, Ba-To and Soui-Nghe. Discussing the matter in the province chief's house afterwards, the delegation chose Soui-Nghe.[3] Thereafter, the delegation reported to its constituency. Several hundred more refugees signed up to be in the first party than actually went; they decided instead to wait.[4] Within a short time, Dr. Dan had received numerous additional requests from social, political, and religious groups in MR-1. The Ministry of Rural Development inquired about the possibility of resettling at least 5,000 RD cadres who were soon to be terminated.[5]

In late April, 1,726 Catholic refugees from Quang-Tin province arrived in the port of Vung-Tau and were taken to the large resettlement area Nui-Le in Xuan-Loc district of Long-Khanh province. Their journey overland was secured by an RF battalion and other troops, and refugees were quickly recruited into PF and PSDF units. At first, water was a problem, with only three of eight dug wells producing marginal amounts. A request had been made for a deep-well rig. The refugees were pleased with the quality of the land alloted to them, and expected to be agriculturally self-sufficient in six months, barring unforeseen difficulties. Both the province chief and the district chief were interested and helpful, particularly because the refugees were occupying an important tactical area.[6] Later others joined them, and the area was divided into a number of settlements with different names.

Seventeen hundred twenty families with 9,328 people, were resettled in four "Dong-Tam" ("To Be in Agreement") sites in Long-Khanh province during the period from May to September 1972. The 522 families in Dong-Tam I had come from Chu-Lai, Quang-Tin province, where they had become unemployed with the closing of the US base. They were led by a Catholic priest. By early October they had built a seven-room school; water had been reached in the deep well; and both a sawmill cooperative and a carpentry cooperative had been established. All the people had built their houses, and 110 hectares of farm land had been cleared. That was not much, but heavy rains had delayed the clearance of the total 261 hectares—one-half hectare per family. The refugees were impatient to have the land distributed. With them temporarily, in 51 large tents, were 444 Cham refugee families from Phuoc-Long, Binh-Long, and Binh-Duong, who had been in the An-Loi camp. They were to settle in Dong-Tam IV as soon as land was cleared. The 515 families in Dong-Tam II were from Quang-Ngai, led by two Catholic priests. All had built their homes and cultivated gardens. They established a temporary school by self-help. The latest arrivals were 239 families from the northern districts of Quang-Tri, who had been in Da-Nang, Xuan-Loc, and Nha-Trang. They were in temporary houses made of saplings and tarpaulins, and were starting to build their homes.[7]

Our IGA inspection team visited these sites and Soui-Nghe on October 11, 1972, and found that the reports prepared for us had not exaggerated their progress. All the centers had a good deal of land around them, but most of it was not cleared, and none had been distributed. We found the same situation at the LDHB sites we visited in Region 2, where Vietnamese had encroached on Montagnard settlement land. Delays in making land available to the settlers constituted the one point of our criticism concerning the program. Our report recommended that agricultural land promised to the resettled refugees should be distributed as a matter of urgency and that land reserved for the Montagnards be protected from encroachment.

Some of the Vietnamese repatriates from Cambodia were also settled under the LDHB program. Early in February 1972, Dr. Dan and other officials, together with Franklin Stewart and Carole Steele of CORDS WVD, visited two sites in Kien-Phong province where repatriates had recently settled. They observed the dredging of overgrown canals, and then saw the astonishing transformation the refugees had wrought in what had been quiet little outpost areas. The people had built houses, were keeping chickens and ducks, and some had shops. Others were fishermen, to whom Dr. Dan distributed token nylon string to make nets (more was to come later). In one hamlet each family was preparing to cultivate five hectares of floating rice as soon as the rainy season arrived.

One of the repatriate resettlement hamlets was Tan-Thanh, where 3,500 settlers had moved from an unsatisfactory site in November 1972. Already a school, a maternity-dispensary, a police station, and other public buildings were being built by the refugees. Eighteen hundred twenty-five of the settlers had been assisted by the GVN to move; the others had moved themselves, and more settlers were expected.[8]

However, in April 1972, Tan-Thanh, which turned out to be on a Communist main-force line of communication, became insecure, and 2,300 people fled from it. In November, the corps commander declared that it was secure again and the people could return home. They disagreed strongly, and requested to move to Soui-Cat in Long-Khanh under the LDHB program. At two successive meetings of the CPDC Central Recovery Committee, the top GVN representatives—in the second meeting, General Hon—said that, in view of the corps commander's declaration, there was no basis for further assistance or for their move to Soui-Cat.[9] However, the refugees and Dr. Dan won. Late in December, 1,870 of them traveled by truck and bus to Soui-Cat, where temporary shelters had been constructed in advance and their home sites had been cleared.[10]

There were other transfers to LDHB settlements in 1972, but the larger movement did not get under way until Dr. Dan was formally put in charge of return to village and resettlement of refugees in the spring of 1973.

RESETTLEMENT AND RETURN TO VILLAGE OF EASTER OFFENSIVE WAR VICTIMS AND OTHER REFUGEES

As the months since the massive surge of refugees from the NVA Easter offensive rolled by, the temporary camps that had been hastily made ready for them steadily deteriorated. Moreover, the refugees in the Da-Nang camps and most other camps in MR-1, as well as those in the Phu-Tai camps in Binh-Dinh, could not become self-supporting in those locations. However, it became clear, after Quang-Tri city (then a heap of rubble) had been recaptured on September 16, 1972, that most of that province would remain in enemy hands. Plans were formulated by the province government-in-exile to return some of the war victims to their home in the southern part of the province, but those who had come from the areas still under NVA control would have to be settled elsewhere. President Thieu had already ordered that the camps should be cleared rapidly, and in September 1972, General Truong wrote to the Prime Minister asking that as many refugees as possible be taken out of the region. It was a politically painful recommendation, but a sound one. At that point, Dr. Dan was put in charge of a small interministerial committee to find resettlement sites, and to urge the MR-l refugees to go south (chapter 12). However, in the light of the findings and recommendations of our IGA inspection team, and in the expectation that the Paris negotiations would soon bring about an end to the war, the energies of the GVN and CORDS/USAID were applied principally to upgrading the camps, using the impact teams. In retrospect, had we known what the cease-fire agreement would bring, we should have recommended emptying the camps and resettling the refugees where there was sufficient land. More months passed before that conclusion was drawn.

It was only on March 14, 1973, that the Prime Minister created the Interministerial Committee in Charge of Return-to-Village and Resettlement of War Victims, with Dr. Dan as chairman and Dr. Phieu as vice chairman (chapter 12). This body had responsibility for and authority over the whole gamut of functions necessary to reestablish war victims, principally the regular resettlement program under Dr. Phieu and LDHB under Dr. Dan. On it were represented all the agencies whose services would be needed to accomplish its work.[11] It had a monumental task. There were 661,300 registered war victims in camps throughout the country, of whom 255,600 were in 34 sites in Da-Nang alone and 163,000 in the rest of MR-1. The second military region counted 187,200, of whom 137,900 were in Binh-Dinh. Region 3 had 52,000 refugees, of whom 31,600—mainly from Binh-Long—were still in camps in Binh-Duong. There were only 3,500 refugees in MR-4, all of them at one site in Chau-Doc. Some of the in-camp populations were victims of the post-cease-fire fighting. The committee planned to resettle 250,000 and return the remainder to their homes by year-end. The RTV projection was less than the 209,418 returned in 1972 plus the 663,113 in RTV process at the end of that year, but the War Victims Directorate of the USAID considered these estimates probably unreachable. It expected that at least 100,000 refugees would still be in camps at the end of 1973.[12]

Dr. Dan's committee operated under the general direction of the Guiding Council for National Rehabilitation, which President Thieu established on June 4, with himself as chairman and the Prime Minister as secretary general. This group was to determine broad policies for the recovery of the whole economy following the cease-fire agreement and to mobilize the necessary resources. It published a strategy for healing the wounds of war, resettling war victims, reconstructing war-damaged facilities, increasing production, and establishing a comfortable life for every stratum of the population.[13] That was a noble dream which, however, was frustrated by both the continued aggression of the Communists and the warlike policies of the GVN itself.

The GVN in consultation with the US Mission had budgeted 42.0 billion piasters for war victim relief and reestablishment (at 475 = $88,421,000 US) in 1973, of which about half for the MSW and half for the LDHB program. This was much more than had originally been planned, because there had been 25% inflation in 1972 and more inflation was expected in 1973. Furthermore, the GVN had decided to cease subsidizing the price of rice, thereby almost doubling its cost. Finally, the extension of territorial security had been less than expected, which meant that more refugees would remain in camps or be resettled in other locations, a more expensive process than return to their home villages. Almost all the budgetary requirement would have to be met from the American AID Chapter (counterpart funds).[14]

The committee set to work with a will. There was the closest cooperation among Dr. Dan, Dr. Phieu, and Nay Luett, Minister for Ethnic Minority Development. The Ministries of Agriculture and Public Works lent technical assistance but provided little budgetary support. The MSW and LDHB program had to supply the material resources. The USAID named Raymond Fontaine as its principal liaison officer, and later sent representatives of its agriculture, economics, logistics, transportation, and other staffs to serve under his direction. They saw to it that necessary material support was provided.

Every week saw more refugees returning home and others being resettled, some in the new hamlets, most in the regular centers. Those from the Da-Nang camps and other MR-1 sites generally moved to settlements in MR-3, although some went to a new site in Ninh-Thuan province (MR-2); the refugees in MR-2 and -3 were resettled within their own regions.[15] However, this was not a job that could be accomplished overnight.

At the same time, surveys to find and eliminate ghost refugees were conducted constantly. In July 1973, nearly 20,000 were eliminated from the Da-Nang camp rolls. Another 1,300 were stricken from the rolls in August. In December, 35,000 more were eliminated from the Da-Nang camp rosters as a result of a survey conducted primarily by university students from Saigon and confirmed by special administrative cadres assigned to the camps. Seven camp chiefs were arrested and sent to Saigon for investigation, and two more were sought. All this was announced at a press conference by Dr. Dan and the Minister of Education in Saigon. They both praised the sincerity and efficiency of those who had made the survey, and declared it a major victory over corruption. Then they turned the press conference over to the students and their teachers. One of the students said that the camps must have held the world record for having given birth to twins; some families had declared as many as three sets. Other fraudulent practices by both the refugees and the officials were described.[16]

Although the in-camp refugee population was greatly reduced by resettlement, return to village, and elimination of ghost refugees, it still remained substantial in mid- and late 1973. Some of the camps were miserable places, even worse than when our inspection team had seen them in October 1972. At the August 1, 1973, hearing of the Senate Refugee Subcommittee, Wells Klein, who had been a member of a study mission to Viet-Nam, reported:

By the time of our visit the temporary success of the emergency relief effort had deteriorated into the miserably overcrowded squalor, with its attendant lethargy, that these now permanent refugee camps evidence. This has been the history of the Vietnam refugee program. Time and again reasonably effective response to an immediate crisis has been followed by almost total neglect. We have seen a decade of "temporary" refugees living in "temporary" quarters.

Klein cited the Da-Nang and Phu-Tai camps, as well as others in Hue, Quang-Ngai, Chu-Lai, Qui-Nhon, "and in the highlands where Phu Bon, Pleiku, and Kontum present the special problem of Vietnamese discrimination against the Montagnard, discrimination unfortunately either tacitly condoned or overlooked in the administration of a refugee assistance program." He singled out a camp in Phu-Cuong, capital of Binh-Duong province, as a welcome exception. However, the An-Loi camp in the same province for highlanders from Binh-Long reportedly had the highest death rate of any camp in the country, despite extensive aid from the GVN, the United States, and voluntary agencies. He said of its inhabitants, "One has the impression that they are disintegrating as a people in prolonged refugee status."[17]

The American Consul General in Da-Nang visited Camp Books about a year after the IGA team had been there. Years later, recalling his visit, he wrote:

Conditions in the camp were sickening: over-crowding, filth, and lethargy. Newborn babies were lying side by side with dying adults. Individual cooking fires filled the airless tents with dense smoke. The hapless souls huddling together in their misery in this hell on earth didn't even have the energy to complain or protest. This description may seem over-dramatic, but, believe me, what I saw there left me aghast.[18]

This was no inexperienced novice writing. The Consul General had served in Viet-Nam, Laos, Cambodia, Taiwan, and Hong Kong in the 1950s and again in Laos in 1961–62. He was a Chinese-language officer, and had come to Da-Nang after being chief of the East Asia-Pacific division of the State Department's Intelligence and Research Bureau.

So the people were moved to resettlement sites, some well planned and some not. The VC, threatened by the new settlements on formerly vacant land which they had been accustomed to regard as their own, attacked the LDHB and regular refugee sites constantly. Some of the settlers fled, but they usually returned as soon as security was reestablished. Others, particularly the Catholics, fought back, and more often than not, drove off the attackers. They had been compelled to flee too many times, and now they were not going to be driven out of their homes again.

The official statistics for 1973 showed that 354,000 refugees had returned home that year and 496,900 (some of whom had returned in 1972) had received all their RTV benefits; 213,100 were still in the RTV process at year-end, meaning that they had returned home but had not been fully paid. The majority in all three categories were in MR-1. These figures included about 43,000 refugees who had been generated prior to the 1972 offensive.

Some 214,363 refugees had been resettled away from their homes, 48,356 of them in MR-1; 105,380 in the second region; 60,401 in MR-3; and 220 in the fourth region. However, 234,000 refugees remained in camps at the end of 1973, and 197,400 were still in camps in mid-March 1974, when these statistics were compiled. Thus, although the committee's targets for 1973 were largely met, and in the case of RTV were probably exceeded, there was still a large camp population. This was because the cease-fire agreement of January 1973 did not bring an end to combat and the generation of new refugees; instead, the fighting increased for many months.

An astonishing 484,200 in-place war victims had filed claims in 1973 for houses damaged. Thirty-one hundred had been killed, and 3,200 had submitted claims for wounds. Altogether, 631,300 were paid in 1973 for houses damaged in that year or before, 7,700 survivors were paid death benefits, and 6,200 were paid for wounds.[19] All these payments were made by the provincial SW services of the Ministry of Social Welfare.

As part of a cabinet reshuffle in February 1974, Dr. Dan was appointed Deputy Prime Minister in charge of social welfare, refugee relief and resettlement, and land development and hamlet building. He was concurrently Minister of Social Welfare. Dr. Phieu retired from the government and went into private practice as a physician.[20] It is interesting that all the top officials of the GVN in charge of refugee relief and resettlement, beginning with Dr. Nguyen Phuc Que in 1966–68 (chapter 5), continuing with Dr. Tran Lu Y in 1968–69, Dr. Tran Nguon Phieu in 1969–74 (chapter 9), and finally Dr. Dan in 1974–75, were physicians.

On March 29, 1974, Prime Minister Tran Thien Khiem and Dr. Dan led a delegation of Vietnamese and foreign dignitaries for the inauguration of a new Quang-Tri provincial headquarters in Hai-Lang district town. The United States and many other foreign countries and voluntary agencies had contributed funds and materials for the reconstruction and new buildings in the city. Some 83,000 refugees had returned to that district and the neighboring districts of Mai-Linh and Trieu-Phong.[21]

Charles W. Browne, Jr., chief of the War Victims Division of Region 1, was decorated with the Medal of Merit by President Nguyen Van Thieu on June 22, "International Aid Day." He was one of 11 recipients, each nominated by the embassy of his country. No other of the many American refugee advisors over the years had received this high award. Charlie Browne had begun his Viet-Nam service in 1966 as a deputy district advisor in Lai-Thieu, where I first met him in 1968. He had succeeded George Klein as III CTZ refugee chief, and in 1973 was transferred to MR-1. Charlie was 42 at the time of the award.[22] He was an opinionated—150% anti-Communist and pro-GVN—plain-spoken and practical but compassionate man, one of the very best. He died of cancer in October 1976.

Although there were still 3,900 people awaiting final instructions on movement, the last of the MR-1 refugee camps was officially closed in the second week of July 1974. At the same time the final group of 800 refugees from Binh-Long left the camps in Binh-Duong province. Forty-six thousand eight hundred refugees were left in camps in the country.[23]

WHAT HAPPENED TO THE LAND?

Dr. Dan personally went all over the country looking at land that belonged to the government, was not occupied, was reasonably secure, and could be cultivated. Members of his small staff and of the MSW did likewise. Then, in consultation with corps commanders and province chiefs, he gradually gathered commitments to make this land available for resettlement. Thus, for example, in September 1973 Dr. Dan met with Brigadier General Nguyen Vinh Nghi, commander of MR-4, and his land reform and agricultural experts. They identified seven provinces with land that was thought to be available for immediate development and others that might furnish resettlement opportunities in the future. It was agreed that 100,000 hectares of land would be set aside for the LDHB program, 55,000 hectares of which in the seven provinces. In Binh-Tuy province, Region 3, another large tract was being prepared for 30,000 refugees from Quang-Tri. A total of 500,000 hectares, plus 1,500,000 hectares of main living areas for Montagnards, was promised.[24] However, the provincial authorities were very slow in clearing and distributing the land, and around such settlements as Buon Jat in Darlac province (a joint project of the MSW and the Ethnic Minorities Ministry), Vietnamese encroached on the land reserved for the Montagnards.[25]

Dr. Dan has said that he ran into serious problems with the Vietnamese generals. "As soon as we opened a resettlement site, they took the neighboring land and the province chiefs were not allowed to reveal their names. . . . It was a tough fight to try getting those lands back for the refugees."[26] One general grabbed 15,000 hectares of land. Dr. Dan took this up at a cabinet meeting, but could not get it reversed.[27]

Indeed, the provision of land remained the weak point in both the LDHB program and the regular refugee resettlement program. In mid-1973, for instance, Irwin Hamburger, the USAID land reform advisor for the central Highlands, and L. J. Van Wagoner, the chief refugee advisor of MR-2, both experienced AID foreign service officials, protested the movement of 12,000 Sedang people from the Mary Lou camp in Kontum to Plei M'nang (not an LDHB site) in Phu-Bon, which was surrounded by Jarai land. That was much too large a group of hill tribespeople (who were accustomed to living in small, widely scattered villages) to put in one place. The first thing the new arrivals asked was, "Where is our land?" Hamburger and Van Wagoner said there were sites that were more accessible than Plei M'Nang, and that the move should not have been made during the rainy season.[28]

A survey of 118 Montagnard refugee resettlement centers with 198,413 people in nine provinces made by the Land Reform Office of USAID in September 1973 revealed that only 13.5% of the resettled tribespeople in 36 sites were cultivating enough land that they could raise a 12-month rice supply and graze their cattle. Twenty-two-and-a-half percent of the people in 37 centers could raise enough rice for a 6-to-12-months' supply, and had restricted grazing. Most of them had outside employment. The other 64% could raise less than a 6-months' supply of rice, and over a third of them had little or no outside employment. That meant that they were destitute. The survey found that all but two or three of the settlements were on borrowed land; that is, land that was not their own and that they had no written permission to use. Outside employment usually meant wage labor for neighboring Vietnamese, service in the military, or gathering of forest products.[29]

Reports prepared by USAID Saigon in October 1973 and obtained by the Study Mission of the Senate Refugee Subcommittee document the lack of sufficient land for the LDHB and other refugee settlers in Regions 2 and 3. Tables 13 and 14 summarize the data for representative samples of the sites. Part of the problem in the LDHB centers was that many people who were not chosen for them moved in after they learned how pleasant they were, thus overcrowding the land. Other sites were simply occupied by people impatient to get out of the camps and move as close to their home villages as possible. Still others were selected by province chiefs, sometimes for strategic reasons, with little regard as to how the settlers would support themselves. In most of these cases, either Dr. Dan or Dr. Phieu and their services had to continue supporting the refugees with rice or money.

Late in 1973, a USAID team assessing the proposal to set aside 55,773 hectares in the Delta for refugee resettlement which had been agreed to by General Nghi in his September 1973 meeting with Dr. Dan, found only 4,000 hectares that were suitable, aside from 20,000 hectares on Phu-Quoc Island which the USAID considered impractical. Dr. Dan agrees that very little land could be resettled immediately. To make much of the available land in the Delta usable, drainage canals would have to be dredged. This had been done in some cases, but it was time-consuming and expensive. Dr. Dan had been approached by a number of dredging companies, some of them American, and he probably could have obtained funding had there been time.[30]

Some better land could have been used if it were secured, according to Richard Holdren, the former chief refugee advisor of MR-4; this was a matter of determination on the part of the corps commander and province chiefs. They lacked the interest and the will to do what would have been necessary, he asserted. The fact that securing the areas would have violated the cease-fire agreement was not a matter of concern to the GVN officers, said Holdren.[31]

By 1974, the situation had improved for some settlements. However, as of June 1974, only 1,830 (2.1%) of the 84,000 families who had been resettled by the programs in 1973 and 1974 had received temporary land titles. No permanent titles had been issued to them, since they were required to cultivate and improve the land for two years before receiving them. This was intended to prevent land speculators from buying land from the refugees and thus disrupting their resettlement. Thirty-seven hundred more temporary titles were being processed. However, according to Embassy Saigon, the lack of titles did not seem to have dampened the enthusiasm of the settlers to clear and develop the land.[32]

Table 13
Official Description of Resettlement Sites, Region 2, as of October 17, 1973

Province	Name of site	Population	Land Available	Problems
Binh-Dinh	1. Hoai-Thanh	3,376	None	Minimal security prevents farming in nearby areas.
	2. Hoai-Hao	3,238	"	"
	3. Hoai-Chau	1,260	"	"
	4. Duc-Huu	1,971	"	"
	5. An-Dong	8,113	"	"
	6. Phu-Duc	3,097	"	"
	7. Long-My	3,453	7-800 ha.	"
		24,508		
Binh-Thuan	Go-Boi	1,230		
Cam-Ranh	Vinh-Linh*	943 families/5,867	800 ha.	Land not adequate for present needs. Water, irrigation major needs. 1,647 add. settlers recently approved. Large scale land clearance needed.
Darlac	1. Buon Hang 2	3,618	4,000 m^2 per family (2/5 ha.)	
	2. Buon Cu Kpam	3,173	1/3 ha. per family	
Kontum	1. Kongu (Dakkam)	1,984	Have cleared small areas, planted rice	Need land clearance for 600 ha. reportedly available. Unexploded ordnance in area.
	2. Plei Klau Klah (Plei Sar)	1,290		

Province	Name of site	Population	Land Available	Problems
	3. Plei Broch	1,317	GVN est. 900-1,000 ha.	Do not have means to develop.
	4. Plei Klet	288	120 ha.	"
	5. Tan-Phu	795	Limited	Land available but need assistance from nearby hamlet.
	6. Tan-Phu Ext. (Desomai)	3,488	None	Crowded living area.
	7. Ngok Long (Plei Rohai)	870	Limited	
Lam-Dong	1. Tan-Rai*	944/3,314	3-4,000 ha. of public domain forest	VECCO and ARVN respon. for clearing majority, but have not begun.
	2. Minh-Rong*	2,268/7,926		

Province	Name of site	Population	Land Available	Problems
Ninh-Thuan	1. Ninh-Binh*	1,192	1 ha./family to be allocated	Access to farming area, bridge needed for heavy equipment.
	2. Tra-Giang*	863		
	3. Quang-Thuan*	9,603		
	4. Song-My*	3,552		
		15,210		

Province	Name of site	Population	Land Available	Problems
Phu-Bon	1. Buon Hoai	2,684	Only small garden plots have been allocated to each family	Crowded site will need large land clearing effort.
	2. Plei M'Nang	6,963		
Pleiku	1. Plei Bak	674/1,999	150 ha.	On a previously established main living area (MLA)
	2. Me Kuk	729/2,347	240 ha.	Land belongs to tea plantation.
	3. Le-Chon	952		Resettled on established MLA.
Quang-Duc	Sung-Duc	627		

Source: USAID Saigon, published in US Senate, *Relief and Rehabilitation of War Victims in Indochina: One Year After the Ceasefire,* a Study Mission report prepared for the use of the Subcommittee to Investigate Problems Connected with Refugees and Escapees, of the Committee on the Judiciary, United States Senate, Ninety-third Congress, Second Session. January 27, 1974, 20.

*These sites were identified as Land Development and Hamlet Building (LDHB) centers by Dr. Phan Quang Dan, November 10, 1987.

Table 14
Official Description of Refugee Resettlement Sites, Region 3, as of October 1973

Province	Name of Site	No. of Settlers	Land Reserved	Problems
Phuoc-Long	Phuoc-Tin*	1,250 families/5951	3,120 ha.	Limited secure farm areas.
Binh-Duong	Soui-Dua	44/264	130 ha.	Limited secure farm areas.
Binh-Tuy	Phuc-Am	696/3,914	1,120 ha.	High incidence of malaria Accurate survey has not been done, leading to boundary dispute with neighbors.
	Nghia-Tan	996/6,001	1,600 ha.	
	Binh-Ngai	547/3,628	880 ha.	Delays in releasing funds from province for dev. projects.
	Dong-Den*	233/1,212	4,240 ha.	
Phuoc-Tuy	Soui-Nghe*	1,738/9,482	1,494 ha.	Delays in distrib. of land. Settlers were promised 3 ha. per family, but presently not enough land is available.
Long-Khanh	Dong-Tam*	698/4,473	2,088	See below
	Trung-Nghia*	679/4,473	1,860	"
	Xuan-Da*	542/3,171	838	"
	Xuan-Hiep*	495/2,068		"
		375/1,794 remain	1,887	"
	Quang-Xuan*	285/1,700	Undetermined	"
	Soui-Cat 2*	384/2,068	1,176	"

287

Problem areas in Long-Khanh sites:

1. Delays in distribution of food and housing allowances.

2. Delays in clearing and distribution of farm land.

3. Some of farmland is too rocky for cultivation.

4. Groundwater is very deep in many areas.

5. At the sites where food allowances have been terminated (Dong-Tam, Trung-Nghia, Xuan- Da), many of the settlers are still not producing enough for a satisfactory income.

6. Fund allocations for rice continue to be computed at rate before value added tax was enforced. Since present cost is 50% more, province does not have sufficient funds to purchase amount required for distribution.

---

*Land Development and Hamlet Building (LDHB) centers, identified by Dr. Phan Quang Dan November 10, 1987.

Source: USAID Saigon, published in US Senate, *Relief and Rehabilitation of War Victims in Indochina: One Year After the Ceasefire*, 20–21.

Dr. Dan asserted that most of the LDHB settlements had sufficient land that their inhabitants could make a living. He said that at the beginning of 1974, an American committee surveyed both the RTV and the land development sites and found most of them viable.[33] Data on the Ninh-Thuan LDHB settlements as of September 1974 confirmed that they had acquired and were farming much more land than they had a year before. Additional centers were planned for the province.[34]

Reporting on July 18, 1974, to the Senate Refugee Subcommittee on the findings of a new study mission, Wells Klein said that the resettlement program had made remarkable progress since the previous mission had viewed it more than a year earlier. There were problems, such as the length of time it took to clear land, delays in granting titles, and inadequate support by the Ministries of Agriculture, Health, and Public Works. However, Klein said, those were operational rather than conceptual problems and, if they could be dealt with, it should be a successful program.[35] As it turned out, not all the problems could be dealt with, especially the lack of land in central Viet-Nam, where most of the refugees were located.[36]

Although the refugee resettlement and Land Development programs did indeed make great progress, I conclude that most of the settlements did not become viable before the final North Vietnamese offensive in 1975 overran them. That was in part because the program did not have time to solve the land problem, a lengthy process at best, which was made more difficult by the greed and heartlessness of some generals and officials, as well as by the encroachment of Vietnamese on Montagnard lands.

VICTIMS OF THE STRUGGLE FOR TERRITORY AND PEOPLE, 1973–75

In the two days and nights before the cease-fire provided in the Paris accords was to become effective (8 A.M. Viet-Nam time, January 28, 1973), Communist forces occupied more than 400 hamlets across the country, 144 of them in the provinces around Saigon. Some of them had been contested for a long time, but others, especially on major highways, were normally GVN-controlled. Part of Tay-Ninh city was one of these. Then, in the days after the "cease-fire," the GVN forces counterattacked and took back virtually all the locations. In other places, such as Quang-Tri province, the government forces had tried to seize Communist positions the same way, and were also beaten back. By the second week of February, the fighting died down, but it soon resumed.[37] Armed clashes never ceased from then on to the end of the war.

The cease-fire agreement had mandated an accommodation between the GVN on the one hand and the North Vietnamese and their puppets, the Provisional Revolutionary Government (PRG) on the other (chapter 4, articles 9–14). This accommodation did not occur for even one moment. The GVN, which had signed under US duress, never recognized the legitimacy of the PRG or the right of

Communist forces to be on South Vietnamese soil. The Communists regarded the agreement as only a step toward their conquest of the entire country. Under those circumstances, the elaborate machinery for truce supervision and political conciliation set up by the Paris agreement was a mockery. The war went on. Only American soldiers were out of it.

By mid-June 1973, some 360,700 new civilian war victims had been generated by post–cease-fire combat, of whom 319,100 were in their home areas, either having stayed there as in-place war victims who had been wounded or whose houses had been damaged or destroyed, or enabled to return home after a short period. The other 41,600 were refugees who had fled from their home areas.[38] The numbers kept rising thereafter.

Chapter 4 of the Paris agreement had said: ''The two South Vietnamese parties will . . . ensure the democratic liberties of the people: personal freedom, . . . freedom of movement, freedom of residence.''[39] Neither side honored these provisions. Quite to the contrary, both sides used civilians as instruments to assert control of territory.

The areas held by the Communists were virtually without population, because almost all of the previous inhabitants had fled or been evacuated. In order to establish plausible claims to those areas, the North Vietnamese moved some of their civilians down the Ho Chi Minh trail into them. Some went to the central highlands. In MR-3 they not only brought in northerners but also returned southerners who had fled into Cambodia from Tay-Ninh and Binh-Long provinces. Many northerners, including young women, were brought in to base areas in all regions to construct roads and other installations and to settle there.[40] In August 1973, Embassy Saigon reported that the DRVN was sending down considerable numbers of settlers, including a recent contingent of 1,000 women ''admonished, no doubt, by whatever is the Marxist equivalent of the old Biblical injunction to 'go forth and multiply.' ''[41]

GVN corps commanders and province chiefs often resettled refugees at the edges of contested areas, sometimes with tragic consequences. Embassy Saigon reported, in answer to a *New York Times* article, that territorial expansion had never been mentioned in the Interministerial Committee, nor was it ever the reason for the Committee's selection of a site for resettlement. The sites were in abandoned or virgin land, where the VC may have roamed freely in the past, but the embassy asserted that in no case were there Communist forces that had to be driven away to enable refugee settlement to proceed. However, the embassy admitted that the province chiefs of Binh-Dinh and Quang-Ngai ''have been so eager to reduce camp populations that they have hastily executed a few RTV and resettlements in an unsatisfactory manner. Advisory and Ministerial effort is correcting the situation.''[42] It needs to be understood that any area not under the firm control of one side or the other was contested during the entire Viet-Nam conflict, and the Communists often attacked even places clearly in GVN hands, as we have seen. Conversely, VC areas were regarded as free strike zones by the GVN. As a result, no part of South Viet-Nam was ever completely secure.

Involuntary Resettlement and Return to Village

There is little controversy about the facts, at least as regards the Binh-Dinh settlements. Fox Butterfield of the *New York Times* had reported that refugees had returned, under government prodding, to Hoai-Tan village in Binh-Dinh, but had been furnished no food and no seeds to plant, and were constantly caught in the crossfire between GVN and Communist troops, each camped only a few hundred yards away. Some 40,000 in all had been taken out of the camps by ARVN trucks and dropped off along Route 1 near their old villages. Butterfield wrote:

Saigon's objectives in this move, according to United States and Vietnamese officials here, are to reduce the burden of feeding so many people and to repopulate the area so that the Government will control the majority of votes in any future election. But at the same time it appears that the Government is alienating many of the refugees by coercing them into moving and failing to provide even the most elementary relief supplies and security.[43]

A few months later, Thomas W. Lippman of the *Washington Post* visited other refugees in the same area. They had not come from camps but had been removed from villages near Bong-Son, when almost 20 square miles of Communist-held territory west of QL-1 was retaken by GVN forces. Lippman claimed that, "Wrenched from their rice fields at harvest time, they are now camped in wretched huts along highway 1, more bewildered than angry, watching the continuing war." The American Consul General in MR-2, while confirming that the military action did occur at harvest time, said that the villagers came to the GVN side at their own initiative.[44]

Edward L. Block, a member of the USAID War Victims Directorate, had visited Quang-Ngai in June 1973, where, he said, none of the refugees he saw had volunteered to move to the resettlement sites selected by the GVN. They were in a battle zone. On September 26, two civilians were reported killed and four were wounded in Tu-Cung village, where My-Lai hamlet was located. The embassy said that about 1,200 My-Lai refugees had left camp on June 16, 1973, but were unable to return home because of poor security, so they stayed in the nearby hamlet of Tu-Cung. They were cultivating about 200 acres of their own fields, but were still receiving allowances as refugees. A year later some were able to cultivate their own land and were reportedly nearing self-sufficiency, but others who had temporarily resettled in Tu-Cung were in dire straits.[45] Dr. Dan had visited Quang-Ngai in mid-September 1973, and had cautioned the province chief not to rush RTV or resettlement but to concentrate on developing those sites already populated, for which money would be sent. He disapproved plans to resettle in the province the remaining 4,000 in-camp refugees.[46]

One of the saddest cases of forced repopulation of contested areas occurred in Kontum province. The inhabitants of Polei Krong village, all highlander

tribespeople, had been forcibly relocated there in the 1960s. The nearby Vietnamese Trung-Nghia village had been a land development center in the Diem
years for people forcibly moved from coastal Quang-Ngai and Binh-Dinh. Both
villages were evacuated in April 1972 during the Easter offensive, and the
inhabitants were taken to camps in Pleiku province. In September, the Kontum
province chief ordered that all refugees be returned to the province, and late in
the year the people of the two villages returned home to start rebuilding. However, they were forced to flee again when the villages were attacked at the time
of the cease-fire. When GVN forces regained the area, they were ordered back
against their will and against the counsel of the USAID refugee advisor. Then,
on June 7–8, 1973, the Communists, who claimed to have been in possession
of the area on cease-fire day, attacked again with three battalions of NVA and
VC troops, and the people fled to the Ngok Long (Mary Lou) camp, where
Arnold Isaacs interviewed them. They were determined not to repeat the experience again, and asked to be resettled where it would be safe.[47]

Other examples of forced resettlement could be cited, but those recounted
above are sufficient to establish that the practice was not infrequent in 1972–
74.[48] It had the same unfortunate consequences as the earlier forced relocations.
Wells Klein, in reporting to the Senate Refugee Subcommittee on August 1,
1973, said:

It was the Study Mission's observation that the refugees were very much voiceless pawns
in a political and territorial tug-of-war between the GVN and the PRG. They represent
an important bloc of votes in the event of an election and perhaps more important, besides
the army, they represent the only available potential for establishing de facto territorial
control in the recently intensified struggle now focusing on land as well as people.[49]

These involuntary resettlements were done at the corps and provincial level,
without the approval of Dr. Dan, Dr. Phieu, or Nay Luett. The three Ministers
tried to prevent such abuses, but rarely succeeded against the military officers
heading corps and provinces.

Evidently their protests had some positive results, however. In mid-1974,
Wells Klein told the Senate Refugee Subcommittee that:

One of the more important things we observed is that there seems to be no indication
that the GVN is systematically using refugee resettlement for territorial acquisition or
population control purposes. You will remember that this was one of our concerns last
year.

Likewise, and I think we are at some difference of opinion with our Embassy in Saigon,
we saw no indication that the PRG or the NVA are specifically targeting refugee sites
although refugee resettlement and return to village sites are periodically caught in the
war, and there are refugee areas which are occasionally and almost arbitrarily attacked.
However, there does not seem to be a purposive attempt by the other side to disrupt
refugee resettlement.[50]

Forcible Retention of People in GVN Areas

Although Dr. Dan and Dr. Phieu were prepared to allow people to return to villages in PRG territory if they wished, the GVN officials in many provinces made no pretense of abiding by this provision of the Paris agreement. Despite the protestations of US officialdom that no cases where people had requested to return and been refused were known, there were such instances, and the mission was aware of some.[51] Daniel Southerland of the *Christian Science Monitor* had reported one case, in a hamlet only 35 miles from Saigon, where the people, who had been forcibly evacuated by the Americans some years earlier, now wanted to go home to PRG territory and were forcibly prevented from doing so.[52]

In November 1973, Thomas Lippman of the *Washington Post* reported a case that reminds us of an earlier time. He had visited the refugee village of Thanh-Thuy in Quang-Nam province, near the Marble Mountain, to which over 2,200 people had been forcibly relocated in 1969. This was actually the Ngan-Cau refugee camp, one of a pair that had been burned by the VC in April 1970 (chapter 11). It was a desolate site, and the refugees wanted to return to their homes which were about a kilometer away, but the GVN prevented it, as the district chief frankly said.[53]

As deputy to Frank Kellogg, Special Assistant to the Secretary of State for Refugee and Migration Affairs, I wrote to Robert Wenzel, Director of the Viet-Nam Working Group, referring to my earlier query concerning the Binh-Dinh movements, and asking about the Lippman article. I said:

It was my experience, when I was in the CORDS refugee program from 1967 to mid-1970, that forced relocation of people and their enforced retention in so-called secure areas frequently brought Communist sympathizers into GVN territory and made Communist sympathizers out of others who had not previously been partisans of the Viet Cong.

I recognize the complexities of the situation. . . . However, since January 27, 1973, forced relocations and enforced residence of people are deprived of whatever justification they may have had previously by the exigencies of the war and are specifically in violation of Article 11 of the cease-fire agreement. Moreover—and in this respect they are of direct concern to this office—such forcible locations of people contravene Article 13 of the Universal Declaration of Human Rights.[54]

Wenzel sent the memo to the embassy, and in due time I received a "Dear Lou" letter from Ambassador Martin expressing surprise at my reaction to the two reports. He said, "As a matter of fact, I had looked into them and determined that in both cases there had been no basic deviation from the current policy of the RVN against 'forced relocation.' " He continued that he was surprised at my language indicating that the "exigencies of war" no longer existed. (He was quite right; the war had never ceased.) In his typical manner, the Ambassador turned the issue into a suggestion that S/R (the Special Assistant to the Secretary of State for Refugee and Migration Affairs) help in bringing Hanoi to the bar of world opinion for its terrorist acts.[55] After more correspondence, he declassified a number of reports of terrorist incidents, which we passed on to the voluntary agencies.

Asked to comment on the Lippman article, Charlie Browne bitterly attacked its author but confirmed its substance. He admitted that the people of the settlement were not allowed to RTV ''because there is still heavy V.C. activity . . . There are special security measures for Thanh Thuy: A. Residents must get permission from the village chief when they leave the village. B. At night there is a curfew between 1900 hours and 0600 hours.'' Ninety-five percent of the families had relatives with the VC, said Browne. He agreed that the village was not self-sufficient, and that rice was expensive. He concluded:

There is no question that Thanh Thuy Village is an unfortunate place. It is a hard core area where people are pro V.C. No wonder the people are controlled by the GVN. . . . Bob Lanigan, Director of the Quang Nam office of the Consulate General, states that Lippman could not have picked a worse place than Thanh Thuy to write about. He states that it's a rough place. Also he firmly states that it is by no means typical of Quang Nam. . . . I guess about all I can say is that these guys—these mercenary, narrow thinking so called reporters—are still running around Vietnam digging up unfortunate situations to write about.[56]

Charlie Browne was nothing if not blunt. His attitude toward the provisions of the Paris agreement was widely shared among officials of the US Mission and Embassy at all levels, as well as by many GVN officials. From their point of view, there was no possibility of reconciliation with the Communists, and therefore the Vietnamese people, including the refugees, must be kept on a war footing. The North Vietnamese rulers reciprocated this view.

However, in testimony on July 13, 1974, before the House Foreign Affairs Committee, Robert Nooter, Assistant Administrator of AID for Supporting Assistance, said that when he had been in Quang-Tri recently, he learned that a couple of villages had moved to PRG territory. Nooter added that there was no feasible way for the GVN to restrain people who wanted to move across to the other side.[57]

Renewed NVA/VC Offensive in 1974

Beginning in May 1974, there were renewed NVA/VC attacks all over the country, which generated a new wave of war victims. By mid-August, 329,000 people had become refugees, of whom 256,000 required GVN relief. Nine of Viet-Nam's 243 districts, in Quang-Tri, Binh-Dinh, Kontum, Phuoc-Long, and Binh-Long, had been left in Communist hands after the Easter offensive of 1972. Now two more were taken, Thuong-Duc in Quang-Nam and Minh-Long in Quang-Ngai.[58] The United States did not intervene. These setbacks further depressed the morale of the civilian population.

WHAT DID THE REFUGEE AND LAND DEVELOPMENT PROGRAMS ACCOMPLISH?

By December 31, 1974, some 699,653 refugees who had been inadequately resettled before 1972 plus those generated in the Easter offensive were returned to their home villages; and 570,806 more were resettled in 173 sites in all four regions. Moreover, 539,524 new refugees and in-place war victims generated by the cease-fire fighting of 1973 and the 1974 Communist offensive were cared for.[59] Altogether this was a remarkable achievement. Although some were re-located involuntarily, most of those who were reestablished at home and in resettlement centers moved voluntarily.

The 39 LDHB hamlets were carefully planned and prepared, which was a principal reason why there were so few of them. Many of the communities were led by Catholic or Cao-Dai priests, Protestant pastors, or Buddhist monks, who were experienced in looking after the material as well as spiritual needs of their flocks. Dr. Dan did not move people until basic facilities and supplies were in place at the centers—roads, water sources, temporary housing, marked plots for permanent houses and gardens, food, and health facilities and personnel. The settlers' household possessions were moved with them. At destination they were provided with tools, seeds, and other necessities. Dr. Dan was even able to help build churches and pagodas, since some suppliers gave 10% more roofing and other building materials than were purchased.

Land remained a problem throughout. With the never-ceasing battle for territory that made so much of South Viet-Nam insecure and contested, the search for arable land that was not already occupied, on which refugees could be settled, was difficult. It was made more difficult by the greed of some generals and by Vietnamese farmers who encroached on Montagnard land. One cannot escape the conclusion that weak and corrupt GVN officials collaborated in the land-grabbing.

The LDHB administration contracted for machine-clearing of land, but this proceeded slowly. Some of the settlers cleared their own land with hand tools and small machine tillers or plows and buffaloes. This occurred at some of the regular settlements also, although less frequently.

The USAID saw to it that resources were available, and Dr. Dan personally oversaw their use in the LDHB settlements. How well they were utilized in the other sites depended on the province and district chiefs; materials and money did not always get where they were supposed to go.

What about the attitudes of the settlers in the two programs? Except for the survey at Ap Binh-Hoa in 1972 (chapter 7), no attitude studies of refugees were conducted after 1970, so we must rely on anecdotal examples and informed conjecture. All the settlers in the LDHB centers were volunteers, many of them under the guidance of religious leaders. They were anti-Communist nationalists but, according to Dr. Dan, they were not partisans of the Thieu regime. Although the GVN had abolished village and hamlet elections during the 1972 emergency and never restored them, the LDHB settlers kept their original leaders. Moreover, in the absence of adequate military security, they organized their own defense as best they could, which in some cases was effective and in others was not.

At the other end of the spectrum, the involuntary settlers and refugees who were not permitted to go to homes in PRG territories were clearly anti-GVN, and some, like those at Thanh-Thuy, were pro-Communist. Keeping those people in GVN territory did not contribute to its security. To the contrary, it required the diversion of security forces from more important duties and provided convenient rest and recuperation centers for VC cadres inside the GVN lines.

The bulk of the refugees fell somewhere in between those extremes. If they were treated well and assisted, they tended to favor those who had been good to them. If they were mistreated, they became enemies of those who were bad to them. Most were not pro-GVN, but neither were they pro-Communist.

Table 15, taken from Dr. Dan's January 1975 report, shows how the RTV and resettlement sites were divided among the Military Regions. In aggregate, it was not an ideal distribution, either as between return-to-village and resettlement, or by regions. Although it is understandable that people would want to go back home, the security situation in Region 1 was such that fewer people should have returned to their home villages and fewer should have been resettled there. As we have seen, some of this was not voluntary, and it led to dissatisfaction with the GVN, and to later flights from Communist attacks that could not be held off.

In Quang-Tri, 93,542 refugees returned to their home villages, and 87,709 were resettled, a total of 181,251 people, or much more than half the pre-1972 population of the province, in two small districts and part of a third. That can not have been a viable situation. One wonders whether all those refugees went there willingly. Dr. Dan had recommended that no people be allowed to return to Quang-Tri, which he proposed to turn into a vast land-mine.[60]

One hundred ten thousand refugees had returned to their home villages in Thua-Thien during 1972. Only 26,979 were resettled in that largely pacified province, about half in four rural centers and a fishing village organized by Catholic priests and recognized post facto as LDHB sites.

As we have observed, there was much forced return to home villages and resettlement in the three lower provinces of Region 1. A total of 328,318 refugees were reestablished there. That was far too many for the carrying capacity of those insecure provinces. There were no LDHB centers.

Similarly, 113,273 refugees were returned to home villages and 70,566 were resettled in precarious Binh-Dinh (a total of 183,839). Many of them did not go voluntarily. No LDHB center was put in that insecure province.

The 7,575 refugees reported as having returned to village, and 14,214 resettled in Kontum were too many for that province, much of which was in enemy hands.

However, 47,216 refugees, of whom many were highlanders, were settled in viable LDHB centers in Region 2.

By contrast, the 192,913 resettled in MR-3 (most of them in LDHB sites)

Table 15
Return to Village, Land Development Centers, and Regular Resettlement, as of December 31, 1974

Refugee Return to Village			
Regions	No. of villages	No. of families	No. of people
I	187	65,291	356,028
II	96	27,907	147,537
III	28	4,071	24,855
IV	338	26,184	171,233
Totals	649	123,453	699,653

Refugee Resettlement in LDHB Centers			
Regions	No. of villages	No. of families	No. of people
I	5	2,423	12,735
II	18	9,147	47,216
III	21	20,233	113,398
Totals	44	31,803	173,349

Refugee Resettlement in Regular Centers			
Regions	No. of villages	No. of families	No. of people
I	74	33,036	170,196
II	39	30,019	143,752
III	16	14,159	79,515
IV	5	802	3,994
Totals	134	78,016	397,457

Source: Dr. Phan Quang Dan, *Refugee Relief & Rehabilitation, Land Development & Hamlet Building* (Saigon: January 15, 1975), 213–60. The English language edition mistakenly listed all the resettlement centers as LDHB sites. In a meeting with Raymond Fontaine and me on November 10, 1987, Dr. Dan corrected the translation and identified the Land Development sites.

were less than the region could have accommodated if the land had not been grabbed by others.

And the fact that only 3,994 refugees were resettled in MR-4 indicated that little suitable land was offered in that rich agricultural region.

As 1975 began, Dr. Dan declared that his program was now open to unemployed and underemployed people. Six hundred thousand families with 3,000,000 people had applied. The NVA's "Great Spring Offensive" of that year put an end to their hopes.

After the fall of South Viet-Nam on April 30, 1975, the Communists turned the Land Development Centers into "new economic zones," but without the extensive assistance the LDHB program had provided to help the people get reestablished, and with many more people in the sites. They became in effect vast concentration camps, in which thousands died of overwork, disease and hunger. What a dismal sequel to a noble program!

14

North Viet-Nam

If the arrival of over 900,000 refugees from the North in 1954–55 was a mixed blessing for South Viet-Nam (chapter 1), their departure was not an unmitigated loss to a North Viet-Nam that was in the process of being Communized. Most of those who left were strong Catholics, who were unlikely to collaborate with the Ho Chi Minh regime, and the leaders of the Democratic Republic of Viet-Nam (DRVN) knew it. Although they brutally obstructed the flight of the refugees, largely because their sheer numbers exposed the unpopularity of the socialist society they were building, it is not unlikely that they were somewhat relieved to see such a group out of the way. Moreover, the exodus made about 200,000 hectares of precious land available for redistribution, despite assurances that it would be held in escrow, most of it in the Red River Delta. Furthermore, it relieved the tight food situation of a population that was growing at the rate of 3.5% a year.[1]

LAND REFORM AND MASS EXECUTIONS

The regime inflicted a grievous wound upon its society, with few if any compensating advantages, by the clumsy and ruthless way it implemented land reform, which started as early as 1953 in Viet-Minh controlled areas and reached its height in 1955–56. From the standpoint of strict equity, redistribution of the land was largely unnecessary since, unlike the situation in the Mekong Delta, few families owned more than two or three hectares, and in the Red River Delta, about 98% owned the land which they tilled. However, the more prosperous peasants would be opposed to collectivization of agriculture, which was the real if hidden aim of the redistribution. Therefore, just as the Soviet Union in the 1930s exterminated millions of "kulaks," the North Vietnamese rulers made "enemies of the people" out of the property-minded peasants and physically eliminated them. This was done through the class demarcation regulations of March 1953 and the Population Classification Decree of March 2, 1955, which provided for classification of the whole population into landlords, rich peasants, middle peasants, poor peasants, and landless workers. Some tortured reasoning was necessary to fit urban professionals, shopkeepers, and artisans into these classes, but that was done without casualties.

The decrees also created criminal subcategories of landlords and rich peasants: traitors (that is, collaborators with the French), despots, and reactionaries. In the countryside, "People's Agricultural Reform Tribunals," made up of poor peasants and agricultural workers under the guidance of party cadres, tried persons in the first two classes for all sorts of trumped-up charges and handed out sentences of death, prison, or exile to concentration camps. The process had many of the attributes of the worst years of the French Revolution devouring its children in the 1790s, in that many who were convicted had fought in the Viet-Minh against France, some even as members of the Lao-Dong Party. Estimates of the numbers who were executed ranged from 3,000 to 500,000. The actual total was probably somewhere in the lower range, although none of the calculations was solidly based. At least 100,000 were sent to prison or forced labor camps. It got to the point where people were afraid to speak to each other, disobedience and hatred of the regime spread, and the leaders realized that they faced a crisis. Then Ho Chi Minh himself in August 1956 declared a halt and admitted that errors had been committed. In a published letter to the compatriots he promised that those who had been wrongly classified would be reestablished with honor, and shortly thereafter the official newspaper extended that pledge even to Catholics, saying that some churches and their priests would be restored.[2]

The correction of errors came too late, however, to avert a peasant revolt in Nghe-An province, Ho's birthplace, in the heart of Interzone IV, which had been thought to be the most loyal to the regime. On November 2, 1956, while Canadian members of the International Control Members were in the area, a group of peasants presented a petition to some of them asking permission to go south. Viet-Minh soldiers tried to drive the farmers away but were beaten. The entire 325th Division was brought in to quell what had become a full-scale revolt, and almost 6,000 peasants were deported or executed. The incident passed almost unnoticed by the world press, which was preoccupied with the simultaneous Soviet crushing of the Hungarian revolution and the fighting in the Suez area. However, Ho Chi Minh abolished the land reform tribunals as of November 8, and removed the Secretary General of the party and the Minister of Agriculture. In the "campaign for the rectification of errors," thousands were returned from prisons and concentration camps—and some took revenge against their erstwhile oppressors.[3]

In South Viet-Nam, a succession of shocks to the society like these would probably have brought down the government, but in the Communist dictatorship of the North, which was prepared to use the most ruthless methods of control, the people were gradually molded into instruments of production. The whole society became a disciplined engine of war against its sister republic, and over the next years endured privation, the loss of hundreds of thousands of its men, and periods of intense American bombing, never faltering in the regime's quest for victory.

Although 702,000 hectares, plus almost two million farm implements and over 100,000 draft animals were redistributed to 1,500,000 families by the land reform, the result was only to spread rural poverty more evenly, and that was evidently a principal objective of the program: to show that individual ownership and cultivation of land was not feasible. Soon the smallest farmers fell out, augmenting the tiny proletariat for the government's program of rapid industrialization and furnishing labor for its irrigation projects. The establishment of agricultural production cooperatives began in earnest late in 1958, and by the end of 1960 there were 41,404 of them, taking in over 85% of all farmers. The later consolidation of the cooperatives reduced their number but steadily increased the percentage of participants.[4]

MOVEMENT OF VIETNAMESE INTO THE MOUNTAINS, AND HIGHLANDER RESETTLEMENT

Even with these measures, the Red River Delta was still overpopulated, while the mountainous regions were thinly peopled and had much uncultivated land. Of the 15,900,000 inhabitants counted in the 1960 census, 2,388,565 were members of ethnic minority tribes, over three times the number of Montagnards in the South. The coastal and Delta provinces had an average density of over 800 people per square kilometer, while it was 17 people or less in the autonomous regions of the mountains.[5] At the Third Congress of the Lao-Dong Party in September 1960, Le Duan in his political report proposed a comprehensive program of resettling "hundreds of thousands of people from the plains to the mountainous areas to work in industry and agriculture, building industrial zones, State farms and State forest enterprises." The resolution adopted by the Congress ratified this plan.[6] The motives were the same as in Ngo Dinh Diem's land development program in the South: to move surplus populations, including troublesome elements (who in the North were private traders, vagrants, and petty thieves) from the coastal plains; strengthen control in areas that were inhabited by the less patriotic ethnic minorities, ultimately producing a Vietnamese majority; increase security in the very regions that had been used by the Viet-Minh as sanctuaries during the French war; and open up previously uncultivated land.[7] The plan was to resettle one million people (300,000 agriculturalists, 700,000 dependents) and bring a million hectares into cultivation during the five-year plan for 1960–65; also to reform the lifestyle of the ethnic minorities, forcing them to live in permanent settlements and to collectivize their agriculture. It got under way in late 1960, under the administration of the Bureau of Land Reclamation, whose Director, Le Quang Ba, was a member of the Party Central Committee.

It was not easy to induce either the city people or the peasants to resettle in areas which they considered to be primitive and dangerous, but the regime used intensive propaganda and other means of persuasion. By mid-1966, the government claimed that its goal of transferring a million people to the Highlands had been achieved, but said that hundreds of thousands more would have to be moved.[8]

At first the newcomers were settled among the tribespeople, but there were such frictions that many of the latter moved away. Then separate settlements and collectives were established, but the highlanders still had to provide initial housing, food, and other necessities. This was the source of many grievances, as was the arrogant attitude of many lowlanders. Since it was difficult to develop the new settlements to the point of self-sufficiency—and, indeed, food production in the new communities did not meet requirements even as late as 1969, the government had to provide foodstuffs, other necessities, and loans and grants. The fact that many of the settlers were city people, unfamiliar with agriculture to say nothing of pioneering in undeveloped regions, made progress even slower. Thus, rather than improving the country's economic situation, the program was a drain on the already strained lowland economy. Some of the settlers secretly returned to their native villages, although stringent travel controls kept this to a low level.[9] In any event, the program of moving Vietnamese into the Highlands seems to have been quietly abandoned, except for some party cadres, frontier troops, and experts of various sorts.

However, the effort to get the highland tribes to regroup into larger villages and to abandon slash-and-burn agriculture for settled farming of paddy rice and other crops was continued. In part, this was motivated by the realization that the traditional farming methods of the highlanders were denuding the mountains of forests, wasting timber, and causing erosion, floods, droughts, and other problems. At the same time, the highlanders were to be organized into cooperatives and their farming plots collectivized. For years the official and party press were full of articles about how various tribespeople were brought to sedentary agriculture, with positive results for their living standards.[10]

The resettlement and collectivization went slowly—much more slowly than the regime wanted. The first directives and resolutions of the Lao Dong Party Central Committee were issued as early as 1955; however, by 1969 only 100,000 "nomadic" people had built experimental production installations and settlements, and only 60% of this group had entered agricultural cooperatives. In reporting this, Le Quang Ba said that over 500,000 mountain people still did not have permanent production installations (sedentary agriculture) or residences. (Ba in fact understated the total number of highlanders by a factor of four.) He added gloomily that a number of lowlanders who had come to take part in the economic development of the region were also burning forests and cultivating in a migratory way. Ba reiterated that settlement and collectivization must be vigorously carried out, to be completed in 1970, and he outlined the steps toward that objective.[11]

A month after Ho Chi Minh's death in September 1969, Ba called upon the revered leader's name in again urging the highlanders to abandon their nomadic ways and to collectivize their agricultural production. He wrote that Ho had been much concerned with the migratory farmers, "whose life was insecure and miserable. He often reminded the party and state organs that they should actively work for the settlement of such farmers and improve their economic and cultural conditions and living standard." Ho was said to have kept a clipping file on the subject, to have been happy over any success, and to have made recommendations to overcome shortcomings. Ba continued, explaining that on 17 July 1979, more than a month before his death, Ho had listened to a report. "He reiterated that it was necessary to apply the principle of voluntary acceptance, to have good cadres . . . to arouse enthusiastic response among the masses, and most ideally to use either cadres from the minority groups themselves or those cadres who could speak the tribal dialects."[12]

It was apparent that the North Vietnamese regime, perhaps mindful of the consequences of excessive haste and brutality in its earlier land reform program, was proceeding gingerly with the highlanders. They in turn were in no hurry to settle down and form cooperatives.[13] As late as 1973, it was reported with some rejoicing that the 1972 campaign had enlisted over 60,000 highlanders in three provinces to resettle and develop sedentary production. However, they had cleared and planted only about 1,720 hectares of rice and other grain and some 1,640 hectares of tea and other industrial crops. Nonetheless, it was claimed that they had built over 1,000 kilometers of roads, 97 new schools, and 64 public health stations.[14]

Aggregate data are not available on the total number of highlanders who were resettled according to the Communist Party's prescription, but it would appear that in general they were not forcibly regrouped as they were in the South. There were many accounts of their joining the armed forces and otherwise supporting the DRVN's war objectives, and it seems that, willy-nilly, they did.

US BOMBING AND POPULATION DISLOCATION

American bombing of North Viet-Nam began with reprisal raids in August 1964 in the wake of attacks against two US ships in the Gulf of Tonkin. There were no more strikes until February 1965, and daily bombing began only in March. Thereafter the "Rolling Thunder" operations continued until October 31, 1968, with some interruptions ordered by President Johnson to induce the DRVN to come to the bargaining table. There were a few strikes in 1969, 1970, and 1971, and then two series of intense operations in 1972 and a few strikes in January 1973, ending with the cease-fire of January 28.[15]

Less than one-third the bomb tonnage that was dropped in South Viet-Nam was inflicted on the North, and it was done in a more intermittent manner (table 16

Table 16
Comparative Tonnages in US Aerial Warfare

Year	North Viet-Nam	South Viet-Nam
1965	33,000*	31,540
1966	128,904	237,332
1967	247,410	467,245
1968	227,039	807,275
1969	659	632,341
1970	832	252,123
1971	1,842	113,788
1972	218,883	538,062
1973**	15,347	40,914
Totals	873,916	3,120,620

*This figure is from Guenter Lewy, *America in Vietnam* (New York: Oxford University Press, 1978), 381.

**January 1973 only. No US bombs were dropped on either North or South Viet-Nam after January 27, 1973.

Source: US Senate, *Relief and Rehabilitation of War Victims in Indochina*, Part III: North Vietnam and Laos, hearing before the Subcommittee to Investigate Problems Connected with Refugees and Escapees of the Committee on the Judiciary, United States Senate. Ninety-third Congress, First Session. July 31, 1973, 24. The source was the Department of Defense. Data in 1965 for South Viet-Nam included only tonnage dropped by B-52s.

shows this). In every year that American troops were in Viet-Nam (assuming that considerable tonnage was dropped on South Viet-Nam by fighter-bombers in 1965, which were not included in the statistics for that year), and even when the US combat troops had departed, the bombing in South Viet-Nam was much heavier than in the North. It was also more continuous, which meant that those exposed to it, especially civilians in contested areas, rarely had time to recover in South Viet-Nam, while there were several years from late 1968 until 1972 during which the North Vietnamese had the opportunity to recover and rebuild. They were, however, left in uncertainty as to when bombing would resume. The very heavy bombing in both the North and South in 1972 was mainly a response to the NVA Easter offensive, but the later sorties that year were intended to break the logjam in the Paris truce negotiations.

There was no ground combat in North Viet-Nam. Attempts were made to infiltrate GVN and US sapper squads, but these were quickly discovered and wiped out. There was also relatively little naval gunfire from the allied side. Consequently, the bombers were the only weapons of destruction unleashed against the North. Mostly they were fighter-bombers, which came in at relatively low levels; B-52s were not used in large numbers until 1972. The pilots were under strict instructions to hit only military targets, which included railroads, airfields, bridges, petroleum depots, heavy industry, power plants, vehicles, ferries, barges, and so forth. Initially, targets that were in heavily populated areas were to be avoided. Geographically, the areas that could be hit were gradually extended northward, but until mid-1966 they did not include the immediate Hanoi-Haiphong metropolitan region. Later, especially in 1972, greater latitude was given, including targets in Hanoi and those designed to take out the port of Haiphong. The northeast quadrant near China was always off limits.

The North Vietnamese mounted the most fearsome air defenses that American pilots had ever experienced, including the most advanced Soviet missiles and MIG fighter planes. Dodging the flak sometimes threw off the aim of the bombers, which accounted for some of the civilian damage inflicted, as did the fact that the antiaircraft guns and missile launchers were often emplaced in populated areas. Likewise, many other military targets, especially factories, railroads, and petroleum storage, were located next to housing, hospitals, and so on. It was only in 1972, with the advent of "smart bombs," which were radar- and laser-guided, that it became possible to pinpoint military targets and avoid most nonmilitary installations near them.

So the bombing caused widespread damage to civilian installations, especially in the southern panhandle, where cities, towns, and villages were completely wiped out. Even in 1972, the "Linebacker" attacks were not able to avoid inflicting harm to civilian areas, especially from the B-52s, which flew at 30,000 feet. Many American visitors were taken by DRVN officials to view that destruction in selected areas, and were given propaganda mixed with information about the places they could not visit. Some, including Ramsey Clark and the Senate Refugee Subcommittee study mission headed by Dr. Nevin Scrimshaw, brought back pictures. One of the most publicized installations was the 1,000-bed Bach-Mai Hospital in Hanoi, which was almost totally destroyed in 1972 by three bombs that had escaped the bomb train and one rocket. What most reporters failed to mention was that the hospital was about 1,000 yards from the Bach-Mai airstrip and military barracks, which were prime targets. It was also close to a heavy machine factory which was hit.

Some of the damage was caused by fragments of antiaircraft shells and missiles falling back to earth.

A number of observers visiting Hanoi after the bombing had ceased were surprised that the civilian destruction was much less than earlier alarmist reports had implied.

However, what caused much of the adverse publicity was the fact that the ordnance used included pellet bombs and other antipersonnel devices, including some designed to explode after some delay. When these fell in civilian areas, they caused grievous casualties to men, women, and children. Also, there was much dispute as to whether flood-control dikes were deliberately bombed with a view to curtailing food production and flooding habitations. The consensus seems to be that, although some dikes were damaged, rice production was not adversely affected, and no inhabited areas were flooded because of dike destruction.[16]

The air war destroyed many of North Viet-Nam's military installations, factories, electric power plants, petroleum stores, and transportation facilities. However, the country learned how to make rapid repairs and to decentralize production and distribution, and its economy was never in danger of collapsing. It was estimated that between 475,000 and 600,000 of its people were mobilized during the period 1965–68 for repair, dispersal, and transport, most of them intermittently as circumstances necessitated. One hundred thousand military personnel were employed full-time and thousands of civilians worked part-time on air defense.[17] Other means, which will be described below, were utilized to keep the economy and the war machine going, and they were successful. The bombing did not halt or appreciably reduce the flow of men and materiel to the South. Soviet and Chinese aid more than made up any economic and military losses, and, if anything, the air war solidified the people behind their government and the war effort.[18]

Evacuation of Cities and Dispersal of Industry

The DRVN government issued its first order on February 28, 1965, to evacuate from the major cities all except those occupied in production or combat. This affected mainly children and the aged. At that time the only government help was the issuance of certificates entitling the evacuees to a 30% reduction of train fares and 20% reduction on buses and ships. The villages would have to provide housing aid to the new inhabitants. Only in the cities of the southern panhandle, like Vinh, where life simply could not go on, did the government give money to the evacuees. It was reported that about 50,000 people had left Hanoi by the fall of 1965, but they began to drift back, mainly because of financial strain. People coming up from the panhandle were stopping over in Hanoi for up to two weeks to buy supplies before going out into the countryside.[19] Schools at all grades, including universities, were evacuated after stray bombs hit some of them in 1965.

On June 29, 1966, the government ordered the evacuation from Hanoi of all who were not "truly indispensable to the life of the capital." Petroleum (POL) dumps were struck that very day. A few days later, a sterner order was issued, and that one was enforced. There was a street-by-street census, and ration cards were marked with the status of each person. The entire government, except for the President and a few other high officials, was also ordered to move to locations outside the city. A number of factories, weaving handicraft shops, small printing shops, and most other shops were dispersed out of the capital in the summer of 1966. During July, about 10,000 people a day left Hanoi. Estimates of the total number who departed ranged from one-third to three-quarters of the 1,000,000 inhabitants of the city.[20]

The evacuations of Hanoi, Haiphong, and other cities were carried out under the authority of the administrative committees of those municipalities (equivalent to city councils), and the evacuees remained under their authority. This was done on the assumption that the relocations were to be temporary, as in fact they were for most people. Some people, however, were moved to rural areas in connection with the dispersal of their factories, not just as a wartime precaution but also to develop local industry permanently.[21]

At that time, a government subsidy was provided to those who moved. Camps were established for those without relatives in the countryside, mostly in the cooperatives, which also provided schools and jobs for the youngsters. Inducements were offered to villages accepting urban schools. The relocated institutions of learning were placed in scattered buildings to further reduce the risk from bombing, and trenches, and shelters were built near them. The central government assumed a greater proportion of the cost.

There were additional evacuations in 1967, but some major factories had to remain in Hanoi, and they were attacked. The evacuation of Haiphong was less drastic, because the operations of the port could not be moved. However, the children were sent out. The most intense bombing of Hanoi occurred in the year from March 1967 to March 1968, and again in 1972. Most of the factories in Haiphong were destroyed, and during 1967–68 there were shortages of just about everything.

Other cities, particularly in the southern panhandle, were hit even harder than Hanoi and Haiphong, and where possible they were evacuated. Combat villages were created in the country, tightly controlled by the party. People were encouraged to report on those who did not cooperate. However, the bombing caused such disruption of communications and food distribution in May and June 1966 that, according to an Italian journalist who visited at the time, there were peasant uprisings in Nghe-An and Thanh-Hoa provinces, an assault on the military warehouses in the port of Dong-Hoi, and a mutiny of an army detachment in the area of Dien-Bien-Phu which had not received supplies for a week.[22] Most hospitals and clinics were dispersed into the countryside, and their number was expanded to cope with casualties and increased illness.

Though the principal POL facilities were destroyed, petroleum products were stored everywhere, in deep underground depots, and in small tanks and 55-gallon drums scattered about, even in rice fields. Trucks were parked along many of the roads under trees, and moved at night. Bomb craters in the roads and bomb damage to railroads were rapidly repaired.

No figures are available on the total number of people dislocated in this manner. However, it was certainly a good proportion of the urban population. The movements created many social and economic problems: crowding, lack of privacy, disease caused by unsanitary conditions, separation of families, loss of production, and shortages. People were told that the sacrifices were necessary for the war effort and the survival of the country in the face of American aggression, and they endured.[23] However, at least in the earlier stages of evacuations, there were severe tensions between the evacuees and the people among whom they were settled, sometimes even affecting public order and security. This seems to have especially involved evacuees settled in the mountain regions. The party admonished both the evacuees and their provincial hosts to respect each other's customs and to maintain peace and order. On the other hand, the evacuees were welcomed in some rural areas as an additional source of manpower, both in the fields and in such public works projects as building or repairing dams. In some instances the evacuees shared their rations with their hosts, and they lived together.[24]

Unlike many of the refugees in South Viet-Nam, the evacuees in the North never lacked employment. The very bombing that made evacuation necessary also created many of the jobs for the evacuees. Mention has been made above of the large numbers of people mobilized for repair work and civil defense. When the people went into the countryside, most factories, shops, government offices, schools, and other employment-generating activities went with them. Women and children were pressed into service to replace the men fighting in the South. As mentioned, farms were always in need of labor to make up for the machines and other resources that were lacking. As a result, nobody was ever in the position of enforced idleness or of feeling unneeded. That undoubtedly was a prime factor in the high morale of the population despite the hardships.

The first emergency for the major cities ended on April 1, 1968, after President Johnson terminated the bombing north of the 20th parallel. In fact, after the first week of April, no bombing occurred north of the 19th parallel, thus sparing about 90% of the country's population. On November 1, all bombing ceased, by the President's order. Repair and recovery proceeded rapidly, and people filtered back into the cities. Factories were reassembled closer to their markets. There were elections (Communist-style) for the National Assembly in April 1971, the first since 1964. New housing complexes were built. However, the schools, with some 4,000,000 children, for the most part remained in the countryside.[25]

People and economic enterprises were again sent out of Hanoi, Haiphong, and other centers when bombing resumed in 1972. If anything, bombing was resumed on an even greater scale than during the earlier years.[26] The mayor of Hanoi said that two-thirds of the city's population of 720,000 (1,200,000 with its suburbs) had been evacuated when the bombs struck in December that year.[27]

Although the Lao-Dong Party organizations and people in the areas to which evacuees were sent were made responsible for supplying many of the necessities, and were constantly admonished that they must uphold the spirit of mutual affection and love in assisting their guests, the party and administrative organs of the sending cities and the central government had primary responsibility to see that the evacuees had food, water, air raid shelters, wells, bathrooms, latrines, and so on. The evacuated people of course had to pitch in to provide the labor. The service sectors of the capital and other cities were mobilized to extend their activities to the areas to which their clients had been sent, as did the mass organizations of women, youth, and others. Special provisions were made so that evacuees could use their ration stamps in their new home neighborhoods, rather than having to return to their previous locations, and the period of validity of the stamps was extended when new ones could not be issued.[28]

In 1972, new allowances for evacuees were established for evacuees from Hanoi, Haiphong, and Nam-Dinh, formalizing by categories of adults and children the eligibility for assistance which had originally been set up in 1965. The allowances were meager. Families of war dead and wounded, both military and civilian, were included.[29]

Air Raid Shelters

Some 34 million individual shelters, thousands of group shelters, and about 30,000 miles of trenches were constructed in the years 1965–68; and these, along with the evacuations, greatly reduced casualties from the bombing. The individual shelters were round holes about four or five feet deep, just big enough for one person to crouch in. Many were lined with concrete pipes specially made for the purpose and had lids of woven bamboo. The goal of the government was to have at least three shelter places for each individual, one at his home, one at the work place, and one in between. The collective shelters were of reinforced concrete, some with double roofs covered with earth. Revetments of earth were constructed around many buildings and small POL dumps. Countless dispersed factories and shops were located underground.

In the southern panhandle, whole communities lived and worked underground for several years. Facilities were built underground for sleeping, bathing, and other daily functions. Factories, shops, schools, movie houses, libraries—all were underground. Shelters and trenches were dug even in rice fields. It was learned that certain vegetation kept snakes away from the shelters.

When air raid sirens first sounded, people were instructed to go to the shelter location. As the people were warned by radio or loud speakers that enemy planes were close, they were to go into the shelters. Gradually the people in the cities became somewhat blasé. Visitors have described how many residents of Hanoi would ride their bicycles to shelters, sit there reading newspapers until the planes were almost on top of them, and then dive into the one-person shelters. This was sufficient in most cases. Diplomats observed some instances where air-to-surface missiles hit within four feet of a one-man shelter and the occupant still survived.

The government required that shelters be cleaned and maintained regularly, even in periods when no air raids occurred. Each person was responsible for this task. New shelters were built and the old ones cleaned even after the bombing halt of October 31, 1968.

There were home-guard civil defense groups who were trained in such things as rescuing people buried in shelters, treating injuries, and fighting fire. The whole country was mobilized to keep life going under the bombs.[30]

CIVILIAN CASUALTIES AND HEALTH SERVICES

North Viet-Nam did not publish aggregate data on civilian war casualties. The US National Security Study Memorandum No. 1 of 1969 (the "Kissinger Memorandum") contained an estimate that about 52,000 civilians were killed in the period 1965–69 by American air strikes.[31] The North Vietnamese journal *Vietnamese Studies* published some figures in 1970 showing that the number of people wounded by the bombing increased by 26% to 1,201% in each of four regions from 1965 to 1967; and that the number killed per raid ranged from 0.16 to 15, depending on the area and year; but it did not give totals. It recounted how medical people increased their knowledge and skill in treating the different injuries caused by steel-pellet bombs, rockets, explosive bombs, phosphorus and napalm, burying alive, shock, and infections.[32]

Dr. Tran Duy Hung, mayor of Hanoi, said that a preliminary count of casualties from the December 1972 bombings of the city showed 1,318 killed and 1,261 wounded. He attributed the small number to the fact that most of the people had been evacuated. Ha Ngoc Que, an official of the DRVN "War Crimes Commission," pointed to the 1:1 ratio of killed to wounded as very unusual (which it was) and as something that the North Vietnamese were studying very carefully. He said that the normal ratio was 1:6 or 1:7; in Dresden during World War II it was 1:4 or 1:5, he asserted. He attributed the high ratio to carpet bombing, in which the Americans mixed heavy and light bombs, some of which exploded underground. He said that all members of many families were killed by concussion, blast, or building collapse.[33] Despite the paucity of data, it seems that the number of civilian war casualties in the North was far less than in the South. American physicians and other visitors saw injured patients in various North Vietnamese hospitals.[34]

North Viet-Nam had a well-developed but somewhat antiquated health system, starting with over 6,000 cooperative and village medical stations and going up by stages to excellent tertiary-care hospitals, many of which were destroyed or damaged by bombing but still functioned. There was strong emphasis on preventive medicine, including maternal and child health, immunizations, and sanitation. A study mission of the Senate Refugee Subcommittee, headed by Dr. Nevin Scrimshaw, Professor of Human Nutrition at the Massachusetts Institute of Technology, and including two other physicians, which spent a week in the country in March 1973, found essentially no evidence of malnutrition and was impressed by the general health of the population. The group had visited Hanoi, Thai-Binh, and Nam-Dinh, in all of which health facilities and other civilian structures were heavily damaged. They were informed that the country had over 7,000 physicians, or one for every 3,500 people, and 20,000 assistant physicians. The latter received three years of medical education after completing the full 10 years of general schooling. They functioned at the level of the village medical stations. In addition, there were nurses and other personnel, whose numbers were not given. The study mission found a good emergency medical system. The team saw little evidence of war casualties, probably because considerable time had passed since the end of the bombing, and because they did not obtain information on the number of amputees.[35]

The numbers of physicians and physician assistants reported to Dr. Scrimshaw and his colleagues seems high for an underdeveloped country of about 21,500,000 people that had been at war for over 25 years. The inspection of the South Vietnamese public health system that a colleague and I conducted in April and May 1972 collected figures from the Ministry of Health showing that in 1971 there were approximately 2,000 physicians, 5,914 nursing employees, and about 11,000 other health professionals, including Oriental medicine practitioners, in that population of 18,000,000. They were products of a training system that had received extensive and sophisticated American aid for a number of years.[36] It seems likely that the North Vietnamese figures were inflated. However, it was agreed on by many observers that the health care system in the North was more than adequate for both the ordinary and the emergency needs of the population.

ASSISTANCE TO MILITARY DEPENDENTS, WAR CASUALTIES, ORPHANS, AND THE ELDERLY

North Vietnamese soldiers fighting in the South were not allowed to take their families with them. This gave rise to homesickness and anxieties as to the welfare of the dependents, especially since mail was slow and uncertain, but it freed the soldiers from the kinds of concerns about families in combat areas that had so often led to desertions and panic among South Vietnamese Government troops, the so-called "family syndrome." North Vietnamese soldiers in South Viet-Nam could maneuver and retreat if necessary without worrying about loved ones in the vicinity. The party and government in the North took special care to implement measures of care for the military dependents.

As in the case of evacuees (who included most of the military families) much of the responsibility was placed on the local official and economic organs and on the people themselves. Involving the populace in the care of its less fortunate members was a deliberate part of North Vietnamese party and government policy. The wives and mothers of soldiers were exalted as heroines, and the children also had a special status. Praise was given to local organizations and people who gave material and moral help to servicemen's families, and criticism was meted out to those who did not. Evidently there were enough of the latter category that the Council of Ministers decided on September 4, 1968, that the subsidy policy of the party and government, which had been decreed in November 1965, must be imposed everywhere, so that military personnel would not have to worry about their families. "There must be absolutely no family left without care or help," the council declared. Preference was to be given to dependents of workers and government employees serving in the armed forces. If those persons had received subsidies, their dependents must receive the same amounts. When one parent was in the armed services and the other died, the children were to receive specified subsidies. Other benefits were also provided. The Ministry of Internal Affairs and the General Trade Union were assigned enforcement responsibility. A month later, an even stronger and more specific circular was issued. It demanded that "Absolutely no military's family is left without care, not a single military's family with difficulty without adequate help, and no wife of a military with ability to work is left jobless."[37]

Care of wounded and disabled soldiers and their families was made an important task of the people, mass organizations, and cooperatives; and numerous examples of generous assistance were publicized. People were urged to adopt orphans. There were allowances for the families of war dead and for orphans. Of course, all survivors who could work were expected to do so, and they received help in getting jobs suitable to their capabilities.[38]

At the end of 1972, when the US bombing was just concluding, the Hanoi Administrative Committee adopted rules for allowances and other aid to victims of the bombing, including coffins, payment of hospital costs of the injured, food, clothing, and household utensils for those who had lost their homes.[39]

When the bombing was all over and the Paris truce agreement was about to be signed in January 1973, the Hanoi Administrative Committee adopted a program much like Operation Recovery in South Viet-Nam after the Têt offensive of 1968. Declaring that over 8,000 houses had been destroyed and more than 9,000 heavily damaged, the city announced that temporary housing was to be built rapidly. Partial subsidies were to be given to home-owners to buy building materials—bamboo, tar paper, and so on. In the outskirts and parts of the central city the people themselves were to rebuild permanent housing, assisted where necessary by carpenters furnished by the townships and districts. On certain streets, multistory housing was to be constructed by the city.[40]

In sum, after losing over 900,000 of its most energetic and able people to the South in 1954-55, the North Vietnamese regime caused severe social and psychological damage to its remaining rural population with a brutal Communist-style land reform program, but then adopted a more moderate course. In the 1960s, it relocated perhaps a million people to the highlands for social and economic reasons; and it tried, evidently with limited success, to collectivize the Highland tribes. American bombing inflicted grievous suffering in the North, although nowhere near as much as the war had caused year after year to the population of the South. The assistance given to war victims was evidently not as systematized as in the South, and responsibility was divided among the government, the party, the mass organizations, and the people themselves. In general, it seems to have worked. Under their totalitarian system and in the conviction that their cause was just, the people of the North survived and continued to support the war with a unity and determination that were not duplicated in the South. The bombing may have contributed to bringing about the Paris agreement of January 1973, but it did not prevent the ultimate victory of the DRVN.

15

The Final Offensive of the North Vietnamese

While the January 1973 cease-fire agreement brought peace to North Viet-Nam and the opportunity to repair the bomb damage, combat continued without letup in the South, and the Communists made preparations for an even larger war. They built a wide all-weather road within western Viet-Nam from the Demilitarized Zone down to the vicinity of Saigon, with branches extending eastward, over which they funneled huge quantities of equipment and ammunition. No longer were scanty supplies transported on bicycles or human backs; now they moved in convoy on trucks, immune from bombing. A petroleum pipeline was constructed along a nearby route. Preparations for a major assault went on night and day. The only thing left open was the timing.

The number of new victims of the fighting in 1974 had outstripped the number who were fully reestablished, although many others were in the process of receiving the benefits due them. Some 417,300 new "temporarily displaced war victims" (previously called refugees) were generated during the year, and 179,600 casualty and property damage claims of in-place war victims were submitted, the bulk of them for damage to houses. Two hundred fifty-five thousand eight hundred people were resettled in 1974, and another 62,000 received partial payments, including some who had resettled in prior years; 99,300 returned to their home villages, and another 130,200 were in process of being paid at year-end, including some who had returned to village in prior years. In addition, 131,040 in-place war victims were paid, of whom 55,051 had made claims in 1974.[1]

In the latter part of 1974, the Communists were attacking all over the country, not just to destroy GVN forces, but to "liberate the people and hold the land," in the words of North Vietnamese General Van Tien Dung.[2] They battered the First ARVN Division severely around Hue. In the provinces of MR-1 south of

Da-Nang they took back almost all the territory that the GVN had seized in its 1973 pacification campaign. In the western Highlands, the Communist forces overran the remaining GVN enclaves. Only Kontum city remained in government hands in that province. Communist gains were registered also in MR-3 and MR-4, the Mekong Delta. At the end of the year, the VC had control of over 500 hamlets in the Delta with about 750,000 people, more than at any time in the previous five years.[3]

The North Vietnamese Politburo decided in early October 1974 in its "Resolution for 1975" to undertake a phased offensive, the success of each phase determining the timing and magnitude of the next. The first phase, to begin in December, would identify South Vietnamese vulnerabilities.[4]

Just at Christmas 1974, the North Vietnamese launched an attack in Phuoc-Long province, most of which was already in Communist hands, and on January 6, the capital, Phuoc-Binh (formerly Song-Be) was captured. It was the first province capital to fall into enemy hands since the Easter offensive of 1972. Refugees began filtering through the jungle to Quang-Duc province on the north and down into Binh-Duong province on the south. A simultaneous assault in Tay-Ninh province gained ground, including Nui-Ba-Den, the well-known Black Virgin Mountain.[5] Tanh-Linh district in Binh-Tuy also fell, including three return-to-village sites. Tens of thousands of refugees poured out of all three areas. Fighting near the Gia-Ray resettlement site in Long-Khanh province forced nearly 80% of the 7,500 inhabitants to flee. In MR-4, it was estimated that over 100,000 new temporarily displaced war victims had been generated, almost all in Vinh-Binh and Kien-Giang provinces. Only 3,800 had been registered by January 8. During the next week, 15,000 were newly registered in Kien-Tuong province.[6]

Even though the Communist offensive was only in its initial stage, the GVN realized that its effects would overstrain Vietnamese resources for assisting the victims. At a press conference on January 8 to announce the fall of Phuoc-Long province, the Ministry of Foreign Affairs distributed a telegram signed by Deputy Prime Minister Phan Quang Dan addressed to the International Committee of the Red Cross (ICRC), the League of Red Cross Societies (LICROSS), the UNHCR (United Nations High Commissioner for Refugees), and UNICEF, saying that the large-scale attacks by North Viet-Nam in blatant violation of the Paris agreement had left thousands of civilians, including women and children, in dire need of shelter, food, and medicine. The message appealed for international aid.[7]

UNICEF had given modest assistance to Viet-Nam before, notably for the National School of Social Work, and the UNHCR had assisted the resettlement of refugees from Cambodia in 1970 and thereafter, but otherwise international organizations (except voluntary agencies) had not given significant aid for the relief of Viet-Nam's war victims, who were considered a domestic problem. That began to change in 1974, when the UNHCR developed a program, estimated to cost $12,500,000 US, for assistance to uprooted and displaced persons in

North Viet-Nam, Laos, the territories of the Provisional Revolutionary Government (PRG) in South Viet-Nam, and the territory of the GVN. The United States was prohibited by law from making any appropriated funds available for North Viet-Nam and its policy precluded aid to the PRG, but AID granted funds to the UNHCR fund for refugees in GVN-controlled territory and Laos, increasing its contribution gradually from $500,000 to $2,000,000.[8] Evidently in response to the GVN's appeal of January 8, part of the broader program was merged into the Joint UNHCR/UNICEF Emergency Relief Operation, which collected $17,185,438 from donors and spent $14,150,795. That operation made available to South Viet-Nam over 20,000 tons of food, more than 45 tons of medicaments, over 1,500 tons of roofing sheets, and other supplies. The most urgent shipments were sent by air. (It is not known how much arrived before the Communist takeover.) Thereafter, $4,628,205 was spent for agricultural aid in South Viet-Nam, and the balance of the funds was transferred to the general UNHCR Indochina program, to be spent, by agreement with the donors, principally in the southern region of the Socialist Republic of Viet-Nam.[9]

THE SPRING OFFENSIVE IN THE CENTRAL HIGHLANDS

Early in February, General Van Tien Dung, Chief of Staff of the NVA, arrived in South Viet-Nam to take command of what was to be the Great Spring offensive, which ended in the conquest of Saigon on April 30. The first target selected by the Politburo was Ban Me Thuot, the capital of Darlac province, headquarters of the 23rd ARVN Division, and a major city of the central Highlands. The NVA began by cutting the major roads leading to the city. On March 10, 1975, an overwhelming NVA force attacked Ban Me Thuot, which was defended by only one of the 23rd Division's regiments and principally by its own territorial forces, since Major General Pham Van Phu, the II Corps commander, had expected the principal attack to occur against his headquarters in Pleiku. Within two days the capital was taken. Among those captured were the US Consulate General team headed by Paul Struharik and a group of American missionaries. They were released some months later.[10]

The Regional and Popular Forces, most of whom were Montagnards, did not fight the North Vietnamese at Ban Me Thuot, although a Rhadé ARVN officer commanding a highlander unit near Ban Me Thuot was trying to organize a defense against the Communist troops. Some Montagnard forces turned their guns against the ARVN troops. Agence France Presse correspondent Paul Léandri (who was later killed by Saigon police) reported that they were FULRO troops, who were independent of the GVN units, and a Montagnard leader cited by Gerald Hickey confirmed that. However, highlander leaders now in North Carolina dispute this. They pointed out that the Viet-Cong Iron Division was made up largely of Montagnards and was commanded by a highlander colonel. It participated in the NVA attack. A former FULRO leader agreed, however, that the FULRO forces did not help either to defend or to attack Ban Me Thuot. NVA tanks carried FULRO banners, which allegedly were faked.[11]

The capture of the city demoralized the other two regiments of the 23rd Division because their families were in the city, and many of the soldiers left their posts to find their relatives. Units of the division had been airlifted into a village on Highway 21 east of the city in order to relieve the defenders, but when they were reunited with family members who had fled there from Ban Me Thuot, some officers and men threw away their weapons and uniforms and headed toward Nha-Trang on the coast.[12]

President Thieu had already concluded that it was necessary to abandon most of the Highlands, and at a meeting in Cam-Ranh on March 14 with Prime Minister Khiem, ARVN Chief of Staff General Vien, and General Phu, he ordered the II Corps commander to retreat from Pleiku and Kontum to the coast. There the troops were to be regrouped in order to recapture Ban Me Thuot. The President directed that the withdrawal be kept secret from the territorial forces and the people. Of course it couldn't be.

That afternoon, General Phu notified his immediate subordinates, warning that Thieu had ordered that neither the province chiefs nor the territorial forces were to be informed of the decision to withdraw. According to one of his top commanders, he said, "The regional forces are all montagnards, let's give them back to the mountains."[13] Then he turned over command to his deputy and the next morning evacuated himself and his family from Pleiku to Nha-Trang. This started a chain reaction; the acting commander and many of his staff and field commanders collected their families and fled, abandoning their men and the civilian population. The Vietnamese Air Force had begun its evacuation on the evening of the 14th. Panic ensued, and soon as many as 200,000 people, soldiers and civilians all mixed up together, were in flight down Route 7B, an old logging road which was in disrepair but which had been selected for withdrawal. It wound through Cheo-Reo, the capital of Phu-Bon province and thence over streams and rivers to Tuy-Hoa, the capital of Phu-Yen province on the sea. Most never made it. When NVA General Dung learned of the retreat, he ordered his commanders to stop it, and they did so, with utmost ruthlessness. His troops overran the Cheo-Reo airstrip, while a number of Montagnard soldiers joined them in firing on ARVN troops. Indeed, there had been fighting between Communist and anti-Communist highlander forces in Thuan-Manh district of Phu-Bon even before the NVA attack on Ban Me Thuot. East of the town, the NVA intercepted fleeing refugees and poured fire on them. There also rebel highlanders armed with both American and Communist weapons fired into the refugee convoy, according to a respected Vietnamese journalist who was with it. Other parts of the refugee column were caught at other choke points and were decimated by Communist fire, being run over by GVN military vehicles, drowning in the rivers, and sheer exhaustion. Demoralized ARVN soldiers robbed many of the civilians. The GVN Air Force bombed some by mistake. Most of the survivors were captured by the North Vietnamese.

During the awful trek, GVN Army helicopters had flown up to 80 missions a day, dropping bread, picking up the wounded, and giving fire support. However, many of the refugees had eaten nothing but leaves and roots during the last days of their journey. Eleven days after the retreat began, about 45,000 pitiful survivors straggled into Tuy-Hoa, where Dr. Dan, the province chiefs of Phu-Yen and Ninh-Thuan, the deputy corps commander (Brigadier General Le Van Than, former province chief of Thua-Thien), and the Deputy Minister of Interior (Colonel Pham Van Chung, former province chief of Quang-Nam) had improvised some camps and provided some food. It was quite disorganized, as most of the local officials and the city's population had fled. At that time, Dr. Dan started the evacuation of refugees to the South. By March 31, Tuy-Hoa itself came under North Vietnamese fire.[14]

Columns of refugees from Kontum and other highland locations made their way to Nha-Trang; there were perhaps 60,000 in all. Those from Ban Me Thuot and other parts of the southern highlands arrived in Dalat, where 90% of its population fled on March 21, even though there was no military threat to the city.[15]

The catastrophic flight from the Highlands was a shameful blot upon the honor of the once-proud armed forces and government of Viet-Nam. The top military commanders in MR-2 had abandoned the territorial forces and the population *at the order of President Thieu* and commanders at all levels had abandoned their own troops. Leaderless, the soldiers gathered up their families and fled precipitously, often killing the unarmed civilians in their path. Few Vietnamese emerged with honor from that debacle.

The Consulate General (ConGen) in Nha-Trang and the other agencies under its wing did what they could to bring in from the highland provinces their own field personnel, the voluntary agency volunteers, and the Vietnamese who were their employees and associates, and there were some heroic acts by young officials rescuing their Vietnamese and tribal employees and friends. Consul General Moncrieff (Monty) Spear, Pleiku ConGen Chief Earl Thieme, Walt Martindale in isolated Quang-Duc, and Edmund Sprague, the tribal-language-speaking representative in Phu-Bon deserve special mention for their help to the Vietnamese and Montagnards for whom they assumed responsibility. However, in the crush of panic-stricken people at the airports they were unable to take out many who were in peril. Those who were rescued were regrouped in Nha-Trang.[16]

THE OFFENSIVE IN THE COASTAL AREAS

On March 8, just as the NVA was preparing to attack Ban Me Thuot, other units probed GVN positions in Quang-Tri and Thua-Thien. That was sufficient to set off the flight of about 50,000 people from the northernmost province, heading toward Hue. Then President Thieu, as part of his "Light at the Top, Heavy at the Bottom" concept, decided that Quang-Tri would have to be given up, and he ordered corps commander General Ngo Quang Truong to send the

Airborne Division to Saigon as a strategic reserve. After winning a short reprieve, I Corps withdrew the division from its positions west of Hue and Da-Nang and embarked it on March 16. One of its three brigades was landed at Nha-Trang; the other two went on to Saigon. General Truong then pulled the Marine Division out of Quang-Tri, triggering a general evacuation of civilians as well as the military.

President Thieu vacillated over whether to defend Hue, and that, coupled with news of what was happening in the Highlands, broke the morale of the ARVN First Division and other units, sending their soldiers and families in flight toward Da-Nang, despite General Truong's efforts at organizing an orderly retreat. Truong redeployed a brigade of the Marines toward the Thua-Thien coast on March 23–24, but NVA ambushes killed, wounded, or captured four-fifths of them.[17]

Meanwhile, Prime Minister Khiem, Dr. Dan, and other members of the cabinet came up to Da-Nang on March 19 to confer with General Truong about the "Light at the Top" strategy and to decide what to do with the enormous refugee mass it was creating. The decision was to send to the south those from Quang-Tri and others if necessary. That was before the mass exodus from Hue. Dr. Dan formed a task force to plan the relocation of up to one million refugees to Cam-Ranh, Ninh-Thuan, Binh-Thuan, and similar locations. Shortly thereafter, he brought Colonel Ton That Khien, a member of his staff, to Da-Nang to take charge of the relief program. Colonel Khien had been province chief of Quang-Ngai, Quang-Tri, and then Thua-Thien, so he knew the region. He was honest, dedicated, and competent. He had with him a check for 800 million piasters (about $1.1 million US at 725 in 1975). However, conditions in the city soon became so chaotic that Colonel Khien could accomplish nothing. He was evacuated on a ship at the end. A crash estimate by Embassy Saigon that a program to care for one million refugees from April 1 to December 31 would cost $140 million US was also quickly overtaken by events.[18]

The new Chief of Naval Operations, Vice Admiral Chung Tan Cang, sent every available vessel to the north. His action came none too soon. Not only were the remnants of the Marine brigade at the small river port of Tan-My in Thua-Thien province, but a good part of the population of Hue soon converged there. The Marines fought with both militia personnel and civilians, killing many of them, to get on the overcrowded vessels.[19] This was a spectacle often and widely repeated in the following days.

The North Vietnamese hoisted their flag over the Citidel at Hue on March 26. They had already begun shelling the column heading down Route 1 toward Da-Nang.[20]

On March 24, Quang-Tin and Quang-Ngai provinces fell without a fight. The province chief of Quang-Tin and the higher ranking military officers in both provinces were the first to flee; then came the soldiers, heading toward Da-Nang in the north or the Chu-Lai base in Quang-Tin. However, the NVA overran both provinces so fast that few civilians were able to get out.[21]

By March 24, Da-Nang was the unwilling host to at least 500,000 refugees, civilian and military, and possibly many more. The number kept increasing. They were not registered, and, unlike in 1972, there was little organized care for them, despite Colonel Khien's efforts. The city refugee office was vacant, the officials having fled. The former US bases that had been used as refugee camps in 1972–73 had long since been pulled down. Consequently, the refugees took shelter at schools, temples, and on empty lots—anywhere they could find room—and they roamed around looking for missing family members. Dennis Brown of CARE organized a makeshift relief operation, but it was a drop in the bucket of need. After NVA rockets hit the airbase and a nearby settlement on March 26, panic spread, with looting and robbery by armed soldiers, some of them drunk. Before the end of the week, utter chaos reigned.[22]

Ambassador Graham Martin had fought hard for increased American aid to the beleaguered GVN, and maintained an optimism that the US Government would not allow Viet-Nam to go down before the North Vietnamese onslaught. However, he left it to his Consuls General to decide when to evacuate their American and Vietnamese employees and families from endangered outposts, while cautioning against precipitate action that might lead to the very collapse of the Vietnamese military and civilian authorities he was trying to avoid. At the time of the MR-2 and MR-1 debacles, he was on medical leave in the United States, and his deputy, Wolfgang Lehmann, the Chargé, maintained Martin's policy. In mid-March, Monty Spear had pulled his field people and some of their Vietnamese associates in to Nha-Trang. Consul General Albert Francis in Da-Nang withdrew his people from the outlying posts ahead of the NVA at about the same time. Lehmann, reporting this, asked Washington to think in terms of a possible sealift to move large numbers of refugees to the south. On March 24, Al Francis determined that the time had come for evacuation from Da-Nang. He sent a message to the Saigon Embassy requesting that the contingency plan to have US Navy forces stand offshore be initiated, and that an airlift sufficient to remove 40,000 refugees be commenced. His requests were granted, and within hours the first chartered World Airways 727 arrived. Over a hundred passengers were ferried to Cam-Ranh. Other aircraft followed. In the subsequent days, increasingly unruly mobs of soldiers and civilians rushed the planes as they landed, often pushing past those who had been ticketed by the Consulate General, and the airport guards were unwilling or unable to maintain order. On Friday, March 28, the flights had to be stopped. However, Edward J. Daly, the rough-and-ready chief executive officer of World Airways, was not to be daunted. The next day he personally took a plane to Da-Nang. It was mobbed by frantic soldiers the minute it landed, and the pilot had to take off with his rear door, loading steps and wheels still down because men were hanging onto them. Altogether 330 people were carried to Saigon on the damaged plane; all but 10 of them were soldiers. It was the last of the airlift; fewer than 1,200 refugees had been evacuated in a program intended to take 40,000.[23]

Meanwhile, in addition to the Vietnamese Navy vessels sent by Admiral Cang, the American Defense Attache General Homer Smith procured tugs, barges, and cargo ships to evacuate the ARVN troops and materiel, and civilian refugees. In order to avoid violating the War Powers Act, he utilized only civilian craft chartered to the Military Sealift Command. A meeting of the National Security Council in Washington on March 25 ratified this action. Then, at the suggestion of Ambassador Martin, who was in Washington, President Gerald Ford, with the advice of Secretary of State Henry Kissinger, decided to send US Navy vessels as well, instructing them to stay in international waters. They were given authority to pick up evacuees, both civilian and military. President Ford notified congressional leaders on March 29. The purpose of these decisions was primarily to rescue the Vietnamese armed forces so that they could fight again, but in the process of implementation, civilian refugees also benefited. Having returned to Saigon with Army Chief of Staff General Frederick Weyand, Martin requested that the fleet use air cover and naval gunfire to keep the NVA at bay while a massive evacuation went on, but this suggestion was not accepted. President Ford also ordered that military supplies on order for Viet-Nam be delivered immediately. The Australian government sent its air force C-130s to assist, after notifying Hanoi; and ships of Korea, Taiwan, Australia, Great Britain, and the Philippines joined the rescue operation.[24]

At the same time (March 29) the President appointed AID Administrator Daniel Parker as his Special Coordinator for International Disaster Assistance, with the mandate to do everything possible for the Vietnamese refugees fleeing from the Communist armies.[25] AID had a superb disaster assistance office, equipped with instant worldwide communications and the logistical and financial capability to respond rapidly to emergencies wherever needed. The appointment of Parker put these resources at the service of the Viet-Nam war victims, and brought the military vessels and aircraft already mobilized under expert civilian guidance. However, this was not enough to save most of the refugees from being enveloped by the North Vietnamese.

The United States government had asked United Nations Secretary General Kurt Waldheim to appeal to the North Vietnamese with a view to allowing an extended opportunity for the evacuation of civilian refugees. This was done contrary to the view of Frank Kellogg, Special Assistant to the Secretary for Refugee and Migration Affairs (and my immediate chief), who knew that the United Nations agency would not be able to intervene in a conflict where two of the major-power members were arrayed on opposite sides. This was especially the case where GVN soldiers were mixed up with the civilians. The UN Secretary General declined to intercede, and thereby incurred the unjust wrath of powerful US officials, who retaliated by delaying consideration of his appeal for contributions for humanitarian aid within Viet-Nam, including those portions under Communist control.[26]

On March 28, the 13,532-ton freighter SS *Pioneer Contender* was off the coast of Da-Nang, and several tugs and barges went in. Over 6,000 refugees, one-fourth of whom were soldiers, were loaded onto the ship in a relatively orderly fashion. By the time it steamed away for Cam-Ranh, the USNS *Andrew Miller* had arrived, and took on 7,500 passengers. Other ships followed. However, as the North Vietnamese forces neared the city, the crowds awaiting evacuation became more unruly, and hundreds were drowned while attempting to board the barges or were crushed between the vessels and the docks. Scenes like those at Tan-My were repeated. Al Francis and his few remaining staffers and volunteers managed to get many of their Vietnamese employees, families, and associates evacuated, including a reluctant General Truong, but many also were left behind in the crush. Altogether, about 90,000 refugees made it to the south by sea; 16,000 of them were soldiers. They were all that were saved of the entire I Corps forces. A few more people were flown out on Air America planes from the Marble Mountain strip. As many as a million people were left in Da-Nang.[27]

Da-Nang was in North Vietnamese hands by March 30, and the NVA kept going down the coast with all speed. In Binh-Dinh, the 22nd ARVN Division and territorial forces had been fighting hard for weeks, but they then gave up and fled. Qui-Nhon was evacuated on March 31 and was in enemy hands the next day. No refugees reached any of the US vessels waiting offshore.[28]

General Phu fled from Nha-Trang on April 1 once again, as he had done in Pleiku, without notifying his subordinates. Consul General Moncrieff Spear, Earl Thieme, Walt Martindale, and other officers had sent many Vietnamese out to the South. On April 1, at the express order of George Jacobson in Saigon, Spear and his remaining staff left. The evacuation was chaotic and, according to Arnold Isaacs, Frank Snepp, and others, many of the Consulate General's employees were abandoned. It seems, however, that some of them were rescued in the following days. This was possible since the Communist troops were diverted to the south; the capture of the city was announced only on April 5. Cam-Ranh was given up on April 3, but the NVA seized it only on the 4th— with all the equipment that had been saved from the North. Many refugees from Phan-Rang were picked up by US ships on April 3 and 4; that city was not taken by the North Vietnamese until the 16th.[29] However, by mid-April, General Dung's forces were closing in on the approaches to Saigon.

The refugees who had earlier been dropped off at Cam-Ranh and other sites were now carried to such places as Vung-Tau and Phu-Quoc Island. By the end of the first week of April, American ships had lifted 95,612 people and foreign-flag vessels had carried an estimated 40,000 more. In addition, at least 750,000 people were fleeing the Communists on coastal and river craft, land vehicles, or on foot.[30]

At Phu-Quoc Island, an insensitive Vietnamese Navy commander kept thousands of refugees offshore for days, where many died of privation and the heat, while he and his men conducted elaborate security screening as a trickle was allowed to land. Finally the US Embassy got higher headquarters to break the logjam, and some 40,000 refugees were offloaded. Ten thousand military personnel among them were transferred to the mainland, but most of the rest remained on the former prison colony until it too was captured by the Communists.[31]

SOME ASPECTS OF THE DUAL DISASTER

To analyze all the factors in the defeats in both MR-2 and MR-1 is beyond the scope of this study. The books by Snepp and Isaacs (Snepp, *Decent Interval*, and Isaacs, *Without Honor*: see Bibliography) contain thorough accounts and analyses, and for those who know how to read "Communese," the book by General Dung is also valuable (*Our Great Spring Victory*: see Bibliography). Relevant to our study are the following:

1. The ambivalence of some GVN and FULRO Montagnard troops and the strength and determination of those on the Communist side at Ban Me Thuot and in Phu-Bon resulted in considerable part from the forced relocations and other acts of mistreatment by the South Vietnamese over the previous years. At least two of the highlander leaders had turned to the Communists some time before the final NVA offensive, and few of the tribal people had any reason to love the GVN. General Westmoreland thought that the defections at Ban Me Thuot were evidence that "the wily Montagnards" had decided to cast their lot with what appeared to be a tide of victory of the North Vietnamese (see note 11). The weight of evidence recounted by Gerald Hickey (*Free in the Forest*: see Bibliography) and Montagnard leaders now in the United States would indicate otherwise. In past years, Montagnard troops had fought valiantly against the Communists, even in some situations where they were sure to lose. However, the visible and pervasive contempt with which most Vietnamese officials and others regarded the highlanders, the senseless relocations into wretched camps while Vietnamese farmers stole their land, and other indignities, finally were repaid in the only way the Montagnards knew how. While the Montagnard territorial forces and FULRO troops probably could not have saved the day at Ban Me Thuot, if they had put up the stubborn resistance of which they were capable, it might have inspired the ARVN soldiers to do no less. At worst, the military forces fighting the NVA would have been defeated with honor. After the defeat, many highlanders again fought the Communists, but then it was too late.

2. The "family syndrome" was a major cause of the disintegration of military units in both regions. The long-standing ARVN practice of allowing, and indeed, encouraging families to live close to the troops, was intended in part to motivate the soldiers to fight to protect their loved ones. However, it practically guaranteed that when military-dependent housing areas were threatened, the troops would look after their loved ones first. That happened during the 1972 NVA offensive, and it happened on a wider scale in 1975. In the Vietnamese culture, when a choice had to be made between loyalty to the state and family loyalty, the latter would almost always win. During the retreats in the two regions, this was not

a factor for the Airborne and Marine divisions or the Navy, since the dependents of those mobile forces were all in and around Saigon. However, it was the dominant factor for the other soldiers and officers. For some reason, evacuation of military dependents had never been part of strategic or tactical planning; it was left to the families and soldiers themselves, and commanders recognized and respected this.

Nonetheless, it was inevitable that mixed flights of soldiers and civilians would make them targets of enemy assault. They were not legitimate targets, because the invasion itself was an egregious violation of the 1973 cease-fire agreement, but in the light of what had happened in 1972, it was to be expected that the NVA would attack the retreating military and civilian refugees. It was normal for a warring party to take whatever military action might be necessary to prevent the escape and possible regrouping of enemy troops. Whatever harm to civilians might ensue was considered one of the hazards of war.

3. Fear of the Communists was the dominant reason for refugee flight in 1975. Especially in MR-1 but also elsewhere, the memory of the VC massacres at Hue in 1968 was a powerful reason to fear what a new Communist conquest would bring. Three experienced researchers who had conducted some of the Human Science Research refugee surveys in 1966–68, assisted by some university students, some of whom had also participated in those studies, interviewed 70 heads of families at three refugee sites near Vung-Tau on April 8–10, 1975. Two of the camps were run by the GVN, the other one being administered by a Catholic agency. The refugee sample was not at all representative of the total population of South Viet-Nam, but it was the best that could be collected in the last few weeks of the RVN. Forty of the respondents (57.1%) were Catholics, and 29 (41.5%), not necessarily all Catholics, gave North Viet-Nam as their native region; that included the descendants of families born in the North. Thirty-nine of the family heads (55.7%) said they came from central Viet-Nam. Actually almost all had fled from that area in the spring of 1975, including those who had come down from the North in 1954–55. They came from 19 provinces and the autonomous cities of Hue, Da-Nang, Nha-Trang, and Dalat. The largest number came from Quang-Tri, followed by Binh-Tuy and Binh-Thuan. At least 30% were from urban centers. There was a disproportionate number of merchants, soldiers, police, and civil servants among the refugees (41.4%), while only 21.4% had been farmers. They were mainly lower or lower-middle class, presumably because the wealthy had been able to get to Saigon by private means.[32]

By contrast with earlier movements surveyed by members of this team, these refugees tended to give relatively simple and clear-cut reasons for their flight. Most gave only one reason; the 70 people gave only 103 responses. Forty-one and four-tenths percent feared Viet-Cong reprisals, and 28.6% were unwilling to live under Communist control—a total of 70% who cited the Communists as the cause of their becoming refugees. Some gave graphic facts and fears about

Communist killings of family members to support their responses on that point. There was no significant difference between Catholics and non-Catholics in their fear of or aversion to the Communists. Thirty-seven and one-tenth percent of the sample cited fear of fighting, shelling, or bombing; 28.6% said they saw others leaving and panicked. Only three family heads (4.3%) said they had been ordered to leave by GVN authorities.[33]

4. Although the flight from the invading North Vietnamese was the largest single refugee movement in the RVN's history, the great majority of the people in the territories which were overrun did not flee, either because the invasion was so rapid that they could not or because they decided not to. Most of the highlanders were probably in the latter group, although they had no more love for the North Vietnamese than for the Southerners. An American observer who was living with and studying the people of one village in Thua-Thien reported that about 95% of the inhabitants of that village, which had been pro-NLF, chose to remain, as did most other rural residents in the province.[34] It seems likely that many people were tired of the fighting and fleeing and decided to await whatever might come. As in all refugee movements throughout history, it was those who had the most to fear from the conquerors who took flight; the ordinary peasants and urban poor simply wanted to be left alone to work and live as they always had.

5. The absence of GVN relief efforts for the refugees in Tuy-Hoa, Da-Nang, and Cam-Ranh, which was noted above, was symptomatic of the general disintegration of the Vietnamese Government, which felt itself abandoned by the United States in the face of the North Vietnamese offensive. In all previous emergencies, at least since the Têt offensive of 1968, the GVN with American help had responded quickly and effectively. This was the case during the Easter offensive of 1972, whose magnitude was scarcely less in its opening phases than the final offensive of 1975. A proven GVN apparatus, procedures, programs, financial means, and commodity stockpiles had been in place throughout the country. In 1975, even though American civilian aid was available on as generous a scale as in 1972, the GVN officials who would administer the relief efforts had abandoned their posts, in some cases well before the enemy approach. Thus, when the tattered refugee band finally made it to Tuy-Hoa, the local GVN officials were gone. When Colonel Khien showed up in Da-Nang, he found nobody to work with. This was as disgraceful as the abandonment by General Phu and other military officers of their men and the people whom they were to protect. Local GVN refugee-assistance personnel were also absent at Cam-Ranh, a planned evacuation point for refugees from MR-1 when officials from Saigon, the corps, and two provinces came to assist. After Prime Minister Khiem's government resigned on April 2, Dr. Dan and a few other leaders at the center, with a small number of brave subordinates like Huynh Thanh Hu'ng, valiantly tried to cope with the chaotic situations in Regions 1 and 2, an impossible task. Personnel did remain on duty at Vung-Tau and on Phu-Quoc Island.

OPERATION BABYLIFT

Beginning in 1974, significant numbers of Vietnamese children were being adopted by American parents (1,352 in that year), and several licensed adoption agencies were functioning in Viet-Nam in cooperation with the Ministry of Social Welfare. The number of children who were adoptable was not large, since they had to be full orphans (that is, with both parents dead) or be legally given up for intercountry adoption by their parents. The overwhelming majority of the estimated 880,000 full or partial orphans in the country, of whom over 500,000 were children of dead soldiers, were cared for by their extended families; only about 21,000 were in orphanages, and few of them were adoptable.[35]

By the spring of 1975, the crowded condition of orphanages and increasing pressure from prospective parents in various Western countries and governments on their behalf combined with the parlous condition of Viet-Nam to induce a speedup of the normally slow procedures for intercountry adoption. Lauralee Peters of the US State Department's East Asia Bureau, who had worked on the problem in the consular section of Embassy Saigon, brought the matter to the attention of her superiors, and on April 1 an interagency meeting chaired by Daniel Parker of AID and including Frank Kellogg, the Special Assistant to the Secretary of State for Refugee and Migration Affairs (S/R), the Bureau of Security and Consular Affairs (SCA), and the Immigration and Naturalization Service (INS) of the Justice Department agreed that those children whose processing had established their eligibility for immigration and adoption should be airlifted and "paroled" into the United States. This was Mr. Parker's only action concerned with the movement of people out of Viet-Nam; his official responsibility was normally for assistance within foreign countries, while the State Department had responsibility for international migration and refugee movement. However, since AID was providing assistance to child welfare within Viet-Nam and had the expertise, Mr. Parker developed the orphan airlift, with the concurrence of the other agencies concerned. Attorney General Edward H. Levi approved parole, and Mr. Parker set "Operation Babylift" in motion the next day.[36]

Although some of the orphans were shipped out on commercial flights, the first official flight of the operation was on an Air Force C-5A Galaxy on April 4. Two hundred forty-three children and 62 accompanying adults—wives of embassy and AID personnel, nurses, and voluntary agency people, were loaded onto the two decks, and the giant plane took off from Tan-Son-Nhut airport. However, a short distance out the rear cargo doors blew out, and the plane crashed in a muddy rice field. All those in the lower deck were killed, but almost all of those above survived.[37] The world was shocked by the tragedy, but the airlift went on.

Many of the children slated for adoption had received special care and feeding at a unit of the Seventh Day Adventist Hospital near the airport administered by the International Rescue Committee, but it was recognized that the long journey to the United States would be extremely stressful. The children were given medical examinations before departure, and the Babylift flights stopped over at Clark Field in the Philippines, where additional examinations were conducted and those with illnesses or weakness were hospitalized. By April 8, some 1,348 orphans had been lifted to Clark, of whom 1,311 went on to Travis Air Base in California. President Ford met one of the flights, and was covered by news photographers.[38] By April 28, some 2,700 children had been carried to the United States by the operation.[39]

Given the anxiety of the Vietnamese about the advancing North Vietnamese, it was inevitable that there would be abuses. Both on the official flights and on those arranged by some adoption agencies on commercial planes, children who were not orphans and adults who were the wives or girlfriends of Americans were carried. However, Operation Babylift was a success, and it created sympathy not only for the children but also for stricken Viet-Nam, as evidently had been intended.[40]

THE COLLAPSE OF THE GVN: VIETNAMESE BECOME INTERNATIONAL REFUGEES

Initial Planning and Evacuations of Refugees

During the many trials and tribulations of the Vietnamese people over more than 30 years of war, including occupation by the Japanese and the war against the French, few had left their native land. Now that the North Vietnamese were quite clearly about to conquer South Viet-Nam, however, it was apparent that large numbers of endangered people would have to escape from the country by one means or another. Experience in the North and in those parts of the South where the Communists had established their rule showed that religious people, Catholic, Buddhist, and Protestant alike, would be persecuted. Landowners and capitalists, even small proprietors, would be considered hostile elements. Those who had worked for and with the Americans, military and civilian leaders, and high civil servants of the GVN, would all be enemies. Editors and writers of the "puppet" press, as well as academic and other intellectual persons who had not been Communist apologists, were in danger, and of course there were tens of thousands of dependents of Americans, both official and private, and of other foreigners who had been working in the country, as well as the extended families of many who had already left. The number of those who were at risk was very large.

The problem of saving the endangered people was complicated by the fact that the adjacent areas of Laos and Cambodia, the only countries with which South Viet-Nam had land borders, were in Communist hands.

The American Embassy and the other agencies under the Ambassador's direction had been compiling lists of their Vietnamese employees, their families, and their contacts who should be removed from the country. The total was somewhere between 200,000 and one million, depending on how the cutoff point was calculated. A few were secretly gotten out on military planes in the first three weeks of April, along with the Vietnamese wives and girlfriends of American military and civilian personnel. However, although in his meetings with Kissinger and others toward the end of March, Ambassador Martin had asked for parole covering about 250,000 Vietnamese, the authority was slow in coming (as will be discussed below), and this placed severe restrictions on the numbers who could be evacuated and brought into the United States.

Other than the United States, France had the largest number of potential refugees to be concerned about, even though thousands, including Vietnamese with French nationality, had left when the country was divided at the 17th parallel in 1954. In South Viet-Nam there were large French-owned plantations of rubber (Michelin, for instance—a favorite hideout of the VC), coffee, and other products. French-owned businesses were numerous and wealthy, including the breweries which produced the famous "33 beer." Prestigious French educational and cultural institutions continued to function. Thousands of Frenchmen and their families quietly left on the daily Air France flights, along with Vietnamese who had French citizenship.

There was a huge Chinese colony in Saigon-Cholon, most of which had remained carefully neutral, protecting its pervasive commercial interests. However, some thousands had identified themselves with the GVN cause. Beginning early in April the Embassy of the Republic of China (Taiwan) issued 1,400 passports and 3,500 certificates of identity, but because the GVN did not provide exit visas, most could not get out before the end. The ROC also made clear that it would take care of over a thousand Vietnamese students and others already in the country.[41]

In Washington, Frank Kellogg's office (S/R), in which I was the deputy, quietly began planning for mass evacuation of Vietnamese and also Cambodians (since the Khmer Rouge were closing in on Phnom Penh even faster than the NVA was moving) early in 1975. Chris Pappas and Ferris (Dick) Jameson obtained space in the State Department's Operations Center (a splendidly equipped area with instant communications worldwide, as well as excellent communications with the White House, the Pentagon, the CIA, and other agencies). They gathered officers from the Department's East Asia Bureau, AID, and the Pentagon. It was all low-level and informal, but needs for transport and other necessities were calculated. We were not informed that Ambassador Martin had requested parole authority late in March. We were thinking at first in terms of evacuating temporarily to neighboring countries in East Asia while resettlement modalities were worked out. The US Mission in Geneva was instructed to request UNHCR and ICEM assistance, to which both agencies responded positively. We also drafted a circular telegram to the US Ambassadors in the Asian countries asking them to approach the governments to which they were accredited in strictest confidence with the request that they receive evacuees in staging areas. Clearances were delayed while parole and the embassy's evacuation plans were being considered, and our telegram was sent only on April 19. The message was repeated for information (not for action) to Saigon. (Ambassador Martin told me years later that he had been skeptical of its chances of success.)

The initial responses were surprisingly positive. All the governments said that they would be willing to receive refugees temporarily, provided that they were given assurances that the refugees would be resettled in other countries. Even Lee Quan Yew of Singapore offered to put at our disposal an incompleted housing block which could take 2,000 families. Taiwan said it would take ethnic Chinese for permanent stay. However, in the absence of broad US parole authorization or firm guarantees of resettlement elsewhere, the assurances could not be given, and most of the Southeast Asian nations refused to accept people whom the United States evacuated. There is no tradition of brotherly acceptance of each other's refugees in populous East Asia, as there is in Africa, Latin America, Europe, and parts of South Asia. However, a number of Vietnamese who got to the neighboring non-Communist lands on their own were allowed to stay temporarily, and some permanently.[42]

A formal Interagency Task Force had been formed on April 2, chaired by Philip Habib, Assistant Secretary of State for East Asia and the Pacific (EA), with Deputy Assistant Secretary Robert Miller as his alternate. Frank Kellogg and Leonard Walentynowicz, Director of the Bureau of Security and Consular Affairs, were the other principal State Department members, and Frank Wisner of the Public Affairs Bureau, who had served in Viet-Nam, quickly took a leading role. The AID contingent was headed by Arthur Gardiner, Assistant Administrator for East Asia. Leonard Chapman and his deputy James Greene represented INS. General Chapman had previously been commandant of the Marine Corps and was well acquainted with Viet-Nam. The Department of Defense (DOD) and the Joint Chiefs of Staff, which were to play a major role in the evacuation and in the reception of refugees on United States territory, was strongly represented. CIA and the Defense Intelligence Agency (DIA) provided the necessary intelligence that told the task force how much time it had. The task force took over a good deal of the State Department's Operations Center and functioned on a 24-hour-a-day schedule. Our S/R:ORM office supplied people around the clock, principally Chris Pappas, Dick Jameson, and Eleanor Green, our public affairs advisor (who was shortly coopted full-time).

On April 5, Frank Kellogg sent a memorandum to Acting Secretary of State Robert S. Ingersoll recommending that he send an attached letter to Attorney General Levi asking that he use his parole authority to admit refugees from Cambodia and Viet-Nam who would face death or persecution from the Communists. The letter said, "We estimate there are conservatively 200,000 to whom the United States has an obligation and the number may run to many times that number. We hope that many will be able to resettle in third countries but that may not be possible." Ingersoll signed and sent the letter.

Six days later, on April 11, the Attorney General replied that the Immigration Service had already decided that it would not require the departure of South

Vietnamese or Cambodians who were in the United States. As to those in third countries that were signatories of the Convention relating to the Status of Refugees, he suggested that the United States request those governments to permit them to remain. Those in other countries would be treated in the same manner as those in their countries of origin; the total of both categories had been estimated to be as high as 865,000. Subject to the President's approval, the Attorney General was prepared to exercise his parole authority for 67 South Vietnamese in the Philippines and 2,000 Cambodians in Thailand. The request to parole the larger number raised questions as to "our immediate and long range capacity to employ, house, school and otherwise support varying numbers of refugees and the proper programs to do so." He proposed consultation with the Congressional Judiciary Committees and said that the President's approval would be necessary.[43]

For his part, Ambassador Martin had no doubt that the United States would have to bring out large numbers of Vietnamese if the military situation within the country could not be stabilized. However, he felt that substantial American military and economic aid would enable Viet-Nam to survive, and he did not want actions taken that would undermine that chance. He was irritated at what he considered ill-advised interference by the East Asia Bureau (EA) of the State Department, and obtained a special channel to Kissinger and his NSC (National Security Council) deputy, Brent Scowcroft, bypassing the EA task force.[44]

On April 10, in an address to a joint session of the Congress, President Ford gave the first public indication that the United States was prepared to assist in the evacuation of not only Americans and their dependents but also of what came to be identified as "high-risk" Vietnamese. He said:

I must, of course, as I think each of you would, consider the safety of nearly 6,000 Americans who remain in South Vietnam, and tens of thousands of South Vietnamese employees of the United States Government, of news agencies, of contractors and businesses for many years whose lives, with their dependents, are in very grave peril. There are tens of thousands of other South Vietnamese intellectuals, professors, teachers, editors and opinion-leaders who have supported the United States, to whom we have a profound moral obligation. . . .

And now I ask the Congress to clarify immediately its restrictions on the use of U.S. military forces in Southeast Asia for the limited purposes of protecting American lives by ensuring their evacuation if this should be necessary. And I also ask prompt revision of the law to cover those Vietnamese to whom we have a very special obligation, and whose lives may be in danger, should the worst come to pass.[45]

The President immediately sent the necessary written communications and draft legislation to the Congress.

It is not clear why action to obtain parole authority for what came to be called "high-risk" Vietnamese was so long delayed. The concerns expressed by Attorney General Levi in his letter of April 11 about problems of employment, housing, schooling, and so forth, of the refugees to be brought to the United States were being addressed within the task force, which drafted legislation providing money for the voluntary resettlement agencies and the states for these purposes (see the next subsection for details). The different interests and perceptions of the cabinet departments, various Congressmen and Senators, and bureaucratic rivalries played a part. Thus, Secretary of Defense James Schlesinger and the Joint Chiefs of Staff were reluctant to send American forces back into Viet-Nam to protect an evacuation, and Schlesinger evidently had little interest in getting Vietnamese out, even though the Defense Attaché (DAO) in Saigon was strongly committed to his associates and intelligence sources. On the other hand, Henry Kissinger and Central Intelligence Director Colby felt that the United States owed an obligation to rescue the many Vietnamese at whose side Americans had fought for so long. (Colby, however, in accordance with his concept that the CIA should be an objective source of intelligence and analysis, refrained from taking a position in policy debates.) Chairman Joshua Eilberg of the House Immigration Subcommittee, Congressmen Jack Brooks, Elizabeth Holtzman, Bella Abzug, Senator Edward Kennedy, and others were, for widely divergent reasons, unenthusiastic about bringing masses of Vietnamese refugees into the United States.

The clear expression of presidential intent and the Kellogg Initiative led to approaches by the Interagency Task Force to the Congressional committees for consultation on parole. The embassy's highly classified revised evacuation plan was sent on April 9, listing 197,200 Vietnamese who would be most endangered, including cabinet officers, legislators, high civil and military officers, employees of the US government, and their families. Thereafter, the less-classified daily reports included in the high-risk category only mission employees and their dependents.[46] Other estimates of the embassy and Washington agencies ranged up to over a million, but around 200,000 was considered most reasonable. However, disharmony among Washington agencies and between Washington and Saigon caused the task force to delay in presenting a clear case to the congressional committees, thus losing valuable time and contributing to unnecessary confusion.

On April 14, Mr. Habib, accompanied by Messrs. Kellogg, Walentynowicz, General Chapman, and Greene, appeared before the House Subcommittee on Citizenship, Immigration and International Law, chaired by Joshua Eilberg, to discuss the proposals for parole. The hearing quickly went into executive session for the specifics. Eilberg said that the subcommittee had no objection to the request received the day before to parole about 3,000 immediate relatives of American citizens for prompt removal. Habib said that plans for the other categories of Vietnamese were not complete, but would be by the 18th. He said there were 17,600 Vietnamese employees of the American Mission, including all civilian and military agencies, and that they might have as many as seven or eight family members each. That could add up to 150,000 people. He asked for the subcommittee's advice on the high-risk category, without giving any figure. Then Mr. Greene reported that there were about 13,000 Vietnamese who were lawful permanent residents of the United States, plus 5,000 American citizens of Vietnamese origin; he gave a "ballpark" estimate of 30,000 of their immediate relatives to be brought in. He reminded the members of the subcommittee that the President had asked authorization to use troops in the evacuation, saying that a small contingent had been employed successfully in Operation Eagle Pull, which had evacuated the embassy and high-risk Cambodians from Phnom Penh.

In answer to the chairman's question as to the possibility of a bloodbath, Habib said that about 5,000 people had been executed by the Communists at Hue in 1968. After the March 1975 conquest of Da-Nang, he added, GVN policemen were beheaded, groups of soldiers were tied together and killed with grenades, and GVN security personnel were being systematically liquidated.

To Eilberg's questions about other countries that might grant temporary or permanent asylum, Kellogg responded that Brazil, Colombia, and Venezuela had very informally indicated their possible availability for limited resettlement. (As it turned out, none of them did take the Vietnamese.) Some Southeast Asian countries might take evacuees temporarily, he said.[47]

The next day, Habib and his colleagues appeared before the full Senate Judiciary Committee, where Senator Edward Kennedy was in the chair, even though the committee's regular chairman, Senator James Eastland, was in attendance. Kennedy opened with a statement saying that, even though the hearing was to consider the President's evacuation plan, the millions within Viet-Nam who were in need of relief and rehabilitation should not be forgotten.

Habib led off by saying that the President had requested authority to use the armed forces to assist evacuation and that he had requested $250 million for emergency humanitarian relief within Viet-Nam. Kennedy asked whether the government could request UN Secretary General Waldheim to use his good offices in working out the safety of the threatened population within Viet-Nam, to which Habib replied that Waldheim had been asked to bring about a cessation of hostilities. That led into an argument about the US request that Waldheim intervene to permit the evacuation of people from Da-Nang, and Kennedy then asked why the United States hadn't responded to the Secretary General's March 31 appeal for humanitarian aid. Senator Charles Mathias (Republican of Maryland) said that he had pressed Secretary Kissinger hard on that question at a meeting of the Appropriations Committee which he had just attended, and that Kissinger had showed some flexibility.

Habib then requested that the committee go into executive session to consider the parole proposal, and that was done. Thereupon he listed the categories to be evacuated, as follows:

Alien dependents of American Mission personnel	1,870
Key Vietnamese working for US companies	400
US Mission local nationals	17,600
With dependents	130,000

These were characterized as the high-risk category. Habib mentioned but gave no figures for GVN officials, military, political and intellectual leaders, and similar groups. He said that the total would be around 200,000, not counting diplomats of other countries and other third-country nationals to be repatriated. These figures were somewhat different from those given to the House Subcommittee, and neither enabled the two committees to make a judgment on the full parole numbers that would be needed.

Habib said that the United States intended to approach the UNHCR and ICEM for help in internationalizing the resettlement of the evacuees, and listed some countries which might take some for temporary or permanent asylum (as recounted above). He reported that the fleet of vessels that had been assembled for evacuation from Da-Nang and other coastal locations within the country was still standing by; it could move 100,000 people in about five days, and twice that number in 10. However, he said, President Thieu was not interested in evacuation; he wanted to stabilize the situation in a truncated Viet-Nam.[48]

Because of the potentially large number of relatives of Americans or permanent resident aliens who could be paroled, the Attorney General had been unwilling to have those figures brought before the congressional committees until they could be discussed at a cabinet meeting on April 16. Furthermore, the Immigration and Naturalization Service took a firm position that no more than 50,000 high-risk Vietnamese, or 40% of those actually evacuated (whichever was less), should be absorbed by the United States.[49] This was totally unrealistic; as it turned out, almost all the high-risk people who were evacuated or escaped ended up in the United States.

While the hearings were going on, the Defense Attache's Office (DAO), with the connivance of some of the civilians in the embassy and other agencies and the knowledge of the Ambassador, was quietly moving out some high-risk people with whom they had close connections on the cargo planes which were still bringing in military supplies. In the absence of parole authority, the evacuees were piling up in the Philippines, which eventually protested to the United States.[50] Other "black" flights brought some evacuees to American bases in Thailand. However, the total numbers of non-Americans counted as evacuated by this means was only 3,153 by midnight April 21. Most of the space on the returning military planes was empty.

Down to the Wire—Evacuation in Earnest

On April 17, the Senate Armed Forces Committee voted not to support the President's request for additional military aid to Viet-Nam, and Kissinger acknowledged that the debate was over and that the administration would accept the verdict of the Congress. That had more a psychological than a practical effect, since North Vietnamese forces were already closing in on Saigon, but afterwards a number of Vietnamese and Americans blamed that rejection for the defeat of South Viet-Nam.

The next day the President appointed L. Dean Brown head of a new Interagency Task Force (IATF) to take charge of the evacuation of Americans and Vietnamese, succeeding the one headed by Philip Habib. The appointment meant that the task force was to have a full-time chief; Habib had been compelled to take more time than he wished away from his broad regional responsibilities. It also raised the level of authority. As the President's representative, Brown had command authority over the various agencies and their resources. Dean Brown, who had retired from the Foreign Service and his previous position as Deputy Under Secretary of State for Management and was President of the Middle East Institute, was a soft-spoken but tough administrator, who also had wide diplomatic experience. He knew how to function in the maze of Washington bureaucracy. He quickly enlarged the top staff, appointing James M. Wilson, Jr., a senior Foreign Service Officer who was an East Asian expert, as his deputy; bringing in Clayton McManaway, who had been chief of program and budget in CORDS and was then serving in the Pentagon; and coopting Julia Vadala Taft, Deputy Assistant Secretary for Human Resources in the Department of Health, Education and Welfare (HEW). Frank Wisner became Brown's special assistant. Brown set about getting the financial resources necessary to support what was to become a vast operation. At first only $5 million was available from Frank Kellogg's emergency fund; that had already been tapped by Presidential Determination. Another Presidential Determination was obtained for $98 million in AID funds appropriated for postwar humanitarian assistance in Viet-Nam. Draft legislation requested $507 million more, most of which would go to the Defense Department for the evacuation by air and sea and for transit and reception centers in Guam and the continental United States, since it was decided that most of the evacuees would have to be brought straight onto US soil. Seventy-eight million dollars of the appropriation was to go to the State Department's Office of Refugee and Migration Affairs (ORM) to indemnify voluntary agencies for part of their resettlement expenses, and $125 million was to reimburse states for welfare, education, and public health costs of the new refugees—the concerns Attorney General Levi had pointed out.[51]

Ambassador Martin, concerned to avoid the panic that had plagued the air and sea evacuations from Da-Nang, but determined to move large numbers out of Viet-Nam if the worst case came to pass, searched for the best means of evacuation from Saigon, and also for alternatives. He asked that John Thomas, then Director of ICEM, come out to consult. (The request was never passed on to Thomas.) At his request, Admiral Noel Gayler, the CINCPAC, sent Rear Admiral Hugh Benton to help in the planning. Benton produced a plan that could move 200,000 persons in one day from the beaches of Vung-Tau and from other points, primarily by ship. Many more could be taken out if several days were available—which they were. Martin decided that the mission's local national employees would have to make their own way to Vung-Tau, and his telegram saying so convinced some people in Washington that the plan was not serious. Also, it was based on assumptions that the NVA/VC would not interfere with the evacuation and that the GVN would cooperate. In fact, the Vietnamese Marines, some of whom were already in Vung-Tau, were prepared to protect the operation and to control crowds. There were then over 200,000 refugees, mainly from MR-1 and MR-2, in Vung-Tau, and the road from Saigon was still open. The plan had been coordinated with CINCPAC and the US Special Advisory Group (USSAG) in Thailand. However, CINCPAC then vetoed it, perhaps because Admiral Gayler did not want to risk a large fleet of ships and aircraft in the face of the rapidly advancing NVA.[52]

After the President had set the policy for the administration—and reiterated it strongly in a meeting with the Senate Foreign Relations Committee in the Oval Office on April 14,[53] Henry Kissinger, as the President's Assistant for National Security Affairs sent a seemingly contradictory telegram via "Martin channels" to the Ambassador on April 17. It said:

We have just completed an interagency review of the state of play in South Vietnam. You should know that at the WSAG [Washington Special Action Group, a high-level body chaired by Kissinger in his role as Assistant to the President for National Security Affairs] meeting today there was almost no support for the evacuation of Vietnamese, and for the use of American force to help protect any evacuation. The sentiment of our military, DOD, and CIA colleagues was to get out fast and now.

The back-channel message went on to deplore the Congressional situation and concluded that the US Mission must accelerate its reduction of Americans.[54] This telegram has subsequently been quoted to show erosion of support for the Vietnamese people even at the highest level of the US government. It did reveal some divisions in Washington, principally about sending troops back into Viet-Nam, but clearly did not reflect the President's policy on evacuating Vietnamese, a policy which was very soon carried out with the loyal and efficient participation of US military forces and other elements of the administration.

That same day Kissinger, as Secretary of State, sent another telegram via "Martin channels" saying that "in the unanimous view of the Washington agencies represented [in the WSAG] the situation in Viet-Nam is rapidly and irretrievably approaching the worst case" (complete defeat of the GVN). As a result, the pressure for immediate evacuation of US personnel has become irresistible. The Secretary then asked Martin's view about a possible approach to the Soviet Union and the People's Republic of China "in order to work out some arrangement which would permit the departure of substantial numbers of Vietnamese who would be endangered and to whom we are most deeply obliged." The message concluded, "You are doing a fantastic job. Warm regards."[55] This was followed up by a telephone conversation between the Secretary and Ambassador Martin. Then Kissinger met with Soviet Ambassador Anatoly Dobrynin and handed him a note from the President to General Secretary Leonid Brezhnev saying that his overriding concern was to achieve controlled conditions for the evacuation of Americans and selected Vietnamese. To that end, the United States was prepared to discuss both a cease-fire and political problems.[56]

Evidently as a result of the approach to the Soviets, the North Vietnamese secretly agreed to allow some time for the American evacuation. It was only on April 29 that they began firing on the Tan-Son-Nhut airport. General Dung, however, continued his inexorable march toward Saigon, hindered for only a few days by strong resistance at Xuan-Loc. Dean Brown intensified the logistical preparations for the evacuation and reception of the refugees, but until the parole categories were extended, execution was restricted. Although Ambassador Martin had much respect for Dean Brown, there was friction between the task force and the Ambassador, as, for example, when the IATF questioned the plan to use Vung-Tau as an evacuation point. Martin also rejected its suggestion that he discuss evacuation with President Thieu, and he refused to allow refugees to be put aboard some Military Sea Transport Command vessels at the Saigon Newport docks, saying that to do so would precipitate panic. At that time there was plenty of room on returning military supply planes, in any case.[57]

Meanwhile, agreement on steadily broadening parole categories was slowly achieved in correspondence and conversations between General Chapman and Attorney General Levi and the chairmen of the Congressional Judiciary Committees; but it was only on April 21 that 50,000 GVN officials, political and intellectual leaders, and others in the high-risk category and their families (although not nearly as many as were needed) were formally authorized parole, bringing the authorized total to 130,000. This was 16 days after Acting Secretary of State Ingersoll had requested parole for 200,000 at-risk Cambodians and Vietnamese. Embassy Saigon was notified of this in the morning of April 22, Viet-Nam time, in a telegram that failed to mention that families were included in the 50,000. Ambassador Martin adopted a "John Marshall broad construction" of the message and sent families out with the principals.[58]

Also on April 21, President Nguyen Van Thieu resigned with an angry speech denouncing the United States for deserting its ally, and turned over the power that he had held for eight years to aging Vice President Tran Van Huong. Two nights later, Frank Snepp drove Thieu to the airport, where Ambassador Martin bade him farewell and he and his family were flown to Taiwan.

At that point, the air evacuation of both Americans and Vietnamese swung into high gear, achieving up to 7,500 a day on military and chartered aircraft, plus others on commercial planes. The embassy set up a processing facility at DAO headquarters on the edge of Tan-Son-Nhut airport and persuaded the Ministry of Interior to put some personnel issuing exit permits there also. Considerable pressure, using the promise of evacuating the officials and their families, and frequently outright bribery, were necessary to get and hold the cooperation of the Vietnamese civil and military personnel, and both American and Vietnamese rules were often bent. American civilian and military personnel went about the city picking up their friends and persons on the lists made up by the various sections of the mission and delivering them to the airport. It was more than a little chaotic, because there was so little time to move so many people out. The operation went on day and night until April 29, when the North Vietnamese began shelling the taxiways and runways, thus halting the evacuation by fixed-wing aircraft. By that time, at least 44,920 people, about 5,600 of whom were Americans, had been flown out to Clark Field and Guam. The Vietnamese evacuees included wives and children of Americans, orphans, families of military, police, political officials, employees of the US Mission, business enterprises, voluntary agencies, bar girls, and others. Most fell into the categories for whom parole was authorized, but many did not. Moreover, many whom the evacuation was intended to get out were unable to make it.[59]

There was some daring freewheeling that saved a number of high-risk people who might not have escaped otherwise. One example of this was the rescue operation of Foreign Service Officers Lionel Rosenblatt and Craig Johnstone. Both had served in Viet-Nam earlier. Rosenblatt was in the CORDS Refugee Division in 1967, and then was a liaison officer to the GVN's "Phung Hoang" program, with an emphasis on coordinating intelligence about the VC infrastructure among GVN and US agencies. In 1975, he was special assistant to Deputy Secretary of State Robert Ingersoll, in whose office he was in contact with the whole Viet-Nam picture, having access to the most highly classified communications. As plans for the evacuation from Viet-Nam developed, he was the acknowledged leader of a group of young officers, including Frank Wisner and Everett Bumgardner, pressing for more aggressive and timely action. This group concentrated initially on sensitizing the bureaucracy to the large number of Vietnamese who had worked for or cooperated with the United States, some of whom were working in responsible civil or military positions within the GVN. After seeing that hundreds of these high-risk people, including employees of the consulates in Da-Nang and Nha-Trang, were left behind in the panicked evacuations from Regions 1 and 2, and noting what he considered the casual way with which the national high-risk problem was being treated, Lionel became increasingly convinced that the evacuation plans would leave behind many endangered people, particularly in the middle and lower ranks.

Johnstone, who spoke Vietnamese, had served in the CORDS evaluation unit; I first met him when he evaluated the relief program for the victims of Têt 1968 in Saigon. Serving in the Department's Operations Center in 1975, he also had access to information about the Viet-Nam situation and plans, and shared Rosenblatt's appraisal. At the instigation of the two activists, Dean Brown's task force (where both had been among the earliest assigned) queried the embassy to see whether it wished any help in evacuation planning on the ground by task force officers; Ambassador Martin demurred. Reading Martin's message on the Admiral Benton plan cited above, which said that the mission's local nationals and their families would have to make their own way to Vung-Tau, galvanized the pair to action. On April 20, they both left the task force and boarded the last Pan American flight to Saigon. There they quickly reestablished contact with Vietnamese and American friends, rented vehicles, and began bringing to the airport Vietnamese who were not likely to get out in the normal way. One of these was Nguyen Thi Hue, a Catholic employee of the USAID War Victims Division, who had served under my direction in 1968-69 (see chapter 1). After gathering up her own family of 26, Hue helped the two young officers by typing up the necessary papers for processing their clients through both Vietnamese and American formalities. Altogether over 200 people were put aboard planes by Rosenblatt and Johnstone. When they returned to Washington, haggard and unkempt late in the month, Secretary Kissinger almost fired them, since they had run the risk of capture and interrogation to extract the highly classified information in their brains. However, after scolding them severely, he made clear his personal admiration for their courage and effective compassion.[60]

With the airport shut down, "Frequent Wind," a previously prepared plan for rotary wing evacuation of the remaining Americans, allied diplomats, and Vietnamese in danger, was set in motion on April 29. It was a combined operation of the Marines, the Navy, and the embassy, which had the responsibility for selecting those to be extracted and getting them to the DAO area at the airport, several roof-top helicopter pads, and the landing area in the embassy compound. Once again, many were rescued and many were left behind; Ambassador Martin had been promised more helicopters than were sent. The operation was militarily almost perfect, with the choppers braving small arms, antiaircraft, and surface-to-air missile fire, but what Americans and the rest of the world saw on their television screens were scenes of frantic Vietnamese being pushed back from the embassy wall by the Marines. In a little over 24 hours, operating night and day, Frequent Wind evacuated 6,968 people, most of them Vietnamese, and landed them on US aircraft carriers off shore. One of the last to go was Ambassador Martin, who had spent many sleepless hours overseeing the evacuation and pleading with Washington to complete it.[61] That same morning, General Van Tien Dung's troops entered Saigon.

There were too many heroes among the civilian and military officers of all components of the mission and the military forces taking part in the evacuation, beginning with Ambassador Graham Martin, to name them all here. Lacy Wright, Ray Fontaine, Mel Chatman, Shep Lowman, and Kenneth Moorefield are only a few among the many.

As the American choppers were making their tireless rounds between the ships and the landing pads, many Vietnamese helicopters also landed on the US Navy aircraft carriers. There was not room to keep them; as soon as their crews and passengers disembarked, the valuable craft, paid for by American military assistance, were pushed overboard.

Another small helicopter lift was being conducted by Air America helicopters under the direction of Consul General Terry McNamara, from Can-Tho in the Delta to the Seventh Fleet and to the refugee camp on Phu-Quoc Island. This was preempted when on April 29 the embassy ordered the helicopters to join Operation Frequent Wind, and then a previously developed plan to evacuate the remaining employees, their families, and others, by boat down the Bassac River.

When the Vietnamese pilots failed to show up, McNamara took over the lead "mike" boat himself and led the convoy, with several hundred refugees aboard, down the river and out to sea, where they boarded US Navy ships.[62]

In Saigon, some tugs and barges were left at the Khanh-Hoi docks. At the last moment, when buses failed to show up for a number of people waiting at safe houses under the control of Shep Lowman, he got the refugees to go down to the docks, where they were able to board the barges without being mobbed because armed police also boarded. A large number of refugees from the Bien-Hoa area, led by Joseph Langlois, Charles Lahiguera, and Vu Bich Hien of the Consulate General, were among the passengers. The barges picked up more passengers at Phuoc-Le, the capital of Phuoc-Tuy province, and then were towed out to sea, where the refugees boarded the SS *Miller* for the voyage to Subic Bay.[63]

The Khanh-Hoi dock bargees and McNamara's band were by no means the only ones to escape by this means. Hundreds if not thousands of Vietnamese craft of all descriptions put out all along the coastline searching for the American ships. Among them were many who had been advised by the embassy to go to Vung-Tau. The US Navy's orders were to pick up their passengers and crews, and that it did. Some startled fishermen, out on their normal occupation, were told to "climb aboard," and when they next saw land, it was Guam!

All told, about 140,000 Vietnamese left their homeland during those last weeks, of whom about 131,000 entered the US immigration system. Almost 5,000 went on to third countries, and 2,425 requested repatriation to Viet-Nam.[64]

The evacuation was far from accomplishing its goals. Many thousands of mission employees and their families, and additional thousands of high-risk people, including Vietnamese officials; intellectual, religious, labor, and political leaders; intelligence sources; journalists identified with the GVN cause; and others, were left behind. Only about 55,000 of those who were evacuated or escaped fell within the approved parole guidelines. On the other hand, the bulk of the escapees were soldiers, small merchants, farmers, fishermen, housemaids, bar girls, and others who by no stretch of the imagination could be characterized as high-risk. On May 6, INS Commissioner Leonard Chapman wrote to Senate Judiciary Committee Chairman James Eastland saying that the Secretary of State had requested parole for additional groups, as follows: (1) Approximately 69,000 Vietnamese evacuated at the last moment, picked up at sea, or presently on Vietnamese vessels; the choice, wrote Chapman, was to force them to return, leave them at sea, or accept responsibility for them; (2) About 3,000 Vietnamese and Cambodians who had fled to third countries, some of which were threatening to return them; and (3) Vietnamese stranded in third countries; their number was unknown. A further letter of July 15 said that approximately 10,000 Vietnamese and 7,000 to 9,000 Cambodians were stranded in third countries, and parole was requested for them as well. That letter added a new category: 3,000 to 5,000 Laotian refugees. After further exchanges of correspondence, the Attorney General authorized parole for these and other categories.[65]

The conclusion is inescapable that, from the standpoint of getting the right people out, the evacuation was too long delayed, poorly prepared, and badly executed, despite the excellent performance of the US military forces and of many individuals in Washington, the Saigon Mission, and the Vietnamese community. That it brought out many thousands who were not seriously at risk is understandable and not a tragedy. What is harder to understand and to excuse is that so many genuinely endangered people were left behind to be killed or imprisoned by the Communists. The causes of failure were manifold and complex. The inordinate delays in seeking and being granted Congressional consent to parole were a principal reason. The data and analyses presented to back up the requests were belated, sloppy, and unrealistic. Conflicts and jealousies among Washington agencies and between them and Saigon were partly responsible for that. There were forlorn hopes that the United States would provide additional military and economic assistance which would save part of Viet-Nam and, when that failed, that negotiations through the French Ambassador and the Hungarians would lead to a coalition government.

The refusal of the GVN until the last days to grant exit permits to its citizens was an important obstacle, which Ambassador Martin felt he couldn't defy, although in practice it became little more than a lucrative source of bribes to Vietnamese officials. Had Martin been willing to consult with Thieu, as Washington repeatedly urged him to do, that obstruction might have been eased and the evacuation might have become a joint effort instead of an American enterprise. That would also have facilitated the internationalization of both initial asylum and resettlement. There was also the fear, based on the experiences at Da-Nang and Nha-Trang, that precipitate action would trigger panic and the collapse of the GVN, and nobody knew how much time was left before that happened. In fact, the delays did not slow General Dung's conquest, although he did allow some days for the evacuation to proceed, and they did not prevent the disintegration of the South Vietnamese Government and armed forces. However, they did obstruct what could have been a quiet and orderly process of getting out those whom the Communist takeover would put in grave jeopardy. The retention of the Seventh Fleet off the coast of Viet-Nam for several days after April 30 to pick up refugees saved what would otherwise have been a disaster.

Some Who Were Rescued

Fortunately, many of the Vietnamese leaders whose work has been discussed in this book were able to get out in April 1975, but some of them and many family members were left behind.

Early in the morning of April 26, Ray Fontaine of the USAID brought to Dr. Phan Quang Dan an urgent message from Ambassador Martin that the French Ambassador and members of the International Control Commission had assured him that the Communists would organize a tripartite coalition government with

Dr. Dan as the only representative of the Vietnamese nationalists. The Communists had much consideration for Dr. Dan as a sincere patriot and dedicated humanitarian. Ambassador Martin suggested that he agree to stay and participate in such a government; however, it would be up to Dr. Dan to decide. Dan immediately replied that, entrusted with full power in the GVN, he would stay and fight the Communists but would not cooperate with them. The following day he was flown to Guam with his wife, his younger son, and his eldest son's family.[66] John Thomas made him a consultant at Camp Pendleton, California, for four months, after which he practiced medicine in St. Thomas, Virgin Islands until 1987, when he and his wife moved to Florida. Dr. Dan has been active in campaigning for the freedom of the three Indochina countries, and for working in close cooperation with Laotian and Cambodian nationalists against the Vietnamese Communists.

Dr. Tran Nguon Phieu, with Ray Fontaine's help, departed at the very end of the evacuation with his daughter Lan Chi and the three children of Dr. Cao Xuan An, who had been his secretary general in the MSW and decided to stay in Viet-Nam. Dr. Phieu's wife was unable to get to the airport, however. He went to Austin, Texas, with the four children, was sponsored by a friend in the US Navy, and took a job as an orderly at the state mental hospital. The International Rescue Committee (IRC) and the US Catholic Conference gave him some help, but basically he made it on his own. He took the short course organized by HEW to prepare for the medical examinations allowing him to get a residency, and passed. Now, as Dr. Phieu N. Tran, he has a successful practice in Amarillo; some 1,000 Vietnamese and 3,000 Lao in the city are his principal patients. His wife joined him in 1981.[67]

As has been recounted in chapter 9, John Thomas encountered the irrepressible Dr. Tran Lu Y at Camp Pendleton in 1975. However, since the doctor's wife was already in France, he joined her there and is practicing medicine in a suburb of Paris. He is also backing some projects for rescuing boat people and is active politically.[68]

After completing a psychiatric residency at St. Elizabeth's Hospital in Washington, D.C., Dr. Ton That Niem, who had been the last Minister of Health in Viet-Nam, moved to California with his family and is practicing in the midst of the huge Vietnamese community in Santa Ana. He is also Director of Medicine at the nearby state mental hospital.

I first met Tran Quang Thuan at the IRC Los Angeles office in 1976, where he was the chief caseworker. He is now chief of the unemployment insurance section of the state employment security agency in a large district of Los Angeles County.[69]

Touneh Han Tho and his family were evacuated with the help of the Papal Delegate. He is now the owner of two successful bakeries in Sacramento, California.[70]

These are only a few of the former officials involved in refugee and social welfare care who were able to get out in the 1975 evacuations. There were also many refugees from other parts of the GVN, and most of the top generals. Some of those wrote thoughtful books under the auspices of the US Army Center of Military History, which have been cited in this study.

Some of the Many Who Were Not Rescued

As mentioned above, Dr. Phieu's wife was not able to reach the airport in time to be evacuated. She had been a teacher of zoology at Saigon University, and the Communist regime kept her on. Indeed, she was sent to some of the "new economic zones," which were expansions of Dr. Dan's settlements; the Communists said that she was to bring some science to them. She found them miserable places. In 1981 she was permitted to rejoin her husband under the Orderly Departure Program.

Nay Luett and Paul Nur were among those left behind. They both died in reeducation camps. Pierre Toplui K'Briuh, Secretary General of the MDEM, spent four years in a reeducation camp, was released in 1979, and managed to escape by boat in 1983. However, his wife and eight children were left in Kontum. He is now in North Carolina. R'Mah Dock was jailed by the Communists on April 6, 1975 in Pleiku. He escaped in 1978 and is now also in North Carolina.

Reverend Ha Cillpam had arranged air evacuation for 300 Montagnard students at the MDEM school in Saigon, but the Ministry refused permission for them to leave. K'Briuh says that he was absent when the pastor's telephone request came in; he would have facilitated their departure.

Very few other highlanders were able to get out. Aside from the 250 or so in the United States, a group of 300 were landed in Denmark, and that is all. As this is written, some 4,000 highlanders being held by the Khmer Rouge inside Kampuchea are trying to escape.

Dr. Cao Xuan An had decided to stay, but he and his wife later came to the United States, where he is practicing medicine in San Diego, California. Their children joined them there.[71]

Huynh Than Hu'ng also decided to stay and continue to help his people. However, he was put into a reeducation camp, for more than six years, until being released with his family to his son in West Germany in October 1982. When I first saw him and his wife in April 1984 in Washington, his health was still impaired from the experience, but he has since recovered. He has an especially retentive and precise memory and has been extraordinarily helpful to me in this study.

Dr. Nguyen Phuc Que, who had a number of relatives in rather high positions in North Viet-Nam, has been allowed to continue practicing medicine in Ho Chi Minh City (Saigon). Dr. Phieu's wife saw him and his wife frequently.

Colonel Ton That Khien was released from reeducation camp only early in 1988, after over 12 years of incarceration.[72]

Lt. Colonel Le Van Ba remains in Viet-Nam, but his assistant, Nouyen Van Hien, died of cancer there a few years ago.

Thich Nhat Thien, the former head of the Buddhist social welfare organization, was still in jail as of December 1987. In the last days of the RVN, he and Tran Quang Thuan went to Dr. Niem, then Minister of Health, asking that the organization's orphans be evacuated, and the Minister appealed to Prime Minister Nguyen Ba Can. However, the Defense Minister blocked their evacuation until it was too late.[73]

A community of Catholic refugees who had come from North Viet-Nam in 1954–55 and founded Xuan-Ninh hamlet in Cam-Ranh had worked on the American base until it closed out, then took other work or cultivated the extensive land that had been allocated to the hamlet. In 1975 about four-fifths of them fled south, some being evacuated to Phu-Quoc Island. The Communists encouraged them to go home, but then settled North Vietnamese on their land. About 100 families escaped on boats in 1979 and came to Amarillo, Texas, where Dr. Phieu N. Tran is their physician. Later, some fishermen among them moved to Louisiana with their families and resumed their original occupation.[74]

After the Fall

Since those fateful days in 1975, all the Vietnamese people, so many of whom had tried to stay neutral in the struggle between the GVN and the Communists, have experienced Communist rule at first hand. About 983,000 refugees had arrived in other countries as of April 30, 1988, over and above the 140,000 who came out in 1975. More than a quarter of the refugees came directly from North Viet-Nam, mostly to the People's Republic of China. In addition, it is estimated that at least 500,000 drowned or died from other causes at sea. The flight continues.[75]

16

Some Conclusions and Lessons

During the period 1954 to April 30, 1975, well over half the people of South Viet-Nam were uprooted, some more than once, over 900,000 were wounded in the conflict between the nationalist government and the Communists, and about a quarter of a million were killed. Table 17 summarizes this. The traumas that such tremendous dislocations inflicted on the victims and the society of the Republic of Viet-Nam, whose population had barely reached 20 million by the time it was taken over by the North, have been described historically in the previous chapters. Unfortunately, aggregate sociological data are not available to reveal fully what the experience did to the people as a whole, although we know pretty well what it did to the war victims, and how they reacted.

Additional millions were displaced in North Viet-Nam, some by the actions of their government, but most by the war.

The refugees who came down from the North in 1954–55, often at the risk of their lives, gave up everything to flee the newly victorious Communist regime. They embodied an iron determination to live in the traditional way. Those 928,000 largely Catholic refugees became an important element, if not the backbone, of all succeeding regimes in the South. They were the only refugees who rose to such important roles. Most of those who were displaced later suffered the opposite fate; they became an under-class, displaced from their land, the graves of their ancestors, and many of their possessions, living among often-hostile strangers, and sometimes dependent on the uncertain charity of the government and private voluntary agencies. The sample surveys summarized in this book document the extent to which their standard of living had declined, and they show that even the voluntary refugees in the 1960's had a deeply pessimistic view of their present living conditions and relatively little hope for the future.

There were exceptions. Some of those whom the Diem regime moved under

Table 17

Refugees, Evacuees, and Other War Victims in South Viet-Nam, 1954–75

Years and Type of Cases	Number of Persons
1954-55, Refugees from the North[1]	928,000
1955-62[2]	
Land Development relocatees	210,000
Highlander resettlers	90,000
Agroville relocatees	20,000
1961-64	
Strategic hamlet relocatees[3]	873,700
1964-65, refugees and evacuees[4]	510,000
1966, refugees and evacuees	980,000
1967, refugees and evacuees[5]	698,000
1968, refugees and evacuees[6]	787,000
Têt and May Offensive victims[7]	1,072,000
1969[8]	
In-camp refugees and evacuees	140,000
Newly registered out-of-camp refugees	476,000
1970[9]	
Refugees and evacuees	129,000
Refugees generated previously, newly registered	281,000
Repatriates from Cambodia	200,000
1971, refugees and evacuees[10]	198,200
1964-72, unregistered refugees in Saigon[11]	574,500
1969-72, in-place war victims[12]	650,000
1972, refugees from the NVA Easter Offensive[13]	1,289,000
1973[14]	
Refugees and evacuees	818,700
In-place war victims	490,500
1974[15]	
Refugees	417,300
In-place war victims	179,600
1975, to April 30, internal refugees, estimate[16]	2,000,000
of whom 140,000 became international refugees[16]	
TOTAL	14,012,500

Table 17 (*continued*)

Years and Type of Cases	Number of Persons
Minus refugees possibly double-counted from the 1972 and 1975 offensives	<u>-3,000,000</u>
	11,012,500
Displaced persons in PRG areas and others not registered from 1972 offensive[17]	<u>700,000</u>
Adjusted total	11,712,500
Civilian war casualties 1965-74[18]	
Hospital admissions	570,600
Estimated lightly wounded	342,400
Estimated deaths	<u>247,600</u>
Total	1,160,600
Population of South Viet-Nam[19]	20,100,000

---

[1]Chapter 1.

[2]Chapter 2. I assume that half of the 40,000 agroville inhabitants were relocated.

[3]Chapter 3. The Diem regime claimed that 8,737,000 citizens were in strategic hamlets by July 1963; this figure was highly exaggerated. I have divided it by two, and accepted Colonel John E. Arthur's estimate that 20% of inhabitants were relocated from their homes.

[4]1964–65 and 1966 figures based on reports of the Special Commissariat for Refugees compiled by CORDS.

[5]My calculations, based on data in chapter 5.

[6]Based on MSWR data.

[7]Chapter 8, peak numbers.

[8]My calculations, starting with MSWR registrations; 25,000 unrecognized refugees in I CTZ added to registered refugees.

[9]Saigon COMUSMACV telegram 311129 Z Jan 71, and chapter 10, including Nooter statement May 8, 1972 to the Senate Refugee Subcommittee.

[10]COMUSMACV telegram 162003 Z Feb 72. I have added to the 135,700 new refugees 62,500 persons relocated in MR-2 during 1970–71 but not recognized as refugees (chapter 11).

[11]My calculations in chapter 4.

[12]US Senate, *Relief and Rehabilitation of War Victims in Indochina: One Year After the Ceasefire*, a Study Mission Report, prepared for the Senate Refugee Subcommittee, January 27, 1974, 6.

[13]Chapter 12.

[14]Chapter 12 and 13; Saigon 3527, March 18, 1974.

[15]Chapter 15.

[16]Chapter 15.

[17]US Senate, *Relief and Rehabilitation of War Victims*, 7.

[18]Guenter Lewy, *America in Vietnam* (New York: Oxford University Press, 1978), 442–46. I consider that his estimates are as accurate as can be derived from the incomplete raw data. The Senate Refugee Subcommittee estimated that 1,005,000 were wounded and 430,000 killed from 1965 through 1973 (*Relief and Rehabilitation of War Victims*, 9). An unknown number of the wounded and dead were included in the statistics of in-place war victims; their families did not always submit claims.

[19]Estimate, 1974, Arthur S. Banks, ed., *Political Handbook of the World: 1975* (McGraw Hill, 1975), 387.

its land development program, especially resettled refugees from the North, did rather well for a time—although at the expense of the Montagnards and others whose land they took. However, as the insurgency took hold in the Highlands and other parts of the countryside in the 1960s, many of them fled again, ending up in Saigon and other cities. There some of them made new lives and even prospered. The same was true of many who were able to find employment on US military bases or other types of work for the wealthy Americans, but that artificial prosperity disappeared with the departing American troops in the 1970s. Only a few, who had the good fortune to be settled in those of Dr. Dan's new hamlets that had adequate land, were reestablished in a more durable way.

GENERATION AND MOTIVATION OF RELOCATEES, REFUGEES, AND WAR VICTIMS

The Diem regime's experiments in social and political engineering: land development, highlander resettlement, agrovilles, and strategic hamlets, accounted for 1.3 million people who were displaced in the years 1955 to the end of 1963. They comprised loyal anti-Communists, simple peasants, and some elements who were considered unreliable. Land development moved people *into* territory held or claimed by the guerrillas; the other two programs consolidated peasant hamlets and villages in both GVN and contested areas. The great majority were moved involuntarily. All these experiments failed, and their legacy furnished an impetus to the burgeoning guerrilla movement in the subsequent years.

However, as the Communists gained strength from 1963 to early 1966 and were themselves in a position to exploit and oppress the people, hundreds of thousands of refugees fled from them. The first to go were the landlords, wealthier peasants, merchants, artisans, Catholics, and others ideologically opposed to Communism. The insurgents initially encouraged the departures, in order to get rid of troublesome elements and to over-burden the government's capability to care for them. Later, some ordinary peasants, tired of the burdensome taxes, corvée labor, endless political indoctrination, and military service imposed on them, also fled from areas dominated by the guerrillas, and this hurt the Communists economically. Most of the 510,000 who became refugees in 1964–65 were in that category. As more and more people left, the Communist terror became harsher and more indiscriminate in both insurgent territory and areas controlled by the GVN. Refugee sites were especially targeted, in an effort to induce their inhabitants to return to their homes. During these years most of those who fled could rightly be called refugees from Communism (Ty-nạn Cộng-sản). They presented an opportunity for the government to win this important body of displaced people over as loyal adherents, by hospitable care and effective socioeconomic rehabilitation programs combined with political work among them. This was what the energetic and perceptive Dr. Que and his dedicated successors tried to bring about. Unfortunately, both the way the GVN and the

Americans fought the war and the inadequate care that government officials provided its victims dissipated that opportunity.

Once American troops were present in large numbers (starting in late 1965), the character of the war changed radically, and with it the manner in which most refugees were generated. The Americans had already trained and equipped the Vietnamese forces to fight a conventional war against massed enemy troops, even though the insurgency was for years almost entirely a guerrilla war; and now the American forces themselves used a strategy and tactics that had been learned in Europe and Korea. They were not effective against the elusive enemy in Viet-Nam, and the search-and-destroy strategy and the massive and indiscriminate use of firepower in populated areas inflicted terrible destruction upon the people and their property, especially in the countryside, but also, during the Têt and May offensives of 1968, in the cities. The Communists and the Allies were both responsible for that urban devastation.

Artillery, bombing, and ground sweeps of American, Korean, and Vietnamese troops became the leading generators of refugees and civilian war casualties in the countryside. Few among them were fleeing from Communist oppression; it was the war that dislocated them. Often, however, the able-bodied men stayed behind, either to till their fields or because they had been drafted by the VC. The proportion of men in the working ages was always lower among refugees than among the general population. Those people who fled went to areas where they could have relative safety. Communist terror pursued them to their new habitations, inflicting further casualties, but that was seen as the lesser danger. Forced relocation by the Americans and the GVN added to the number of refugees generated by conditions of war.

After American strategy and ARVN turned from search-and-destroy to clear-and-hold, and pacification began to succeed (1969–71), refugee generation declined, and more refugees went back to their homes than were newly created. The results were dramatic. Many other constructive developments, both economic and political, became possible, and for a time the people were happy.

It was just these successes that motivated the North Vietnamese to invade the South openly with massive conventional forces in 1972. That caused a new wave of refugees, who this time were fleeing from both the fighting and the Communists, some with the VC massacres at Hue and elsewhere during Têt 1968 fresh in their minds. But with the "cease-fire" fighting in 1973 and intensified NVA incursions in 1974, it was the war that once again was the generator of flight and evacuations, with no clear ideological cause that could create a patriotic spirit among the victims or the general public. For that and other reasons, lassitude and war weariness settled over the land. By the time of the final NVA offensive of 1975, multitudes of people and soldiers alike thought only of panicked flight.

Thus, anti-Communist ideology was responsible for the 1954–55 exodus from the North and for the flight of some groups later. Others moved to escape Communist oppression. Those people were "voting with their feet." However, the great majority of refugees and evacuees during the years 1966 to 1972 were escaping from artillery, bombing, and ground combat, without commitment to either side.

However, the experience of Hue in 1968 was burned deeply into the memories of Vietnamese everywhere. That, perhaps more than anything else, accounted for the enormous refugee flows in 1972 and 1975. Did that mean they were voting with their feet? Yes, it did, in the sense that the experience with Communism in the flesh was something that instilled a lasting fear among city people and many peasants alike.

WAR VICTIM RELIEF AND RESETTLEMENT

Despite the remarkable success of the relief, movement, and resettlement of the 1954–55 refugees from the North, its lessons had been largely forgotten when the new problem of internal refugees in the South arose almost 10 years later. It took several more years of painful experimentation and development of new programs and procedures before a reasonably satisfactory system of relief for the millions of refugees, evacuees, and in-place war victims was put in place. However, it was done, and with steadily increasing inputs of American material and human resources, the successive Ministries responsible for social welfare and refugees became ever more proficient in coping with large and small emergencies. During and after the worst crises, such as at Têt 1968 and the 1972 NVA offensive, the whole government pitched in to help the victims and achieve recovery. The reestablishment of the urban war victims in 1968 was particularly effective. In between such major emergencies, the Refugee Ministry was left pretty much alone, but the United States provided adequate resources, and both the Ministry and CORDS/REF developed the various skills and capabilities to do what was necessary. By and large, the system worked. Nobody starved, there were no epidemics, people were given shelter and were assisted in rebuilding.

For those refugees who could not return to their homes quickly, however, there were serious flaws in the relief system, and even more damaging inadequacies in the mechanisms for resettlement. It had been assumed that the relief period would be short, no more than two or three months, and that no more than six additional months would be required for resettlement if the people could not go home. These assumptions frequently proved to be unrealistic. As more and more of the countryside fell under Communist control or became zones of conflict, increasing numbers of refugees were compressed into areas that were already inhabited and cultivated, especially in the crowded northern provinces. This meant that few of the refugees, most of whom were peasants, could again be placed on cultivable land in their own region. Other sources of livelihood would have to be found, such as employment with the Americans, which generally meant that the refugees would have to be induced to change their occupations and be retrained. In the meantime, they would have to be supported and their camps upgraded. That carried with it the danger of developing a dole mentality, and the continued provision of relief, contrary to the regulations that had been laid down, required improvisation and invited corruption.

Delays in making payments, caused by the highly centralized system and sometimes also by corruption or what John Thomas called the "hamster syndrome," caused hardship and resentment. Many thousands of refugees lived for years in miserable camps that had been constructed as temporary residences and then converted by a stroke of the pen into resettlement sites. In some of the larger and more visible camps, such as Cam-Lo, as many as three successive six-months' rice rations were given and elaborate upgrading projects were carried out. However, this still did not make them viable.

Over the years, the payment system was gradually decentralized and speeded up, but neither it nor the methods of providing for the other needs of the camps ever became truly responsive. In too many camps the refugees took little interest in maintaining or improving their facilities. They became passive recipients of a dole. It would have been better to involve the refugees more in the administration of payments and the expenditure of resources for their needs, in much the same way as the village self-development funds were administered.

Fortunately for many of the refugees, the huge American military and civilian presence and our generous aid to Viet-Nam, supported by billions of dollars, opened up hundreds of thousands of job opportunities, skilled and unskilled. Indeed, for several years skilled jobs were going begging. For those refugees who were placed near US, Korean, or RVNAF bases, or in cities, there were jobs and other economic opportunities for men, women, and children. Even when relief rations ran out, these war victims suffered little or no hardship—except being away from their homes, land, and the graves of the ancestors.

However, those who were not near such job opportunities and whose camps had insufficient land, were inadequately cared for by the relief and resettlement system, and were condemned to sterile lives of enforced idleness. No amount of camp upgrading could make up for this. The problem was concentrated in such places as Cam-Lo, Ha-Thanh, the three lower provinces of I CTZ, and Binh-Dinh. Several hundred thousand refugees were in that situation during the years from 1965 on.

The problem was perceived at the time, and two complementary solutions were proposed. Ambassador Komer pressed the military commanders to limit the generation of refugees, who were overwhelming the capability of the GVN to provide care, and to assume temporary responsibility for those they created. The US force commanders in I and II CTZ were particularly resistant to his suggestions, and went on generating refugees with little regard to what would become of them. The second approach, first proposed by Dr. Que, was to resettle refugees from the overcrowded northerly provinces to areas in other zones where there was vacant land or where job opportunities existed. As we have seen in chapter 5, two such movements from Phu-Yen and Binh-Dinh to Cam-Ranh and Ninh-Thuan province occurred in 1966, and they were highly successful. However, further transfers were then vetoed at higher levels in the GVN as possibly creating the impression that the government was planning to give up the upper part of the country in a peace settlement. A small interzonal resettlement from Quang-Ngai to Cam-Ranh took place late in 1968, but, partly on my advice, that was the last such resettlement until Dr. Dan's program took hold in 1971–72. In retrospect, we should probably have tooled up much earlier for substantial voluntary interzonal movement, instead of spending so much effort and resources trying vainly to make many of the northern camps self-sufficient.

During the period 1968–71, what I have called the flowering of pacification enabled a million and a half refugees to go home. Then the Ministry, together with some imaginative and concerned province chiefs, CORDS, and the refugees themselves, cooperated in rebuilding houses and public facilities, clearing and plowing long-neglected and overgrown land, planting and harvesting, and restoring commerce. Return of refugees (whether internal as in Viet-Nam or international) to their homes and fields is always the best solution.

Most of those gains were reversed by the North Vietnamese offensive of 1972 and the fighting of the next two years, and that faced the refugee assistance system with new challenges it was unable to meet. Over a million and a quarter refugees were generated in 1972, many of them people who had returned to their homes during the preceding years. That occurred at the same time as the American troop drawdown was nearing completion, reducing job opportunities for refugees and ordinary citizens alike. We on the US side and the officials in the Ministry of Social Welfare had hoped that the cease-fire negotiations in Paris would lead to a settlement that would permit the refugees to go home in peace, and therefore we wasted much time in a futile attempt to upgrade camps when we and the Ministry should have been pressing harder for the acquisition of more land for voluntary resettlement under the Land Development and Hamlet Building Program.

Just before the 1973 cease-fire agreement was signed, both sides engaged in military operations to take and hold more territory, and then both pushed people to return home or settle in their zones, including contested areas. (North Vietnamese were brought into the PRG zones.) That was a far cry from the generous and constructive program that Dr. Dan was unfolding. As had happened during the earlier period, most of what was called resettlement was fictitious, since the refugees were not in viable situations. The data in chapter 13 make that clear. Only in some of the new hamlets of Dr. Dan's Land Development Program and at Nay Luett's Buon Jat and a few other highlander settlements did the refugees have enough land to be self-supporting. Moreover, many of those who returned to their homes, especially in Quang-Tri, the lower three provinces of MR-1, and Binh-Dinh, were in unviable and dangerous situations. There was some increase in the amount of land available to the Land Development hamlets, but not enough. It was not the Paris cease-fire agreement that stood in the way, since both sides disregarded it, but rather the changing power balance between the South and the North. Consequently, increased refugee numbers, crowded into shrinking GVN-controlled territory, exceeded the capacity to reestablish them. Some wanted to return to their homes in Communist-held areas, as the Paris cease-fire agreement had provided, but the GVN prevented this wherever it could. It would have done better to let them go home, since they remained a festering sore where they were held; in the end, they probably helped the invading NVA.

In sum, although the GVN's refugee assistance program handled emergency relief situations very well and kept millions of war victims from starvation or epidemics, it could not reestablish all of them in viable circumstances because sufficient secure agricultural land was not available, except during the few years when pacification flowered; other employment opportunities shrank with the departure of the Americans. For too long the military and civilian policy-makers in both the Vietnamese and the American governments failed to appreciate the implications of these limitations and to take the necessary corrective measures.

EFFECTS UPON THE OUTCOME OF THE WAR

I conclude that both the ways in which most persons were displaced in South Viet-Nam and the inadequacies of their care created or perpetuated attitudes that exerted an adverse influence on the outcome of the war against the Communists.

If all the displaced persons had "voted with their feet" by escaping from the Communists, as those who came down from the North in 1954–55 did, their situation would have been similar to that of refugees from the Communist parts of divided countries, such as Germany, Korea, and China. Those refugees were strong opponents of the regimes from which they fled and effective supporters of the regimes that gave them asylum. Indeed, in Taiwan they took over the government and have resisted absorption by their huge motherland ever since.

It takes only a moment's reflection to realize just how different the refugee situation in South Viet-Nam was. There, only a minority of the refugees had fled from Communism, and it was a divided minority. The original Catholics from the North often oppressed the Buddhists, both Southerners and Northerners, and many of both groups oppressed and exploited the Montagnards. Over time, the majority of the refugees had not voted with their feet against an ideology or an authority, but had fled, with great reluctance, from war. More than one-tenth of the people who were displaced during the life of the Republic were not refugees at all, but were forcibly moved or evacuated, most of them from contested areas or territory controlled by the insurgents. There was no unity among these diverse groups, even though all were cared for by the same government.

Let us examine these diverse groups one at a time.

Refugees from the North

The refugees who came down from North Viet-Nam in 1954–55 made notable contributions to the economic development, military strength, and public administration of their new homeland, and provided much-needed skills in medicine and other areas as well. They were a varied population, made up of simple peasants and workers in addition to leaders in many fields. (The democratic humanitarian Dr. Phan Quang Dan and military politician Nguyen Cao Ky were also Northerners, but they came to the South at different times and under different circumstances.)

However, many of the Northern Catholics who rose to positions of power under Diem and his successors—and there were thousands of them in national, provincial, and district government and in the numerous quasi-official organizations—played a large role in the polarization of South Viet-Nam's society and body politic. They helped to develop and enforce the GVN's uncompromising stance against any accommodation not only with the Communist North, but also with the democratic left opposition and the insurgents in the South, many of whom were not Communists but nationalists who were seeking such social-justice measures as genuine land reform. A number of Northern Catholics were also willing participants in the persecution of the Buddhists, left-wing youth groups, and other segments of the population. These refugees thereby helped to exclude from the community many potential leaders and their followers, including landless and poor peasants who might have been mobilized in the national cause. By the time comprehensive land reform and other democratic measures were enacted in 1970 and thereafter, many of the alienated people were either already committed to the other side or neutral at best.

Thus, the presence of the Northern refugees had both positive and negative effects on the outcome of the war, and it is hard to say which outweighed the other.

Southern Refugees from Communism

Those who fled from VC oppression within South Viet-Nam after the level of insurgent violence became a threat in the early and mid-1960's were potential participants in the national effort. However, not all supported the GVN. Why? At first they were considered VC sympathizers by many GVN officials and military commanders, and were often denied entry into GVN-controlled villages and towns. If they were able to stay, they received little or no help. When a refugee assistance program was established, most were housed in camps that ranged from adequate to miserable, and were lucky if they could find jobs. These were people who had given up everything—their land, the family graves, and frequently all their possessions—to come to the GVN side. Beginning with Tran Quang Thuan and Dr. Que, the Ministry stressed that these anti-Communist refugees were potential assets to the national cause and should be given hospitable care. Eventually that was done. Where they were able to cultivate land, principally in the Delta, or where they had good employment, they were likely to be anti-Communist, although not necessarily pro-GVN. The excellent Cao-Dai B camp in Quang-Ngai (chapter 11), which had only 0.5% unemployment when it was surveyed in 1970, is an illustration of this. Its 3,183 inhabitants had a lack of confidence in the government, no clear attitude toward the Allies, and enmity toward the VC. Eighty percent of those strongly motivated people were found to be energetic nationalists, 18% neutral, and only 2% pro-Communist. Most of the refugees were not so fortunate, and that affected their attitudes toward the contending parties. At the Chon-Tam refugee settlement in Hoa-Khanh village of Quang-Nam, just outside Da-Nang, where 27 of the 50 respondents said they had fled VC oppression (the others having fled fighting and bombing), 40% of the 6,554 refugees were unemployed. In that camp there were almost equal numbers of males and females. Forty-five percent of its people were adjudged to be energetic nationalists, 47% neutral, and 8% pro-Communist.[1]

Refugees from the War

The largest group of refugees was composed of those who had fled from the war itself: artillery and bombing or ground combat. The American, Korean, and South Vietnamese troops all made massive and indiscriminate use of firepower, on populated as well as unpopulated areas, and for several years that was the major cause of war casualties and refugees (chapters 4 and 6).

Superficially, persuasive arguments could be and were made for fighting this way. First, it was said to save the lives of American and Allied troops. The people were usually warned (but sometimes not sufficiently in advance) to get out of VC or contested territory before it was bombarded, so any who remained were considered VC and were fair game. Depopulating enemy or contested territory and inducing the people to come into GVN areas was intended to free the Allied troops to find and destroy the enemy without worrying about killing civilians. It also was supposed to deny the population and its resources to the enemy. Moreover, it increased the number and percentage of the population under GVN control, a point of pride as the hamlet evaluation system was graded. More refugees were considered indicators of increasingly successful pacification; they were counted as having voted with their feet, even when they were only trying to escape death.

In fact, however, this method of fighting caused terrible suffering to the people and prolonged the war. The peasants of Viet-Nam were deeply attached to their land and the graves of their ancestors. Sometimes they stayed, even when the rain of destruction from the skies forced them to live underground, as on the Batangan peninsula and other parts of Quang-Ngai. Where the VC/NVA were using the populace and its habitations as shields, it appears that both peasants and city dwellers were reasonably understanding of the use of Allied firepower to dislodge the enemy, although in many instances it was excessive, and they often blamed the VC for their suffering. However, when no Communist soldiers were present—as was so often the case, or when only a few snipers fired from dwellings, churches, and so on, and then left, people did not understand, and they were deeply resentful. The depredations of Task Force Oregon and other units in I CTZ caused awesome destruction and created strong resentment against the Americans. Also, such practices as B-52 bombing in the densely populated Mekong Delta, where the presence of the VC was especially difficult to detect, undoubtedly multiplied the numbers alienated from the anti-Communist cause. Civilian war casualties mounted, and far too many were inflicted by Allied bombs and shells. Resentment meant that the people would not inform the Allied troops about enemy movements or cooperate in other ways. In a people's war, hearts and minds were lost to the GVN side and sometimes gained by the enemy. The Viet-Cong and the North Vietnamese lost no opportunity to make propaganda, both in Viet-Nam and in the wider world, out of Allied destructiveness.

Although both the Geneva Conventions and the rules of engagement of the United States armed forces imposed strict limitations on the use of firepower against unarmed civilians, it seems clear that those regulations were commonly and widely ignored or violated. The incidents described in chapters 4, 6, and 11 illustrate this. The cultural gap between the American military personnel and the Vietnamese whom they were sent to defend was partly responsible. There had been no Vietnamese immigrants in the United States from which soldiers or even interpreters could be recruited. There were no Vietnamese studies programs in American universities or military schools until the late 1960s, and there was little indoctrination of either soldiers or officers before they were shipped out. Too many American soldiers regarded the Vietnamese, especially in the countryside, as subhuman; they described them as "gooks," "slopes," or "dinks," or in other derogatory terms. The belief was common that for the Orientals life was cheap; it never seems to have occurred to many Americans that a Vietnamese mother grieved just as much over the loss of a child or a husband as an American mother did. Although troop-community relations were sometimes quite good, they could deteriorate quickly under battle conditions when guerrillas hid among the people. Some soldiers openly admitted without any remorse that they had killed civilians, and airmen were directed to strafe peasants in the fields simply because they were running away or attempting to hide. Without means of communicating with the people, except through the few ARVN interpreters, US troops had no way of distinguishing guerrillas from the ordinary peasants among whom they often lived. Rarely before in US history had American soldiers been put into such an alien and frightening cultural environment, and one for which they were so ill-prepared. Consequently, they tended to regard all Vietnamese as enemies. The incident at My-Lai, as well as what Jonathan Schell and Honda Katsuichi saw in Quang-Ngai, become understandable under such circumstances. They were nonetheless not to be excused, and the lack of command attention to those dangers was a grievous and costly fault, as General Peers pointed out.

The movement of large numbers of people from their land into refugee camps or the cities imposed a heavy social and economic burden upon the GVN and the US, for which they were ill-prepared. The programs to cope with the refugees, admirable as they were, could not make up for the fact that thousands of hectares became unavailable as a source of support for the population and that hundreds of thousands of people were now crowded into restricted areas without alternate land on which to grow their food. Substantial resources had to be diverted from both economic and military assistance to care for the refugees. Enormous destruction in the cities during the Têt and the May offensives of 1968 added to the economic burden, as well as to human suffering.

Many voices, Vietnamese and American, were raised in warning to the US and Vietnamese governments over the years against the counterproductive effects of their strategy and tactics. Some outstanding experts in fighting insurgencies were among those advocating more sensitive approaches. For too long their voices cried out in vain. General Abrams's order of July 1968, which was issued only after Dr. Lu Y and Robert Komer requested it, seems to have been fairly effective in reducing indiscriminate use of firepower in populated areas by US forces, and the new emphasis on clearing and pacifying areas rather than making violent sweeps further reduced destruction of villages by the Americans. Even after the official policy changed in 1968–69, however, ARVN and the Koreans especially continued their destructive ways. It is not possible to count how many enemies of the anti-Communist cause were created in this manner, but they were numerous indeed. When GVN assistance was not provided or was inadequate, the adverse reactions were intensified.

The sample surveys summarized in previous chapters reinforce the unscientific observations of many Vietnamese and Americans who were involved with refugee assistance or evaluations, to the effect that the great majority of refugees who fled from armed combat were resentful against the side perceived as responsible for generating them, usually the GVN or the Allies, and were neutral with regard to the conflict itself. They neither supported nor opposed the Communists, but few were supporters of the GVN. A number of refugees joined the territorial forces but, as Dr. Phieu noted, this was principally because they were paid.[2] It must be presumed that they entered their units with the same attitudes as the people from whom they came. There is no evidence that they were particularly effective, even in defending refugee camps. When their sites, including such Land Development hamlets as Soui-Nghe, were attacked by the VC, the refugees fled; they did not stand and fight, as the Hoa-Hao peasants of the Delta or the FULRO villages in the Highlands (until 1975) did.

Forcibly Relocated People

Of all the causes of refugee movement in South Viet-Nam, forcible relocation was the one most certain to bring in or make enemies for the GVN and converts for its foe.

The same arguments used for employing firepower to depopulate contested areas were employed to justify forced movement of people from insecure to "secure" territory. Relocations were said to have the added advantages that the locations to be vacated and the people to be moved could be carefully selected, and then the evacuations could be conducted with surprise, as in the case of

358 Victims and Survivors

Ben-Suc, or after warning, as in the DMZ movement, so that everybody would be removed from the territory. The facts proved otherwise. In all the relocations studied by evaluators, some of which have been summarized in this book, significantly fewer men in the military-age groups were found than in the voluntary refugee populations. In a number of the operations, the planned aggregate numbers of people were discovered to be overstated, indicating that many managed to escape movement. At Ben-Suc, VC activity was observed a few days after all the people were supposedly evacuated and the extensive network of tunnels and underground headquarters and storage installations were destroyed. On the other hand, the evacuations brought into GVN territory virulent nests of VC dependents, who in turn gave access to the cadres and guerrillas, as was demonstrated at Lai-Thieu during Têt 1968, at Cam-Lo, and in other relocation sites.

We have seen that those involuntarily moved in the Diem regime's experiments were alienated from the government and that many of them cooperated with the Viet-Cong, for example in supplying them from land development centers and opening the gates of strategic hamlets. The surveys made by Human Sciences Research in 1967–68, by the Pacification Studies Group in 1970, by the defoliation teams in 1972, and by CORDS evaluators and other experts throughout that period abundantly documented that forcibly evacuated people had a more pessimistic view of their present conditions and lower expectations for the future than voluntary refugees. Furthermore, those negative attitudes were long-lasting. Some of the studies showed that involuntary evacuees had a significantly higher proportion of "pro-Red" members than refugees who chose to come out on their own (see chapters 7 and 11).

In 1974–75, Gary Murfin, one of the original Human Sciences Research investigators, used scientific methodology to go over the previous data and some additional surveys to see whether there was any difference between the degree of stress experienced by those persons forcibly evacuated and those who moved voluntarily. He found that:

1. Persons forced to move by the government of Vietnam or other Allied forces actually experienced high levels of stress. These levels were significantly higher than those experienced by voluntary refugees.

2. Forced relocation produced stress that worked to inhibit the sociopolitical support of the government by the evacuees and produced a predominantly negative outlook among those who were moved that was equally unsupportive of the GVN.

Murfin said:

From the facts, I have concluded that forced relocation was a counter-productive effort which produced stress that worked against the government's political goal to gain the support of the people. The overall effect was to work against GVN aims of establishing itself in the countryside and meant that evacuees were unlikely to be sympathetic to the government's cause. . . .

Some of the results of this study suggest that people can be moved in such a way that stress can be considerably reduced. This is not a recommendation or suggestion I make lightly, since it is filled with considerable risk. The results do indicate, however, that *if* prior warning can be given and time allowed to prepare for movement and *if* appropriate resettlement planning is done and the right assistance is provided (e.g., money, housing, food, employment), then there is a good chance that stress can be reduced.[3]

The only forced relocation studied by Human Sciences Research that came close to meeting Murfin's criteria for reducing stress was the Hung-Quang regroupment in Quang-Nam province (chapter 7). However, those regrouped people rated their present circumstances at only 1.90 on the Cantril scale (well below the DMZ evacuees), compared with 4.57 for their past and 3.00 for their future. Those are not indicators of reduced stress, even though the people were close enough to their fields to continue cultivating them and had been assisted with housing and other necessities. Another well-planned relocation, which may have been forced (although the people had evidently wanted to escape from the VC), moved people and their possessions from Tuyet-Diem on the Batangan Peninsula of Quang-Ngai to Son-Tra II, where they could continue fishing and cultivating their fields (chapter 6). The stress level of those relocatees was not measured.

With the small human and material resources that had to be spread among so many genuine refugees, it simply was not possible to do all that would have been necessary to reduce stress among all the people who were involuntarily relocated in South Viet-Nam.

One thing that was not mentioned by Murfin was the lack of political work among the involuntary evacuees, yet that was one of the most important reasons why they remained a danger to the nationalist cause. Having recognized that the relocations were bringing VC dependents and partisans into its territory, the GVN should have been much more thorough in screening out the Communist infrastructure, and then in educating and indoctrinating the people in nationalist and democratic doctrine. It would have required the same kind of intensive political education that the Communists conducted, and it would have to be continued for years. Presumably the children who went to school got that, but the parents did not, and it seems probable that their influence outweighed that of the often poorly trained and ideologically unmotivated teachers. The RD cadres were no match for the Communists in that kind of contest for hearts and minds, and in any case they did not stay long enough in one location. Where the relief and resettlement assistance promised by the government was not delivered, its message was further discredited. The plain fact was that the GVN was not equipped to do what was necessary for all the people the Americans and ARVN brought into its territory.

How many people were there? It seems that the largest identifiable numbers of Vietnamese (as distinguished from Highland tribespeople) were moved forcibly during the Diem regime: I estimate about half of those in the land development program and the agrovilles, or roughly 125,000 and almost all of the

873,700 who were relocated in the creation of the strategic hamlets, mainly in the Delta. The forced relocations discussed in chapter 7 moved 44,300 people. Those in the coastal areas of I CTZ during 1968–69 that were reported relocated about 37,000 people. Part of the problem was that most forced movements were not reported as such, especially after they had to be approved in advance by the Central Pacification and Development Council. However, the total involuntarily relocated was certainly over 10% of all the refugees and other war victims listed in table 17.

After a great deal of reporting and pressure by me and others, which then got backing from Ambassador Colby and General Abrams, the GVN, beginning late in 1968, issued increasingly strict instructions to bring forcible relocations under control. Although they achieved some reduction of the practice, it never really ceased, even after the cease-fire of 1973, though then the tendency was to compel refugees to move back to their homes or other locations in contested areas in order to show the flag. Those involuntary movements caused the same kind of disaffection and alienation from the GVN as the earlier relocations. When the relocatees were prevented from leaving their camps, like the people of Thanh-Thuy, they became a festering sore within GVN territory—and a source of derogatory information for reporters. It is clear that the forcibly evacuated and forcibly retained people were a dangerous liability to the GVN and an asset to the enemy.

In North Viet-Nam it seems likely that most of the one million or so peasants who were relocated from the Red River Delta to the Highlands moved involuntarily. That campaign was conducted with much publicity and Lao Dong Party involvement at all levels, being portrayed as a contribution by all concerned to the national economy and social advancement. Government and party controls were strict enough that we shall probably never know how the resettled people or their hosts reacted—or even how many stayed in the remote areas.

Regrouped Montagnards

All the mistakes that were made in forcibly relocating South Vietnamese were compounded in the various groupments of the Highland tribes by the incursions of Vietnamese on their lands. Indeed, land grabbing seems to have been an important, if not the most important, motive for moving and consolidating highlander villages.

Each one of the successive programs, beginning with Diem's highlander resettlement effort, compressed the Montagnards into a smaller space. The justification was that the traditional swidden agriculture practiced by many tribes took much more land than sedentary agriculture, and also denuded the forests. However, the more advanced tribes practiced sedentary agriculture that was at least as efficient as that of the lowland people. In some places, they had built elaborate terraces to hold water for paddy rice and to prevent erosion. Their fruit, tea, and other tree crops were often exemplary. However, their land also was often taken by Vietnamese, along with that that had been devoted to slash-and-burn cultivation.

Montagnard land rights were traditional and not written down in legal form. The highlanders did not need such forms; they knew the tribal and village boundaries, and passed the knowledge down through the generations. Their tribal courts settled disputes.

For the Vietnamese, those customs had no legal force. In their theory, the entire Highlands had been the property of the Bao Dai, and when his rights passed to the Republic, it was for the GVN to apportion them as it chose. Although some Americans in the USOM and then the USAID, aided by such experts as Gerald Hickey, fought for recognition and codification of Montagnard land rights, the dominant view within both the GVN and the American AID Mission for many years was that they did not exist. By the time main living areas and other land rights were acknowledged, most of them had already been taken away by the Vietnamese. It was somewhat like the treatment of the American Indians by the whites in our country.

In a number of cases, recounted in chapter 11, after highlanders were relocated, ostensibly to bring them from insecure to secure territory, Vietnamese moved onto their former lands and either cultivated or logged them. They also encroached on the new lands that had been allocated to the displaced Montagnards. Moreover, the unsophisticated tribal people were frequently the victims of unscrupulous contractors hired by provincial and district authorities to build their houses or perform other services. Furthermore, as in the case of the Bru in the Cua Valley of Quang-Tri, Vietnamese troops and their neighbors found other ways to make life dangerous for the relocated highlanders. It is no wonder that FULRO and other tribal movements, as well as the Viet-Cong, won converts among the exploited Montagnards, and that many escaped from GVN areas back into the forest.

In 1971, Nay Luett, the Minister for Ethnic Minority Development, and Gerald Hickey, estimated that at least 65% of all Highland villages had been relocated for one reason or another since 1945. Depending on which estimate of highlander population is accepted, that meant that between 397,000 and 570,000 of the tribal people had been uprooted.[4] Many more were forced to move during the NVA offensive of 1972 and the "cease-fire" fighting of 1973–74.

This enormous dislocation and compression of a whole people changed their society and culture fundamentally. In past years, although they distrusted all Vietnamese, many of the proud and independent highlanders in the territorial forces had fought bravely against the Communists, especially when they were led by American Green Berets. Montagnard leaders now in the United States recognize that regrouping brought some benefits, principally location on main roads and access to Vietnamese schools, health facilities, and other amenities. (However, as I was able to observe, the Vietnamese province hospital in Kontum so discriminated against the highlanders that most went to the overcrowded and poorly equipped hospital of Dr. Pat Smith.) On the other hand, with insufficient land for cultivation, the relocated people became wards of the state, dependent on official refugee rations and the charity of voluntary agencies. In their new locations they also learned to lie and steal, something they never did in their original homes. They were impoverished mendicants—their pride and independence were gone.[5]

A perspicacious and sympathetic former district senior advisor of CORDS who served in both Le-Thanh (Thanh-An) and Le-Trung districts (which comprised two-thirds of Pleiku province) observed that the relocated highlanders behaved like the pawns they were, passive and neutral. Their movements were restricted by the designation of areas around their camps as free fire zones. He never saw any move toward self-defense on their part, whereas a number of normal Montagnard villages requested and were assisted in creating armed self-defense forces.[6] After they were forcibly relocated by the GVN, they became indifferent at best; many escaped and returned to VC territory, where they were used as laborers and suppliers of food. Thousands of Katu and other tribespeople who had been kidnapped by the Communists helped, willingly or not, to build and maintain the Ho Chi Minh Trail. There were increasing numbers of highlanders with the VC, in two divisions and many guerrilla units. At the end, when Ban Me Thuot and then the rest of the Highlands were attacked, few Montagnard troops helped the GVN, and some joined with the North Vietnamese.

Whether for this reason or because nobody helped them to escape, very few Montagnards were among the evacuees and escapees from Viet-Nam in April–May 1975, and even today only about 600 are in western countries. However, once they found that the North Vietnamese discriminated against them even more than did the Southerners, thousands of FULRO adherents fought the new oppressors in the forest for some years, until their situation became hopeless. Then some thousands escaped to Kampuchea and were in the process of trying to get out to Thailand as these lines are written.

This brief summary, which derives from the information in the preceding chapters, demonstrates that most refugees and evacuees, including many who were nominally resettled, were poorly adjusted psychologically, and hostile or indifferent to the GVN, and that this affected the outcome of the war. The constructive programs developed and carried out by the succession of able and compassionate Ministers and their dedicated staffs, with the help of American advisors, mitigated but did not overcome the adverse effects of the traumas inflicted by the ways refugees were generated or the structrual obstacles preventing the reestablishment of most of them in durable and viable situations. Except for the forced evacuees and some of the Montagnards (who themselves had been forcibly relocated), most war victims did not actively work or fight for the enemy. What counted was that the great majority did not support or help the government, and in the face of united and fanatical Communist forces and cadres, that lack of support from so large a part of the population meant that the GVN was bound to lose. I do not share the belief that the Viet-Nam War was won within Viet-Nam until the withdrawal of American aid opened the way for invasion from the North. The war was being steadily lost in the hearts and minds of the Vietnamese people, and in their refugee camps and villages, except for those brief years between the Têt offensive and late 1971; the decline was never reversed after the 1972 Easter offensive of the NVA. Refugees and evacuees were both passively and actively involved in that decline.

Moreover, the frequent violence and heartlessness with which many refugees were generated and the all-too-frequent neglect and exploitation of these people at the local level were widely publicized in the United States through the hearings of the Senate Refugee Subcommittee and countless reports in the media. The negative aspect was stressed, while constructive humanitarian achievements were often overlooked. There is no doubt that this contributed significantly to the erosion of popular and congressional support of the war effort. That American boys were involved in the brutal killing of civilians and burning of their homes, and were losing their own lives in the process, made the people of the United States determined to bring them home. More and more Americans also came to feel that a Vietnamese government that evidently mistreated the most unfortunate of its population and whose own people were not united in resisting the Communists could not win and was unworthy of the blood and material resources the United States was expending.

Special mention of the "family syndrome" is needed. In both 1972 and 1975, thousands of ARVN troops deserted under fire in order to bring their families, who were living near the Army encampments, to safety. When that occurred, it of course opened the way for enemy advances, and it meant that troops and civilians were mixed up together in disorganized flight. The North Vietnamese attacked these frantic masses, both to decimate the troops and to demoralize the people. It was not abnormal for Communist forces to behave this way—they had often done so in the past—and it should have been anticipated. The failure of both the joint General Staff and its American advisors to appreciate the dangers inherent in the practice of housing dependents near potential invasion routes, and to plan in advance for their orderly evacuation was a costly error.

It has been pointed out that many troops of the US Seventh Army in Germany are presently in a similar situation, in that their families also live on potential battlefields.[7]

THE FINAL EVACUATION

There were two aspects to the efforts to bring to safety people who would be at risk (or who thought they were) from the advancing North Vietnamese: flight and evacuation within the country, and evacuation and flight out of Viet-Nam. The latter was by far the more complex, but both presented difficult policy and practical questions. In both cases a balance had to be found between, on the one hand, keeping government, the economy, and other vital functions going as long as there was a prospect that territory and people could be defended and, on the other hand, saving endangered people. If key officials and those necessary to the economy were removed too early, those functions would collapse, there could be panic among the people generally, and the morale of the troops could be impaired. However, removing some endangered and surplus people in a careful manner could be a prudent way of clearing a battlefield and actually helping the defense. On the other hand, if evacuating at-risk personnel was delayed too long, they would be captured and some would be killed. That actually happened throughout Viet-Nam.

In fact, these questions had never been thought through by the GVN or its US advisors before the final emergency was upon the country, and that was a grievous fault. There had been no civil emergency planning such as has been done in the United States and NATO Europe. That lacuna stemmed in part from President Thieu's determination until the end to hold on to every square meter of Vietnamese territory. As the refugee program had developed over the years, it included plans to cope with emergencies, such as stockpiling food and other supplies in province capitals, and both the US and GVN military became quite adept at extracting people from insecure areas (willingly or unwillingly). However, the removal of GVN officials and other high-risk individuals was seen as a responsibility of the national government. What happened to many of them in Hue during the Têt offensive of 1968 should have alerted the GVN and its American advisors to the need for planning.

During the 1972 offensive, which overran Quang-Tri and threatened other whole provinces, both military officers and civilian officials fled, sometimes abandoning their troops and the people, but they were able to return later. This time it was different, in that whole regions were abandoned. Thieu's sudden decision after the NVA conquest of Ban Me Thuot in March 1975 to institute the "light at the top, heavy at the bottom" policy was made not only without any plan for orderly military withdrawal, but also without thought for the civilians who would be captured by the Communists, including the government officials. Indeed, Thieu directed that the province chiefs in the Highlands of MR-2 not be informed, and they were not. In MR-1 also no provision had been made for orderly withdrawal of endangered civilians. Under those circumstances, it was no wonder that panic ensued in both regions and relatively few endangered people got out. On the other hand, many military officers and local GVN officials evacuated themselves before there was a need to, deserting their troops and the people, including refugees, entrusted to their care.

When, late in March 1975, the possibility arose that all of South Viet-Nam would fall, it brought with it, for the first time in the nation's history, the need to think in terms of moving the country's political, military, intellectual, and other leaders, and specially endangered citizens into exile abroad. Normally when such a catastrophe threatens a nation, its own government takes the lead in preparing flight and evacuation, and that is not considered cowardly or shameful. Usually friendly neighboring countries receive the refugees. That happened in Poland and a number of Western European countries in World War II, with the result that governments in exile and de Gaulle's Free French forces were able to establish themselves outside of Hitler's grasp, mainly in England. It was also the case when the Soviets crushed the Hungarian revolution in 1956, and it has happened frequently in Africa and Latin America. The evacuations have not always been models of effectiveness, but by and large they have gotten out the most threatened people.

In Viet-Nam it appears that President Thieu and most of his top associates were immobilized by unrealistic hopes, and never gave thought to saving the flower of their country's civilization until the last days. Fortunately, some concerned and courageous Americans, headed by President Ford, were prepared to assume responsibility for rescuing those to whom we owed a moral obligation. For the reasons set forth in chapter 15, decisive actions were unduly delayed, with the result that many who should have been brought out were caught by the North Vietnamese. I believe that the problem should have been discussed with Thieu no later than the end of March 1975, when Da-Nang fell. It was obviously a painful subject, but it had to be faced. If he had been brought to address the awful prospect early enough, Thieu himself could have asked the neighboring countries to receive Vietnamese refugees and could have enlisted the UNHCR and ICEM to help. That would have avoided the awkward situation, in which the United States found itself, of appealing on behalf of a government that was not willing to state its own case, and the rescue effort would have been a cooperative one instead of an American operation.

As it turned out, the evacuation did rescue many thousands of the nation's leaders among the 140,000 Vietnamese who came out. It was not enough, however, and all governments who might find themselves in a similar situation should learn from the experience.

SOME LESSONS ABOUT PEOPLE-FACTORS IN PROTRACTED WARFARE

Although much that happened in Viet-Nam was unique to that country, many of the experiences and the lessons that can be drawn from them are transferable to similar situations elsewhere, as in El Salvador, Nicaragua, Ethiopia, and Angola. There have been many such conflicts before, and there will be more. We can learn much about people-factors and how best to deal with them from the Viet-Nam experience.

Some killing, injury, and displacement of civilians are inevitable in wars, as people are caught in sudden combat or flee from battlefields. Beyond that, however, the amount of damage to civilian populations and their property, and the generation of refugees, are controllable by the belligerents, depending on the strategies and tactics they adopt. Furthermore, if the harm done is perceived by the victims as excessive or disproportionate to legitimate military purposes—which people on the spot are often quite capable of judging—it produces resentments that may make an operation or campaign unproductive.

Communist terror, whether selective against individuals or indiscriminate against crowds (rocketing, mortaring, grenades, mines, and so forth) is always deliberate. It is turned on and off as party leaders dictate. While selective assassinations seem to be effective in cowing actual or potential opponents, indiscriminate terror frequently creates anger and stimulates resistance. Such tactics by anti-Communist guerrillas have similar effects. Massacre of large groups, as was done by the Viet-Cong and North Vietnamese at Hue in 1968, can change a whole population into enemies of the perpetrators, but it also generates mass flight should the aggressors sweep forward again, as they did in 1972 and 1975. Whether the Communists thought that far ahead in 1968 is not known. In any case, mass slaughter of civilians is an option that is not open to the forces with which the United States is allied.

Careful and observed bombardment of an identified military target will generally be perceived as legitimate, even when some nearby civilians are killed, injured, or forced to flee. However, indiscriminate bombing or artillery fire on populated areas which may or may not contain enemy forces will probably be seen as unwarranted and cruel by the victims, as well as outside observers, and will cause resentment against those responsible. If refugees are thereby generated, they may flee deeper into enemy territory or abroad, or under some circumstances may come for safety to the side with the bigger guns, but in that case they will be an alienated and uncooperative element. Chances are that most of the able-bodied men will remain with the enemy, willingly or unwillingly. The Allies found that out in Viet-Nam, and the Soviets have found it out in Afghanistan.

It is generally best to leave people on their land, even in enemy-held areas. Although they will be used as food-suppliers and laborers by the enemy, such exploitation, especially if it becomes excessive, will probably alienate the people from their oppressors. Intelligence nets can be established, and these communities can become the friendly water in which guerrillas fighting the enemy can swim and be nourished.

Defoliation to destroy crops in enemy-held areas is never appropriate. Quite apart from environmental damage, its result will be to starve civilians, because enemy forces will always take whatever food they need.

It must never be forgotten that war victims are human beings, with the same feelings, capacity for grief, and aspirations as their neighbors. In a people's war, callous or inhumane generation of refugees and other war victims is not only morally wrong; it is counterproductive. If the United States is a party to the conflict, even indirectly, as in El Salvador or Nicaragua, American public opinion will not long tolerate such behavior on the part of American troops or those the United States is supporting. Indiscriminate employment of mass-destruction weapons in populated areas, especially when few or no enemy soldiers are fighting there, is an example of military tactics that must be effectively prevented.

Forced relocation of people to bring them to "security" or deny them to the enemy is likely to be counterproductive everywhere, except when it removes them temporarily from an active battlefield—and usually force will not be required to get people to escape from active combat. The reasons given above with respect to Viet-Nam have validity elsewhere as well.

If forced relocation (except for a short time under battlefield conditions) is proscribed, how is a friendly force to find and defeat the enemy without harming civilians? Father Nguyen Lac Hoa, Roger Hilsman, and other experts have given the answer (chapters 4, 6, and 7): by fighting guerrillas with guerrillas, and by careful fixing of a massed enemy on the ground before attacking him. This means using trained and culturally sensitized men and officers as fighters, rather than indiscriminate firepower. It may cause more friendly casualties at first, although this has been doubted, but it is more likely to shorten a war and result in fewer military casualties on the friendly side over its duration. It needs also to be remembered that people are people, whether soldiers or civilians, and life is life. Each human life has infinite value. This is not only a moral imperative; it has practical importance in any war.

If refugees come out on their own, fleeing enemy terror or oppression, they should be welcomed and cared for as brothers and sisters. The decision to leave their land, family graves, and possessions will not have been taken lightly. Their motives and their potential as allies in a just cause demand respect. They should be hospitably received, given succor, and assisted to become self-supporting again.

However, all refugees are an economic and social burden to the party on whose territory they take refuge. For this reason, as well as those discussed above, the generation of refugees by friendly governments and forces should be held to a minimum. If the territory from which they came remains insecure or in the hands of the enemy, the crowding of more people into limited ''friendly'' areas, unless there is plentiful cultivable land or alternate employment opportunities, increases the difficulty of reestablishing the refugees. They may then become a continuing drain on scarce resources. In any conflict in which the United States is a party, and in some where it is not, American public opinion demands that humanitarian assistance be provided, and Americans are willing to pay a generous part of the cost; however, that will not always be sufficient to bring the victims to a self-supporting state.

The creation and operation of large refugee assistance programs makes demands on the limited pool of skilled human resources in underdeveloped countries, and in conflicted areas this may also require the help of military units, whose often-unsympathetic commanders usually do not take kindly to what they consider distractions from the business of fighting the war. Such programs are an invitation to corruption and diversion of money and commodities, especially if they come from abroad. Yet if assistance to the war victims is not prompt, effective, and sufficient, human suffering is prolonged, and the resentment of the victims against the indigenous authority is increased. In these days of instant, worldwide communication, the inadequacies of a relief effort, especially when it is supported by foreign money, are shown on television screens and in the other media everywhere, and this may weaken support for the party perceived to be responsible.

Both developed and underdeveloped nations with large populations of indigenous war victims often need and frequently welcome expert advice and assistance from abroad. International voluntary agencies are the best and most incorruptible sources of such aid. United Nations agencies such as UNICEF and the UNHCR, as well as ICM (which with its smaller and more homogeneous membership can respond quickly), may be called on as appropriate. The foreign aid agencies of the United States, Canada, the Scandinavian countries, and some others, now have or can call on many experts in refugee and disaster assistance, including former Ministers and other officials of Viet-Nam, to help the requesting government. The aim should be full reestablishment of the war victims economically, socially, and politically as functioning members of their community. Human dignity should at all times be protected and enhanced.

In a people's war, troops must at all times be under the firm control of officers who are educated in the political as well as the military aspects of the war, respectful of human dignity, and culturally sensitive. The soldiers must be led to behave as friends of the people. It will require changes in the training and indoctrination of American troops and US military advisors if they are to be employed in such situations. Moreover, and this is paramount, an enlightened, humanitarian policy on the part of the government of the affected country, and proper care for the civilians, including displaced persons, is a sine qua non to win such a war. If the United States is involved, even the best behavior of its troops and generous assistance cannot make up for persistent failures of an indigenous government and its military forces to respect the dignity and aspirations of their people.

These recommendations are no more than what common sense would dictate, but they are not easy to follow, especially in the heat of battle. Furthermore, my stating them will have no effect upon the Communist world, whose troops and partisans, as we have seen, are capable of brutalities toward civilians equal to or exceeding any that the free world has inflicted. "Low-intensity wars" especially seem to bring out the beast in men on both sides. A neutral humanitarian presence seems to be needed to curb excesses.

The International Committee of the Red Cross (ICRC) has traditionally played that role, acting under the Geneva Conventions on land warfare and on the protection of noncombatants. Two additional Protocols to those Conventions, the first relating to the protection of victims of international armed conflicts, and the second on protection of victims of noninternational conflicts, were drawn up in 1977 and have been ratified by 71 and 64 nations respectively. They are much more specific than the 1949 Geneva Conventions in the acts against civilians that are proscribed, and the second protocol extends protection to civilians caught in civil wars. Among things that are protected, in addition to human lives, are the crops, livestock, and other property of civilian noncombatants. Mass bombing and other attacks on civilian populations are not permitted. Protocol II prohibits the forcible displacement of civilian populations unless their security or imperative military reasons so demand. Guerrillas taken as prisoners are to be recognized as prisoners of war if they have distinguished themselves from civilians at least by carrying arms openly during combat. The United States participated in drafting the Protocols, and its delegate signed them, but it has withheld ratification.[8] I agree with the governments of the various nations that have ratified that the safeguards against giving rights to combatants who do not clearly identify their presence are sufficient. The United States would contribute to the protection of innocent civilians around the world by ratifying the protocols.

An official of the UNHCR has suggested that the United Nations expand its role of protection and assistance to international refugees to encompass displaced persons within their own countries as well, when the concerned governments request it.[9]

By these or other means, an international humanitarian presence, which could be respected by the contending parties, should be inserted into all low-intensity and high-intensity wars to protect refugee civilians and other noncombatants. The United States should take the lead in developing a system for doing this.

Let us hope that lessons from the Viet-Nam conflict will lead not only those of us on both sides who were touched by it, but also the coming generations, to a new respect for the dignity and worth of our brethren everywhere, including the humblest among them.

Notes

For a description of date notation styles used in these notes, please refer to the preface.

CHAPTER 1. VIET-NAM: EXODUS FROM THE NORTH AND MOVEMENT TO THE NORTH, 1954–55

1. George Naidenoff, "Migration Creates Upheaval in Vietnam Church," *Migration News* 5, no. 2 (March–April 1956): 19.

2. Vietnam Directorate General of Information, *Operation Exodus: The Refugee Movement to Free Vietnam* (Saigon: Directorate General of Information, n.d. [1959]).

3. Nguyen Thi Hue, interview with author, May 2, 1984. Hue's family, which was close to the Bao Dai, was forced to move out from a town in Thanh-Hoa province in 1946 and to flee from French bombing and fighting to Hanoi at the end of 1951, leaving their land. They then moved to Hue. In 1956, the family moved to Nha-Trang, where all of Hue's brothers joined the National Army.

4. See American Embassy Bangkok despatch 93, August 25, 1954. Unless otherwise stated, this and the other official communications cited in this chapter were studied in the National Archives of the United States, file group RG 59 NA, files 751 g. 00 and 851 g. 411.

5. See Peter A. Poole, *The Vietnamese in Thailand: A Historical Perspective* (Ithaca, N.Y.: Cornell University Press, 1970).

6. Saigon telegram 2873, June 22, 1954; Saigon 2891, June 25; Hanoi telegram 763, June 27; Saigon OARMA telegram MC 353–54, July 1; Hanoi telegram 2, July 1; Saigon 60, July 5, 1954. These messages give somewhat divergent accounts of the withdrawals, but it appears that the French evacuated about 10,000 to 12,000 Vietnamese civilians also, mostly by sea.

7. Telegram 32, July 2, 1954, from American Embassy Paris, reporting a conversation of Ambassador Douglas Dillon with the Prime Minister.

8. Khuyen Baccam, conversation with the author, Washington, D.C., November 17,

1986. A member of one of the prominent families, Baccam's father had been executed by the Communists in 1947 or 1948, when Khuyen was three years old. His oldest brother, a village chief, was executed by the Communists in 1952. Two others joined the French army; one of them was captured during the battle at Dien-Bien-Phu and has not been heard from since then.

9. Telegram 4853 from the Department of State to Embassy Paris, June 28, 1954, United States Department of State, *Foreign Relations of the United States, 1952–54*, vol. 16 (henceforth referred to as *FR*), 1256–58. See also Joseph Buttinger, *Vietnam: A Political History* (New York: Praeger, 1968), 374.

10. Paris telegram 32, July 2, 1954, cited in note 7.

11. Office of the Secretary of Defense Task Force, final report, *United States–Vietnam Relations, 1945–1967*, bk. 2 (Washington, D.C.: Government Printing Office, 1971), 12. This 12-volume report, prepared for the Armed Forces Committee of the House of Representatives, is the official and most complete version of the Pentagon Papers, and will henceforth be cited as the Pentagon Papers. Two other versions, one published by the *New York Times*, and the other published at the request of Senator Mike Gravel, will be cited under those names.

12. Pentagon Papers 2:16.

13. Ibid., 2:17–18.

14. Jeffrey Race, *War Comes to Long An: Revolutionary Conflict in a Vietnamese Province* (Berkeley: University of California Press, 1972), 32.

15. Pentagon Papers 2:17.

16. US Consulate General Hanoi telegram 111, August 2, 1954, citing *Vietnam Presse* of July 31; Embassy Saigon despatch 114, September 23, 1954, enclosing a list of violations prepared by the GVN; Saigon despatch 184, December 6, 1954, enclosing a report by Father Patrick O'Connor, correspondent of the National Catholic Welfare Service. A memorandum to Secretary of State John Foster Dulles from Walter S. Robertson, Assistant Secretary of the Far East Bureau, dated November 18, 1954, stated that reports from the French and eye-witness accounts from escapees left no doubt that thousands of refugees were fleeing at the risk of and in the face of Viet-Minh intimidation and threats, as well as forcible prevention, in violation of Article 14(*d*) of the accord and paragraph 8 of the Conference Declaration. Saigon despatch 191, December 11, 1954, reported as yet unpublished articles by AP/Reuters correspondents Corley Smith and Jacques Mootsamy on the mass of evidence that the Communist government in Hanoi had organized concerted actions to stop the exodus of hundreds of thousands of Buddhist and Catholic peasants fleeing from the Red River Delta. They gave a number of examples.

17. Thomas A. Dooley, *Deliver Us from Evil* (New York: Farrar, 1956).

18. Ibid., 10–11. At the end of his 10-month service in Viet-Nam, Lt. Dooley was decorated by Prime Minister Diem as an Officier de l'Ordre National de Viet-Nam (see Commander in Chief, US Pacific Fleet, to Chief of Naval Operations, "The Role of the US Navy," in *Viet-nam: The First Five Years, an International Symposium*, ed. Richard W. Lindholm (East Lansing: Michigan State University Press, 1959), 75.

19. Dooley, *Deliver Us from Evil*, 22, 181.

20. Ibid., 142.

21. Embassy Saigon telegram 1262, September 28, 1954.

22. Major General Nguyen Duy Hinh and Brigadier General Tran Dinh Tho, *The South Vietnamese Society* (Washington, D.C.: US Army Center of Military History, 1980), 21.

23. Dooley, *Deliver Us from Evil*, 150–53.

24. US Embassy Saigon telegram 2997, July 23, 1954.

25. Saigon 342, July 27, relaying Hanoi's 107; Saigon 352, July 28, 1954.

26. Saigon 458, August 5, and 478, August 6, 1954.

27. US Department of State telegrams 491 and 492 to Saigon, August 7, 1954; CINC-PAC msg. 120236Z August 1954 to Secstate. (Military messages were identified by date-time group, with "Z" meaning Greenwich mean time.)

28. Bui Van Luong, "The Role of Friendly Nations," in *Viet-Nam: The First Five Years*, 49. Luong had been the Commissioner General of the Refugee Commission until 1957 and at the time of the symposium was the Commissioner General of Agricultural Development. See also Commander in Chief, US Pacific Fleet, to Chief of Naval Operations, "The Role of the US Navy." ch. 6.

29. Directorate General of Information, *Operation Exodus*, 6, 13–20.

30. Joseph Buttinger, *Vietnam: A Dragon Embattled*, vol. 2 (New York: Praeger, 1967), 856. See also his later book, *Vietnam: The Unforgettable Tragedy* (New York: Horizon Press, 1977), 17–19.

31. Hinh and Tho, *South Vietnamese Society*, 22.

32. Pentagon Papers 2:12.

33. Commander in Chief to Chief of Naval Operations, "The Role of the US Navy," in *Viet-Nam: The First Five Years*, 70.

34. An address at a conference on America's Stake in Vietnam, at the Willard Hotel, Washington, D.C., June 1, year not stated, probably 1956. This document is in the papers of Joseph Buttinger, which were given to the Harvard Yenching Library. Bernard B. Fall made the same point in his commentary on Luong's presentation ("The Role of Friendly Nations") in *Viet-Nam: The First Five Years*, 54.

35. Directorate General of Information, *Operation Exodus*, 20.

36. Rt. Rev. Msgr. Joseph J. Harnett, "The Work of the Catholic Groups," in *Viet-Nam: The First Five Years*, 80–82; idem, "Critique of the Program for the Economic Integration of Refugees," 86.

37. Jean Le Pichon, "Commentary on Father Harnett," in *Viet-Nam: The First Five Years*, 96–97, 99. Le Pichon was a French civil servant who was technical expert for COMIGAL, 1955–57.

38. Buttinger's Saigon diary, pp. 4–19, in the Harvard Yenching Library.

39. Joseph Buttinger, speech, January 29, 1955, at the Buttinger home in Pennington, New Jersey. Text in the Buttinger papers (Harvard Yenching Library).

40. Although Buttinger did not say so, Charles Sternberg, former Executive Director of IRC, wrote in a personal letter to me, August 26, 1985, that Joe Buttinger supplied the initial funds needed for the assistance work. Buttinger's wife, the psychiatrist Murial Gardiner, a remarkable woman who had helped his underground work in Austria in the years 1934–38, was an heiress to the Swift meatpacking family fortune; together they funded many worthy causes.

41. Joseph Buttinger also devoted most of the next 14 years to writing scholarly histories of Viet-Nam, which became standard reference works in English: *The Smaller Dragon* (New York: Frederick A. Praeger, 1958); then the massive two-volume *Vietnam: A Dragon Embattled*; and a condensation of both works, *Vietnam: A Political History* (New York: Praeger; 1968). These books were also published in Europe in French and German. In 1977 he published *Vietnam: The Unforgettable Tragedy* which was more polemical than scholarly, reflecting Buttinger's disillusionment with both Ngo Dinh Diem

(to whose regime he had contributed notable support in earlier years) and American war policy.

42. Edward Geary Lansdale, Maj. Gen., USAF (Ret.), *In the Midst of Wars, An American's Mission to Southeast Asia* (New York: Harper & Row, 1972), 169–70. Lansdale assisted Philippine Minister Magsaysay in his successful campaign to defeat the Huk insurgency.

43. Leland Barrows, Director of USOM/VN before the Viet-Nam National Committee for Foreign Aid, statement, June 14, 1956 (paper in the Buttinger collection). Harnett, "Critique of the Program for Economic Integration of Refugees," in *Viet-Nam: The First Five Years*, 83–87. Harnett asserted that $35 million had been appropriated by Congress for the temporary shelter phase, but that at the end of February 1956, none of this had reached the refugee villages. In his commentary on Msgr. Harnett's presentation, Alfred L. Cardinaux, who had been Chief of the USOM Refugee Resettlement Division, said that USOM released funds without delay upon approval of individual village projects, but that the antiquated Vietnamese fiscal system (inherited from the French) delayed payments, in ibid., 88.

44. Directorate General of Information, *Operation Exodus*, 20–21.

45. Ibid., 34; Cardinaux, "Commentary on Father Harnett," in *Vietnam: The First Five Years*, 88–90; Barrows statement, June 14, 1956. It should be noted that most of the US refugee assistance funds were provided in piasters derived from the Commodity Assistance Program, under which dollar-funded commodities were imported by Vietnamese merchants or manufacturers, who paid piasters into accounts in the Central Bank, under the joint control of the GVN and USOM. Also see the following reports by the Michigan State University Vietnam Advisory Group: *Research Report: Field Study of the Refugee Commission* (Saigon: MSU, 1955); *Review of Recommendations Concerning Proposed Field Organization of the Commissariat for Refugees of September 20, 1955* (Saigon: MSU, 29 June 1956); *Final Report Covering Activities of the Michigan State University Vietnam Advisory Group for the Period May 20, 1955-June 30, 1962,* (Saigon: MSUG, 1962) 1, 6. The sending of the MSU Group in the fall of 1954 had resulted from the long-time association between the university, particularly Professor Wesley R. Fishel, and Diem, dating from the time when Diem was a refugee from the French in the United States.

46. Le Pichon, "Commentary on Father Harnett," 97, 99.

47. Directorate General of Information, *Operation Exodus*, 22–43. General O'Daniel wrote a colorful book about Cai-San and other resettlement centers, *The Nation that Refused to Starve: The Challenge of the New Vietnam* (New York: Coward-McCann, 1960). See also John D. Montgomery and the National Institute of Administration (NIA, Viet-Nam) Case Development Seminar, *Cases in Vietnamese Administration*, Saigon: MSUG, 1959.

48. Bernard Fall, "Commentary on Father Harnett," in *Viet-Nam: The First Five Years*, 94.

49. Gerald Cannon Hickey, *Free in the Forest* (New Haven and London: Yale University Press, 1982), 17; Harnett, "The Vietnamese Refugees Five Years Later," *Migration News* 8, no. 5 (September-October 1959): 40–41.

50. Fall, "Commentary on Father Harnett," 94; Cardinaux, "Commentary on Father Harnett," 87; Hickey, *Free in the Forest*, 19.

51. Luong, "The Role of Friendly Nations," 52–3; Dr. Ly Trung Dung, "Integration

of Refugees in Viet-Nam," *Migration News*, Geneva: International Catholic Migration Committee (ICMC) (July-August 1958): 11–12.

52. Naidenoff, "Migration Creates Upheaval," 19–20.

53. William K. Hitchcock, letter to author, September 8, 1984.

54. Pentagon Papers 2:15–16.

CHAPTER 2. LAND DEVELOPMENT, HIGHLANDER RESETTLEMENT, AND AGROVILLES, 1957–62

1. The most authoritative work on the highlanders during the period 1954–76 is the ethnohistory by Gerald Cannon Hickey, *Free in the Forest* (New Haven and London: Yale University Press; 1982).

2. Interviews of Gerald Cannon Hickey with Vice President Nguyen Ngoc Tho and Bui Van Luong, both summarized in *Free in the Forest*, 7–8 and 17.

3. Ibid., 10.

4. Ibid., 18, citing the RVN Commissariat General for Land Development report, *The Work of Land Development in Vietnam up to June 30, 1959*, 3–7. Also see John D. Montgomery, *The Politics of Foreign Aid* (New York: Praeger, 1962), 72–73.

5. Montgomery, *Politics of Foreign Aid*, 73–80. A statement of the aims of the GVN, and data on 25 land development sites were presented in Republic of Viet-Nam, Commissariat for Land Development, *Briefing on Central Highlands Land Development Area*, undated, evidently 1958 (in the Michigan State University [MSU] Archives).

6. Ibid., 81–2; William Henderson, "Opening of New Lands and Villages: The Republic of Vietnam Land Development Program," in *Problems of Freedom*, ed. Wesley R. Fisher (Glencoe: Free Press, 1961), 123–27; Department of Rural Affairs, *1960 Vietnam Agricultural Statistics*, October 1961, reprinted in the *Economic Newsletter of American Friends of Vietnam*, April 16, 1962. The October 1962 population figures are in Maynard Weston Dow, *Nation Building in Southeast Asia* (Boulder, Colorado: Pruitt Press, 1966), 153. However, Hickey (in a telephone conversation, December 14, 1987) said that ramie and the other fiber products raised on the settlements were too costly to compete with Philippine products.

7. Embassy Saigon despatch 279, March 2, 1959, printed in *Foreign Relations of the United States, 1958–1960*, Volume 1, *Vietnam*, 162–63 (henceforth referred to as *FR Vietnam*); letter from the Consul in Hue (Heavner) to the Deputy Chief of Mission in Vietnam (Elting), October 15, 1959 (*FR Vietnam*, 244–45).

8. William A. Nighswonger, *Rural Pacification in Vietnam* (New York: Praeger, 1966), 38. The land development centers in the Mekong Delta were located in Kien-Phong and Kien-Tuong provinces, some of them very close to the Cambodian border (map, Republic of Viet-Nam: Locations of the Various Land Development Sites 9/59, in Vietnamese MSU Archives).

9. Dennis J. Duncanson, *Government and Revolution in Vietnam* (New York and London: Oxford University Press: 1968), 247.

10. Montgomery, *Politics of Foreign Aid*, 82. In Pleiku, many of the sites were right up against the Cambodian border (map of the sites, 9/59), where they were especially vulnerable to VC attacks.

11. Henderson, "Opening of New Lands," 128–29.

12. "Policy Regarding Land Development Projects," in Hickey, *Free in the Forest*, 19.

13. "Agrarian Reform in Free Vietnam," *Viet-Nam in World Affairs*, Special issue, 1960, 158, cited by Hickey, *Free in the Forest*, 19.

14. Ibid., 42–44. The Field Administration Division, MSU Vietnam Advisory Group, in *Preliminary Research Report on the PMS*, June 1957 (MSU Archives), identified "land grabbing" and the fear of it as one of the primary causes of Mountaineer discontent. The report was prepared by Hickey with the assistance of Frederic Wickert.

15. Hickey, *Free in the Forest*, 45, 62.

16. Bernard Fall, "South Vietnam's Internal Problems," *Pacific Affairs*, February 1958, 252; William A. Nighswonger, *Rural Pacification in Vietnam* (New York: Praeger, 1966), 38; Pentagon Papers 2:29.

17. Han Tho Touneh, interview with author, December 5, 1987. Some of Touneh's father's rice paddy land in the Don-Duong district of Tuyen-Duc province was taken for the Vietnamese.

18. Fall, "South Vietnam's Internal Problems," February 1958, 252. Stanley Karnow, *Vietnam: A History* (New York: Viking, 1983), 234, tells of an example of corruption he encountered when visiting a resettlement site in Kontum.

19. Dennis Duncanson, *Government and Revolution in Vietnam* (New York and London: Oxford University Press, 1968) 247. This was confirmed by Everett Bumgardner, an experienced, Vietnamese-speaking member of USOM at the time (lecture to the CORDS training course at the Foreign Service Institute, October 23, 1967).

20. Han Tho Touneh, December 5, 1987. On December 14, 1987, Hickey confirmed that making highlander land available for Vietnamese resettlement was a primary motive for the highlander resettlement program, at least in some provinces. On the other hand, Dr. Ton That Niem, whose father was Diem's delegate in the Central Highlands and who himself was a public health officer there, doubts that it was government policy at the central level to relocate highlanders in order to make land available for Vietnamese settlers, though this might have occurred locally in some instances (Interview with Dr. Niem, December 6, 1987).

21. Hickey, *Free in the Forest*, 45 and 63, citing *Seven Years of the Ngo Dinh Diem Administration* (Saigon: Information Printing Office, 1961), 115. Also see Pentagon Papers, 2(4):29.

22. Hickey, *Free in the Forest*, 71–72.

23. Touneh, December 5, 1987.

24. "Resettlement of Highlanders in Binh-Tuy Province," an unsigned, undated memorandum, probably written in 1958, in the MSU Archives.

25. Hickey, *Free in the Forest*, 47–60. See also Fall, "South Vietnam's Internal Problems," 252.

26. Nighswonger, *Rural Pacification*, 28–29; Embassy Saigon despatch 278, March 7, 1960 (*FR Vietnam*, 308).

27. Joseph J. Zasloff, *Rural Resettlement in Vietnam: An Agroville in Development*, MSU Advisory Group, AID contract, ICA c 1126, 1961(?), (Saigon: MSU, 1963) 6–7. Officials of the Democratic Republic of Viet-Nam (DRVN) revealed to Stanley Karnow in 1981 that Pham Ngoc Thao had been a Communist agent (Karnow, *Vietnam*, 38 and 257). Truong Nhu Tang, who himself rose to become the Justice Minister in the Communist-dominated Provisional Revolutionary Government (PRG), confirmed that his friend Alfred Pham Ngoc Thao was a Communist agent (Truong Nhu Tang, with David

Chanoff and Doan Van Toai, *A Vietcong Memoir* [San Diego, New York, London: Harcourt Brace Jovanovich, 1985], 42–62).

28. Joseph J. Zasloff, *Rural Resettlement in Vietnam: An Agroville in Development*, 1–11. Zasloff and a Vietnamese colleague made an intensive investigation in the spring of 1960 and visited three agrovilles, two of which are described in this thorough and objective report.

29. Ibid., 11–37; Pentagon Papers 2:30. Everett Bumgardner, in a lecture to the CORDS training course on October 23, 1967, said that old women and men were worked to death building the agrovilles, which were in reality forced labor concentration camps (my notes on the lecture). Duncanson said that the agrovilles were created for 43,000 unreliable families after Diem had been to Malaya to study the New Villages (Duncanson, *Government and Revolution*, 261). This is not entirely correct. A mixture of reliable and unreliable elements was regrouped. For example, the province chief of Long-An created an agroville on the Cambodian border as a strategic barrier, and lavished public money on a hospital, schools and loans to the farmers. He considered the settlement a success; Diem visited it, but it collapsed after Diem's fall (Jeffrey Race, *War Comes to Long An: Revolutionary Conflict in a Vietnamese Province* [Berkeley: University of California Press, 1972] 53–55). *Vietnamese Studies*, Hanoi, volume 1, 1964, contained a denunciation of the agrovilles and strategic hamlets, and published the appeal of the NLF to abolish the "prosperity zones" as part of the NLF program.

30. US Embassy Saigon despatch 251, February 16, 1960 to the Department of State (*FR Vietnam*, 285).

31. Saigon despatch 278, March 7, 1960, transmitting a report on the internal security situation (*FR Vietnam*, 302).

32. Saigon telegram 2622, March 10, 1960 (Ibid., 326–27).

33. Despatch 426, June 6, 1960 (*FR Vietnam*, 485–89). Phong-Dinh province was later divided, and Vi-Thanh (earlier called Vi-Thuan) became the capital of Chuong-Thien province.

34. Saigon despatch no. 157, October 15, 1960, transmitting the English text of the memorandum (*FR Vietnam*, 598–602).

CHAPTER 3. THE STRATEGIC HAMLET PROGRAM, 1961–64

1. Pentagon Papers 2:3, citing State Department Briefing Paper *The North Vietnamese Role in the Origin, Direction, and Support of the War in South Vietnam*, n.d., iv; and State Department, Bureau of Intelligence and Research (INR), RFE-3, Nov. 1, 1961, *Communist Threat Mounts in South Vietnam*, 4–5.

2. Ibid., citing National Intelligence Estimate (NIE) 50–61, 28 March 1961, *Outlook in Mainland Southeast Asia*, 7.

3. Ibid., 4–7.

4. Ibid., 7–10.

5. Milton Osborne, *Strategic Hamlets in South Vietnam: A Survey and a Comparison*, Data Paper number 55 (Southeast Asia Program, Department of Asian Studies, Cornell University, 1965), 6.

6. Malcolm W. Browne, *The New Face of War* (Indianapolis and New York: Bobbs-Merrill, 1965), 4–8.

7. Roger Hilsman, *To Move a Nation* (Garden City, N.Y.: Doubleday, 1967), 437–

38. Hilsman had himself been a member of Merrill's Marauders in Burma during World War II.

8. Ronald H. Spector, *United States Army in Vietnam: Advice and Support, The Early Years* (Washington, D.C.: Center of Military History, US Army, 1983) has an excellent brief summary of how the traditional Vietnamese society had been altered by both the Viet-Minh experience and the Diem regime, and of how the US military advisors misunderstood the implications of these changes (pp. 335–37). See also pp. 353–54 on the beginning of counterinsurgency studies at the US Army Special Warfare School at Fort Bragg and the introduction of Special Forces into Viet-Nam.

9. In an impromptu interview with me on May 7, 1984, Ambassador Durbrow, an old friend, said that although he had advised Diem to pay peasants for their forced labor and to remedy other grievances at the agrovilles, he did not believe in 1984 that peasant dissatisfaction was a significant factor in the growth of VC strength. This is contrary to his frequently expressed belief when he was Ambassador. I think Durbrow was right in his earlier assessments, and may have forgotten some facts over the intervening years.

10. Pentagon Papers 2:10–11, citing Sir Robert Thompson to President Diem, 27 October 1961, Appreciation of Vietnam, November 1961-April 1962, and letter from Lt. Gen. Lionel C. McGarr to Secretary of Defense, 20 November 1961, Sec Def control nr. 2654.

11. Sir Robert G. K. Thompson, *Defeating Communist Insurgency: The Lessons of Malaya and Vietnam* (New York: Praeger, 1966), 121–27; Pentagon Papers 2:11–12, citing the Thompson memorandum and letter to Diem enclosed with Embassy Saigon despatch 205, November 20, 1961. Thompson drew up a draft Government of Viet-Nam (GVN) National Security Council Policy Directive entitled "Delta Plan," a copy of which is in the Roger Hilsman Papers, John F. Kennedy Library.

12. Roger Hilsman, "A Strategic Concept for South Vietnam," February 2, 1962, in National Security Files (NSF), also in the Roger Hilsman Papers, both at the John F. Kennedy Library; Pentagon Papers 2:12–15; Hilsman, *To Move a Nation*, 438–39.

13. Browne, *The New Face of War*, 89–90. See also Dennis Duncanson, *Government and Revolution in Vietnam* (New York and London: Oxford University Press, 1968), 315; and Douglas Blaufarb, *The Counterinsurgency Era* (New York: Free Press, 1977), 105.

14. Blaufarb, *Counterinsurgency Era*, 105.

15. Ibid., 104–5, 109–12; Duncanson, *Government and Revolution*, 312–18.

16. William A. Nighswonger, *Rural Pacification in Vietnam* (New York: Praeger, 1966), 54–55, 61; Osborne, *Strategic Hamlets in South Vietnam*, citing the GVN *Vietnam Presse*, weeks ended 24 and 30 July, 6 August, and 3 September 1961.

17. Dow, *Nation Building in Southeast Asia*, 156.

18. John C. Donnell and Gerald C. Hickey, *The Vietnamese "Strategic Hamlets": A Preliminary Report* (Rand Corporation, Santa Monica, California, Memorandum RM-3208-ARPA, August 1962), vii-viii, 1, 7–16. This report was based on a field trip in January to April 1962 centering on villages close to Saigon and nearby provinces. It was concerned with social, economic, and political aspects as seen by the peasants. Both authors had spent several years in Viet-Nam previously. They did not go into the military aspects. See also Pentagon Papers 2:15–16.

19. Donnell and Hickey, *Vietnamese "Strategic Hamlets,"* 16–29.

20. Lionel C. McGarr, Lt. Gen., USA, Chief, MAAG, letter to Secretary of Defense Robert McNamara, 6 December 1961, enclosing letter of 6 December, McGarr to Admiral H. D. Felt, CINCPAC. On 2 December General McGarr had addressed a letter to President

Diem commenting on Sir Robert Thompson's 11 November paper and enclosing an outline of MAAG's "Concept and Measures for Counter Insurgency Operations in the Delta," which proposed military, psychological, and socioeconomic actions to win over and protect the people. First priority was stated to be the Saigon hinterland, including Zone D, Phuoc-Thanh province. At his Honolulu Conference in December, Secretary Mc-Namara suggested that the Zone D plan be studied and that perhaps another area should be selected first (MAGAR-OT, 18 December 1961, Memorandum for Chief, MAAG, Subject: Trip Report–SecDef Conference). These documents are in the Center of Military History (henceforth called CMH), US Army, Washington, D.C.

21. H. H. Eggleston, Brig. Gen., USA, Acting Chief, Army Section, MAAG, Lessons Learned No. 6, MAGAR-OT (OP), 11 April 1962. Also Pentagon Papers 2:16. It is not altogether clear that this relocation was officially part of Operation Sunrise, since it took place outside the area approved by President Diem.

22. Hq. US Army Section, MAAG, Subject: Lessons Learned No. 19, MAGAR-OT (OB), 31 July 1962, encl. Special Projects Group, CPNS & TNG Div., US Army Sec., MACV-MAGAR-OT (SPC), 11 May 1962, Operation Sunrise, information as reported by Captain Bich 10 May; Special Projects Group, Memorandum for the Record, 17 May 1962. Subject: Status of Relocation Effort, Operation Sunrise, 15 May 1962. Also Pentagon Papers 2:22, citing Homer Bigart, "US Helps Vietnam in Test of Strategy," *New York Times,* March 27, 1962, and "No Win," *The New Republic,* April 1962. On April 5, 1962, John Kenneth Galbraith, then Ambassador to India, who visited Viet-Nam from time to time at the request of President Kennedy, wrote to the President enclosing a memorandum on Viet-Nam. He said, among other things:

The political aspects of some of the measures which pacification requires or is believed to require, including the concentration of population, relocation of villages, and the burning of old villages, may be damaging to those, and especially to Westerners, associated with it. . . . We should dissociate ourselves from action, however necessary, which seems to be directed at the villagers, such as the new concentration program.

These papers are in NSF, at the John F. Kennedy Library.

23. Institute for Defense Analyses, International and Social Studies Division, *The American Experience with Pacification in Vietnam,* Report 185, vol. 3, by Chester L. Cooper, Project Leader, with Judith E. Corson (henceforth referred to as IDA-185), 183.

24. MACTN-BH, 25 July 1962, After Action Report, Operation no. 15, by elements of 5th Infantry Division . . . 16–22 July.

25. Hq. US Army Section, Lessons Learned no. 19, 3–5.

26. Thompson, *Defeating Communist Insurgency,* 129.

27. Blaufarb, *The Counterinsurgency Era,* 114. At a meeting of his National Internal Security Council on October 9, 1962, Diem criticized Operation Sunrise, saying that the results did not justify the amounts of money and troops used (Status Report on Southeast Asia, October 3, 1962, prepared by the Task Force, Southeast Asia, Department of State, NSF, John F. Kennedy Library).

28. IDA-185, 184–86.

29. Pentagon Papers 2:23–24.

30. John B. O'Donnell, "The Strategic Hamlet Program in Kien Hoa Province, South Vietnam: A Case Study in Counterinsurgency," in Volume 2 of *Southeast Asian Tribes, Minorities, and Nations,* edited by Peter Kunstadter (Princeton, N.J.: Princeton University

Press, 1967), 704–7. O'Donnell was the USOM Province Representative (Prov Rep) in Kien-Hoa from December 1962 to August 1964, and also for a time in Long-An. As Stanley Karnow and Truong Nhu Tang reported (chapter 2, n.27), Colonel Thao was a secret Communist agent.

31. O'Donnell, "Strategic Hamlet Program," 707–44. He concluded this excellent account with some cogent conclusions and recommendations regarding strategic hamlets and counterinsurgency programs in general. Donnell and Hickey in their survey report of August 1962, *The Vietnamese "Strategic Hamlets,"* 6–7, said that the Kien-Hoa province chief believed that fortification of all hamlets with ditches and walls was excessively expensive and not effective. Therefore, fortifications were limited to the military posts. A similar system prevailed in Vinh-Long.

32. O'Donnell, "Strategic Hamlet Program," 721–23; Dow, *Nation Building in Southeast Asia,* 164, citing Hedrick Smith, *New York Times,* January 12, 1964. Smith reported that more than half of those relocated left their hamlets. Nighswonger, *Rural Pacification,* 96–105, gives details about the strategic hamlets in Quang-Tri and Quang-Nam, which were sometimes referred to by knowledgeable Americans as "paper hamlets." A special effort was made to set up the hamlets around the An-Hoa coal mine in western Quang-Nam, forcing over 2,000 people to move. The province chief embezzled much of the funds. When the Second ARVN Division left the area, security collapsed. All told, according to Nighswonger, over 8,000 Quang-Nam citizens were relocated in 1963, and more than half of those moves were not reported to USOM or MACV until March 1964.

33. Pentagon Papers 2:24–28.

34. Nighswonger, *Rural Pacification,* 73, n.28; Blaufarb, *Counterinsurgency Era,* 115.

35. Osborne, *Strategic Hamlets,* 33–36.

36. Pentagon Papers, Senator Gravel Edition, 2 (117): 684–88.

37. Thompson, *Defeating Communist Insurgency,* 130–33.

38. Dow, *Nation Building in Southeast Asia,* 158–64.

39. Dennis Duncanson, *Government and Revolution in Vietnam* (New York and London: Oxford University Press, 1968), 319.

40. Ibid., 321.

41. Douglas Pike, *Vietcong* (Cambridge, Mass.: M.I.T. Press, 1966), 251.

42. Hickey, *Free in the Forest,* 70–71; MAAG III Corps, MAGTN-III C-3, to Chief MAAG Saigon, 23 January 1963, Response to message asking information on progress or lack in US efforts to bring VC under control.

43. Osborne, *Strategic Hamlets,* citing *Vietnam Press,* 21 April and 7 July 1963. Osborne remarked, "On the basis of the figures provided for the lowland areas, these reports must be assumed to be far too optimistic."

44. Pentagon Papers, Gravel Edition, 2 (119): 690–701; Gareth Porter, ed., *Vietnam: The Definitive Documentation of Human Decisions,* 2 vol. (Stanfordville, N.Y.: Earl M. Coleman Enterprises, 1979), 2:169–74.

45. Hilsman, *To Move a Nation,* 451–67; Memorandum for the President, undated (evidently February 1963), signed by Michael V. Forrestal, Pentagon Papers, Gravel Edition, 2 (120): 717–25.

46. Thompson, *Defeating Communist Insurgency,* 133–37.

47. Report to General Harkins, 14 March 1963 (from the Westmoreland files at the CMH).

48. Paul D. Harkins, General, USA, letter, 12 April 1963, to Admiral H. D. Felt,

CINCPAC, Comments requested by your 20 March message on Colonel Serong's address (CMH files).

49. CMH files.

50. In his paper, "Pacification: The Overall Strategy in South Vietnam," submitted 22 April 1966 at the Army War College, Lt. Col. Robert M. Montague, who had served in Viet-Nam and later became a principal assistant to Robert Komer in the pacification program, recounted the mistakes made in the strategic hamlet program and said, "The hamlets, which were supposed to be anti-Communist centers of resistance, frequently turned out to be more anti-government than anti-Communist." He said that American advisors, including himself, found fraudulently reported successes. After the coup that overthrew Diem in November 1963, the VC stepped up their offensives, and, according to Montague, nearly 80% of "completed" hamlets crumbled. Robert Scigliano of Michigan State University, a dedicated student of Viet-Nam, wrote that between 1961 and mid-1963, the program in Central Viet-Nam did help to restore a favorable balance of power for the government. However, in the Delta the program was jeopardized, both because the settlements were more spread out and because the government pushed the program too fast and established hamlets in pro-guerrilla territory. "In An Xuyen province on the Camau peninsula, for example, the guerrillas control practically all the strategic hamlets, and in Long An and Dinh Tuong provinces, just south of Saigon, they control between 80 and 90% of them." See R. Scigliano, "Vietnam: Politics and Religion," *Asian Survey*, 4, no. 1 (January 1964): 672.

51. An appendix to Osborne, *Strategic Hamlets*, contains a translation of Memorandum No. 58/CV of the NLF, dated 5 August 1963, outlining what had been done in combatting the strategic hamlets and setting out tasks for the future. The document was captured in Tay-Ninh, August 15, 1963. Volume 1 of *Vietnamese Studies*, published in Hanoi in 1964, contains reports on the struggle against the program. "Special War and Liberation Struggle in South Vietnam," by Moc Vien (pp. 76–96) was especially significant.

52. Thompson, *Defeating Communist Insurgency*, 138–39.

53. Hilsman, *To Move a Nation*, 502–5. Also Memorandum of Conversation, White House Meeting, September 10, 1963, recorded by Roger Hilsman (Hilsman Papers, Kennedy Library), and National Security Council Executive Committee Conference with the President, September 10, 1963, recorded by Bromley Smith (NSF, Kennedy Library). See also USOM Rural Affairs Division, Second Informal Appreciation of the Status of the Strategic Hamlet Program, 1 September 1963; this report by the division that Rufus Phillips headed was even less optimistic than his remarks at the President's September 10 meeting. For example, this passage:

Progress has been best in the II Corps in completing the *establishment* phase of the program. However, even in this area by conservative estimates, no more than 50% of the hamlets constructed can be considered satisfactory from the point of view of possessing a true will to resist the Vietcong. Continued effort stressing hamlet development to give the hamlet people an economic and political stake worth defending, is absolutely essential if the program is to succeed.

54. These documents are in CMH. The Memorandum for the President of 2 October 1963, reporting on the visit of Robert McNamara and General Maxwell Taylor to Viet-Nam, said that there were lags in the economic and civic action of the strategic hamlet program and that:

Without this element, coupled with effective hamlet defense measures, what are called "strategic hamlets" may be only nominally under GVN control. We were particularly struck by some evidence that a hamlet's readiness to defend itself often bears a direct relation to whether the Province Chief, with U.S. help, has managed to make a convincing start on civic action.

The two high officials reported the view of the vast majority of military commanders consulted that military success might be achieved in the I, II and III Corps areas by the end of 1964, but that victory in IV Corps would take longer—at least well into 1965. They recommended that about 1,000 US personnel be withdrawn by the end of 1963. The report is in NSF and the Hilsman Papers at the Kennedy Library. JCS to CINCPAC 118 05/1945 Z Oct 1963 (NSF, Kennedy Library) reported that the President had approved the military recommendations. It directed that the military campaign be completed in I, II, and III Corps by the end of 1964, and in IV Corps by the end of 1965. It said (as McNamara and Taylor had) that the emphasis should be on clear-and-hold instead of terrain sweeps, and on consolidation of the strategic hamlet program.

55. Karnow, *Vietnam*, 257.

56. Hilsman, *To Move a Nation*, 522–23.

57. Duncanson, *Government and Revolution in Vietnam*, 327, 339.

58. William E. Colby and Peter Forbath, *Honorable Men: My Life in the CIA* (New York: Simon and Schuster, 1978), 175–78, 203–4, 218, 222.

CHAPTER 4. THE BEGINNINGS OF THE REFUGEE PROBLEM

1. Chapter 3.

2. International Voluntary Services (IVS) Annual Report 1962–63, 12. Dan Whitfield later became the USOM province representative in Quang-Tri. In his testimony before the Senate Refugee Subcommittee on September 28, 1965 (Hearing record, 304–15) he described a military operation in the Ba-Long Valley next to Laos which brought 2,500 anti-Communist refugees to secure territory. Whether these were the same as the people mentioned in the IVS report is not known.

3. Edmundo Navarro, USOM province representative in Tay-Ninh, testimony at Senate Refugee Subcommittee hearing, September 28, 1965, 293–304.

4. Senate Subcommittee Hearing, July 14, 1965 (Hearing Record 56–63).

5. Dr. Stephen F. Cummings, interview, December 19, 1986, with author. Cummings was USOM refugee advisor in Binh-Dinh province from December 1965 to October 1966, and went on to become the regional advisor for IV Corps in the Mekong Delta. After this he was the liaison officer of the CORDS Refugee Division with the Ministry of Social Welfare and Refugees until mid-1969. See also the statement on July 13, 1965 of Edward M. Kennedy, Chairman of the Senate Refugee Subcommittee (Hearing record, 2).

6. Senate Refugee Subcommittee Hearing record, July 13, 1965, 5–6.

7. *Final Report of the Research Project: Conduct of the War in Vietnam* (US Army, May 1971). The quotations are from pp. 24 and 34. This document is in the Center of Military History (CMH), Washington, D.C.

8. Hundreds of such American newspaper reports were compiled by Seymour Melman in his book, *In the Name of America: The Conduct of the War in Vietnam by the Armed Forces of the United States, as Shown in Published Reports* (New York: Dutton, 1968).

9. Danny Whitfield, testimony to the Senate Refugee Subcommittee, September 28, 1965, Hearing record, 307.

10. Senate Refugee Subcommittee Hearing record, September 28, 1965, 294–5, 298.

11. Ibid., 298, 300.

12. Malcolm W. Browne, *The New Face of War* (Indianapolis and New York: Bobbs-Merrill, 1965), 165–66. Browne gave no further details of this incident.

13. Jack Shulimson and Major Charles M. Johnson, USMC, *U.S. Marines in Vietnam: The Landing and the Buildup 1965* (Washington, D.C.: US Marine Corps, 1978), 37–39, 47–48.

14. Ibid., 62–65; also see Guenter Lewy, *America in Vietnam* (New York: Oxford University Press, 1978), 54–55. The commentary is Lewy's.

15. Shulimson and Johnson, *U.S. Marines in Vietnam*, 69–83; Lewy, *America in Vietnam*, 54–55.

16. *Interviews Concerning the National Liberation Front of Vietnam*, Rand File No. DT-135(1), Part Two, 136–40, 183–85.

17. Lewy, *America in Vietnam*, 57–59; Stephen Cummings, conversation with author, December 19, 1986.

18. Neil Sheehan, "Vietnam Peasants Are Victims of War," *New York Times*, February 15, 1966.

19. Rand Corporation File No. AG-402, interrogation report, March 2 and 3, and April 1, 1966, 13–18.

20. Rand File No. AG-402 Suppl. (NVA), interrogation report, August 24, 1966, 26–27, 29–30.

21. Browne, *The New Face of War*, 119.

22. *The War in Vietnam*, Film A-428, Reel 4, Honolulu Conference, 1966, in the Lamont Library of Harvard University.

23. Thich Nhat Hanh, *Lotus in a Sea of Fire*, with a foreword by Thomas Merton (New York: Hill and Wang, 1967), 109–12. The book deals with the damage that the war, and especially the Americans, were doing to Vietnamese society and morals. The author was received by Pope Paul VI on July 16, 1966, and the book contains a summary of Nhat Hanh's remarks on that occasion.

24. Lewy, *America in Vietnam*, 61–62.

25. Bernard Fall, "Commentary on Bui Van Luong," in *Viet-Nam, The First Five Years*, ed. Richard W. Lindholm (East Lansing: Michigan State University Press, 1959), 55.

26. Ibid, 59.

27. Allan E. Goodman, Lawrence M. Franks, and Nguyen Thi Huu, *The Causes and Consequences of Migration to Saigon, Vietnam* (New York: SEADAG, Asia Society, August 1973).

28. Ibid., 25.

29. The April 1972 Special Manpower Survey of the National Institute of Statistics, as cited by Allan Goodman, found that 32.8% of the estimated 1,759,480 people in the Saigon Prefecture were migrants, of whom 16% (92,338) had come from North Viet-Nam. Goodman reported finding clusters of Northerners who had originally settled in Central Viet-Nam but then fled when their areas became insecure, but he did not say how many there were. They would be included in the aggregate figure of Northerners. Projecting the percentages to the entire metropolitan area but excluding the Northerners yields a figure of 574,469 war-related migrants from Central and South Viet-Nam (32.8% migrants, of whom 62.7% were war-related). This calculation is admittedly tenuous,

since the Manpower Survey was not limited to migrants who arrived in 1964–72. Goodman did not estimate the total number that his sample represented.

30. Hung Thanh Huynh, in a telephone conversation with the author, March 7, 1987.

31. "Humanitarian Problems in Indochina," Senate Refugee Subcommittee hearing, July 18, 1974, 13.

32. Chien Thang Plan (CMH files).

33. Paul E. Suplizio, Major, USA, "A Study of the Military Support of Pacification in South Vietnam, April 1964-April 1965," a thesis presented to the Faculty of the US Army Command and General Staff College for the Master of Military Art and Science degree. Ft. Leavenworth, Kans., 1966. Suplizio later became an advisor in CORDS.

34. Shulimson and Johnson, *U.S. Marines in Vietnam*, 115–16, quoting from a letter to McNamara, 11 November 1965.

35. Ibid., 133–41. Lt. Colonel William R. Corson, USMC (ret.), who was named commander of the CAP in February 1967, has written a passionate but informative account of it in his book, *The Betrayal* (New York: Norton, 1968), 174–98.

36. Lewy, *America in Vietnam*, 62–63, citing the after-action report (AAR) of operation Lanikai and Office of the Assistant Secretary of Defense (Special Action) (OASD [SA]), SEA *Analysis Report*, January 1967, 15.

37. This paper is in the files of the International Rescue Committee at the Hoover Institution on War, Revolution, and Peace, Stanford University, Palo Alto, California.

38. Dr. Stephen F. Cummings, conversations with the author, December 19, 1986, and January 14, 1987.

39. Richard C. Holdren, End of Tour Report, May 19, 1968. Holdren had arrived in Da-Nang as USAID Regional Refugee Advisor early in 1966. However, General Thi, who was exiled to the United States for siding with the Buddhists during the Struggle Movement later in 1966, told me on November 11, 1986, that he didn't have many refugees and that he did not believe in moving people around. His view was that the government had to protect people, not move them away from their ancestral homes. He did help to move 15,000 from Chu-Lai when the American base was established there. He also said that he had not allowed any defoliation in I CTZ while he was Corps Commander in 1964–66.

40. Lt. Col. Ngo Thanh Tung, Province Chief of Quang Nam, memorandum of conversation with Richard Burnham, USOM Saigon, September 7, 1965 (CMH).

41. Philip Geyelin, "The Vietnamese Refugee Problem," *The Reporter*, 33 (September 23, 1965): 43–45.

42. Sector Advisor, Quang-Ngai sector, to Senior Advisor, MACV, 30 August 1965, enclosing the report of the two officers (CMH).

43. Jeffrey J. Clark, Captain, USAR (MOBDES), "Historical Project, Army Civil Affairs Operations in Southeast Asia," DAMO-ODS Memorandum for the Record, January 25, 1974, CMH.

44. Senate Subcommittee Hearing record, July 13, 14, 20, 27, August 4, 5, 10, 18, September 17, 21, 28, 30, 1965, especially 1–15, 39–84, 87.

45. Ibid., 163–65.

46. Ibid., 169–70.

47. Ibid., 320–27.

48. Ibid., 331–35.

49. 89th Congress, 2nd Session, Senate Report No. 1058, *Refugee Problems in South Vietnam*, March 4, 1966, 15.

50. Richard Eder, "U.S. Refugee Plan for Vietnam Set," *New York Times*, August 31, 1965.

51. American Council of Voluntary Agencies for Foreign Service, Inc., "Notes on Meeting of September 2, 1965 with AID/Washington and Voluntary Agency Personnel on Recent Developments in Vietnam."

CHAPTER 5. THE BEGINNINGS OF A REFUGEE AND WAR VICTIMS RELIEF PROGRAM, 1964–67

1. *Vietnam Statistical Yearbook 1964–65*, volume 12, National Institute of Statistics, 1966, 263 (exchange rates) and 286–87, 294 (budget estimates, furnished by the Directorate General of Budget and Foreign Aid). The Vietnamese fiscal year was the calendar year.

2. Ibid., 296–97.

3. Tran Quang Thuan, interviews with the author, October 6, 1976, and December 8, 1987 in Los Angeles.

4. Ibid. Also, Hung Thanh Huynh (his Anglicized name), interview with the author, in Stamford, Connecticut, May 24, 1985.

5. Interview with Mr. Thuan by the author, October 8, 1976, telephone interview March 14, 1987, and interview December 8, 1987; interview with Mr. Hung, May 24, 1984.

6. John Thomas, letter to the author, March 17, 1987.

7. John Thomas, unpublished manuscript.

8. GAO (General Accounting Office) report of October 1967 concerning the Refugee Program for Vietnam, costs (Senate Refugee Subcommittee Hearing record 1967), 287.

9. Ibid., 285.

10. John Thomas manuscript.

11. Ibid.

12. Embassy Saigon telegram 2725, January 27, 1966.

13. This material is from the Lyndon Baines Johnson Library and was studied on Film A-428, Reel 4, *The War in Vietnam*, Honolulu Conference, 1966, at the Lamont Library of Harvard University.

14. Ordinance 22-SL-HP-VP, February 22, 1966.

15. GAO Report, 285–86. The GVN fiscal year allows an additional five months for the expenditure of operating funds and up to three years for capital funds. It is not known whether the GAO took account of those "complementary periods."

16. The copy that I brought back from Viet-Nam and used in the writing of this book was about three inches thick.

17. Special Report for the White House, *Refugee Programs*, August 15, 1966, no attribution, presumably by AID.

18. Hung Thanh Huynh, interview with the author, May 24, 1985. Mr. Huynh accompanied Dr. Que on some of those trips. He said that this policy had been enunciated by Minister Thuan and Minister Lieng earlier, but had evidently not been explained by them to the field commanders.

19. Eric M. Hughes, Refugee Coordinator, ORC Bulletin 25, November 4, 1966, transmitting in English and Vietnamese *Policy Guidelines for Assistance to Refugees— 1966*, issued by the GVN Special Commissioner for Refugees, 11 pages.

20. Asia Training Center, University of Hawaii/AID, *Debriefing of a Refugee Coordinator: Vietnam 1965–66*, No. 86612, 11–14. The coordinator was Eric Hughes.

21. *Vietnam Statistical Yearbook 1969*, 379.

22. Presidential Ordinance 005-a-TT-SLL, November 9, 1967.

23. General Accounting Office, "GAO Supplemental Inquiry Concerning the Refugee Relief Program for Vietnam," in *Civilian Casualty and Refugee Problems in South Vietnam, Findings and Recommendations*, ed. Senate Refugee Subcommittee, May 9, 1968, 55–56. In 1967, the exchange rate was 118 piasters to the dollar.

24. Special Report for the White House, *Refugee Programs*, August 15, 1966, 3.

25. Ibid., 3.

26. Ibid., 3.

27. Edward Marks, interview with the author in New York, October 2, 1986.

28. GAO Report, Senate Refugee Subcommittee, 1967 Hearing record, 286.

29. Draft unsigned memorandum of conversation (CMH).

30. Richard C. Holdren, "The Refugee Situation in I CTZ," Briefing Paper for III MAF Staff Meeting, 26 July 1967; idem, Regional Refugee Advisor of CORDS, End of Tour Report, May 19, 1968.

31. Holdren, End of Tour Report.

32. State Department telegrams 17923, August 8, and 18618, 19619, and 19244, August 11; Saigon telegram 2966 EXDIS, August 12, 1967; all in CMH.

33. Ambassador Robert W. Komer, memorandum to Lt. General Robert E. Cushman, Jr., August 15, 1967, transmitting copies of the letter.

34. State 21579, August 16, 1967, "Confidential, Eyes Only" for Komer. There was a tendency in both Washington and Saigon to overclassify communications. All these messages have since been declassified.

35. Nguyen Phuc Que, Minister, letter to Ambassador Komer, August 22, 1967.

36. Saigon TOAID 2856, September 16, 1967. This and the weekly telegraphic situation reports (sitreps) are at the CMH.

37. Holdren, End of Tour Report, 10.

38. Senate Refugee Subcommittee, 1967 Hearing record, 94–108. The Hearing record gave the name of the AID accompanying officer as Dr. Arthur Branscomb, but Mr. Holdren, who received the group in I CTZ, says it was Dr. Martha Branscomb. She became a good friend of both of us.

39. Senate Refugee Subcommittee, *Civilian Casualty and Refugee Problems in South Vietnam: Findings and Recommendations*, May 9, 1968, 33–38.

CHAPTER 6. MOUNTING COMBAT AS A GENERATOR OF WAR VICTIMS

1. Douglas Pike reported that in the years 1960–66, the VC had killed many unpopular and corrupt officials, but had also ruthlessly wiped out virtually the entire class of natural village and hamlet leaders (that is, those who, by virtue of age, wisdom, or strength of character, were turned to for advice or leadership by the people). These were village elders, school teachers, religious leaders, and the like. He said: "Many villages by 1966 were virtually depopulated of their natural leaders, who are the single most important element in any society. . . . By any definition, this NLF action against village leaders

amounts to genocide.'' Douglas Pike, *Vietcong* (Cambridge, Mass.: MIT Press, 1966), 248.

2. Human Sciences Research, Inc., *The Refugee Situation in Phu-Yen Province, Viet-Nam* by A. Terry Rambo, Jerry M. Tinker, and John D. LeNoir. (McLean, Virginia: Human Sciences Research, Inc., July 1967). In addition to the general survey, 23 family heads were asked more detailed questions designed to bring out changes in rural conditions resulting from insurgent and counterinsurgent activities, 24 were asked questions relating to the economic aspects of the problem, 13 GVN officials were interviewed, 49 nonrefugee family heads who had remained in their hamlets were surveyed, and a number of refugees who had resettled at Cam-Ranh Bay were interviewed.

3. Ibid., 5–27, 176–99.

4. Ibid., 34–51.

5. Ibid., 52–57, 60–67.

6. Ibid., 75, 77, 83–84, 92–99, 107–8.

7. Ibid., 111–120.

8. Human Sciences Research, Inc., *The Refugee Situation in Dinh Tuong Province,* by Jerry M. Tinker, Field Research Memorandum No. 6, August 1967, vii, 1–7, 22–35.

9. Ibid., 10–12.

10. Ibid., 13–21.

11. Ibid., 8–10.

12. Ibid., 36–52.

13. Human Sciences Research, Inc., *Refugee Movement in Revolutionary Warfare: A Study of the Causes and Characteristics of Civilian Population Displacement in Viet-Nam,* by A. J. Rambo, Gary D. Murfin, and David De Puy. Research and writing completed August 31, 1968.

14. Ibid., iii–iv, 1–9. I question some of these generalizations about revolutionary warfare in Viet-Nam. The GVN, after the Diem regime, did not demand total commitment, and was not able to enforce even its more limited demands. I and some others who had been involved in insurgency and counterinsurgency are firmly of the opinion that both insurgents and those trying to defeat them should, for both moral and practical reasons, be subject to the restraints of international humanitarian law, which does make a distinction between combatants and noncombatant civilians. In Viet-Nam we could not influence the behavior of the VC/NVA in this respect, but some of us could and did influence the behavior of the US and Vietnamese governments.

15. Ibid., 47–56.

16. George Goss, Chief, CORDS/REF briefing of COMUSMACV, 8 September 1967; *Vietnam Statistical Yearbook*, National Institute of Statistics, 1969, p. 379.

17. Donald A. Henderson, Major Henry J. Lewis, and Tri, Task Force Oregon Operations, MACCORDS Evaluation Report, 13 September 1967, 1–7; The CORDS Research and Evaluation Division (RE) was created by Ambassador Komer. The military and civilian evaluators, American and Vietnamese alike, were carefully chosen and trained to report and analyze objectively, without fear or favor. Their reports constitute probably the most reliable information on military and pacification developments in Viet-Nam.

18. Ibid., 5, 7, 8, and 11.

19. Jerry L. Dodson, ''Evaluation of Refugee Handling Operations in Quang Ngai Province,'' MACCORDS-RE, 4 September 1967.

20. ''Task Force Oregon Operations,'' 8–9, and Inclosure 2, Report by Tri, 4, MACCORDS Evaluation Report, 13 September 1967.

21. Jonathan Schell, *The Military Half* (New York: Vintage Books, 1968), 182–96.

22. A translation of almost all the *Asahi Shimbun* reports was published under the title, ''Villages in the Battlefield, The Vietnam War and the People,'' in the *Japan Quarterly*, 15 (April-June 1968): 159–79. It is from this article by Honda Katsuichi that I have taken this account.

23. Ibid., 160–71.

24. Schell, *The Military Half*.

25. Ibid., 10, 12–13, 14–15, 50, 83, 105, 127.

26. Ibid., 131–38.

27. Ibid., 51 (Second ARVN Division), 165 (complaint of an ARVN captain).

28. Paul Nitze, who had been Deputy Secretary of Defense, in *The Lessons of Vietnam* edited by W. Scott Thompson and Colonel Donaldson D. Frizell (New York: Crane, Russak, 1977), 199. This was the proceedings of a seminar on the subject with a number of prominent participants and experts on the war. Nitze confused the Schell articles and the book with *The Village of Ben Suc* by the same author, which will be discussed later in this chapter. As the discussion proceeded in the seminar, Professor Ithiel de Sola Pool, referring to Nitze's remarks, said the fact that Robert McNamara was so badly shaken by the manuscript ''means that the level and penetration of understanding of the realities of Vietnam were deplorable.'' Pool pointed out that some, like Sir Robert Thompson, General Lansdale, and Gerald Hickey understood Vietnamese society, but their views were not brought into the control structure (Ibid., 274–75).

29. James D. Hataway, Jr., memorandum to the Ambassador, ''Subject: House Destruction in Quang-Ngai and Quang-Tin,'' December 12, 1967, originally Secret.

30. Comments on the Schell manuscript, 16 December 1967, 16 pp., originally Secret.

31. James D. Hataway, Jr., memorandum to the Ambassador, ''Subject: Destruction in Quang Ngai and Quang Tin,'' January 26, 1968, originally Confidential.

32. General William C. Westmoreland, *A Soldier Reports* (Garden City, N.Y.: Doubleday, 1976), 287–88. The general was badly misinformed about the territory east of Route 1. There were in fact scores of farming and fishing communities in that stretch of land in both Quang-Ngai and Quang-Tin provinces, as the other reports cited above have made clear. During the period of the heaviest Allied military campaigns, thousands of people in southern Quang-Ngai literally went underground, living in tunnels and rooms dug into the hard ground (interview with Dr. Stephen F. Cummings, November 4, 1987). That was also the case on the Batangan peninsula, as was discovered during Operation Russell Beach later. I visited a number of hamlets and refugee camps in that area during 1969 and 1970.

33. DepCORDS flag memorandum, 7 August 1967, to Chief/REF.

34. R. W. Komer to Chief of Staff, ref.: Acting AC of S memorandum 6 September; subject: ''Evaluation of Refugee Handling in Quang Ngai,'' 16 September 1967, Dodson report.

35. Walter T. Kerwin, Jr., Major General, USA, Chief of Staff, memorandum for Deputy COMUSMACV for CORDS, 12 October 1967.

36. Combined Campaign Plan, 1968, AB 143, Annex C, Refugee Support.

37. Saigon TOAID 4026, October 14, 1967.

38. R. W. Komer, memorandum for General Westmoreland, ''Subject: Refugees,'' 28 November 1967 (enclosing copy of the message to LTG Cushman).

39. Lt. Gen. Cushman, Msg PO102254Z Dec 67, Secret, for Ambassador Komer, MAC Eyes Only.

40. Charles T. Cross, Acting Deputy for CORDS, I CTZ, memorandum, Personal, to Ambassador Komer, 7 December 1967.

41. H. L. T. Koren, Deputy for CORDS, III MAF, to Ambassador Komer, memorandum, Subject: "Refugee Situation in I CTZ, in Preparation for Kennedy Visit," 14 December 1967.

42. The Joint Chiefs of Staff, Office of the Special Assistant for Counterinsurgency and Special Activities, the Joint Staff, "Subject: After Action Report—Field Trip, Vietnam 22 November-3 December 1967, to review refugee progress," 13 December 1967 (CMH).

43. Seymour J. Deitchman, *The Best-Laid Schemes: A Tale of Social Research and Bureaucracy* (Cambridge, Mass. and London: MIT Press, 1976), 337–39.

44. Ibid., 340–42.

45. Guenter Lewy, *America in Vietnam* (New York: Oxford University Press, 1978), 245, 276.

46. Thomas C. Thayer, *War without Fronts: The American Experience in Vietnam* (Boulder and London: Westview Press, 1985), 47–48.

47. *Vietnam Statistical Yearbook*, National Institute of Statistics, 1969, 332–33 (source: Ministry of Health).

48. GAO Supplemental Inquiry Concerning Civilian Health and War-Related Casualty Program in Vietnam (B-133001), February 1968, Appendix to *Civilian Casualty and Refugee Problems in South Vietnam: Findings and Recommendations*, Senate Refugee Subcommittee, May 9, 1968, 40–41.

49. Robert H. Nooter, Deputy Coordinator, Bureau of Supporting Assistance, Agency for International Development, statement before the Senate Refugee Subcommittee, May 8, 1972, cited in Thayer, *War without Fronts*, 126.

50. Senate Refugee Subcommittee Hearings 1967, 217–22.

51. Dr. F. J. L. Blasingame, chairman of the team, Executive Director, American Medical Association; Dr. John Knowles, Director General, Massachusetts General Hospital; and Dr. Alvin J. Ingram, professor of orthopedic surgery, University of Tennessee, testifying October 9, 1967 (Ibid., 5, 21).

52. Dr. Theodore Tapper, resident in pediatrics, University of Pennsylvania, Philadelphia; and Dr. John Constable, plastic surgeon, Boston; accompanied by Dr. Herbert Needleman, Committee of Responsibility, Philadelphia; and Mrs. Esther Smith, Executive Director; testifying on May 18, 1967 (Ibid., 235, 238–39).

53. Ibid., 223.

54. Ambassador W. E. Colby statement to the Senate Refugee Subcommittee, April 21, 1972, 41 and Annex K, cited in Thayer, *War without Fronts*, 130. Neither Colby nor Nooter explained the discrepancy between Colby's total of 43,849 and the figure of 48,734 given by Nooter to the same subcommittee a couple of weeks later (Thayer, *War without Fronts*, 126).

55. AID Administrator William S. Gaud, statement, October 16, 1967, and General Humphreys, statement May 10, 1967 (Senate Refugee Subcommittee 1967 Hearing record, 153–56, 234).

56. General Humphreys said he had operated on people referred by Viet-Cong hospitals (Ibid., 222).

CHAPTER 7. ONCE AGAIN, PLANNED FORCIBLE RELOCATION OF PEOPLE

1. Lt. General Bernard William Rogers, *Vietnam Studies, Cedar Falls—Junction City: A Turning Point* (Washington, D.C.: Department of the Army, 1974), iv-vii, 15–77, 158. Colonel Hoang Ngoc Lung, *The General Offensives of 1968–69* (Washington, D.C.: US Army Center of Military History, 1981), 5. General Rogers and Colonel Lung are the principal sources of the information about the military operation, and about the return of the enemy to the Iron Triangle shortly after the operation. Also see Jonathan Schell, *The Village of Ben Suc* (New York: Knopf, 1967), 1–77. This had originally been an article which had taken up most of one issue of the *New Yorker* (Bernard Fall, *Last Reflections on a War* [Garden City, N.Y.: Doubleday, 1967], 247–49).

2. Rogers, *Vietnam Studies*, 39; Fall, *Last Reflections*, 250.

3. W. C. Westmoreland, General, United States Army, Commanding, memorandum for the Record, 17 January 1967, subject: "Meeting with General Thieu on 13 January 1967 at his Office in the Palace," originally Top Secret (CMH).

4. Saigon telegram 15790, 171200Z January 1967; COMUSMACV telegram 04072 to CINCPAC, Info SECDEF and CJCS, 030300Z Feb. 67. Also see Schell, *Ben Suc*, 77–132.

5. Memorandum to the Director, Region III OCO, Bien-Hoa, from the Province Representative, Binh-Duong, 20 February 1967, "Subject: After Action Report, Operation 'Cedar Falls.' "

6. Human Sciences Research, Inc., *A Study of Mass Population Displacement in the Republic of Viet-Nam*, Part I, *Analysis of the Forced Relocation Process*, by A. T. Rambo, D. Brown, and P. Estermann, research and writing completed May 15, 1968, 7, 13, 15, 16, 41, 48, 51, 59, 87. Also see MACCORDS-RE, 26 September 1967, "Evaluation of Lai Thieu Refugee Resettlement Project."

7. Dr. Stephen F. Cummings, in a conversation with the author on November 4, 1987, perceptively analyzed the lack of GVN political work among refugees.

8. This information comes largely from reports of the IRC team to its New York headquarters, which has made its files available to me. Nick Price, a Vietnamese-speaking "generalist," was particularly insightful about what the evacuees and refugees were thinking (compare his letters of October 21 and December 16, 1967). Also see the monthly reports of the team, beginning May 1, 1967.

9. Human Sciences Research, Inc. (HSR), *A Study of Mass Population Displacement in the Republic of Viet-Nam*. Part II. *Case Studies of Refugee Resettlement*, by David A. DePuy, Philip L. Esterman, and Dale K. Brown. I have used the Review Draft of May 1968, hereafter called HSR Case Studies. Pages 3–45 cover the DMZ evacuation and the Cam-Lo resettlement. Also see Major Henry J. Lewis and Jerry J. Dodson, MAC-CORDS-RE: Evaluation Report, Cam Lo Resettlement Project, 14 August 1967, 8 pp., hereafter called Cam-Lo Evaluation.

10. HSR Case Studies, 7–8. AD/RDW to Ambassador Komer, Memorandum, 20 May 1967, with a covering memo 25 May from Barry Zorthian to Komer. David A. DePuy, "Cam-Lo Refugee Census Report," Memorandum for the Record, 15 August 1967.

11. HSR Case Studies, 14, 16.

12. Cam-Lo Evaluation, 6–7, 8.

13. HSR Case Studies, 16–17.

14. Cam-Lo Evaluation, 2, 4.

15. Ibid., 4–5; HSR Case Studies, 18–24. The HSR *Study of Mass Population Displacement*, part I, 14, said that 70% of the DMZ evacuees were unemployed.

16. Cam-Lo Evaluation, 5–6; HSR Case Studies, 37–45.

17. Senate Subcommittee, Hearing record, October 9, 1967, 73. Mr. Luce at the same time questioned whether the Cedar Falls evacuation had been necessary.

18. Human Sciences Research, Inc., *A Study of Mass Population Displacement in the Republic of Viet-Nam*, parts I and II.

19. HSR Case Studies, 89–121. HSR Part I, 7, is the source of data on the number of families in each site and the number surveyed.

20. HSR Case Studies, 49–79.

21. Ibid., 131–35, 148, 154.

22. Ibid., 136–38, 155.

23. Ibid., 140, 142–43, 166.

24. Ibid., 179–83, 203.

25. Ibid., 183–84, 202.

26. Ibid., 188, 195, 215, 217.

27. Ibid., 231–36, 245, 247, 250–53, 257–58.

28. HSR Part I, i-xi, 3–50. The 14 other countries where this test was administered were the United States, the German Federal Republic, Yugoslavia, Poland, Japan, Brazil, Nigeria, India, Israel, Egypt, Cuba, the Dominican Republic, Panama, and the Philippines. A group of American Negroes interviewed in 1959, part of the US sample, felt that the present was slightly worse than the past, but the difference was not significant.

29. Ibid., 51–52.

30. Ibid., 73–86.

31. Ibid., 90.

32. Jerry Dodson, Field Evaluator, MACCORDS-RE, 22 July 1967, Memorandum for the Record, subject: "Edap Enang Resettlement Project," July 22, 1967. Also see Gerald C. Hickey, *Population Relocation in the Highlands*, 20 March 1969 (CORDS Information Center), and Gerald Hickey, *Free in the Forest* (New Haven and London: Yale University Press, 1982), 165–66.

33. Dodson, "Edap Enang Resettlement Project," 6.

34. L. Wade Lathram, Assistant Chief of Staff (AC of S), CORDS, memorandum, July 27, 1967, to Ambassador Komer, transmitting the RE evaluation; George I. Forsythe, Maj. Gen., USA, assistant deputy for CORDS, memorandum for AC of S, CORDS, 28 July 1967.

35. Hickey, *Population Relocation in the Highlands*, 11–14.

36. DTG 111242 Z Jan. 1968 from LTG Rosson, CG I FFV for Komer in response to your MAC 00365.

37. Peter Rosenblatt, memorandum to Ambassador Komer, 30 January 1968, subject: "Edap Enang."

38. MACCORDS/REF/RE: Memorandum, 21 January 1967, for Lathram; Robert E. Matteson, memorandum for Lt. Gen. William B. Rosson, "Subject: Report on 20 January Visit to Edap Enang."

39. George Goss and Col. A. H. Ringler, MACCORDS/RE/REF: Memorandum for the Record, "Subject: Edap Enang Resettlement Project." These papers are in the CMH.

40. Author's handwritten notes on the visit. I reported my findings to Goss and Lathram.

41. Telegram from PSA Pleiku 29 Jan. 68 to I FFV/SA CORDS, attn Ref. Off. Nha Trang, info. ref. Saigon. The message and Komer's note are in CMH.

42. M. G. Forsythe, MACV telegram 05917, DTG 281150Z Feb 68, to CG I FFOR-CEV/SA II CTZ, from MACJOIR for DepCORDS, "Subject Edap Enang." No reply was in the CMH file.

43. Hickey, *Population Relocation in the Highlands*, 14–17; CORDS Pleiku Province Reports, April and May 1968. John F. Thomas, Chief, Refugee Division, MACCORDS-REF: Evacuation of Montagnards in Pleiku Province, to AC of S, CORDS. This memorandum, drafted by L. A. Wiesner, expressed agreement with the objectives of a paper prepared by the Mission Ethnic Minorities Sub-Committee, "which are to assure the greatest possible freedom of movement, consistent with military security, to the Montagnards in question and to elicit a decision that they are not to be forcibly kept at Edap Enang." Also see Maj. Bill Reiff, MACCORDS-REF, 26 June 1968, to Mr. John Thomas, Field Trip I CTZ, II CTZ.

44. Hickey, *Population Relocation in the Highlands*, 16–17; Pleiku Province Report, May 1968.

CHAPTER 8. THE COMMUNIST TÊT AND MAY OFFENSIVES OF 1968

1. Colonel Hoang Ngoc Lung, *The General Offensives of 1968-69* (Washington, D.C.: U.S. Army Center of Military History, 1980), 33–37, wrote that Resolution 13 of the North Vietnamese Politbureau directing preparations for a General Offensive/General Uprising had been acquired in October 1967, and that other captured documents indicated planning for the offensive, but the GVN did not take these reports seriously. Until late January 1968, the US military had given no greater credence to such reports. Neither ally was able to discover when the planned offensive was to take place.

2. Ambassador Komer, memorandum to AC of S CORDS, 16 December 1967.

3. Ambassador Komer, "1967 Refugee Situation" (Year-end Summary), 28 December 1967, talking paper.

4. MACCORDS-REF, Year-End Report, 4 January 1968; Memorandum from AC of S CORDS to CofS, "Outline of CY 68 Refugee Resettlement Program," undated; W. C. Luken, "Refugee Situation Report," January 1968, undated, drafted 10 Jan. 1968.

5. Don Oberdorfer, *Tet!* (Garden City, N.Y.: Doubleday, 1971), 117–20.

6. I had refrained from telling my wife about the attacks in my letter of January 28, but did give her an account of them in my letter of February 4. She saved these letters.

7. Lung, *The General Offensives*, 43–44.

8. Ibid, 46–50; Oberdorfer, *Tet!*, 121–31.

9. Oberdorfer, *Tet!*, 116–17. Much of Oberdorfer's dramatic but well-researched book deals with the attacks on Saigon and the other cities and with the defensive actions of the Vietnamese and US troops.

10. CORDS/REF Disaster Relief, Situation Report (Sitrep), 3 February 1968.

11. Samuel L. Popkin, "Pacification, Politics and the Village," *Asian Survey* 10, no. 8 (August 1970): 669.

12. Harvey Meyerson, *Vinh Long* (Boston: Houghton Mifflin, 1970), 13–34; also see Oberdorfer, *Tet!*, 153–54.

13. MACCORDS-RE, Trip Report. Visits 22–28 February by John C. Lybrand, Capt.

David A. Pabst, David Kenney, and Binh Huy Giam; Trip Report, by LTC Hurd and Capt. Donald C. Cox 20–25 February 1968; CORDS/REF Sitrep, 5 March 1968.

14. Oberdorfer, *Tet!*, 184.

15. Bill Vale, letter to Carel Sternberg, Saturday afternoon, February 24, and Sunday, February 25, 1968.

16. Sitreps, February 7-April 26, 1968.

17. *Status of Recovery*, 4 April 1968, a memorandum probably by Clayton McManaway (CMH); RVN, Prime Minister's Palace, Central People's Relief Committee, "Relief Information Synopsis" of July 15, 1968. Some of the data collected by this committee differed from those of the MSWR.

18. MACCORDS-RE, Evaluation Report, "Refugee Affairs in Tuy Phuoc District, Binh Dinh," 6–7. The evaluation was conducted April 24–27 by LTC William A. Donald, USMC, and a Vietnamese evaluator.

19. A. H. Ringler, Col., GS, Chief, RE, to Clayton McManaway, "Evaluation of the Refugee Situation in Phong Dinh," 18–21 April conducted by LTC Hurd.

20. Dorothy Selves (nurse), letter, to IRC New York, February 11, 1968.

21. Oberdorfer, *Tet!*, 129–30.

22. Ibid., 202–32. Oberdorfer gave details of a number of executions and burials. Also see Lung, *The General Offensives,* 80–82.

23. Truong Nhu Tang, with David Chanoff and Doan Van Toai, *A Vietcong Memoir*, (San Diego, New York, London: Harcourt Brace Jovanovich, 1985), 154–55.

24. Allan E. Goodman, "The Dynamics of the United States-South Vietnamese Alliance: What Went Wrong," in *Vietnam as History: Ten Years After the Paris Peace Accords*, A Wilson Center Conference Report, ed. Peter Braestrup (Washington, D.C.: University Press of America, 1984), 94.

25. Samuel Popkin, "Commentary: The Village War," *Vietnam as History*, ed. Braestrup, 102–3.

26. MSWR Message No. 93-XH-TN/TN/CT/1, February 3, 1968.

27. MSWR Message No. 452-XH-TN/KTN/CT, February 14, 1968.

28. I am indebted to Lt. Col. (ret) Harry T. Johnson, who was a key member of the Joint Recovery staff, for this analysis. (Interview with the author, May 22, 1978, at Johnson's home.)

29. Saigon telegram 39547, October 5, 1968, "Subject: Final Report on Project Recovery," drafted by William M. Stewart, approved by R. W. Komer.

30. Oberdorfer, *Tet!*, 182.

31. Saigon 39547, October 5, 1968, "Final Report on Project Recovery."

32. Sitrep, 4 March 1968.

33. Sitreps, 8 and 21 March 1968.

34. Sitrep, 27 June 1968.

35. Sitrep, 25 April 1968.

36. C. E. McManaway, Memorandum for Minister Cang, 29 April 1968, "Subject: Acceleration of Tet Evacuee Relief and Resettlement."

37. Lung, *The General Offensives*, 93–99; LTC. Le Van Duong, J-5 (Joint general Staff, RVNAF, 1969), Senior Editor, *Series of Combat History: The Viet Cong "Tet" Offensive (1968)* (Saigon: Joint General Staff, 1969), 191–93.

38. Sitrep, 9 May 1968.

39. Sitrep, 16 May 1968.

40. CORDS Binh-Duong Province Report, June 1968.

41. John C. Russell, CORDS/NLD, Memorandum for Mr. Clayton McManaway, "Subject: Meeting with Dr. Ho van Minh," 16 May 1968.

42. Lung, *The General Offensives*, 100–102.

43. DTG 291204 JUL 68 (CONFIDENTIAL) msg no. 21952 to CG's USARV, COM-NAVFORV, III MAF, I FFORCEV, II FFORCEV, SA IV CTZ, CO 5th SF Grp. Abrams sends. This message was covered by memoranda from Major General Corcoran, Chief of Staff and from Komer, referencing a memcon with Lu Y. For an explanation of AB 143, see pp.145–46.

44. Sitreps, 23 and 30 May, 6 and 27 June, 8 August, and 20 September 1968.

45. Sitrep, 6 June 1968.

46. Sitrep, 27 June 1968, and my personal observation.

47. Saigon telegram 39547, Final Report on Project Recovery, October 5, 1968.

48. CORDS Refugee Division, *Assessment of Refugee Program*, 1968, 2–4.

49. See, for example, the Quang-Tri Province Report May 1968; Monthly Refugee Field Program Report, IV CTZ, period ending July 31, 1968; and Monthly Refugee Field Program Report, I CTZ, Period 1 through 31 August 1968. The September 1968 refugee figure is from MACCORDS/REF: The Refugee Problem, September 30, 1968.

CHAPTER 9. THE COMING OF AGE OF THE REFUGEE–WAR VICTIMS PROGRAM

1. CORDS Refugee Division, "Status of Refugees," 21 March 1968.

2. Ibid., 28 March and 2 May 1968.

3. Saigon telegram 26718, May 8, 1968, drafted by L. A. Wiesner, concurred in by J. F. Thomas, approved by W. E. Colby.

4. Unpublished manuscript by John Thomas, 10–12.

5. Ibid., 16–17.

6. Ibid., 22–23.

7. John F. Thomas, Chief, Refugee Division, CORDS, letter to Nguyen Phuc Que, Minister, May 22, 1968.

8. Republic of Vietnam, Ministry of Health, Social Welfare and Relief, August 13, 1968, No. 6732/YTXHCT/2/KCT/VP, Communiqué from Dr. Tran Lu Y, Minister of HSWR: "Definition of a Refugee."

9. Stephen F. Cummings, GVN Liaison Officer, MACCORDS/REF, 10 September 1968, Memorandum for Record, "Subject: Memorandum of Conversation with Mr. Huynh Thanh Hung, Assistant to MHSWR for Refugees and Relief."

10. Refugee Census Report (blue card); W. Luken, MACCORDS/REF: "Resettlement of Refugees, to Corps Refugee Advisors from Chief, REF/REP," 28 June 1968.

11. An amusing sidelight: As we were being driven from the Can-Tho airport, we passed the large plant of Brasseries et Glacieres d'Indochine (Breweries and Ice Makers of Indochina, a French company which produced the popular "33" beer). One of the computer experts observed, "I understand the law says they've got to wear 'em."

12. Because of crowded conditions which were strange to the peasant refugees (who had normally washed and bathed frequently), and lack of training in how to cope with sanitation and personal hygiene when water and open space were scarce, many camp water wells quickly became polluted, and the group latrines (one for each five families)

were not cleaned and frequently were not used. Small children usually ran around naked and without sandals, picking up parasites from feces and other litter on the ground and skin diseases from lack of cleanliness. From the Viet-Nam experience, governmental and private agencies learned some lessons about sanitation and health education that have been applied in refugee camps since 1975.

13. Sitrep, August 8, 1968. Also see William C. Luken, Reports Officer, to Preston Hogue, Liaison Special Assistant, Memorandum, "Survey of Out of Camp Refugees," August 15, 1968.

14. Sitreps, 4 and 19 October 1968; CORDS Refugee Division, *Refugee News*, October 1968, 1.

15. MHSWR Communiqué 6805/YTKHCT/KCT/CTNNCC, "Nationwide Refugee Registration Plan," November 4, 1968.

16. Dr. Tran Lu Y, Minister of HSWR, "Census of Out-of-Camp Refugees and Relief Assistance Provided for this Category of Refugees," MHSWR Relief Branch, March 13, 1969, No. 2394/YTXHCT/2/KCT.

17. Thomas, manuscript, 17–18.

18. Sitrep, 18 July 1968; author's notes on a conversation with Hung Thanh Huynh, May 24, 1985.

19. S. T. Cummings; memorandum of conversation with Dr. Lu Y, June 6, 1968.

20. Sitrep, 15 August 1968.

21. CORDS/REF, Sitreps, 22 August and 19 October 1968.

22. CORDS Refugee Division, Assessment of Refugee Program 1968, 11.

23. World Relief Commission, *World Relief Reporter* (Long Island City, NY), Spring 1968; Sitrep, 4 October 1968.

24. CORDS/REF, "Significant Issues" for Period 15–21 November 1968.

25. CORDS III MAF, I CTZ, "Monthly Refugee Field Program Report," period 1 through 30 June 1968, 5, and period 1–31 August 1968, 7.

26. Sitrep, 22 August 1968.

27. Survey by the 29th Civil Affairs Company, August-September 1969. The survey found health and other facilities substandard in the Vietnamese camp, and the company's Eighth platoon worked with Revolutionary Development (RD) cadres to improve them. Also see Department of the Army, 29th Civil Affairs Company, "Periodic Civil Affairs Report." AVCA DNG-B-29, 11 October 1969, 3.

28. Author's notes on the visit, December 27, 1969; Agriculture Advisor to Chief, Refugee Division, "Trip Report—Quang Tri Jan. 26–30, 1970," Memorandum, February 2, 1970.

29. C. D. Crocker, Special Assistant for VSD, memorandum to Alexander Firfer, DepCORDS/I CTZ, "VSD Field Trip Report—I CTZ," memorandum April 28 to May 21, 1970, 2.

30. Chief of the Province, Quang-Tri, to MSW, Official message, May 1970.

31. John D. Miller, Summer Institute of Linguistics (SIL), Danang, letter to author, May 14, 1970. The SIL was engaged in producing written versions of the various tribal languages. Mr. Miller spoke and wrote the Bru language. Also see author, "DFC Weekly Staff Meeting, Refugees," memoranda to the Deputy for CORDS, 19 and 27 June 1970.

32. Crocker, "VSD Field Trip Report," 2; EMA/REF ADV, report, undated (but apparently June 1970), "Development of the Cua Bru," enclosing "Memo of Record regarding Discussion with Land Service Chief 18 June '70"; Claude F. Raffin, CPT, Signal Corps, Commander, Eighth AA Platoon, 29th Civil Affairs Co., Memorandum

20 June '70, to Province Chief, Quang Tri Province, through Province Senior Advisor; Le Van Nghiem, Quang Tri Ethnic Minority Service Chief, "Huong Hoa District—Brou Problem; and Economically (*sic*) Development Plan to Up-Grade the Self-Help Development Village for Montagnard Bru in Cua valley, Huong Hoa," 6 June 1970.

33. Author's notes on the visit, June 22; author's memorandum to DFC, 27 June 1970.

34. CORDS XXIV Corps, Refugee Report, June 21 through July 20, 1970, 2–3.

35. Ibid., August 21 through September 20, 1970, 4; CORDS War Victims Division, I MR, Quang Tri Province as of October 20, 1970, "Narrative Province Overview," 2; Ibid. as of December 1970, 1–2; ibid. as of April 20, 1971, 1.

36. Social Development and War Victims Division, CORDS, Headquarters FRAC, Report, period 21 Dec–20 Jan. 1971–72, 5.

37. Martha Barnhill, administrator of CORDS/REF I CTZ, (who coordinated the move), letter to author, March 18, 1986.

38. Dr. Tran Lu Y to General Lam, Memorandum 4590/YTXHCT/KTN/CT, July 13, 1968; General Lam to Minister of HSWR, letter no. 80-DV-XDNT, July 29, 1968; Dr. Lu-Y to Lt. General, I Corps Commander, (concurrently GRVN Delegate) memorandum 6355/YTXHCT/2/TNCS/DC, October 9, 1968.

39. Thomas, manuscript, 19–20.

40. CORDS Refugee Division, *Refugee News*, October 1968, 3; Dr. Lu-Y, memorandum of October 9, 1968 to General Lam.

41. L. Wiesner, Memorandum, "Subject: Meeting with Dr. Lu Y," December 31, 1968.

42. Author's notes on the visit to the three settlements, March 19, 1969.

43. DEPCORDS II CORPS NHA, Megellas to Hitchcock, message 7751–10–69, Oct. 6, 1969; CORDS/REF-SGN, Hitchcock to Megellas, message 10–2235–69. However, officials of the Ethnic Minorities Ministry (MDEM) were under the impression that 6,000 Vietnamese had actually been moved onto the Nam-Phuong plantation in Lam-Dong in December 1968 or January 1969 (Hickey, *Free in the Forest*, 193–94). I visited the plantation in May 1969, when the only Vietnamese there were the administrators and 38 inmates of the institute for beggars. 14,000 roofing sheets were still being held in the province warehouse for the interzonal project, which did not materialize.

44. CORDS Refugee Division, "Cam Lo Reservoir Completed," *Refugee News* 2, July 1968, 3.

45. RCS, MACCORDS MR I, "Refugee Report," period 21 April–20 May 1971, 2.

46. Author's notes on the visit, December 27, 1969.

47. War Victims Advisor, Quang-Tri, to War Victims Division, "Update on Cam Lo and Ha Thanh Resettlement Areas," Da Nang, 9 March 1971; Thomas E. Estrada, Chief, War Victims Division, CORDS, XXIV Corps, letter to author, 29 April 1979.

48. Report of conversation of Quang-Tri refugee advisor Ellsworth Amundson with deputy province chief Dien, January 22, 1970; RVN No. 20/VP/HDTS Cam Lo District, Report of the ordinary meeting of the village council of Truong-Son, April 8, 1970.

49. Special Assistant to the Dep CORDS, Rural Survey Program, "Survey of the Attitudes of Refugees in Twelve Selected Camps in I CORPS," April 11–27, 1970.

50. Social Development and War Victims Division, CORDS XXIV Corps; Report, period November 21-December 20, 1971, 1, 3; Saigon telegram 0474, 12093Z Jan 72.

51. Saigon telegram 7483, section 1 of 3, 200942 Z May 72.

52. Food for Peace Officer, memorandum to Chief, Refugee Division, "Subject:

Inspection of Ha Thanh Camp, Quang-Tri, Meeting in Quang-Tri,'' Ref. FFP, 2 February 70.

53. Author's notes on the various meetings and conversations.

54. Food for Peace Officer, Memorandum to Chief, Refugee Division, Trip Report—Hue and Quang Tri, 1/20–22, 1970.

55. Author's notes on conversations; Update on Cam Lo and Ha Thanh Resettlement Areas, 9 March 1971, op. cit.; letter, 29 April 71 from Thomas E. Estrada to the author.

56. General Tran Thien Khiem, Deputy Prime Minister to P&D, "Subject: Planning for Permanent Resettlement and Homecoming of Refugees," CPDC/CC Circular No. 1294/PThT/BDXD, August 13, 1969; Dr. Tran Nguon Phieu, Minister of Social Welfare, "Subject: Relief and Normalization of Refugees," Communiqué No. 8924-BXH-KCT-TNCS-TT, September 23, 1969.

57. Refugee Division, Hq. XXIV Corps; period 21 May through 20 June 1970, 4–5.

58. Senate Refugee Subcommittee, *Refugee and Civilian War Casualty Problems in Indochina, a Staff Report*, September 28, 1970, 3, 6.

59. Sitreps, 18 July and 20 September 1968; "IRC Poultry Raising Project a Marked Success," *Refugee News*, no. 4 (September 1968); "Social Welfare Medals for IRC Team Members," *Refugee News*, no. 7 (December 1968).

60. Sitrep, 4 October 1968; Cecil B. Lyon, "Report on Vietnam and Hong Kong," 1/15/70, 5–6.

61. Peter Giehrl, International Rescue Committee, report on Lai-Thieu, June 4, 1968; Francoise Queneau, IRC Director in Vietnam, letter to Garret Ackerson, June 10, and her memorandum to Carel Sternberg, June 16, 1968.

62. Report, Queneau to Sternberg, October 14, 1968.

63. Report from Queneau, October 24, 1968.

64. Jane M. Murphy, Gary D. Murfin, Neil L. Jamieson III, A. Terry Rambo, Jeary Adrian Glenn, Leroy P. Jones, and Alexander H. Leighton, "Beliefs, Attitudes, and Behavior of Lowland Vietnamese," in *The Effects of Herbicides in South Vietnam*, vol. 18 (Washington, D.C.: National Academy of Sciences, 1974), ch. 8: 14–29, 31–33.

65. Ibid., ch. 8: 45.

66. International Ministerial Level Conference on Social Welfare, United Nations, New York, September 3 to 12, 1968: Ministry of Health, Social Welfare and Relief, "Social Services in Viet Nam," 7, 17–20.

67. Robert Johnson, USAID/ADLD, and Louis Wiesner, Acting Chief, CORDS/REF, memorandum to J. P. Robinson, Acting Director, USAID/VN, and W. E. Colby, AC of S, CORDS, "Transfer of Functions, Personnel, Equipment and Records of Social Development division from USAID/ADLD to CORDS/REF," 29 May 1968.

68. Thomas manuscript, 20–22.

69. Minister of Health, Social Welfare and Relief, memorandum to the Director of DGBFA (Directorate General of Budget and Foreign Aid), "Draft of American Aid Budget," September 21, 1968.

70. L. A. Wiesner, Acting Chief, CORDS/REF, memorandum to all USAID II personnel, "Subject: Orphanage Visits," 28 Sept. 1968; Sitrep, 19 October 1968.

71. Thich Nhat Thien, "Report," October 25, 1968 (Buddhist Social Welfare Center).

72. Wells Klein, *Vietnam refugee program and related concerns*, unsigned, undated report prepared for the Senate Refugee Subcommittee (and published as an appendix to *Refugee and Civilian War Casualty Problems in Indochina, A Staff Report*, September

28, 1970), September 1969, 6–7. The subcommittee omitted this and other complimentary passages.

73. Chief, CORDS/REF to AC of S, CORDS, 21 January 1969, enclosing a memorandum to Chief of Staff with a draft memorandum from Colby to Ambassador Bunker.

CHAPTER 10. THE FLOWERING OF PACIFICATION, 1969–72: MILITARY DOCTRINE AND CIVIL ADMINISTRATION SUPPORT PEOPLE'S WAR

1. Prime Minister, Communiqué 4306-XDNT-51, October 19, 1968.

2. Darwin D. Harbin, Lt. Col., Infantry, Deputy Sector Advisor, Military, "Operation Lam Son 260/Nevada Wager, Vinh Loc District-Thua Thien Province," undated; Civil Operations and Revolutionary Development Support, III MAF, I CTZ, Danang, Monthly Refugee Field Program Report—I CTZ, period 1 through 30 September 1968, 1. Page 6 of the Field Program report gave the number of returned refugees as 8,000.

3. Speech by Major General Cao Hao Hon to the Central Pacification and Development Council, 11 September 1970, 2.

4. Dr. Tran Lu Y, Minister of HSWR, Communiqué No. 919-YTXHCT-2-KCT-TT, November 20, 1968. It was commonly referred to as Communiqué 919.

5. John Nesvig, CORDS/NLD Sadec, *Return-to-Village—Sadec's Experiences*, July 1969, edited by Tom Scygiel, CORDS/REF Saigon, October 1969; L. Wiesner, memorandum, "Subject: Meeting with Dr. Lu Y, December 31, 1968," January 1, 1969, enclosing a memorandum to Dr. Tran Lu Y, "Draft of Proposal to Extend Benefits under MHSWR Communique 919."

6. Raymond Fontaine, memorandum to John Thomas, "Minister Tran Lu Y's Visit to Sadec," CORDS/REF, *Significant Issues for Period January 1 through 9, 1969*, 2.

7. CORDS/REF, *Significant Issues*, January 1 through 9, 1969, 2.

8. "Combined Campaign Plan 1969," AB 144, and its Annex C ("Refugee Support"); "1969 Pacification and RD Plan" and its Annex IX ("Refugee Relief Program"), December 15, 1968; RVN Prime Minister's Office, (Central Pacification and Development Council) (CPDC) 15 February 1969; Circular 142 from Huynh Van Dao, Minister attached to the Prime Minister's Office, concurrently Secretary General of the CPDC, "Subject: Implementation of 1969 P and D Plan," February 15, 1969.

9. Richard A. Hunt, "Strategies at War: Pacification and Attrition in Vietnam," in *Lessons from an Unconventional War*, edited by Richard A. Hunt and Richard H. Shultz, Jr. (New York: Pergamon Press, 1982), 34–36.

10. Author's notes on a conversation with Mr. Megellas, May 17, and on a briefing by Colonel Franklin, Deputy Commander, 173rd Airborne Brigade, at LZ English, May 19, 1969. I had briefed the officers on the refugee program. However, when the 173rd finally did leave in 1971, the province and district officials and territorial forces, which had depended very heavily on the Americans, did not muster the necessary energy and courage to prevent the enemy from filling the gap (CORDS Binh-Dinh Province Reports, 3 June and 1 September 1971).

11. Author's notes on a meeting of II CTZ refugee officers, May 3, 1969.

12. Author's memorandum, 10 October 1969, to DFC, "Return of refugees to home village in Binh Dinh Province, II CTZ"; author's notes on Firfer staff meeting, October 17, 1969.

13. Stephen F. Cummings, memorandum for the record, "Trip Report—MHSWR Visit to Quang Tin, Quang Nam, Da Nang, Binh Dinh, August 10, 11, 1969''; author's notes on a statement by Dr. Phieu at meeting of regional refugee officers, August 18, 1969.

14. Staff report, September 28, 1970, 7.

15. See, for instance, author's memorandum for the record, 21 March 1969, "Subject: Meeting of Regional Refugee Officers at the Refugee Directorate, Saigon, March 14–15, 1969."

16. Dr. Lu Y's speech delivered at the closing ceremony of the seminar for III and IV CTZ SWR Service Chiefs, undated, translated by CORDS-REF, 9 January 1969.

17. Annex IX to 1969 Pacification and RD Plan (Refugee Relief Program).

18. Author's notes on the regional refugee officers' meeting of July 17 in Saigon and the II CTZ refugee officers' meeting of July 19–20, 1969, in Nha-Trang.

19. S. F. Cummings, draft memorandum on a conversation of William K. Hitchcock with Dr. Lu Y, 2 July 1969.

20. Stephen F. Cummings, memorandum for the record, "Subject: Conversation with Minister of HSWR Tran Lu Y," 25 June 1969.

21. Prime Minister's Office, CPDC/CC, Circular No. 1294/PThT/BDXD, "Subject: Planning for Permanent Resettlement and Homecoming of Refugees," August 13, 1969.

22. Dr. Tran Nguon Phieu, Minister of Social Welfare, Communiqué No. 8924-BXH-KCT-TNCS-TT, "Subject: Relief and Normalization of Refugees," September 23, 1969.

23. CORDS REF, III MAF, Monthly Refugee Field Program Report (I CTZ), 1–31 December 1968; "Quang-Tri Refugee Program August 1968—August 1969," an undated, unsigned report in the files of the US Army Center of Military History, 24, 30–31; author's notes on the February 17, 1970 ceremony at Gia-Dang.

24. An example was recounted in Report No. 390-XH-TT-VI, dated May 4, 1970, prepared by Vo Trong Khoa, SW Controller of I CTZ, on his visit to Kim-Ngoc return-to-village (RTV) hamlet of 45 families, Nam-Hoa district, Thua-Thien province. Khoa said the RTV'd refugees still owned their land: "There was no question of dispute to get it back." The refugees were also given equal portions of public land.

25. I CTZ Refugee Field Program Report, period 21 November 69 through 20 December 69, 2, and 21 December 69 through 20 January 70, 7. For reasons that were not clear, the SWR (Social Welfare and Relief) service had reported only 35,114 refugees returned home in Thua-Thien, while the US narrative had shown 128,158. After examining the data, CORDS/REF I CTZ decided that the US narrative was correct. This meant that the national RTV figure should be increased accordingly, to 581,264. A story about the Kubota tractors ("Modernization Churns Up Village Life") was published in the *Stars and Stripes*, December 10, 1969, 7.

26. The Senate Refugee Subcommittee staff report cited above (n. 14) charged that the refugees settled along the Street Without Joy were far from their original homes. I found no evidence to confirm this.

27. Author's notes on meetings with Firfer; notes on author's visit to Quang-Nam, October 20, 1969, including conversations with refugee advisor James Ready, PSA Lt. Colonel Blakely, Colonel Tin, and Le Van Thai, SWR service chief; memorandum from author to Chief Economic Development Division, CORDS II MAF, 19 December 69: "Dong Tien Project (Go Noi Island Plan)," (Quang Nam Province); note on author's

visit to the island, February 19, 1970; Quang-Nam SWR Service, "Estimation of Establishment the Phu Ky RTV Area—Dien Ban, Quang Nam," approved by Le Tri Tin, Province Chief, 17 March 1970; Message 467 from I CTZ SW inspector representative Pham Huu Nhan to Quang-Nam SW service, 21 May 1970; notes by Thomas E. Estrada and author on briefings at II MAF 28 May, 9 and 13 June 1970; War Victims Division, CORDS—MR-1, report, period 21 September through 20 October 70, 5–6.

28. Refugee Field Program Report, I CTZ, 21 November through 20 December 69.

29. Refugee Field Program Report, II CTZ, 10 August 69, 1–2.

30. Table, page unnumbered, in William K. Hitchcock's Opening Statement, Senate Foreign Relations Committee, Hearings on Vietnam, February 17–20, 1970.

31. Ibid.; CORDS/REF, *Refugee Population*, December 1969, 4.

32. Author's notes on regional refugee officers' meeting in Saigon, December 11–12, 1969.

33. Author's notes on a visit to Quang-Ngai, October 24–25, 1969.

34. Author's notes on the I CTZ province plans; Hq. XXIV Corps, CORDS Refugee Field Program Report, period 21 January through 20 February 1970, 5–6.

35. W. E. Colby, DEPCORDS/MACV, memorandum for AC of S, CORDS, "Subject: Refugees," 10 May 1970.

36. CORDS/REF, "Explanatory Notes on Refugee Population Figures," May 25, 1970; General Accounting Office, *Refugee and Civilian War Casualty Problems in Vietnam*, prepared for the Senate Refugee Subcommittee, December 14, 1970, 17. The GAO said: "We believe that the above figures . . . are misleading and significantly understated as to the true number of people in need of assistance."

37. Robert H. Nooter, Deputy Coordinator, Bureau for Supporting Assistance, AID, statement presented to the Senate Refugee Subcommittee, May 8, 1972, 38. His tabulation had reduced the number of refugees returned home the year before (1969) to 189,000, while increasing the number resettled to 821,000. No explanation was given for those changes, and I doubt their correctness.

38. Joseph Buttinger, *Vietnam: A Political History* (New York: Praeger, 1968), 43, 50–51.

39. Senate Refugee Subcommittee, *Refugee and Civilian War Casualty Problems in Indochina, a Staff Report*, September 28, 1970, 35, 37–38; Various articles from the American press, April-May 1970, reprinted in the Senate Refugee Subcommittee hearing record of May 7–8, 1970, 95–103; author's notes on remarks of Norman Firnstahl at regional refugee officers' meeting in Saigon, May 26, 1970. Also author's interview with Dr. Phieu N. Tran in Amarillo, Texas, November 22, 1987.

40. CORDS-DMAC-MR 4, "1970 DEPCORDS Annual Report," War Victims Division, 6–10; Franklin R. Stewart, Director, War Victims Directorate, CORDS, memorandum for Johannes Hoeber, Chief, Refugee and Social Welfare Staff, Bureau of Viet Nam, AID/Washington, 6 February 1971, "Successful Resettlement of Cambodian Repatriates."

41. United Nations General Assembly, 1 September 1970, Executive Committee of the High Commissioner's Programme, "Note on Allocations from the Emergency Fund for Refugees in the Republic of Viet-Nam."

42. Charles Stewart Callison, *Land to the Tiller in the Mekong Delta* (Berkeley: University of California Press, 1983). Collison got the distribution statistics from "Terminal Project Appraisal Report" for land reform, AID Washington, October 7, 1975. See also Brig. Gen. Tran Dinh Tho, *Pacification* (Washington, D.C.: US Army Center

of Military History, 1980), 142–44. Jeffrey Race, *War Comes to Long An* (Berkeley: University of California Press, 1972), 272–73, was skeptical of the political benefits, but he seems to be in the minority.

43. Nooter, statement to subcommittee, 38.

44. "War Victims Division," CORDS, MR-1, period 21 May-20 June 1971, 3–4.

CHAPTER 11. THE DARK SIDE

1. Lt. Gen. W. R. Peers, USA (Ret.). *The My-Lai Inquiry* (New York and London: W. W. Norton & Co., 1979), 180–81. General Peers had been commander of the 4th Division and was responsible for establishing Edap-Enang. Afterwards Peers became deputy commander and then commander of all US forces in II CTZ and senior advisor to the Vietnamese Corps commander. The inquiry arrived at "a very conservative figure of 175 to 200"; the Criminal Investigation Division conducted a census-type evaluation and came up with the figure of 347 killed.

2. Ibid., 230–31.

3. Ibid., 234–37.

4. For example, Joe McGinnes, "Writer Finds GIs in Viet Defend Civilian Killings, Say War is War," *Chicago Tribune*, April 10, 1971; Charles A. Anderson, *The Grunts* (San Rafael, California: Presidio Press, 1976), 177–85.

5. Tran Van Don, *Our Endless War: Inside Vietnam* (San Rafael, California: Presidio Press, 1978), 156–57.

6. Chief, CORDS/REF to AC of S, CORDS, 2 Sept 68 (items provided for AC of S Information Book). The memorandum listed the incidents in July and August.

7. See for instance CORDS/REF to AC of S, CORDS, 6 March 1969, "Assessment of Priority Programs for the Month of January, 1969," item 1b.

8. Message cite TTHI/REF 108363 TO DFC/REF/III MAF DANANG, 2 Jan '69.

9. "Summary of VC Attacks Generating Refugees, 2/28/69"; "Summary of VC Attacks Generating War Victims as of 1200 hours 10 March 1969." Both documents were unattributed, but probably were compiled by the CORDS Refugee Division, Saigon. The casualty figures for Kon Horing have been revised in the light of my notes during a visit on September 3, 1969.

10. Decree No. 1025-ND-TNCS, June 13, 1966, by the Chairman of the Central Executive Committee, signed by Major General Nguyen Cao Ky.

11. CORDS Refugee Directorate, "Significant Issues for the period 27 February through 5 March 1969."

12. CORDS, "Significant Issues for the period 5–11 April 1969," 2.

13. CORDS, "Significant Issues for the period 11–17 May 1969," 1-2.

14. So said Dr. Tran Nguon Phieu, Minister of Social Welfare, at a meeting of regional refugee officers on December 12, 1969, according to my notes on the meeting.

15. Security Officer, memorandum 26 January 1970, to Chief, Refugee Division, I CTZ, and messages on 7, 16, and 19 January and 2 February 1970 from PSA Refugee CORDS Quang-Ngai and Quang-Nam.

16. Message cite QNAM/DEV 04–02–70, 10 APRIL '70, to DFC/I CTZ.

17. Message cite PSD/QNAM 05–06–70, msg. undated, but each incident dated.

18. See message cite QNAM/REF 06–04–70 to DFC/REFUGEE/CORDS/XXIV CORPS/DANANG, 11 June '70; and I CTZ SW Insp. Representative message No. 534/XH/TT/VI dated 12–6–70 to Minister of SW Saigon and others, signed Pham Huu Nhan.

19. Author's notes and pictures on the visit.

20. "War Victims Division-CORDS MR-1," period 21 May–20 June 1971, 1 and tables.

21. Huynh Van Dao, Minister attached to the Prime Minister's office, concurrently Secretary General, CPDC, circular no. 142, 15 February 1969.

22. CPDC Postal Msg. No. 408/PTL.T/BDXD, April 17, 1969; JGS/RVNAO-J8 message No. 810-1/TTM-P3-BD, 24, April 1969, "Subject: Specification of Different Cases Concerning Population Movements, Refugee Temporary Relocation and Resettlement."

23. CORDS/REF, "Significant Issues for the periods January 17–23, January 24–30, and January 31-February 6, 1969."

24. Significant Issues for the period 7–13 February 199.

25. Significant Issues for the period 19–27 February 1969.

26. Report of Dr. John Levinson, who visited the area in April-May 1969, printed in the hearing record of the Senate Refugee Subcommittee, Part 1, June 24 and 25, 1969, 46; David Hoffman, "Statistics Are Hiding Refugees," *Washington Post,* December 14, 1969.

27. SWR Service Chief Quang Ngai, Le Dam, message No. 3166 TNCS/2, dated 12 Dec 1969, to the Pacification and Development Council and the Inspector MSW I CTZ; Vo Trong Khoa, Assistant Inspector Rep. MSW I CTZ, message No. 1161/XH/TT/VICT/CD dated 18 Dec 69 to Cabinet Office and Vice Minister (relief).

28. Inspector SW I CTZ, Memorandum No. 51/XH/TT/VI, 23 January 1970, to Dr. Minister of SW, Saigon, and Commanding General I CTZ concurrently Chairman of Pacification and Development Council, Danang, "Subject: Living Conditions of the Repatriated People in the Batangan Campaign, Quang Ngai."

29. Louis A. Wiesner, Chief, Refugee Division, memorandum, 29 January 70, to DFC, CORDS, III MAF, "Subject: Shortage of Food on Batangan Peninsula, Quang Ngai"; my hand-written notes on the visit, and my photos. Also see Tong Quyen, Letter No. 73/XH/TT/VI dated 28 Jan 1970, to the province chief and Dr. Minister of MSW Saigon; General Hoang Xuan Lam, I Corps Headquarters, message No. 135/BTL/QD I/VICT to Second Infantry Division, 4 February 1970.

30. B. J. Trout, Capt., USMC, to REF, CORDS, XXIV Corps, 11 June 70, "Subject: Trip Report to Quang-Ngai Province."

31. CORDS Refugee Division, Quang-Ngai province, War Victim Report, as of Apr. 20, 1971, 3–4.

32. I CTZ Refugee Field Program Report, period 21 November through December 20, 1969, signed by Louis A. Wiesner; J. A. Gaugush, Capt. USMC, Resettlement OFF/REF, CORDS III MAF, memorandum, 24 November 69, to C/REF, "Subject: Unrecognized Refugees, I CTZ."

33. Alexander Firfer, Deputy for CORDS, memorandum to Commanding General, III MAF, "Subject: Briefing of General Lam on Refugee Problems," 6 January 1970.

34. Hitchcock, memorandum, 21 January 1970, to Colby, "Subject: Generation of Refugees."

35. COMUSMACV, DTG 081628 Z Feb 70, to VMAC [all subordinate commands] Conf 19/70 (CORDS), "Subject: Generation of Refugees."

36. Prime Minister, Circular 857-PThT/BDPT/TU/TT, 2 March 1970.

37. W. E. Colby, memorandum of conversation, "Subject: Generation of Refugees," Participants: Lieutenant General Hoang Xuan Lam, CG, I CTZ, and Ambassador W. E. Colby, date: 9 March 1970, signed by W. E. Colby.

38. CORDS, Refugee Field Program Report, period 21 February through 20 March 1970, 4.

39. General Tran Thien Khiem, Prime Minister and Secretary General, CPDC, Circular 1166-PThT/BDPT/TU/TT, 18 April 1970, "Subject: Temporary Evacuation and Gathering of People for Hamlet Building."

40. DFC, CORDS, I CTZ, memorandum, 14 May 1970, to Director, REF, CORDS; William E. Colby, letter to Prime Minister Khiem, June 13, 1970.

41. I CTZ, Refugee Field Program Reports, period 21 February through 20 March 1970, 4; 21 March through 20 April 1970, 3–4; 21 April through 20 May 1970, 7; PSA Refugee CORDS, Quang-Nam, messages to DFC Refugee, CORDS, Da-Nang, 6, 7, and 12 March 1970; Louis A. Wiesner, report on meetings of 23 April 1970, at Hoi-An, with Mr. Hu'ng, the province chief, and others; P. J. Brown REF/Volag Officer, memorandum, 1 May 1970; Nguyen Huu Bich, Head of Relief Committee, Central Christian Youth Social Service, Da-Nang, *Relief News*, 24 April 1970; Vo Trong Khoa, I CTZ SW Insp. Representative (acting), memorandum to Director of Cabinet, MSW, Saigon, "Subject: Refugee Evacuees of Phu-Lac 6 and Chau-Son II of Quang-Nam Province", CORDS War Victims Division Reports, as of October 27, 1970, 1; as of December 29, 1970, 1; Quang-Nam War Victims Division Report, as of April 26, 1971, 2.

42. REF, Thomas E. Estrada, Memorandum to DFC, 14 May 1970, "Report of Visit to Quang-Ngai Province, 13 May 1970."

43. Author's notes on Firfer's staff meeting, May 22; John M. Welty, Chief, PPR, memorandum for LTC Nguyen Binh Thuan, Chief, I CTZ P&D Council Coordinating Center, "Subject: Proposal of Quang-Ngai Province to Relocate People in Mo-Duc District"; Refugee Division, period 21 May through 20 June 1970, 8.

44. Refugee Division, hq. XXIV Corps; period 21 May through 20 June 1970, 8–9.

45. Rural Survey Program, "Survey of the Attitudes of Refugees in Twelve Selected Camps in I Corps," April 11–27, 1970. The narrative report had 5 pages; there were 28 pages of tables.

46. W. E. Colby, DEPCORDS/MACV, letter to His Excellency Tran Thien Khiem, Prime Minister, June 13, 1970.

47. State Department telegram 123185, 310010 Z Jul 70; Saigon 12402, Aug 3, 1970; State 135409, 200105 Z Aug 70. The Department gave as its reason for the upgrading that fact that the report could damage relations with the GVN. That had been overtaken by events, since Colby had already sent it to the Prime Minister, but Saigon agreed to the upgrading.

48. Tad Szulc, "New Drives Swell Number of Vietnam War Refugees," *New York Times*, March 13, 1971; Clarke T. Baldwin, BG, GS, Director, International and Civil Affairs, ODCSOPS, memorandum for Deputy Chief of Staff for Military Operations, 23 March 1971, "Subject: War Victims in RVN."

49. CORDS Refugee Division, Quang-Ngai Province: Province Update Form, as of 20 April 1971, 1–2.

50. Henry Kamm, "Hopes Dim for the Millions Adrift across Indochina," *New York Times*, April 21, 1971, 1, 16; author's interview with Cushing in Washington, D.C., November 1986.

51. Gerald Cannon Hickey, *Free in the Forest* (New Haven and London: Yale University Press, 1982), 194; Maj. Bill Reiff to Mr. John Thomas, 26 June 1968, Field Trip I CTZ, II CTZ.

52. John G. Rogers, DPSA CORDS/Pleiku, to Refugee Division Chief, CORDS Re-

gion II, 19 March 1969, "Status of Plei Ring De Montagnard Refugee Resettlement Center."

53. Author's Draft Memorandum for Record: Trip Report—Pleiku Province—April 25–28, 1969. The final report must have been classified, because it is not in my files.

54. Author's draft trip report; Rogers's memorandum on Plei Ring De.

55. Author's draft trip report; author's outline for briefing of the Fourth Division.

56. CORDS Province Report, Kontum Province, period ending December 31, 1970.

57. Author's notes on the visit, June 28, 1969.

58. Hickey, *Free in the Forest*, 221-23; Harry T. Johnson, Jr., LTC, GS, Chief, CPDC Liaison Group, memorandum for the record, 4 May 1971. "Subject: Action Taken by CPDC/CC to Resolve the Problem Concerning the Relocations of Both Montagnards and Vietnamese (March–April)," enclosing a table showing each relocation, and other documents. Also, General Accounting Office (GAO). *Followup Review on Assistance to War Victims in Vietnam*, a report prepared at the request of the Senate Refugee Subcommittee, May 3, 1972, 22–24. The proposal for the initial relocation in Darlac had been referred to President Thieu, who approved it with the condition that only pacification funds be used, not those of the MSW, "since this is not a refugee problem." This was specifically cited in the Prime Minister's communiqué 1166 of April 18, 1970 and was one reason for its issuance.

59. Dr. Gerald C. Hickey, memorandum for the record, "Subject: Unlearned Lessons of History: Relocation of Montagnards," February 13, 1971, printed in the record of the Senate Refugee Subcommittee hearing of April 22, 1971, Part III, "Vietnam," Appendix III, 61–62; Hugh Manke, Viet-Nam Director, IVS, "Montagnard Relocation: A Summary," Subcommittee Senate Refugee hearing record, April 22, 1971, 63–66; Land Reform Office, USAID Saigon, memorandum "Describing Reasons for Montagnard Relocation," Appendix III, 67–72; Hugh Manke, "Ha Lan Village: The Story of One Relocation," Senate Refugee Subcommittee hearing record Appendix III, 72–73; Henry C. Bush, Control Data Corporation, Report on "Montagnard's Desiring to Return to Original Hamlet Sites and Vietnamese Farming Within Montagnard Hamlets," Appendix III, April 22, 1971, 73–75.

60. For example, an unnamed American missionary cited by Manke, "Montagnards Desiring to Return," 66. Manke's statement for the hearing said, "However, the Montagnards and many American observers believe that the *primary factor behind the relocations is to get the Montagnards off the land so that the Vietnamese can claim it.*" Release copy, (mimeographed), April 22, 1971, 3.

61. Lamar M. Prosser, Program Evaluation Officer, CORDS/MACV, "Final Report of Investigation: Montagnard Refugee Deaths, Pleiku Province, December 1970–April 1971," undated, 17 pp. The report was transmitted to Robert Nooter, AID Washington, by George D. Jacobson under cover of a letter dated 5 August 1972.

62. Col. Le Huy Luyen, MR 2 Assistant Commander, memorandum to MR 2/Deputy for CORDS, Nha-Trang, "Subject: Request for Support for the Implementation of 'Gathering People for Hamlet Establishment' Plans from Pleiku, Phu Bon and Darlac Provinces," February 17, 1971; Douglas Cozart, Chairman, Council of Voluntary Agencies, letter to Dr. Tran Nguon Phieu, Minister, March 15, 1971 (both printed in the record of the Senate Refugee Subcommittee, April 22, 1971, 54–56).

63. Hickey, "Unlearned Lessons of History," 62.

64. Author's interviews with Dr. Phieu, November 22, 1987, and with Han Tho Touneh, December 5, 1987.

65. Harry Johnson, "Action taken by CPDC/CC," 1–2.

66. Hickey, letter to Ambassador Colby, 22 February 1971.

67. Prime Minister, Communiqué No. 1412-PThT/BDPT/KH 11, May 12, 1971.

68. CORDS Province Reports, Pleiku, period ending 31 August; Binh-Thuan, periods ending 30 June, 31 July, and 30 September 1971.

69. CORDS Pacification Studies Group, "The People of the U-Minh Forest Area: A Survey of their Attitudes in the Context of Past and Present VC/GVN Activities," 26 pp. plus tables, undated, covered by a Disposition Form from MACCORDS to Chief of Staff, 18 June 1971, and a handwritten note from Colby to General Abrams initialed by the General.

CHAPTER 12. THE NORTH VIETNAMESE EASTER OFFENSIVE OF 1972

1. Truong Nhu Tang with David Chanoff and Doan Van Toai, *A Vietcong Memoir* (San Diego, New York, London: Harcourt Brace Jovanovich, 1985), 219–20.

2. Brigadier F. P. Serong, Australian Army (ret.), "The 1972 Easter Offensive," *Southeast Asian Perspectives*, Summer 1974, 25–26, 27–28; Lt. Gen. Ngo Quang Truong, *The Easter Offensive of 1972* (Washington, D.C.: U.S. Army Center of Military History, 1977), 29. These are excellent military accounts of the offensive. General Truong, who had been commander of MR-4 and before that, commander of the First Division, was named by President Thieu to be commander of MR-1 on May 3, 1972, after the fall of Quang-Tri, replacing Lt. Gen Hoang Xuan Lam.

3. US Embassy Saigon telegrams 4778 and 4823, April 7, 1972; telegram 4882, April 8, 1972.

4. Truong, *Easter Offensive*, 46; Serong, "1972 Easter Offensive," 34; Sir Robert Thompson, *Peace Is Not at Hand* (New York: McKay, 1974), 41. Also see a number of graphic articles with photos in *Stars and Stripes*, May 4 and 6, 1972.

5. Saigon telegrams 6470 (2 parts), May 5; 6582 (3 parts), May 6; and 7039 (2 parts), May 14, 1972; unsigned memorandum (probably by CORDS Social Development and War Victims Division of MR-1), "Relief for War Victims," May 18, 1972. In the frantic atmosphere of the time, refugee figures were by no means precise. Even many months later, GVN and US officials were still trying to figure out how many people in Quang-Tri had been overrun and gone north and how many had gone south as refugees. Cf. section 1 of Saigon telegram 16885, December 1, 1972.

6. Directorate for Refugee Affairs, CORDS, FRAC, RVN, "Population of MR-1 Refugee Sites, as of 26 May 1972," with penned notes updating to 29 May; Saigon 8239 (2 parts), June 5, and 8567, June 9, 1972.

7. Truong, *Easter Offensive*, 64–71.

8. Henry Kamm, "Horde of Ghost Refugees Get U.S. Food in Vietnam," *New York Times*, March 8, 1973.

9. Saigon telegram 04901, section 2, March 24, 1973.

10. All the year-end refugee statistics for 1972 in this chapter are from Garnett A. Zimmerly, AID, Acting Chairman, 34th weekly report of the Ad Hoc Vietnam War Victims Committee in Washington, January 3, 1973.

11. General Truong, *Easter Offensive*, 86–105; Serong, "1972 Easter Offensive," 31, 36, 41, 47–49.

12. Saigon telegram 6470, section 1, May 5, 1972; Saigon telegram 7483, May 27, 1972; Saigon telegram 8567, June 9, 1972.

13. Serong, "1972 Easter Offensive," 44–46; Truong, *Easter Offensive*, 105.

14. Saigon telegram 8567, June 9, 1972; Saigon telegram 11870, August 11, 1972.

15. Truong, *Easter Offensive*, 112–136. Also see William A. Stofft, Major, Armor, Field Evaluator, MACCORDS-PSG: Evaluation, Binh-Long Refugees, 1 May 1972, 10pp. This is a survey report on 43 refugees who were interviewed by evaluators of the Pacification Studies Group at a camp in Phu-Cuong, Binh-Duong province. Stofft, now a Brigadier General, later became Chief of the US Army Center of Military History.

16. Saigon telegram 6470, section 2, May 5, 1972.

17. Stuart A. Herrington, *Silence Was a Weapon: The Vietnam War in the Villages, A Personal Perspective* (Novato, California: Presidio, 1982), 126–133.

18. Truong, *Easter Offensive*, 144–155.

19. "Dinh Tuong: Hell in a Small Place," *Time*, September 11, 1972, 24.

20. Ad hoc Inter-agency Washington Committee on Vietnam Refugees, Thirty-fourth Weekly Report, January 3, 1973.

21. Raymond G. Fontaine, Chief, Refugee Division, CORDS/War Victims, MAC-CORDS-WV-R, 13 Oct. 72, Memorandum for the Record, "Subject: Chronology of Events Related to the Relief of War Victims, 1972"; Prime Minister, Decree No. 419-ND-ThT-BDPT, May 15, 1972; Donald Bremner, "Saigon Faces Big Decisions on Refugees," *Los Angeles Times*, June 7, 1972.

22. Saigon telegram 7483, Section 3, May 20, 1972.

23. Ad Hoc Vietnam War Victims Committee, Initial Report, AID/W, May 18, 1972.

24. Minister of Social Welfare, Circular No. 1188-BXH/KCT/NNCC/TrC/TT, "Subject: Regulations and Rates of the War Victims Relief," August 2, 1972.

25. Fontaine, "Chronology"; John R. Mossler, Director, MACCORDS, memorandum to Brig. Gen. James A. Herbert, Deputy Director, MACCORDS, "Subject: Project Agreement Revision for Project 307 War Victims Relief and Rehabilitation," June 20, 1972; Saigon telegram 12168, August 18, 1972.

26. Fontaine, "Chronology"; extracts from Cabinet minutes, weeks of September 17 and 24, 1972.

27. My notes on the Ad Hoc Committee meeting in Saigon chaired by Norman Firnstahl September 26, 1972.

28. Saigon telegram 13548, September 15, 1972.

29. Saigon telegrams 16004, November 10, 1972, and 17562, December 15, 1972.

30. James S. Ready, Acting Chief, SD&WVD, CORDS, FRAC, memorandum for the record, for ADFC MR-1, Danang, "Subject: Report of sub standard rice issue for Camp Books War Victims," October 2, 1972.

31. Anthony Faunce, Acting Inspector General of Foreign Assistance, memorandum to the Honorable John A. Hannah, Administrator, Agency for International Development, "Subject: Inspection of War Victims Program in Vietnam," December 6, 1972, 31.

32. Author's interview with Mr. Hu'ng in Stamford, Connecticut, August 15, 1987.

33. Ibid.; unsigned memorandum for the record, "Subject: Refugee Officers Meeting—October 10, 1972"; Consulate Da-Nang telegram 0256, November 6, 1972.

34. Henry Kamm, "Saigon Aides Suspended in Rice Scandal," *New York Times*, November 6, 1972.

35. MACCORDS-WV-R, memorandum for the record, "Refugee Officers Meeting—

October 10, 1972''; Faunce, "Inspection of War Victims Program," 5–7, 15–19, 29, 30–32.

36. Faunce, "Inspection of War Victims Program," 8.

37. Ibid., 11–12.

38. Ibid., 10–11, 19–30, 32–33.

39. AIDAC to Saigon, State telegram 193373, October 24, 1972.

40. Robert H. Nooter, Assistant Administrator, letter to George D. Jacobson, DEP-CORDS, and John R. Mossler, Minister-Director, November 8, 1972, enclosing the Preliminary Trip Report, November 8, 1972, from SA/VN/OP, William F. Mulcahy and SA/TCD/LD, Donald L. Goodwin.

41. Saigon telegram 16604, section 2, November 24, 1972; Saigon telegram 16885, section 1, December 1, 1972; and Saigon telegram 17917, December 22, 1972. Tad Szulc in his article misleadingly headlined, "State Department Urges End of Pentagon Role in Pacification," *New York Times*, December 24, 1972, gave a good summary of the IGA report, but said nothing about the remedial actions.

42. State telegram 015885, January 27, 1973, AIDAC.

43. Saigon telegram 01230, January 30, 1973.

44. John A. Hannah (signed by Maurice Williams, Deputy Admin.), memorandum for the Honorable Joseph S. Brown, Acting Inspector General of Foreign Assistance, "Subject: Inspection of War Victims Program in Vietnam," March 8, 1973; Louis A. Wiesner and D. B. Kraft, "IGA Inspectors Accomplishment Report," March 13, 1973.

45. Washington Ad Hoc Vietnam War Refugee Committee, Forty-fifth Weekly Report, March 19, 1973.

46. Thomas W. Lippman, "Quang-Tri Refugees Go Home," *Washington Post*, March 19, 1973; Ad Hoc Committee, Forty-sixth Weekly Report, March 26, 1973.

47. Ad Hoc Committee, Forty-seventh, Forty-ninth, Fiftieth, Fifty-second, and Fifty-fifth Weekly Reports.

48. Ad Hoc Committee, Fifty-eighth and Final Weekly Report, June 18, 1973.

49. Ibid.

50. Richard H. Shultz, "Vietnamization-Pacification Strategy 1969–72," in Richard A. Hunt and Richard H. Schultz, eds., *Lessons from an Unconventional War* (New York: Pergamon Press, 1982), 60–117.

CHAPTER 13. RESETTLEMENT AND RETURN OF REFUGEES TO HOME VILLAGES, 1972–74

1. Denis Warner, "Return to Mother Earth," *Asian Affairs*, 5 (May-June 1974), 332–45; Dr. Dan, letter to author, with enclosures, November 30, 1987.

2. Dr. Dan, letter to author, April 8, 1985.

3. Raymond Fontaine, memorandum to Franklin R. Stewart, "Subject: Trip to Phuoc Tuy for Relocation of Quang Tri Refugees," November 29, 1971.

4. American Embassy Saigon telegram 0474, January 12, 1972; James S. Ready, Acting Chief, Social Development and War Victims Division, CORDS, XXIV Corps, letter to author, March 2, 1972.

5. Saigon telegram 2050, February 12, 1972.

6. John C. Buchanan, Major, Infantry, Field Evaluator, MACCORDS-PSG, 8 May 1972, "Evaluation, Nui Le Catholic Refugee Resettlement—Long-Khanh Province."

7. Fact Sheet, "LD&HB in Long Khanh and Phuoc Tuy Provinces," probably prepared by CORDS WVD; Edward L. Block and Lucielo C. Ramirez, CORDS/War Victims, Refugee Division, "Report on Community Development Survey of Settlers Living in Dong Tam I, a Land Development and Hamlet Building Site in Long Khanh Province," October 10, 1972. A draft letter of October 12 from Dr. Dan to ADWV said that the Chams destined for Dong-Tam IV had come from Chau-Doc, Tay-Ninh, and Binh-Long. Dan asked for a financial commitment to support further moves.

8. Carole Steele, Memorandum to Franklin R. Stewart, through Raymond C. Fontaine, "Subject: Kien Phong Field Trip," 7 February 1972.

9. Jean A. Sauvageot, Major, USA, Special Assistant to the Director of CORDS, notes on CPDC Central Recovery meetings of 24 November and 8 December 1972. Sauvageot spoke fluent Vietnamese.

10. Dr. Dan's draft letter of 12 Oct 72; C. Steele, "Report on War Victim Problems and Progress," December 28, 1972.

11. The Prime Minister's Mission Order 448/PThT/HDTUC TTTPH, 20 February 1973, created a small interministerial group to examine the resettlement problem. The Prime Minister's Decree No. 259 ND/ThT/PC3, March 14, 1973, created the War Victim Resettlement and Rehabilitation Interministerial Committee, with Dr. Dan as chairman, Dr. Phieu, Minister of Social Welfare, vice-chairman, and the Ministers of Ethnic Minority Development, Agriculture, and Public Works, and the Undersecretaries of Interior and National Defense as members.

12. Saigon telegram 04343, section 1, March 17, 1973; Saigon telegram 05347, April 2, 1973; Saigon 05624, April 4, 1973.

13. Robert H. Nooter, Assistant Administrator for Supporting Assistance, Agency for International Development, statement before the Senate Judiciary Subcommittee on Refugees, August 1, 1973, 7–9.

14. Saigon telegram 05930 (2 sections), April 9, 1973; Saigon telegram 06156, April 12, 1973; State telegram 098560, AIDAC, May 23, 1973.

15. See, for example, Saigon telegrams 09289, May 25, 1973; 09806, June 2, 1973; and 10822, June 16, 1973.

16. Saigon telegrams 13169, July 21, 1973; 14509, August 11, 1973; and 21313, December 21, 1973.

17. Wells Klein, Member of the Senate Refugee Subcommittee Study Mission to South Vietnam and Executive Director, American Council for Nationalities Service, New York, statement, August 1, 1973. This statement was expanded and made part of *Relief and Rehabilitation of War Victims in Indochina: One Year after the Ceasefire*, A Study Mission Report prepared for the use of the Senate Refugee Subcommittee, January 27, 1974.

18. Retired Foreign Service Officer Paul Popple, letter to author, February 25, 1986. Quoted with permission of the writer.

19. Saigon telegram 3527, March 18, 1974. The number of civilians paid for wounds was only a fraction of those admitted to hospitals with war wounds.

20. Saigon telegram 2227, February 20, 1974.

21. Saigon telegram 4220, April 3, 1974.

22. Saigon telegram 08337, June 25, 1974.

23. Saigon telegram 9107, July 10, 1974.

24. Saigon telegram 16483, September 17, 1973; Dr. Phan Quang Dan, Deputy Prime

Minister of the Republic of Vietnam, *Refugee Relief & Rehabilitation, Land Development & Hamlet Building* (Saigon: January 15, 1975), 198.

25. Anthony Faunce, Acting Inspector General of Foreign Assistance, memorandum to the Honorable John A. Hannah, Administrator, Agency for International Development, "Subject: Inspection of War Victims Program in Vietnam," 19.

26. Dr. Dan, letter to author, April 8, 1985.

27. Dr. Dan, conversation with the author, New York, June 17, 1986. Dan did not name the general. Dr. Phieu in a conversation with the author on November 22, 1987, confirmed that the generals moved in on the land around Dr. Dan's settlements.

28. Takashi Oka, "Viet Refugees: U.S. Aid Misfires?" datelined Nha Trang, *The Christian Science Monitor*, July 16, 1973.

29. "Economic Condition and Availability of Land at Montagnard Resettlement Sites," Report of a Survey made by USAID/ADLR September 1973, in the Study Mission report, *Relief and Rehabilitation of War Victims in Indochina*, Appendix IV, 188–91. The nine provinces surveyed were Kontum, Pleiku, Darlac, Phu-Bon, Lam-Dong, Tuyen-Duc, Quang-Duc, Binh-Dinh, and Phu-Yen.

30. Edward L. Block, statement before the Committee on Foreign Affairs, House of Representatives, July 2, 1974, on the President's (Fiscal Year 1975) Foreign Assistance Request, 569–80. State telegram 146922 summarized this testimony. Saigon telegram 9802 (two sections), July 11, 1974, replied to it. Also relevant are the author's conversations with Raymond Fontaine and Dr. Dan, November 10–11, 1987, in Tampa, Florida.

31. Richard C. Holdren, letters to the author, September 17 and (postmarked) October 27, 1987.

32. Saigon telegram 7888, June 14, 1974.

33. Dr. Dan, letter to the author, June 19, 1987.

34. Ministry of Social Welfare and LDHB, *Song Pha Resettlement Sites in Ninh Thuan* (Vietnamese and English) (Saigon: September 1974), 3, 6–9.

35. "Humanitarian Problems in Indochina," Hearing before the Senate Refugee Subcommittee, July 18, 1974, 12–13.

36. Dr. Phieu, who had been Minister of Social Welfare from 1969 to 1974, told me on November 21 and 22, 1987 that not many refugee settlements had sufficient land, especially in the Center. Dr. Dan did get land for his LDBH sites, but they encompassed only a minority of the refugees needing resettlement. This confirms the other information reported above.

37. Arnold R. Isaacs, *Without Honor: Defeat in Vietnam and Cambodia* (New York: Vintage Books, 1983), 8–11, 70–71, 78–79, 81–82.

38. Saigon telegram 10822, June 16, 1973. By the end of July the number of post-cease-fire war victims had climbed to 461,300, of whom about 250,000 had been displaced from their homes at some time (Saigon telegram 13621, July 28, 1973).

39. Isaacs, *Without Honor*, 66.

40. Colonel William E. LeGro, *Vietnam from Cease-Fire to Capitulation* (Washington, D.C.: Center of Military History, 1981), 34.

41. Saigon telegram 14910, section 2, August 17, 1973.

42. Saigon telegram 12550, July 12, 1973.

43. Fox Butterfield, *New York Times*, June 5, 1973, quoted in State telegram 112023, June 9, 1973.

44. Thomas W. Lippman, "Saigon Fights to Regain Land, People," datelined Bong-

son, *The Washington Post*, September 30, 1973, A13; Moncrieff J. Spear, Consul General, Nha Trang, letter to Robert H. Wenzel, Director, Viet-Nam Working Group, Department of State, November 14, 1973.

45. State telegram 146922, July 8, 1974, reporting on Block's testimony to the House Foreign Affairs Committee, and Saigon telegram 12550, July 12, 1973, both cited above; Saigon telegram 7887, June 14, 1974.

46. Charles W. Browne, Jr., Chief, ERB/CG-1, memorandum to Daniel L. Leaty, Chief, Regional Development Office, CG-1, "Dr. Dan's Visit to MR-1–15 thru 17 Sept," September 18, 1973.

47. Isaacs, *Without Honor*, 87–88; Saigon telegrams 10822, June 16, 1973, and 12550, July 12, 1973.

48. Nan Borton, who was serving in the highlands for Catholic Relief Services from 1973 to 1975, told me on November 17, 1986 (when she was Executive Director of International Voluntary Services) that it was fairly common for villagers, especially Montagnards, to be forced back to their villages. This was a cynical GVN action to create buffer zones. Then many of the settlements were attacked, and the people had to flee again.

49. Klein statement of August 1, 1973, Senate Refugee Subcommittee Hearing record, 9.

50. Senate Refugee Subcommittee Hearing record, July 18, 1974, 13–14.

51. For example, a communication from Dr. John Hannah, Administrator of AID, July 31, 1973, to the Senate Refugee Subcommittee, released by Senator Kennedy September 24, 1973 under cover of Kennedy's statement calling for an end to US support of forced relocations. Hannah transmitted Saigon's answers to the subcommittee's questions. The mission said: "The other option open to refugees is to return to PRG-controlled territories. This option is neither proffered nor supported by the GVN. Although the Mission knows of no case where any group of refugees has requested return to PRG territories and been refused, this might occur without our knowledge." (p. 6 of the replies).

52. Daniel Southerland, "Saigon Curbs Homeward-bound Refugees," datelined Trung Lap, *The Christian Science Monitor*, March 16, 1973.

53. Thomas W. Lippman, " 'Let Us Go Home,' Viet Villagers Ask," datelined Thanhthuy, *The Washington Post*, November 23, 1973.

54. S/R—Louis A. Wiesner, memorandum to EA/VN—Mr. Robert H. Wenzel, "Subject: Generation and Treatment of Refugees in Viet-Nam," November 23, 1973.

55. Ambassador Martin, letter to author, January 9, 1974.

56. Charles W. Browne, Jr, Chief, RRD/CONGEN-1, memorandum to Mr. Edward G. Ruoff, ADRR/USAID/Saigon, "Comments on 'It's War—Still—For Than Thuy,' an article by Thomas W. Lippman, Bureau Chief/Saigon office of *The Washington Post*."

57. Hearing before the House Committee on Foreign Affairs, July 13, 1974, 278.

58. Saigon telegram 11070, August 22, 1974; Major General Nguyen Duy Hinh, *Vietnamization and the Cease Fire* (Washington, D.C.: Center of Military History, 1980), 173–79.

59. Phan Quang Dan, *Refugee Relief and Rehabilitation, Land Development and Hamlet Building* (Saigon: January 15, 1975), 200, 208, 213–14.

60. Dr. Dan, conversation with the author, November 10, 1987.

CHAPTER 14. NORTH VIET-NAM

1. Bernard B. Fall, *The Two Viet-Nams: A Political and Military Analysis*, Second Revised Edition (New York: Praeger, 1967), 154–55. Joseph Buttinger and others observed the same advantages for the DRVN.

2. Fall, *The Two Viet-Nams*, 154–56. Fall said that the best educated guesses were that probably close to 50,000 were executed in connection with the land reform and that at least twice that number were arrested and sent to forced labor camps. He was well acquainted with all parts of Viet-Nam and spoke the language. Joseph Buttinger, *Vietnam: A Political History*, (New York: Praeger, 1968), 426–29. He put the number executed at 10,000 to 15,000. In a lecture to my CORDS class at the Foreign Service Institute October 12, 1967, Richard Smyser of the National Security Council staff said that the Communists had killed between 50,000 and 300,000 during the land reform. Edwin E. Moise, *Land Reform in China and North Vietnam: Consolidating the Revolution at the Village Level* (Chapel Hill: University of North Carolina Press, 1983), 170–280, a scholarly analysis of the land reform. Moise calculated the number executed at between 3,000 and 15,000 (217–222). President Nixon asserted that 500,000 were executed and another 500,000 died in slave labor (*New York Times*, July 28, 1972, 10, cited by Moise).

3. Fall, *The Two Viet-Nams*, 156–58; Buttinger, *Vietnam*, 428–29. Though citing Fall, Buttinger put the number killed during the revolt at 1,000. Moise (*Land Reform*, 258) gave the same figure.

4. Fall, *The Two Viet-Nams*, 158–60. Moise, in *Land Reform*, said the land reform expropriated 702,544 hectares in 3,314 villages with 10,514,000 people (189). That came to only 67 square meters per person. His account stopped short of the formation of the cooperatives.

5. Charles N. Spinks, John C. Durr, and Stephen Peters, *The North Vietnamese Regime: Institutions and Problems* (Washington, D.C.: American University Center for Research in Social Systems, April 1969), 42, 57. This study relies heavily on official North Vietnamese statements and publications, but also uses reports of foreign journalists and other visitors.

6. Ibid., 57–58, citing Le Duan, "Political Report of the Central Committee of the Viet Nam Workers' Party," *Third National Congress of Viet Nam Workers' Party*, Vol. I (Hanoi: Foreign Languages Publishing House, undated), 131–34, 234–35.

7. Ibid., 56, 58–59; Jon M. Van Dyke, *North Vietnam's Strategy for Survival* (Palo Alto, Calif.: Pacific Books, 1972), 126.

8. Spinks, Durr, and Peters, *The North Vietnamese Regime*, 60; Van Dyke, *North Vietnam's Strategy*, 126. Another North Vietnamese source cited by Spinks, Durr, and Peters gave a figure of 730,000 migrants by early 1966, of whom 540,000 were said to be engaged in land reclamation and 190,000 in farming and forestry production. In a totalitarian country it is difficult to go behind the claims and statistics of its government.

9. Spinks, Durr, and Peters, *The North Vietnamese Regime*, 61–67.

10. See, for example, Nguyen Tuan, "Party Committee Leads Sedentary Living of Muong Te Mountain District," *Nhan Dan* (The People), Hanoi, 18 January 1968. This was translated by the Joint Publications Research Service (JPRS) of the US Department

of Commerce under the heading "Translations on North Vietnam." The items will be identified by the JPRS catalogue number or the Readex microtext number. This translation is on Readex 1968 microtext 6280–48, card 12. See also "Nghe An, Quang Ninh Peasants Improve Labor Organization; Son La Enlarges Scale of Cooperatives," *Nhan Dan*, 30 November 1968, JPRS, Readex 1969–2048–19, card 13; Si Do, "Frontier Forces Help Minorities' Resettlement," *Quan Doi Nhan Dan*, 13 December 1969, JPRS, Readex 1970–5722–25, card 6.

11. Le Quang Ba, "Satisfactorily Carry out the Campaign for the Settlement of the Nomads in Conjunction with the Collectivization of Nomadic People," *Hoc Tap* (To Learn), Hanoi, No. 5, May 1969, 37–43, JPRS, Readex 1969–12875–24, card 16.

12. Le Quang Ba, "People in the Highlands, Forever Grateful to President Ho, Pledge to Properly Carry out the Campaign for Settlement Combined with Cooperativization," *Nhan Dan*, 6 October 1969, JPRS, Readex February 1970–1980–25, card 3.

13. See for example, *Nhan Dan*, 18 October 1970, JPRS 51795; and *Nhan Dan*, 7 November 1970, JPRS 52049.

14. "More than 60,000 Mountain Region Compatriots Are Settled," *Nhan Dan*, April 25, 1973, JPRS, Readex 1973–27618–13, card 12.

15 Van Dyke, *North Vietnam's Strategy*. Most of the book deals with the bombing and DRVN defensive measures. Also, Guenter Lewy, *America in Vietnam* (New York: Oxford University Press, 1978), 374–417.

16. Millions of words have been written and spoken about the effects of the bombing on civilians. The most balanced presentation, in my opinion, is that of Guenter Lewy, *America in Vietnam*, 375–417. Van Dyke covered the bombing in the period 1965–69 extensively in *North Vietnam's Strategy*. The Senate Refugee Subcommittee devoted much attention to the bombing, with testimony from both US Administration witnesses and those, including Ramsey Clark and its own study mission headed by Dr. Scrimshaw, who described in detail damage to civilian installations such as hospitals. See especially the hearings of August 16 and 17 and September 28, 1972, July 18 and 31, 1973, and *Relief and Rehabilitation of War Victims in Indochina: One Year after the Ceasefire*, A Study Mission Report for the Senate Refugee Subcommittee, January 27, 1974, 46–71. Among the more objective newspaper reports is that of Peter Ward in *Baltimore Sun* of March 25, 1973: "In Hanoi There is an Air of a City in Victory." He wrote: "Hanoi has certainly been damaged, but evidence on the ground disproves charges of indiscriminate bombing. Several bomb loads obviously went astray into civilian residential areas, but damage there is minor, compared to the total destruction of selected targets." Malcolm W. Browne and his Vietnamese wife were part of a group admitted to witness the release of American prisoners of war. In the *New York Times* of March 31, 1973, "Hanoi's People Still Curious and Likable," Browne wrote, "The damage caused by American bombing was grossly overstated by North Vietnamese propaganda, and many westerners' reports have similarly overstated the dilapidation of buildings caused by an impoverished economy over the years. In fact, Hanoi remains a beautiful and bustling city." Maria Grebnec wrote similarly in *The Nation* of Bangkok, on March 22, 1973. These and many other newspaper reports were reprinted in Appendix I of the Senate Refugee Subcommittee hearing record of July 31, 1973.

17. Excerpts from National Security Study Memorandum No. 1 of 1969, "U.S. Bombing of North Vietnam, 1965–1969," reprinted as Appendix VII of the Senate Refugee Subcommittee Hearing record, *Problems of War Victims in Indochina*, Part III, *North Vietnam*, August 16–17, 1972, 178, 184. This will henceforth be referred to as the

Kissinger Memorandum. Also see Lewy, *America in Vietnam*, 390, citing Sam B. Barrett (Aerospace Studies Institute), "The Air Campaign against North Vietnam," October 1969, 14.

18. However, one person in the North, who must remain anonymous, wrote to a relative at the time that people cheered the Christmas 1972 bombing and hoped and prayed that it would continue, because a few more days would cause the regime to collapse. There is some but not much substantiation for this report. Another source said that the Christmas bombing caused panic and fear that the Americans would invade.

19. Van Dyke, *North Vietnam's Strategy*, 126–28.

20. Ibid., 128–30.

21. Spinks, Durr, and Peters, *The North Vietnamese Regime*, 70.

22. Jouri Piethukoff of *Il Messaggero*, cited by ibid., 74.

23. Van Dyke, *North Vietnam's Strategy*, 130–59. He used a number of North Vietnamese sources and foreign journalists' reports to document these findings. Also see Peter Arnett, "Close-Up of North Vietnam at War: Everything Moves at Night," *New York Times*, October 3, 1972, and Peter Arnett, "Focus on Hanoi's 'Ant Power,' " *Christian Science Monitor*, October 3, 1972; both articles were reprinted in an appendix to the Senate Refugee Subcommittee hearing record of September 27, 1972, 84–87.

24. Spinks, Durr, and Peters, *The North Vietnamese Regime*, 71–74. See also "Relocated Families are Helped by Local People," *Nhan Dan*, November 17, 1968, JPRS, Readex 1969–2048–19, card 12.

25. Van Dyke, *North Vietnam's Strategy*, 11, 21, 133–4, 150. He cited among others the reports of Michael Maclear of the Canadian Broadcasting System, who visited North Viet-Nam late in 1969 and again in early 1971. Also the *New York Times*, January 3, 1970 (city edition) 3, and January 13, 1971 (city edition) 1, 6, cited by Van Dyke.

26. "Mill Evacuates Nonessential People," *Hanoi Moi* (New Hanoi), 21 April 1972, JPRS, Readex 1972–9915–16, card 8; Editorial: "Organizing Production Well in the New Situation," *Hanoi Moi*, 26 April 1972, JPRS, Readex 1972–9915–16, card 8. There were many more similar reports in the press.

27. Murray Marder, "North Vietnam: Taking Pride in Punishment," *The Washington Post*, February 4, 1973, reprinted in the Senate Refugee Subcommittee hearing record, July 31, 1973, 86.

28. Editorial, *Hanoi Moi*, 3 May 1972, JPRS, Readex 1972–9915–16, cards 10–11; "T. Mine in Quang Ninh Provinces Organizes Workers' Lives in the Evacuation Areas," *Nhan Dan*, 15 July 1972, JPRS, Readex December 1972–15030–24, card 11; "Ministry of Internal Trade Notice on Sale of Goods to Evacuated Compatriots," *Hanoi Moi*, 29 December 1972, JPRS, Readex 1973–23511–14, card 3.

29. "Questions Concerning Evacuation Allowances Answered, Explaining the Measures" column, citing Circular No. 8, TC/MCVX of the Ministry of Finance May 5, 1972 and other circulars of 1965 and 1972, *Phu Nu Viet Nam*, No. 296, July 1, 1972, JPRS, Readex December 1972–15030–24, card 17.

30. Van Dyke, *North Vietnam's Strategy*, 67–77, 207–8; Kissinger Memorandum, 189; John A. Sullivan, Associate Executive Secretary, American Friends Service Committee, testimony, in Senate Refugee Subcommittee hearing record, August 17, 1972, 29–30.

31. Kissinger Memorandum, 191.

32. "25 Years of Health Work," *Vietnamese Studies*, Hanoi, No. 25 (1970): 131–32.

33. Murray Marder, "North Vietnam: Taking Pride in Punishment," *Washington Post*, February 4, 1973, reprinted in Senate Refugee Subcommittee hearing record of July 31, 1973, 84–90. These particular references were on pp. 86 and 89.

34. For example, Dr. George A. Perera, formerly Associate Dean of the College of Physicians and Surgeons, Columbia University, who accompanied John A. Sullivan: Senate Refugee Subcommittee Hearing record, August 17, 1972, 36.

35. Senate Refugee Subcommittee Hearing record, July 31, 1973, 3–49.

36. Anthony Faunce, Acting Inspector General of Foreign Assistance, memorandum to John A. Hannah, Administrator, Agency for International Development, "Subject: Inspection of Public Health Program in Vietnam," July 11, 1972, 9–10.

37. "Council of Ministers' Notice to Supplement the Policy of Families of Military Personnel," *Nhan Dan*, 30 October 1968; "New Policy Issuance Favors Kin of Servicemen," editorial, *Quan Doi Nhan Dan*, 31 October 1968, JPRS, Readex 1969–2048–19, cards 1 and 3.

38. "Regarding Policies Toward Families of War Dead," *Thoi Su Pho Thong* (Propaganda Notebook), No. 6, June 1971, JPRS, Readex 1971–16823–14, card 12. "Thanh Linh Township Organization in Nghe An Province Provides Good Leadership in Carrying Out Policies Relating to Wounded Soldiers and Dependents of War Dead," *Quan Doi Nhan Dan*, July 27, 1971; "Job Priorities, Pensions for Soldiers and their Families," Readers' column, *Thoi Su Pho Thong* 7 (July 1971): 70–75; "Elderly in Gia Lam Care for the Families of the Wounded and the War Dead," *Hanoi Moi*, 8 July 1971. All in JPRS, Readex 1971–16823–14, card 8.

39. "Municipal Administrative Committee Passes Resolution on Assistance to Families of Bombing Victims and to Evacuees," *Hanoi Moi*, 6 January 1973, 1, 4, JPRS, Readex 1973–23511–14, card 8.

40. Excerpt from report by the Hanoi Municipal Administrative Committee at an unscheduled meeting of the Hanoi People's Council on 16 January 1973: "The Guidelines for Resolving the Housing Problems of Families Who are Victims of U.S. Bombs," *Hanoi Moi*, 17 January 1973, JPRS, Readex 1973–23511–14, card 9.

CHAPTER 15. THE FINAL OFFENSIVE OF THE NORTH VIETNAMESE

1. Saigon telegram 1527, February 7, 1975. The data were those available at the time; an update was promised when all provincial reporting was completed. The NVA offensive, however, overran some provinces before they could finish their reporting.

2. Arnold R. Isaacs, *Without Honor* (New York: Vintage Books, 1983), 327, citing General Van Tien Dung, *Our Great Spring Victory* (New York: Monthly Review Press, 1977). Isaacs used the text translated by the Foreign Broadcast Information Service, FBIS Supplement 38, June 7, 1976 and Supplement 42, July 7, 1976. I have used Dung's book as published by the Monthly Review Press of New York in 1977, and the rest of my citations will refer to that edition.

3. Isaacs, *Without Honor*, 327–28.

4. Frank Snepp, *Decent Interval: An Insider's Account of Saigon's Indecent End Told by the CIA's Chief Strategy Analyst in Vietnam* (New York: Random House, 1977), 122.

5. Isaacs, *Without Honor*, 331–33; Saigon telegram 0240, section 2, January 8, 1975.

6. Saigon telegrams 0229, January 8, 1975, and 0516, January 15, 1975.

7. Saigon telegram 0231, January 8, 1975.

8. Department of State airgram A-7682, October 8, 1974, to the US Mission to the United Nations, containing the testimony of Robert Wenzel on July 18 to the Senate Subcommittee on Refugees concerning international organization assistance; State telegram 253383, November 16, 1974, to US Mission Geneva AIDAC; Geneva telegram 7063, November 20, 1974, listing contributions from other nations totaling $5,005,026; State telegram 270502, December 10, 1974 to Geneva AIDAC; and State telegram 025661, February 4, 1975 to Geneva AIDAC.

9. United Nations General Assembly document A/AC.96/526, 16 August 1976, Executive Committee of the High Commissioner's Programme, Twenty-seventh session, *Report on UNHCR Assistance Activities in 1975–1976 and Proposed Voluntary Funds Programme and Budget for 1977,* Submitted by the High Commissioner, 106–8.

10. Isaacs, *Without Honor,* 346; Denis Warner, *Not with Guns Alone* (Richmond, Vic.: Hutchinson of Australia, 1977), 37. Warner, an Australian correspondent, reported that the VC and NVA murdered about 300 soldiers and civilians whom they had taken prisoner in Ban Me Thuot. This was based on his interview in Saigon with a Buddhist monk who managed to escape the massacre.

11. General William C. Westmoreland, *A Soldier Reports* (Garden City, N.Y.: Doubleday, 1976), 399, wrote that the Montagnard RF and PF troops manning the outposts around the town did not warn of the impending attack. Gerald C. Hickey, in *Free in the Forest* (New Haven and London: Yale University Press, 1982), 273, indirectly cited Léandri, and also recounted that a Montagnard leader had observed from a helicopter that the tanks entering Ban Me Thuot had the legend, "Front for the Liberation of the Ethnic Minorities" on their sides. The leader, Y Jut Buon To, also said that many FULRO forces joined the attack, and that the Rhadé Regional Forces made no effort to resist. Olivier Todd, largely on the basis of information obtained from Paul Léandri, asserted that some of the FULRO members acted as scouts for the North Vietnamese (*Cruel Avril, 1975: La chute de Saigon* [Paris: Editions Robert Laffont, 1987], 147–48). In an interview on December 5, 1987, former Montagnard leader Han Tho Touneh said that only a small minority of the tribespeople, a few hundred, who had deserted the territorial forces, joined the NVA attack under the leadership of the pro-Communist Kpa Koi. The bulk of the Montagnard troops, he said (about 15,000), went into the forest and continued fighting the North Vietnamese until 1981, when the remnant of the force tried to escape across Cambodia to Thailand. Only 214 made it; they are now settled in North Carolina. One of them, Reverend Ha (Jimmy) Cillpam, told me on February 13, 1988 that Kpa Koi, whom he had seen three days before the attack, withdrew his troops into the forest. According to Reverend Cillpam, Kpa Koi might have come to an agreement with the Iron Division that neither force would fight the other. Y Yok Ayun and Pierre K'Briuh were also aware of the Iron Division and another VC division.

12. Isaacs, *Without Honor,* 346–47.

13. Dung, *Great Spring Victory,* 97. The North Vietnamese got this information from the interrogation of Colonel Pham Duy Dat, the Ranger commander at II Corps headquarters. Isaacs, (in *Without Honor,* p. 350), reported almost exactly the same words.

14. Isaacs, *Without Honor,* 342–45, 347–56; Snepp, *Decent Interval,* 193–206, 213; Westmoreland, *A Soldier Reports,* 399–400; Colonel William E. Le Gro, *Viet-Nam from Cease-Fire to Capitulation* (Washington; D.C.: Center of Military History, 1981), 151–54; Denis Warner, *Not with Guns Alone,* 60–63. Olivier Todd, in *Cruel Avril,* said that

about 60,000 civilians and 5,000 soldiers made it to Tuy-Hoa (175). Pierre K'Briuh and R'Mah Dock told me on February 13, 1988 about the fighting in Phu-Bon. R'Mah and his family got as far as that province in the refugee column, where the VC took their jeep. After three weeks, during which R'Mah's wife had a baby in the jungle, they made their way back to Pleiku. David Butler, *The Fall of Saigon* (New York: Simon and Schuster, 1985), 101–7, quoted news dispatches which Nguyen Tu, who traveled with the refugee convoy for four days, wrote for the serious popular Saigon newspaper *Chinh Luan*. He sent the reports out on the helicopters that assisted the refugees and finally escaped on one of them. On November 10–11, 1987, Dr. Phan Quang Dan recounted his experiences with the refugees from Pleiku.

15. Isaacs, *Without Honor*, 355–56.

16. The best account of the American evacuations is by Snepp, *Decent Interval*, 180, 182–3 (the unsuccessful attempt to rescue Paul Struharik and companions in Ban Me Thuot and their capture), 190–91, 197–203. Also see Moncrieff Spear's letter to me postmarked June 28, 1985, which contains some details of the evacuation from the Highlands and then from Nha-Trang.

17. Isaacs, *Without Honor*, 356–63; Snepp, *Decent Interval*, 206–8, 210–13.

18. Snepp, *Decent Interval*, 210; Isaacs, *Without Honor*, 358–59. Warner, in *Not with Guns Alone*, said the Khiem visit occurred on the 17th (65); it was he who reported that the meeting concentrated at first on the refugee problem. This was confirmed by Bui Vien, former Assistant Minister of Defense and Secretary of State in the Prime Minister's Office (Stephen T. Hosmer, Konrad Kellen, and Brian M. Jenkins, eds., *The Fall of South Vietnam: Statements by Vietnamese Military and Civilian Leaders* [New York: Crane, Russak, 1980], 221). This book will henceforth be referred to as Hosmer, Kellen, and Jenkins, *The Fall of South Vietnam*. Moncrieff Spear, in an interview on April 25, 1977, told me about Dr. Dan's task force and the evacuation plans, which Dr. Dan confirmed on November 11, 1987. The Prime Minister and his party had stopped over in Nha-Trang. Hung Thanh Huynh, who had been Colonel Khiem's superior in the Ministry of Social Welfare, gave me the information about the attempted relief program in Da-Nang, in a conversation on November 2, 1987. Dr. Dan confirmed this in a letter on November 30, 1987. The embassy's estimate was contained in Saigon telegram 3708, March 28, 1975.

19. Snepp, *Decent Interval*, 210; Isaacs, *Without Honor*, 359.

20. Isaacs, *Without Honor*, 358, 360–61. Hue was almost completely empty when it was taken. Dung's assertion that the masses rose up and helped the NVA troops in various ways is not credible (*Great Spring Victory*, 103).

21. Isaacs, *Without Honor*, 361–63.

22. Isaacs, *Without Honor*, 363–66. Snepp, on page 214 of *Decent Interval*, asserted that the number of displaced persons in MR-1 had already exceeded 2,000,000 by the third week of March, but on page 230 he said that over 500,000 had converged on Da-Nang, bringing its population to nearly 2,000,000. The 2-million population figure was also stated by Bui Vien (Hosmer, Kellen, and Jenkins, *The Fall of South Vietnam*, 221. Nobody really knew how many frightened people left their homes or how many arrived in Da-Nang. Warner, *Not by Guns Alone*, reported that no preparations had been made in Da-Nang to receive the refugees and no shelter or supplies were available for them (68). However, Theresa Tull, who was in charge of the Da-Nang Consulate General until Albert Francis returned from medical evacuation late in the third week of March, was

impressed by the way the people of the city helped the refugees (interview with the author in Washington, D.C., May 31, 1977).

23. Author's conversations with Graham Martin at his home, February 10, 11, and 12, 1988; Saigon telegrams 0674, March 18, 1975, and 0675, March 19, 1975, from Lehmann, Martin channel, to Brent Scowcroft, pass Martin; Danang telegram 0298 to Saigon, March 24, 1975; Isaacs, *Without Honor*, 366–71; Snepp, *Decent Interval*, 224, 257.

24. Saigon telegram 3698, March 28, 1975; State telegram 9905, 282257 Z Mar 75; Saigon telegram 4329, 291135 Z Mar 75; Snepp, *Decent Interval*, 224–25, 231, 235–36, 256; Todd, *Cruel Avril*, 205.

25. Daniel Parker, testimony before the House of Representatives Subcommittee on Citizenship, Immigration and International Law, April 8, 1975. Hearing record, Serial No. 43, 4–5.

26. Saigon telegram 3776, March 30, 1975, expressed Ambassador Martin's strong view that Waldheim should be pressed to intervene with Hanoi in the name of Article 13 of the Universal Declaration of Human Rights. Senate Refugee Subcommittee, *Indochina Evacuation and Refugee Problems*, Part II: *The Evacuation*, Hearing, Tuesday, April 15, 1975, 17–18, records an exchange of (opposite) views on this matter between Assistant Secretary of State Philip C. Habib and Senator Kennedy. In his testimony before the House Subcommittee on Citizenship, Immigration and International Law on April 8, 1975, Aid Administrator Daniel Parker said, "I must say I have not been favorably impressed by the Secretary General's decision to put political responsibility above what I consider moral responsibility in seeking to intervene amongst the parties to let the affected individuals determine whether they want to live, seek safety" (20–21) A French journalist reported that, while supporting a PRG appeal for aid, North Viet-Nam charged that the US Government "has brought pressure on the U.N. secretary general to ask him to take part in the schemings which consist of forcing the population to evacuate" territory taken over by Communist forces (Jean Thoraval, Agence France Presse, "Hanoi Appeals for Aid to Vietcong-Held Areas," *The Washington Post*, April 4, 1975, printed in Senate Subcommittee Hearing record of April 8, 1975, 124–25). In the absence of the State Department documents, which have not been released in response to my Freedom of Information Act request, I rely partly on my memory for the manner in which the request to Waldheim was made and S/R's reaction to it.

27. Isaacs, *Without Honor*, 374–79; Snepp, *Decent Interval*, 245–61; author's interview with Theresa Tull, May 31, 1977. 34,600 of the 90,000 evacuated by ship were on American vessels.

28. Isaacs, *Without Honor*, 378–81.

29. Ibid., 381–85; Snepp, *Decent Interval*, 264–72. Monty Spear said that he and his staff had gotten very substantial numbers of Vietnamese out secretly in the period before the collapse of the region. Then, about 2,000 Vietnamese were evacuated from Nha-Trang by the evening of April 1, and another 3,000 were picked up the next day by a Military Sealift Command transport. From Saigon, Spear sent flights back to some of the MR-2 towns even after that (interview with the author, April 25, 1977; letter to the author, June 28, 1985).

30. Daniel Parker before the House Subcommittee on Citizenship, Immigration and International Law, April 8, 1975, Hearing record, 4.

31. Isaacs, *Without Honor*, 385–90.

32. Le Thi Que, A. Terry Rambo, and Gary D. Murfin, "Why They Fled: Refugee

Movement during the Spring 1975 Communist Offensive in South Vietnam," *Asian Survey*, 16 (1976): 855–59. All of the protocols of the survey were abandoned during the evacuation of the authors; the article was written from the working notes carried out in a rucksack by one of them.

33. Ibid., 859–63.

34. James Walker Trullinger, *Village at War* (New York: Longman, 1980), 199–201.

35. Testimony of Lauralee Peters of the State Department and John Thomas, Director of ICEM, before the House Subcommittee on Citizenship, Immigration and International Law, April 8 and 9, 1975, Hearing record, 37–53, 95–96.

36. Daniel Parker and Edward B. Marks of AID, Leonard Walentynowicz, Director of the Bureau of Security and Consular Affairs, State Department, and Lauralee Peters, testimony before the House Immigration Subcommittee, April 8, 1975, Hearing record, 5–7, 23, 35–37. Under section 212(D)(5) of the Immigration and Nationality Act, the Attorney General has authority to admit provisionally by parole certain persons for emergent reasons. This power had been used for groups of refugees whose numbers exceeded the conditional entry (seventh preference, 10,200 a year) quota or when there was an emergency precluding normal immigration procedures. Thus, some 40,000 Hungarians had been paroled in after the Soviets suppressed the revolution there in 1956. By 1975, about 675,000 Cubans had been paroled following Castro's assumption of power in 1959. Fifteen hundred Uganda Asians were paroled when Amin expelled them in 1971 (testimony of General Leonard Chapman, Commissioner of the Immigration and Naturalization Service [INS], before the Senate Refugee Subcommittee, April 15, 1975, Hearing record, 43). Parole is administered by INS, after consultation with the Judiciary Committees (or their subcommittees) of the two Houses. The orphans were not technically refugees, but there was a need for haste. Staff members of the appropriate Congressional subcommittees were notified of the decision.

37. Parker, Senate Refugee Subcommittee hearing, April 15, 1975, 7; Butler, *The Fall of Saigon*, 223–26; Isaacs, *Without Honor*, 395–96.

38. Parker testimony, House Immigration Subcommittee hearing record, 8–9; Isaacs, *Without Honor*, 396–97.

39. Department of the Army, After Action Report, *Operation New Life/New Arrivals, US Army Support to the Indochina Refugee Program 1 April 1975–1 June 1976*, prepared by Operations and Readiness Directorate, Office, Deputy Chief of Staff for Operations and Plans, January 25, 1977, ix.

40. Isaacs, *Without Honor*, 396–97.

41. Much of the foregoing paragraphs is based on my memory. The information about Taiwan was given to Dorothy Parker, Minority Counsel of the Senate Refugee Subcommittee during her visit to that country on May 19–22, 1975 (*Indochina Evacuation and Refugee Problems*, Part IV, *Staff Reports*, June 9 and July 8, 1975, 86–87).

42. Assistant Secretary Habib discussed preliminary third-country offers of asylum before the Senate Refugee Subcommittee in Executive Session, April 15, 1975, hearing record, 32–33. State telegram 087849, 170309 Z Apr 75 instructed the mission in Geneva to approach the UNHCR and ICEM. Geneva telegram 2634, April 17, 1975 reported their positive responses. State telegram 090485, 190051 Z Apr 75 NODIS (no distribution beyond addressee) was the circular telegram to East Asia posts asking the Ambassadors to approach the governments about staging areas. I have had to rely on my memory about the responses and further exchanges, because the State Department has withheld copies of those documents in response to my Freedom of Information Act request submitted in

December 1986. Ambassador Martin is the source of the information that the US refused to give the assurances demanded by the East Asian nations.

43. S/R–Frank L. Kellogg, Action Memorandum to the Acting Secretary, "Parole of Refugees from South Vietnam and Cambodia," April 5, 1975, enclosing a letter from Ingersoll to the Attorney General. The memorandum was drafted by F. Jameson, and cleared by the Bureaus of Security and Consular Affairs (SCA), East Asian Affairs (EA), Congressional Relations (H), and the Office of the Legal Adviser (L). The letter was signed by Ingersoll on April 5, 1975. The letter from Attorney General Edward H. Levi was dated April 11, 1975.

44. For instance, State telegram 073051, April 1, 1975, drafted in EA and approved by Secretary Kissinger, asked Embassy Saigon's views on a range of contingency actions, including accelerated evacuation of dependents and nonessential personnel (with regular status reports), early withdrawal from more exposed positions in MR-2 (which had already been done) and possibly in MRs 3 and 4, inclusion of high-risk Vietnamese in the Embassy's emergency and evacuation (E&E) plan, etc. State telegram 074874 of April 2, 1975, said that the Secretary wished by the opening of business April 3 a detailed, mission-coordinated breakdown by categories of those Vietnamese whom the US had a moral responsibility to evacuate. It appears that Martin did not reply to these messages, but expressed his anger by telephone calls to Kissinger and Scowcroft. Had he furnished the data that the Department requested, we could perhaps have initiated parole consultations with the Congressional committees sooner. In State telegram 077668, April 5, "Eyes only for the Ambassador from the Secretary," Kissinger said:

I am not at all pleased by the way we are approaching the difficult question of Viet-Nam evacuation. If we lose our composure—be it in Washington or wherever—we will lose much more as well—lives, national dignity and a common sense of confidence. . . . Everyone is under stress, but this need not lead to the disintegration of discipline or clearheadedness that I believe is engulfing us.

Therefore, Kissinger established new procedures, which provided for direct and identifiable orders from him to Martin after getting the Ambassador's views and plans. This was the parallel "Martin channel," by-passing the task force and the Department of State's regular communications.

45. Gerald R. Ford, *Public Papers of the Presidents of the United States*, 1975, Book I, January 1 to July 17, 1975 (Washington, D.C.: United States Government Printing Office, 1977), 463–64.

46. Saigon telegrams 4527, 090045 Z, and 4528, 090145 Z Apr 75, both highly classified and NODIS, contained the evacuation plan, including the estimate of 197,200 Vietnamese of all categories in danger; 126,000 of them were US government employees and dependents. It estimated that 15% of them might elect not to go, reducing the total to be evacuated to 167,620. Saigon telegram 5009, April 15, 1975, Confidential, gave the figure of 175,107 total Americans and aliens and broke it down. 167,000 of the alien evacuees were US Mission local national employees and their dependents. Saigon telegram 5303 of April 19, 1975, raised the total of potential evacuees to 203,925, explaining that the increase was due largely to revised estimates of relatives of American citizens, and alien employees and dependents connected with US firms and organizations. State telegram 090591, 192126 Z Apr 75 from Dean Brown authorized the embassy to plan for the evacuation of other high-risk Vietnamese.

47. House Immigration Subcommittee Hearing record, April 14, 1975, 144–85.

48. Senate Judiciary Committee Hearing record, April 15, 1975, 1–43.

49. SCA–Leonard F. Walentynowicz, briefing memorandum to the Deputy Secretary, "Status Report: Question of Parole of Cambodian and South Vietnamese," April 16, 1975.

50. Isaacs, *Without Honor*, 399–400. I recall the telegrams from Ambassador Sullivan relaying the Philippine government's protests.

51. My memory of the transition to the IATF. A letter, April 25, 1975, from President Ford to the Speaker of the House enclosed a Presidential Determination transferring $98 million of Indochina postwar reconstruction funds for the evacuation costs (a similar letter went to the president of the Senate). Dean Brown's testimony before the House Immigration Subcommittee, May 5, 1975, 9–10, gave details of the requested appropriation. The amount actually appropriated was reduced to $405 million.

52. Saigon telegrams 5111 and 5112, April 16, 1975, transmitting and analyzing the Benton plan. Shep Lowman had warned the Ambassador that an organized procession to the port city would invite a North Vietnamese attack like that on the columns from northern MR-1 and from Pleiku (telephone conversation with the author, February 26, 1988). That may have been the reason why the plan called for the mission employees to make their own way to Vung-Tau. Memorandum from Thomas Polgar [CIA Station Chief] to the Ambassador, April 24, 1975, reporting a conversation with Major General Bui The Lan, Commandant of the Vietnamese Marines. Lan asked in return that 250 family members of the Marines be evacuated, and that was done. The rest of the Marines escaped by boat during the last days.

53. Snepp, *Decent Interval*, 359–60.

54. Nguyen Tien Hung and Jerrold L. Schecter, *The Palace File* (New York: Harper & Row, 1986), 328. Butler, in *The Fall of Saigon*, 263, quoted the same telegram. The State Department made this message available to me under the Freedom of Information Act. It was WH 50717, April 17, 1975.

55. Telegram WH50718, April 17, 1975, from the White House to Ambassador Martin from Secretary Kissinger. This telegram and others were furnished in response to my Freedom of Information Act request.

56. Snepp, *Decent Interval*, 371–2; Secretary Kissinger to Ambassador Martin, WH50736, April 21, 1975.

57. State telegram 088999, April 18, 1975; Saigon telegram 5448, April 22, 1975; my conversations with Graham Martin, February 10–12, 1988; Butler, *The Fall of Saigon*, 299.

58. Letters from Senators Kennedy and Eastland to Attorney General Levi, April 17, 1975; letter from L. F. Chapman, Jr. to Senator Eastland, April 18, 1975; letter from Chapman to Eastland, April 21, 1975; letter from Chapman to Eastland, April 22, 1975; letter from Levi to Eastland, April 22, 1975. The last letter confirmed a telephone conversation the previous evening when they had discussed a request from Kissinger for immediate parole of: "1. Up to 50,000 'high risk' Vietnamese refugees, and their families. These would include past and present U.S. Government employees, Vietnamese officials whose cooperation is necessary for the evacuation of American citizens, individuals with knowledge of sensitive U.S. Government intelligence operations, vulnerable political and intellectual figures and former Communist defectors"; (2) 10,000 to 75,000 immediate relatives of American citizens and resident aliens; (3) Vietnamese already at Clark AFB, "provided they qualify as high risk individuals"; (4) and (5) approximately 1,000 Cambodians in Thailand and approximately 5,000 Cambodian diplomats. Levi continued:

"We were advised that it was deemed essential to begin at once to assist the departure from Vietnam of appropriate individuals if such an effort were to be orderly and successful." He said that this was discussed with Senator Eastland and ranking minority member Hruska, both of whom concurred, as did their counterparts in the House. He had accordingly exercised his parole power. Further letters from Chapman on April 24 and 28 added more detailed categories, including 2,000 more orphans. This correspondence was printed in the Appendix to the Senate Refugee Subcommittee Staff Reports of June 9 and July 8, 1975, 161–68. As early as April 19, Kissinger authorized Martin to begin moving out high-risk Vietnamese (WH50728 and a supplemental telegram from Brent Scowcroft, April 19, 1975). However, State telegram 091723, 220238Z Apr 75, conveying the parole authorization for high-risk persons, did not mention that families were included. The embassy sent the families out anyhow, as Graham Martin testified to the Special Subcommittee on Investigations of the House International Relations Committee on January 27, 1976 (hearing record, 544).

59. The best accounts of the evacuation are Snepp, *Decent Interval*, 373–490; Isaacs, *Without Honor*, 408–60; and Butler, *The Fall of Saigon*, 25–39, 267–452. A tabulation provided by Ambassador Martin on January 27, 1976, to the Subcommittee of the House International Affairs Committee (page 589 of the hearing record) gave airlift statistics from April 6 to 30; data for the first five days of the month were unavailable.

60. Snepp, *Decent Interval*, 406–7; author's interviews with Lionel Rosenblatt, May 25, 1977; November 13, 1986; and by phone in February-March 1988; and author's interview with Nguyen Thi Hue, May 2, 1984.

61. Brigadier General Richard E. Carey (the commander of the operation) and Major D. A. Quinlan, "Frequent Wind," three articles in the *Marine Corps Gazette*, February, March, and April 1976; Snepp, *Decent Interval*, 508–62; Isaacs, *Without Honor*, 464–77; Butler, *The Fall of Saigon*, 409-52; many telegrams between Martin and both Washington and CINCPAC, for example, Saigon telegrams 291400Z and 291420Z Apr 75 to White House Flash, "I repeat, I need 30 CH53's and I need them now! Warm regards Martin," and telegram 291442Z Apr 75 to Martin from Brent Scowcroft: "Defense promises 30 CH53's on the way. Warm regards." They never arrived; 19 CH46's with lower capacity came instead; so several hundred people including 130 members of the Korean Embassy were left in the US Embassy compound. President Ford ordered Martin to leave on the last chopper.

62. Snepp, *Decent Interval*, 504–5.

63. Author's Interview with Shepard Lowman, November 12, 1986; author's interview with Hien Bich Vu (Vu Bich Hien), November 14, 1986.

64. Frank Wisner, letter to Congressman Martin A. Russo, June 1, 1975; prepared statement of Julia Taft, July 17, 1975, both printed in the Hearing record of the House Subcommittee on Citizenship, Immigration and International Law, Serial No. 43, 219, 237.

65. Chapman, letters May 6, July 15, July 31, and August 4, 1975, to Eastland, printed in the Appendix to Senate Refugee Subcommittee, *Indochina Evacuation and Refugee Problems*, Part IV, *Staff Reports*, June 9 and July 8, 1975, 169–73.

66. Author's interview with Dr. Dan, November 11, 1987 and further correspondence; author's interviews with Raymond Fontaine, October 30 (by telephone) and November 11, 1987; and a letter from Fontaine, November 11, 1987.

67. Author's interviews with Dr. Tran by phone at various times from 1975 to 1986, and in person, November 21-22, 1987.

68. Letters to author, March 10 and May 26, 1987.

69. Author's interview with Tran Quang Thuan, December 8, 1987.

70. Author's interview with Han Tho Touneh (Touneh Han Tho), December 5, 1987.

71. Author's Correspondence with Dr. An and interviews with Dr. Phieu N. Tran.

72. Dr. Dan, letter of February 26, 1988.

73. Author's interviews with Dr. Niem and Mr. Thuan, December 6 and 8, 1987.

74. Author's interview with Mao Tien Trinh, his 87-year-old mother Vu Thi Tam, his brother-in-law Nguyen Van Dau, and Dr. Tran in Amarillo, Texas, November 22, 1987.

75. Data from the US Committee for Refugees, June 23, 1988.

CHAPTER 16. SOME CONCLUSIONS AND LESSONS

1. Rural Survey Team, Office of the Special Assistant to DepCORDS, "Survey of the Attitudes of Refugees in Twelve Selected Camps in I Corps (April 11–27, 1970)."

2. Both Dr. Dan and Dr. Phieu had observed the antipathy of most refugees to the GVN, and they both tried to do something about it, for example, training local refugee leaders and organizing defense, but they were unable to get the support they needed. Dr. Phieu said there was a real difference between refugees and other people. Unfortunately, however, those differences were not systematically studied.

3. Gary D. Murfin, *War, Life and Stress: The Forced Relocation of the Vietnamese People*, a dissertation submitted to the University of Hawaii for the Ph.D, December 1975 and accepted as satisfactory, v, 211–212.

4. Gerald C. Hickey, *Free in the Forest* (New Haven and London: Yale University Press, 1982), 228, 302. The Special Commission for Highland Affairs estimated that there were 610,314 members of highland ethnolinguistic groups in 1965-67; FULRO estimated 792,635; and unofficial sources (Hickey, missionaries, and others) came up with a figure of 877,000. Except for the 90,000 relocated under Diem's highlander resettlement program and 62,500 moved in 1970–71 by General Ngo Dzu, I have assumed, in order to avoid double counting, that the others relocated during the period 1954–75 were included among the registered refugees.

5. So said a group of Montagnard leaders in Greensboro, North Carolina, in conversation with me on February 13, 1988. My own observations of numerous highlander refugee camps from 1968 to 1970 and again in 1972 confirmed this analysis.

6. George Shepard, telephone conversation with the author, February 26, 1988.

7. General Bruce Palmer, Jr., *The 25-Year War: America's Military Role in Vietnam* (Lexington: University Press of Kentucky, 1984), 147. General Palmer wrote that more than one American on duty in Germany has asked himself what he would do if war suddenly broke out and his wife and children were in danger.

8. Francoise Bory, *Origin and Development of International Humanitarian Law* (Geneva: International Committee of the Red Cross, 1982), 15–37; lecture at Harvard University Law School by Professor George Abi Saab, April 6, 1987; *Geneva Conventions of 12 August 1949 and Additional Protocols of 8 June 1977, Signatures, Ratifications, Accessions and Successions, as at 31 December 1987* (Geneva: International Committee of the Red Cross, n.d.), 9. For the texts of the two Protocols see Adam Roberts and Richard Guelff, ed., *Documents on the Laws of War* (Oxford: Clarendon Press, 1982), 387–463.

9. Luise Drüke-Bolewski, "US Policy in Vietnam and Massive Displacement of Peo-

ple,'' an unpublished paper presented to the Faculty of Arts and Sciences of Harvard University, January 1987, 33–36. Ms. Drüke-Bolewski was an official of the UNHCR on leave for advanced study. The paper represents her views and not necessarily those of the UNHCR.

Select Bibliography

GENERAL WORKS

Asian Survey 10, no. 8 (August 1970): 627–764. This issue, edited by Joseph Zasloff, contains nine papers growing out of a conference of the Council on Vietnamese Studies in New York, April 24–25, 1970, about issues of social and political development in the countryside. The paper by Samuel Popkin, "Pacification: Politics and the Village," is of particular value.

Braestrup, Peter, ed. *Vietnam as History: Ten Years after the Paris Peace Accords.* Washington, D.C.: University Press of America, 1984. Contains some excellent papers and commentaries.

Buttinger, Joseph. *The Smaller Dragon: A Political History of Vietnam.* New York: Frederick A. Praeger, 1958.

———. *Vietnam: A Dragon Embattled.* 2 volumes. New York: Praeger, 1967.

For many years, these two books were the standard scholarly works in English on Vietnamese history. They are still of great value. Buttinger expresses strong but well-documented views, especially about social and economic issues.

———. *Vietnam: A Political History.* New York: Praeger, 1968, is a condensation of Buttinger's two larger works.

Callison, Charles Stuart. *Land-to-the-Tiller in the Mekong Delta: Economic, Social and Political Effects of Land Reform in Four Villages of South Vietnam.* Berkeley, Calif.: Center for South and Southeast Asia Studies, University of California, 1983. A scholarly study including important political implications of land reform.

Colby, William, and Peter Forbath. *Honorable Men: My Life in the CIA.* New York:

Simon and Schuster, 1978. Contains significant chapters about Colby's involvement with the strategic hamlets and other programs during the Diem era and his later service as pacification chief in Viet-Nam.

Cooper, Chester L. *The Lost Crusade, America in Vietnam*. New York: Dodd, Mead & Co., 1970. Foreword by Ambassador W. Averell Harriman. Cooper had a lengthy and important role with respect to Viet-Nam in the US government.

Corson, William R. *The Betrayal*. New York: W.W. Norton & Co., 1968. Colonel Corson, who commanded the Combined Action Program (CAP) of the US Marines and the Vietnamese territorial forces, wrote angry and usually accurate but unsupported words about US-Vietnamese relations. Surprisingly little about the CAP.

Fall, Bernard B. *Last Reflections on a War*. Garden City, N.Y.: Doubleday, 1967. A number of reports and essays by the dean of Viet-Nam historians, collected by his widow.

Thich Nhat Hanh. *Vietnam: Lotus in a Sea of Fire*. New York: Hill and Wang, 1967. A leftwing Buddhist view of the war, the Vietnamese government, and US involvement.

Hilsman, Roger. *To Move A Nation: The Politics of Foreign Policy in the Administration of John F. Kennedy*. Garden City, N.Y.: Doubleday, 1967. This is a very valuable account by a former influential advisor to President Kennedy. Hilsman lost his influence to McNamara and the military, however, after Kennedy was killed.

———. "Vietnam: The Decision to Intervene." In *The Superpowers and Revolution*, edited by Jonathan R. Adelman. New York: Praeger, 1986.

Nguyen Duy Hinh and Tran Dinh Tho. *The South Vietnamese Society*. Indochina Monograph Series. Washington, D.C.: US Army Center of Military History, 1980. An insightful study based on the first-hand experience of the two generals.

Karnow, Stanley. *Vietnam: A History*. New York: The Viking Press, 1983. This large book, which is the companion to a 13-part documentary film series for the Public Broadcasting System, is based on both extensive research and the journalist's own long experience. It contains a great deal of information on high-level decision making in Washington, Saigon, and Hanoi, but relatively little on what was happening at the "rice roots" in Viet-Nam.

Lacouture, Jean. *Vietnam: Between Two Truces*. New York: Random House, 1966. Translated from the French by Konrad Kellen and Joel Carmichael. Introduction by Joseph Kraft. Useful.

Lake, Anthony, ed. *The Legacy of Vietnam*. New York: New York University Press, 1976. Interesting essays on the broader issues of international politics, military policy, and foreign aid.

Lansdale, Brigadier General Edward G. *In the Midst of Wars*. New York: Harper & Row, 1972. A good account of the author's personal experiences as advisor on counterinsurgency to Magsaysay, Diem, and successive American ambassadors.

Luce, Don, and John Sommer. *Viet-Nam: The Unheard Voices*. Ithaca and London: Cornell University Press, 1969. Forward by Senator Edward Kennedy. Somewhat emotional but based on personal experiences in the countryside of these two International Voluntary Services (IVS) leaders, who spoke Vietnamese.

Melman, Seymour. *In the Name of America: The Conduct of the War in Vietnam by the Armed Forces of the United States, as Shown in Published Reports*. New York: Dutton, 1968. A voluminous collection of newspaper articles, gathered by a member of Clergy and Laity Concerned.

Oberdorfer, Don. *Tet! The Story of a Battle and its Historic Aftermath*. Garden City, N.Y.: Doubleday & Co., 1971. A meticulous history of the crucial Communist offensive and its effects upon public opinion and the Johnson administration, but with little on the effects within Viet-Nam.

The Pentagon Papers. This was the popular name for *United States-Vietnam Relations, 1945–1967*, a document-rich study in 12 books by the Office of the Secretary of Defense Task Force, which was leaked by one of the researchers. Washington, D.C.: Government Printing Office, 1971. An invaluable source on US Government decision making. Two abridged versions were published: *The Pentagon Papers*, the Senator Gravel Edition, 5 volumes, Boston: Beacon, 1971–72; and *The Pentagon Papers: As published by the* New York Times, one volume, New York: Quadrangle Books, 1971.

Pike, Douglas. *Viet Cong*. Cambridge, Mass.: The Massachusetts Institute of Technology Press, 1966. Still the definitive work.

Porter, Gareth, ed. *Vietnam: The Definitive Documentation of Human Decisions*. 2 volumes. Stanfordville, N.Y.: Earl M. Coleman Enterprises, 1979. Contains some documents also printed in the Pentagon Papers, and translations of many documents in Vietnamese.

Scigliano, R. "Vietnam: Politics and Religion," *Asian Survey*, 4, no. 1 (June 1964): 666–73. Mainly discusses Diem's conflict with the Buddhists, but contains some useful observations about strategic hamlets.

Shaplen, Robert. *The Lost Revolution*. Revised edition. New York: Harper & Row, 1966. A remarkably perceptive account of what happened on the ground as well as in high places.

Truong Nhu Tang, with David Chanoff and Doan Van Toai, *Vietcong Memoir*. San Diego, New York, London: Harcourt Brace Jovanovich, 1985. A revealing autobiographical history by one of the highest National Liberation Front officials, who became disillusioned after the North Vietnamese took over the South.

Taylor, Telford. *Nuremberg and Vietnam: An American Tragedy*. New York: Quadrangle Books, 1976. On the international law applicable to military strategy and tactics in Viet-Nam, by a former US prosecutor at Nuremberg. Controversial.

Thompson, Sir Robert G. K. *Defeating Communist Insurgency: The Lessons of Malaya and Vietnam*. New York: Praeger, 1966.

———. *No Exit from Vietnam*. London: Chatto & Windus, 1969.

———. *Revolutionary War in World Strategy, 1945–1969*. New York: Taplinger, 1970.

———. *Peace is Not at Hand*. New York: McKay, 1974.

These four books by the former security chief in Malaya and head of the British Advisory Mission to Viet-Nam provide a penetrating if controversial analysis of the evolving conflict and what the United States should do. His gloomy predictions in the last book were realized.

US Department of State. *Foreign Relations of the United States*. Washington, D.C.: United States Government Printing Office. Several volumes on Viet-Nam, including the Geneva Conference of 1954. The most recent is *Vietnam*, Volume 1, 1961.

Vietnam, Monthly Bulletin of Statistics. National Economy Department, National Institute of Statistics, 1957–74. Text in Vietnamese, French, and English.

Vietnam Statistical Yearbook, 1957–74. National Institute of Statistics.

Warner, Denis Ashton. *Not with Guns Alone*. Hawthorn, Victoria: Hutchinson of Australia, 1977. Excellent eye-witness account, with much useful information.

1954 PARIS AGREEMENT, REFUGEES FROM THE NORTH, AND PROGRAMS OF THE DIEM REGIME

Donnell, John C., and Gerald C. Hickey. *The Vietnamese "Strategic Hamlets": A
    Preliminary Report*. Santa Monica, California: The Rand Corporation, Memorandum RM-3208-ARPA, August 1962.
Dooley, T. A. *Deliver Us From Evil: The Story of Viet-Nam's Flight to Freedom*. New
    York: Farrar, 1956. A personal account of the exodus from North Viet-Nam and
    Lt. Dooley's part in it. Highly emotional but factual.
Dow, Maynard Weston. *Nation Building in Southeast Asia*. Boulder, Colo.: Pruett, 1966.
    A study of resettlement projects in Malaya, the Philippines, and Viet-Nam. Useful.
Duncanson, Dennis. *Government and Revolution in Vietnam*. New York and London:
    Oxford University Press, 1968. Duncanson was a member of the British Advisory
    Mission under Sir Robert Thompson. He considered the strategic hamlet program
    a success, despite faults that he recognized.
Ly Trung Dung. "Integration of Refugees in Viet-Nam," *Migration News*, July-August
    1958, 11–12. Geneva: International Catholic Migration Committee. A good factual
    article.
Harnett, (Msgr.) Joseph J. "The Vietnamese Refugees Five Years Later," *Migration
    News*, September-October 1959, 39–43. Msgr. Harnett was head of the National
    Catholic Welfare Conference program in Viet-Nam.
Hooper, Edwin Bickford, Dean C. Allard, and Oscar P. Fitzgerald. *The United States
    Navy and the Vietnam Conflict*. Vol. I: *The Setting of the Stage to 1959*. Washington, D.C.: Naval History Division, Department of the Navy, 1976. Contains
    a good account of Operation Passage to Freedom in 1954–55.
Bui Quang Khanh. "The Organization of Hamlets and Their Transformation into Strategic
    Quarters in Vietnam," *E.R.O.P.A. Review*, June 1963, 51–71. Explains the government theory of hamlet development.
Lindholm, Richard W., ed. *Viet-Nam: The First Five Years, an International Symposium*.
    East Lansing: Michigan State University Press, 1959. Proceedings of an international symposium with American, Vietnamese, and French experts. Very valuable. Much information on refugee reception and resettlement.
Michigan State University, Vietnam Advisory Group. *Research Report: Field Study of
    Refugee Commission*. Ralph Smuckler, Research Coordinator, Walter W. Mode,
    Frederick R. Wickert, Saigon, September 1955.
———. *Recommendations Concerning Proposed Field Organization of the Commissariat
    for Refugees*, by a team composed of Walter W. Mode, Frederick R. Wickert,
    and Ralph Smucker, Saigon, 1955.
———. *Review of Recommendations Concerning Proposed Field Organization of the
    Commissariat of Refugees*, Saigon, 1956.
———. *Review of Recommendations Concerning Proposed Reorganization of the Commissariat for Refugees of August 6, 1955*, by Walter W. Mode and Roland Haney,
    Saigon, 1956.
———. *Final Report, Covering Activities May 20, 1955–June 30, 1962*. Saigon, 1962.

Montague, Robert M., Jr., Lt. Col., Artillery. *Pacification: The Overall Strategy in South Vietnam*. Carlisle Barracks, Pa.: US Army War College, 1966. Covers agrovilles, strategic hamlets, and the oil-spot policy after the fall of Diem. Colonel Montague later became a top aide of Ambassador Robert Komer.

Montgomery, John D. *The Politics of Foreign Aid: American Experience in Southeast Asia*. New York: Praeger, 1962. Some details on refugee assistance, 1954–56. Good account of the land development program, 1956–58.

Montgomery, John D., and the N.I.A. Case Development Seminar. *Cases in Vietnamese Administration*. Saigon: MSU Vietnam Advisory Group, 1959. Contains three cases pertaining to the strategic hamlet program.

National Catholic Welfare Conference. *Terror in Vietnam: A Record of Another Broken Pledge*. Washington, D.C.: National Catholic Welfare Conference, 1955. Instances of Viet-Minh violations of the armistice agreement relating to those who wished to move to South Viet-Nam.

O'Daniel, J. W., Lt. Gen. (ret.). *The Nation That Refused to Starve: The Challenge of the New Vietnam*. New York: Coward-McCann, 1960. History of the resettlement of refugees from the North at Cai-San, by the former chief of the US Military Assistance Advisory Group. Well-written; uncritically laudatory of Diem.

O'Donnell, J. B. "The Strategic Hamlet Program in Kien Hoa Province, South Vietnam: A Case Study in Counterinsurgency." In Peter Kundstadter, ed. *Southeast Asian Tribes, Minorities and Nations*. Princeton: Princeton University Press, 1967. Excellent, detailed account, based largely on the author's experience as USOM province representative.

Osborne, M. E. *Strategic Hamlets in South Vietnam: A Survey and a Comparison*. Data Paper no. 55, Southeast Asia Program. Ithaca, N.Y.: Cornell University, April 1965. Disappointing. Some good information, but only conjecture about peasant reactions.

Samuels, Gertrude. "Passage to Freedom in Viet Nam." *National Geographic*, June 1955, 858–874. Good article; excellent pictures.

Schaad, Carl W., Col., artillery. "The Strategic Hamlet Program in Vietnam: The Role of the People in Counterinsurgency Warfare." Student thesis at the US Army War College, Carlisle Barracks, Pa., 1964. Concludes that in most areas where a concentrated civil-military effort took place, the program contributed significantly to improve security and resistance of the rural population to the Communists.

Smith, Major W. A. "Strategic Hamlets in Vietnam," *Military Review*, 44, no. 5 (1964): 17–23. Major Smith served in the Strategic Hamlets Division of the MAAG. The article contains some good advice, which was ignored.

Viet Nam, Commissariat General for Refugees, Saigon. *An Historic Exodus in Viet Nam*. Undated. Good information. This was reprinted as an Appendix to the Senate Judiciary Subcommittee on Refugees hearing record of July 13–September 30, 1965. See the listing under Congressional Hearings and Reports.

Viet Nam, Directorate General of Information. *Operation Exodus: The Refugee Movement to Free Vietnam*. Saigon: Directorate General of Information. Undated, probably published in 1959. Good factual account, pro-Diem and pro-Catholic. Very useful.

Zasloff, Joseph J. *Rural Resettlement in Vietnam: An Agroville in Development*. Saigon: Michigan State University, Viet Nam Advisory Group, 1963. The best account of the agrovilles.

MILITARY STRATEGY AND TACTICS, PACIFICATION

Anderson, Charles R. *The Grunts*. San Rafael, Calif.: Presidio Press, 1976.
———. *Viet-Nam: The Other War*. Novato, Calif.: Presidio Press, 1982.
    Well-written and insightful autobiographical works by one of the "grunts."
Blaufarb, Douglas. *The Counterinsurgency Era*. New York: Free Press, 1977. One of
    the best analyses of how insurgencies were combatted in Viet-Nam and Laos, by
    a former CIA station chief in Laos.
Browne, Malcolm W. *The New Face of War*. Indianapolis and New York: Bobbs-Merrill,
    1965. Penetrating account by a journalist on Vietnamese tactics against insurgency
    before the arrival of American combat troops.
Deitchman, Seymour J. *The Best-Laid Schemes: A Tale of Social Research and Bureauc-
    racy*. Cambridge, Mass.: MIT Press, 1976. A unique description by a Defense
    Department insider of how the bureaucracy and the military managed and reacted
    to social science research. Very useful.
Herrington, Stuart A. *Silence Was a Weapon: The Vietnam War in the Villages*. Novato,
    Calif.: Presidio Press, 1982. An honest personal account of Captain Herrington's
    experiences as a Phoenix advisor in Hau-Nghia province, 1971–72. He spoke
    fluent Vietnamese. Good material on effects of military operations on people,
    including refugees.
Hunt, Richard A., and Richard H. Shultz, editors. *Lessons from an Unconventional War:
    Reassessing U.S. Strategies for Future Conflicts*. New York: Pergamon Press,
    1982. A collection of well-researched analyses by experts in unconventional war-
    fare. Chapter 2 by Dr. Hunt is especially good. Professor Shultz's analysis of
    hamlet evaluation system aggregates by hamlets (instead of population), despite
    some arithmetical errors, presents a convincing picture of pacification which is
    gloomier than the conventional wisdom.
Institute for Defense Analyses. *The American Experience with Pacification in Vietnam*.
    3 volumes. Washington, D.C. Report 185, IDA Log No. HQ72–14047, March
    1972. Chester L. Cooper (author of *The Lost Crusade*), Project Leader; Judith E.
    Corson, Laurence J. Legere, David E. Lockwood, and Donald M. Weller. Thor-
    ough. Considerable new information.
Katsuichi, Honda. "Villages in the Battlefield: The Vietnam War and the People," *Japan
    Quarterly*, 15 (April-June 1968): 159–179. Eye-witness reports of US operations
    in Quang-Ngai, from *Asahi Shimbun*. Grim reading.
Komer, Robert W. *Bureaucracy at War: U.S. Performance in the Vietnam Conflict*.
    Foreword by William E. Colby. Boulder and London: Westview Press, 1986. A
    distillation of the findings and lessons for US policy and administration which the
    author has drawn from his high-level service concerned with the Viet-Nam War
    and as Under-Secretary of Defense.
Lewy, Guenter. *America in Vietnam*. New York: Oxford University Press, 1978. A
    meticulously documented, fair-minded, factual, and analytical account of the
    evolution of American strategy and tactics and of their consequences, including
    effects upon Vietnamese civilians. This is certainly one of the most important
    works on US involvement in the Viet-Nam war.
Littauer, Raphael, and Norma Uphoff, eds. *The Air War in Indochina*. Revised edition.
    By the Air War Study Group, Cornell University. Boston: Beacon Press, 1972.
    Full of facts; good analysis.

Hoang Ngoc Lung, Col. ARVN. *Strategy and Tactics*. Washington, D.C.: US Army Center of Military History, 1980.

————. *The General Offensives of 1968–69*. Washington, D.C.: US Army Center of Military History; 1980.
   Colonel Lung was the J-2 of the Joint General Staff. Honest, straightforward, acknowledging both GVN and US mistakes.

National Academy of Sciences. *The Effects of Herbicides in South Vietnam*. 20 volumes. Washington, D.C.: National Academy of Sciences–National Research Council, 1974. An exhaustive study by many natural and social scientists. Commissioned by the Secretary of Defense pursuant to Public Law 91–441.

Nighswonger, William A. *Rural Pacification in Vietnam*. New York: Praeger, 1966. Solid, well-documented.

Palmer, General Bruce, Jr. *The 25-Year War: America's Military Role in Vietnam*. Lexington: University Press of Kentucky, 1984.

Schell, Jonathan. *The Military Half: An Account of Destruction in Quang Ngai and Quang Tin*. New York: Vintage Books (Random House), 1968.

————. *The Village of Ben Suc*. New York: Alfred A. Knopf, 1967.
   Both these stark eye-witness reports were originally published in *The New Yorker*.

Scoville, Thomas W. *Reorganizing for Pacification Support*. Washington, D.C.: US Army Center of Military History, 1982. Straightforward, based on official documents.

Serong, Brigadier F. "The 1972 Easter Offensive," *Southeast Asian Perspectives*, no. 10, Summer 1974. Brigadier Serong was chief of the Australian Military Mission in Viet-Nam. Useful.

Shulimson, Jack, and Charles M. Johnson, Major USMC. *U.S. Marines in Vietnam: The Landing and the Buildup*. Washington, D.C.: History and Museums Division, Hq. U.S. Marine Corps, 1978. Some information on pacification and the CAPs.

Spector, Ronald H. *United States Army in Vietnam, Advice and Support: The Early Years, 1941–1960*. Washington, D.C.: Center of Military History, 1983. A first-rate, broad-gauge study, recognizing the importance of political, social, and economic factors in revolutionary warfare, and the failure of US military leaders at the time to reckon with these forces.

Summers, Colonel Harry G. *On Strategy: The Vietnam War In Context*. Carlisle, Pa.: U.S. Army War College, 1981. Reprinted, Novato, Calif.: Presidio Press, 1982. An influential book. The author outlined ideas on how to fight insurgencies; he discounted pacification as something the US armed forces should not engage in.

Suplizio, Paul E., Major, USA. "A Study of the Military Support of Pacification in South Vietnam, April 1964-April 1965." A thesis presented to the faculty of the Command and General Staff College, Fort Leavenworth, Kansas, 1966, for the Master of Military Art and Science degree. Principally discusses the Chien Thang plan of the GVN. Major Suplizio later served in CORDS.

Telfer, Major Gary L., Lt. Col. Lane Rogers, and V. Keith Fleming, Jr. *Fighting the North Vietnamese, 1967*. Washington, D.C.: History and Museums Division, Hq. U.S. Marine Corps, 1978. Another volume in the official Marine Corps history, which contains reports on Operations Lam Son 54, Beau Charger, Hickory, and Prairie IV.

Thayer, Thomas C. *War without Fronts: The American Experience in Vietnam*. Boulder, Colo. and London: Westview Press, 1985. Thayer was chief of the operational analysis division of the Defense Department's Advanced Research Projects Administration in Viet-Nam, and then in Washington, D.C. The principal source of the profuse statistical data in the book is the computer file in the Defense Department National Military Command Support Center.

Tran Dinh Tho, Brigadier General, ARVN. *Pacification*. Washington, D.C.: Center of Military History, 1980. Another in the series by former leading ARVN officers. General Tho was Assistant Chief of Staff for Operations in the RVNAF Central Logistics Command. This is an upbeat but balanced and insightful analysis.

Thompson, W. Scott, and Donaldson D. Frizell, eds. *The Lessons of Vietnam*. New York: Crane, Russak, 1977. Proceedings of a symposium with General Westmoreland, Paul Nitze, Robert Komer, and other authorities. Excellent, full of cogent ideas.

Ngo Quang Truong, Lt. General, ARVN. *The Easter Offensive of 1972*. Washington, D.C.: Center of Military History, 1980. Well-balanced record by the man who was appointed MR-1 commander in the midst of the offensive. He credits US air support for much of RVNAF's success.

————. *RVNAF and US Operational Cooperation and Coordination*. Washington, D.C.: Center of Military History, 1980. Sensitive and honest.

Westmoreland, William C., General, USA. *A Soldier Reports*. Garden City, N.Y.: Doubleday, 1976. Contains much material on Viet-Nam.

Whiteside, Thomas. "A Reporter at Large (Defoliation)," *The New Yorker*, February 7, 1970, 32–69. An important article on the damaging effects in Viet-Nam and Cambodia of US aerial spraying of herbicides; one of a series on the subject by Whiteside.

REGIONAL AND LOCAL STUDIES

Goodman, Allan E., Lawrence M. Franks, and Nguyen Thi Huu. *The Causes and Consequences of Migration to Saigon, Vietnam*. New York: SEADAG, Asia Society, August 1973. Based on sample surveys in greater Saigon, plus data from other cities from the National Institute of Statistics. The authors, however, did not take into account the GVN's definition of a refugee, and therefore misinterpreted their results.

Hickey, Gerald Cannon. *Free in the Forest: Ethnohistory of the Vietnamese Central Highlands, 1954–1976*. New Haven and London: Yale University Press, 1982. Enormously valuable. Based both on the author's long personal experience and on extensive scholarly research. A definitive work.

Meyerson, Harvey. *Vinh Long*. Boston: Houghton Mifflin Co., 1970. Penetrating eyewitness account, which demolished the illusion of pacification both before and after Têt 1968.

Race, Jeffrey. *War Comes to Long An*. Berkeley: University of California Press, 1972. Good insights at the "rice roots" in a province that was a testing ground for successive pacification theories.

Trullinger, James Walker. *Village at War*. New York: Longman, 1980. The author, who spoke Vietnamese, lived in the pro-VC village of My-Thuy-Phuong in Thua-Thien province from November 1974 until its capture by the North Vietnamese at the end of March 1975, interviewing and observing the inhabitants.

REFUGEES AND OTHER WAR VICTIMS

American Council of Voluntary Agencies for Foreign Service. *Report on Vietnamese Refugees and Displaced Persons*. New York: American Council of Voluntary Agencies for Foreign Service (ACVA), October 1965. By a delegation from ACVA.

Dr. Phan Quang Dan. *Refugee Relief & Rehabilitation, Land Development & Hamlet Building*. Saigon: Office of the Deputy Prime Minister of the Republic of Vietnam, January 15, 1975. A comprehensive report, listing all resettlement and land development sites (but not separating them), and containing maps by province. Dr. Dan corrected the list in November 1987. See table 15.

Geyelin, Philip. "The Vietnamese Refugee Problem." *The Reporter*, 33 (1965): 43–45.

Human Sciences Research, Inc., McLean, Virginia. A series of sample surveys of refugees in 1967 and 1968, done under contract with ARPA (Advanced Research Projects Agency, Department of Defense).

———. *The Refugee Situation in Phu-Yen Province*, by A. Terry Rambo, Jerry M. Tinker, and John D. LeNoir. 1967.

———. *The Refugee Situation in Dinh-Tuong Province*, by Jerry Tinker. Field Research Memorandum no 6. August 1967.

———. *Refugee Movement in Revolutionary Warfare: A Study of the Causes and Characteristics of Civilian Population Displacement in Viet-Nam*, by Gary D. Murfin and David DePuy. 1968. This survey was conducted in Thuong-Duc district of Quang-Nam.

———. *A Study of Mass Population Displacement in the Republic of Vietnam*, by A. T. Rambo, D. A. DePuy, D. Brown, and P. Estermann. Part I: *Analysis of the Forced Relocation Process*. 1968. Part II: *Case Studies of Refugee Resettlement*. 1968. This was a study at four sites of forcibly evacuated people and five sites of voluntary refugees.

The Human Sciences Research studies were the most thorough surveys of the characteristics, motivations, economic and social situations, and attitudes of evacuees and refugees ever conducted in Viet-Nam.

Marks, E. B. "Saigon: The Impact of the Refugees," *The Reporter*, 36, no. 1 (1967): 33–36. By the second American Refugee Coordinator in Viet-Nam.

Mead, T. *Proposal for a Resettlement Program*. Saigon: Joint Development Group, 1967. The group did postwar planning under contract with AID. This interesting proposal evidently did not materialize.

Murfin, Gary Dean. *War, Life and Stress: The Forced Relocation of the Vietnamese People*. Honolulu: University of Hawaii, 1975. A doctoral dissertation by one of the Human Sciences Research investigators, based on those and other studies. A convincing demonstration of the effects of forced relocation on the psychological adjustment and attitudes of the victims.

Rural Survey Program, Office of the Special Assistant to the Deputy for CORDS, I CTZ. "Survey of the Attitudes of Refugees in Twelve Selected Sites in I Corps (April 11–27, 1970)." Unpublished report, mimeographed. 1970. Confirms and amplifies findings of the Human Sciences Research studies.

Thomas, Liz. *Dust of Life*. New York: Dutton, 1978. The personal experiences of a volunteer in a Saigon orphanage, who also helped refugees during the 1972 and

1975 North Vietnamese offensives. Good vignettes about dealings with the GVN
bureacracies.

NORTH VIET-NAM

Fall, Bernard B. *The Two Viet-Nams: A Political and Military Analysis*. Second revised
    edition. New York: Praeger, 1967.
————. *The Viet-Minh Regime: Government and Administration in the Democratic Re-
    public of Vietnam*. Revised and enlarged edition issued jointly with the Southeast
    Asia Program, Cornell University. Westport, Conn.: Greenwood Press, 1975.
        Both are sound works by a master of the subject.
Joint Publications Research Service. United States Department of Commerce. Translations
    on North Vietnam. A running translation service, covering newspapers and other
    periodicals. Microfilm items are identified by JPRS catalogue numbers; microtext
    by Readex card numbers.
Moise, Edwin E. *Land Reform in China and North Vietnam: Consolidating the Revolution
    at the Village Level*. Chapel Hill: University of North Carolina Press, 1983. Good
    academic scholarship.
Spinks, Charles N., John C. Durr, and Stephen Peters. *The North Vietnamese Regime:
    Institutions and Problems*. Washington, D.C.: American University Center for
    Research in Social Systems, 1969. Useful on relocation to the Highlands and
    evacuations from the cities.
Thompson, James Clay. *Rolling Thunder: Understanding Policy and Program Failure*.
    Chapel Hill: University of North Carolina Press, 1980. On the bombing of the
    North.
Van Dyke, Jon M. *North Vietnam's Strategy for Survival*. Palo Alto, Calif.: Pacific
    Books, 1972. Well documented and useful.
Vietnamese Studies. Hanoi, 1964–79, appearing irregularly. Some interesting material.

FROM THE CEASE-FIRE NEGOTIATIONS TO THE NORTH VIETNAMESE CONQUEST OF THE SOUTH

Butler, David. *The Fall of Saigon: Scenes from the Sudden End of A Long War*. New
    York: Simon and Schuster, 1985. A good journalist's report, based in part on
    previously classified telegrams.
Carey, Brigadier General Richard E., and Major D. A. Quinlan. "Frequent Wind,"
    Marine Corps Gazette, February, March, and April 1976. On the planning and
    execution of the helicopter evacuation from Saigon, April 29–30, 1975, by the
    commander of the Ninth Marine Amphibious Brigade.
Van Tien Dung. *Our Great Spring Victory*. Translated from the Vietnamese by John
    Spragens, Jr. New York: Monthly Review Press, 1977. The official history by
    the commander of the North Vietnamese forces in 1975.
Hawthorne, Leslie, ed. *Refugee: The Vietnamese Experience*. Melbourne and New York:
    Oxford University Press, 1982. Twenty personal histories recounted by refugees
    who went to Australia.

Herrington, Stuart A. *Peace with Honor? An American Reports on Vietnam, 1973–75*. Novato, Calif.: Presidio Press, 1983. A personal account. The author believes in retrospect that the political and military collapse of South Viet-Nam occurred in 1974, for a variety of reasons. Highly critical of the American Embassy's performance during the final evacuation, in which the author participated.

Hosmer, Stephen T., Konrad Kellen, and Brian M. Jenkins. *The Fall of South Vietnam: Statements by Vietnamese Military and Civilian Leaders*. A Rand Corporation report prepared for the Historian, Office of the Secretary of Defense. New York: Crane, Russak, 1980. A useful synthesis, but lacks interviews with Thieu or Khiem. The leaders tended to blame the United States, but some were frank in admitting Vietnamese failures.

Nguyen Tien Hung and Jerrold L. Schecter. *The Palace File*. New York: Harper & Row, 1986. Although its main subject is the efforts of the Vietnamese government to get the United States to provide the military and economic assistance promised in secret letters by President Nixon, the book also contains significant information on the final evacuation in 1975. Worth study.

Isaacs, Arnold R. *Without Honor: Defeat in Vietnam and Cambodia*. New York: Vintage Books (Random House), 1983. An excellent, if somewhat passionate, account of what went wrong and why. Good analysis of US and GVN policies and actions, as well as those of North Viet-Nam. Well documented.

Kissinger. Henery. *White House Years*. Boston, Toronto: Little, Brown and Company, 1979.

————. *Years of Upheaval*. Boston, Toronto: Little, Brown, 1982.

   The books contain exhaustive details on the cease-fire negotiations and the aftermath, including how Watergate and Congressional inhibitions prevented the US from responding to North Vietnamese violations of the agreement. They end with Nixon's resignation in August 1974; therefore do not cover the final defeat.

LeGro, Col. William E. *Vietnam from Ceasefire to Capitulation*. Washington, D.C.: Center of Military History, 1981. Colonel LeGro was the Defense Attaché's chief intelligence officer. A detailed military history, with some useful information on refugees.

Le Thi Que, A. Terry Rambo, and Gary D. Murfin. "Why They Fled: Refugee Movements During the Spring 1975 Communist Offensive in South Vietnam," *Asian Survey*, 16 (1976): 855–63. Results of a survey in three refugee camps, April 8–10, 1975. Based on working notes carried out in a rucksack, since the original protocols were lost during the evacuation.

Snepp, Frank. *Decent Interval: An Insider's Account of Saigon's Indecent End*. New York: Random House, 1977. Snepp was a top strategy analyst in the CIA Saigon station. The book used classified documents and the author's personal recollections, without CIA clearance. A good if highly critical history.

Todd, Olivier. *Cruel Avril, 1975, La chute de Saigon*. Paris: Editions Robert Laffont, 1987. Mainly vignettes of happenings during the last month of the war, but contains political and diplomatic history, especially on the abortive negotiations for a coalition government.

General Cao Van Vien and Lt. Gen. Dong Van Khuyen. *Reflections on the Vietnam War*. Washington, D.C.: Center of Military History, 1980. An honest, straightforward book by two of the highest ranking officers of RVNAF.

CONGRESSIONAL HEARINGS AND REPORTS

By far the most thorough and continuous inquiries into the refugee and war victims situation and the assistance efforts in the three Indochinese countries were conducted for ten years (1965–75) by the Senate Judiciary Subcommittee to Investigate Problems Connected with Refugees and Escapees (Senate Refugee Subcommittee), chaired by Edward M. Kennedy. The Subcommittee heard witnesses from the US Departments of State and Defense, AID, and their missions in the three countries, voluntary agencies, various physicians, and other interested parties. It sent study missions to the countries, and stimulated General Accounting Office investigations. Its hearing records are replete with newspaper reports and other material, and altogether make up an unequaled treasure of information. Senator Kennedy himself evolved from an attitude initially in tune with that of the Johnson policies to an ever-stronger opposition to the war, as is shown by his statements. Although he always gave the administration a fair hearing, his selection of other witnesses and information and the reports of the subcommittee's staff tended to reflect his changing views. Some of the most significant hearings and reports are listed below.

Senate Report 59, 89th Congress, first session. *First Special Report of the Subcommittee*, February 9, 1965.

Senate Report 371, 89th Congress, first session, June 25, 1965.

Refugee Problems in South Vietnam and Laos. Hearings, July 13–September 30, 1965.

Report, March 4, 1966, pursuant to Senate Resolution 49, 89th Congress, first session, together with individual views.

Civilian Casualty, Social Welfare, and Refugee Problems in South Vietnam. Hearings. May 10–October 16, 1967.

Civilian Casualty and Refugee Problems in South Vietnam: Findings and Recommendations. May 9, 1968.

Civilian Casualties, Social Welfare, and Refugee Problems in South Vietnam. Hearings, part 1, June 24–25, 1969.

Refugee and Civilian War Casualty Problems in Indochina, a Staff Report, September 28, 1970.

War-related Civilian Problems in Indochina. Hearing, part 1, April 21, 1971.

War Victims in Indochina. Reports prepared for the Subcommittee by the General Accounting Office, May 23, 1972: Followup Review on Assistance to War Victims in Vietnam (B-133001), and Civilian Health and War-related Casualty Program in Vietnam—One Year Later (B-133001).

Problems of War Victims in Indochina. Hearings, part 1, May 8, 1972.

Relief and Rehabilitation of War Victims in Indochina. Hearings, Part 2, Orphans and Child Welfare, May 11, 1973. Part 3, North Vietnam and Laos, July 31, 1973.

Relief and Rehabilitation of War Victims in Indochina: One Year After the Ceasefire. A Study Mission Report, January 27, 1974.

Humanitarian Problems in Indochina. Hearing, July 18, 1974.

Humanitarian Problems in South Vietnam and Cambodia. Report to the Subcommittee, 1975.

Indochina Evacuation and Refugee Problems. Hearings, part 1: Operation Babylift and Humanitarian Needs, April 8, 1975. Part 2: The Evacuation, April 15–30, 1975. Staff reports, June 9 and July 8, 1975.

Several Committees of the House also took an interest, including the following:

Committee on Government Operations, Subcommittee on Foreign Operations and Government Information: Hearings, U.S. Assistance Programs in Vietnam, July 15, 16, 19, 21, and August 2, 1971.
International Relations Committee, Hearings: Part 1, Vietnam Evacuation and Humanitarian Assistance, April 9, 15–16, and May 7–8, 1975. Part 2, The Vietnam-Cambodia Debate, March 6, 11–13, and April 14, 1975. Part 3, Evacuation: Testimony of Ambassador Graham A. Martin, January 26, 1976.
Subcommittee of the Judiciary Committee on Immigration, Citizenship and International Law: Hearings: April 8, 1975–February 5, 1976, regarding Indochina Refugees (evacuation, reception, and resettlement).

DOCUMENT COLLECTIONS

The US Army Center of Military History in Washington has an outstanding collection of documents from the armed services, AID, CORDS, and other sources on military policy and operations and pacification, with a great deal of information on refugees and other war victims. It possesses the papers of Robert Komer, William Colby, and Clayton McManaway, and certain papers of General William Westmoreland.
Documents of the Department of State which have not yet been published have to be obtained under the Freedom of Information Act. The process is cumbersome and slow.
The National Archives has papers of all government agencies and permits researchers to study declassified documents, which are usually 30 or more years old.
The Yenching Library of Harvard University has the papers of Joseph Buttinger, including correspondence with Ngo Dinh Diem and members of his government, diaries, drafts and finished copies of Buttinger's speeches, correspondence, and publications, materials of American Friends of Vietnam, and so on. Very useful.
The files of the International Rescue Committee on Viet-Nam from 1965 to 1975 are in process of being transferred to the Hoover Institution at Stanford University.
Catholic Relief Services in New York has an archivist, who is now in process of cataloguing its voluminous files on Viet-Nam.
Michigan State University has the papers of the MSU Advisory Group, which was in Viet-Nam from 1955 to 1962.
The presidential libraries have rich collections, some of which have been microfilmed and are in other libraries. For example, I have studied at Harvard material from the Lyndon Baines Johnson Library.

Other archives around the country no doubt have documents related to the subject of this book. I do not pretend that my research has exhausted them. There are still gaps, as the reader will readily detect. I myself brought back from Viet-Nam many unclassified papers, and collected more while I was in the State Department. Many of the telegrams, reports, and policy documents of the GVN ministries that I have cited in this book are in my collection. I have also been able to study the private files of other officials who served in Viet-Nam.

Unfortunately, most people, American and Vietnamese, who escaped in 1975 had to leave their papers behind.

Index

About the Author

LOUIS WIESNER, a retired Foreign Service officer, is an international authority on refugee assistance. He held important posts connected with refugee aid to Viet-Nam and other countries and served as counselor and medical programs administrator with the International Rescue Committee following his retirement from the State Department.